Families Today

Fourth Edition

Connie R. Sasse, CFCS

McGraw-Hill **Glencoe**

New York, New York   Columbus, Ohio   Chicago, Illinois   Peoria, Illinois   Woodland Hills, California

Copyright © 2004, 2000, 1997, 1994 by The McGraw-Hill Companies, Inc.

Send all inquiries to:
Glencoe/McGraw-Hill
3008 W. Willow Knolls Drive
Peoria, IL 61614-1083

ISBN 0-07-829840-7 (Student Edition)
ISBN 0-07-829841-5 (Teacher Wraparound Edition)
Printed in the United States of America.
4 5 6 7 8 9   027 08 07 06 05

Technical Reviewers

Steven A. Hamon, Ph.D.
Licensed Clinical Psychologist
The Antioch Group
Peoria, Illinois

Linda D. Ladd, Ph.D., Psy.D CFLE
Family Development Specialist
Texas Cooperative Extension
College Station, Texas

Teacher Reviewers

Sabrina Bennett, M.Ed., CFCS
Family and Consumer Sciences Instructor
Madison County High School
Danielsville, Georgia

Nancy M. Carter, M.A., CFCS
Family and Consumer Sciences Teacher
Wolfson High School
Jacksonville, Florida

Tommy Sue Garrett, M.A., CFCS
Early Childhood Education Careers Teacher
Metro Nashville Public Schools
Nashville, Tennessee

Jill Tolleson
Family and Consumer Sciences Teacher
Delight School System
Delight, Arkansas

Patti A. Tubbs, M.Ed.
Family and Consumer Sciences Educator
Merrillville Community School Corporation
Merrillville, Indiana

Jennifer K. Wede
Family and Consumer Sciences Teacher
Carrington High School
Carrington, North Dakota

Catherine T. Whichard
Family and Consumer Sciences Teacher
Beaufort County Schools
Washington, North Carolina

Darlene E. Yoquelet, M.S., CFCS
School-Age Parent Educator
Garland High School
Garland, Texas

Judith Zaunbrecher, M.Ed.
Family and Consumer Sciences Teacher
Iowa High School
Lake Charles, Louisiana

Contents in Brief

Contents

Unit 2: Strengthening Relationships 105

Building Character

Balancing Work & Family Life

Career Success Stories

Tips & TECHNIQUES

SKILLS CHECKLIST

Highlighted Topics

Focus On ...

UNIT 1

The Family Foundation

Teen Views

What one word best describes what family means to you?

Martin

"It's hard to pick just one, but I'd say 'supportive.' Whenever things aren't going well, somebody's there for you—like when my father had his heart attack. We all stood by each other. I remembered all the times when my dad had told me not to give up. I kept hearing those words, and I even said them to him after the surgery. I thought he was asleep, but later he told me that he heard."

Mary Fran

"I guess I'd pick 'caring,' since I think that fits my family. Even when we say things we shouldn't have, it's okay. We still care. Sometimes I yell at my sister for something silly. When I hurt her, I can see it in her eyes, and then I feel bad, so I try to make it up to her. Last night we went to the mall together and had a good time. She's only nine, but I think she knows I care."

What's your view?

What other words would you use to describe families?

25

Families, Society, and You

Why Study Families?

OBJECTIVES

After studying this section, you should be able to:

- Explain what you can gain by studying families.
- Identify the functions of the family.
- Identify skills that contribute to successful family life.
- Describe a helpful attitude to have when learning about families.

TERMS TO LEARN

functions
conflict resolution

When asked to name what means the most to them in their lives, people often respond, "My family." The care of families is obviously too important to be left to chance. How much do you know about families? Simply living in a family doesn't make anyone an expert on them. Turning to the expertise, knowledge, and experience of others in order to build a strong family makes good sense.

You may be surprised to discover all that you can learn and put to good use in your life after studying about families. Take a look.

APPRECIATING FAMILIES

Sometimes the most important things in life are taken for granted—families, for example. Can you think of reasons why this might be true? Families are an everyday part of life for most people. Sometimes it's easy to lose sight of the importance of anything that is simply there all the time.

By studying about families, you can learn why they are so important. As you will read in the chapters to come, families provide many **functions**, or purposes, yet their job is not always easy.

Families add value and structure to individual lives and to society. What new appreciation might you have for the family you belong to as you learn more about families?

So much can interfere as families work to fulfill their functions. You might never have thought about all that families provide. The functions of the family include:

- Love and affection.
- Protection.
- Education.
- Teaching values.
- Economic support.
- Procreation.
- Guidance.
- Socialization.
- Recreation.

As you read this text, you'll also have new insights into what it means to be a family. You'll see that many different kinds of families exist and that both similarities and differences can be valued. As your understanding of families increases, your appreciation for them is likely to also. Valuing something makes you more likely to take good care of it. Families are supposed to last for a long time. Taking good care of them is a worthwhile goal.

LEARNING ABOUT YOURSELF

What you learn about families will give you a better understanding of yourself. In a sense the family is a mini version of the world. As you relate to family members, you learn what it takes to get along with other people. The more you understand about family relationships, the better equipped you are to make them work.

Love and support for each other is the foundation of family relationships. How could you show support and love for each member of your family?

The knowledge and skills you gain transfer to the larger world. In time you'll be able to take all that you've learned about relationships and use that knowledge when you're on your own.

Within the family, you grow and develop. You discover the kind of person you are and that you want and need to be. As you study families, you'll see the critical link between families and individuals. You may even look inward to find ways to strengthen that link in your own life.

Building Your Skills

Any study of the family would not be complete without learning and practicing skills that family members need. Successful family living depends on these skills:

- **Communication skills.** Communication heads the list. Without good communication, families can easily have problems. Misunderstandings may occur when feelings are not made clear. Learning to communicate well can be a key to family harmony.
- **Problem-solving and decision-making skills.** Learning to make sound decisions is another basic skill. Problems are often approached by making a series of careful decisions. Families must decide how to raise children, how to spend their time, and how to relate to each other. The ability to use these skills well makes life go more smoothly within the family.
- **Management skills.** The ability to manage is another needed skill. Everything from managing family finances to household schedules depends on this skill. Learning to manage well helps bring order to family life.

You communicate with your family not only with words, but also with attitudes and actions. How might you improve communication with your family?

- **Conflict-resolution skills. Conflict resolution** is an approach to settling disagreements. Since disagreements do happen, people need appropriate methods for solving them. Too often arguments in the family get out of hand when people react with their feelings rather than their minds. Practicing good conflict-resolution skills helps family members get along better with each other.

As you study the family, you'll learn about all of these skills—and others. You'll see why they are important to families, but even better, you'll discover ways to put them to practical use in your life. As Derrick said, "One important thing I learned in my family life course is that I'm not a very good listener, but I'm working on it. Now I'm starting to see how much better I get along with people when I make an effort to listen to them."

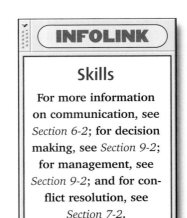

INFOLINK

Skills

For more information on communication, see *Section 6-2*; for decision making, see *Section 9-2*; for management, see *Section 9-2*; and for conflict resolution, see *Section 7-2*.

Every family faces problems. Strong families work together to solve them. Do you sometimes help your family solve problems? How?

Building Character

Responsibility: A Quality That Counts

Responsible people make families stronger. That's because they do what they're supposed to, allowing people to trust and count on them. Responsible people back up their words with actions. If something goes wrong, they aren't afraid to take charge and even accept blame when they make a mistake. Responsible people recognize a need when they see it. Often they don't have to be asked to act. A teen could show responsibility by:

- Caring for a younger sibling when a parent is ill.
- Doing assigned family chores promptly and competently.
- Using some part-time earnings to help with the grocery bill.
- Deciding to avoid certain friends who tend to get into trouble.
- Offering to pay for a scale the teen broke at work.
- Completing school assignments on time.

QUESTIONS

1. How does a person learn to be responsible?
2. What happens in relationships when a person is not responsible?
3. How do you show responsibility in your family?

STRENGTHENING YOUR FAMILY NOW

Your study of the family can serve another purpose. You can learn to make the family you live in stronger.

You may know teens like Jordan, who struggles to get along with his parents, or like Megan, who argues with her stepsister. Both teens want a smoother family life, but they need tools to help them.

This course will increase your knowledge about what happens in relationships, both inside and outside the family. Using what you learn, you can strengthen your own family. The power of your family now depends, in part, on you. Great and small, your contributions can make a difference.

Solving Problems

Families today face many challenges. Some are more complicated than others. Work schedules may have to be meshed with family time. Many families have to cope with economic difficulties, death, drug problems, abuse, and crime. Some families face the challenges presented by divorce and remarriage. A changing world with scientific advances and new patterns of living must be handled. All of these affect families. Any of these could affect you in some way.

Few, if any, families can say they are problem-free. Having problems is just part of life. Even strong families have problems.

They cannot be strong, however, if they can't find ways to manage and solve their problems. What, then, do families need when it comes to problems? They need to know:

- That problems can be solved.
- That change is possible.
- How to solve problems.
- Where to get help.
- That a commitment to family comes first.
- That every family member contributes to the family.

STRENGTHENING YOUR FUTURE FAMILY

Studying the family can give you a foundation for what lies ahead. If you form a family in the future, you have the ability to make it what you want it to be.

In Luke's family, love and affection was absent. He missed the closeness they had when he was younger, but it had been gone for several years, and the pattern just wasn't changing.

If you learn now what a family needs to be strong, you can apply that knowledge right from the beginning when you build a family of your own. You'll recognize what can go wrong and how to react so that problems don't get bigger or go on indefinitely. You can prevent many mistakes from happening. With foresight, skills, and knowledge, you can shape family life to be what you want it to be.

You see many types of families in everyday life. Each aims to build a strong family foundation for the members within.

WORKING WITH FAMILIES

As you study the family, you may even find that your interest extends beyond your own personal life. Some people find careers that enable them to work with families. Others use political avenues to influence public policies and laws that affect families. Many people simply become volunteers who give their time to provide services for families. You will read more about all of these possibilities in this course.

BEGINNING YOUR STUDY

When Jennifer began a course on relationships and family living, reading about families made her think about those she knew. Some were similar to hers, but many were quite different. Something her teacher said the first day of class stuck in her mind.

As Mrs. Ashley put it, "While we study the family, let respect be your guide. In other words, remember to speak and act thoughtfully. Just as your family's important to you, others feel the same way. Families don't all look and act the same, but they have some very clear similarities. As you'll learn, families want many of the same things for their members, but the methods they use and the obstacles they face may be different. Despite their differences, the value of all families to people and society can't be denied."

Like Jennifer, you're about to study the family. Her teacher's words are just as significant for you to remember.

SECTION 1-1 REVIEW

Check Your Understanding

1. Why are families sometimes taken for granted?
2. List the functions of the family.
3. Complete this sentence in your own words: "Good communication is a basic skill needed by families because . . ."
4. How can the family you might form in the future benefit from your study of the family now?
5. What are three ways in which your interest in families can extend beyond your personal life?
6. **Thinking Critically.** What might happen if students who are studying the family show little respect for each other and their family situations?
7. **Problem Solving.** Carrie's family is troubled. Their problem has been growing for weeks until Carrie now feels that the situation is hopeless. She believes that nothing can be done to make things better. Based on what you have read, what would help Carrie and her family at this point?

The Need for Strong Families

OBJECTIVES

After studying this section, you should be able to:

- Explain why society is concerned about families.
- Summarize the impact that family laws can have on individuals and families.
- Identify who is responsible for making families strong.
- Explain why society needs strong families.

TERMS TO LEARN

pessimist
optimist

If you unravel a rope, you see that individual strands are woven together to form a whole. If you cut or remove a strand, the whole rope becomes weaker. In much the same way, individuals, families, and the larger society are intertwined in complicated ways.

With people, every action or reaction in one area has an impact on others. For example, when Alex was on a county-wide, all-star baseball team, his travel and games affected his family's schedule. Street crime, a problem in the city where Karla lives, affects the daily routine of her family members. If families don't teach members the skills and values they need to get along, other individuals and society feel the lack.

Society is much more complex now than ever before. Many communities are struggling to find ways to help families and individuals with problems. Society, however, can't correct every problem that comes along. Families and individuals must look inward for some of their own solutions. Simply longing to change the world, or expecting it to change, isn't enough.

THE SITUATION IN SOCIETY

Where society and families are concerned today, the news is both good and bad. Although looking at the negative side may not be pleasant, it is necessary. Problems can't be fixed if they are ignored. Solutions aren't likely to

Broken lives can lead to broken families—and vice versa. Do you see solutions?

be found if you and others in your generation don't identify what needs improvement and then take steps to make things better. When you accept responsibility for making your family's life better, you help make a better society.

Statistics About Families

Statistics show that many U.S. families today face tough situations. Here's some evidence:

- There are over a million divorces annually. The likelihood of a new marriage ending in divorce is over 40 percent.
- Over one-fourth of all children live with only one parent.
- About 20 percent of all children live in poverty. Children who live in poverty are at a disadvantage compared to children whose basic needs are met.

- Over half of children who live with only their mothers are living in poverty.
- One out of every three births is to an unmarried mother. A majority of single mothers with children under six have never been married. Single mothers who have never been married are more likely to be poor than divorced single mothers.
- More than 500 babies are born each day to mothers 15-17 years old. Eighty-five percent of the mothers are unmarried. Seventy-five percent of all teen mothers are unmarried.
- More than three children die every day due to parental abuse. Over three-fourths of those who die are under five years of age.
- At least two million children between the ages of five and thirteen take care of themselves for some portion of the day while parents are working, according to the U.S. government census.
- One child in eight has an alcoholic parent.
- The first use of alcohol typically begins around the age of thirteen. Those who begin drinking before age fifteen are four times more likely to become an alcoholic than those who begin at age twenty-one.
- One of the leading causes of death among young people ages fifteen to nineteen is killing by firearms.

- Youths age twelve–seventeen are nearly three times more likely than adults to be victims of serious violent crimes, including assault, rape, robbery, and homicide.

All of these statistics point to problems in society today. Although some of these problems have existed for a long time, they have increased over the years. What you see in your life and in your community may or may not be part of this picture. Chances are, however, that at least some of these situations are apparent to you.

As gloomy as the picture painted by these statistics seems, a positive side to the situation of families in society can be seen in several ways. Not only is there a growing desire for society to address family problems in a more active way, but there is also an awareness that families and individuals can do much to help themselves if they are willing to try. Just as important is an increasing recognition of the many strengths that families have.

Society Cares About Families

CONCERN FOR FAMILIES

A surge of interest and concern for families is apparent today. You can find examples in newspapers and magazines as well as other media. People want changes in society that will benefit families, easing their problems and worries.

Family Law

Laws of all types have an effect on families. Policies and laws that concern families are continually under scrutiny. As society changes, the laws that people live by change, too. New problems and situations must be addressed.

Laws protect both individuals and families. Laws that deal with taxes and interest rates influence how much money a family has to spend. The poor and unemployed are affected by laws that set up and control programs that help them. State and federal laws affect the education children receive. Since society includes a growing number of older people, laws must be aimed at their needs.

Family strength comes from within, but it often grows stronger with help from the outside. In what ways does society show support for families?

Family values and family laws are topics of debate in the courtroom. Individual freedoms are weighed against societal good.

Stay informed by reading and listening to the news and sharing ideas with others. Letters and phone calls to legislators can make a difference.

Social Security laws, for example, have great impact on older family members.

Laws deal with all aspects of family life. Some control the circumstances for marriage and divorce. Child support and paternity laws help make sure that both parents support the children they bear. When Rene's former husband stopped paying child support, she used the law to get him to accept his financial responsibility to his children.

Some laws relate to specific situations in families. Laws deal with child, spouse, and elder abuse as well as neglect. Children who get in trouble with the authorities are dealt with under special laws for juveniles.

Your Role in Family Law

The responsibility for laws lies not just with legislators. People have to remember that laws are made and changed under public pressure. You owe it to yourself, your family, and all families to take interest in legal processes and express your opinion.

Business and Industry

People are also urging business and industry to look at their family policies. Family and work lives affect each other. When one is strained, so is the other.

Business leaders are recognizing that they have much to gain by addressing family needs. Employed parents have a difficult time taking care of all the needs of children—health, school, and otherwise—without some flexibility and cooperation from employers. When employers work with employees to create helpful family policies, both sides benefit. Home life is better, making people happier and more effective employees.

Community Involvement

Many agencies have been created to help families with their concerns. Social service agencies help people who have everything from financial problems to diseases, disabilities, and troubled relationships.

Education is another means of community involvement. Even the course you are taking now is an indication that family life is worth examining. People are realizing more and more that families need support from all corners of society in order to function well.

TAKING RESPONSIBILITY

In many ways, society works hard to help families with their needs and problems. Schools do more than just teach the basics. They handle discipline problems, deal with hunger, and provide additional knowledge—about the hazards of drug use, for example. Law enforcement agencies deal with family arguments and young people who run away or become involved in dangerous and illegal activities. Social agencies provide a wide array of services.

Although these and other resources are helpful and necessary, many families need to take a more active role themselves. Society cannot be expected to do it all. By recognizing their own power and strengths and taking on more responsibility, families can relieve some of the pressure on a society that is already overburdened.

THE POSITIVE VIEW

If you pour water into a glass to the halfway point, is the glass half empty or half full? Someone with a negative point of view, the **pessimist**, might say "half empty." In contrast, the **optimist**, a person who looks at the positive side of an issue, might say "half full." People do look at situations in different ways. The positive view of families today takes the focus off weaknesses and puts it on strengths.

When families look within their framework, they can find many ways to build strengths. What do you think they might discover?

Family Fun. Spending time together as a family is one way to strengthen family ties. Fun, however, doesn't mean creating financial hardships. How can you have fun on less money? Here are some suggestions to try:

- Walk, hike, or bike on public trails or swim at public beaches.
- Do routine chores (walking the dog?) or creative projects (cooking?) together.
- Take advantage of the low admission costs of school- and town-sponsored events.
- Watch for bargain days or times for reduced admission to commercial sports or amusement centers, movies, or other entertainment.
- Enjoy special dining at noon when meals are less expensive and eating places are likely to have "specials."

Try It Out. Talk with members of your family about what they like to do. Work together to plan a low-cost or free outing that all of you will enjoy.

Finding Family Strengths

Healthy families have many good qualities, or strengths, that work for them. They communicate by listening and sharing feelings. They support each other. They spend time together, working and playing. They care. These are some of the qualities that are characteristic of strong families.

Describing strong families is not easy. There is no magic line that is crossed when a family becomes strong. Instead, families are at all levels of strength. Because no family is perfect, each can find ways to improve upon the strengths it has.

A family's strength lies not so much in how well it provides as it does in how well the family tries. When Soo-Ling's father became ill, everyone in the family pulled together to make the best of a bad situation. Without his income, they struggled, but their spirit pulled them through. The measure of success for Soo-Ling's family didn't depend on what they had. Instead, it relied on the support they gave each other. The family looked for strengths—and found them.

Often you will hear strong families described as healthy families. In general, these are the families that fulfill the needs of their members to the best of their ability. They identify the strengths they have and need, and they work to develop them. When problems arise, large or small, they look for ways to cope and try to find solutions. If this means getting help from people outside the family, they're willing to do so.

INFOLINK

Strong Families

For more information on strong families, see *Section 8-1.*

Writer John Beecher said, "Strength is a matter of the made-up mind." To be strong, then, what must a family do?

Society needs strong families. When families are functioning well, they are a buffer against many of life's problems. Their strength combines with that of other families to make society strong, too.

When people are asked to describe or talk about themselves, they often point out all their flaws first. For some reason, they forget to look for the good in themselves. People can just as easily overlook what is good about families. From the optimist's point of view, however, the family bag of strengths is more likely half full than half empty, and with effort it can fill even more.

SECTION 1-2 REVIEW

Check Your Understanding

1. What are four reasons why many families face tough situations today?
2. How can an individual affect the laws concerning families?
3. Why should business and industry be interested in families?
4. What makes families strong?
5. Should a strong family be able to solve all of its own problems?
6. **Thinking Critically.** Scott's family is moving because of increasing run-down property and crime in the neighborhood. Is their view optimistic or pessimistic? How might a person with the opposite view tackle the situation of a declining neighborhood?
7. **Problem Solving.** Mimi's ten-year-old son was picked up by police after two instances of school vandalism. Mimi told authorities that he gets in trouble because he doesn't like school. They don't treat him right, she says, so she can't do anything about it. What is your reaction to her comments? Will her attitude help the problem get resolved?

Chapter 1
Review and Activities

CHAPTER SUMMARY

- The functions of the family are: love and affection; protection; education; teaching values; economic support; procreation; guidance; socialization; recreation.
- Successful family living depends on family members having a variety of skills.
- Strong families have learned how to cope with the problems every family faces.
- There is a growing concern about the well-being of families and how this affects individuals and society.
- Families face many tough situations today that call for them to be skillful in handling them and knowing where to go for help.
- Interest in families is shown through laws that affect families, the practices of business and industry, and community involvement in helping families.
- Families must take responsibility for staying strong and healthy. They must recognize their strengths to get through tough times.

REVIEW QUESTIONS

Section 1-1
1. What are three things you can gain from studying families?
2. What basic skills are needed for successful family living?
3. Should family members expect to have a problem-free life? Why?
4. Demario is getting married soon. How might a family living course help him strengthen the family he builds in the future?
5. What is a respectful attitude like? Why is it important when studying families?

Section 1-2
1. What do statistics indicate about families today? What are five ways laws affect families?
2. How does society help families?
3. Should people rely heavily on society to make sure that families are strong? Explain your answer.
4. Why does society need strong families?

BECOMING A PROBLEM SOLVER

1. Another holiday is approaching and Jim isn't looking forward to it. His mother and aunt don't get along well, and Jim's cousin is a pest. Jim would like the day to be fun for all, and he wants to do something to help make that happen. What would you suggest?

2. Over the years, Tina's family has grown apart. They live in different states and seldom see each other. Even the letters and phone calls have lessened greatly. Tina sees the closeness other families have and misses that in hers. What could she do?

THINKING CRITICALLY

1. **Analyzing Cause and Effect.** Do you think that family problems cause problems in society or that problems in society cause problems in the family? Defend your reasoning.
2. **Predicting Consequences.** What could happen if a family does not learn to solve the problems that it faces? What consequences could this have for individual family members and society?
3. **Drawing Conclusions.** How much impact do you think a teen can have in improving family life? Explain your reasoning.
4. **Drawing Conclusions.** Why do you think focusing on family strengths is more important than concentrating on weaknesses?

MAKING CURRICULUM CONNECTIONS

1. **Social Studies.** Find the name and address of the member of the United States House of Representatives from your area and of your United States Senator. Do the same for your state political figures.
2. **Language Arts.** Write a letter to a government official describing how you think a current law affecting families could be improved. Outline your reasoning for suggesting this change.

APPLYING YOUR KNOWLEDGE

1. Select a law that affects families. What was the purpose of the law you have chosen? Has the law fulfilled its purpose? Evaluate whether you think the law has had a positive effect on families.
2. With your classmates, collect newspaper and magazine articles about families. Categorize them as to their tone—are they optimistic or pessimistic? Which category seems to present the stronger case? Why?

Family & Community Connections

1. Identify at least three careers that exist in your community that are related to working with families. How do people in these careers strengthen families?

2. Contribute to the family strength of people in your neighborhood. With your classmates, arrange to provide child care at an elementary school during parent-teacher conferences. This will give parents the opportunity to meet with teachers without the distraction of young children or worrying about alternative child care arrangements.

Chapter 2

Families Make a Difference

WORDS FOR THOUGHT

"A happy home is more than a roof over your head—it's a foundation under your feet." *(Anonymous)*

IN YOUR OWN WORDS

In what ways does a happy home provide a person with both a "roof" and a "foundation"?

Families Meet Many Needs

OBJECTIVES

After studying this section, you should be able to:

- Define and give examples of emotional support.
- Summarize the impact emotional support has on the family and its members.
- Identify how families meet physical needs.
- Explain what lessons are part of the socialization process.
- Explain the impact of family on intellectual development.
- Compare how needs and wants affect families.

TERMS TO LEARN

needs
emotions
emotional support
high self-esteem
low self-esteem
personality
socialization
independence
wants

In order to become well-adjusted, productive members of society, what do people need? The answer is the family. Families are the supportive structure designed to take care of people throughout life. They supply what children need to grow and develop. A family's culture influences just how these functions are fulfilled.

Needs are required for a person's survival and proper development. Families fulfill needs that are emotional, physical, social, intellectual, and moral.

PROVIDING EMOTIONAL SUPPORT

When someone says something nice to you, what's your reaction? Like most people, you probably have a good feeling that lifts your spirits. You may want to return the good feeling or pass it along to someone else.

What Are Emotions?

All the feelings you have in response to thoughts, remarks, and events are called **emotions**. Emotions are usually thought of as positive or negative, depending on the way they make you feel. In general, positive emotions, such as joy and love, are thought to be good feelings; negative emotions, such as anger and fear, tend to be considered unpleasant.

Labeling an emotion as negative doesn't mean the emotion is wrong. After all, people can't help the way they feel. When negative emotions are felt too often, however, they are a symptom of emotional pain that can complicate lives. Even worse, sometimes people harm themselves or others when they react to negative emotions. They may hurt people in their own family.

In any family each person feels many different emotions. That's not unusual. For the well-being of the family, however, the key is to promote positive emotions and manage negative ones. One way to promote positive emotions in the family is through emotional support.

The Need for Support

Everything that families do to help meet the emotional needs of each member is part of giving **emotional support**. When you make someone feel good, you contribute to that person's emotional health. Sincere compliments help others feel positive about what they've done. Listening helps someone who is trying to solve a problem. Helping ease another's concerns gives emotional support.

Receiving emotional support from your family has many benefits. It does everything from shaping your self-confidence to helping you get through difficulties.

Developing Self-Esteem

One important role of families is to raise self-confident children who see themselves as capable and of worth. Those with such feelings have **high self-esteem**. People who doubt their abilities and worth have **low self-esteem**.

Self-esteem is built on all the experiences a person has in life, but it is first shaped in the family. If a young child is continually called "bad" or "stupid," the child begins to believe this label. Children and adults with low self-esteem do not believe in themselves and their own capabilities. Those with high self-esteem are willing to try new things—and even fail at them.

"A time to laugh, a time to cry..." A family meets many emotional needs. How have you met the emotional need of one family member today?

Expressing Emotional Support

With the right words and actions, you can support your family and friends.

For at least a week, try these and similar ideas. What effect do your efforts have on your relationships?

Handling Difficult Times

Families also provide emotional support to help people get through tough times. Handling problems is easier if you don't have to deal with them alone. Family members are usually the first to be there when something goes wrong.

Shortly after Kim began driving, she was involved in a minor traffic accident. Although there were no injuries, she was extremely shaken by the experience. Admitting to her mother that she had made a mistake was not easy for Kim, but her mother's presence and reassuring arm around her shoulders were welcome.

Emotionally supportive families offer shelter from the outside world. Sometimes it feels good to get away from the pressures and responsibilities of work and school. People usually feel that they can be themselves in the family. Even when problems are only the day-to-day ones that people routinely face, families can provide a supportive place to be.

Tips & TECHNIQUES

Creating a Family Bond

Emotional links in a family are usually lasting. As other relationships come and go, family ties remain. A sense of belonging exists. Family members are likely to keep their interest in your life, just as you do in theirs.

Within the family, people receive affection from each other simply because they are family, not because of talents and skills they have. Ideally, family members accept and love each other without

conditions. This doesn't mean that you will always get along perfectly with other family members. It does mean that underneath the day-to-day problems of living, there is love and affection.

"Look at these pictures of Grandma and Grandpa." "No wonder you're so handsome, Dad." How often do you think to compliment the people in your family?

Some personality traits are inherited. Can you think of friends who share similar characteristics to their parents? Were the qualities learned, inherited, or possibly both?

Shaping Lives in the Family

Whether people eat steak or hamburger at home doesn't really have much impact on their lives. What they experience emotionally, however, does.

Within the family, personalities are shaped. All the characteristics that make a person unique make up **personality**. You might describe a classmate as fun-loving, outgoing, and caring. These are part of personality.

Although personality comes about in many ways, the family influence is very strong. Often the traits developed or learned in the early years are kept for life. With positive emotional support from the family, people are more likely to develop personality traits that serve them well. This in itself is reason enough to make emotional support a priority of family life.

Similarly, family interaction plays a major role in how each member sees himself or herself—self-esteem. When children are praised for their efforts and made to feel they have value, they develop confidence. This encourages them to try new things. Many areas of development are enhanced. On the other hand, children who are made to feel that they are bad, incapable, or worthless develop more slowly. You will learn more about personality in Section 22-1.

Taking the First Step

Providing emotional support is a two-way street. One person cannot always be the giver and someone else always the receiver. Adults need emotional support as much as children and teens do. Closeness in a family depends in part on both giving and receiving emotional support.

Think about the actions you take in your family. Do you often have something positive to say? Do you offer to help before you're asked? By taking the first step, you can be the one who gets the cycle of good feelings rolling.

You can show emotional support in many ways. Even when family time is limited, you can still find ways to show you care. You'll discover that good feelings come with giving emotional support as well as receiving it.

MEETING PHYSICAL NEEDS

People need food, shelter, and clothing in order to survive. These are physical needs. Providing these basics is a struggle for some families today. Most families do the best they can. When family members see this, they value the caring and the effort that is made. How much they have or don't have seems less important.

Usually certain family members are employed to earn money for what the family needs. When jobs are not available, some families seek outside help through friends, relatives, and government programs.

The skills you learn at home will be useful when you're on your own someday. **What skills do you need to master?**

Protecting Family Members

Physical needs include more than just providing food, housing, and clothing. Family members also protect each other.

Health care is one example of protection. Simple health care is usually handled at home, where illness and minor injuries are treated. For more serious problems, routine checkups, and preventative care, family members go to doctors and other health care workers.

Families protect in other ways, too. The rules that families set help protect children from dangerous situations and ones that they may not be able to handle. One of the first rules Josh learned was that he was not supposed to touch the range. Later, he learned not to leave the apartment without another family member. Rules were made to keep him safe in and around his home.

As a teen, you probably have rules to follow. For example, rules about curfews and telling your family where you will be while away from home are aimed at keeping you safe. Caring families set rules. Remembering this makes following rules easier.

BUILDING SOCIAL SKILLS

Have you ever seen the child's toy that has pegs of different shapes that must be placed in the matching holes? In a sense people are like these pegs, searching for a place in life where they fit. Families help people learn how to get along in society. This process is called **socialization**.

Many small lessons are part of the socialization process. Through socialization, you learn:

- **How to get along with others**. Learning to share a toy was one of your early lessons in getting along with others. Cooperating while playing a game was another. People who learn lessons like these from family members later find that getting along with friends and the people they work with is easier.
- **What behavior is acceptable where you live**. In the family, people learn social rules. In order to function well in society, they need to know what is expected and be able to act accordingly.
- **How to be independent**. Two early lessons about **independence**, the ability to take care of yourself, came when you learned how to put on your own clothes and how to cross streets alone. As a teen, you are learning how to make decisions that are in your best interest. Your goal is the eventual ability to manage successfully on your own.
- **What responsibilities you have to your world**. Responsibilities are first learned as children clean up after themselves and help others in little ways. These lessons are gradually broadened to include the world outside the family. Concern for such issues as protecting the environment and preventing crime begin in the family. Families have a responsibility to look beyond their own interests and instill a community spirit in their members.

When families prepare people for life, getting along is easier. Through the socialization process, people find that, like the pegs of varied shapes, they fit well into the world around them.

Responsibility begins at home. Where does it go from there?

PROMOTING INTELLECTUAL GROWTH

Throughout life, people develop their minds. They not only gain knowledge, but they also learn ways to improve their thinking skills. Over time, wisdom, in the form of good sense and insight, may grow as well. Families contribute to the intellectual development of all family members, but their impact on the children is especially important.

The family is a child's first teacher. Many of your first lessons in life were probably learned from members of your family. With a good start, children have a better chance of doing well in school and throughout life.

If you have a younger brother or sister, you may have helped your sibling grow intellectually. All family members can help in this area. For example, Wendy influenced her brother's intellectual development without even realizing it. By playing with him and talking to him when he was still just an infant, she helped Eric learn to speak. As he grew older, she read stories to him and took him to the park where he could see people and activities. Wendy's efforts, combined with those of the rest of her family, were very important to Eric.

Families need to be involved in a child's formal education. Any teacher will tell you that students are more likely to do well when adult family members take an interest in education. This means going to conferences, talking or writing to teachers and administrators, supporting teachers in their efforts, monitoring schoolwork, and attending special events.

MEETING MULTIPLE NEEDS

Suppose Carlos helped his younger sister write the alphabet on index cards. Then he used them as flashcards to help her learn the letters. Which function of the family was served? Most people would say "intellectual." That's true, but is there more? Carlos and Rosa are likely to benefit emotionally, too. Carlos feels rewarded as Rosa learns. She feels his concern for her. If she gives him a hug or thanks him, he feels appreciated. Social needs are also met as they learn to work together and get along.

As you can see, the functions of the family are linked. Even simple actions can meet more than one need. The methods used don't matter as much as making sure that love and consideration provide the backdrop.

Family games bring people together and promote learning at the same time.

"We're off! Just think—two weeks of fun ahead of us." Family togetherness can be the foundation for getting along with others in your life.

NEEDS VERSUS WANTS

In thinking about what families "need" to provide, remember that "wants" are something different. **Wants** are desired but not essential. The people in your family need food to survive. If you all get a craving for ice cream, however, that's a want. Although your life might not be as pleasant without the ice cream, you can survive.

Motivation from Needs and Wants

Needs motivate family behavior. An unmet need commands attention and effort until filled. After a long holiday weekend away, for example, one family needed rest. Their tiredness showed in many ways. They could hardly wait to get a good night's sleep.

In another family, the father was on an overseas military assignment. Missing each other made the family's need for love, affection, and closeness extremely strong. How might this situation have affected their actions?

Wants are motivators too. A family that wants a new television set might find ways to save for one. A family that wants to have fun together might plan a trip to a theme park.

Confusing Needs and Wants

Needs and wants can cause problems for families who confuse the two. For example, will buying a new television or taking a trip to a theme park cure the problems of a family that has grown apart? It isn't likely. These items are not what count the most in family life, since they are wants rather than needs.

People must recognize what is truly essential for building a strong family. They may find that simple methods are just as effective as expensive, elaborate ones. Helping your family recognize real needs and then meeting them is part of being a family member.

THE POWER OF FAMILIES

The family has been important for thousands of years. Many times throughout history, critics have said that the family was in trouble and would soon vanish. Despite this, families have continued to exist. No replacement has yet been found that could fulfill the functions a family serves.

Because families are the foundation of society, they may change as society changes, but they are unlikely to disappear. Without a doubt, families have the power to make a difference—to individuals and society. It is this power that must be preserved and strengthened, and you can play a part in that effort.

SECTION 2-1 REVIEW

Check Your Understanding

1. What are the major functions of families?
2. Define emotions.
3. How do families influence the self-esteem of family members?
4. Explain this statement from the text: "Providing emotional support is a two-way street."
5. Name at least two ways in which families protect their members.
6. Why is the socialization process important?
7. Where do people usually begin their intellectual development?
8. **Thinking Critically.** It has been said that you should never deny a person his or her emotions. What do you think this means?
9. **Problem Solving.** Brendan's older brother and sister have moved away from home, which has left him feeling very lonely. When he talked to his father about the way he felt, his father bought him some new computer games. A couple weeks later Brendan still feels the same way. Why didn't the father's solution solve Brendan's problem? What should Brendan do now?

Families Teach Values

OBJECTIVES

After studying this section, you should be able to:

- Explain what values and a value system are.
- Explain the impact of values.
- Identify ways that families teach values.
- Describe what influences values.
- Give guidelines for developing a value system.

TERMS TO LEARN

values
value system
moral code

Have you ever made paper airplanes? Although some sail smoothly through the air, others spin immediately to the ground. Successful flight, like life, depends to a great extent on the rudder. On an airplane the rudder is a moveable part at the back of the plane. It controls the direction of flight. What is the rudder in life that controls a person's direction? Values are probably at the top of the list.

WHAT ARE VALUES?

Values are beliefs and principles that are based on ideas about what is right, good, and desirable. Individuals and families decide which values are important to them. These values may vary from one person or family to another.

The set of values that you have is called your **value system**. How you spend your time, energy, and money indicates your values. You prefer certain activities. You choose words that reveal your attitudes about what's important. You behave according to what you believe. You may feel that some principles are worth standing up for, even fighting for, yet others don't interest you at all. You adopt qualities that you admire and believe are right for you. Together, these make up your value system.

Family values are what the members believe in and put into their actions. What would you describe as a value held by this family?

With values like these, you choose according to your own preferences. Your decision has no harmful effects on anyone.

A Moral Code

Many choices you might make could have harmful effects for you or for others. That is why cultures teach that some core values should apply to all people. Common values, such as honesty and responsibility, guide decisions and behavior in positive ways. When these values are embraced, life is better for individuals, and society is strengthened.

Common values are also reflected in documents and laws. For example, the Declaration of Independence and the Constitution set forth certain values like freedom and equality.

Families have value systems, too. The adults in a family provide leadership in establishing a value system. Their agreement helps build a reliable value system.

The Impact of Values

As you think about values, you'll notice that some have more impact than others. Charlie values privacy and likes to spend time alone, while Lisa values companionship and wants to be with people. Because Kristin values a challenge, she likes difficult jobs. Brent, who values security, prefers jobs without risk.

A moral code guides actions. Suppose someone drove this car over the speed limit—or even stole it. What can be said about the person's moral code?

Once you learn a value, you can teach it to someone else. What value is this teen teaching his younger sister?

The idea that people are valuable and worthy of respect says that the way you treat others should reflect the way you want to be treated yourself. This concept can be found in many of the world's religions. Such values as compassion and courage are an outgrowth of this principle.

Personal beliefs of what is right and wrong become your **moral code** and guide your behavior. How do you know what to include in your moral code? You have many opportunities to learn these values.

LEARNING VALUES

Values are first learned within the family. Families are responsible for their members' moral development—by teaching values that belong in a person's moral code. These lessons are passed along to children, who eventually pass them along to their children. Even when children don't adopt a value right away, they often do eventually.

Adults in a family need to express what their values are, so that young people can grow up with a sense of what is right and good. This training gives a feeling of security. Guiding principles are always there and ready for use. Otherwise young people may have an unsure feeling about what to do, especially when problems occur.

Families teach values in several ways:
- **Example.** Older family members demonstrate values to younger ones. For instance, when Mrs. Hassim shoveled snow for a sick neighbor, she gave a lesson without words. Ahmad saw that it's right to care for others in need.
- **Direct teaching.** Often lessons are taught by simply telling younger family members what is right. Loren teaches a direct lesson by holding his son's hand and saying, "You may not hit people. It hurts them."
- **Religious training.** In many families religion supplies principles to live by. Religious principles include core moral values.

Building Character

Helpfulness: A Quality That Counts

You've got a problem and you need someone to talk to. You're in a panic and you want support. What you need is someone helpful, and sometimes others need the same from you. A helpful person shows regard for others by offering service, assistance, or support. Help can be physical or emotional. A helpful teen might:

- Help a younger brother solve a computer problem so he can finish an important paper.
- Fix dinner so a parent can talk with a visiting friend.
- Check the bus schedule for a grandfather who isn't clear about how to find that information.
- Write encouraging notes to a friend who is lonely in a new city.
- Comfort an older sister whose baby was stillborn.
- Encourage a friend to apply for a position that has opened up at work.

QUESTIONS

1. Is it easier to give physical or emotional help to others? Explain your answer.
2. How could too much helpfulness cause problems?
3. How do you show helpfulness in your family?

DEVELOPING A VALUE SYSTEM

Families provide the foundation for a value system, but many other influences also have an effect. Friends can impact a person's values. This is especially true during the teen years. Although you can learn from friends, they may pressure you to go against your values.

Your values are tested every day in many other ways, too. The media—movies, television, magazines, and newspapers—suggest all sorts of values, not all desirable ones. Smoking and drinking are made to look appeal-ing. Beauty and good looks are empha-sized. Violence is a common theme. Your own good sense and a strong value system can help you identify and resist negative influences.

Many other influences affect your thinking in both positive and negative ways. These include people at school and in the community. It's important to stay true to the core values in your moral code.

As you become more involved with people and events outside your family, you will be more aware of ways people's values seem to conflict at times. How will you know what's right?

Some values can cause debate. Reaching agreement on controversies is not easy. It may even be impossible.

Many issues are not clear cut. You may not be sure what's right. You may see reasons that support both sides of an issue. You may even question why some people believe as they do when your opinion is just the opposite. How will you reach a conclusion?

Guidelines to Follow

As you develop a value system, you need to be prepared to preserve, defend, adjust, and strengthen your values. Good judgment will help you. Turning to family values for guidance is important.

It pays to be cautious as you absorb other ideas into your thinking. When tackling new issues, consider how your core values apply. Are your attitudes reasonable and logical?

Here are some guidelines to use as you develop a value system that will serve you well throughout life:

- **Follow the rules of society**. Rules and laws were created by people who realize that without order there is destruction. The rules of society are based on values that respect life, property, and truth. Thus, such acts as killing, stealing, and cheating are not allowed. Taking the laws of the land seriously builds strength into society. It also makes you a stronger person. People who follow the laws gain respect and

opportunity in society. Laws, of course, are changed when necessary. Keeping informed about issues, voting, and writing to legislators can all bring about change.

- **Choose right over wrong**. Even though answers are not always clear, you'll often know deep inside what is right. You may be tempted to push an important value to the side. Take time to think about what's really best for you and others. Challenge what you see and hear. If you're not sure, ask yourself these questions: "Is it illegal? Will it be harmful to me or anyone else? Will I regret it later?"

- **Learn from others**. Observe what goes on around you. The mistakes and experiences of others can help you strengthen your own values. Evaluate each source of information carefully to see whether an influence is positive. Talking to an adult you trust—a family

Some issues provoke controversy. Can you think of some that are difficult for people to settle?

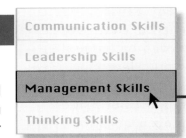
member, teacher, or school counselor, for example—can also help you clarify your principles.

- **Know what you value**. When you know clearly what your values are, they'll be there when you need them.
- **Contribute to the family value system**. Your actions and words can strengthen the value system of your family. In Becca's family living course at school, she learned that sharing leisure time is good for a family. She began to think about how often the people in her family went separate directions to follow their own interests. At Becca's suggestion, the family planned an evening of games and popcorn. Her idea helped the family renew a value that had been recently overlooked.

ACTING ON VALUES

Values mean nothing without action. That's the way it is with values. First you learn them, and then you live by them. You are thoughtful only if you pay attention to the feelings of others. You are honest only if you act that way, even when no one is watching. No matter what you say, people soon see your real values through your behavior. As you examine your value system, ask yourself if your actions match your beliefs. If not, why? What can you do to act on important beliefs?

The same principle is true of the family value system. People in a family can say that they believe in togetherness, but unless they find ways to share time, it isn't true. If a family values cooperation, they must solve problems together. If they value education, they must help younger members learn and encourage them to do well and stay in school. A family value system can help keep the family and its members moving in the right direction. It will only be as strong as family members make it.

A family has the responsibility to teach positive values. As a family member, you have the responsibility to help put those values into action.

What you consider to be right reflects your value system. You may try to encourage others to "do the right thing." Make a private list of your own values—ones you know you want to abide by for life.

SECTION 2-2 REVIEW

Check Your Understanding

1. In what ways does your value system become apparent to others?
2. Give two examples of values that are a matter of preference and two examples of common values.
3. What is the basis for a moral code?
4. Why do adults need to express their values to children?
5. Why are values sometimes confusing?
6. What three questions could you ask yourself to help figure out what is right and wrong?
7. Can you have values without showing them?
8. **Thinking Critically.** If common values were missing in society, how might that affect you?
9. **Problem Solving.** Elena and a group of her friends have tickets to a concert. Elena discovers that the concert is the night before she is to take her college entrance exam. Doing well on the exam is important because a high score will qualify her for scholarship aid. How can values help Elena decide what to do?

Chapter 2
Review and Activities

CHAPTER SUMMARY

- Families must meet members' needs in many ways. The methods used are less important than meeting them with love and consideration.
- Providing emotional support means helping meet the emotional needs of others.
- Families meet many physical needs, such as food, housing, clothing, and protection.
- Families meet social needs by teaching family members how to fit into society.
- Intellectual needs can be met when a family provides a stimulating home environment and takes an interest in a child's education.
- Values are beliefs about what is important. Some values in society are generally accepted as right for all people.
- Values are learned first in the family.
- There are many influences on values in addition to the family, some positive and some negative.
- Values are meaningless unless they are a guide to behavior and action.
- Strong families build strong communities by teaching positive values.

REVIEW QUESTIONS

Section 2-1
1. What is emotional support? How is emotional support linked to self-esteem?
2. What effect does emotional support have on personalities within the family?
3. Why do families set rules for children and teens to follow?
4. Identify four lessons taught for socialization.
5. Why must families meet the intellectual needs of family members?
6. Why must families examine their needs and wants carefully?

Section 2-2
1. What are values?
2. Compare a personal value system with a family value system.
3. How do common values affect people and society?
4. Identify three ways that families teach values.
5. How are values influenced?
6. What are five guidelines to follow when developing your value system?

BECOMING A PROBLEM SOLVER

1. Gary's friends are going to a movie that Gary knows his parents would not like because it contains violence and bad language. If he tells his parents his plans, he knows they'll forbid him to go. He wants to go to the movie with his friends. What should Gary do?

2. Hannah loves cola soft drinks. Her mother has refused to buy them anymore, saying that it isn't healthy for Hannah to drink so much cola. She suggests water or juice as more healthful beverages. What should Hannah do?

THINKING CRITICALLY

1. **Drawing Conclusions.** Of the needs a family meets, choose the one that you think is most important and explain why.
2. **Recognizing Assumptions.** What assumptions are reflected in the saying, "Actions speak louder than words"?
3. **Recognizing Inferences.** What is implied in the following ad slogan for a luxury car: "It blurs the lines between needs and wants"?
4. **Recognizing Values.** What do you think are the two most important common values a society can have? Why?

MAKING CURRICULUM CONNECTIONS

1. **Political Science.** Read the Declaration of Independence and list at least five values promoted by the writers of this document.
2. **Language Arts.** Write a short essay describing a time when your value system helped you make a difficult decision.
3. **Social Studies.** Summarize the functions of families found in this chapter. Then, research how families in another culture handle these functions. Write a report comparing that culture's families to those of American society. When all students have presented information on the cultures they researched, discuss reasons for similarities and differences.

APPLYING YOUR KNOWLEDGE

1. Observe students in your school as they interact in the halls and lunchroom. What conclusions can you draw about their socialization? What rewards or benefits do the students receive (from each other or adults) for acceptable behavior?
2. While you watch your favorite television show, identify the values shown through the plot, conversation, setting, or the relationships of the characters on the program. Are these values that promote strong families and strong communities?

Family & Community Connections

1. Plan an activity with a child that will help meet at least three of the four basic needs. For example, a walk in the park meets: physical needs as you walk or run in the park; social needs as you move and talk together; intellectual needs as you point out information about leaves, plants, or trees to the child; and emotional needs as you support and encourage the child's exploration of the park. If possible, carry out the activity.

2. In your community newspaper, find an article about a person or event that shows or reflects a specific value. Give a brief report to the class, identifying the value and explaining how the value (or the lack of it) is illustrated by the article.

Family Characteristics

"Call it a clan, call it a network, call it a tribe, call it a family. Whatever you call it, whoever you are, you need one."
(Jane Howard)

IN YOUR OWN WORDS

Do you think there are people who don't need a family? Explain your reasoning.

Looking at Family Structures

OBJECTIVES

After studying this section, you should be able to:

- Explain why the images people often have of family are not always realistic.
- Describe various family structures.

TERMS TO LEARN

images
ideal
nuclear family
blended family
extended family
adoptive family
legal guardian

As you think about families, you may see certain **images**, the mental pictures of what you believe something is like. Can you create an image of what a family is? If you're having trouble coming up with an answer, don't think you're alone! This is difficult, even for experts.

IMAGES OF FAMILIES

Where do your images of what a family is come from? Some come from families portrayed in the media—in television, videos, and movies. Other images come from the real families you see around you.

Families in the Media

On television or in movies, you can see families portrayed every day. Some television families solve complex problems in 30 minutes. Some family members are incredibly witty, including the two-year-old. Some families are unusually attractive. Some are simply ridiculous. Still others show an **ideal**, or a perfect, image.

A family in a movie can have a flawless holiday—with the relatives, food, decorations, gifts, and sharing all coming together at just the right moment. The realities of a messy kitchen, an overcooked turkey, a tired cook or two, and a cranky Uncle

The "Ozzie and Harriet" show from early TV and the "Family Matters" TV show of recent years depict a marked contrast in family life. In what ways do current TV shows reflect the families of today? What differences do you notice?

Ned may not be shown. Scriptwriters aim to entertain you. They need a story line and an ending. Time puts limits on what they can do. In real life, the story line is long, complicated, and sometimes even boring.

The media can influence your thinking more than you realize. What you see on the screen begins to seem like the way real life is for others. You may think your life and your family don't measure up. You need to guard against such feelings. Real families are very different, from each other and from the media images. When you understand this, reality is easier to accept.

Real-Life Families

You may have heard the saying, "The grass is always greener on the other side of the fence." In other words, what others have may look better to you than what you have. Even the real families you know,

however, may not be what you think they are. Most families don't show "real" life to outsiders. What you see may look wonderful, but your picture is incomplete.

You may wish you had a family similar to a friend's. You might be surprised to discover the friend admires characteristics of your family. If you switched families, you both might discover that the "other side of the fence" isn't as green as you thought.

Nothing is wrong with looking for ways to improve family life. In fact, you should. On the other hand, trying to live up to images that are false or out of reach never works. This is both pointless and frustrating.

Your family may not be like the ones on television or the rest of the families you know, yet you can find something special there. The reality is that different doesn't necessarily mean better or worse. It simply means different.

FAMILY STRUCTURES

Families come in all shapes and sizes. How many different family structures, or forms, can you identify? The form that a family takes has impact on the way the family functions.

Single People

Although single people may live alone, most maintain family bonds with parents, brothers and  sisters, and other relatives. A single person who has no close family may turn to friends to fulfill the needs normally met by family members.

Single people often have freedoms that others don't have. Many come and go as they please without having to coordinate with anyone else's schedule or needs. Time to devote to a career and interests, as well as community involvement, may be more readily available.

Most singles need to link with other people. By making an effort to include friends in their lives, singles can add to their feeling of contentment.

When people think of "family," different images come to mind. This family has recently added a new member.

Couples

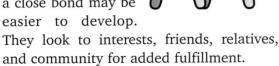

Couples with no children in the home have an opportunity to focus on each other. With just the two of them, a close bond may be easier to develop. They look to interests, friends, relatives, and community for added fulfillment.

Income for a couple can also be an advantage. With only two people in the family, money doesn't have to spread as far. They may be lucky enough to have money for special activities and interests, such as travel.

One problem couples can have is career conflict when both partners are employed. For example, what do Cliff and Janelle do if one of them is offered a job in another town? Will the other one stay behind, look for a new job, or quit working? Such decisions aren't easy to make.

Nuclear Families

A **nuclear family** consists of a mother, father, and their children. In nuclear families, household as well as child-raising responsibilities can be shared. Families need to work out a fair way of sharing.

For the partners in a nuclear family, simply having another adult around can be positive. Good times are fun to share, and bad times can be easier to get through when someone else is right there.

For children in a nuclear family, having both parents present gives them the support of both. They can learn firsthand what it means to be a mother and father. Parents can share the time they have to spend with children. They may have more energy for this than a single parent might.

Sharing the responsibilities of raising children is common in families today. The close interaction of family members benefits each person.

Single-Parent Families

A single-parent family consists of one parent and his or her children. Single parents enjoy the rewards of parenting that come to anyone who loves raising children.

Single parenting, however, is usually a challenge since all the responsibilities must be juggled alone. Many single parents provide and manage all the income for the family and typically take care of all household tasks. Finding the time and energy to do everything is seldom easy. Sometimes relatives and friends help out.

Like other parents, single parents must regularly set aside some special time for children. Giving them love and guidance strengthens the relationship between parent and child. Children need contact with other adults, too, so they can learn the roles of both men and women. Volunteers with the Big Brothers-Big Sisters organization serve this purpose.

Single parents need contact with other adults. Some communities have single-parent organizations where people can socialize and share concerns.

> **INFOLINK**
>
> ## Blended Families
>
> For more information on getting along in blended families, see *Section 13-2*.

Blended Families

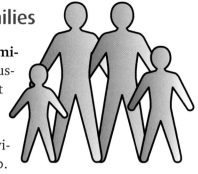

A **blended family** consists of a husband and wife, at least one of whom has children from a previous relationship. A blended family can include the children of both spouses as well as new children born to the couple.

Growing up in the same family is different from suddenly being part of a new one. Adjustments are needed by both adults and children. Extra effort, combined with patience and understanding, makes new routines and relationships work.

Extended Families

An **extended family** includes relatives other than parents and children. Grandparents, aunts, uncles, and cousins are all part of your extended family, whether you live with them or not.

Extended family members, regardless of where they live, can be an important resource. Most relatives expect to be there for each other when they are needed. It's just part of being a family. As Denise said, "My father lives almost 2000 miles away, but he says he's coming after our baby is born. He says nothing can keep him away!"

A family can be a real mixture of different personality types. For this reason, getting along with relatives may be a challenge at times. You may know of families whose disagreements have kept them apart for years. Everyone loses in such a situation. Working together to keep the bonds close is worthwhile. Most people feel that nothing can replace family ties.

Adoptive Families

Adopted children are not biologically linked to their parents. That is, they were not born to them. Instead, the parents have gone through a legal process to make 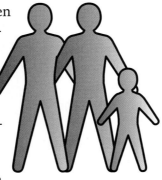 the children part of the family, creating an **adoptive family**. The adopted child usually takes the family's last name and is legally protected by all the same rights that a birth child has.

When an infant is adopted, parents have the greater adjustment. If the child is older, the child has to adjust, too. Memories and experiences the child has had may cause fear and insecurity. Parents need to be patient and understanding as they make the child feel safe and secure.

Legal Guardians

Sometimes parents die or can no longer take care of children for some reason. A relative or close friend of the family may wish to take care of the child. The courts can make this person a **legal guardian**, one who has financial and legal responsibility for the care of a child. The child's last name doesn't change when this occurs.

Foster Families

A foster family takes care of children on a temporary basis. Foster children may be waiting for an adoption to take place. They may need a place to live while family problems are solved.

Foster parents are usually licensed by the state. They are screened by social workers and often provided with some training. They receive a small amount of money from the state to help pay the child's expenses.

Foster parenting is rewarding for many people. It can be trying, however, if a child has difficult problems. Becoming attached to children who will eventually leave is a special concern for foster families. They learn to accept the idea that the arrangement is temporary. They must give love but be willing to let go when the time comes.

MANY VARIATIONS

Many families have two or more relatives living with them in a multigenerational household. As you can see, families are as varied as the people in them. What truly counts in any family is what goes on inside. Within the family, people gain skills, strength, and knowledge that enable them to cope in society and build new families to carry on.

Career Success Stories

Hector Dias: *Adoption Coordinator*

"When placing children in permanent homes and foster care, I work with the children, the birth parents, families who adopt, and foster parents. The children, however, are my *first* priority. Finding the right 'fit' for everybody is seldom easy. Counseling and follow-up services help smooth the transition for both child and family.

"Finding new homes for babies is part of my job, but I spend much more time locating homes for older children. Sometimes I'm surprised by what happens. Jess is an example of that. At age ten, he had been in several foster homes. One family planned to adopt him, but the mother got sick, so it didn't work out. That was really hard on Jess. Many times I wished I could just take him home with me.

"Then one day after running a road race, I bumped into another runner coming through the finish line. We talked and ended up having lunch together. When she found out what I do for a living, she became really interested. To make a long story short, it was her family that finally adopted Jess. He was real insecure for a while and showed it, but now they're all doing well. I'm real happy for Jess and kind of glad that I'm a runner, too."

CAREER PROFILE

Education and training: master's degree preferred

Starting salary: about $25,000

Job prospects: government and private social service agencies; community and religious organizations; hospitals

Important qualities: emotionally mature; sensitive to people and their problems; able to work independently; good communication skills

Plan Ahead

Careers that provide help to people are called human services careers. Check resources to find others beside adoption counselors. What skills are needed in these careers? Through what classes and activities could these skills be learned?

A foster family is a temporary way to provide care for children. The love given is *not* temporary—it is the reason behind foster care.

Check Your Understanding

1. How do families shown in movies and television differ from real families?
2. Identify two freedoms often enjoyed by single people.
3. What advantages do couples sometimes have over other family types?
4. What is an extended family?
5. Explain the difference between adoptive families and foster families.
6. **Thinking Critically.** Compare nuclear and blended families. How are they similar and different?
7. **Problem Solving.** Greg's grandfather is coming to live with them. Greg has been told he must give up his room to his grandfather and share his brother's room. He and his brother don't get along very well, so Greg doesn't want to move in with him. What should Greg do?

Family Personality

OBJECTIVES

After studying this section, you should be able to:

- Describe characteristics that contribute to a family's personality.
- Summarize ways that families make decisions.
- Discuss the role of interdependence, dependence, and independence in healthy families.

TERMS TO LEARN

autocratic style
democratic style
interdependence
dependent
goal

What have you noticed about different families? Do you feel more comfortable with some than with others? As Emily said, "For a long time I felt uncomfortable when visiting at my friend Kate's home. The people in her family were always hugging each other, but at my home no one does that very often." You may be surprised to discover how differently families operate.

WHAT IS FAMILY PERSONALITY?

Just as you have a personality, a family does, too. All the characteristics that combine to make a family unique give the family a personality. The atmosphere in the home, the way the family makes decisions, how members relate to each other,

and the family's values and goals are all part of its personality.

Different Family Atmospheres

After spending some time in a family's home, you become aware of the atmosphere. Because people are all so different, family atmospheres are, too. The pace may be relaxed and organized, casual and friendly, or formal and distant.

The Bartolo family is loud. They laugh as easily as they cry. Displays of affection are common. Family members like to tease, and each has learned to give as well as take in this kind of exchange. Everyone is quick to reveal emotions. Arguments are frequent, but short. When they are over, they are forgotten.

The atmosphere in a home can be seen as well as heard. What clues in this setting tell you something about the atmosphere?

The Williams family is quiet. They share conversation, but joking is not their style. Although they care about each other, they don't openly show much affection. Family members are more likely to display how they feel by doing things for each other without mention. Arguments, if they take place at all, are in the form of discussions. Family members are uncomfortable with anything that sounds angry, so they settle disagreements gently.

Your family may not be like either the Bartolo or Williams family. Yours may be a combination or something different altogether, depending on the characteristics of those in your family. As long as people feel loved and secure, the atmosphere doesn't matter. In healthy families, the atmosphere allows people to make the best of themselves and each other.

Family Decision Making

A family's personality is linked to how they make decisions. Not all families decide in the same way. The way people make decisions reflects, in part, how they relate to each other.

One Person Decides

In some families one person makes most of the decisions for the family. Decisions about spending money, routines within the household, and activities are controlled mostly by one individual. Some minor decisions may be handled by others, but the responsibility for major decisions is in one person's hands. This is the **autocratic style** of decision making.

Rachel Simon's family, for example, uses the autocratic style. Her father makes most of the major decisions for the family. Rachel's mother doesn't care for this kind of responsibility. If Mrs. Simon preferred to be involved in more of the decisions, she and her husband would have to talk about how to manage in a different way.

Shared Decision Making

Another method of making decisions is common in families. With the **democratic style**, decision making is shared. Decisions are made by more than one person. Abilities are taken into consideration when deciding who will take care of what.

Leon's family operates with the democratic style. Because his mother is a good money manager, she pays the bills each month. Both of his parents participate in major decisions, such as purchasing a car and making their budget. When a vacation is planned, everyone helps decide what to do. They also work together to set up a schedule of household duties to share. As you can see, Leon's family takes advantage of personal strengths and interests when deciding what each person will contribute.

In a family that operates democratically, the opinions and feelings of children are included and valued. That doesn't mean that children will necessarily get a vote in all matters. Parents are responsible for using adult judgment. Their experience and knowledge contribute to good decision making, which is in the best interest of the whole family.

INTERDEPENDENCE IN THE FAMILY

Families want members to become close. Knowing you can rely on each other feels good. Called **interdependence**, this feeling of mutual reliance is healthy. Family members spend time together, sharing feelings and activities. They feel secure.

Two votes for the beach! Families that operate democratically might decide on vacations as a group. Does each person have an equal vote on every decision?

In families that function well, interdependence is valued. Family members are close, but each member is still open to the outside world. In healthy families, members are encouraged to make decisions for themselves and to explore relationships with others. The family provides a link to many opportunities and experiences.

Finding a Balance

In healthy families people rely on each other, but too much or too little reliance can be a problem. A good balance between independence and dependence is the goal.

Dependent people rely too heavily on others. With little trust in themselves, they want decisions made for them, and they avoid taking action on their own. Too much dependence is confining. When family members are overly dependent, they do everything together. Their needs blend, making them less aware of their own individuality. They may shy away from the outside world, which increases their dependence on each other. In situations like these, children don't easily learn to take care of themselves.

In a family with very independent members, maintaining family bonds can be a problem. If family members follow their own path all the time, closeness can't develop. These families miss out on the joys and pleasures of a satisfying family life.

Families that function well blend the best of dependence and independence. All members learn to stand by each other while developing an ability to participate in the outside world.

FAMILY GOALS

All families, as well as individuals, have hopes and dreams. Many of these become goals that influence what goes on in the family. A **goal** is something you plan to be, do, or have, and you are willing to work for it. The goals that drive your family are probably different from those of other families.

Jackson's family would like to move to another part of the country. They want to live closer to his grandfather, who is ill and needs their support. They are making plans that will take them in this direction.

Elizabeth's family would like to buy a house of their own someday. For this they are willing to make sacrifices along the way. Goals affect what goes on in each of these families.

A person can be shy without being dependent. Do you think a person can be dependent and not be shy?

Building Character

Trustworthiness: A Quality That Counts

"I trust you. I really do." What do these words mean? When you trust, you believe that you won't be rejected, betrayed, or hurt by someone. The person who earns your trust is considered trustworthy. You can count on him or her to act with your best interests in mind. Without trustworthy members, a family can't be interdependent. Families become stronger through trust. A teen could show trustworthiness by:

- Following the rules at home even when alone.
- Being honest with parents about where the teen is going to be and with whom.
- Obeying traffic rules and speed limits when driving.
- Not revealing confidential information told by a friend.
- Completing school assignments and jobs at work as expected.

QUESTIONS

1. In each of the examples above, what might happen if the teen is not trustworthy?
2. Describe an experience of broken trust that you've had. How did it make you feel?
3. In what specific ways could you demonstrate trustworthiness in your family?

Goals are based on the unique values and needs of every family. Families make value decisions every day. Many are casual and aren't particularly harmful or helpful. For example, a family can choose an afternoon of picnicking, shopping, reading, or working a puzzle. Different families make different choices. These decisions aren't critical.

Other kinds of goals, however, have greater impact. Will the family save money for a trip or save for a child's education? Will they spend free time on community work or an extra job? As you can see, goals can be set on many levels, from simple to complex. In other words, some have a much greater impact on the family than others do.

A COMBINATION OF QUALITIES

A family is like a puzzle with hundreds of pieces. So many different factors come together to make the whole. Each person brings a special personality to the group. The combination creates a unique result. Family personalities are as interesting as they are complex.

Families set goals for themselves. They may be as simple as spending more time together or as complicated as learning to live on less income.

Check Your Understanding

1. What makes an atmosphere healthy in a family?
2. How does interdependence help families?
3. Elena is a thirty-year-old who has always lived with her parents. She relies on them for almost everything. What word in the text describes her and why?
4. How do goals affect families?
5. **Thinking Critically.** What might happen if one parent prefers a democratic approach and the other an autocratic one in a family? How could such situations be resolved?
6. **Problem Solving.** Patrick's father was a member of the Air Force, and he expects Patrick to enlist after high school graduation. Patrick has no interest in the military and wants to become an apprentice electrician. Because his father is autocratic, Patrick is afraid he's headed for the Air Force. What should Patrick do?

Stages of Family Development

OBJECTIVES

After studying this section, you should be able to:

- Describe the stages of family development common to many families.
- Identify the concerns and challenges of each stage of development.
- Identify exceptions to the typical pattern of family development.

TERMS TO LEARN

launching
empty nest

Social scientists describe a basic pattern of family development that follows predictable stages as a family moves from life as a couple, through parenting, and into the later years. This pattern is often called the family life cycle. Not everyone labels each stage within the cycle the same way, but the basic pattern is the same. Because the cycle is a general one, however, many exceptions exist.

STARTING AS A COUPLE

The first stage of family development begins with a couple. Having grown up in different settings, two young people adjust to their early years together. They are moving into uncharted territory with each other. Because these years can set the stage for life, young couples need to walk carefully.

Many couples find that having some time to themselves—without children—is helpful. They can get to know each other better before another person shares life with them.

As a couple, two people learn to think and act as a team. Daily routines involve two people, not just one. They learn to rely on each other and yet maintain their individuality. As they make plans, their ability to work together and communicate is tested. Allowing some time to build a solid foundation for life is a good idea.

A young couple is in the beginning stage of the family life cycle. They have many decisions to make. What decisions will affect the direction their life takes?

Adjusting to their own relationship is only part of the picture. A young couple must work out relationships with others, too. Each has an extended family. Learning how to get along with them and include them may take some effort. The same is true of friends. Would you, as a young wife or husband, share former friends or make new ones? How might you involve friends in your life?

Making Decisions Together

Many decisions face a couple in the beginning stage of the family life cycle. Decisions that were made alone before must now involve another person. Couples have to consider:

- **Housing.** Where to live is one of the first issues. How close should they live to other family members? Living too close may increase dependency. Living too far away may be uncomfortable. Because people are very mobile today, decisions on where to live may come up often.
- **Furnishings.** Part of getting established means gathering all the furnishings and equipment needed in a household. Doing so can be expensive, especially when you have very little to start with. Mitsu and Hiro used items donated by family members. They also found bargains at garage sales and discount stores to help them get started.
- **Education and careers.** Career plans are often a major concern at this stage. Careers have a direct impact on finances. Any decision made about education and careers will affect the family for many years. For example, while her husband was in college, Marta worked in a clerical job to support them. After Dave graduated, they had their first child. Marta stayed home to raise the family. A divorce nine years later left Marta with no education or training to support herself

and her children. Marta went into marriage thinking she would be taken care of for life. In the real world, that seldom happens.

- **Money.** Deciding how to manage the finances is an ongoing question first addressed in the beginning stage. Often two incomes are involved. Decisions that couples make include these: Will they have separate checking and savings accounts or have them in both names? If separate, who will be the manager? Who will pay the bills? What purchases will they make? As you can imagine, money can be a source of problems if decisions are not made carefully, with the wishes of both people considered.
- **Children.** A decision about having children shouldn't be made lightly. Discussions before marriage are worthwhile. When a couple decides to have children, they are ready to move out of the first stage of family development. Some couples remain childless, either by choice or circumstance.

THE PARENTAL STAGE

A society needs children in order to survive. Families that follow the typical stages of development fulfill this need. When children enter the picture, the couple moves into the parental stage.

During the parental stage, families raise children to be productive, independent adults. The parental stage lasts until children are financially on their own. This stage is a long one in the life of a family and has three parts: the expanding years, the developing years, and launching years.

The Expanding Family

During the first part of the parental stage, sometimes called the expanding years, new members are added to the family. While children are small, most families are very focused on home and family life. Young children require a great deal of time and attention from parents. Parents may feel tied down at times. The number of activities that the couple can share alone together usually drops drastically.

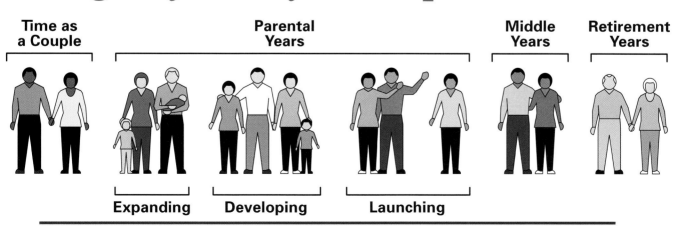

Stages of Family Development

Time as a Couple

Parental Years

Middle Years

Retirement Years

Expanding   Developing   Launching

As Cassie put it, "Jason and I used to enjoy all kinds of activities together. Our children, who are two and four, have brought such joy into our lives, but our lifestyle sure has changed. Now we go to the park, rent videos, and ride our bikes around the neighborhood with the children in bike seats. We love doing things as a family, but sometimes we have to try hard to find a few moments just for us."

Children place a heavy financial obligation on a family. Everything from basic food and clothing needs to medical, education, and entertainment expenses must be met. If child care is needed, one more expense is added to the budget.

The Developing Family

As children grow older, the parental stage moves into the developmental years. Children enter school, and more activities focus outside the home. As children move into their teens, this period becomes very different from the earlier years. Teens are gradually getting ready to leave the family, learning the skills they will eventually need to be independent.

While raising children, the family pace is often busy. The time needed to get everything done is limited. People need to share duties and manage well to prevent pressures from building. Sometimes they also have to realize that not getting every job done—and done perfectly—is okay.

Launching

The end of the parental stage is marked by the exit of children from the family home. Called **launching**, this process sends children out on their own.

In some families the parental stage lengthens when adult children return home. Often the reasons are economic. The adult child may be saving money to buy a house or paying off a college loan, for example. In the Ortega family, Raul returned home at age twenty-three when he decided to enroll in a community college. Over half of young adults age twenty to twenty-four live with their parents.

A family can be in more than one stage of the family life cycle at the same time. Could that be true of this family?

Reaching Out. The people in your extended family are in different stages of family development. Each person could be having problems and adjustments that are typical with the stage. What could you do to make life a little better for them? You could start with these ideas:

- Read and write letters for an elderly relative who would like to keep in touch with others.
- Spend some time with young children to relieve a harried parent in your family.
- Call and boost the spirits of a relative who lives alone.
- Send an e-mail message to a family member who is away at college or in the military.
- Help a younger brother or sister with homework to improve a grade as well as an attitude.

Try It Out. What strengths and skills can you offer to support family members as they manage at each stage? Choose one family member and make a plan of specific ways to reach out to that person at least once a month. Carry out your plan.

THE MIDDLE YEARS

When the children have grown up and left home, the family becomes a couple again. A new stage, the middle years, is entered. As the population ages, many people are finding added years during the middle years of life.

The feelings of the middle years can be positive as well as negative. The **empty nest** (the home with children grown and gone) leaves some parents feeling lost and without purpose. Other people love the new-found freedom after years of focusing on others. If the nest fills again with children who return home, adjustments may be needed.

This stage can be a time of questioning. Careers that have already peaked may feel less challenging. Most people work through these feelings by finding new goals and new purposes in life. If time is available, volunteer work is meaningful. Simply having time to enjoy hobbies can be a pleasure that was missed for many years. The couple may question their own relationship if it has been neglected. They can work to renew the companionship and sharing that they enjoyed when they were starting out.

Income pressures often decrease during this stage. As people hit their career peaks, their incomes are probably at an all-time high. If children are independent, they're no longer an expense. Therefore, couples may have more money to spend as they wish and save for retirement.

The middle years may find people caring for aging parents. Since women have traditionally been caregivers, this responsibility often falls upon their shoulders. If they're still raising children, balancing all the family responsibilities may be quite difficult.

THE RETIREMENT YEARS

The final stage of family development is the retirement stage. Not everyone views retirement in the same way. Some people eagerly look forward to time for travel, hobbies, or just relaxation. If they have planned for retirement and are financially secure, positive feelings are more likely.

Other people fear retirement. They may wonder what they will do with themselves. These are usually the people who have not developed interests outside their jobs. The end of a career means the end of everything.

The retirement years can be good ones. People who have led a full life are usually prepared for their later years. They adjust to aging and slowing down and discover simple pleasures that they never noticed before. They reflect on the past and are willing to share the wisdom that life has given them.

OTHER PATTERNS

Of course, not every family fits neatly into the stages of family development just described. Just think of all the reasons why people follow different patterns. Divorce is one. Remaining childless is another. Becoming a couple at an older age and raising a grandchild are two more.

The stages of family development may be different lengths in families. For example, one family may have two children, raise them to the teen years, and then have another child. Obviously, the parental stage for this family is especially long. The stages may even overlap in certain ways. A retired couple might take in a foster child. Many possibilities for variation exist.

Despite the many exceptions, the basic pattern continues in society. Children grow up in families and then raise families of their own. This is the way it has been and probably will be in the future.

"Slowing down" isn't everyone's idea of retirement. Do you know any grandparents who live a lively pace and have a spirited outlook?

Focus On ...

Grandparenting

Becoming a grandparent is a special pleasure for many people in the middle years and later. They enjoy their grandchildren in ways that they couldn't with their own children.

Sometimes people take care of grandchildren on a regular basis. Two common reasons for taking on this responsibility are family problems and parents who are employed full time. Many grandparents today are providing a safety net for children who might otherwise have difficult times.

USING YOUR KNOWLEDGE

Lena needed to go back to work after her son was born. Her mother Betty, recently retired, had no everyday commitments. When Lena brought up the idea that her mother might take care of the baby during the day, Betty looked troubled. What do you think was going through Betty's mind? Why?

SECTION 3-3 REVIEW

Check Your Understanding

1. Explain this statement from the text: "As a couple, two people learn to think and act as a team."
2. How does the family focus change from the expanding years to the developmental years? What causes this change?
3. What does launching mean as it relates to family development?
4. What does the term "empty nest" mean?
5. Why do income pressures often decrease in the middle years stage?
6. What are some ways people can prepare for an enjoyable retirement?
7. **Thinking Critically.** Why might adjustments be needed in a family when a young adult moves back into the family home after launching?
8. **Problem Solving.** Gretchen is a young single mother who lives at home while finishing high school and working part time. She will be full time after graduation. Her parents are encouraging her to move out and she wants to live on her own with the baby, but she doesn't know how she'd manage financially. She hopes to take one evening college class per semester. What should Gretchen do?

Chapter 3
Review and Activities

CHAPTER SUMMARY

- Real families differ from each other and from those shown in the media.
- Families take many different forms, each with special concerns and benefits.
- A family's personality is made of many characteristics that make each family unique.
- Decision making varies from family to family, with one person making decisions in some families and shared decision making in others.
- Interdependence is a quality of healthy families. Too much dependence or independence can lead to problems.
- Family goals are individual and distinct, reflecting the family's values and personality.
- Families go through predictable stages of development, each bringing characteristic changes and challenges.
- A family pattern of development depicts routine stages that families go through.

REVIEW QUESTIONS

Section 3-1
1. Why are the images that people have of families not necessarily realistic?
2. How can comparing your family to families shown in the media cause problems? What is a more realistic approach?
3. What are some benefits and drawbacks of each family structure?

Section 3-2
1. What makes up family personality?
2. Distinguish between the ways different families make decisions.
3. Why is too much dependence or independence a problem in some families?

Section 3-3
1. What are the major stages of family development?
2. Identify the basic decisions young couples must make as they begin life together.
3. In what ways are the middle years a time of questioning for a couple?

BECOMING A PROBLEM SOLVER

1. Sixteen-year-old Brittany lives with her mother and her ten-year-old brother. Brittany's mother, who is a single parent, works in the accounting department of a hospital and constantly seems tired. Brittany is expected to supervise her brother after school and help out at home. She is concerned about her mother and discouraged by all her responsibilities. What should she do?

2. Sarah has always admired the lively, fun-loving atmosphere in her friend Amanda's home. They play games, ride bikes, rent videos, and generally have a good time together. Her own family is much more serious. Sarah wants her family members to be more relaxed and enjoy each other more. What could she do?

THINKING CRITICALLY

1. **Drawing Conclusions.** What advantages and disadvantages can you identify for children in single-parent families? How might single-parent families deal with the disadvantages you have identified?
2. **Assessing Outcomes.** What do you think adult life might be like for a person who never learns to be independent?
3. **Predicting Results.** Which stage of family life do you think would be the most difficult for people? Why? Explain which one you think would be the easiest.

MAKING CURRICULUM CONNECTIONS

1. **Social Studies.** Compare various family structures to the structures of a community organization, a city government, a state legislature, a U.S. Senator's staff, and the U.S. Supreme Court. How are family structures similar to those of the government? What does this say about the role of families in our society?
2. **Language Arts.** Think of an exception to the stages of family development that might occur for a person. Write an explanation of how that person's stages of development are different from the expected pattern.

APPLYING YOUR KNOWLEDGE

1. Write a one page description of the family personality you would like if you have a family in the future. Consider atmosphere, decision making, values, and goals.
2. As a class, make a list of popular television shows that portray family life. For each, identify the main family pattern and the stage of development the family is in. Do you find a wide variety of families and stages on television? If not, which are most popular? Why do you think this occurs?

Family & Community Connections

1. Write a short essay about the goals you feel are important to your family. How can you help your family to achieve these goals?

2. Investigate your community to learn about programs that are available to families in various stages of family development. What activities are available for those in each stage? Who sponsors them? Is there a fee? Which of these activities might appeal to you as you create a family?

Chapter 4

Families in a Changing World

WORDS FOR THOUGHT

"A single arrow is easily broken, but not ten in a bundle."

IN YOUR OWN WORDS

How do you think this quotation relates to families?

Society's Trends Affect Families

OBJECTIVES

After studying this section, you should be able to:

- Identify trends in society that affect families.
- Explain the effects of trends on families.

TERMS TO LEARN

trend
service industries

Families today live amidst rapid change, and the pace just gets steadily faster. When looking at changes in society, people identify trends. A **trend** is noted when a detectable change takes place over time. Trends tell you what might happen to you and your family in the future. Since you have ideas about what to expect, you can be better prepared for what's ahead.

CHANGES IN SOCIETY

Society has changed considerably over the years. Many changes directly impact families.

The Aging Population

Due to medical advancements and better nutrition, people are living longer than they used to. "Baby boomers," born during an increase in birth rates after World War II, are adding to the aging population as they reach their older years.

As they grow in number, the aging segment of society gains a stronger voice in politics and the media. Their concerns need to be addressed. What happens to them has strong impact on you and your family. Can families provide the financial support and daily care that elderly people often need? How will society help with medical care, housing, and transportation? These questions need answers.

Lifelong Education

Another trend in today's society is the move toward lifelong education. Formal education is no longer just for the young. People of all ages attend college or get other training. Some want more education to qualify for a promotion or career change.

Returning to school can mean adjustments for families. They may need to get by on less income and share more household chores as the new student becomes busier. On the plus side, when someone in a family is stimulated by a return to school, the rest of the family shares the good feelings.

Many retired people find they have time for more education. Community colleges often have special classes and activities for older adults. What opportunities for lifelong education are available in your area?

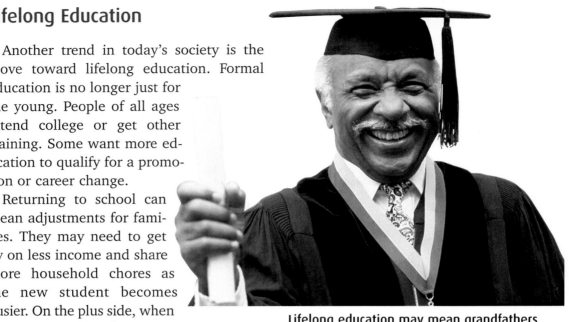

Lifelong education may mean grandfathers graduating from college with grandsons. What a wonderful example of persistence and values!

CHANGES WITHIN THE FAMILY

In addition to the broad trends in society, you can also see family trends. Some show how family patterns have changed.

Family Patterns

You already know that families come in different shapes and sizes. These variations have come about through social change, as you can see here:

- **Single people.** The number of single-person households is growing. Waiting to marry at older ages contributes to the number of singles. There is less social pressure to marry than in the past, and some people remain single.
- **Couples.** Couples make up a large segment of households today. More couples than in the past postpone having children, have fewer of them, or have none at all. Because people live longer, there are more couples who have already raised and launched their children.
- **Nuclear families.** In recent years, the nuclear family has been threatened by high divorce rates. A growing concern for families, however, points to the value of the many nuclear families in society. Children need stability for proper growth and development, and many people believe that healthy nuclear families offer the best environment for raising children.
- **Blended families.** In the 1970s, the divorce rate started to increase. Although

the rate has been going down in recent years, many divorces still take place. Since many divorced people with children remarry, a large number of blended families have resulted over the years.

- **Single-parent families.** Divorce and the rise in births to women who are not married account for growth in the number of single-parent families. Although most single parents are women, about fifteen percent are men. The struggles that many single parents face in raising children alone reinforce the need for strong nuclear families.
- **Extended families.** Many extended families are living together today. Adult children, alone or with their own children, often move in with parents. Older relatives may move in with younger ones to provide child care or because they need care themselves.

Financial Challenges

Many families today struggle financially to make ends meet. Many are not able to buy homes of their own. The soaring cost of college means that families may not be able to send their children to college. To receive education or training, many students must rely on financial aid, student loans, and work income rather than family help.

Focus On ...

Yesterday's Families

What would life in pioneer days have been like? Living on a farm came with much hard, physical labor. People did much for themselves: raising and preparing food, building homes, and making and caring for clothes. Families were usually large, and everyone pitched in to get the work done.

From studying history, you know that many families moved to urban areas during the 1800s. Farming declined as industry flourished. Life in urban areas was not easy either. In many families, every member, even small children, had jobs to support the family.

Although the lifestyles of yesterday's and today's families were different, there were certain similarities. Families have always worked to provide for their members. Their basic needs haven't changed much. The primary difference is in what people and society do to meet those needs.

USING YOUR KNOWLEDGE

Emma and Jake were teens in the late 1700s. What would you say to describe to them how life has changed for families since their lifetime? Try writing one of them a letter.

In general, females have had a particularly difficult time earning an equitable wage in the workforce over the years. Although their earnings have increased overall, progress is still needed. Many women who make a living wage now do so because they have received the education and training they need to get a good job. Stacy was one of the lucky ones. As she said, "I got into a special program for women in the construction trades. I work for a company that builds malls, and now I earn enough to provide a good life for my children." Unfortunately, many women are not in this category.

Women who are single parents are particularly at economic risk. Often they receive little or no financial support from the fathers of their children. Many have no job or earn low pay. If they've prepared themselves to be independent wage earners, however, they may be able to support their children alone.

An increasing number of households now have two or more wage earners. Many families need two incomes to survive today, and some count on extra income from teens and extended family members in the home.

Child Care

Watch for trends in the area of child care. Controversy exists over how well children do when both parents are employed. Even though child care programs are improving, some parents want creative ways to be home with young children in particular.

CHANGES IN THE WORKPLACE

Changes in society and the family affect the workplace, and vice versa. Rapid change can be seen in the workplace, often spurred by technology.

New Jobs and Environments

Far fewer workers are needed for industrial jobs today. Computers and robots do tasks that people once did. Computers have also increased the ability to process and distribute information. Technological skills are

Financial costs of having, providing for, and educating children may lead to more "only" children in families. Do you know families who decided to have only one child? What part do you think costs played in the decision?

Career Success Stories

Rita Eberley: *Employment Counselor*

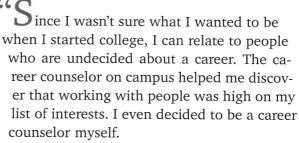

"Since I wasn't sure what I wanted to be when I started college, I can relate to people who are undecided about a career. The career counselor on campus helped me discover that working with people was high on my list of interests. I even decided to be a career counselor myself.

"People want employment counseling for lots of reasons. Like me, some of them don't know how to choose a career path. Some aren't happy with their current career and want to make a change. I sometimes help people see that their current job is actually where they want to stay.

"I don't always get to see the long-range results of my work, but one recent experience made me feel really good. John is a middle-aged man who came to me two years ago after being laid off from a manufacturing job. His self-esteem had hit rock bottom, and his whole family was hurting. We worked together for several weeks, getting John some computer training so he could get back on track. I just ran into him the other day. John loves his new job and is doing great. Now he actually sees the job loss as something positive in his life—and he said that I had been too. You can bet that made my day."

CAREER PROFILE

Education and training: master's degree preferred

Starting salary range: $18-25,000

Job prospects: colleges and universities; job training, career development, and vocational rehabilitation centers; and counseling and social service agencies

Important qualities: strong interest in helping others; good interpersonal skills; communication skills

Plan Ahead

Employment counselors look at personal traits, interests, skills, and work history. With a classmate, have a career planning session, with each of you taking turns as the employment counselor. What careers would you suggest for each other? How can you prepare for these careers?

Many people now work from home computers. What effects do you think home work will have on the family over the next few years?

essential for these jobs. Tasks that were once done with a file of index cards now use computerized databases. How else have computers changed the job market?

Another change is the shorter time people spend in a particular job. Typical Americans have had eight jobs by the time they are thirty-two years old. You may have already held more jobs than your grandparents did in their lifetime!

You may hold jobs in the future that don't even exist today. Many people need retraining when jobs are changed or eliminated. Others need new skills to reenter the workplace. When Trudy needed a job after the plant where she worked closed, she studied computerized records administration at a community college. Her new career is totally different from before.

Service Industries

Over three-fourths of Americans who are employed now work in **service industries**. These careers provide assistance to others for a fee. In general, service industry jobs tend to pay low wages.

Many services have resulted from changes in society. Catalog shopping, house cleaning, food catering, and home maintenance are all service areas that have expanded in recent years. Creative people continually think of new services to fit people's needs.

A Global Workplace

The workplace has become global rather than local. Products and services are developed in one country and sold in another. People and companies from other countries may own businesses in your area. Decisions about work and employment in your community may actually be made on the other side of the world.

As the world becomes even "smaller," through improved communication and transportation technology, links with other countries will continue to increase. Families are likely to live and work with people of all ethnic backgrounds. Learning to understand and get along will be increasingly important.

Building Character

Adaptability: A Quality That Counts

It's been one of those days. Nothing goes as planned. Do you let it get you down, or do you adapt? An adaptable person makes the best of a situation. When you alter your habits or priorities to fit changes, you have adaptability. A teen could show adaptability by:

- Calling a friend for a ride when the family car isn't available.
- Doing the family laundry when a parent starts taking college classes in the evening.
- Learning helpful Spanish phrases when a family from Mexico City moves next door.
- Changing weekend plans to be home when relatives visit.
- Opening a can of soup for lunch after the leftover pizza is gone.

QUESTIONS

1. What are two advantages to being adaptable?
2. What personality traits make it easier to adapt to new situations?
3. Are there times when a person is better off not adapting? Explain your answer.

SECTION 4-1 REVIEW

Check Your Understanding

1. What is a trend? How can information about trends be used?
2. Why is the population aging?
3. What has happened to many of the people who formerly worked in manufacturing industries?
4. In what way is the world becoming smaller?
5. **Thinking Critically.** Do you think change is stimulating or frustrating for people? Why?
6. **Problem Solving.** Ginny is thinking about quitting her dispatch job because she's worried about learning to use the new computer the company has installed. She loves doing dispatch and has heard that all dispatch jobs are now being run with computerized systems. Ginny could find other work, but wouldn't be able to earn as much money. What should Ginny do?

Living in a Diverse World

OBJECTIVES

After studying this section, you should be able to:

- Demonstrate an awareness of and respect for cultural diversity.
- Define culture and give examples of cultural qualities, similarities, and differences.
- Describe and tell how to avoid the dangers of ethnocentrism.

TERMS TO LEARN

diversity
culture
enculturation
subculture
culture shock
assimilation
cultural heritage
ethnocentrism

When you sit down to eat a meal, do you sit on the floor? A chair? A mat? What utensils do you use? A fork? Chopsticks? Your fingers? Some of these options may seem unusual and others familiar. Each, however, is common in some part of the world. This shows that you live in a world of **diversity**, where people are all different in one way or another.

Wherever people live, they need to learn what is customary. Getting along in any community and in life depends on knowing the conventions of that particular society.

WHAT IS CULTURE?

Everything about a specific group of people, including their common traits and customs, is called **culture**. Culture can be seen in what people believe as well as how they act. Economic conditions, as well as knowledge, art, and technology, affect what a culture is like. As members of a society, people develop a culture that is shared by the group.

If you had the opportunity to travel around the world, you would see many diverse cultures. What qualities make each culture unique? Language could be one. Attitudes, customs, and daily routines might also be different. Styles of dress could be another. Jillian's grandmother lives in Afghanistan. When her grandmother goes out in public, she wears a chador (CHUH-dur). This traditional Muslim garment is a long loose robe that covers the body.

Cultures are complex. When social scientists talk about cultures, they describe the qualities that make up the whole culture. These are called cultural traits. A common gesture, such as a handshake, is one trait. A custom, such as a ritual followed when someone dies, is another.

Traits combine to make a cultural pattern. For example, all the customs that are followed when a couple marries make up a pattern that is character-istic of their culture. If you've ever attended a wedding of people from another culture, you've observed how cultural patterns can differ.

Cultural Similarities

When describing cultures, it's easy to focus on the obvious differences. Actually there are many similarities. Regardless of where they live or how they live, people all around the world have the same basic needs.

First of all, people need a place to live and food to eat. In any culture, these are priorities. People need ways to protect themselves. They establish and practice religion in some form. Through artistic methods, they express themselves. Can you think of any other similar needs that different cultures have?

Living in society means that some system of order must be developed. People need methods for settling differences. Power and responsibility must also be assigned. Leadership comes in many forms, a president, prime minister, queen, or king, for example. Decisions are also made about who will make the laws and how they will do so.

Families teach culture to younger generations. How could you learn more about the different cultures of people in your community?

People may look different, but they all experience the same basic emotions. How else are they similar?

Wherever you go around the world, you will find another similarity. Each society has a family system of some type. Although the people may live together in different patterns and styles, families are the foundation of each society. Families around the world fulfill the same functions, though in various ways. In addition, they are important to each society because they help preserve the culture as well as make the society strong.

Cultural Differences

Differences make cultures interesting. Differences can be seen in how people meet basic needs. People are not necessarily able to choose the methods they use. Many come about simply because of necessity. For example, people who live in tropical climates wear lighter-weight clothing and less of it than those who live in cold climates. Fibers that are readily available are used to make clothes.

What people eat is also determined by what is available. If rice grows well in a wet climate, then rice is likely to become a staple in the diet of people who live where it rains heavily. In another climate rice may not grow well, but wheat and corn do. These, then, become the basis for foods and eating habits in another culture.

Cultural differences have come about naturally. When people live together in one society but separate from other societies, they develop their own individual ways of doing things. The patterns and beliefs become ingrained and carry on through the society's history.

Tips & TECHNIQUES

Respecting Other Cultures. People sometimes lack respect for what they don't understand, including unfamiliar cultures. Respect for cultures can be learned and shown in many ways. You could try these to build your own sensitivity:

- Make friends with someone from another ethnic background. Friendship is one of the quickest ways to understanding.
- Give a child in your family a toy or book that represents another culture. Help the child learn more about the culture represented by your gift.
- Watch what you say. Your positive language about other cultures will show the respect you feel.
- Check out a foreign foods cookbook from the library and find an unfamiliar ethnic dish to prepare for your family.
- Read the television listings to find programs that teach about other cultures. Watch one of them.
- If there are ethnic neighborhoods in your community, visit a store that features ethnic groceries and choose an unfamiliar food to prepare. Ask a clerk for help.

Try It Out. Invite a foreign exchange student to speak to your class about what life is like in his or her country. What is the biggest cultural difference he or she has observed?

FAMILIES TEACH CULTURE

Families are the main teachers of culture in any society. Each generation passes along what it has learned to the next as the culture carries on. This process is called **enculturation** (in-KUL-chur-A-shun).

You may have grown up hardly aware that you were learning the ways of a particular culture, but you were. Without enculturation, people would have a hard time functioning in society. They would not know what behavior is acceptable and what is not. This is the societal equal to the socialization that occurs in the family.

You can sometimes identify a cultural uniqueness visually. What visual evidence identifies this teen as coming from a Thai culture?

Your country also has many subcultures, which you may or may not be linked to. A **subculture** is a culture shared by a group of people who live within a larger, different culture. For example, Amy's parents are Chinese. She grew up in the United States and lives as an American, but she has also learned and practices many customs and traditions of the Chinese subculture.

BLENDING CULTURES

Have you ever seen a movie in which a character enters a culture never experienced before? What happened? Probably, **culture shock,** the difficulties and feelings of uneasiness that people have when they are exposed to another culture. In general, people are most comfortable with what is familiar to them. In your own culture, you know what behavior is expected and approved. You might not be so sure in another culture.

The boundaries between cultures today are not as distinct as they once were. With advanced methods of communication, travel, and doing business, people of different cultures are finding more opportunities and reasons for getting together. Often people move from one culture to live in another. As they adopt the culture of the new environment, they may put aside many of the habits, customs, and patterns they knew before. This is called **assimilation** (uh-SIM-uh-LAY-shun).

If cultural heritage isn't passed along to children, it will be forgotten. What do you know about your own heritage? Talking with older family members about your ancestors might reveal interesting information that you'll be glad to have someday.

CULTURAL PRIDE

Culture is a source of pride for many families. It's part of history. For this reason families want to preserve culture, not lose it. Many families take pride in teaching young members about the beliefs, customs, and traits that have been important to their ancestors and continue to be for them.

Called **cultural heritage**, this set of information about a group of people is often carefully preserved within families. Anna's mother taught her how to make stuffed cabbage, a traditional Hungarian food. This dish is a favorite at dinners with her extended family.

Feelings about cultural heritage are often very special. Some people carry their feelings too far, however, thinking that their own culture is the best, or the most natural. When this attitude is extreme, called **ethnocentrism** (eth-no-SEN-triz-um), it is dangerous because it can lead to acts of hatred and violence. Nothing excuses such behavior. As you have just read, different cultures developed because of circumstances and environments. Each one came about naturally in its time and place.

Every family's heritage, regardless of what it is, can be valued. Cultural heritage is a source of pride but never a reason to look down on others. You can feel good about your own heritage while appreciating the heritage of others at the same time. Families are responsible for teaching their own culture to their young, but they must also teach respect for other cultures as well. When people of different cultural backgrounds live side by side, the society cannot be strong without understanding and respect for each other.

SECTION 4-2 REVIEW

Check Your Understanding

1. What is diversity?
2. What qualities make cultures unique?
3. In what ways are cultures different from each other?
4. How are cultures taught in society?
5. What attitude should people have toward their own and other cultures?
6. **Thinking Critically.** Relate the meaning and order of the following terms to the discussion in the text: different; unfamiliar; fear; dislike; hate; violence.
7. **Problem Solving.** When a family from Korea moved into her neighborhood, Madison was interested. While spending time with them, she enjoyed the conversation and learning about their customs. She couldn't believe her ears one day when a friend said, "So, you're hanging out with foreigners these days. You must be pretty hard up for friends." How do you think Madison might respond?

Chapter 4
Review and Activities

CHAPTER SUMMARY

- Many trends affect family life.
- The population is aging. This brings new concerns and adjustments for families.
- Lifelong education is a trend today.
- The numbers of single-person households, couples, blended families, and single-parent families are growing.
- The number of dual-income families continues to increase.
- The workplace has become global, leading to a need for better understanding among people of different nationalities.
- In societies people often develop a shared culture.
- Circumstances make cultures different, but no one culture is better than another.
- Families pass along culture to each generation through enculturation.
- Ethnocentrism is a natural feeling, but can be dangerous if taken to extremes.

REVIEW QUESTIONS

Section 4-1
1. What are four trends that affect families?
2. What needs and concerns have arisen from the aging of the population?
3. Why has lifelong education become a trend?
4. Choose three family patterns and describe the trend associated with each one.
5. In general, how do women fare in the workplace? How can they improve their status?
6. What is a disadvantage of the trend toward more service industries?

Section 4-2
1. What is culture?
2. Why are people who live in a subculture typically familiar with another culture?
3. Are various cultures around the world more alike or different? Explain.
4. What causes culture shock?
5. Why is ethnocentrism dangerous? What attitude is helpful in combating it?

BECOMING A PROBLEM SOLVER

1. Rebecca will miss some school because of the Jewish holidays celebrated by her family. An important standardized math test is scheduled for one day when she will be gone. It's important to her family that she participate in their religious observance. What should Rebecca do?

2. Blake has been invited to the wedding of a friend from India. He has no idea how he should dress, what will happen at the wedding, and what he should do about a gift. What should Blake do?

THINKING CRITICALLY

1. **Recognizing Alternatives.** If you were a business person or community leader, what would you do to help older people with these problems: lack of medical care; lack of housing suitable for seniors; reduced ability to read small print and signs; inability to drive; clothing that doesn't fit the shapes of aging bodies?

2. **Predicting Consequences.** What skills will become more important as the number of service industry jobs grow?

3. **Analyzing Behavior.** Why do you think some people have trouble coping with change? What attitudes or skills can help overcome this problem?

4. **Recognizing Alternatives.** When people of different cultures live together in a community, which is more important—blending the cultures or preserving them? Why?

MAKING CURRICULUM CONNECTIONS

1. **History.** Suppose you were a textbook writer in the eighteenth or nineteenth century. Research what family life was like in a time of your choosing. Then rewrite one of these parts of Section 4-1 as it might have appeared then: Changes in Society; Changes Within the Family; Changes in the Workplace.

2. **Social Studies.** Choose one family function. Research and report on how that function is met in three cultures.

APPLYING YOUR KNOWLEDGE

1. Given the trends in today's society, what do you think families will be like in the future?

2. Survey the family types represented by students in your class. Relate the results to the information in this chapter. What conclusions can you draw?

3. With your classmates, discuss the impact of diversity on society. Do you think diversity strengthens or weakens society? Why? How will diversity change society itself? Change the family?

Family & Community Connections

1. Many young people choose technical schools in order to get training for the skilled labor force. Check your telephone directory under schools to see what opportunities exist in your area. Contact at least one program to find out what is offered.

2. Using newspapers, the Internet, or other media, find examples that show how your community or state is linked to cities and businesses in other countries. What are the positive and negative aspects of this trend?

UNIT 2

Strengthening Relationships

Teen Views

What helps you the most in getting along with your family?

Ashley

"A year ago, I would've said that nothing helps. My mom and I never agreed on anything. When we started talking instead of arguing, though, that made a big difference. You don't really hear what somebody else is saying when you're mad. When my mom and I decided to change, we started listening—and then talking. I just feel better inside when we handle things this way, and I think she does, too."

Ramon

"Getting along isn't a big problem in my family. When things get tense, we do a lot of joking around. Like the time I kind of lost it with my dad over something that really didn't matter at all. He stared at me for a long time with this serious look on his face, and then he just grinned and said, 'You're just like the buttons on my shirt. You pop off at the wrong time.' I'm glad he has a sense of humor."

What's your view?

What ideas do you have that could help teens get along better within the family?

Chapter 5

Roles and Relationships

WORDS FOR THOUGHT

"We must learn to live together as brothers or we will perish together as fools." *(Martin Luther King, Jr.)*

IN YOUR OWN WORDS

How can you relate these words to your own life?

The Importance of Relationships

OBJECTIVES

After studying this section, you should be able to:

- Explain why relationships are valuable in life.
- Compare the different kinds of relationships.
- Demonstrate the qualities of good relationships.
- Relate rewards and costs to success in relationships.
- Identify signs of weak relationships.

TERMS TO LEARN

relationships
mutuality
trust
self-disclosure
rapport
empathy
exploitation

Probably no part of life affects you more than your **relationships**, or connections with other people. Helping a friend can leave you in good spirits. On the other hand, arguing with a family member can leave you feeling low. When relationships have such an impact, isn't learning about them and improving them a worthwhile goal?

A NEED FOR OTHERS

A person may have many relationships or a few, but everyone needs *some* relationships. Quality counts more than quantity.

Relationships should be satisfying. A pleasant encounter with a store clerk can set the tone for the rest of your day. Pleasant encoun-ters with those who are close to you can set the stage for life.

Positive relationships serve significant functions in your life. They:

- **Meet emotional needs.** You feel loved and accepted.
- **Enrich life.** People share experiences, feelings, and ideas.
- **Help you get things done.** What you accomplish often depends on help and support from others.

KINDS OF RELATIONSHIPS

Everyone has built-in relationships: through family. Few bonds are stronger or more important than those between family members. Their value and influence can last a lifetime. Most people have relationships

Family relationships usually last a lifetime. Friendships and casual relationships may come and go.

A society full of people who are all the same seems unappealing, even boring. Fortunately, you live in a society that blends all sorts of different people—old and young, ethnically diverse, and with many points of view. Exchanges with them can enrich your life.

Although familiar things and people may make you feel comfortable, they can be limiting. Differences make people interesting. Relationships with many people can make *you* more interesting.

that extend beyond the family. They form friendships, often including people of different ages and backgrounds. Some friendships are almost as strong as family ties.

Beyond family and friends are many casual relationships. A classmate you work with on a school committee and a cafeteria server may be your *acquaintances*—people you know but aren't particularly close to.

Some relationships are *voluntary*. That is, you choose them. Others, such as those with most family members and coworkers, are *involuntary*. They are not chosen.

Diversity in Relationships

"I saw an old science fiction movie where everyone was alike. They thought the same way and even acted the same, too," Beth recalled. "Talk about strange!"

Relationships with people who are different from you provide you with a broader view of life.

Positive relationships enrich your life. What qualities build strong relationships?

RELATIONSHIP QUALITIES

Which of these two statements is true: "Relationships are satisfying and a source of growth" or "Relationships are disappointing and painful"? You might say that both statements are true—sometimes. No relationship is entirely wonderful. On the other hand, no relationship should bring only pain. To a great degree, relationships are what you make of them.

What makes a good relationship? A few of the many qualities are described here.

Mutuality

A good relationship has **mutuality** (myoo-chu-WAL-ut-ee). That is, both people contribute to the feelings and actions that support the relationship. They understand what they want from each other.

Mutuality is satisfying because the exchange between partners is balanced, even if not always equal. You might give more to the relationship one time, and receive more at another. The closer the relationship, the more willing people are to give without getting an immediate return.

Mutuality is shown and felt in many ways. For example, after a long day with her active one-year-old son, Kerry felt that she did nothing but give and give to him. Then Quentin smiled his big one-tooth grin and cuddled in her lap for a bedtime story. Kerry knew that she was receiving something priceless.

What can you learn from people who are different from you? Older people can tell you what life used to be like and provide insights about living. Children can remind you of how exciting simple discoveries are. People from other cultures have information to share. Whether food, music, clothing, or art, you can discover something new.

If you're adventurous and have an open mind, you can become a more well-rounded person by broadening your relationships. The rewards will be many. You will prepare yourself for the work world, where understanding all kinds of people is essential. You will learn to be relaxed with many different people. You will have knowledge, ideas, and experiences that help build your mind and awareness. All of this can come just from reaching out to the people around you.

Building Character

Loyalty: A Quality That Counts

Loyalty is faithfulness to a cause or person. People who are loyal don't let misunderstandings or pressure from others sway them in their beliefs or relationships. They offer support even when it doesn't seem appreciated or when things go wrong. A teen could show loyalty by:

- Walking away when a group starts to speak unkindly about a friend.
- Standing and singing the National Anthem at a school assembly.
- Making an effort to get to work when bad weather has kept many employees at home.
- Standing by a family member who is in trouble.

QUESTIONS

1. Is loyalty found only in long-standing relationships? Explain your thinking.
2. What actions might show loyalty to oneself?
3. Some good friends ask your support for a cause you don't believe in. How do you respond?
4. To whom or what do you show loyalty? How do you show it?

Trust

The belief that others will not reject, betray, or hurt you is called **trust**. Trust expects acceptance and support and is needed in all relationships, both casual and close. Cast members of a school play trust each other to attend practices and learn their lines. Friends and family members trust each other to keep personal discussions private. In what other relationships do you see trust?

Self-Disclosure

The willingness to tell someone personal things about yourself is called **self-disclosure**. Sharing with at least one other person is vital to good mental health.

The information you disclose says a lot about a relationship. People generally reveal the same type and amount of information they receive, telling more about themselves as the relationship deepens. When two people are very close, they feel free to talk about their hopes, joys, fears, and sorrows. Trust strengthens when people self-disclose and honor confidences.

For Marcy, self-disclosure helped her build a closer relationship with Heidi. At first they talked about schoolwork, their favorite television shows, and other everyday things. They began to talk about career goals and personal dreams. One day, Marcy told Heidi about something troubling that had happened to her. Because Marcy trusted Heidi, she could reveal this information.

Rapport

Good relationships develop as people build **rapport** (ra-POR), a feeling of ease and harmony with another person. As Lindsey put it, "No matter what we're doing, I'm comfortable with Ty. He's easy to be with. Whether we're talking or quiet, we understand each other. We can usually tell how the other one will react to something. Even when we disagree, there's no tension."

Empathy

When you have the ability to put yourself in another person's position, you show **empathy** (EM-puh-thee). You set aside your own ideas in order to understand the other's point of view. People who have empathy are particularly tuned in to feelings. An empathetic person knows when someone else is hurting, and wants to help.

Shared Interests

Suppose one teen likes skateboarding and biking, and another likes to read and listen to classical music. Can they form a close relationship? They might, although people who share at least some interests have a better chance. Shared interests form a strong base for building a relationship.

HOW RELATIONSHIPS WORK

Browsing through the newspaper, Howard read that an old friend had become an Eagle Scout. We used to be good friends, Howard thought. Now I never think of him. I guess we just drifted apart.

Relationships often build when people share an interest. Would two teammates become close because they both enjoy softball or because they spend so much time together?

Showing appreciation for parents helps strengthen family relationships. How could you use your time, energy, and talents—instead of money—to strengthen the relationships in your family?

If you've had a similar experience, you may wonder why some relationships endure and prosper, yet others wither and die. Experts who study relationships ask the same question: What makes relationships last? One theory suggests that relationships survive based on rewards and costs.

Rewards are what bring pleasure and satisfaction in a relationship. Some people look for material benefits that meet physical needs and wants. Others want emotional support, excitement, or love. A relationship is rewarding when people feel it meets certain needs.

Costs are the physical, mental, and emotional contributions you make to a relationship. Some costs are expected. For Kendall, being a parent costs the time and energy to fix lunch for his son every day.

Other costs are painful, even punishing. When Megan's friends didn't show up after promising to attend her cello recital, Megan was hurt. Her disappointment was a cost she paid in her friendship.

Relationships that have the qualities described in this chapter are rewarding ones. Shared interests, rapport, and trust make a relationship last. A relationship that lacks these qualities is short-lived.

Not everyone accepts the costs-and-rewards theory. Some think emotions have more impact on relationships. There is no doubt, however, that a relationship thrives when it is satisfying, and suffers when it isn't.

SIGNS OF WEAK RELATIONSHIPS

Just as strong relationships have identifiable qualities, weak ones have "danger signals." Staying alert for these signs can help you make repairs and improvements or leave relationships that are too costly.

Imbalance of Costs and Rewards

When there is a lopsided exchange of costs and rewards, a relationship suffers. You might see this more in involuntary relationships, where partners can't easily end the association.

Stan noticed this type of problem in his relationship with his boss Jay. Jay often made unreasonable demands and lost his temper if they weren't met. Stan didn't complain because he wanted to keep his job. Faced with this dilemma, what would you do?

Stan decided to change his expectations. He accepted that working with Jay would be difficult. He did what was asked and didn't take his boss's outbursts personally. He showed his coworkers that he valued their help. Stan learned to make the best of an unrewarding relationship.

Changes in Quality

When necessary qualities weaken, a relationship may not last. Taylor's friendship with her college roommate Victoria suffered when trust was lost. One day Taylor noticed some money missing from her nightstand. Later, Taylor walked into the dorm room to find Victoria reading Taylor's mail. Taylor's sense of trust in Victoria was shaken. What do you think happened?

If you think about the other qualities of good relationships, you can see that problems with any of them can signal trouble in the relationship. What might a lack of rapport or self-disclosure indicate?

Exploitation

As you've read, you need certain things from a relationship. However, a relationship can be poisoned by **exploitation**, using another person unfairly for personal benefit.

"Carla, this is the last dollar I can loan you this week." When a friend doesn't pay back debts, how do you prevent exploitation?

Getting to know many people teaches you lessons about relating to others. Why do some people you know get along well with others, yet some don't?

How can you tell if someone is taking advantage of a relationship? Exploiters tend to be self-centered. They have little trust in others. An exploiter thinks: Everyone else is out to get all they can for themselves; I'll use them before they use me. Using this idea of "fairness," they feel no guilt about failing to give equally to a relationship.

Shelly fits the description of an exploiter. She shows no regard for people's feelings. She borrows her sister's clothes without asking. She cancels plans at the last minute if something more "fun" comes up. What do you think is the cost-and-reward balance in a relationship with Shelly?

WALKING AWAY

Ending any relationship, even a troubling one, can feel like defeat. It's hard to admit you were wrong about someone. Remember, though, that you can end voluntary relationships. You don't need people in your life who use, intimidate, or hurt you in some way. Walking away from a re-

INFOLINK

Communication Skills

Section 6-2 gives tips on communicating effectively. See *Section 7-2* for more information on the role of communication in conflict resolution.

lationship that isn't in your best interest is your responsibility and your right.

Since most family and work relationships are involuntary, people usually try to maintain them. Still, exceptions exist. One teen sought counseling after being sexually abused by a relative. It took courage to take action against a destructive relationship, but emotional anguish is too high a cost for any relationship.

LEARNING TO BUILD RELATIONSHIPS

Like everyone else, teens need good relationships in their lives, but sometimes building and keeping them isn't easy. Hunter quit trying to make friends because his family moved so often. Always leaving friends behind was painful. Cal spent time at his computer instead of making friends.

That seemed easier to him. Maureen was simply frustrated by relationships that weren't enjoyable. Am I doing something wrong, she wondered?

Like these teens, you may wonder how to make quality relationships part of your life. This text gives many ideas. You will read about helpful relationship skills that you can develop: communicating well; resolving conflicts appropriately; reaching out to others; and many more. Reading other books and magazine articles can add to your understanding.

You can also benefit from the knowledge and experience of those around you. Learn from counselors and other adults. Watch people who get along well. What do they do to make their relationships work?

Above all, learn to look beyond yourself. Relationships are more likely to thrive when you focus on others and their point of view.

SECTION 5-1 REVIEW

Check Your Understanding

1. What are relationships?
2. How can knowing diverse people help you?
3. Why is mutuality essential in a good relationship?
4. How do trust and self-disclosure contribute to a relationship?
5. What is empathy? Give an example of showing empathy in a relationship.
6. Darla thinks of Shaun as her friend, but he rarely talks to her unless he needs help with an assignment or a last-minute date. How would you characterize their relationship?
7. **Thinking Critically.** What causes rewards and costs in a relationship to get out of balance?
8. **Problem Solving.** Jody thought her friend Carmen had been avoiding her all week. When Jody asked for an explanation, Carmen said, "I can't talk about it, but I need some space right now. Just be patient a while, okay?" How should Jody respond?

Examining Roles

OBJECTIVES

After studying this section, you should be able to:

- Relate roles to relationships.
- Explain how roles are learned.
- Argue against the use of stereotypes in relationships.
- Relate the concepts of role expectation and role conflict.

TERMS TO LEARN

role
given role
chosen role
role models
role expectation
stereotype
role conflict

"To see Angie in class," Lynn said of her friend, "you'd think she was quiet and shy, but when we get together with Deanne and Charla, Angie's totally different—funny and outgoing. You wouldn't think she was the same person. It just depends on where she is and who she is with."

Like Lynn, you've probably noticed that people don't act the same way in every situation. As you read on, you'll see why.

People who study societies have noted the strong effect of roles on relationships. A **role** is an expected pattern of behavior associated with a person's position in society. No one has just one role; each person has many.

LIFE'S MANY ROLES

Roles help people know how to act in different situations. Do you talk the same way to your friends as you do to your parents? Chances are, you don't, at least not all the time. If you think about it, you'll realize that you change your behavior to suit different situations—you take on different roles.

Try listing all your roles. Are you surprised at how many you have? Within a family, each person has a variety of roles. A woman, for instance, can be a wife, mother, daughter, aunt, sister, and cousin. Which people in your family have the roles of teacher, provider, caregiver, and companion? What responsibilities come with each role on your own list?

This father is often the family chef. What other responsibilities might he have in his role as a parent?

Many other roles occur outside the family. Erving is a student at school and an employee at his part-time job. In society Erving is a citizen and a consumer. He is also a friend to many different people.

Given and Chosen Roles

Roles are either given or chosen. A **given role** is one that is automatically acquired. At birth you became a son or daughter. If your parents have other children, you are a brother or sister. Your roles as student, consumer, and citizen are typically given ones.

A **chosen role** is one that is deliberately selected. People choose to marry and become husbands and wives. They may choose to become parents by having children. They become employees when they decide to take jobs. What other roles might a person choose?

LEARNING YOUR ROLES

Knowledge of roles is not inborn. Like values, roles are usually learned through examples and direct teaching. Families provide much of this information in a child's early years. Later on, other examples and influences can have an impact.

Sabrina, for example, learned about her role as a volleyball team member in several ways. First, her family taught her about teamwork and responsibility by assigning tasks at home. Playing in an after-school volleyball program, Sabrina learned more about getting along with others. She read books and articles about athletes she admired and prepared herself to be a good team member.

Role Models

Sabrina also learned her role as an athlete by watching those who had gone before her. Sabrina admired Mandy, a senior setter on the volleyball team. She watched how Mandy moved on the court and how the older girl showed good sportsmanship.

Observing others is a common way to learn a role. The people you learn behavior and attitudes from are called **role models**. They influence your thinking, giving you examples to copy.

Some celebrities are excellent role models, but many are not. What might happen when they aren't?

Children, for instance, learn what it means to be a father or mother, a husband or wife, by watching their parents. They look to older siblings for examples of "grown-up" behavior.

Role models are also found outside the family. You might learn from a coworker how to soothe an irate customer, or see how a neighbor coaxes a reluctant child into taking a bath.

You, in turn, serve as a role model for others. For example, younger students may watch how you act at a school assembly or sports event. Children in your neighborhood may follow the example you set as you show your level of concern for neighbors and property.

Not all role models are good ones. Just as positive qualities can be mirrored, so too

Tips & TECHNIQUES

Treating Family Like Company. Do you ever feel that "company behavior" is taken out and put away with the good dishes? Persuade your family to join you in an experiment:

- Identify specific qualities of "company behavior." Consider table manners, personal appearance, topics of conversation, tone of voice, and amount of criticism, among other points.
- Schedule at least an hour with your family (a meal or family night) when everyone treats each other like company.
- Carry out your "company" hour.
- Discuss with your family their feelings after the experiment.
- Identify behavior changes that family members are willing to try.

Try It Out. Carry out this experiment with some or all of your family members: Make at least one change toward "company behavior" in how you act toward the others. What are the results of your behavior change?

Balancing Work & Family Life

THE CHALLENGE —

Managing Household Chores

Would you rather wash dishes or watch a movie? Doing the dishes may be boring, but mundane tasks keep a home running smoothly. So the bad news is: household chores are inescapable. The good news? Sharing the load can help your family finish them faster so *everyone* has time to watch that movie.

How You Can Help

To manage chores better and enjoy more free time with relaxed family members, try these tips:

- Make a list of all chores to be accomplished. Ask each family member for input.
- Work with your family to schedule daily jobs for each person. After a week-long trial run, discuss and adjust the schedule. Then post it.
- Volunteer to help a sibling or parent who is especially busy. Encourage others to do the same.
- Keep your home clean by picking up after yourself. Encourage family members to pick up, too.
- With the family, devise a neutral way to prod members who neglect chores. Decide on a warning system with consequences.

---

are negative ones. People must make good decisions about what attitudes and behavior are worth imitating.

Role Expectations

As you learn about roles, you decide how you want to act in different situations. You also form ideas about what other people should be like and how they should behave. The behavior you anticipate from a certain role is called a **role expectation**.

Suppose you expect a doctor to be knowledgeable and organized. If the doctor examining you couldn't answer your questions or find needed medical instruments, you would probably be alarmed.

Stereotypes

At 6'6", Terrance wishes he had a quarter for every time someone asked if he plays basketball. He doesn't. He doesn't even like the game. Thanks to his height, however, he is forever answering that question.

Terrance is feeling the effects of a **stereotype**, a standardized idea about the qualities or behavior of a certain category of people. Stereotypes are inaccurate role expectations. They are generalities that don't apply to all people. Stereotypes are often linked to physical features or ethnic background.

Some stereotypes are just annoying. Others can also be destructive. The stereotype of the "grouchy old man" and the "spoiled, only child," for example, can prevent you from seeing older adults and only children as individuals. If you judge someone on the basis of a stereotype, you're likely to be wrong. If you go one step further and talk about or mistreat that person, you're hurting the individual. That is definitely wrong.

ROLE CONFLICT

When Bailey was young, her father and brother took care of the family car. Bailey and her mother never did these jobs. Bailey grew up believing that auto maintenance was a male's responsibility. In college, she met some young women who maintained their own cars. Bailey's ideas changed, so she learned to change a flat tire and recognize what's under a car hood.

One weekend at home, Bailey started to check the motor oil in her car's engine. "That's my job," her father said, "I'll do that so you can go help your mother."

Bailey and her father had different expectations for the roles of women and men. This differing view of role expectations is called **role conflict**. Role conflict can lead to confusion.

Role conflict isn't likely when people agree on role expectations and are comfortable with them.

An adult who takes care of a parent experiences role reversal. What do you think that means?

One reason role conflicts occur is that roles are learned from many different sources. The ideas about behavior that Bailey found at college were different from those she had learned at home.

Another reason that people view roles differently is that roles change gradually over time. While Bailey's father thought that males should take care of the car, she could see that idea changing in other families. Some fathers were teaching their daughters about car maintenance. Even after some people accept and promote change, the same ideas haven't been considered yet by others. That causes differences in points of view and sometimes disagreements.

People often see roles differently. How might each person here describe the role of "mother"?

Understanding Roles

When serious role conflicts occur, people need to examine the expectations on both sides and resolve them in some way. By communicating role expectations and working through role conflict, people can begin to see how roles affect beliefs and behavior. This understanding improves their relationships with others.

SECTION 5-2 REVIEW

Check Your Understanding

1. What are roles?
2. What is the difference between a given role and a chosen role?
3. Give an example of how a role model has influenced your idea about a role.
4. What is a role expectation?
5. Give an example of role conflict.
6. **Thinking Critically.** Suppose a famous actor with a reputation for reckless behavior declares, "I am not a role model. I have never wanted to be a role model." Does his saying this make it so? What might he really be saying?
7. **Problem Solving.** Vijay's friend told him about a neighbor who had won a full college scholarship. "She's really smart," his friend said, "but then, all those people are." Vijay pointed out that this was a stereotype. "But it's a compliment," his friend replied. What should Vijay say?

Chapter 5
Review and Activities

CHAPTER SUMMARY

- Relationships affect your life in many ways.
- People need positive relationships for several reasons.
- Mutuality signals a balanced relationship.
- In a good relationship people feel close, supported, and accepted.
- Relationships tend to continue when costs and rewards are balanced.
- Recognizing weaknesses in relationships can help you repair or end a poor relationship.
- Every person plays many roles in relationships, either chosen or given.
- People learn about roles primarily through role models.
- Stereotypes unfairly categorize people according to standard ideas about qualities or behavior.
- Role conflict occurs when those involved in a relationship have different role expectations.

REVIEW QUESTIONS

Section 5-1
1. Why do people need good relationships?
2. Give examples of voluntary and involuntary relationships.
3. What are six qualities of a good relationship?
4. How does trust play a role in self-disclosure?
5. Give an example of a cost and a reward in a parent-child relationship, for the parent and the child.
6. What are three signs of weak relationships?

Section 5-2
1. Why are roles useful in different situations and relationships? List examples of given roles and chosen roles.
2. How do people learn roles?
3. Why are stereotypes very destructive to society?
4. What is role conflict and why does it occur?

BECOMING A PROBLEM SOLVER

1. Jan and Lena share a bedroom. Jan ends up cleaning Lena's side of the room because she can't stand looking at the mess. She gets annoyed because she knows Lena now expects her to keep the room clean. What can Jan do?
2. Jacob and Mike are organizing a group of students to join the county Paint-A-Thon, when volunteers paint the houses of older people who have asked for help. Mike suggests asking Suzi to join them. Jacob laughs and says, "Can you see a girl trying to handle a ladder and paint? We need guys who can do their share of the work." What should Mike do?

THINKING CRITICALLY

1. **Compare and Contrast.** How are rapport and empathy similar? How are they different?
2. **Analyzing Behavior.** Of the qualities of a good relationship described in this chapter, which do you think is the most challenging to acquire? Explain.
3. **Predicting Consequences.** What do you think is ahead for these teens and their relationships? Teen A expects to get calls from friends but never makes any. Teen B dominates conversations by talking about many personal problems. Teen C loves humor and avoids all conversations that are serious.
4. **Determining the Strength of an Argument.** Do you agree or disagree that relationships operate on a system of rewards and costs? Why?

MAKING CURRICULUM CONNECTIONS

1. **Language Arts.** Write a short essay discussing the role expectations you think others have for you. Explain how this affects your role expectations of others.
2. **Drama.** Attend a production of your school's drama department. Observe the roles the various actors play. How are the roles in a theatrical production similar to and different from the roles people play in life?
3. **History.** Research how the roles of husbands, wives, and children have changed over time. What has caused these changes?

APPLYING YOUR KNOWLEDGE

1. Complete the following statement in writing: "My idea of a good relationship is…"
2. With classmates, discuss the impact of diversity in the workplace. What relationship qualities will help you get along with people who are different from you?
3. With a partner, write and perform a skit that demonstrates empathy between two friends.
4. As a class, brainstorm a list of ways to help eliminate stereotypes.

Family & Community Connections

1. Interview your parents and grandparents (or other adults of similar ages) about their role expectations for marriage and family relationships. Compare their expectations to your own. What are the similarities and differences between the generations?

2. Choose two people in your family or community who you think show the qualities of a positive role model. Describe the qualities that led you to select them.

Improving Communication

The Communication Process

OBJECTIVES

After studying this section, you should be able to:

- Define communication.
- Explain the importance of communication in relationships.
- Relate the four basic elements of communication to success in communicating.

TERMS TO LEARN

communication
communication channel
verbal communication
nonverbal communication

Why do babies cry? They may be hungry, tired, or need a diaper change. If they could communicate better, they could save themselves and their parents a lot of frustration.

Learning to talk makes expressing yourself easier. However, **communication**, the process of creating and sending messages and of receiving and evaluating messages from others, is a complex skill. The more you're aware of the skills involved in communicating, the better able you are to use them.

AN IMPORTANT SKILL

Effective communication is a cornerstone of every good relationship. Sharing information, ideas, and feelings fosters understanding among people. Today especially, when everyone seems so busy with work, school, and other activities, communication is a vital link. It helps people build relationships and keep up with family and friends.

ELEMENTS OF COMMUNICATION

The communication process includes four basic elements. These are: communication channels; participants; timing; and the use of space. Used well, each of these elements contributes to successful communication.

Communication Channels

A **communication channel** is the way in which a message is passed. One of the main channels is **verbal communication**, or spoken words. You communicate verbally more times than you can count every day, yet

You and your friends probably communicate on the telephone, even after just seeing each other in person. Why does it seem difficult for some teens and parents to communicate?

speech is only one way to share information. **Nonverbal communication**, communication without words, is also effective for making thoughts and feelings known.

Nonverbal communication takes many forms. Facial expressions, gestures, and posture all send messages. Suppose a friend collapses into a chair at the library, sits with shoulders slumped and eyes closed, and sighs. What can you say about your friend's mental state?

Some actions send negative messages. Reba was annoyed when her brother was late picking her up to take her to dance class. He had stopped at a music store first. To Reba, this behavior said that buying a new CD was more important to her brother than being on time for her. She returned a nonverbal message of her own: she slammed the car door as she got out.

Actions can also send positive messages. Seeing her brother Misha rushing to get the lawn mowed, Ivana offered, "I can do that if you want to finish your homework before going to work." By helping Misha finish the job, Ivana communicated caring and support.

Technology, both old and new, may eliminate some or all of the nonverbal aspect of communication. When you write a note, talk on the telephone, or use email, your words must be precise and to the point so you will be understood.

Participants

The participants also affect the quality of communication. The best communication results when all those involved share in the exchange. There is a balance in the give-and-take of ideas.

If you've taken part in small-group discussion at school, you can appreciate the value of balanced participation. One group member may try to dominate the discussion. In contrast, another must be urged to contribute anything at all. Either way, ideas are missed. The whole point of communication is defeated. Like a tennis match, communication works only when participants are ready and willing to receive and return messages.

Timing

True communication occurs only when both sender and receiver focus on the exchange. Choosing the right time to send a message affects how well it's received. Joyce learned this lesson when she asked her sister Janine if she could borrow one of Janine's sweaters. Janine looked up from the letter she was reading and snapped, "You're always borrowing my clothes! Why don't you wear some of your own for a change?" Later Joyce discovered that the letter was a notice turning down Janine's application for a job she badly wanted. Joyce's unlucky choice of time led to some harsh words and feelings between the sisters.

Knowing whether someone is ready and willing to listen to your message takes skill and sensitivity. By first saying, "How's it going?" or "Can I interrupt for a minute?" you get a feel for the other person's mood.

Use of Space

How space is used can affect communication. For instance, would you shout an apology across a crowded room? Such a

Better Communication. Do you ever feel that people in your family don't listen to you? If you watch or read advertisements, you know that a catchy gimmick is as important as the message in getting someone's attention. Have some fun and wake up your "audience" by adding a surprising or playful touch to your communication. Here are some ideas:

- Try hamming it up like a "high-powered" salesperson when you're trying to win over a family member to your point of view.
- Is a young sibling tuning you out? Make a simple hand puppet by drawing eyes and a mouth on a sock. Let the puppet do your talking.
- If you normally yell to express strong feelings, try whispering instead.
- If someone isn't hearing your side of an issue, write it out instead—in a humorous rap or poem, or set to a familiar tune.

Easy? Hardly! Sparking authentic, rather than automatic, reactions, however, can enliven and enrich your conversations and relationships.

Try It Out. Think of an issue where family members don't seem to be listening to each other. Plan a strategy to listen and be heard on this topic. Carry out your plan.

personal communication requires more physical closeness. Likewise, conversation tends to be freer when family members are sitting around the kitchen table than when they are scattered around the living room.

Have you ever had a conversation with someone who seemed to be closing in on you? When you pulled back, the other person leaned closer. Conversation is most effective when both people are comfortable with the distance between them.

Physical viewpoint makes a difference, too. That's why communicating with children is more effective when you get down on their level, rather than "look down" from a position of power. Messages flow more freely when people feel they have equal status.

Nonverbal communication is "saying things" without speaking. This gesture may be "heard" as "Oh, boy, did I goof!" What one nonverbal communication is universal to show a friendly attitude?

BECOMING A SKILLED COMMUNICATOR

Mastering the communication process takes time and practice. You need to pay attention to how you use all four elements.

Becoming a skilled communicator also means learning communication skills and overcoming some obstacles. You'll read about some of these in the next section.

SECTION 6-1 REVIEW

Check Your Understanding

1. What is exchanged when people communicate?
2. Why is communication important in relationships?
3. Why is timing important in communicating?
4. Describe an effective physical distance for communicating.
5. **Thinking Critically.** When might verbal communication be the more effective channel of communication? When might nonverbal communication be better?
6. **Problem Solving.** Grant's family is hosting a Russian foreign exchange student. Grant likes Sergei, but gets uncomfortable because Sergei stands very close when they talk. If Grant takes a step back, Sergei just closes the gap. What should Grant do?

Using Communication Skills

OBJECTIVES

After studying this section, you should be able to:

- Demonstrate good active and passive listening skills.
- Demonstrate techniques for effective speaking.
- Identify and correct problems in communication.

TERMS TO LEARN

passive listening
active listening
assertive
feedback

Relationships thrive on effective communication. Communication thrives when people practice skills that help them send and receive messages accurately. Are you a good communicator? Think about each of the skills described here and decide where you need to improve.

ing. Hearing is a physical response. Listening is a mental activity that lets you receive messages accurately.

Two types of listening skills are useful in communicating with others: passive listening and active listening.

LISTENING SKILLS

Have you ever been daydreaming in class when you felt a strange silence and realized the teacher had asked you a question? You know, then, the value of listening in communication. One study showed that people spend almost three-fourths of their waking hours in communication, and almost one-half of that time listening.

Why, then, is the complaint "You don't listen to me" heard in so many families? Perhaps people confuse listening with hear-

Passive Listening

Passive listening provides responses that invite the speaker to share feelings and ideas. The listener puts aside personal judgments. Such comments as "No kidding?" and "You said it!" show that the listener is focused on the speaker's words.

Lily used her passive listening skills when her foster daughter Gloria came home and announced, "I should have stayed in bed."

Lily stopped folding clothes and pulled a chair to face Gloria. "That doesn't sound good," she said.

Learn to Listen

When you listen well, you use these ideas to focus on the other person. *Why does each technique make a difference?*

Use encouraging words and gestures.

Don't let your mind roam.

Keep eye contact.

Think of a reason to listen.

Don't interrupt.

Lean toward the speaker.

Stay calm and positive.

Good listeners build strong relationships. All people like to know that what they say is being heard and understood—especially in families.

"We had a science test that I completely forgot about," Gloria went on, slumping in the chair. "And at the end of my shift at the drug store, my cash register was $37 off."

"Oh, no!" Lily said. "Thirty-seven?" As Gloria nodded miserably, Lily gave her hand a squeeze. Notice that Lily didn't express any ideas of her own. She just encouraged Gloria to keep talking.

Active Listening

In **active listening** you try to understand the speaker's feeling and the message's true meaning. You make comments that are designed to draw out information.

For example, as Belle told her father about her first basketball practice, his comments included: "I'm sorry you and Val didn't both make the blue team," "Your new coach sounds like she knows her stuff," and "Didn't those wind sprints make you tired?" Craig encouraged Belle by wanting to know exactly what she meant and how she felt.

SPEAKING SKILLS

"Speak clearly, if you speak at all; carve every word before you let it fall." Those lines from American writer Oliver Wendell Holmes contain excellent advice. Words are powerful. Care and self-control are needed to use them for positive communication.

I-Messages

Erica was angry and worried when her best friend Quinn missed their study date without calling her. "You're just impossible, Quinn!" she told him the next day. "You should have let me know you weren't com-

A good communicator often becomes a leader in life. Are all people who do public speaking good communicators? Why or why not?

ing. You made me waste an hour waiting for you. Why can't you be more responsible?" How do you think Quinn responded to this outburst?

Erica was using what are called "you-messages." You-messages blame the other person for the speaker's feelings. They are a direct attack on the person and the actions.

Erica could have expressed her feelings much more effectively with "I-messages." I-messages are those that accurately reflect what the speaker thinks, believes, and feels. They give facts to explain the speaker's reaction.

Using I-messages, Erica might have said, "Quinn, I'm really upset that you didn't call me last night. I was worried that something had happened to you. Besides that, I lost study time I needed. Please call me the next time, okay?"

I-messages are particularly valuable when the speaker is hurt or upset, and feels like lashing out. This is also when they are hardest to send. Practice and self-control help you state feelings calmly rather than venting your anger at someone, even when the other person is at fault.

Assertiveness

When you're **assertive** (uh-SURT-iv), you communicate ideas and feelings firmly and positively. You take responsibility for yourself and your position. An assertive person recognizes others' opinions but isn't overpowered by them.

Assertiveness is not rudeness. Assertiveness differs from *aggression*. Aggressive people push to have their own way, often acting hostile. You can confidently tell your ideas and respectfully let others express theirs.

Eva needed to be assertive when her sister Betty phoned. "My babysitter just called and told me she's sick," Betty said. "Robb and I have tickets to a play tonight. Could you stay with the kids?" Eva explained: "I wish I could, but I've made plans for tonight." Eva didn't apologize or look for excuses; she simply stated her decision.

Feedback

Feedback is a response that shows whether a message was understood. It bridges the gap between listening and speaking. Both a speaker and a listener may ask for feedback to make sure they agree on what was said.

Feedback helped Jack and his son one afternoon at the mall. Jack told his son, "You finish checking out while I get the car. I'll meet you at the door." "Okay," replied Sal. "Do you mean these doors, or the doors where we came in?" "These doors," Jack said, adding, "I'll pull up when I see you waiting, so stand outside under the canopy." Sal and Jack used feedback to clarify their messages and avoid confusion.

Sometimes your feedback should be to stop the person from finishing. If a friend begins to use language you do not approve of, say, "Let's talk about this later."

Tact: A Quality That Counts

Have you ever been hurt by careless words tossed your way by a friend or family member? Tact or diplomacy is the ability to say things in a way that won't hurt people's feelings or turn them off to your message. A teen could be tactful by:

- Calmly asking a parent to talk about a curfew that seems unfair.
- Waiting to be alone to tell a friend that he or she wasn't on the list of students who made the jazz band.
- Setting an appointment with a teacher at a convenient time to talk about a poor test grade.
- Thanking someone who has asked for a date and explaining that staying friends would be more comfortable for now.

QUESTIONS

1. How was tact shown in each of these situations?
2. How can you tell whether something you say is tactful?
3. Describe a time when you had to handle a situation tactfully.

PROBLEMS IN COMMUNICATION

With good communication skills, you can avoid many misunderstandings. Recognizing habits or situations that make communication harder is the first step to overcoming them.

Difficult Subjects

"Why is it that no one wants to talk about the things that matter most?" With that question, one teen summed up the frustration many people feel at handling sensitive topics. In some families, death, divorce, sexuality, and other personal or complicated subjects are off limits. Other families discuss them only with great difficulty. You can probably see why. Can you also see the problems that may arise when sensitive topics aren't discussed?

Difficult subjects demand careful treatment. Including more than two people in the conversation is sometimes helpful. You might open the conversation by referring to something similar that happened to a friend or a character on television. Start with an I-message—in writing, if that's easier.

Silence

Silence can be a pleasant break from conversation. However, you can probably tell

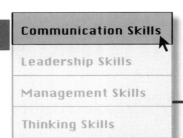

Positive Discussions

Positive discussion can be an opportunity to improve relationships. When people feel put down or criticized, in contrast, the discussion and the relationship take a turn for the worse. Are you a positive influence in discussions? How do you "check out" on the following key points?

✓ I treat everyone with respect.
✓ I encourage others to share their ideas and don't interrupt when they do.
✓ I compliment others on their good ideas.
✓ I keep an open mind to other points of view and don't put down others' ideas.
✓ I share my thoughts and feelings but don't take over the discussion.
✓ I consider how others feel.
✓ I am tactful.

If you can do all of these things, your discussions will be positive and productive.

Using Your Skills

Improving family discussions takes an effort from everyone. Help your family develop a list of rules for constructive discussion. Encourage suggestions from everyone. Put the rules into practice. What effect do they have on your family's communication?

---

the difference between comfortable silence and the silence that conveys disinterest, boredom, or even hostility.

Sometimes, silence signals fear. Sharing feelings can be frightening. In trying to find the right words, a person may fear saying something inappropriate or being laughed at. Communication on sensitive subjects is filled with awkward silence. Among youth and children experiencing family conflict, silence is the most common response.

Pinpointing the reason for the silence helps restart the flow of communication. If someone you know is unusually silent, you might casually point this out. Depending on your relationship, you might ask outright, "Is there something you want to talk about?" You could also send subtle, supportive messages to encourage that person's trust. Some of the techniques for discussing difficult subjects may prove useful.

Occasionally silence indicates a serious problem, such as depression. Getting a person to self-disclose is vital to getting that person needed help.

Interference

Interference, such as the television and loud music, can disrupt communication. Even a light noise, such as a dripping faucet, can be distracting. People who want to communicate well try to eliminate interference first.

Mixed Messages

A mixed message results when different messages are sent over different channels at the same time. For example, Spencer was talking to his stepfather about classes he wanted to take next semester; however, his stepfather kept checking his watch. Spencer finally asked, "Would you rather talk about this later?" His stepfather turned on the television and said, "No, this is a good time to get it settled." How did his stepfather's actions compare to his words?

When a mixed message is sent, the nonverbal message generally reflects the sender's true feelings. A message that is expressed both verbally and nonverbally is much more convincing.

Thinking You Already Know

Lonnie curled up in a corner and quietly watched television, ignoring the spirited discussion going on about him. Watching from the sofa, his brother Joe thought, Lonnie must be mad—not at me, I hope. I'd better stay out of his way tonight.

Was Joe right about Lonnie? He can't be sure. Mind reading—assuming you know what someone else is thinking—often leads to wrong conclusions. Lonnie might wonder, what's wrong with Joe? Is he mad at me?

Why do people use this unhelpful approach? "Mind readers" are sometimes too impatient to hear other people out. Mind reading can be a way to dominate a conversation and another person. People who know each other well may believe they can almost literally read each other's minds.

To find out what someone thinks, pay attention. Ask questions and use feedback to learn what is really going on.

Different Definitions

Some communication problems occur because people have different cultural backgrounds, outlooks on life, or definitions of terms. For example, Linda and her

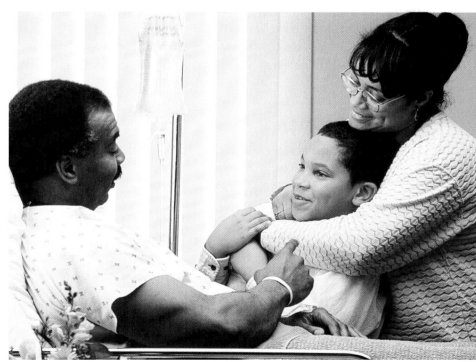

Words are not needed in every situation. Sometimes saying less is best. What words would you use when talking with someone who is seriously ill?

Career Success Stories

Dalisa Parks: *Newspaper Journalist*

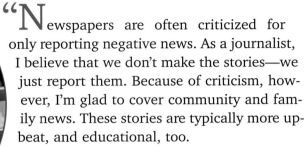

"Newspapers are often criticized for only reporting negative news. As a journalist, I believe that we don't make the stories—we just report them. Because of criticism, however, I'm glad to cover community and family news. These stories are typically more upbeat, and educational, too.

"Recently, I was invited to speak to a middle school class about journalism careers. I found that the students had been using some of my articles in their health class all year long. They were eager to meet me and to see what I looked like because they felt they knew me through my words. That was a great experience! Discovering that my work could be used as a teaching tool was pretty special to me.

"Covering the news means that no two days—or stories—are exactly alike. The deadlines make for grueling days. I spend a good chunk of my time on the phone, touching base with sources and following up on news ideas. I also pick up on trends by using e-mail, online services, and electronic bulletin boards to see what people are talking about. I push myself hard every day and hope that my articles will somehow touch the people who read them, like the students in that middle school class."

CAREER PROFILE

Education and training: bachelor's degree preferred

Starting salary range: $18–24,000

Job prospects: daily and weekly newspapers; magazines; trade journals; freelance writing

Important qualities: excellent communication skills; writing skills; creativity; curiosity; persistence

Plan Ahead

Write an informative article about journalism as a career as if you were a reporter for your school or local newspaper. Find at least two sources of information for your article. Does this career appeal to you?

mother had different ideas about what "clean" was. Linda was to clean her room before she could go shopping with her friends. She hung up her clothes and dusted her dresser. Inspecting her room, her mother said, "Linda, this room isn't clean! It needs vacuuming. Shopping will have to wait a little longer."

To be useful, messages must be specific and clear to everyone. When sending and receiving messages, always be mindful of another's point of view.

WRITTEN COMMUNICATION

Although technology is making instant, spoken communication more common, the written word is still very important. The ability to write effectively is a valuable tool for both work and personal life.

The principles of effective communication described in this chapter also apply to written communication. Choose clear, precise words; avoid mixed messages; and use I-messages for writing as well as speaking.

Some aspects of written communication present certain challenges. The fastest written message is still slower than spoken words, so clarifying a message through feedback takes longer. On the other hand, the added time needed to write and respond to a message can be wisely used to create a carefully worded, meaningful exchange.

You may think of writing as a task for work or school. Writing can also be useful in your personal life. Upset after fighting with a friend, Kayla tried to write her feelings in her journal. As she reflected on the event, she began to see her friend's position more clearly. Her journal entry turned into a note of apology, and the friendship was preserved.

SECTION 6-2 REVIEW

Check Your Understanding

1. Why is listening an important part of communication?
2. Are I-messages or you-messages more effective for communicating? Explain.
3. How does feedback promote good communication?
4. What is meant by assertiveness?
5. How can different definitions interfere with good communication?
6. **Thinking Critically.** What misunderstanding might occur if a speaker wanted you to respond with passive listening, and you used active listening instead, or vice versa?
7. **Problem Solving.** When Lynn and Sadie go someplace together, Sadie usually pays any expenses, such as snacks or movie tickets. Sadie feels that Lynn should return the favor. Whenever Sadie brings up the subject, however, Lynn tells her how good it is to have such a generous friend. Sadie then feels embarrassed. What do you make of this situation? What advice would you give Sadie?

Chapter 6
Review and Activities

CHAPTER SUMMARY

- Communication is an important skill for building and keeping relationships.
- To use the communication process effectively, you need to be familiar with the four basic components.
- Listening is an essential part of good communication.
- Active and passive listening are effective for showing support and interest.
- Using I-messages and being assertive are positive ways to say what you think or feel.
- Feedback is a way to learn whether messages have been received and understood.
- Silence can signal that a person is uncomfortable with a subject or is afraid of a negative response.
- When a person's actions contradict his or her words, the result is a mixed message.
- Communication problems can occur because people don't have the same outlook on life or the same definition of terms.
- Written communication is a valuable skill for many situations.

REVIEW QUESTIONS

Section 6-1
1. What is communication?
2. How does communication affect relationships?
3. What are the basic elements in the communication process?
4. How might someone communicate anger nonverbally?
5. How do time and space affect communication?

Section 6-2
1. Luis asked Mitch, "Are you listening to me?" Mitch replied, "I heard you." Did Mitch answer Luis' question? Why or why not?
2. Suppose you had an exciting experience to relate. Would you prefer a passive or an active listener? Why?
3. What would a positive response be when silence is a communication problem?
4. What are effective alternatives to "mind reading"?
5. Give an example of a mixed message.

BECOMING A PROBLEM SOLVER

1. Jada is talking to a friend who keeps looking away to see what is going on around them. Jada feels that her friend isn't listening. What should she do?
2. Whenever Dale and Paige talk, Paige manages to turn the conversation toward herself. Dale is tired of that subject. How should he respond?
3. Cory sometimes listens so actively that he finishes other people's sentences for them. He knows this habit is annoying, and wants to overcome it. What do you suggest?

THINKING CRITICALLY

1. **Identifying Cause and Effect.** In culture A, people stand very close when they talk to each other, but in culture B they stand farther apart. If one person from each culture talk together, what do you think might happen?
2. **Drawing Conclusions.** How effective is gossip as a form of communication?
3. **Analyzing Behavior.** Do you think males and females communicate differently? Explain your reasoning.
4. **Analyzing Behavior.** Might a person have good reasons for not wanting to communicate? Is not communicating about a subject ever healthy?

MAKING CURRICULUM CONNECTIONS

1. **Art.** Draw a cartoon that illustrates a communication problem.
2. **Literature.** Using written works from different periods, such as novels, journals, or newspapers, show how communication has changed over time. Note changes in word choice and other literary techniques. Write an essay on your findings, perhaps imitating the writing styles you notice.
3. **History.** Create a time line from 1900 to the present, marking technological innovations that have affected communication. How have these developments helped and hindered effective communication? Overall, have these devices improved the quality of communication? Why or why not?

APPLYING YOUR KNOWLEDGE

1. Try speaking the following sentences in ways to convey different feelings, such as sincerity or disbelief: "You sure are a good friend." "Did you say that you're going to the football game with Josh?" Can classmates identify your meaning? Discuss how people express different messages with the same words. Are vocal techniques, such as inflection and emphasis, verbal or nonverbal communication?
2. With a partner, write six you-messages. Change them to I-messages.

Family & Community Connections

1. With your family, list situations that use specialized body language, such as an auction, a religious service, or training an animal. Why is nonverbal communication used in each instance? Are there parallels between each type and body language in general?

2. With a partner, suggest ways that family members can communicate when they can't speak to one another in person. Think of creative ways to use signs, symbols, and various technological devices.

Chapter 7

Resolving Conflicts

WORDS FOR THOUGHT

"You cannot shake hands with a clenched fist."
(Indira Gandhi)

IN YOUR OWN WORDS

What does the fist symbolize in the quote? What does the quote mean?

Understanding Conflict

OBJECTIVES

After studying this section, you should be able to:

- Define conflict and explain its causes.
- Distinguish between constructive and destructive conflict.
- Show how defining the problem, setting limits, and following up are used for successful conflict resolution.
- Demonstrate a process of negotiation and compromise.
- Recognize ways to avoid conflict.

TERMS TO LEARN

conflict
power
control
negotiate
compromise
mediator

When you struggle to push a heavy box across the floor, friction between the box and the floor is part of the reason you have to work so hard. Don't wish for a world without friction, however, because friction also keeps you from crashing into classmates when walking down the hall.

There's another kind of friction that is troublesome but also useful. Friction between people, or conflict, is useful when you are forced to address issues that need attention. It can be troublesome, however, when you must struggle to manage a disagreement.

WHAT IS CONFLICT?

"We had an argument."
"I hate it when we fight."
"We just don't see eye-to-eye on this."

However you say it, you know that **conflict**, a disagreement or struggle between two or more people, is part of any close relationship. In fact, the closer your relationship is, the more heated your conflicts can be. Why do you think this is so?

Conflict is not pleasant, but it doesn't have to be painful. You can learn to handle conflict so that it actually strengthens a relationship.

When you learn to resolve conflicts, relationships improve. How does that affect the atmosphere at home?

TYPES OF CONFLICT

The sources of specific conflicts vary. What your friends and their parents argue about may not be a problem in your family. Conflict in general, however, occurs for a few common reasons. As long as people work and play together, conflicts tend to arise from challenging situations, personality differences, and power struggles.

Situational Conflict

Sometimes a particular situation gives rise to conflict. Situational conflict can occur in all kinds of relationships and in any part of daily life. Living, working, or playing together—all may contain the seeds of situational conflict.

Courtney found herself in such a situation involving her brother. "Whenever it's my turn to use the bathroom in the morning," she complained to her mother, "Jeff is still in there. You'd think he actually has hair on his chin for all the time he spends shaving. Last week I was late for school twice."

"Have you talked to Jeff?" her mother asked. "Maybe he doesn't realize what's happening."

"Oh, he knows, all right. Every time I get upset, he just stays in there longer. He says I spend too much time fiddling with my hair at night, but all he has to do is tell me if he wants in."

Can you see how circumstances created a conflict between Courtney and her brother? They can't control the fact that they must share a bathroom. Still, they can control how they handle the situation. What do you think would help them solve the problem?

Situational conflicts may be intense but are often short-lived. People usually deal with the common problems and move on.

Personality Differences

Another type of conflict may arise from differences in personalities. Each person has a distinct personality, a unique combination of values, traits, and style. Such differences enrich life but can also create conflict. Suppose two sisters share a bedroom. One enjoys reading, and the other likes listening to music. What potential conflict lies in their different tastes?

Conflicts caused by clashing personalities are often over small matters. One person's habits may get on another person's nerves. Sometimes these small quirks, however, build into major battles.

Power Struggles

Power is the ability to influence another person. Power struggles occur when issues are important to both sides. Using power is one way people get others to agree to their terms.

Many arguments between teens and parents are about power and who has the power in certain issues. Conflict over curfew is typically a power concern. A teen's choice of friends may also lead to a power struggle.

A related issue is the desire or need for control. **Control** is the action of directing another person's behavior. When power is the cause of conflict, the desire for control may get in the way of a solution. For example, Andy's new supervisor made some unpopular changes at work. She wouldn't listen to the workers' complaints, however, since she wasn't interested in other points of view. She only wanted to be in charge.

Letting Go of Conflict. You can't always change situations that are causing conflict. So what do you do? You may need to let go of a disagreement or any pain you feel. A ceremony based on one of these ideas could help you put a conflict to rest:

- Let a seed cluster (such as a dandelion) represent the conflict and blow it away.
- Write the issues on balloons. Then pop them.
- Write the issues on paper and ceremoniously shred the paper.
- Write the issues on leaves and set the leaves adrift in a stream.

Letting go is not giving in. Instead, you are making a choice to accept peace of mind in situations you can't change.

Try It Out. Think of a past conflict that still bothers you. Design and carry out a personal "letting go" ceremony to help free you from this conflict.

As you begin to assert yourself in your family, conflicts may arise. You can settle them by attacking the problem, not the family member. **How might a teen negotiate a later curfew time?**

RESOLVING CONFLICTS

Like Emily and Jacob, you can learn to settle differences constructively. Success comes with understanding some basic steps for resolving conflicts.

Define the Problem

Constructive conflict resolution begins when parties agree on what they are arguing about. Each side says, "The problem as I see it is . . ." This step may seem unnecessary. However, people often make assumptions about what others are thinking, even when they agree. When they are at odds, they tend to assume the worst about the other's motives. Putting thoughts into words sets the tone for a calm, orderly discussion.

During discussion, all points of disagreement are brought to the surface. Verbal and nonverbal messages are exchanged. You may have a "game plan," a strategy to help the other person understand your position. To resolve the conflict constructively, you also need to say things that acknowledge the other's point of view in a respectful way, even if it makes no sense to you. This is called *validation*.

Set Limits

To keep a discussion on track, parties need to set limits. They agree on the points to be argued. Other issues and personal attacks are "off limits." Likewise, dredging up a fight from last week doesn't help solve today's problem. It only turns the discussion destructive.

OUTCOMES OF CONFLICT

"Jacob and I were always so quick to fight," Emily recalled. "We'd say some horrible things to each other. When we learned to talk things over instead, we found out what really bothered us, and why. Ever since we learned how to argue, we're much closer than before."

As you can see from this example, conflict can have either a positive or a negative outcome. Positive conflict is *constructive*. People work together to solve a problem and reach a better understanding of each other. They are likely to be satisfied with the outcome and feel positively toward each other.

Conflict can also be negative. In *destructive conflict*, people attack each other rather than the problem. Destructive conflict can doom a relationship.

TRY NEGOTIATING

You may have heard of diplomats negotiating a treaty or an employer and workers negotiating a contract. You probably negotiate, too, when you settle conflicts with family and friends.

To **negotiate** is to deal or bargain with another. During negotiation, people suggest possible solutions and seek points of agreement. More suggestions can lead to more agreement. Gradually, the parties hammer out a solution that is acceptable to all.

Negotiation only works when people are willing to compromise. **Compromise** means giving in on some points of disagreement and having your way on others. You give a little to get a little.

In constructive conflict, the goal of negotiating and compromise is to achieve a "win-win" situation. This means that all parties feel as though they've gotten a fair deal, one that satisfies their needs and concerns.

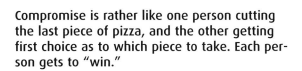

Compromise is rather like one person cutting the last piece of pizza, and the other getting first choice as to which piece to take. Each person gets to "win."

Negotiation is not always successful. Sometimes parties are too far apart on the issues. Each side may be unwilling to give up something the other side wants.

Other times, a "solution" fails because it doesn't really please everyone. One party may accept an agreement just to end the conflict, and even try to make it work. Unless the terms satisfy all those involved, however, the quarrel is apt to crop up again later. A cooling-off period may be needed before further negotiation.

Negotiation requires give-and-take. What happens to negotiation when two people resort to stubbornness?

Career Success Stories

Franco Juarez: *Guidance Counselor*

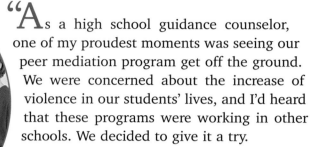

"As a high school guidance counselor, one of my proudest moments was seeing our peer mediation program get off the ground. We were concerned about the increase of violence in our students' lives, and I'd heard that these programs were working in other schools. We decided to give it a try.

"The way our program works, I teach a class to student volunteers, who learn to be mediators. They learn skills in problem solving and negotiation and go through plenty of practice. Then they help students who have conflicts. I schedule the sessions but don't attend them. The mediators are amazingly dedicated to resolving issues, no matter how many sessions it takes. Since our program began, suspension and detention rates have been cut in half. Now I've started teaching others in a university class how to start mediation programs.

"Although I'm a good organizer and very resourceful, my love for kids is really what helps me do my job well. Not a day goes by that I don't have to tackle some problem that a student is having. Some days are quite a challenge, but I try to be resilient and stick to my goals. I guess having a hand in the students' successes makes me feel that I've been successful too."

CAREER PROFILE

Education and training: master's degree

Starting salary range: $25-40,000

Job prospects: public and private elementary, middle, and high schools; vocational-technical schools

Important qualities: communication skills; good organization; sense of humor; enjoy working with young adults

Plan Ahead

Talk with a guidance counselor in your school to find out more about this job. Ask what he or she likes most and least about the career. If you're still interested, find out how to prepare for this career. What courses do you need to take now?

Consider a Mediator

Sometimes outside help is needed to resolve a conflict. A **mediator** is a person who leads those in conflict to solutions without taking sides in the controversy. Mediation can be informal, as when one friend helps two others talk through a dispute. In formal, structured mediation programs, the mediator follows a procedure to help conflicting sides understand each other, negotiate, compromise, and solve their problem. Some schools have peer mediation programs to handle conflict between students.

FOLLOWING UP

Conflict resolution is not complete without follow-up. In follow-up, solutions are put into action. Perhaps more important, negative feelings between the parties are dealt with and managed. Grudges or hurt feelings that are allowed to fester may flare into conflict again. Proper follow-up includes feedback that allows each party to evaluate whether resolution has occurred.

AVOIDING CONFLICT

A conflict that never develops is one you don't have to worry about. How do you avoid conflict? Here are some techniques to try:

- **Don't let others irritate you.** Recognize when someone is only looking for a reaction from you.
- **Focus on the positive.** When you focus on advantages, disadvantages can seem less bothersome.
- **Change the subject.** If you feel things get tense, lead the conversation in a different, less emotional direction.
- **Take a personal stand against serious, and especially physical, conflict.** Let others know that you aren't going to resort to violence.
- **Don't be intimidated or provoked into fighting.** Show your strength by doing what you know is right, not what others may want.
- **Walk away.** Explain calmly, "This is not worth fighting about." You can be proud to show self-confidence in this way.

SECTION 7-1 REVIEW

Check Your Understanding

1. Why do conflicts occur?
2. If conflicts arise from disagreements, how can they be considered constructive?
3. Why does setting limits help people resolve conflicts effectively?
4. What happens in a "win-win" situation?
5. What method for avoiding conflict would work best for you and why?
6. **Thinking Critically.** Why is refusing to fight a sign of strength?
7. **Problem Solving.** When Vince and his brother Terrell bought a car together, they agreed on how to share the costs of upkeep and use of the car. Now Terrell isn't filling the gas tank as agreed and he takes the car when it's not his turn. What should Vince do?

Dealing with Conflict

OBJECTIVES

After studying this section, you should be able to:

- Relate the use of communication skills specifically to resolving conflicts.
- Explain why self-control is essential to effective conflict resolution.
- Determine whether the time is right for dealing with a conflict.
- Distinguish respectful from disrespectful behavior among people in conflict.
- Explain the importance of teamwork to finding lasting solutions.

TERMS TO LEARN

respect
competition

Now you have some good ideas for successfully resolving conflict. However, ideas can help you only if you can carry them out. Think of resolving conflict as trying a new recipe. The picture in the cookbook looks good. Now you need to know what you must do to put the real food on your dinner table.

COMMUNICATION SKILLS

As you know from experience, resolving disputes doesn't come automatically. People who do it well are those who use good communication skills. Like all skills, the ones for settling disagreements constructively improve with practice.

Fortunately, you don't have to wait for conflict to arise to practice these skills. If you work on them every day, in fact, you may find fewer conflicts come your way.

Conflicts cannot be settled without communication skills. You learned about communication in the last chapter. Now take a look at how it relates specifically to conflict resolution.

Listening carefully to another's point of view can help you know what he or she is thinking. You can learn why a conflict has come between you. It may be easier to solve then.

Listening

Listening is so important to good conflict resolution, yet that's just when it can be most difficult. Have you ever been so upset that what someone said didn't register in your mind? When the message sent is a negative one, you may become more upset and more negative. How do you think that affects the other person? What happens to the conflict?

Listening effectively to an opposing view depends on several key communication and relationship skills.

Empathy

During a disagreement, try to listen with empathy. Appreciating the other person's position puts you on track to solve your mutual problem. Thinking only about *your* position and *your* hurt feelings makes it harder to work toward a solution.

Feedback

Misunderstandings are obstacles to any good communication. In solving conflicts, they can add fuel to the fire.

Giving and accepting feedback can help prevent misunderstandings. Asking questions and restating the other person's message show that you're trying to understand. Others appreciate your efforts.

Clarification

Mixed messages can be confusing to the receiver. Sometimes they show the sender's mixed emotions. Sorting out the conflicting messages can lead to greater empathy and self-understanding.

Sorting out a mixed message helped Shana and her father strengthen their relationship. Several times they had talked about whether Shana should go to a party on a night the family had plans. Finally her father said abruptly, "All right . . . all right, Shana, you can go if that's what you want. I don't care." He said nothing more to her that night.

The next morning, Shana said, "Dad, you said I could go to Carrie's party, but you still seem mad about it. Is it really okay with you if I go or not?"

Her father replied, "Yes, it's okay, Shana. I guess I was just hurt that you wanted to be with your friends instead of us. Sometimes I have to remember that you're growing up. That's hard to get used to." By asking for feedback on her father's mixed message, Shana created a chance for a loving exchange.

Watch your own behavior to avoid sending mixed messages yourself. State your feelings honestly.

Talking

No negotiation or compromise is possible if parties don't talk to each other. They must keep communication going.

Using I-messages is especially important in resolving conflict. It's better than lashing out with you-messages, which destroy communication. When both sides use I-messages, they stick to the issues.

Avoid giving the other person "the silent treatment." This ends communication, sends negative nonverbal messages, and builds barriers.

"I felt like I was talking to a brick wall," Carmen said after a heated discussion with her friend. What did she mean?

SHOWING SELF-CONTROL

As you can imagine, resolving conflict is impossible without self-control. The more intense the conflict, the more self-control you need. Unfortunately, people tend to lose control when they need it most. Both emotions and physical reactions must be controlled.

Emotional Control

Feeling annoyed is natural when someone gets between you and what you want. As conflict intensifies, annoyance can turn into "hot" emotions, such as anger and frustration. You can get "so mad you can't see straight." You can't see the other person's position at all.

Keeping emotions "cool" by staying calm lets you use the reason and empathy needed for working out problems between people. If the discussion gets heated, it's wise to call a "time out," a short cooling-off period. Later, you can return and refocus on the problem.

Physical Reactions

Physical reactions are a poor means of resolution. When children fight they may hit, kick, scream, and yell. People who never learn to control their physical impulses often react like children when conflict arises. Physical reactions can cause:

- Hurt feelings, and sometimes, people.
- Damaged or destroyed relationships.
- More violence.
- A still unresolved conflict.

When energy and emotional tension produce conflict, try a constructive outlet. Take a walk or a run, lift weights, vacuum a rug, or wash a car. Clearing your mind and body of frustration and tension can help restore positive energy for finding a solution.

Anger that builds inside a person needs an outlet. If an appropriate outlet like exercise isn't chosen, what might happen?

PICKING YOUR TIME

After a long day at work, Julia walked into the kitchen at home and saw the dirty dishes still in the sink. Derrick was supposed to do those, she thought.

With a sigh, Julia sat down to read the paper. At that moment, Derrick walked in, saying, "Mom, you said I could use the car Saturday night, but Mitch says you told him he could have it." What do you think Julia's response was?

As you can see, not every time is a good time for tackling a problem. The "right" time is when all sides:

- **Are in a proper frame of mind.** They have set aside other concerns to focus on the issues. Mealtime and bedtime are not good choices. Self-control wavers when you are hungry or tired.
- **Have enough time.** If you rush through discussion, for instance, you may miss facts you need to reach a satisfying outcome. Set a time to meet about the problem, if necessary.
- **Are undistracted.** Choose a time when you aren't competing for someone's attention with homework, household tasks, or an interesting television show.

RESPECTING OTHERS

Most people agree that everyone deserves **respect**, showing appreciation or esteem. In a heated debate, however, it's easy to belittle other people and opinions that differ from yours.

Respectful Language

The language used in an argument reflects the degree of respect each person feels for the other. Swearing and name-calling show little respect. Such words raise the emotional level of the quarrel and reduce the chance of reaching a positive outcome.

Respectful Attitudes

Respect is also shown by treating others decently. Conflict between parties who know each other well can be especially hurtful. Each side knows where the other is most vulnerable, but respectful people don't abuse their closeness by taking advantage of this knowledge.

Ben has learned the value of showing respect in resolving conflict. "My brother Chad has a problem with stuttering. I used to tease him. The more I teased, the worse he stuttered and the angrier he got. I was really hurting Chad, but I was hurting myself too. It sure didn't win me any points with him, and it was just plain cruel."

USING TEAMWORK

Too often, people treat conflict as a **competition**, a struggle for superiority or victory. They can "win" the argument only if the other side "loses." The spirit of negotiation and compromise can't survive this "us versus them" mentality.

In successful conflict resolution, people realize that no side wins unless all sides win. They see that everyone is on the same team, with the problem as the opponent to be beaten. They work together as a team to find a solution that everyone can live with.

This teacher knew it would be best to work out a conflict with a student after class rather than disturb a whole class. How can you apply this principle at home?

Building Character

Cooperation: A Quality That Counts

If you had 200 chairs to fold and put away after a school program, how could you do the job quickly? Cooperation would help. With cooperation, people work together, often doing much more than they could alone. Cooperation thrives when spirits are willing and attitudes are positive. Cooperation helps prevent conflict. A teen could show a cooperative spirit by:

- Doing a fair share of preparing for the debate team's competition.
- Agreeing to take a shorter dinner break at work when the boss has a scheduling problem.
- Vacuuming the carpet once a week to help keep the family home clean.
- Going along with the family's weekend plans even though something different sounds more fun.

QUESTIONS

1. What conflicts might have been avoided in the situations described above?
2. What adjectives are the opposite of cooperative? How do you react to people who fit these descriptions?
3. How have you demonstrated a cooperative spirit in the past week?

PRACTICING UNDERSTANDING

"My dad is always telling me how to do things," Yoshi said. "Even stuff I've done hundreds of times, like cutting the grass. It used to drive me nuts, but now I think, 'Why get angry? He's my dad. He's always given me advice to help me do a good job. Someday, he'll see that I can do plenty on my own.' "

Yoshi defused a potential conflict by showing understanding, the ability to see people and situations as they are. He asked himself what he really valued in the relationship and found he could overlook much that was not worth arguing about.

Understanding begins when those in conflict see the similarities in their situations. Yoshi, for instance, realized that he often asked his younger sister if she had her lunch and homework in the morning before leaving for school. Wasn't that similar to how his father treated him? His father's habit still annoyed him, but identifying with his father's position made Yoshi more understanding.

You can be a trendsetter when you use the skills you've learned to make your own world a better place to live. You'll gain friends and influence others.

SETTING AN EXAMPLE

Some of the biggest societal trends start with a single, influential person. An actor might wear a certain type of sunglasses or utter a clever line in a movie. Millions of people buy the same brand of sunglasses and are heard repeating the actor's line.

You can be a trendsetter also. Every time you resolve a conflict constructively, you set an example for at least one other person—the other person involved. Younger siblings, too, can learn by watching your methods. You might work with your peers to spread the practice of nonviolent conflict resolution. Making the commitment today to solving problems constructively can improve the quality of life for you, your family, and friends.

SECTION 7-2 REVIEW

Check Your Understanding

1. What should you remember about listening in order to resolve a conflict?
2. Why are physical actions a poor way to solve conflicts?
3. Should you interrupt a busy, tired person to discuss a conflict? Why or why not?
4. Why is a competitive spirit sometimes a barrier to resolving conflict?
5. Without understanding, what can happen?
6. **Thinking Critically.** What does this statement mean: "A major part of self-control is mouth control"?
7. **Problem Solving.** Jasmine stared at her sister's trophy and saw that same old annoying smile on Jennie's face. Jennie won everything, and Jasmine was about to ruin the moment with a few choice words. What do you think is going on here? How could the situation be improved?

Chapter 7
Review and Activities

CHAPTER SUMMARY

- Conflict in relationships arises from three common factors.
- Conflict can have either constructive or destructive results.
- Setting limits, discussing, negotiating, and compromising are all part of constructive conflict resolution.
- Needless conflict can be avoided.
- Good communication is crucial in resolving conflict.
- Self-control, both emotional and physical, contributes to successful resolution of conflict.
- Choosing the right time can make people more open to resolving conflict.
- By showing respect and using teamwork, those in conflict can find solutions that are agreeable to all.

REVIEW QUESTIONS

Section 7-1
1. What is conflict?
2. Describe three factors that can cause conflict in relationships.
3. What happens when a conflict is resolved constructively?
4. Explain what is meant by setting limits in an argument.
5. What are the purposes of negotiation and compromise in a conflict situation?
6. Give tips for avoiding conflict.

Section 7-2
1. How should you respond when someone sends a mixed message?
2. Why isn't silence a constructive way to resolve conflict?
3. Describe a good time for addressing a conflict.
4. What is respect? Give two examples of how you could show respect for another person during an argument.
5. Describe how understanding can help reduce conflict in a person's life.

BECOMING A PROBLEM SOLVER

1. Kristy and Robert are part-timers in a supermarket. Kristy is frustrated because Robert works hard when the boss is looking and hardly at all the rest of the time. What should Kristy do?
2. When Alex and his girlfriend have a disagreement, she becomes emotional and he stops talking. His refusal to talk makes her more upset and angry. What should they do?
3. April often suggests what she wants to do when she and her friend Maria are making weekend plans. Maria never agrees and pushes until she gets her way. What should April do?

THINKING CRITICALLY

1. **Drawing Conclusions.** When talking about a problem, a person should say things like "from my view," "in my opinion," and "it seems to me that." How do these help?
2. **Predicting Consequences.** What might happen if a person continually holds back anger?
3. **Drawing Conclusions.** Why is it so hard to walk away from a conflict? When would the ability to do this be to your advantage?
4. **Identifying Cause and Effect.** What factors could cause a small disagreement to become a large conflict?
5. **Analyzing Behavior.** Why do some people feel compelled to win arguments?

MAKING CURRICULUM CONNECTIONS

1. **Language Arts.** Write a dialogue that shows how a conflict develops and how it can be constructively resolved.
2. **Social Studies.** Use the Internet or other resources to find statistics on violence in society. Summarize what you learn for the class.

APPLYING YOUR KNOWLEDGE

1. With a partner, make a list of the five most important qualities a person needs in order to be a conflict-resolution expert. Share your list with the class and create a composite list of the top ten qualities.
2. Analyze your own approach to conflict by completing this sentence in writing: "When something makes me angry, I usually . . ." What changes do you need to make?
3. Bring to class comic strips that illustrate conflicts. Evaluate the resolution skills depicted in the comics for the class.
4. With a group of classmates, create a questionnaire that will reveal how well a person is able to handle conflict. Exchange questionnaires with another group and try them out.

Family & Community Connections

1. Think about a recent disagreement you had with someone in your family. Write at least two ways that you could have handled the situation differently in order to improve the outcome.

2. For one week, observe conflicts in your school and neighborhood. Keep notes on your observations. Describe what you notice to your class and share ideas for solutions.

Chapter 8

Building Family Relationships

WORDS FOR THOUGHT

"Humor is the shortest distance between two people."
(Victor Borge)

IN YOUR OWN WORDS

What is the longest distance between two people?

158

Qualities of Strong Families

OBJECTIVES

After studying this section, you should be able to:

- Relate communication to family strength.
- Demonstrate ways that family members show respect for each other.
- Explain what builds unity within a family.
- Suggest traditions that promote family togetherness.

TERMS TO LEARN

affirmation
commitment
traditions

Like a winning team, strong families don't just happen. They work to refine the skills and qualities they need to succeed. A basketball team practices passing the ball; a speech team practices confidence and poise.

In studying families, social scientists have identified qualities and actions that strong ones share. Some of these signs of strength will be described in this section. Many of them grow from the relationship-building skills you've studied in this unit. Not every family has every quality and takes every action discussed here. The more they have and do, however, the better their chance of creating strong family bonds.

COMMUNICATING EFFECTIVELY

Good communication is vital to any relationship, and family ties are no different. Family members need to exchange so much information, from coordinating schedules to sharing dreams and fears. Communicating in the security of the family fills the hunger for intimacy like nothing else can. Good communication is a sign that family members are in touch with each other's feelings and lives.

If you've ever had problems communicating in the family, you know how valuable this skill is. One common barrier to effective family communication is the television. Some people get so wrapped up in the lives of fictional families in comedies or soap operas, they neglect to interact with their own.

When Wanda's family recognized the television problem, they made some changes. They had fallen into the habit of eating supper while watching the news, then leaving the set on until bedtime. The family began weaning themselves by turning the set off after the news, then having supper. They also put a limit on the number of hours each person could watch television daily. They rediscovered conversation, and found that their lives were just as interesting as those on any show. Now Wanda's family controls the television; it no longer controls them.

Affirming Each Other

Suppose you prepared your family a fancy dinner. They ate the food without complaint, but no one mentioned liking it. How would you feel about yourself and your efforts?

As you read earlier, mind reading is no substitute for real communication. When people don't share their feelings directly, however, family members may see no other choice. Guessing that other people care about you is as unrewarding as guessing they liked your meal. You want to be told.

In strong families, people communicate love unmistakably, both verbally and non-verbally. They say, "I love you," "I'm proud of you," and "You did that well." They give hugs, do favors, and find many other ways to show their good feelings toward each other. When you do any of these, you're giving **affirmation** (AF-ur-MAY-shun). You are providing positive input that helps others feel appreciated and supported.

RESPECTING EACH OTHER

Another mark of a strong family is respect for each other. Family members realize that each person is different. They take pride in individual traits and abilities and don't take advantage of anyone's shortcomings. Family members in all stages of life are respected.

Communication and sharing interests are vital skills in family life. You might find yourself spending more valuable time with your family.

Building Character

Humor: A Quality That Counts

Do you have a friend who can always make you laugh, even on your worst days? Humor is the ability to see the lighter side of a situation and to laugh at mistakes. Humor can help smooth the rough spots in relationships if you laugh *with* others, not *at* them. A teen might show a sense of humor by:

- Putting frosting on a cake that flopped and presenting it as "volcano cake."
- Putting a cartoon that poked fun at older siblings on a younger sibling's bedroom door.
- Giving a favorite sweater that shrank in the wash to the family dog to wear.
- Making a large name tag to wear to class after a teacher has repeatedly called the teen by an older sibling's name.

QUESTIONS

1. What might get in the way of developing a sense of humor?
2. Is humor always a helpful approach?
3. How have you used humor to your benefit recently?

Respect for others' opinions requires sensitivity. In a strong family, people respect each other as individuals who are competent to draw their own conclusions. Matthew is developing political views that differ from his parents'. They listen to his opinions. Matthew responds by trying to understand their point of view and the reasoning behind it.

Everyone has a need for privacy at times. Each person needs a safe place for personal belongings and time to be alone. Strong families respect this need. They try to step back and make room for each other, even when living space is small. When Cinda needed privacy to wrap some gifts, her sister took her textbooks from the bedroom they shared and finished her homework in the kitchen.

SHOWING UNITY

While valuing individuality, members of a strong family appreciate the many ways that they are one. They build unity and become a team by sharing commitment, trust, beliefs, and responsibility.

Demonstrating Commitment

A **commitment** is a pledge to support something of value. People who value the family are committed to it. They are willing to work together and sacrifice for the benefit of the family unit. They take genuine interest in the happiness and welfare of each family member.

Trusting Each Other

Trust is as important in family relationships as it is in any other. Family members must know they can count on each other. Children learn trust as infants, when parents supply what they need. Trust builds when parents are caring and true to their word.

Children, in turn, learn to be trustworthy. In strong families, children are given responsibilities suited to their age and ability. When ten-year-old Gerard came home on time for lunch, his grandmother felt confident about letting him play at his friend's house in the future. As he matures, Gerard will be given additional freedoms and opportunities.

The road to trust can be a bumpy one. Children and parents alike can and do make mistakes. Strong families believe in second chances—and in doing better when they are given a second chance.

Sharing Values and Beliefs

Strong families share many values and beliefs. These may range from thoughts about education and politics to religious beliefs and social conditions. A core of beliefs provides stability and a shared outlook on life.

Family Traditions Promote Stability.

Recreation

Traditions can be simple or elaborate. Some are inherited and some created.

A Sunday afternoon outing can be a regular event.

Hobbies

Sharing a hobby or interest is habit-forming.

Many traditions are part of religious practices.

Religion

Many families find strength in their religious beliefs. A belief in a higher power gives the family hope, especially in troubled times. Families who participate in organized religious activities together support each other.

A family may share a commitment to some ideal beyond themselves. Nathan's family believes in caring for the environment. His mother runs a community recycling program, and his father is a biology teacher who feels strongly about the environment. Family vacations are spent backpacking in national parks. This deep sense of concern for nature brings the family together.

Building Strong Morals

Many family beliefs consist of a moral code, principles of right and wrong. Strong families communicate this code clearly. Parents who agree on basic issues are more likely to teach morals. They discuss their beliefs so they can support each other in what they teach their children.

Acting Responsibly

Dan came home from work to find his fourteen-year-old son Patrick heating a casserole in the microwave oven, while four-year-old Megan put up her toys before din-

What traditions take place in your family? What traditions would you like to start?

A picnic in a special place could be an annual event.

Outdoors

Celebrations often turn into family traditions.

Traditions are based on indoor and outdoor activities.

Celebrations

Balancing Work & Family Life

THE CHALLENGE —

Finding Time Together

A quick "hi" as you zip past a parent in the hall while getting ready for school isn't exactly what the experts define as quality time together. Busy schedules keep families apart, yet spending time together forges relationships.

How You Can Help

If time for family togetherness is hard to arrange, try these ideas:

- Record your memories. Ask a different family member to take charge of recording each outing. He or she may take pictures, write a poem, draw a picture, or make a collage. Build a family scrapbook together to hold your memories.

- Make one night a week "Family Night." Ask members which night is most convenient; then set a time. Encourage everyone to reserve the date as they would other appointments.

- Start a new tradition. Eat breakfast with family members every Sunday or pizza together each Monday night.

- Set up a suggestion box. Encourage family members to fill it with ideas for an activity. Then vote on which to do that week.

- Host an "invite a friend" activity so family members meet each other's friends.

---

ner. Each family member was acting responsibly by doing a task that contributed to the smooth running of the home.

Strong families practice and teach responsibility. People learn to do the jobs that are expected of them, without reminders or pressure. Family members also show responsibility by caring for each other and providing support.

Overcoming Problems as a Team

All families experience problems. Strong families develop ways to approach and solve them. They use good communication skills to identify a problem early, when it is most manageable. They are committed enough to the family's survival to work and even sacrifice for solutions.

When serious trouble strikes, strong families pull together as a team. They know that they are stronger together than they are apart. They trust in one another and in their shared beliefs. When problems go beyond their own ability to solve, a strong family looks to outside resources for help.

SPENDING TIME TOGETHER

Can you feel close to people if you rarely spend time with them? Time spent together is both a sign of family strength and a way to build it. Strong families explore common interests and activities. During these times families develop the traits that keep them strong.

In many families, finding time for each other is a struggle. Work, school, volunteering, and other personal activities cut into family time. Everyone needs personal fulfillment, but neglecting family time and responsibilities is like cutting the roots of a plant. The plant cannot thrive.

People need to make a personal commitment to being with family. Sharing at least one leisure activity a week is a goal many strong families achieve. Including another family member in tasks works for others.

Establishing Traditions

Part of a family's time together can be spent establishing traditions. **Traditions** are customs that are followed over time and often passed from one generation to another. They build a bank of common family memories.

WHAT'S IMPORTANT?

While reading about strong families, you may have recognized some of the qualities in your family. Keep building on those. You may have also identified some weaknesses. Remember that any family can improve if they want to. Strong families are found wherever people appreciate those closest to them—and show it.

SECTION 8-1 REVIEW

Check Your Understanding

1. How can television be an obstacle to family strength?
2. How do people affirm one another?
3. How do children learn trust?
4. What kinds of shared beliefs contribute to family unity?
5. Give some examples of traditions a family might follow.
6. **Thinking Critically.** Why is giving affirmation difficult for people in some families?
7. **Problem Solving.** Bethany's family sets aside one night a week as "family fun night," when they pop popcorn, talk, and play games. Fifteen-year-old Bethany feels she has outgrown these rituals, but her parents and twelve-year-old sister still enjoy them. What should Bethany do?

Getting Along in Families

OBJECTIVES

After studying this section, you should be able to:

- Explain what a family system is.
- Offer suggestions for understanding parents and siblings.
- Demonstrate ways to get along with parents and siblings.

TERMS TO LEARN

family system
siblings
heredity
environment

People in families want to get along with each other. When things don't run smoothly, however, they often make a common mistake—they do nothing or they do more of the same. Wishing for change doesn't create it. Doing more of the same brings more of the same. Only when people take action do things improve, but who will take the first step? Why not you?

THE FAMILY SYSTEM

Family members, together with their particular roles and personalities, make up the **family system**. A family system is a web that ties members together. What any person in the system does affects others. Suppose you come home humming cheerfully and offer to make dinner when it's not your turn. What

reactions might you expect from others? How might their reactions, in turn, affect you? In the family system, everything is interconnected.

Getting along within the family system can be a challenge. When people make an effort, however, the family system functions well.

Looking at family relationships usually means first studying what goes on between any two people. Each child has a relationship with each parent and with each other child. If stepparents or extended family members are involved, relationships become more complex. The variety of relationships provides the spark that can cause family relationships to shift and change.

As a teen, you're probably most interested in two types of family relationships—the

You fit into a family system as a sister or brother, a daughter or son, a granddaughter or grandson, and perhaps in other ways as well. **What responsibilities come with these roles?**

one you have with parents and those with brothers and sisters. Understanding and making these work can improve life within the family system.

RELATING TO PARENTS

Most teens have relationships with one or more adults who act in a parenting role with them. These adults may be parents, stepparents, or legal guardians. Whatever your situation, you can apply the principles about parents described here.

Most relationships between parents and teens are loving ones. Surveys of teens show that most get along well with their parents and have good relationships with them. In any close relationship, however, problems can occur.

Understanding Parents

Getting along with people is easier when you understand them. Many books have been written for parents on understanding teens. To make the relationship work well, teens must also understand their parents.

A parent-teen relationship strengthens as mutual understanding grows. If you want your parents to be there for you, then you need to be there for them, too.

> **Affirming Family Members.** Do you enjoy recognition and attention? Schools, employers, and communities all give awards for outstanding contributions and performance—why not families? Try these ideas for recognizing someone's "best supporting role in a family":
>
> - Create awards to affirm family members who make family life more enjoyable. You could recognize a helpful trait, such as dependability or peacemaking, or an accomplishment that contributes to the family, such as getting a raise at work. You might commend a practical action, such as keeping a clean room.
> - Design and print certificates, ribbons, or badges on the computer (use one in the school or community library if you don't have one at home).
> - Plan a presentation ceremony where each family member is recognized, even if some members choose not to participate.
>
> **Try It Out.** Decide how you could show recognition to each member of your family. Set a goal to recognize at least one family member each week. You might even start a new family tradition!

To help understanding, nothing works better than using empathy. Have you ever thought about the job of parenting? Try writing a job description. Few jobs of such length and responsibility are taken on with so little training. Parents are human. They want to do a good job. They don't want to make mistakes, which they and others have to live with, any more than you do. Putting yourself in a parent's shoes can put you far along the road to understanding.

Parents' Concerns

As a teen, you may have a lot of concerns about life. You may forget what is on the minds of others. Parents have plenty to think about. They may be concerned with:

- **Making a living.** Handling the pressures of work can be stressful, especially if the parent is unhappy with the job. In certain times, keeping a job can be a concern.

- **Providing for you.** Most parents want to give children more than they themselves had, and sometimes more than they are able to give.
- **The family situation.** Decisions about caring for older family members and other family problems are a parent's responsibility.
- **Health.** Not everyone enjoys good health. Parents aren't likely to tell children if age has made them a little slower or more tired than before.
- **The future.** No one ever "has it made." Just like you, parents may worry about how they will manage as they get older.
- **You.** You may feel confident in your decision-making ability. Parents, however, often worry about whether they have prepared you well enough to make wise choices, especially in light of the societal problems you may have to face. They've

seen life's challenges and threats. Since you've been such an important part of their lives for so long, is it any wonder that they sometimes act afraid to let you go?

Many other concerns can also affect a parent's behavior. Preoccupation or moodiness, when it happens, often has nothing to do with you. If you were to ask, a parent might say, "I just had something on my mind."

Different Perspectives

Understanding parents also hinges on knowing what motivates them. They don't always see things the same way you do—and for good reason. Parents were raised in a different era. Their experiences and background are different from yours. Diana and her mother, for example, battled over hairstyles until they happened across some old family photos one day. The laughs they had over the hairstyles of 25 years ago helped them put their disagreement in a new light.

Although it comes as a surprise to some teens, most parents do know something. Just as you have knowledge that can be helpful to a young child, parents have experience and wisdom that can be helpful to you. Listening and asking for help and information makes parents feel good. They feel useful and special to you. When you respect their opinions as adults, they see that you are moving closer to adulthood yourself.

Talking to Parents

Adrian cringed to hear her parents say, "I can't believe it; it seems like only yesterday that Adrian was just a baby, and now she's almost grown." When she thought about their words though, Adrian saw how true they were. She had known her parents only as adults, but they had watched her change dramatically. They had adapted to her increasing abilities, even when they weren't sure exactly what those were. Was she ready to ride a bicycle? Was she old enough to stay home alone?

"I didn't know you ran track in high school, Mom. Didn't you hate wearing that funny uniform?" You can feel closer to parents when you know more about them. What parents were like as teens can be an interesting topic to explore.

Most teens want private time to themselves. What may happen if they put up too many barriers?

Their questions didn't end when Adrian became a teen. Was she an adult yet, or did she still need their guidance? Sometimes Adrian didn't know the answer herself. She did know, however, why her parents didn't always treat and talk to her as she thought they should.

As you can see, parents and teens can easily be on very different wavelengths. By talking with each other, they can know each other better. Parents and teens need to talk. They want conversation that is pleasant and helpful, not argumentative. Try these suggestions for improving conversation with your parents:

- **Take time to get to know your parents.** Simple questions about their lives pave the way for more involved conversation.
- **Try a positive attitude.** So often it's not what you say, but how you say it. A short, snippy response sets a negative tone and may even end the conversation.

- **Look for easy approaches to difficult topics.** Talking about a television show, a movie, a book, or something that happened to a friend can ease you into touchy subjects. Parents are just as uncomfortable as you are about some topics.
- **Use humor.** When things start to get heavy, look for ways to lighten up. Sometimes serious points can be made in humorous ways.

Limits and Rules

Parents don't set limits and rules for fun. Enforcing rules is not always easy, but it's necessary—for several reasons. Parents set limits and rules in order to direct family life. They want to be sure the family's values are carried out. Rules can also help children develop positive qualities, such as caring and honesty.

Protection is another reason for setting rules. Rules about crossing the street and curfews are set with safety in mind.

Limits and rules can be a source of conflict for families. As teens become more independent, they may feel that some rules are too restrictive. Teens who feel ready for more freedom find that calmly discussing the subject with parents is the best way to reach agreement.

Parents loosen rules at a pace that they are comfortable with. Teens who have earned trust by acting responsibly are usually rewarded with privileges.

Why Bother?

You have so much going on in your life. You have your own concerns and pressures, so why bother to make an extra effort to get along with your parents? The answer is simple. You need each other and will continue to, probably for a long time. Destructive patterns and habits, once begun, become more and more difficult to break over the years. First steps are often the hardest ones, but someone has to be responsible for taking them. When you look back, you'll know they were worthwhile.

RELATING TO SIBLINGS

Relationships with **siblings**, brothers and sisters, tend to be the longest of all family ties; they last as long as the siblings do. They are also among the most complicated. As you may have noticed, sisters and brothers in a family usually have very distinct personalities. Intrigued at this situation, psychologists have looked for explanations.

Building a relationship with one sibling may take a different approach than is needed with another. What effect does age have?

Heredity and Environment

The family contributes the two major factors that influence personality: heredity and environment. **Heredity** (huh-RED-uht-ee) involves the genetic traits received from parents at birth. **Environment** (in-VY-run-munt) includes the surroundings, people, and experiences that shape development. The combination of heredity and environment makes siblings both alike and different.

Research involving identical twins who were raised apart has shown how heredity affects people. Although raised in different environments, the twins in the studies showed striking similarities that could be linked to their common heritage. From studies like these, most psychologists have concluded that heredity plays a large role in shaping personality.

Even more interesting, however, is the question of environment. Just how much does experience contribute to personality? Environment has an effect, but the process is more complicated than you might expect.

Each child experiences the family environment subjectively. That is, everything is influenced by the child's personality and perceptions. Thus, similar experiences in the family can produce very different results in siblings.

Birth Order

Some psychologists believe that birth order, or the order in which each child is born, is a factor in shaping personality. Birth order strongly affects the family environment for each child. As a first child, for instance, Dana was born to inexperienced parents who gave her their complete attention. When her brother Jared was born, the couple had more confidence in their skills and roles as parents, but less time to spend on a baby. Later, when Rick was born, he entered a family where four people had ongoing relationships with each other.

In a sense, Dana, Jared, and Rick were each born into a somewhat different family. In a different environment, their personalities and ideas about relationships were bound to be different also.

Parents tend to expect a great deal of their first-born. Oldest children tend to grow up responsible, independent, and ambitious. Many become leaders and achievers.

The bond between siblings can last a lifetime if they take good care of it. What do they stand to gain?

Focus On ...

Sibling Rivalry

Where there are siblings, competition between brothers and sisters, sibling rivalry, is common. Children and teens want love, recognition, and to be treated "fairly." Some look for signs of favoritism. Feeling mistreated leads to complaints, fights, and even low self-esteem. If sibling rivalry is a problem for you, ask these questions:

- Do you keep as much track of the "rights" that come your way as you do the "wrongs"? Privileges and special treatment are easily taken for granted and dismissed. A sibling's special moment may come at a different time from yours.
- Is your whole family together all the time? If not, how do you know how every individual is treated? You might be missing something.
- Could parents have reasons that aren't clear to you? Often they do.

- Are you exactly like your siblings? Differences can account for different treatment.
- Do your siblings feel that you are favored? If so, then who's right?

USING YOUR KNOWLEDGE

Jesse is a talented pianist. His younger brother Seth has a long memory of their parents taking Jesse to lessons, going to his recitals, and even buying a piano for him. To Seth, his parents are more involved with Jesse and more proud of him. What might you say to Seth?

Second children are less involved with parents than the older sibling was. Often cheerful and practical, they typically thrive on social activities and friendships. They tend to be peacemakers.

Youngest children must learn early in life to get along with others. The experience can make them popular, fun loving, and generous. If doted on by siblings, however, a youngest child can become self-centered. Growing up in the shadow of older siblings can challenge the youngest to find his or her own identity.

Children without siblings usually get a lot of attention from their parents—and are usually watched more closely than children in larger families. Lacking siblings, they may relate better to adults than to other children. They may try harder to please their parents. Only children tend to be fast learners, good students, and high achievers. They often lead busy, productive lives.

Although it's interesting to look at the possible effects of birth order, not every person fits the profiles. Many influences can cause exceptions.

Managing Sibling Relationships

Studies have shown that siblings do share one trait: they constantly compare how they are treated in the family. Their view of the treatment, however, is not always accurate. Likewise, other studies have found that parents, in general, treat their children in basically the same way at specific ages. They have little control, however, over how their children perceive what they do.

This problem is natural, given a child's point of view. Three-year-old Kaitlyn sees her mother care for one-year-old Ryan. Her mother picks him up and carries him; she fusses over him while feeding and bathing him. Kaitlyn thinks her mother loves Ryan more than she loves her. Kaitlyn actually received the same treatment as an infant. She doesn't need and wouldn't like the constant attention now. Kaitlyn doesn't see that, though. All she knows is Ryan gets different treatment.

Feelings of being "at odds" with siblings are normal, then. Managing those feelings can make family life smoother. If you're looking for techniques for getting along better with siblings, try these ideas:

Time spent on hobbies and interests is a necessary part of life. What could happen, however, if family ties are sacrificed for these activities?

- **Work on settling disagreements with siblings yourself.** Parents may have trouble determining who's right and who's wrong. Asking them to support one of their children against another is unfair. Any decision they make may be held against them.
- **Talk about your feelings.** As a child, your parents had to help you recognize your feelings. Now you must communicate your feelings to them.
- **Look for your own strengths instead of comparing yourself to siblings.** Siblings are as different from you as friends are, so why compare?
- **Avoid serious conflict with siblings.** They will be important people in your life for many years to come. It makes sense to take very good care of the relationships.

ENRICHING YOUR FAMILY SYSTEM

You probably know people who can't or won't get involved with their family. To them, friends or outside activities seem more important than talking and spending time with parents or siblings. No one can tell them what they are missing. They must realize it themselves, and then it may be too late.

Does this description sound at all familiar? If so, now could be the time for a fresh start. Your role in the family can be "new and improved." Remember that how you get along with your family affects how everyone gets along. Be an example for others to follow. Begin now with a personal commitment to family strength and a pledge for action.

SECTION 8-2 REVIEW

Check Your Understanding

1. Why is the family said to be a system?
2. Why do parents often see things differently from their children?
3. What are the purposes of the rules and limits parents set?
4. Briefly explain why birth order may affect a child's personality.
5. What quality do many siblings share?
6. **Thinking Critically.** What problems might arise if parents assume their children will fit the profiles described by birth order theory?
7. **Problem Solving.** Munro's curfew, which his parents think is reasonable, is also one hour earlier than his friends'. Sometimes, at his friends' urging, Munro breaks curfew and his parents punish him. Munro honors the curfew for a time until the pattern begins again. How can Munro and his parents resolve this problem?

Chapter 8
Review and Activities

CHAPTER SUMMARY

- The more traits of strength a family has, the better the chances are that family relationships are healthy.
- Good communication is important in strong families.
- When people respect each other, they show that they understand and accept the differences between them.
- Families build unity by showing commitment and trust; sharing beliefs and responsibility; and overcoming problems.
- Families need to spend time together. Traditions can make time together especially meaningful.
- Understanding parents' concerns and point of view improves parent-teen relationships.
- Rules and limits can be a source of conflict in the family. Talking about them helps create understanding.
- Getting along with siblings is important to family strength and personal fulfillment.

REVIEW QUESTIONS

Section 8-1
1. Why do families need to communicate well?
2. Name two ways that family members show respect.
3. What are five ways families can show unity?
4. How can sharing beliefs benefit a family?
5. Give some examples of how people show responsibility in the family.
6. What role do traditions play in strong families?

Section 8-2
1. What is a family system?
2. What must teens understand about parents in order to get along with them?
3. Give three tips for improving conversations with parents.
4. Should siblings ask a parent to settle their conflicts? Why or why not?
5. Why is it important to avoid serious conflict with siblings?

BECOMING A PROBLEM SOLVER

1. LaTisha has always felt that her sister Ellie gets better treatment from their parents. In anger, she told a friend an embarrassing secret about Ellie. Later, she heard her friend repeat this story to one of Ellie's classmates. How can LaTisha best deal with this situation?

2. Jamie's mother has been noticeably tense and short-tempered for over a week. When Jamie asks if something is wrong, she apologizes and says, "It's nothing to worry about." Jamie's grandmother has been in poor health. He wonders if this is the cause of his mother's moods. What should Jamie do?

THINKING CRITICALLY

1. **Analyzing Behavior.** Why do you think many parents are reluctant to share personal concerns with their children?
2. **Analyzing Behavior.** Seventeen-year-old Kyle spends most of his time in his room with the door shut. He seldom talks to his parents about anything. How might better communication help?
3. **Identifying Cause and Effect.** How might heredity affect personality development?
4. **Recognizing Points of View.** Why might it be easier for a parent to understand a teen's point of view than for a teen to understand a parent's? What can make a parent's understanding difficult?

MAKING CURRICULUM CONNECTIONS

1. **Art.** In the art medium of your choice, illustrate your concept of the family system. You might choose one image that symbolizes the family system to you, or use several images that represent the system's various aspects.
2. **Health.** What do you think is the effect of sibling rivalry on a sibling's mental health? Is such a relationship always negative? Are any positive results possible? Explain your answers.

APPLYING YOUR KNOWLEDGE

1. Working with a group, make a list of five topics on which parents set limits and rules. For each area, have half the group write a few rules that they would establish if they were the parents of teens. Have the others in the group write rules that they as teens think are reasonable. Compare lists. Share your findings with the class.
2. If you could choose, would you be an only child, a child with one sibling, or a child with several siblings? Write a short essay explaining the advantages and disadvantages of your choice.

Family & Community Connections

1. Make a list of television programs that depict parent-child and sibling relationships. Evaluate the reality and the quality of these relationships.

2. Investigate the resources available in your community for strengthening families. Are there classes to help improve communication? Volunteer activities that the whole family can take part in? Counseling services for dealing with family problems? Compile your findings into a booklet that could be distributed to families.

UNIT 3

Managing with Insight

Teen Views

Does a lack of time cause problems for your family?

Yoshiko

"Yes, but we're working on it. Both my parents have weird schedules at work. My father couldn't even get time off for any of my track meets. He was really disappointed when he missed my best time in the distance relay. That's when he talked to his boss. Now he's taking a half day off to come to the city meet."

Jonah

"It used to, but when I got my license, that helped. My mother said she was running in circles trying to get me and my brother and sister all the places we needed to be. Now I do some of the driving. I can tell my mom is really happy about that."

What's your view?

How does your family handle time pressures?

Chapter 9

Solving Problems in Your Life

IN YOUR OWN WORDS

When you have a problem, how can optimism help?

Identifying Problems

OBJECTIVES

After studying this section, you should be able to:

- Explain the levels of impact that problems can have in your life.
- Differentiate symptoms from real problems.
- Explain how attitudes affect your ability to solve problems.

TERMS TO LEARN

problem
procrastination
denial

An old English proverb says: "Every path has its puddle." In other words, no matter where you go in life, you're going to encounter problems. Don't let that thought get you down, however. Problems are inevitable, but when you're in charge, they don't have to ruin your life.

KINDS OF PROBLEMS

What do you think of when you hear the word "problem"? All sorts of images may come to mind. A **problem** is any situation with a dilemma that must be solved or worked out. Great or small, problems need your attention.

Simple Problems

Some problems in life have less impact than others. What if you had to be in two places at the same time? What if you were headed outdoors to shovel snow, and you couldn't find your warm gloves? These are problems, but they're minor. Every day people encounter small problems. They just take them in stride and work them out.

Low-Impact Problems

As problems become more complicated, they have greater impact on your life. They also become harder to handle.

Suppose two friends have placed you in the middle of their disagreement. What will you do? Solving this problem could cost you a friendship, or even two, if not handled well. What if you notice someone you would like to get to know, but you feel uncomfortable about how to approach the person. What do you do?

Problems like these aren't likely to have long-term impact on your life and well-being, but you do feel the effects from them. They need your attention—at least for a while.

High-Impact Problems

By contrast, some problems in life are serious, even critical. What problems can you identify that have high impact? A person who is failing in school or is very troubled by a weight problem, for example, has a more serious problem. Ellen's mother has cancer. How can Ellen cope with this problem?

When ignored or unrecognized, serious problems can threaten your health and well-being. Impacts can last a long time. Dealing with difficult problems isn't easy, but it can be done. You learn to work toward solutions and find ways to manage. You'll learn how in this chapter.

Social Problems

Some problems go far beyond their impact on just you and the people close to you. You may have concerns about people who are homeless. Perhaps environmental issues make a difference to you. If you

The problems you tackle in life can range from simple to difficult. Figuring out what to wear for a special occasion is typically a simple problem. If money isn't available to buy something new, however, what happens to the problem?

Everyone is hurt when emotional problems turn to physical violence. How might this family face their problem together to brighten the future for all of them?

wanted your school to have a new technical center or your neighborhood to have a park, these, too, might grab your attention.

With problems like these, the social implications are obvious. They may not be personal problems, but people who care about others take a personal interest in social problems.

Social problems, such as littering, are both created and solved by people. What can this teen do to prevent a problem for society?

SYMPTOM OR PROBLEM?

When you're sick, you might have a fever. The fever gets your attention, but it's only a symptom. The real problem is the disease and its cause. That's what needs to be treated.

In the same way, people may not see the real problem they face because they look no further than the symptoms. Suppose a parent and teen argue over curfew rules. Is this a symptom or a problem? Think twice. The real issue could be about independence and who's in charge of decisions.

Symptoms are useful because they offer clues that help identify serious problems. If you're confused, concerned, upset, or oppressed, you need to figure out why. When such feelings last, a problem may need to be faced.

In families, frequent arguments signal a problem. A lack of communication can cause families to grow apart, also indicating a problem. Negative behavior, whether disrespectful comments or throwing things, is another sign.

All of these are symptoms of problems. They are not the problem itself. When symptoms occur, you need to ask why. In the feuding family, for example, the problem isn't that they fight too much. The problem is the reason or reasons *why* they fight so often. Be persistent in trying to identify *real* problems. If you solve problems, the symptoms will go away. If you only treat symptoms, the problem is still there and the symptoms will return.

SKILLS CHECKLIST

Communication Skills
Leadership Skills
Management Skills
Thinking Skills

Beat the Procrastination Trap

Even with a goal in mind, procrastination can still be a trap. Use this checklist to help you overcome procrastination:

✓ I have written down when and where I will start working on this goal.
✓ I have identified the tools and information I need.
✓ I have listed the short, easy tasks, and I'll start with them.
✓ I will do my least favorite jobs before easier ones.
✓ I have found support through others who have the same problem.
✓ I have promised myself an appropriate reward once my goal is reached.

Using Your Skills

Using the information above, design a brochure about overcoming procrastination. You can use a computer program that creates brochures or create it by hand. If possible, print the brochure and make copies available in the school counseling office.

Ignoring a problem won't make it go away. You can find time to think about the problems you need to tackle, perhaps while exercising or listening to music. When would be a good time for you?

ATTITUDES TOWARD PROBLEMS

Your attitude toward a problem can sometimes harm you more than the problem itself. Why is that? People react differently to problems. Some reactions can prevent you from finding a solution, and that isn't good.

Procrastination

"I don't know what to do, so I'll just wait." **Procrastination** (pruh-KRASS-tuh-NAY-shun) means putting something off.

People who procrastinate plan to take care of things, but they never do. They may feel uncomfortable or lack confidence, even with a minor issue.

This approach to a serious problem can be very costly. If one day leads to another, the problem doesn't get resolved. As the "mole hill" becomes a "mountain" that gets harder and harder to climb, the effects can cause increasing harm.

Denial

Some people don't want to face the fact that a problem exists. This is called **denial**. Denial makes a person struggle on without ever acknowledging the problem.

Surprisingly, people often spend their time dealing with simple problems that have little importance but let the big problems go. Ignoring an overwhelming problem may seem easier.

Tony started using drugs when he was in junior high school. Several years later, his life was a mess. He hated what had happened, but trying to change things seemed impossible. For a long time, he turned away from his problem because it was too hard to face. Everything kept getting worse, however, until he acknowledged the problem and decided to take some difficult steps to turn his life around.

A tough problem can be hard to face. It's easier to ignore the situation, hoping it will go away, but it doesn't.

Denial can even be subconscious. A person might put an overwhelming problem aside even without realizing. *You* might see the person's problem, but he or she genuinely thinks it doesn't exist. This can be very serious, since the person in denial can't seek a solution to a problem that supposedly isn't there.

Confronting a problem may mean handling unpleasant emotions and situations. A serious look at what could happen often gives people the strength to do what needs to be done.

A Positive Approach to Problems

When you have knowledge and skills, your confidence grows, even when confronted by problems. People need to see problems for what they are: conquerable situations. With this view, you can take positive steps to decrease trouble and pain in your life. You can keep individual and family problems from growing into crises. Learning and practicing problem-solving skills can make your life easier and better.

Here are some coping strategies:
- Recognize that a crisis exists.
- Rely on others for support.
- Analyze possible ways to deal with the crisis.
- Realize that roles and responsibilities may change.
- Eat well, exercise, and get sufficient rest.
- Ask for professional help, if needed.

SECTION 9-1 REVIEW

Check Your Understanding

1. If you spill spaghetti sauce on a pair of old work jeans, how serious is the problem? What if you spill on a new white sweater? What if the sweater was a recent gift from someone special?
2. Why is treating symptoms rather than problems ineffective?
3. Why do some people procrastinate when it comes to problems?
4. Are people always aware that they are in denial? Explain your answer.
5. **Thinking Critically.** Seventeen-year-old Spencer said to a friend: "My folks are always on my case, but hey, no problem. I just get out of the house." How would you evaluate this situation?
6. **Problem Solving.** Jani's grandmother wants to renew her driver's license. She has asked Jani to help her study for the exam. Jani's parents believe her grandmother is becoming a danger to herself and others when she drives. They would prefer that she fail the exam and have asked Jani not to help her. What is Jani's problem? What should she do?

Management Skills

OBJECTIVES

After studying this section, you should be able to:

- Describe how management skills are used in problem solving.
- Explain how to make sound decisions.
- Relate thinking skills to solving problems.
- Explain the impact of ethics on problem solving.

TERMS TO LEARN

management process
long-term goals
short-term goals
resources
prioritize
resourceful
decision
reasoning
ethics

What's the difference between a person who solves problems with ease and someone who doesn't? Often it's the skills they have. With certain skills at your command, you can approach problems with much greater confidence.

part of getting along in life, and they're also useful in problem solving.

MANAGEMENT PROCESS

Have you ever noticed that the busiest people are typically the ones who are able to accomplish the most? That's because they know how to use the **management process**. With this process, people set goals and take carefully planned steps to reach them. They find and use all the resources available. Management skills are a basic

Goal Setting

If you learn to set goals, you can use them in several ways. First, goals help you accomplish tasks. If you decide to read a novel and wash the car over the weekend, for example, you've set two goals. Second, goals channel the direction of your life. You might set goals about education or the family you wish to have. Having such goals encourages you to take early steps toward reaching them. Third, goals can help you solve problems. A goal guides your efforts toward a solution.

To be effective, goal setting should follow certain guidelines:

- **Make goals specific.** State that you will improve your technical drawing grade from a C to a B next semester, not just that you will do better.
- **Establish a time frame for reaching goals.** Decide when you should reach a goal. Goals that take months or years to achieve are **long-term goals**. Career plans and saving for a cross-country trip are long-term. **Short-term goals** require only short periods to achieve. When you make a list of things to do on Saturday, you're setting short-term goals. Sometimes short-term goals help you reach those that are long-term.
- **Show accountability.** If possible, involve someone in your goals. Report what your plans are, so you'll have more incentive to follow through. When someone is watching, motivation increases.
- **Write goals down.** If you write your goals and put them where you can see them often, you'll have a reminder that can help you stay focused.

Identifying Resources

You don't have to solve problems without help. In fact, some problems require help of many kinds. When that's true, what do you do? If you're smart, you'll learn to identify resources. **Resources** are whatever you can use to reach goals and solve problems. Good managers know how to find and use resources.

Resources are typically categorized into three groupings. As you read about the types, think about where you can find these resources in your own life. That way you'll become skillful at identifying them. You'll also be better equipped to find them when you need them.

Human Resources

Human resources are what *people* can offer you, including your own skills, talents, and energy. You gain information, expertise, and sometimes just a willing hand from others. Who helps you when you have a problem? Could you build new associations that might be helpful in the future?

Reaching a goal is like winning a race. What if there were no finish lines? Is living without goals like that?

Focus On ...

Managing Your Time

Good managers often avoid problems by managing well. One of their skills is knowing how to use time effectively. Here's what they do:

- **List and prioritize.** To **prioritize** (pry-OR-uh-tize) means to rank things according to importance. When you make a to-do list, what will you do first and last? Number each item in order of importance to help you see.
- **Schedule your week.** Get a daily planner and divide each day into one-hour blocks. Fill them in with activities you know you'll have, such as school and work. Fill in other activities as you learn of them. Don't forget to leave time for things you enjoy.
- **Double up on activities.** When convenient, do two things at once. Sew on a button while talking on the phone. Think about plans for a school project while cooking dinner.

- **Organize your space.** Keep related items together. Paper, pens, and textbooks could be in a box or drawer near where you study. Place kitchen utensils close to where they're used.

USING YOUR KNOWLEDGE

Kate was worried about the week ahead. She had three tests to study for in addition to two tennis matches. Since her father's birthday was on Wednesday, she and her brother needed to make some preparations. Then her boss at the restaurant called and asked if she could put in some extra hours. What would you suggest to make the next week manageable for Kate?

Here's how the Krause family used human resources for help. With a small home, they had little room for family activities. They decided to turn part of their basement into a family room. Mr. Krause's brother, who is a carpenter, put up paneling and built cabinets for them. Mrs. Krause made curtains and cushions for the room. The whole family pitched in to plan, paint walls, and lay tile. Human resources made their goal come true.

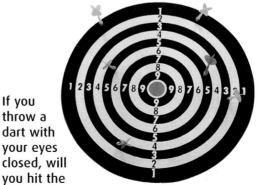

If you throw a dart with your eyes closed, will you hit the bull's-eye? If you aim for goals without resources, will you reach them?

Material Resources

Physical items are material resources. If you were planning a trip, an automobile might be used for travel. If your bedroom needed a good cleaning, you might use a vacuum cleaner, dust cloths, and cleaning solutions. Technology provides many material resources, such as phones and computers.

Money is also a material resource. If your family were moving, you could use money to rent a truck for hauling furniture. If you were taking a class, you could use money to buy books.

Although money can be a useful resource, don't overemphasize it. People who have limited financial resources can still solve problems and reach goals. Creativity and the use of other resources often make up for a lack of finances.

Community Resources

You might have to keep your eyes open to discover all the community resources that are available. Every community has facilities designed for particular purposes. Schools, libraries, museums, and parks are examples.

Communities provide services as well. Government programs supply everything from food stamps to health care. A community service was very helpful to the Cornwell

In her effort to become first violinist in the orchestra, Leah uses human, material, and community resources. Can you identify them? What other resources might Leah use?

family. They wanted to be sure that Mrs. Cornwell's elderly father had lunch every day. He lived with the family, but no one was home at midday to prepare his lunch. The community's senior center turned out to be an excellent resource. Mrs. Cornwell's father could ride a seniors' bus to the center where he could have a hot lunch. Companionship and recreation were added bonuses.

Becoming Resourceful

Suppose you're on the phone and the doctor's office is giving you a message for someone in your family. The telephone notepad is gone. You grab an envelope from the counter and write the message. You were being resourceful—in a simple way.

Resourceful people recognize and make good use of resources. They know how to find them and how to make substitutions. This quality is valuable when you're solving problems. Solutions often rely heavily on locating whatever and whoever can help you.

How do people become more resourceful? They don't give up when something seems like an obstacle. They learn to stop, think, and ask questions. "Since I don't have what I need, what else will work?" Resourceful people dig for answers and approaches.

Resourceful people recognize what can help them. How is this young woman showing resourcefulness?

DECISION-MAKING SKILLS

To make a **decision**, a person considers the possibilities and then selects a course of action or makes a judgment. Every day you make countless decisions that have a wide range of impact on you and others.

What time will you get up? What clothes will you wear? Will you buckle the seatbelt in the car? Will you stop and talk to a friend in the hall before school? Will you read a magazine during study hall or get ready for a test? Although you probably don't spend much time on these decisions, you do put *some* thought into them.

Many decisions you make are more complicated. Decisions are part of the process you use to solve problems. Decisions that help you with problems need to be made with care.

Making Sound Decisions

Making sound decisions hinges on several principles. With these pointers, you can guard against mistakes:

- **Learn to recognize important decisions.** A decision that could impact the lives of you and others needs to be taken seriously. Lateeka looks for the differences in decisions. When a problem or decision has low impact, she thinks quickly about what needs to be done and takes action. On the other hand, in high-impact situations, she isn't afraid to say, "I'll have to think about it."

- **Base decisions on your values.** Ignoring your values can lead to regrets. Ask yourself if what you're choosing is a true need or simply something you want.

- **Avoid impulsive reactions.** Impulse decisions are made too quickly. Emotions rather than thought typically guide them. Allow yourself time to make important decisions. For example, if a dating partner is pressuring you to become sexually involved, you need to think about the possible consequences. Don't act impulsively. The prospects of pregnancy and sexually transmitted disease may be overlooked when impulse overrules good judgment.

- **Make your own decisions.** If you let others make decisions for you, what can happen? You'll be living by their ideas and values, not your own. In the end, you'll have to live with the results. Such decision making can be dangerous, especially if the person who controls the decision is unreliable. For example, Sal stopped at a house with some high school friends on a Saturday night. Although he didn't want any alcohol, he held onto the bottle that a friend urged him to take. Then he drank it. Although this was Sal's decision in the end, he allowed someone else to influence him. What might the outcome be for him?

Tips & TECHNIQUES

Making a Simple Decision. The next time you are stuck on a decision with two possibilities that seem equally reasonable, try one of these techniques. Flip a coin, using "heads" for one choice and "tails" for the other. As an alternative, write each possibility on a piece of paper, put them in a bowl, and select one piece of paper for your choice.

The object of this exercise is to see how you feel about the results you get. If you're happy with the resulting choice, it's evidently acceptable to you. Go with that choice. On the other hand, if you're uneasy with the results, consider your feelings to be a red flag. Perhaps the two possibilities weren't as equal as you originally thought. Your "gut reaction" is telling you to think again.

Try It Out. Use this technique the next time you have trouble making a simple decision. How do you feel about the decision you've made?

"Oh, no! Mom's favorite vase!" What would a responsible approach to this problem be?

- **Make decisions when you are clear-headed.** Postponing a decision is okay if you need to get some rest first. If you're upset, wait until you calm down.
- **Base your decisions on research and facts.** When you're armed with knowledge, it's much easier to make sound decisions.

Taking Responsibility for Decisions

You're responsible for the decisions you make—but why should you be? Wouldn't it be easier to let someone else take the blame when things go wrong? Wouldn't it feel better to look for excuses if you make a mistake? Here are some problems with this kind of thinking:

- Making mistakes is common. By denying your mistakes, you give the impression that you believe you're above making them, yet no one really is.
- People don't respect you when you make excuses. They see excuses as a sign of weakness.
- Others don't want to be blamed for your mistakes, anymore than you want to be blamed for theirs. Blaming others is a quick way to lose friends.
- Logically, if you take credit for what goes right, you have to take responsibility for what goes wrong.
- You can learn from your mistakes. Denying them may cause you to make similar mistakes again.

Owning your decision means saying, "This is what I decided, and I am responsible for the results." When decisions turn out well, taking credit is a pleasure. If they don't turn out well, you show strength when you admit that you made a mistake and try to set it right if possible. People admire that.

THINKING SKILLS

At some point in your life, someone has probably said to you, "Put on your thinking cap." Your "thinking cap" works better when you use reasoning skills, especially when you're trying to solve a problem.

Building Character

Fairness: A Quality That Counts

Have you ever said, "That just isn't fair"? Fairness is objective, impartial, and doesn't discriminate. Honesty and justice help create fair situations. Because you want to be treated fairly, the decisions you make and actions you take should be fair to others. A teen could show fairness by:

- Talking to a friend about a problem rather than ignoring the person or starting an argument.
- Helping two classmates see both sides of an issue when they have a disagreement.
- Letting a brother tell his side of the story before drawing any conclusions about why he didn't show up after work as planned.
- Walking to the end of the ticket line instead of trying to cut in front of others.

QUESTIONS

1. How does a person learn fairness?
2. How do people usually react when faced with unfairness? Is this a constructive response? Why or why not?
3. Why is it sometimes difficult to know what's fair in solving problems?
4. Describe a time when you showed fairness in interacting with another person.

Using Reason

Reasoning means thinking logically in order to reach conclusions. You don't jump to conclusions; you think your way through by collecting evidence, analyzing information, identifying facts, and making predictions.

People who know how to reason have learned how to look at a situation from all angles. They don't just take a person's word for it. Instead, they wonder "why?" They gather all the pieces as if they were putting a puzzle together in order to see the full picture. Before putting each piece in place, they evaluate it carefully for accuracy and sensibility.

TAKING ETHICAL ACTION

Suppose you were confronted with these situations: A classmate offers you a stolen copy of tomorrow's math test. A friend suggests that you both skip school on Friday. Two teammates ask you to stay out past the coach's curfew. You scratch the family car while pulling into the garage. What do you do in each of these situations? Your answers reveal your approach to ethics.

Ethics are the moral rules of society. They are the set of values that help people decide what's right or wrong in order to guide their actions. Ethical thinking takes you beyond yourself. It asks you to consider what happens to others as well as to you. When people behave ethically, they look out for each other in positive ways, so that society is healthy rather than troubled.

To guide your thinking about ethics as you make decisions and solve problems, think about these questions:

- What will happen to you and others over time?
- Would you be willing to change places with those most affected by what you plan to do?
- Would this be the right approach in a similar situation?
- Would there be good results if everyone chose this action?
- Will this solution contribute to the overall well-being of you, your family, and others?

Many decisions you make and problems you solve involve ethics. Would you make fun of a classmate's appearance? This is an ethical decision. What you do reflects on you. If you hurt a classmate, others see that you don't have respect for people. Then what will they think of you?

Some ethical questions are complicated. What if a friend asked you not to tell anyone that she is using drugs? This is an ethical dilemma. You don't want to get your friend in trouble, but you don't want to see her get hurt either. Deciding what to do isn't easy.

The stronger your value system is, the more comfortable you will be in dealing with ethical situations. You can look at such questions with greater confidence. In problem solving, the solutions you reach are likely to be better for you, for others, and for society.

SECTION 9-2 REVIEW

Check Your Understanding

1. What can help you approach problems with confidence?
2. What guidelines can help you set effective goals?
3. As a resource, is money better described as useful or essential? Explain.
4. What pointers can help you make sound decisions?
5. What might be happening when a person says, "But it wasn't my fault"?
6. How can reasoning help you solve problems?
7. **Thinking Critically.** Of the following, who should be the most concerned about making ethical decisions: parents, politicians, medical personnel, journalists, teachers, your friends, or you?
8. **Problem Solving.** When sixteen-year-old Andrea moved to a new school, no one paid attention to her. "They don't like me," she told her older sister. "I'm just ugly and stupid." What would you suggest to Andrea? Is she using strong reasoning skills? Explain your answer.

The Problem-Solving Process

OBJECTIVES

After studying this section, you should be able to:

- Summarize and implement the problem-solving process.
- Explain how to identify and analyze options when solving problems.
- Describe the role of values in problem solving.

TERMS TO LEARN

options
support system
consequences
risk
evaluate

Suppose you're about to make a wooden toy as a gift. The wood, tools, and supplies are on the table. Would you begin by staining and finishing the wood? Not likely, or you'll have to redo it after you saw, nail, and glue. Following the steps shown in the pattern brings better results.

Like the woodworking project, many tasks are accomplished with a step-by-step procedure. Carefully following the steps leads to success. This principle applies to problem solving, too.

To tackle problems effectively, you follow a procedure to put your problem-solving skills to work. On pages 198-199 you'll see the problem-solving process suggested by many experts. Not everyone labels the steps in exactly the same way, but the process is essentially the same. As you read on, you'll learn more about this process and how to make it work successfully for you.

IDENTIFY THE PROBLEM

Identifying the problem is the first step in the problem-solving process. A simple problem may be easy to put into words: "Watching too much television is interfering with my life." Difficult problems may take more effort to identify.

When trying to put a problem into words, you might notice symptoms first. Beth was discouraged because she never had anyone to eat lunch with at school, and she felt that other students seldom spoke to her. These were symptoms of a problem that she needed to identify and tackle. After identifying her problem as shyness, she set out to deal with it.

"My Dad says I can't try out next year if my grades don't get better, but I don't want to quit." How would you state the problem Carey faces?

reached when the problem is solved. For example, if your dog barks during the night and disturbs the neighbors, you might set a goal like this: by June teach Heathcliff not to bark at night. Beth might say, "I will make at least one new friend by May." Achieving exactly what you want may not happen, but you need to know what goal you're working toward.

IDENTIFY OPTIONS

Once you have a clear idea of the problem you want to tackle, what's next? Look for ideas about what you might do. The possible courses of action to choose from are called **options**.

The more options you can identify, the better prepared you are to solve the problem.

Once discovered, some problems seem overwhelming. No problem, however, is too big to handle. You can break a big problem down into parts. Then you can tackle one part at a time. If you discover several reasons for a problem, you can deal with each one as a separate problem if you need to.

Once you've identified a problem, decide what an ideal outcome would be. Set a goal to be

You might list the options you have for solving a problem on paper or computer. How would a word processor be useful in listing and analyzing options?

Write down all the ideas that occur to you, even the weak ones. Good solutions aren't always apparent at first. Even a poor idea can trigger thoughts about better ones.

Remember that two heads are often better than one. What you don't think of, someone else might. As you look for options, you could involve friends you trust, family members, or experts. Ask yourself whose help would be valuable. Then turn to those people.

EVALUATE OPTIONS

Once you have a complete list of options, examine each one. These questions will help you look at the merits of each option:

- What are this option's strengths as a solution? What are its weaknesses?
- Is the choice a realistic course of action for you and your family at this time?
- Would this particular option meet the needs and wants of you and your family?
- Will you be happy with this option later?

The Problem-Solving Process

If you learn how the problem-solving process works with everyday problems, you can later apply it to more difficult ones.

1. Identify the problem.
"I'd like to go to the prom, but is it too late to find a date?"

2. Identify options.
"I know several people who might be able to go."

3. Evaluate the options.
"Well, that eliminates two possibilities."

Gather Information

As you evaluate options, you may need information about them. That means using resources. If you've learned to recognize and locate them, you'll know where to turn.

Finding the right information takes time. You may need to locate books and magazines, search the Internet, or talk to others. The more important the problem is, the more relevant good information becomes.

As you use resources, evaluate information carefully. To help you judge how useful and reliable information is, ask yourself these questions:

- Who is promoting the information?
- What are the credentials of the source?
- Does the source have a special interest in this subject? Is the information biased?
- Is the information current?
- Does the information seem logical?
- Is the information supported by reputable research?

4. Choose the best option.
"Hmmm. Someone fun to be with would be best."

Maria

Jennifer

5. Make and carry out a plan.
"I'll call now—before she goes to work."

"Prom?" "O.K."

6. Evaluate what happened.
"We had a great time, but next year I'll ask earlier."

Balancing Work & Family Life

THE CHALLENGE —

Building a Support System

Busy families today need support—when problems arise and when schedules are rough. Support works in two directions. When you help others, they'll be willing to help you. A **support system** is a group of resources that provide help when a family needs it. Families need to build a support system before problems occur.

How You Can Help

To help your family build a support system, try these ideas:

- Talk with your family about who would help you in a crisis. If you have few options, explore new possibilities.
- Take home a list of family resources prepared by your class and hang it on the refrigerator or bulletin board.
- Check the telephone book or library for lists of community resources.
- Get to know your neighbors. Say hello when you pass and ask questions to start conversation.
- Offer to help a neighbor, friend, or family member. You might say, "I'm pretty good at raking leaves. May I help?"
- Ask for support. If you need help, reach out. You might say, "I'm looking for a job. Do you know anyone who needs a babysitter?"

Consider the Consequences

Imagine that two trains are on the same track. One is headed east and the other west. They are headed toward each other, coming closer and closer. What might the result be?

Unless quick action is taken, a consequence will occur. **Consequences** (KAHN-suh-KWEN-sez) are the results of an action. Some are good. Some aren't. The train derailments in life need to be avoided.

They will create more problems, not solve the ones you already have.

You can prevent serious consequences from happening. As you analyze options, think about their effects on you. Also consider other people. How will your family and friends be affected by each option on your list? What will the impact on society be? These are important questions to ask. The answers must guide what you do.

Sometimes consequences are not clear. You may not know for sure what will happen. For example, when Toshiro started a new business, he had no guarantee that it would be a success. Risk was involved. **Risk** is the possibility of loss or injury. People must weigh risks as they solve problems.

Some people are more willing to take risks than others are. Some risks are more worth taking than others are. Many great successes—and failures as well as tragedies—have followed risk taking. When you don't know exactly what will happen, think carefully about what could.

CHOOSE THE BEST OPTION

Once you have examined your options very carefully, you're ready to choose one. At this point decision making becomes part of the process.

Sometimes the right choice becomes clear as you review options. If the decision is a difficult one, however, you may need to eliminate options until you have only the best one remaining.

When choosing an option, let your principles be your guide. Does the option you are considering agree with your principles? Fewer regrets are likely when you coordinate your decision with the principles you believe in.

MAKE A PLAN

After a decision has been made, your management skills take over as you get ready for action. You need a plan for carrying out the decision. Planning is a way of getting organized and seeing the whole picture before you start to act.

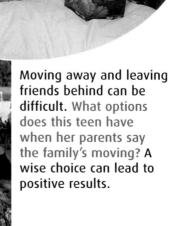

Moving away and leaving friends behind can be difficult. What options does this teen have when her parents say the family's moving? A wise choice can lead to positive results.

Suppose a family bought a car that turned out to be a "lemon." How would evaluating what happened help them avoid the same problem again?

As you plan, the following questions can guide you:

- What steps need to be taken to carry out the decision?
- In what order should the steps be taken?
- What resources will be used in each step?
- Who will take each step?
- How long will each step take?
- When should each step be carried out?

When you know the answers to these questions, write them down. By writing the steps of your plan, you'll be less likely to leave out something important. You'll also be able to check your progress as you move toward the goal.

CARRY OUT YOUR PLAN

After planning, set your plan in motion. Keeping your goal in mind, work through the steps. Use the resources you've identi-

fied. Stick to your plan as closely as you can, but remember to be flexible. Sometimes things happen to make adjustments necessary.

If you've carried out your plan well, a solution will likely be found. You'll feel satisfied that you knew what approach to take and you took it.

Changing Your Mind

Have you ever heard of a bride or groom whose mind changed at the altar? Sometimes changing your mind isn't easy, but it may be the wise thing to do. New evidence and additional thought may suggest a different path of action.

It's far better to admit that you made the wrong choice and face any related difficulties than to live with the long-term effects of a bad decision. Knowing that it's okay to change your mind can give you the courage to do so and lead you to a "new and improved" solution to your problem.

EVALUATE WHAT HAPPENED

A good problem solver doesn't stop yet. Stepping back to look at your level of success gives you knowledge about what to do better the next time. When you **evaluate,** you study the results of your actions to determine how effective they were. Did you solve the problem or not? If you didn't, why not? Here are other questions to ask as you evaluate:

- Did you accurately identify the problem? If not, how did that ultimately affect what happened?
- Was your goal realistic? Did it lead you to a solution?

- Did you identify enough resources? What else should you have used?
- Did you miss any options that might have been better?
- Did you make a good decision?
- Was your plan detailed enough? Did it make good use of resources?
- What improvements would you have made?
- Did you carry out your plan accurately? Did you skip any steps? Did this affect the solution to your problem?
- Did you solve your problem and reach your goal? What did you like and dislike about how your problem was solved?

Evaluating gives you the chance to see what works for you as a problem solver. By evaluating, you can improve your problem-solving skills.

LOOKING TO THE FUTURE

As a teen, you have more opportunities to solve your own problems than ever before. Sometimes a family problem or limited resources, however, can be discouraging. Jackie felt this way until she took charge of her own life. She said, "I can't change what happened yesterday, and today is not particularly good, but I can make tomorrow different." By setting goals, digging for resources, learning to make good decisions, and putting management skills into action, she set out to make a better future for herself—and she did.

No matter what you face, you can do the same. You don't need to let problems overwhelm you. Now is the time to start asking yourself what you want for the future. You have choices. You can think, decide, plan, and act, or you can let circumstances and problems take charge of your life. What will you choose?

SECTION 9-3 REVIEW

Check Your Understanding

1. What should you do if a problem seems too big to handle?
2. Is it better to identify several options or just one when problem solving? Why?
3. What happens to consequences when greater risks are taken?
4. Some people are too proud to admit they were wrong. How might this cause harm when solving problems?
5. What is the purpose of evaluating after solving a problem?
6. **Thinking Critically.** Do you think there are any problems that are unsolvable? Compare your ideas with others.
7. **Problem Solving.** Travis couldn't understand why he always seemed to go along with whatever his friends wanted him to do. As a result, his grades were going down and his father was upset with him. Travis was worried about what his future would be like if he continued on this path. How many options can you think of for Travis as he tries to solve his problem?

Chapter 9
Review and Activities

CHAPTER SUMMARY

- To solve a problem, you first need to be able to identify exactly what the problem is.
- If you don't approach problems with the right attitude, they may not get solved.
- Goal setting helps you keep on track when trying to solve a problem.
- Learning about possible resources helps you identify them when you need them.
- Making good decisions is an important part of solving problems.
- Solving problems ethically means considering others and what may happen to them.
- The problem-solving process is a road map for successfully solving problems.
- Accurate and reliable information is essential in solving problems.
- Thinking through possible consequences can help you choose the best option.
- A written plan helps you get organized and see the whole picture before taking action.
- Evaluation turns problem solving into a learning experience.

REVIEW QUESTIONS

Section 9-1
1. How do problems differ from each other?
2. What could you do to avoid procrastination?
3. Why do people often tackle little problems before big ones?

Section 9-2
1. Describe three types of resources.
2. How do people demonstrate resourcefulness?
3. Who benefits when you and others solve problems ethically?

Section 9-3
1. What are the steps in the problem-solving process?
2. How do you know whether information is reliable?
3. How can using values benefit you when solving problems?

BECOMING A PROBLEM SOLVER

1. Barry is a risk taker. The more danger there is in an activity, the more he likes it. His friends have begun to worry about him. Two of them confront him about his behavior. What should Barry do?

2. Destiny doesn't mind making small day-to-day choices. She hates making important decisions, however. Her parents are pressuring her to choose a college, but she can't decide if she even wants to go. What should Destiny do?

THINKING CRITICALLY

1. **Analyzing Behavior.** Which do you think is a greater difficulty when most people solve problems—trying to achieve too much or too little?
2. **Predicting Results.** Do you think human or material resources are more important in helping a person solve problems and achieve goals? Explain your answer.
3. **Comparing and Contrasting.** Some people "dare to dream" when they think about options. What are the advantages and disadvantages of this?
4. **Evaluating Assumptions.** Making decisions impulsively is usually thought to be bad. Are there ever times when quick decisions are necessary? Explain your answer.
5. **Assessing Outcomes.** Why do you think some people are highly successful even though they had very few resources as they grew up?

MAKING CURRICULUM CONNECTIONS

1. **Language Arts.** Using examples from personal experience, explain in writing how values influence the goals people choose.
2. **Graphic Arts.** Design a chart, graph, or other visual that shows the relationship among goals, resources, decisions, problem solving, and management.

APPLYING YOUR KNOWLEDGE

1. Make a list of emotions that might interfere with problem solving. With your class discuss ways to prevent these emotions from being barriers.
2. Complete these sentences in writing: "The worst decision I ever made was…" and "The best decision I ever made was…" Explain why.
3. With your class, discuss whether procrastination is always negative. Could there ever be a good reason to procrastinate when making a decision or to delay taking action? Explain your answer.
4. Select a problem that you face. Use the problem-solving process to solve it. Be sure to evaluate the results.

Family & Community Connections

1. List helpful resources for each of these goals: learning a foreign language; building a birdhouse; deciding on a career. Identify each resource as human, material, or community.

2. Develop a list of community resources. How could each resource be used to help solve family problems?

Managing Technology

IN YOUR OWN WORDS

What limits do you think computers have?

Benefits of Technology

OBJECTIVES

After studying this section, you should be able to:

- Describe ways that technology adds convenience to living.
- Explain how technology benefits many aspects of life.

TERMS TO LEARN

technology
telecommute

In a general sense, **technology** is using scientific knowledge for practical purposes. Through technology new products and techniques make the world a different place on a daily basis. When you think about the changes, you can see so much that has made life better for people.

LOOKING FOR CONVENIENCE

Convenience has become a requirement today. With busy lifestyles, people hope to make time for everything they need and want to do.

The quest for convenience has spurred many innovations. Proof is in the appliance sections of any department store. What people used to do by hand, they now do in seconds with the right tool. With modern appliances, you can bake bread, clean the air, and compress garbage, all automatically.

For busy people, quick meal preparation saves time. Supermarkets sell foods that are ready for almost instant use. Microwave ovens prepare food in seconds, and dishwashers simplify cleanup.

Handling finances is also convenient. Automatic teller machines provide cash at any time of the day and also make other financial transactions. Convenience can mean paying bills without ever writing a check. Bills are automatically paid and deducted from a bank account through electronic withdrawal or transactions made by telephone or computer. Checks can be automatically deposited in accounts.

Household Conveniences

Technology makes household management easier today. The "smart homes" of the future will practically manage themselves.

In a smart home, computers control many devices. For example, lights turn on automatically when people enter a room. Temperature sensors adjust room temperatures. Light sensors control the window blinds by opening and closing at appropriate times. A telephone call may start the oven or turn off the iron. At some future time, houses may even clean themselves.

IMPROVED COMMUNICATION

When a major event occurs in the world, you know almost immediately. With media coverage, you're often right there, even watching as it happens.

Nowadays, the telephone often replaces letter writing. If you don't want to miss a call, an answering machine records messages. Pagers alert you when someone wants you, so that you can immediately get in touch. Mobile phones allow you to talk

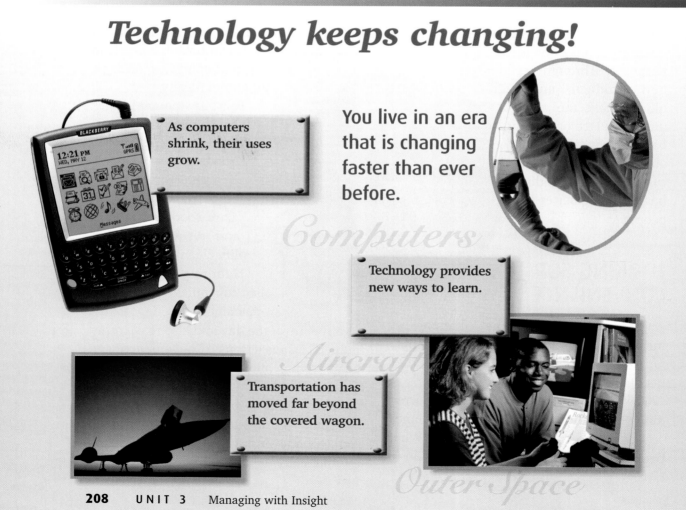

Technology keeps changing!

As computers shrink, their uses grow.

You live in an era that is changing faster than ever before.

Computers

Technology provides new ways to learn.

Aircraft

Transportation has moved far beyond the covered wagon.

Outer Space

almost anywhere. Fax machines and e-mail provide instant communication.

Communication technology helps families. With pagers and cell phones, they can keep track of each other and make sure all is well. Laurie and her grandfather exchange regular messages through e-mail. Until e-mail, Laurie had never gotten a letter from her grandfather.

ACCESS TO INFORMATION

Technology has revolutionized the handling of information. Through computers, and especially the Internet, people have instant access to every kind of information imaginable. From a home computer, you can read a book in a library thousands of miles away. Who would have thought that people would ever be able to exchange information so quickly and conveniently?

ENTERTAINMENT AND TECHNOLOGY

Technology has certainly brought new forms of entertainment into people's lives. VCRs enable you to watch whatever you want, whenever you want. Cable networks and satellite dishes increase viewing choices.

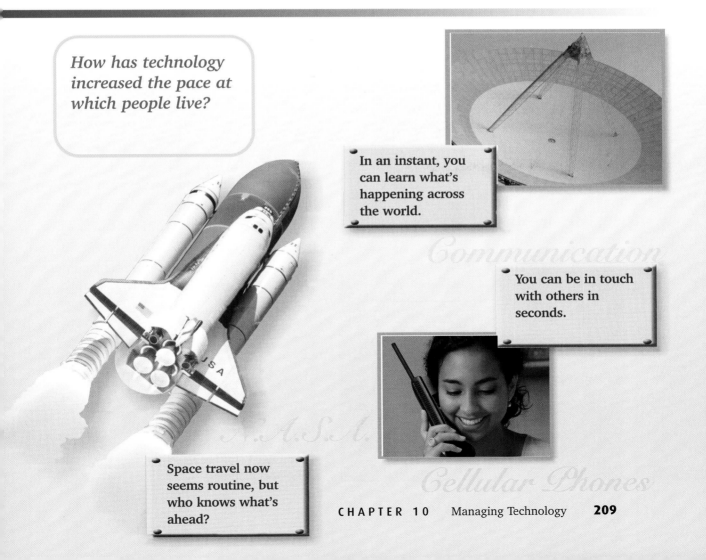

How has technology increased the pace at which people live?

In an instant, you can learn what's happening across the world.

You can be in touch with others in seconds.

Space travel now seems routine, but who knows what's ahead?

Families can listen to the news and learn about current events. Computer games are available at home and in arcades.

Making entertainment increasingly spectacular is a challenge. People go to amusement parks that have bigger and better rides every year. Water parks duplicate ocean waves. Fireworks displays are awesome, artistic creations, sometimes even set to music. Special effects bring lifelike qualities to the movie screen and theater stage. How else does technology dazzle people?

HEALTH AND MEDICAL ADVANCES

Health technology saves, lengthens, and enriches lives. It would be impossible to list all the accomplishments here. They range from simple devices and techniques that make care more efficient to amazing life-saving abilities. You've probably heard of pacemakers, dialysis machines, and laser surgery. What other medical marvels can you list?

Promoting Wellness

Health concerns are also met by new ways of preparing foods for consumers. Synthetic ingredients, which are produced by chemical means, are used in foods. For example, artificial sweeteners reduce calories, and artificial fats help people lower their intake of fat. Meat is leaner, and low-cholesterol eggs are now available. Special preservation, shipping, and handling techniques make fresh fruits and vegetables accessible year-round in most parts of the country.

Interest in exercise has grown over the years, as shown by the development of exercise equipment for use at home and in health clubs. People recognize that they need physical activity in their lives. Families that get children started early promote the exercise habit.

SAFETY AND SECURITY

As the world becomes more complex, technology provides new ways of promoting safety and security. Security systems are installed in homes, businesses, and automobiles. Protective equipment, such as air bags and children's car seats, make travel safer. In an emergency, such as an auto accident or fire, equipment and rescue techniques are available. Victims get the care they need as quickly as possible.

Technology is impacting families in many ways. Home computers can be used for your homework, for entertainment, or for family financial planning.

Career Success Stories

Young Lee: *Disability Accommodations Specialist*

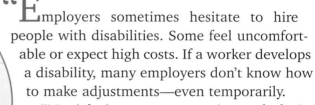

"Employers sometimes hesitate to hire people with disabilities. Some feel uncomfortable or expect high costs. If a worker develops a disability, many employers don't know how to make adjustments—even temporarily.

"My job is to go to a site and design changes for the work environment. These are called work site modifications. I help the client with the disability and the employer see what can be done. Depending on the disability, the change can be as easy as adjusting the office furniture. Other situations are more difficult.

"On a case I just finished, the young woman was in an auto accident and now uses a wheelchair. We ordered a new desk that was taller and rearranged the office to make the aisles wider. Everything she needs to access has been arranged within easy reach. It was actually simpler than she thought it would be. I was happy to see her spirits go up so much after getting back to work.

"Fortunately new technology allows many people with disabilities to work, when they might not have been able to in the past. Special computers and software have opened doors in the workplace. I get plenty of job satisfaction through helping people become productive workers again."

CAREER PROFILE

Education and training: bachelor's degree

Starting salary: around $27,000

Job prospects: private and government rehabilitation services; hospitals; medical supply companies

Important qualities: creative; able to see with a fresh eye; detail-oriented; good communication skills

Plan Ahead

Wherever you work, sensitivity to those with disabilities is necessary. Choose a career that interests you. What work site modifications would be needed for someone with a sight or hearing impairment?

Focus On ...

The Work World

The development of technology has drastically changed the work world. These are some changes you might notice:

- **New tools for work.** Changes occur regularly. New and improved equipment allows people to work faster and more efficiently. Nothing, of course, has had greater impact on work than the computer. Computers that once filled rooms and buildings now fit into briefcases. They perform every kind of function imaginable at great speed, and the capabilities keep expanding.

- **A flexible workforce.** Advances in technology require workers to continually update their knowledge and skills. Remaining open to change is a required skill of workers at every level.

- **New working environments.** More people are working at home today than ever before. Many of them **telecommute.** They use telephone, fax, and computer connec-

tions to do the same work that used to be done at the employer's place of business. Housework, personal interests, other people, and children can distract the home worker. Those who work at home do better if they set aside a certain area as the work location. Some keep specific hours for work only.

USING YOUR KNOWLEDGE

When Judd and Cynthia married, he set up his office in their home. Two children later, he is still working from home while Cynthia is a hospital nurse. Judd is having trouble getting his work done because he must also care for the children at home. What can he do?

CARING FOR THE ENVIRONMENT

Technology has a dual effect on the environment. You've probably heard much about the negative side. Chemical wastes enter the water, earth, and air. Garbage fills dump sites. The more products people create, the more they throw away. Technology uses up energy and natural resources.

Technology is used to solve many of the environmental problems it causes. For example, waste disposal is safer with modern techniques. Recycling technology has helped reduce the amount of trash put into landfills. New ways of cleaning up water have helped restore lakes that were once "dead" due to pollution. More efforts along this line can reduce the negative impact of technology on the environment.

Times have certainly changed. Look what's replaced the lemonade stand of the past.

Many communities make technological resources available to citizens. Libraries have audio and video tapes. They may loan CD-ROMs and computer games. Most have computers and an Internet connection that the public can use.

THE CHALLENGE

As a teen, your view of technology may not be the same as others'. Every person's experiences make an impression. Someone who has lost a job because a robot took over may not feel as kindly toward technology as someone whose cellular phone brought help in an emergency.

What are your thoughts? Is technology an improvement or a challenge—or both? As you complete this chapter, you'll explore some of the problems that accompany technological change. You'll also think about how to manage them well.

IN COMMUNITIES

Many communities use technology to help citizens. Computerized traffic lights control the flow of cars, helping reduce traffic jams and accidents. Information about community services and activities can be distributed through electronic sources.

SECTION 10-1 REVIEW

Check Your Understanding

1. What is technology? How is it used?
2. What will a "smart home" of the future be like?
3. How has technology improved the diets of people?
4. Does technology help or harm the environment? Explain your answer.
5. If you don't own a computer, where in your community might you find one to use?
6. **Thinking Critically.** If you could create new technology, what would you create and what would it do?
7. **Problem Solving.** Many of Antonio's friends have cell telephones. Since Antonio can't afford one, he often feels that he's missing out on something. How should Antonio resolve this situation?

Using Technology Effectively

OBJECTIVES

After studying this section, you should be able to:

- Describe different attitudes toward technology.
- Explain ways that people can manage technology effectively.
- Suggest tips that can help people focus on the positive aspects of technology.

TERMS TO LEARN

futurists
obsolete
intrusive

Over the years **futurists**, people who study and predict what may happen in the years ahead, have talked about the amazing quantity of change occurring in society. Not only do new developments happen on a daily basis, but the rate of change has also accelerated to a bewildering pace. Is it any wonder that some people have trouble keeping up?

machine that can do "everything," or perhaps the latest device for milking a cow.

Technological change isn't exciting to everyone, however. Here's what Katy had to say: "I just can't keep up. Why can't things be simpler? The minute I get familiar with something, it changes and I have to make another decision. Technology is supposed to make life easier. It may allow us to do things faster, but we've got more to do now than ever before."

Technology does come with drawbacks. To get along well with technology, you need to understand what can happen and learn how to manage.

ATTITUDES TOWARD CHANGE

Because technology is so complicated, people's reactions to it are too. If you're a computer wizard, you may keep up on what's happening and eagerly look forward to each new advance. For another person, something else causes excitement—a new drug that treats a disease, a sewing

Adopting New Technology

Attitudes toward change affect how readily people adapt to new technology. Some people want the latest refinement or newest product immediately. Others have to ease into change. Some reject it right from the start. Most people are somewhere in the middle.

INFORMATION OVERLOAD

Is there any way you could learn everything there is to know about a subject, such as geology or botany? While some people might have been able to do that 40 or 50 years ago, they probably couldn't today. The amount of information that has accumulated over the years just keeps increasing.

Annalise was writing a paper on family communication. Her first Internet search produced a list of 675,431 references. Finding what would be useful to her was going to be a challenge.

Over the years, the quantity of information that exists has increased tremendously. As a result, the emphasis today is less on trying to memorize everything about a topic. Instead you need to know how to find information.

Focus On ...

Pressures to Buy

New technology is fascinating, but do you need everything you see? You have to weigh the advantages and also the disadvantages of ownership.

Appliances, for example, cost money, take up space, and use up scarce resources to manufacture, distribute, run, repair, and replace. Some items turn out to be less useful than you thought. Some drain the budget. An item that gets used once or twice, then cast aside, means wasted money. If something will improve your life and is affordable, it may be worthwhile. On the other hand, if a new electronic "toy" isn't needed, it isn't a wise purchase.

Product Obsolescence

Many products, especially electronic devices, become obsolete rapidly. **Obsolete** means being outmoded or replaced by more advanced technology. You may have heard your grandparents complain that "they just don't make things like they used to." That may be true. Many products have a built-in life span today. To get the most for your money, you need to learn how to examine for quality and buy carefully.

USING YOUR KNOWLEDGE

A year after Jamal bought his computer, he realized that it was almost obsolete. The newer models were more powerful and had more features. Jamal's computer was doing what he needed it for, but it wouldn't be long before he would be out of sync with the rest of the computer world. What should Jamal do?

TOO MUCH CONVENIENCE?

While much of technology is aimed at making things easier, can too much convenience be a problem? Some people think so. Immediate access to cash and credit, for example, can cause trouble. Eating on the run can send families in opposite directions. You can learn ways to combat such problems.

Technology enables people to keep homes cleaner than they have ever been. So what happens? Many people develop higher standards for cleanliness. The floor can be not only clean but also sanitized, sealed, and have a glossy shine. What that really means is more work. Convenience isn't really convenience anymore. Set standards that are reasonable for you and your family rather than ones influenced by products and advertising.

"My credit card number is . . ." Some people might finish this sentence by saying, ". . . too convenient." What do you think?

COMMUNICATION CHALLENGES

Communication has been strengthened through technology, but not everything goes well all the time. Here are some typical situations that show the problems:

- Drake's cell phone disturbs others in the theater. When might electronic devices be a problem? Remember courtesy to others when using them.
- Lisa had an accident when using her car phone while driving. Studies show that reduced attention to driving causes many accidents.
- Computer chat rooms sometimes lead to troublesome, even dangerous, relationships. People need to be very cautious about the friendships they build on the Internet.

These are only a few examples. Can you think of other problems connected to communication technology? How can they be managed?

THE COST OF TECHNOLOGY

The monetary cost of technology can be high. Computer equipment costs hundreds, even thousands, of dollars. The newer a technology is, the higher the price is likely to be. As it becomes more commonplace, prices usually go down. Some people wait for that to happen before they buy.

Medical technology adds to the cost of medical care. People want new and better treatments, but they worry about how to pay. Families without insurance can be devastated by the cost of a serious illness. How the costs of new types of medical care will be covered is an ongoing debate.

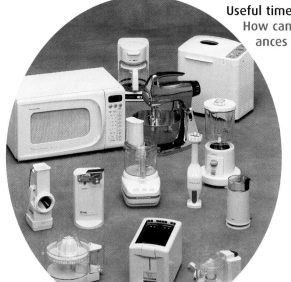

Useful time savers or budget busters? How can you decide which appliances are worth buying?

- Does easy access to modern transportation send family members in different directions too often?
- Do televisions, computers, and video games divide families by capturing attention for hours at a time?
- Does outside entertainment lure family members away from the home more than is reasonable?
- Do people neglect the quiet pleasures of nature, reading, or listening to music because they are conditioned to want much more spectacular entertainment?

People are wise to stay informed about medical care issues. When looking for work, find out what employers offer. The better job may be one that has a health plan. Taking good care of health helps many people avoid the costs of some medical care.

ENTERTAINMENT ISSUES

At first glance, you wouldn't think there would be problems connected to entertainment, but there are. These questions will give you some food for thought. How would you respond?

Often the media need to be controlled to be useful to a family. Television programs address topics that are not suitable for chil-

Some people prefer to rent movies than to go to the theater. What are some of the reasons you rent movies?

Balancing Work & Family Life

THE CHALLENGE —

Using Technology to Help

Technology can help your family prepare quick meals, track schedules, and become better organized. Making such improvements will reward family members with more free time and less stress. Even when technology seems overwhelming or foreign, taking time to use it effectively is worthwhile.

How You Can Help

To use technology to help with home management, try these ideas:

- Use a home or school computer to create a job or scheduling chart or write a form letter to long-distance family and friends.
- Help your family organize finances or recipes, track the family tree, or even write a will on a computer.
- Offer to help start a savings plan for a microwave oven if your family doesn't own one.
- Set up a system for timed telephone use so all family members can make calls.
- Use a cordless telephone so you can do household chores while talking.
- Encourage family members to use automatic timers on such appliances as coffee makers and lights.

dren. The values shown may be offensive. Many of Ted's friends complained about the poor quality of the television programs their children watched. Ted responded this way, "Some pretty bad programs are out there, but you don't have to let your children watch them. We limit our kids on how long they can watch each week. Some programs are off limits. We look for educational and nature programs the whole family can enjoy."

LACK OF PRIVACY

As information spreads across communication systems, people worry about privacy. They don't want their name, address, social security number, and numbers for their telephone, bank accounts, and credit cards to get in the wrong hands. Such information may be used in annoying and harmful ways.

Guarding against identity theft is essential in today's world. Never give personal information out to strangers who call on the phone. Be careful about putting personal data on the Internet. If you order products on the phone, make the calls yourself and only to reputable companies. Make sure computer buying is limited to secure sites. Tear up or shred personal information before throwing it in the garbage. Also, be careful about leaving outgoing mail in your home mailbox.

Intrusiveness

Technology can be **intrusive** (in-TROO-siv). That is, it enters your life without your invitation or willingness. For example, do telemarketing calls aimed at selling you goods over the phone bother your family on a daily basis? Many people are constantly inconvenienced by these calls and feel that their telephone is not for that purpose.

When technology demands your time or is out of your control, you may feel annoyed, yet you do have choices. You can register a complaint with whoever made the call and request that your name be taken off the calling list. You can say that you make it a rule never to make purchases from telephone solicitors and just hang up the phone. Simple solutions can sometimes cure the frustrations that people feel.

HEALTH ISSUES

Good nutrition requires good decision making in a technological world. Fast food, both at home and in restaurants, is readily available. Often such food is high in calo-

---

Building Character

Ethical Behavior: A Quality That Counts

Ethical behavior is based on moral principles and values. It means doing what is right, no matter what the circumstances. Ethical behavior is shown by:

- Purchasing software, rather than copying it illegally from another source.
- Respecting the privacy of another person's computer files or e-mail records.
- Not making unnecessary calls on a cell phone that you recently borrowed in an emergency.
- Keeping a friend's confidences.
- Doing the right thing, even though no one will know if you don't.

QUESTIONS

1. Do you agree that ethical behavior has decreased in society? Why?
2. Does the free flow of information on the Internet make ethics more or less important? Explain your answer.
3. Give an example of a situation when you showed ethical behavior.

ries, fat, and salt. Families need to choose a variety of healthful foods, both at home and in restaurants. Many restaurants now offer meals low in calories, fat, and salt.

Even though many technological advances promote health, health can also be hindered by progress. Technology can lead to a sedentary lifestyle. In other words, many people sit rather than exercise. See for yourself by analyzing how these examples of technology affect physical activity levels: riding lawnmowers, television, computers, automobiles, and garage door openers. Can you think of other examples?

Difficult Medical Decisions

Technology often creates difficult choices in the areas of health and medicine. Some questions, like these, create controversy:

• Should everyone get medical care, whether or not they can pay for it?

• Does everyone have the right to all treatment that is available?

• If a person has a terminal disease, how aggressively should it be treated?

• How should the use of life support systems be handled?

Christy's comments illustrate one dilemma in health care: "My grandmother has heart disease. She could probably live another five to ten years if she had a heart transplant, but that isn't going to happen. There are so few hearts available; they aren't willing to put one in a seventy-year-old woman. I'm really upset—she has as much right to those years as anyone else who needs a transplant." Do you agree with Christy?

ENVIRONMENTAL ISSUES

Unfortunately, some technological advances have negative consequences for the environment. Air and water quality issues or noise pollution may result.

How long do you want the world to exist for future generations? Unless everyone

Great advances in medical science and technology have saved millions of lives. How have people you know been helped by new medical technology?

takes an interest in finding solutions, problems will increase. People recycle items and reduce their consumption of goods. Some write to their legislators. As you help look for solutions and participate in them, you contribute to making a better world for your family and your descendants.

TIPS FOR STAYING POSITIVE

As this chapter points out, technology has both rewards and drawbacks. Technology, of course, is here to stay. You and your family can learn to focus on the benefits if you keep the following thoughts in mind:

- **Have a sense of humor.** Devices fail and strange things happen. Laughing is better than getting upset.
- **Make time for activities that don't involve technology.** Your family can enjoy simple pleasures in life, too.
- **Use only what is important to you.** You may find some real benefits in a relaxed approach.
- **Stay informed.** Technology is fascinating. Knowing something about it can make you feel more comfortable and prepare you for the future.

You can be in control of the technology in your life. You don't have to let it control you. When you think of the many benefits of technology, the negative side stays in perspective. Technology can improve life and help solve problems. As you think about the positive side, you'll see all that you and your family have to gain.

SECTION 10-2 REVIEW

Check Your Understanding

1. What concerns are expressed by people who think there is a negative side to technology?
2. How can convenience be a problem?
3. What is one problem associated with medical technology?
4. What are three examples that show how entertainment technology can cause problems for people?
5. Why do some people have a sedentary lifestyle?
6. What can people do to help with environmental problems?
7. **Thinking Critically.** Why do you think some people are more willing to accept new technology than others are?
8. **Problem Solving.** Larry is frustrated by too much communication. His phone rings constantly—at home, in the car, everywhere. He gets calls from coworkers, telephone solicitors, friends, and family. If it isn't the phone, it's his pager. He feels as though he can't escape. What should he do?

CHAPTER SUMMARY

- Technology affects all aspects of daily life.
- Technology offers many conveniences.
- Through technology, people experience many benefits that make life better for them.
- Not all people view technology with the same degree of interest and excitement.
- When technology is new, it usually costs more than it does later.
- Families need to control their use of media technology in order to preserve its usefulness for them.
- People don't want their name, address, social security number, and numbers for their telephone, bank accounts, and credit cards to get in the wrong hands.
- Technological advances in the fields of health and medicine have created many controversies that are difficult for people to settle.
- When you manage technology well, you prevent it from controlling your life.

REVIEW QUESTIONS

Section 10-1

1. How has technology added convenience to living?
2. What improvements has technology made in the areas of communication and information?
3. How has technology improved the entertainment field?
4. What is one way that technology helps protect people?

Section 10-2

1. Why is memorizing information less important today than in the past?
2. What are two examples that show problems connected with communication technology?
3. How can a person protect against identity theft?
4. What are four ideas that can help people maintain a positive approach to technological change?
5. Why do people need to stay informed about technology?

BECOMING A PROBLEM SOLVER

1. Jesse wants to buy a new computer. The salesperson thoroughly confused him with words and terms about the computer. Jesse had never heard of the brand the salesperson was promoting. What should Jesse do?
2. After his mother's birthday, Jonathan noticed that she was having trouble finding a place to store the new fancy can opener and sandwich maker she had received as gifts. He began to think about all the things their family owned that they seldom or never used: tools in the basement; gimmicky toys; all kinds of appliances. What do you think Jonathan and his family should do?

THINKING CRITICALLY

1. **Analyzing Behavior.** Can you have a "real" relationship with someone whom you have met and interacted with only through the computer? Explain your answer.

2. **Drawing Conclusions.** What courtesy rules would you suggest for people who use cell phones?

3. **Identifying Cause and Effect.** Do you think people can be conditioned to want entertainment that is increasingly more spectacular than what they're used to? What might be the effects on individuals, families, and society?

MAKING CURRICULUM CONNECTIONS

1. **Language Arts.** Using the Internet, find information about futurists and their ideas. Write a report describing something interesting or surprising that you read about what could happen in the future. Present your report to the class.

2. **Science.** Find information about how space technology has contributed to the development of many processes and products used by people every day. Share what you learn with the class.

APPLYING YOUR KNOWLEDGE

1. Investigate an appliance or electronic device. Identify the features that make the product useful. Under what circumstances should an individual or family purchase this product?

2. Over the last century, a person's expected life span has increased dramatically. Discuss with a partner the role that technology has played in this increase. Share two ideas with the class.

3. Use a computer to create a one-page flyer about "managing technology." Make sure you use good grammar and spell words correctly.

Family & Community Connections

1. Interview the parent of a preschooler about the videos the child watches. What control does the parent use over the child's selections?

2. Watch a television program and analyze its content. At what age group is the program directed? How can you tell? What values were illustrated in the plot or format of the program? What impact might this program have on family members of different ages?

Balancing Work and Family Life

WORDS FOR THOUGHT

WORDS FOR THOUGHT

"For disappearing acts, it's hard to beat what happens to the eight hours supposedly left after eight of sleep and eight of work."
(Doug Larson)

IN YOUR OWN WORDS

Who in your family has the most to do during the hours left after sleep and work?

Work and Families

OBJECTIVES

After studying this section, you should be able to:

- Describe two kinds of work that families do.
- Explain how attitudes about who does the work in a family have changed over the years.
- Summarize ways in which jobs affect family life, and vice versa.

TERMS TO LEARN

work ethic
household work
income-producing work

People need time for work, family, and personal activities. When one of these gets routinely slighted, people don't feel right. They sense that all three aspects of life aren't blending the way they should, and they long for harmony.

THE VALUE OF WORK

Every day after school, Molly used to come home and sit in front of the television set. After a couple of hours, she felt more tired than when she first sat down. Molly felt bored and unhappy with herself.

It wasn't until Molly started a volunteer job at the hospital after school that her attitude changed. Having something to do gave her a new outlook. She liked relating to the people and staying busy.

For people like Molly, work is a valuable part of life. Work brings purpose to life. It not only provides something worthwhile to do, but it also brings income and other rewards. You saw some of the rewards that Molly gained. Are there others? You could also point to pride in a job well done and satisfaction in making a contribution.

People often talk about the "work ethic." The **work ethic** is an attitude that says, "I value honest work, and I want to work hard to take care of myself and my family and to have a good life." Some say that the work ethic is what has made this country strong.

Maintaining a home and caring for a family are work. A parent who isn't employed outside the home still has a career as a homemaker. **What does a homemaker have in common with a business manager?**

TYPES OF WORK

Families need work for the same reasons that Molly did—and more. Two basic kinds of work exist for families. One is the work that keeps the household going. The other is the work that produces income.

Household Work

Some work must be done simply for the well-being of people. The work a family does in the home in order to keep up with day-to-day living is **household work**. Although people are seldom paid for this work, it's worthy of value and appreciation.

Have you ever tried to list the jobs that keep a household going? Some are obvious,

but others aren't. Feeding the family is an obvious job. Meals must be planned, food purchased, recipes prepared, and clean up done. Straightening a closet and cleaning the oven, on the other hand, need to be done, but they aren't as apparent as other jobs that need doing.

Some people aren't aware of what others do. If someone else cleans out the refrigerator and wipes up dust, you may not even notice. Nevertheless, someone in a family handles these and other tasks regularly.

Not all household chores are related only to cooking and cleaning. Many families have repairs to make and errands to run. A car may need servicing. These jobs are also important in families.

A Variety of Jobs

Household jobs differ in several ways. For one thing, some are done more frequently than others. Mowing the lawn may be a once-a-week summer job, but unnecessary in winter. In contrast, could a family do the laundry only in the summer or eat only once a week? Most household jobs can be categorized according to how often they need to be done. Daily, weekly, and monthly are common time frames.

Jobs also differ in the amount of time they take. Doing the laundry may take several hours overall, but you can do other things while the clothes are washing and drying. You can't clean the bathroom, however, by setting out the cleaning supplies and walking away.

Some jobs are simpler—even more fun—than others, but you might not get people to agree. While one person may love to cook, another may hate it. What happens if everyone dislikes cooking?

Families have different approaches to household work. What they want and are able to get done depends on attitudes and available time. The willingness of family members to share the load is also a factor.

Income-Producing Work

The other type of work that families do is **income-producing work**. Such work provides money for needs and wants. The amount of time people devote to this work varies.

INFOLINK

Income-Producing Work

For information on preparing for a career, see *Section 29-1*.

In some families one person provides all the income. In many families today, however, multiple family members contribute income. Allan's parents are both employed full-time. Allan and his sister Jayme have after-school and summer jobs. Each person contributes financially to the family.

WHO DOES THE WORK?

Who does the work in a family? This question could cause debate in almost any household.

In the traditional approach to family management, daily care of the home and family was the mother's responsibility. She cleaned, did laundry, prepared meals, and took care of the children. The father's responsibility consisted of providing financially for the family. He also made the main decisions about how money was used, including making major purchases and investments. At home, he did less routine jobs, such as repairing the car and home.

Over the years the way people have handled work has changed. Traditional divisions of work respon-

A strong work ethic produces pride in a job well done. Do you think a person can be as proud of setting up an appealing produce display as someone else is about winning a legal case for a client?

Balancing Work & Family Life

THE CHALLENGE —

Managing Time Well

The day is seldom long enough for busy families. Most feel they need more than twenty-four hours to work, play, eat, and sleep. Managing time well can help your family get things done and still have time for fun.

How You Can Help

To help your family learn how to use each hour wisely, try these ideas:

- Check out a time management book from the library and share tips with family members. You might post one tip on the bathroom mirror each morning.
- Turn off the television during your family's most hectic hours so you can accomplish more in less time.
- Offer to run a family errand or babysit a younger sibling so a parent can have some free time.
- Encourage family members to use spare time to accomplish small jobs. In five minutes you could wash dishes, vacuum a room, or fold a load of clean laundry.
- Break one big job into small parts you can finish in short amounts of time.
- Suggest doing chores together as a family so you can finish quickly and spend time together.

sibilities may not be appropriate for many families today because life has changed. In many families, both the mother and father work outside the home. They also share the household responsibilities. Children and teens also participate to help the family as a whole.

Each family deals with questions of roles and responsibilities in its own way. However, studies have shown that women who are married, have two children, and are employed work an average of about 75-80 hours a week total including at home. Even when husbands share the household work, jobs tend to be assigned differently. Women still do about two-thirds of the everyday jobs at home, including cooking, cleaning, and laundry. Findings showed men are more likely to be responsible for car maintenance, yard work and home repair, paying bills, and household errands. Their work tends to be more flexible. Men often have more control over when they do household work and how much.

Men are more apt to share child care than routine household tasks. Again, however, what men and women do may be different. Men play with, educate, and watch the children more often than feeding them, taking them to the doctor, and other routine tasks.

Younger couples building their families are less influenced by traditional role expectations. They are more likely to view work of whatever kind as something that a family must accomplish together and share responsibilities.

CAREERS AND FAMILY LIFE

A career that produces a family's income is usually a big commitment of time and energy. Household work is too. Combining both can be like having two full-time jobs. Problems come when one person bears too much of the burden. Even when workloads are shared equitably, managing life at home and on the job can still be a challenge.

People once believed that you could separate job and home life. Now they know that home life affects the job, and vice versa. There is a definite interrelationship between job and family life, as you will soon see.

SKILLS CHECKLIST

Communication Skills

Leadership Skills

Management Skills

Thinking Skills

Communicating Effectively

Unless families communicate with each other, they won't know how each person feels about the distribution of work. That can lead to hidden anger and frustration. This checklist will help you determine if your family is communicating effectively about household work:

✓ We know what each family member thinks should be done in the home.
✓ We agree on the household tasks that need to be performed.
✓ We understand family members' feelings and ideas about their part in the family household work.
✓ We listen to suggestions for improving the coordination, timing, and efficiency of family management.
✓ We are aware of each person's time commitments.
✓ We know who is responsible for the supplies needed for household work.
✓ We support each other when there are difficulties.
✓ We know what to do when problems arise.

Using Your Skills

Select one of the items in the list that could be improved in your family. Plan how you could help strengthen communication in this area. Carry out your plan and evaluate its results.

Building Character

Courtesy: A Quality That Counts

When busy and rushed at home or school, how do you act? Do you snap at others or act rude? Courtesy, which is polite behavior and good manners, is most difficult when you are frustrated, stressed, or harried. Consideration and thoughtfulness show courtesy. A teen could show courtesy by:

- Doing an unpleasant household chore without complaint, back talk, or defiant body language.
- Saying "please" and "thank you" to family members.
- Talking calmly to a sibling who has spilled mustard on a borrowed vest.
- Greeting others cheerfully when reporting for work.
- Carrying a neighbor's groceries when she is struggling with three sacks and two small children.
- Being polite to a difficult customer who is making demands that are against store rules.

QUESTIONS

1. What are the advantages of showing courtesy?
2. Why is it more difficult to show courtesy when you are upset or frustrated?
3. In what specific ways could you show courtesy in your family?

Family Life Affects Jobs

Suppose you own a business. You notice that some of your employees have problems. What has happened to them at home is affecting their job performance. Take a look:

- **Lack of family training.** Cal has a poor attitude. He doesn't get along with coworkers and can't take responsibility. Cal is missing certain qualities that he should have learned while growing up.
- **Home pressures.** Allyson is a single parent with two children. She often stays up late to get things done at home. She feels the pressure of trying to manage a busy life. She's tired and not very alert at work.
- **Family problems.** Trevor's wife recently moved out of the family home, taking their son with her. Trevor is depressed, and his emotional state is fragile. He's distracted at work.

As you can see, the job performance of each of these employees is threatened. Employers need workers whose personal lives are healthy and in order.

Jobs Affect Family Life

Just as jobs are affected by family life, family life is also affected by what happens on the job. You can see how in the following examples:

- **Job loss.** Pete lost his job, leaving his family with little income. He's trying to find another one but feels frustrated and worried, which is apparent to his family.
- **Relocation.** Karen has been offered a job transfer. She and her family must decide whether they want to move.
- **Work challenges.** Corbin is an emergency medical technician. Although he likes the work, his family often feels his emotional strain.

- **Difficult work schedules.** As a minister, Rebecca is called to duty at all hours of the day and night. Her family never knows for sure when she'll be around.
- **Work stress.** Tamika works with very tight deadlines on her job. She often carries her tension and frustrations home with her.

Families are heavily influenced by what happens to people on their jobs. For families to function well, they need cooperation from employers who care about them.

LOOKING FOR ANSWERS

When people know how to manage, life is more satisfying. Families and employers are exploring ways to improve the blend of work, personal, and family life. The next section of this chapter will show you how.

Although people often try, separating work and personal life is difficult. Why is that true?

SECTION 11-1 REVIEW

Check Your Understanding

1. What does the term "work ethic" mean?
2. In what ways do household tasks differ from each other?
3. How were household work responsibilities generally divided in the past?
4. What does the phrase "the interrelationship between job and family" mean? Give an example to support your explanation.
5. **Thinking Critically.** What might happen to a society if the work ethic weakens?
6. **Problem Solving.** Sixteen-year-old Dominique's mother has been seriously ill for several months. Dominique has taken over many of the household chores, but her seventeen-year-old sister Isabel won't do any. Dominique feels stressed and her school work is suffering. Any comments she makes to her sister just cause angry words between them. What should Dominique do?

Managing Busy Lives

OBJECTIVES

After studying this section, you should be able to:

- Explain how employers support families.
- Devise and implement a plan for work distribution at home.
- Create tools for managing family life.
- Identify ways that families manage child-care responsibilities.
- Describe a family support system and explain its value.

TERMS TO LEARN

leave of absence
rotation
delegate
reimbursements

When you're very tired, how well do you do in school? Most teens would answer, "Not very well." Adults face a similar situation as they try to balance work and family life. With pressures at home, they may not do well on the job. If the job creates problems, home life may suffer.

The need to balance work and family life gets attention in society today. Frustration and stress levels are rising as people face demands from all areas of life and wonder how to manage.

As a teen, you can help your family manage. When everyone participates, the atmosphere is usually better. Also, the skills you learn can help if you're the leader of a family someday.

EMPLOYER SUPPORT

Traditionally, employers tended to believe that income-producing work should be a person's first priority. That's not true for everyone anymore. One employer saw the change when one of his best employees left for another job despite a substantial raise offer. What did the young man want? He wanted a job that didn't demand excessive hours, including last-minute scheduling for nights and weekends. He wanted time with his family, which was more important to him than a higher income.

As employers continue to realize what people truly want and need, they are making changes. They are creating policies that appeal to people who need to blend family and personal life smoothly with their careers.

Changing Workplace Policies

At one time many corporations commonly moved people on a regular basis. If this caused family problems, the company didn't notice. Eventually, they saw that disrupted families meant disruption on the job. Today many businesses limit transfers or at least give employees options. Workers are not penalized for refusing a transfer, as they once were.

Many companies also offer leaves of absence to workers. A **leave of absence** provides time off from work to use for some purpose. Many employers grant leaves of absence when a child is born or adopted or when a family member is ill. Companies over a certain size are required to offer these benefits. Although these leaves are usually without pay, they do offer workers some job security. Employees know they won't lose their jobs for attending to family responsibilities.

Realizing that personal and family problems affect job performance, some employers offer help. One company, for example, supplies information about smoking, incentives to quit, and support programs. Another company provides counseling for addictions and other personal problems. If possible, concerned employers want to help, rather than let the problem or the employee go.

ALTERNATIVE WORK SCHEDULES

What happens to children when employees are tied to a specific work schedule? Parents miss school conferences. Children may be home alone or unable to get to child care. Doctor appointments are hard to schedule.

Working a set eight-hour shift for five days of the week doesn't always work today. Demands on time include personal business, volunteer work, and family responsibilities. When rigid job schedules don't allow people to do what needs to be done, stress and anger often result.

Although employers have business needs, most want employees to feel in control of their lives. With creative thinking, employers are providing work schedules that ease the lives of their employees. The benefit is a happier, more productive work force.

Some careers require people to work at night. Is this an advantage or a disadvantage for families? Why?

Career Success Stories

Eric Webster: *Human Resources Director*

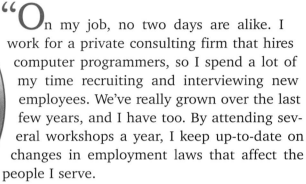

"On my job, no two days are alike. I work for a private consulting firm that hires computer programmers, so I spend a lot of my time recruiting and interviewing new employees. We've really grown over the last few years, and I have too. By attending several workshops a year, I keep up-to-date on changes in employment laws that affect the people I serve.

"The need for child care is an issue I face all the time. Most of our workers are either single parents or from dual-income families, so child care is a major issue. Our flexible sick leave policy allows workers to stay home with their children when they're ill and to use their own sick time for these situations. Otherwise, sick children are often sent to school or child care. We also offer flextime scheduling so people can make up their hours in the evenings and on weekends.

"Another policy I helped develop allows employees to donate their sick time to coworkers. Recently a single parent had a young child with a severe illness. She used up all her sick days and couldn't afford to miss work without pay. With our new policy, several of her coworkers donated hours to her. The five days she gained made a big difference to her. I keep pushing to make things easier for working parents. My ultimate goal is an on-site child-care center."

CAREER PROFILE

Education and training: bachelor's degree

Starting salary range: $25,300–$39,000

Job prospects: all areas of public and private businesses, education, and government

Important qualities: speak and write effectively; demonstrate a persuasive, congenial personality; work well with diverse people

Plan Ahead

Human resources programs include many different ones that employers provide for employees. With a partner, research and list programs that fit the area of human resources. What family policies would help a working parent?

Flexible Work Hours

Some companies have flexible working hours, allowing employees control over the time period that they work. For example, a company might let employees choose any eight-hour work period that falls between 6:00 a.m. and 8:00 p.m. Barbara is a late riser who starts work at 10:00 a.m. Ellis, who cares for his children after school, comes in at 6:00 a.m. Having a choice means that people with different needs and personalities don't have to live and work by the same schedules.

Flexibility has advantages. Giving employees some control over their lives makes them feel better about their jobs and be more productive workers. Less absenteeism is likely. Although employers must deal with complications of scheduling, they often find the effort is worthwhile.

Compressed Work Week

Three-day weekends are another option. An employee who works a compressed work week might work four ten-hour days. The days can be long, but under the right circumstances, such schedules can be very helpful.

Job Sharing

When two people divide the time and responsibilities of one job, they are job sharing. They may each work four hours a day, sharing the salaries and benefits that go along with the full-time job. For people who need time to do other things, this approach can be very satisfying.

WORK DISTRIBUTION AT HOME

A supportive employer isn't the only answer when it comes to balancing work and family life. A balanced life also relies on how the work is distributed at home. Success may hinge on a family following these steps:

1. **Identify all work to be done.** List the frequency and the time each task takes, perhaps in chart form. Note who currently does each task.
2. **Evaluate standards.** Can any household tasks be eliminated, done less often, or simplified?
3. **Determine what each family member could do.** Discuss personal preferences

Even young children can help at home by learning simple tasks. **How can teens help?**

Focus On ...

Benefits of Cooperation

When family members cooperate to get household work done, they enjoy many positive results. Among these are:

- **Less stress.** No one individual has to carry most of the workload when others are available to help. People feel less stress and carry fewer problems away from home.
- **Time for other activities.** When family work is shared, it takes less time to do, leaving time for leisure activities, community involvement, and family fun.
- **New skills.** The skills learned will be useful when teens are eventually on their own. Everyone practices planning, decision-making, and relationship skills.
- **A work ethic.** Family members discover the sense of accomplishment that comes with work. They learn to value such good work habits as neatness, promptness, and thoroughness.

- **Positive feelings.** People receive support, making them happier and more willing to return the same to others.
- **Responsibility.** People give support, making them valued family members and giving them a sense of purpose and commitment to family.

USING YOUR KNOWLEDGE

Mrs. Kane looked at the mess in the living room that she had just cleaned the day before. Now everyone was gone off to have fun, leaving their mess behind. She had planned to sit down and read a magazine before her friend Rosie arrived for a visit. What would you do if you were Mrs. Kane?

as well as what is fair. Consider ages, skills, and strengths. Some tasks can be handled individually. Others can be done as teams. With **rotation** (ro-TAY-shun) people do certain tasks for a specified period and then switch assignments.

4. **Distribute tasks among members.** As family leaders, parents have the final authority. They may **delegate**, or assign responsibilities to others. Make sure every family member has some personal time left.

5. **Set up a schedule.** Show when each task is to be done. Put the final schedule on a calendar or in a chart or notebook and place it in everyone's view.

6. **Periodically, evaluate how the schedule is going.** Is everyone taking responsibility? What changes are needed? Help all family members see the benefits of doing assigned jobs cheerfully. Cooperation and acceptance of responsibility promote positive feelings that lead to better relationships. Teens often gain trust and more privileges.

TOOLS FOR MANAGING

To make family life at home run more smoothly, people create some helpful tools. Although simple, these work best when everyone understands their purpose and agrees to use them.

A Family Calendar

Tony needed to talk to his stepmother about something important, but he didn't know where she was. Julia wanted to schedule a family outing when no one else had plans, but when might that be? An older brother had to pick up a younger one after a field trip, but he forgot the time. A family calendar could solve these problems.

To start a family calendar, find one that's large enough to write on and post it in an accessible place. If all family members learn to enter their own schedule, the calendar becomes a useful information center. With it, a family can quickly see where everyone is going to be and when. They will have an easier time reaching each other and avoiding schedule conflicts.

Family Meetings

Without regular communication, family members have little understanding about what each is thinking. Significant ideas and worries get overlooked when daily life always comes first.

To solve this problem, many families set aside a regular time to meet and talk. They might discuss work loads, complaints, values, and goals.

Team Shopping. Some families use a teamwork approach to grocery shopping. They enjoy the resulting meals more, and shopping gets done more quickly. You might like to try this technique in your family.

- Have each person help keep a running grocery list as supplies run short.
- Encourage everyone to clip coupons that could save money.
- Go to the store together.
- At the store, assign each family member a section for shopping. You might divide the list according to produce, meat, frozen foods, etc., and give one part to each participant.
- At home, put items away together.
- Share a treat to celebrate the cooperative effort.

Try It Out. Ask your family to try the teamwork approach to grocery shopping. Post a piece of paper for a list and put out a box or bowl for coupons. Schedule the shopping trip at a convenient time. How do family members like this way of grocery shopping?

A Family Bulletin Board

Written communication is also necessary for successful family management. Leaving notes for each other is fine, but putting them in a central location on a bulletin board is even better.

Bulletin boards can hold notes, lists, and messages. Kai's family uses the refrigerator door for posting information and lists of things to do. Magnets hold the slips of paper in place.

THE NEED FOR CHILD CARE

When employed parents can't be home to take care of children, what happens? Parents used to ask grandmother, but today she may be employed herself or living far away. Many parents need child care. They want quality at a reasonable price. That combination can be difficult to find.

To locate child care, parents talk to family, neighbors, physicians, and social service workers. Social service agencies often have lists of licensed child-care providers who have met local and state guidelines.

Meal Management for Busy Families

With many hands, a family makes lighter work of meal management.

Who will plan the meal and buy the groceries? This job could be rotated each week.

Groceries

Cooking

While preparing food together, the family can talk about the day's events.

A schedule of cooking assignments allows each family member to take a turn.

Preparing

Three main types of child care are available. These are:

- **In-home care.** This care, the most convenient and often most expensive, is provided in the child's home.
- **Family child-care homes.** The child goes to someone else's home for care. This may be a neighbor or relative's home. The cost varies widely.
- **Child-care centers.** Children are cared for at a special facility that typically has organized activities for children. The care at these centers varies widely. The government regulates child-care centers.

Some have a sliding fee scale that matches the fee to a person's ability to pay.

Alternative Arrangements

Some families use alternatives to child care. They may arrange staggered work schedules so one parent is always home to care for children. Such plans save child-care expenses and let each parent spend time with the children. A drawback is the limited time for two parents to spend with each other or for all family members to be together.

With a partner, plan a menu that an imaginary family could put on the table in 30 minutes. How could duties be divided?

Light conversation makes the mealtime pleasant.

Everyone can have a job, even young family members. Good habits start young.

If one person does most of the preparing, someone else could do the clean up.

Some companies provide child care for the children of employees. How does this help strengthen families and the work force?

Employer Programs

An employee who is worried about children can't work well. Some employers assist workers by helping with child care.

Some companies offer lists of approved child-care facilities. This gives employees some confidence that these facilities have been evaluated and found satisfactory. Companies may offer families **reimbursements** (re-im-BERS-ments), or money paid back, so they can afford child care of their own choosing.

A few companies, mostly large, have child-care facilities at the place of business. Parents and children can arrive and leave together. Some parents are able to spend their breaks and lunch periods with their children. These facilities may also have a sick bay for children. This type of child care benefit is quite expensive for a company. On the other hand, it reduces absenteeism and keeps employee turnover low.

School-Age Children

Once children are in school, child-care concerns don't end. Supervision after school is a concern. Transportation to activities is another need. Many youngsters are unable to participate in activities because they simply have no way to get there.

Many parents who want after-school care can't afford it or find it. Children who stay alone at home after school need to learn skills to keep them safe. They may be supervised by telephone from the parent's workplace. One mother's words described her concerns: "I know I'm not a very good worker after 3:30 p.m. when Traci gets home from school. I worry about what she's watching on TV, whether she has friends over when she's not supposed to, and whether she'll be safe fixing a snack in the kitchen. There's never been a problem—she's very independent and capable for a ten-year-old—but I still worry."

BUILDING A SUPPORT SYSTEM

Recognizing, developing, and using a support system can make life run more smoothly for a family. Common sources of support are extended family, neighbors, friends, and community services.

Neighbors and friends are a good resource. Many families find ways to exchange with others in order to manage. One family, for example, formed a car pool with neighbors so that their daughters could get to Girl Scout meetings. Another family exchanged babysitting hours with friends so that the parents in each family could have some time away without the expense of a babysitter.

Although not every family can afford it, some pay to get the support services they need. A family might hire someone to do housecleaning or yard work. They might pay for a diaper service. Latoya hires a home health aide to stay with her elderly mother who needs companionship and care.

A VIEW FROM ALL SIDES

When you think about managing family life, you need to put yourself in someone else's shoes. Often family members quietly harbor feelings that no one else is aware of. Do you know who *feels* the most burdened in your family? Do you know who *is* the most burdened in your family? Finding out may be the first step to better family management. It may also be the first step to a happier family life.

SECTION 11-2 REVIEW

Check Your Understanding

1. Why are employers doing more to support families these days?
2. Why can't all employees easily follow traditional job schedules?
3. What are three scheduling methods employers use to help employees manage better?
4. Cheyenne hates to wash dishes. How will rotation be of benefit to her?
5. Why is communication an important part of family management?
6. What are the advantages to families and employers when employers offer child care at their place of business?
7. **Thinking Critically.** What might happen if some family members don't enter their schedule and schedule changes on the family calendar?
8. **Problem Solving.** Isaiah is the owner of a small company that employs fifteen people. Several of his best employees are parents who have trouble managing the schedule that Isaiah requires of everyone. A few single employees have grumbled about having to cover when one of the parents leaves for family problems. Isaiah needs people at work in order to stay profitable. What should he do?

Chapter 11
Review and Activities

CHAPTER SUMMARY

- Work is a valuable part of life that brings rewards to people.
- Work serves different purposes for people.
- Attitudes about who does certain work in a household have changed over the years.
- There is an interrelationship between jobs and family life. Each affects the other.
- Families need support from employers to manage their multiple responsibilities.
- Employers use creative methods of scheduling and policies to help employees.
- Sharing the workload in a family means no one is overly burdened or stressed.
- Child care is an ongoing concern of families with children who need care.

REVIEW QUESTIONS

Section 11-1
1. Why is work valuable?
2. What are two basic kinds of work that families do?
3. How have the ways families divide household work changed over the years?
4. Courtney is a legal secretary and a single mother with two young children. How might her home life affect her job performance?
5. What are five job situations that could have negative effects on family life?

Section 11-2
1. What is a leave of absence?
2. What are the benefits of flexible scheduling on the job?
3. What steps can a family take in order to distribute the work fairly?
4. What are three main types of child care?
5. How can a family keep from taking advantage of the people in their support system?

BECOMING A PROBLEM SOLVER

1. Every Sunday, Tom's mother gives him a list of chores to do. He hates the list and usually doesn't finish it. When Tom asks his mother for the car and other privileges, she often says no, which upsets Tom. What should he do?

2. Cara's son Josh has awakened with a slight temperature, a sore throat, and a runny nose. Cara can't afford to miss more work. She knows, however, that the child-care center will not take Josh if they know he is sick. What should Cara do?

THINKING CRITICALLY

1. **Recognizing Values.** Do you think a "work ethic" is alive and well where you live? Explain your answer.
2. **Analyzing Behavior.** Why do you think some people are unaware of many of the household tasks that need to be done?
3. **Recognizing Alternatives.** Do you think standards of cleanliness need to be lowered for busy families? Explain your answer.
4. **Predicting Results.** What might be the short- and long-term effects on a grade-school child who must routinely stay alone after school?

MAKING CURRICULUM CONNECTIONS

1. **Math.** As a class, make a list of household jobs. Compare ideas on how much time would be needed to carry out each responsibility. Assign a time to each task and calculate the average time needed for all household work per week and month.
2. **Language Arts.** Write a letter to your imagined future mate, describing how you would like to divide household responsibilities.

APPLYING YOUR KNOWLEDGE

1. With your classmates, debate the value of work that provides income as opposed to work that does not.
2. Who should decide what jobs family members do? Explain your point of view.
3. With your classmates, make a list of basic indoor and outdoor household jobs. Survey the class to find out who does each job in the students' families. Is there much variation among families? Why or why not? What conclusions can you draw from this activity?

Family & Community Connections

1. If money were no object, what three appliances would you want the most if you were running a busy household? Explain your answer.

2. With a partner, create a set of five to ten rules for household management. Share your list with the class.

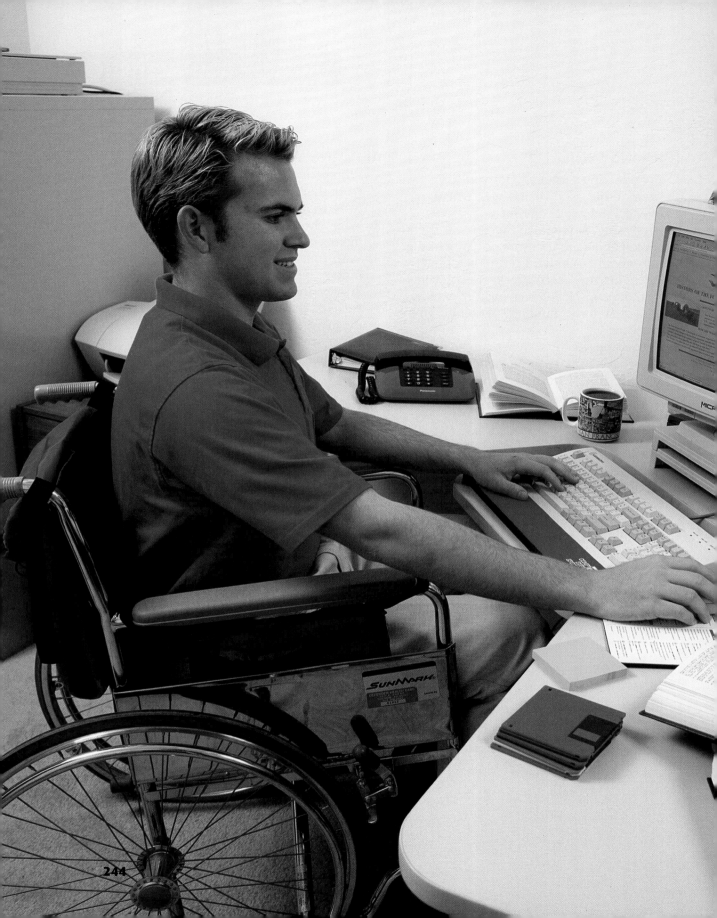

UNIT 4

Supporting Family and Friends

Teen Views

Do you think families face tougher problems today than they used to?

Seneca

"My father says things are a lot tougher for people today, and I guess I agree. If one of my friends mentions the security guard we have at school, Dad just shakes his head. They didn't need security guards when he was in school, and I know it makes him worry. He says that's a sign of the times."

Kent

"I think things aren't really tougher, just different. Families have always struggled. Look what the early settlers went through. They had lots of babies because so many of them died young. Going across the country in a covered wagon in all kinds of weather—that was real hardship. We've got it a lot better than that."

What's your view?

How would you compare the problems families have today to the past?

Chapter 12

The Challenge of Change

WORDS FOR THOUGHT

"My motto is the same as my blood type: B positive."

(Cynthia Nelms)

IN YOUR OWN WORDS

Do you think a positive attitude can get you through every challenge you face in life?

Facing Change

OBJECTIVES

After studying this section, you should be able to:

- Explain what change means in people's lives.
- Compare and contrast the effects of various life changes on individuals and families.
- Distinguish helpful techniques for dealing with a move.
- Plan strategies to help individuals and families cope with financial problems, unemployment, and natural disasters.

TERMS TO LEARN

economize
creditors
bankruptcy
unemployment
identity

Change is a fact of life. Life, in fact, *is* change. Some changes are expected; others catch you off guard. Change can bring gain or loss, joy or frustration. No matter what, you can count on change.

What changes do people face in life? Some are fairly common. If your dentist retires, you have to find and adjust to a new one. If the bus routes are altered, you have to find another way to get around town. These are simple changes that most people take in stride.

Other changes have a greater impact. Moving to another city and experiencing a divorce in the family are not simple events. They alter life significantly. Changes such as these are the focus of this unit.

If not handled well, a change can cause problems, sometimes serious. To enjoy life, you need to know what to expect and how to react.

MOVING

You live in the most mobile society ever, but that doesn't necessarily make moving easy. Moving to a new place, a family is apt to feel sad about leaving and anxious about the unfamiliar environment. They also feel the strain of making all the arrangements that moving involves.

A move within the same neighborhood is usually the easiest kind. You have the physical labor of packing and resettling in a different home, but that's probably the worst part. A long-distance

move takes much more. In addition to a different home, you must also adapt to changes in school, friends, community, and perhaps job.

How difficult do you think moving frequently would be? People who move often may be reluctant to settle in. Alexis began to feel this way after her family moved three times before she was thirteen. She wondered, "Why should I make friends when I'll just have to leave as soon as I start feeling like I'm part of things?"

Alexis learned to cope with frequent moves by changing her attitude. She decided to see each move as an opportunity. What could new experiences and relationships teach her? Now Alexis takes moving in stride and sees adventure in new situations. She has a broader view of life and also interesting stories to share. Through e-mail and phone calls, she continues to enjoy friendships long-distance.

When moves are frequent, however, attitude can't solve the problem of interrupted schooling. School districts teach subjects on different schedules. Students who come in during the middle of the year may miss important concepts that have already been taught. Parents need to work with teachers to see how to make up for any educational gaps.

Preparing for a Move

Before a move, families should discuss their plans openly and honestly. If possible, visiting the area helps everyone feel more comfortable. A city's Chamber of Commerce may have useful information about the community. Studying the material gives a head start on adjustment. You can learn whether the city has a swimming pool and where the library is located. Identifying points of interest provides incentive for exploring the new community as you settle in.

To start learning their way around, children and teens might also visit their new schools before the move. Meeting a new neighbor or classmate also helps.

Taking part in moving eases anxiety by giving a sense of control over the event.

Children can pack toys and arrange items in their new room. A teen might take care of a few practical details, such as filling out a change-of-address card at the post office. Parents need to make arrangements for telephone and utility services, newspaper subscriptions, and personal financial matters.

Adjusting to a Move

No matter how well you prepare, you can't expect a place to feel like home right away. As strange becomes familiar, however, feelings of insecurity fade and a sense of belonging takes their place.

Making an effort is part of adjustment. People who have a job are likely to adjust quickly. Others may need to look for ways to get involved. Community newcomer clubs are a good resource. Parents can help a child make friends by meeting other parents in the neighborhood and introducing their children.

Moving can be an exciting family challenge. It can draw a family closer and provide new experiences that help members grow as individuals.

Welcoming Others

A move is easier on newcomers when others welcome them. When someone moves to your school or neighborhood, help them get off to a good start. You can:
- Introduce yourself to newcomers as soon as possible.
- Take a housewarming gift or make some other friendly gesture.
- Offer to help in some way. You might loan a temporarily missing item or share needed information about the school or neighborhood.
- Include someone new in an activity.

You can be the answer to another teen's adjustment to a move. Introduce new students to your friends. If their family lives near you, ask your family to make them feel welcome, too.

FINANCIAL PROBLEMS

People can't always predict life's events; financial problems can occur. The loss of a job is one cause of money problems. Overspending and misfortune are others. The Jordans were paying off a car loan and credit card bills for a vacation when Mr. Jordan needed emergency heart surgery. Their financial situation became critical.

People feel threatened when finances are in doubt. Some are quick to blame others in the family: "If you didn't spend so much on clothing…" "I told you we couldn't afford to keep up this house." When the problem is not caused by something beyond a person's control, however, it's usually due to an entire family's spending and saving habits. One person is rarely to blame.

When parents sense that their finances are slipping out of control, they can take measures to prevent serious problems. Community colleges and the Cooperative Extension Service may offer classes in money management. A financial counselor can suggest a realistic family budget.

Coping with Financial Problems

Preparing for financial difficulties is one of the best ways to prevent them. Experts suggest having savings to cover up to three months of living expenses as a buffer against hard financial times.

Another way to avoid, and also deal with, financial difficulties is to **economize**, or find ways to spend less money. Some expenses are necessary and unchanging, but others can be controlled or postponed. For example:

- Eat homemade meals. Meals made from scratch can be cheaper than restaurant meals or prepared, store-bought dishes. Watch the ads and compare supermarkets to find the best buys.
- Repair clothing instead of buying new articles. You might also find well-cared-for items in shops that sell used clothing at low prices.
- Look for free or low-cost entertainment. Check out library books and videos. Tour a museum exhibit. Attend a free concert in the park.

Medical bills after a serious illness can be overwhelming. Working together can make it easier for families to decide how to cover the added expenses.

Strength: A Quality That Counts

Becoming psychologically strong takes work, but it's worth the effort. This kind of strength lets you confront difficulties with minimal stress. You can act despite fears and work with others to solve problems. Strength is invaluable for facing situations that involve major changes in your life. To show strength, a teen:

- Gives up the expense of going online without complaint when a parent is laid off from work.
- Makes new friends and joins a club at a new school.
- Ignores thoughtless comments about personal appearance.
- Becomes a teen counselor on a crisis hot line.

QUESTIONS

1. How does each of the actions described above show strength?
2. Is strength a trait of males, females, or both? Explain your answer.
3. Can a person be strong and still show emotions? Explain.
4. Describe some ways that you have shown strength.

- Do tasks yourself that you normally pay to have done. Learning to do routine car maintenance yourself, for example, can save money.
- Exchange services or items with other families.
- Sell possessions that you don't need, especially if they require costly upkeep or insurance.

When money is tight, families may need to change not only their behavior but also their outlook on life. Solving financial problems often means sacrifice. When family members are willing to put aside their own wants in favor of others' needs, getting through tough times is much easier.

Getting Help

If financial problems become unmanageable, a family may need outside help. Credit counselors are a source of advice. They are listed in the telephone directory Yellow Pages under Consumer Credit Counseling Services. These nonprofit organizations can assist you with your problems. Professional companies that seem to offer help, however, can cost more in the end.

Most **creditors**, those to whom a debt is owed, will help people find ways to pay. They might agree to smaller payments or accept property instead. In extreme cases, however, **bankruptcy** (BANG-krupt-SEE)

Waiting to be interviewed in an unemployment office can be difficult. This young mother may feel that all eyes are on her. **How might her family boost her morale?**

lem in society. "We've lived on the edge for years," Jenny explained. "Two months after the rent was raised, my daughter and I were living in my car. It was two weeks before I could find a place I could afford."

People in Jenny's situation often turn first to family and friends for help. Shelters supply temporary housing until people get back on their feet. In some areas, social service organizations work with churches to house and feed homeless families while providing job training, child care, and transportation to and from work.

UNEMPLOYMENT

Of all the reasons for financial problems, **unemployment**— not having a job—is one of the hardest on families. When people need a job and don't have one, life isn't easy.

Effects on the Unemployed

Losing income is only part of the unemployment problem. As you read earlier, work is very important to people for many reasons. Not having work can be very difficult for the person who lost a job.

Unemployment can damage a person's **identity**, your view of yourself as a person. Losing a job can make people feel as though they have failed. They may begin to doubt themselves and grow anxious or depressed.

The longer unemployment lasts, the stronger its effects. If the lack of income causes the family serious financial problems, the jobless person may feel guilty and

---

may be an option. This legal process declares a person unable to pay debts. Any assets the person has may be used to pay part of what is owed. Bankruptcy should be a last resort only. It legally eliminates debts but seriously hurts a person's ability to get credit in the future.

For families in serious financial trouble, a state's Department of Public Aid is a resource. Public assistance, including child care and food programs, is available if needed.

Loss of Home

As a result of dire financial straits, some people are no longer able to afford a place to live. Homelessness is an increasing prob-

react harshly. Some become irritable and sensitive to criticism. Others withdraw into themselves. Some turn to alcohol to dull their feelings, only to find that it makes them feel worse.

The stress of unemployment can cause the jobless person health problems, too. Ulcers, headaches, upset stomachs, and high blood pressure are a few common complaints. If these problems become severe, they can strain an already tight financial picture.

Ultimately, these physical and emotional effects can make finding a new job harder. A job applicant who is depressed, anxious, ill, and filled with self-doubt is unlikely to make a good impression on prospective employers. The person may even think that looking for a job is pointless.

Effects on the Family

While the jobless person is suffering, the family is too. The financial and personal effects of unemployment can cause drastic changes in family life.

In some families, working together to overcome the problems of unemployment often brings members closer at first. Over time, however, the demands may strain family ties to the breaking point. Conflict can flare as families make hard choices about what to do in order to survive. Long-term unemployment can cause a family breakdown.

Young children are often hardest hit by the loss of a parent's job. They tend to get sick more often than children of employed parents. They are less able to understand what is happening and have fewer friends and outside resources for support than older children do.

A teen's life is affected in other ways. When Hannah's mother lost her job, Hannah increased her hours at her part-time job. This cut into her free time and social life. Hannah grew protective of her family. She gave her younger brother small treats to reassure him. She gave extra support to her mother by doing more chores at home. Sometimes she felt unfairly burdened.

The experience opened Hannah's eyes to some hard realities about work. She saw her hard-working mother, through no fault of her own, lose an important part of her identity. Hannah was old enough to see how the lack of work could be more damaging to a parent than the lack of money.

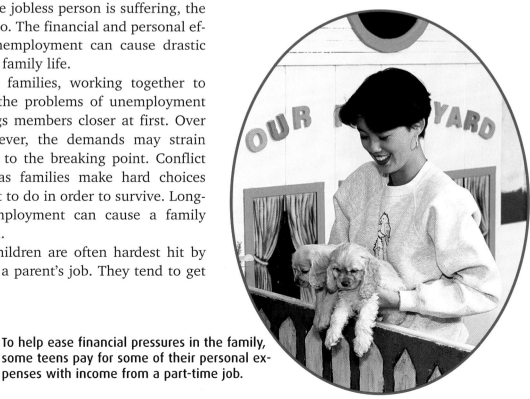

To help ease financial pressures in the family, some teens pay for some of their personal expenses with income from a part-time job.

Coping with Unemployment

Unemployment is a family problem. The family can be its own best resource for coping. Besides economizing, families use other strategies.

Most workers are eligible for some type of unemployment insurance. Insurance generally covers only basic expenses, however, and lasts only about one year. It won't make up for not having savings.

Therefore, the unemployed person needs to be persistent in looking for work. An employment agency or the state job service office can offer job listings and sometimes job counseling. Temporary work, though it may not be the person's first choice, might get the family by until a permanent position is found. Most people who lose their jobs do find new ones.

Older children can contribute something too. They can babysit, run errands, and help with housecleaning or yard work. The feeling of taking action, of not being helpless, is a bigger benefit than any money they bring in.

Teens can work to increase the family income also. Showing support and understanding, however, may be more valued by the unemployed parent. A parent already feels bad about being unable to provide. Blame and accusations only deepen the hurt. Caring, love, and encouragement are far more helpful.

A family can take advantage of community resources as well. Medical clinics provide low-cost services, and government agencies offer free financial advice.

Families should also find a support system. Sharing feelings with other families who are dealing with unemployment can help ease some of the emotional problems. Talking to those who know what unemployment is like can provide needed advice.

Are you and your family at risk of any particular natural disaster where you live? What precautions could you take to prevent loss from a fire?

NATURAL DISASTERS

Fortunately, the worst damage that most people ever experience from severe weather is a broken window or water in the basement. Depending on the part of the country, however, floods, fires, tornadoes, and hurricanes are real concerns. A rising river can be just as effective as unemployment at costing a family their home and wiping out their savings.

You can't control the forces of nature, of course, but planning for dangerous weather is worthwhile. The family's physical safety is the first concern when natural disaster strikes. Many families wisely practice fire drills and other emergency responses at home.

Planning for life after a disaster is just as important. For example, is the family's home or property insurance adequate for the most likely disasters? Does the family have a safe supply of food and water in case of emergency? Where would they stay if they had to evacuate their home? What financial assets are available if their bank were unable to operate? Learning the answers to questions like these may make sense for your family, even if you never need to use that knowledge.

YOUR REACTIONS

How do you handle the changes in your life? Depending on the event, you may have little trouble or a lot. As you will see in the next section, reactions to change can be very strong, sometimes harmful. Such reactions can, and must, be managed.

SECTION 12-1 REVIEW

Check Your Understanding

1. How does change affect people's lives?
2. What are some suggestions for helping a family prepare for a move?
3. List ways to make someone new feel welcome in your school or neighborhood.
4. What is the benefit of economizing
5. Why should bankruptcy be used only as a last resort?
6. What are some suggestions for a family that must deal with the problem of unemployment?
7. **Thinking Critically.** What are some positive and negative results of relying on a job for identity?
8. **Problem Solving.** Shannon's family will be moving in six months, at the end of her junior year in high school. She has worked hard to keep up her grades and is counting on her high school record to get into college. Shannon is worried that changing schools with only one year before graduation might hurt her chances. What can she do to ease her concerns?

Stress Management

OBJECTIVES

After studying this section, you should be able to:

- Explain the causes of stress.
- Describe how stress can be helpful.
- Explain how to recognize stress.
- Describe ways to keep stress from occurring.
- Summarize actions to take in response to stress.

TERMS TO LEARN

stress
stress management
epinephrine

What happens if you leave a teapot full of water on the range to warm? As the heat increases, the pressure inside the teapot rises. Left unattended, the water boils over. People are like the teapot. Pressure can build up inside until they "boil over." The cause isn't heat. It's **stress**—physical, mental, or emotional strain or tension.

To keep a teapot from boiling over, you turn down the heat, let some steam escape, or remove the pot from the burner. Likewise, people must act to prevent stress from becoming a problem in their lives.

CAUSES OF STRESS

Many everyday situations cause stress. Being late, misplacing a textbook, and getting caught in traffic can be stressful. Crowds and noise bother some people. Difficult working conditions and strained relationships with friends or family cause stress to build.

Even pleasing events can be stressful. Would accepting an award before an audience make you tense? What about playing a sport?

Troublesome events cause significant stress in people's lives. The situations described in this unit are typically accompanied by highly stressful feelings.

Even happy events such as a wedding can bring stress to a family. What stresses might you feel when an older sibling gets married?

Personal Reactions to Stress

Everyone feels stress. That's just normal. Not everyone feels stress in the same ways, however. When you take a test, for instance, the tension you feel is different from what other classmates feel. Why is test taking more stressful to some than others?

The amount of stress you feel is partly determined by personality. Terri likes change. She looks forward to new experiences and to learning new skills. Change is less stressful to her than it is to Luke, who prefers the familiar and the routine.

On the other hand, Luke is patient. He doesn't get upset about waiting in line or for appointments. Terri is more impatient, wanting things to happen quickly. How do you think impatience affects Terri's stress level?

THE POSITIVE SIDE OF STRESS

Do you long for the stress-free life? That might not be as good as it sounds. When properly handled, some stress is like the spring in a wind-up toy: it puts you in motion and keeps you going.

The urge to create and accomplish something is positive stress. Some people need a little push. Those who say they work best under pressure are acknowledging that stress motivates them.

STRESS OVERLOAD

Even though winding up a toy makes it go, if you wind too much, you'll break the spring. In the same way, excessive stress can cause both physical and mental disease. The higher your stress level becomes, the more prone you are to illness.

After fifteen-year-old Mattie's parents divorced, she lived with her mother. Her father moved out of state. Mattie missed him so much that she lost interest in food and lost weight. She withdrew from friends and began to feel physically and emotionally exhausted. After Mattie found help from a counselor, she was able to recover slowly from the stress she felt.

UNDERSTANDING STRESS MANAGEMENT

You don't need to be overwhelmed by stress. Learning to manage stress can control the negative impact on your life. You can learn techniques that will help you cope responsibly and comfortably with the demands of life. This is called **stress management**.

Stress management rests on several principles. First, you need to recognize your own stress and its causes. Second, you need to limit stress. Third, you need to know what to do when stress is troublesome.

Focus On ...

What Stress Feels Like

Not everyone feels stress in exactly the same way. Stress strikes where you are the weakest, and your weaknesses are not the same as everyone else's. Here are some signs of stress:

Irritable or depressed
Pounding heart
Rash
Impulsive behavior
Emotionally unstable
Inability to make decisions
Urge to cry or hide
Unable to concentrate
Weakness or dizziness
Afraid but not sure why
Tense
Trembling; nervous tics
Easily startled
Nervous laughter
Speech problems
Grinding teeth
Nail biting
Hair pulling
Tapping fingers and toes
Can't sleep or sleep too much
Sweating
Headaches
Frequent urination
Menstrual problems
Neck and back pain
Appetite loss or overeating
Use of nicotine and drugs
Nightmares
Accident prone

USING YOUR KNOWLEDGE

As Nate sat waiting with legs crossed, his right foot bobbed up and down in the air. He glanced at the clock repeatedly, feeling his heart racing. He gripped the arms of the chair, raised up slightly, and then slumped back down and sighed, shaking his head in disgust. What do you think is going on with Nate?

Balancing Work & Family Life

THE CHALLENGE —

Reducing Stress in Busy Families

Busy schedules make people rushed and impatient. When family members are working, keeping appointments, making meals, and maintaining the home, there's not much time to relax and relate. Instead of battling short tempers, take steps to reduce stress so your family can communicate without anger and frustration.

How You Can Help

For strategies to reduce the stress in your home, try these ideas:

- Lower expectations. Talk with family members and set priorities for what needs to be done.
- Post jokes, schedules, inspirational messages, and notes on a family bulletin board.
- Offer to help family members when you can.
- Choose one personal issue that causes you to fight with family members and either implement a solution or drop the issue for one week.
- Pitch in with family members to accomplish tasks quickly. Make lunches assembly-line style or clean one room together to ease the load.

Recognizing Stress Signals

You won't know how to deal with stress unless you identify what causes it for you. Certain signals show that you're under stress. Many of these are listed on page 258. If you pay attention to these physical and emotional cues, you can link them to the causes. Then you can take action to deal with the problem.

Limiting Stress in Your Life

If you know that lateness makes you tense and upset, what should you do? Eliminate the causes of lateness, right? The simple principle of cause and effect can be applied in order to cut down on the stress in your life. Here are two ways.

Maintain Good Health

Teens who aren't fit have a harder time coping with stress. They may even create stressful situations. If you were tired, how would you react to teasing from a family member? An overreaction could lead to problems.

Low levels of energy and mental alertness signal a problem, often with fitness. Staying fit isn't really that difficult. Do you eat a balanced, nutritious diet, including breakfast? Do you get at least eight hours of sleep each night? Do you exercise regularly and maintain a healthy weight? Do you stay away from drugs and tobacco products? These are strong physical defenses against stress. As further insurance, you can get regular physical checkups to catch any problems early.

Manage Your Life Well

When you don't know what's going to happen to you, the feeling creates stress. Gaining a sense of control increases confidence and reduces stress. The good management skills you learned earlier enable you to take charge of your life. You set goals and make plans to meet them, using the resources you've identified.

Learning to Relax

Learning to relax makes tough times easier. When you feel stressed, try these ideas for easing the moment.

Imagine . . . that you're in a safe and beautiful place.

Talk . . . to someone.

As part of good management, you plan for the unexpected. Learning to change a tire, for example, makes getting a flat less trying. Saving money gives you a financial cushion in an emergency.

Managing time according to your priorities also puts you in charge. Wasting time is a stress creator, just as time pressures can be. Satisfaction, instead of stress, comes when you feel good about how your time is spent.

INFOLINK

Time Management

Review *Section 9-2* **for tips on time management.**

Reacting to Stress

No matter what you do, some stress is inevitable in life. How can you minimize the negative effects? Several techniques are useful.

Put Events in Perspective

Have you heard of people who "make something out of nothing"? Their view makes a situation seem worse than it is. Many situations aren't worth worrying

Some people try to hold stress-ful feelings inside. Why could this be harmful?

about. Give each incident in life no more or less weight than it deserves. Remember, too, that other people have survived worse.

While walking with his uncle, Caleb became angry when mud from the wheels of a passing car splashed on his jacket. "There are more important things to get upset about, Caleb; we can wash it," Uncle Charlie said quietly. As Caleb thought of the recent death of his aunt, he realized that Uncle Charlie spoke from experience.

Use Your Support System

Faced with a stressful situation, which would your reaction be: confide in someone or keep your worries to yourself? Stress creates feelings you need to talk about. Sharing your problems and emotions with someone who can be supportive lightens the burden. A parent or older sibling has probably been through something similar. Sometimes it takes courage to ask for advice or assistance, but the effort is worthwhile. People want to help, just as you would if someone confided in you.

Take Appropriate Actions

Carriage horses wear blinkers along their eyes to keep them from being frightened by things they encounter. What they don't see doesn't bother them. Blinkers, however, aren't recommended for you.

When a stressful situation looms, look it squarely in the eye and take action. Research shows that taking charge lowers production of **epinephrine** (ep-uh-NEF-rin), the human hormone responsible for the physical reactions to stress.

What action you take depends on the situation. For everyday stress that is bothering you, you may be able to ease the symptoms right away. When you feel pressures, breathe deeply for a while. Try to relax by using the ideas on pages 260-261.

Taking constructive action to remedy a stressful situation may also be necessary. If you're worried about a speech you have to give, practice it well. If you're nervous about taking a driver's test, do something that will distract you before you go. If a serious problem is causing stress, turn to the problem-solving process to take action.

Release Emotions

Did you know that crying may actually be a good way to deal with tension? Science points out that emotional tears are chemically different from those caused by such irritations as onions. Stress-related tears have more protein and often contain high levels of minerals and hormones. Crying can bring relief by ridding the body of these chemicals. People who cry to relieve anxiety seem to have fewer stress-related diseases than those who don't cry.

The myth that tears are only for females is slowly breaking down. Both males and females cry at times. As males become more in tune with their emotions, they find that occasional tears show their sensitive side as well as help release tension.

Tears are not the only emotional outlet for stress. Some people have feelings so strong that they need to release them in some nondestructive way. Those who feel like lashing out can hit a pillow or release tension with exercise.

Use Positive Self-Talk

All people talk to themselves, about themselves, in their mind. This "self-talk" increases stress when it's negative. Waiting her turn at bat in a softball game, Emilia thought, "I'll probably strike out again. I'll never be any good at this game." What do you think Emilia's anxiety level was like as she stepped up to the plate?

Positive but realistic "self-talk" increases confidence instead of tearing it down. Positive "self-talk" eases the moment and often leads to success. Those who master the art of positive "self-talk" can condition themselves to think in a different, more optimistic way. This is one more way to reduce stress in your life.

SECTION 12-2 REVIEW

Check Your Understanding

1. What is stress?
2. What causes stress?
3. Is eliminating stress a worthwhile goal? Why or why not?
4. What can happen if a person is overloaded with stress?
5. What principles are the basis for stress management?
6. Why is crying believed to be a good stress reliever?
7. How can "self-talk" help a person deal with stress?
8. **Thinking Critically.** What do you think the Scottish proverb, it's "better to bend than break," means?
9. **Problem Solving.** Gina's full schedule includes school and work, plus volunteer work. Since her mother's illness, all family members must take on extra tasks at home. Gina is starting to feel stress. What can she do?

CHAPTER SUMMARY

- Change, large and small, is a fact of life.
- Moving requires making many adjustments. Planning and a positive attitude can help.
- Financial problems occur for different reasons. A family needs to take money-saving measures to get back on their feet.
- Homelessness can result when people have very serious financial problems.
- Unemployment takes a financial and emotional toll on the jobless person and the family.
- Family members can help each other cope with the problems that unemployment can cause.
- Stress is a common reaction to change and problems. Uncontrolled, it can cause physical and emotional complications.
- Several techniques can help people manage stress in their lives.

REVIEW QUESTIONS

Section 12-1

1. How does attitude make a difference in dealing with a move?
2. How could you help prepare younger siblings for a move?
3. What can a family do when financial problems threaten?
4. When Chan's father lost his job, Chan heard him say, "Sometimes, I wonder who I am." Why might he say this?
5. What options do families have for getting out of debt?
6. Suppose you lived in an area where tornadoes often form. What should you do?

Section 12-2

1. Identify six signs of stress that you think are very common.
2. What are two ways to limit stress in your life?
3. How would a realistic attitude help you manage stress?
4. When faced with a stressful situation, should you keep the problem to yourself or involve others? Why?

BECOMING A PROBLEM SOLVER

1. Adrienne has begun to suspect that her father has lost his job. Although he follows the same routine each day, things Adrienne has seen and heard lead her to think he's looking for a job. How should Adrienne approach this situation?

2. Ty's family is moving to a different city soon. His father is already working there and living in their new home. Ty's mother is against the move and hasn't done much to prepare for it. What should Ty do?

THINKING CRITICALLY

1. **Compare and Contrast.** Explain whether you think moving is easier for young children or for teens.
2. **Drawing Conclusions.** Why might having a job to go to make adjusting to a move easier?
3. **Predicting Results.** Do you think anyone who tries hard enough can find a job? Explain your answer.
4. **Analyzing Behavior.** What might be some advantages and drawbacks of having a personality that seeks out stress, change, and challenge?
5. **Recognizing Values.** Studies show that women cry about five times more often than men do. Why do you think this is so? Should the genders be more alike in willingness and ability to cry? Explain your response.

MAKING CURRICULUM CONNECTIONS

1. **Language Arts/Art.** Design and create a brochure for young children on coping with change. What changes are they most likely to encounter? What general information about change would be helpful? How can you present this information so a child can understand and use it?
2. **Biology.** Research information on the stress hormone, epinephrine. Report your findings to the class.
3. **Civics.** Investigate the bankruptcy laws in your state. What is the process for declaring bankruptcy? What are the penalties? Why do you think the number of bankruptcies is rising nationally?

APPLYING YOUR KNOWLEDGE

1. Find out what is done to help new students in your school feel welcome. With your classmates, plan an activity that would contribute to this effort. What could you do to make friends with newcomers and help them feel at home?
2. With a partner, describe situations that cause you both the most stress. Offer each other ideas for reducing this stress.
3. Many people have favorite stress relievers, such as playing the guitar, shooting baskets, and talking to a friend on the phone. With classmates, compile a list of these in a handout that can be distributed to students or placed in the school newspaper.

Family & Community Connections

1. With help from family members, develop a stress test that people could take to find out how well they handle stress. Ask questions related to the principles of stress management.

2. Investigate whether there is a homeless problem in your community. What steps has local government taken to solve this problem? Are there shelters? Places where free meals are served? What services do you think should be provided to homeless people?

Chapter 13

Divorce and Remarriage

WORDS FOR THOUGHT

"Failure is not sweet, but it need not be bitter."
(Anonymous)

IN YOUR OWN WORDS

Do you think bitterness is an inevitable part of divorce?

When Marriages End

OBJECTIVES

After studying this section, you should be able to:

- Explain why and how a marital relationship can deteriorate.
- Compare ways of ending a marriage.
- Describe decisions that must be made when divorce occurs.

TERMS TO LEARN

divorce
invalidation
annulment
adversarial divorce
grounds
divorce mediation
custody
alimony

When a couple marries, they traditionally vow to stay together "til death do us part." Sadly, many circumstances can arise that make keeping this vow almost impossible. A couple in a troubled relationship may look at the growing problems between them and see the painful option of divorce as the only solution.

Divorce is a legal action that ends a marriage. If current trends continue, about two-thirds of all new marriages in a year will end in some way other than the death of a spouse. Divorce will account for most of those untimely endings. Dissolving a marriage brings major changes in the lives of family members. Even the most civil breakups can cause a great deal of pain, stress, and confusion.

WHY MARRIAGES END

How does a relationship that began in love and high hopes end in painful disappointment? Marriages fail for a number of reasons. Sometimes partners grow in different directions. They no longer share the interests that once drew them together. Partners may not communicate well enough to maintain a relationship. A specific difficulty, such as financial, sexual, and role problems, may wear down a marriage. Physical or mental cruelty can also contribute to a breakup.

Not every troubled marriage is destined for divorce. Couples often seek counseling for help in resolving the problems between them. Many couples have successfully built, or rebuilt, a strong marriage.

Divorce is a major problem for families. What can people do to prevent so many divorces from taking place?

• **Invalidation. Invalidation** (in-val-uh-DAY-shun) means partners respond negatively to each other. They criticize, rather than affirm, each other and grow defensive as accusations increase. Negative feelings build up and feed on each other. For example, Ben told Lucy, "What kind of mother are you? Can't you even keep that kid in clean clothes?" How do you suppose Lucy reacted to Ben's remarks?

• **Betrayal. Betrayal** is the feeling that trust has been broken. The support each spouse expected from the other is no longer there.

The critical act in the breakdown of a marriage is the decision to separate and seek a divorce, rather than the divorce itself. Emotions are rawest and most painful at the time of separation. How families handle a divorce at this point has a strong effect on all family members, especially the children.

PULLING APART IN STAGES

Marriages seldom end without warning. Most breakups are about two years in the making. Over this time, the relationship unravels through three basic stages:

• **Isolation.** The couple becomes isolated from each other. Partners withdraw emotionally and no longer share intimacy or closeness. They may act like strangers, holding polite conversations about neutral subjects.

INFOLINK

Building a Strong Marriage

For information on building a strong marriage, see *Section 32-1*.

ENDING A MARRIAGE

A marriage that can't be saved may be ended legally in one of three ways: annulment, legal separation, or divorce. Sometimes one spouse simply leaves, or deserts, the other. Desertion may end the relationship, but the legal marriage remains.

Annulment

An **annulment** (uh-NULL-ment) decree states that a legal marriage never took place due to some prior condition. The marriage contract is not legally binding because it wasn't entered in good faith.

Laws concerning annulment vary among the states. Common causes of annulment include concealed or falsified pregnancy; insanity; bigamy (being married to more than one person); and forced marriage. If one partner used fraud or tried to cheat the other, the court may annul the marriage.

Annulments are sometimes sought when a couple's religious beliefs forbid divorce. Divorced partners are not allowed to participate fully in their church. Getting an annulment enables them to continue in their faith.

Legal Separation

Some couples obtain a legal separation, which allows them to keep separate homes but not to remarry. The partners make a legal agreement to live apart.

Legal separation can be a stepping stone between marriage and divorce. For some, however, it's a permanent arrangement. Mark and Dee's religion doesn't accept divorce. An annulment isn't possible. Mark owns a business, which would be crippled by the financial effects of a divorce. So far, the couple agree that legal separation is best for them.

Focus On...

Predictors of Divorce

Certain signs indicate whether a marriage will last. These conditions don't ensure a happy or unhappy marriage, but studies show that they affect the chances for one outcome or the other:

- **Age.** The younger a couple is when they marry, the more likely they are to divorce. The risk increases if the bride is pregnant. Teens and young adults often lack the maturity and experience to handle the responsibilities of marriage and parenthood.
- **Income.** Unemployment and financial problems are closely linked to marital troubles that can lead to a breakup. One exception is that women who earn high incomes are more apt to end a marriage than women with low or no incomes. Why do you think this is true?

- **Success of the parents' marriage.** Those whose parents divorced are more apt to end their own marriage.
- **Other factors.** People who are active in a religion are more apt to stay together, as are couples who knew or dated each other for a long time. Also, the more children a couple has, the less likely they will divorce.

USING YOUR KNOWLEDGE

Jake and Missy started dating at age fourteen. By age eighteen, they felt ready to marry. They planned to get jobs as soon as possible and live with Missy's stepmother in the meantime. What do you think their chances are for a strong marriage?

Divorce

By far the most common outcome of marital breakdown is divorce. Divorce rates doubled between 1960 and 1980, a period when divorce laws across the country changed dramatically. Divorces hit a peak in 1981 and have declined slightly since that time.

Like annulment, divorce is regulated by each state. Laws vary considerably. Some states no longer use the term divorce, instead calling the legal action the "dissolution of marriage."

There are two basic ways that couples file for divorce. One type is known as **adversarial divorce** (add-ver-SAIR-ee-uhl). With this, spouses become legal opponents. One partner accuses the other of some marital "crime," such as mental or physical cruelty, desertion, adultery, and insanity. The crime is called **grounds** for divorce. If the accused partner is judged guilty, a divorce is granted.

In the second type of divorce, called *no-fault divorce*, partners simply claim that the marriage relationship has broken down, with neither one to blame. A period of separation may be all the proof needed that a breakdown has occurred. Most couples file for no-fault divorce. The simpler legal process adds fewer burdens to an already distressing ordeal. A sim-

pler procedure, however, doesn't solve the many problems couples face as they untangle their lives.

Coming to Agreement

Ending a marriage means making many decisions, some quite difficult. A couple must agree on everything from how to divide child care responsibilities, to who gets a favorite piece of furniture. The final authority rests with the divorce judge. If the couple reach an agreement, the judge simply legalizes their decisions. When partners cannot agree, the judge makes decisions for them.

Most couples need help in settling major divorce decisions, especially if children or complex financial affairs are involved. Often each spouse is represented by a lawyer, meaning that the spouse with the better lawyer may end up with the better side of the agreement. About half the states have established a procedure called **divorce mediation**, in which an impartial

Children and teens are hurt by divorce. Parental love and support, however, give them a better chance to come through without serious effects.

Focus On ...

Custody Arrangements

The care of children is handled in several ways after divorce. These are the possible legal arrangements:

- **Sole custody.** One spouse retains all legal parenting rights and responsibilities. The other usually has visitation rights, ensuring a certain amount of time with the children. While more fathers are seeking and gaining sole custody today, most decisions favor the mother.
- **Split custody.** Each parent has sole custody of one or more of the children. This arrangement can make the divorce harder on siblings who want to stay together.
- **Third-party custody.** Someone else, often a relative, is appointed as the children's legal guardian. The children may also be placed in a foster home.
- **Alternating custody.** Children live first with one parent for a long period of time, perhaps a year, then with the other. Each parent has decision-making power during that time.
- **Joint custody.** Parents share equally in decisions about the children. Children live mostly with one parent or split their time equally in each parent's home. Joint custody is allowed by most states and preferred in many. Parents are legally bound to work together for the children's welfare; former spouses must be on good terms to make it work.

USING YOUR KNOWLEDGE

The three Staunton children don't want to split up after their parents' divorce, but neither parent wants to be left alone. What might work?

---

third person helps a couple work out a solution. In some states a couple must see a mediator before going to court. In other states, mediation is an option.

Mediation works only for couples who demonstrate a spirit of cooperation. Couples who go through successful mediation are usually happier with the results than those who rely on a judge's decision.

CHILD CUSTODY

When a couple has children, the divorce decree states how the responsibility of their care will be handled. **Custody** is the legal right to make decisions that affect children and the responsibility to provide their physical care. Different custody arrangements are possible, as shown above.

FINANCIAL MATTERS

Marriage is usually a financial union as well as an emotional one. Divorce means dividing property and, if needed, arranging for the financial support of children and a former spouse.

Property Settlement

Most couples have accumulated property during their marriage: a home and furnishings, cars, savings accounts, and investments. In most states, no-fault divorce calls for dividing property equally. Otherwise, a spouse who has been economically dependent on the other may be at a disadvantage.

If spouses can't reach a settlement that seems fair to both, the judge divides their property. Most judges consider what each has contributed to the marriage. Women may be entitled to part of their husband's Social Security or pension, depending on the length of the marriage and other circumstances.

Child Support

The custody arrangement determines how child support is handled. In single-parent custody, the noncustodial parent usually pays a certain amount each month to help support the children. Financial arrangements vary in joint custody.

Since most children live with their mothers, fathers usually make child support payments. This is the case in over three-fourths of all divorces. About one-fourth of these men pay on time and in full. A father who has a good income and who was involved with his children before the divorce is most likely to pay. Even full child support usual-

Children of divorced parents with joint custody live with one parent for a time, then with the other. This requires cooperation among all family members.

ly covers less than half the cost of raising a child, however.

In contrast, time and physical and emotional distance can all lessen a parent's sense of duty to pay child support. Some refuse because they can't influence how the money is spent.

The problem of unpaid child support is a difficult one. The government has programs to locate parents who owe child sup-

Career Success Stories

Teresa Flores: *Government Investigator*

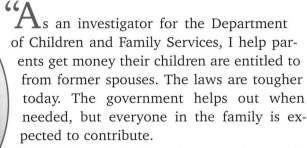

"As an investigator for the Department of Children and Family Services, I help parents get money their children are entitled to from former spouses. The laws are tougher today. The government helps out when needed, but everyone in the family is expected to contribute.

"I'm like a detective who never leaves the office. Typically, I don't see the people I'm investigating—everything is done on the telephone and the computer. I locate them, find out where they work, and have money taken out of their paycheck without any face–to–face contact.

"On my job I have to be tough and compassionate at the same time. I try to deal with facts, not judgments. Parents have a million excuses for not paying, but the bottom line is the children suffer, and I can't let that happen.

"I just finished a case that was like so many others. Janelle came to our office for financial assistance. She said she was having a tough time making ends meet. While we talked about how she was living, I had a feeling there was more to the story. Eventually I learned that her former husband hadn't been paying child support for months. I helped change that."

CAREER PROFILE

Education and training: bachelor's degree

Starting salary range: $24,200–29,600

Job prospects: federal and state government agencies that deal with children and family services

Important qualities: curious; persistent; assertive; good communication skills

Plan Ahead

This career is one of many in government. How could you find a government career in your area? Begin by looking under "employment" in the Yellow Pages of the telephone directory. What contacts might you make?

port and deduct the money from their wages. Parents can be jailed or lose their driver's license. Offenders who are in jail or who lack transportation can't earn wages, however, so punishment is a partial solution at best. Many mothers feel it isn't worth the effort to jail a father for lack of child support.

Spouse Support

Financial support of an ex-spouse is called **alimony** (AL-uh-moh-nee) or maintenance payments. The spouse with more financial resources helps support the other. Very little long-term spouse support is awarded. Some women receive spouse support until they find a job or finish job training.

QUESTIONING DIVORCE

Society has grown more tolerant of divorce over the years. Newer, more flexible laws make divorce less burdensome. Is this change entirely for the better? Certainly no responsible person wants a spouse to feel ashamed for leaving a destructive, even dangerous, marriage.

On the other hand, many people believe that if divorce is too easy to obtain, couples have less reason to work at solving their problems. The effects of divorce are serious. If couples start on this path without weighing the consequences to families, that *is* a reason for concern.

SECTION 13-1 REVIEW

Check Your Understanding

1. What are four common predictors of divorce?
2. How does invalidation harm a marriage?
3. What are the options for ending a marriage? Which options are legal?
4. What are some possible consequences of not paying child support?
5. What is divorce mediation?
6. How does sole custody differ from split custody?
7. **Thinking Critically.** What might be some advantages to children of each type of child custody?
8. **Problem Solving.** Joel and Melissa married at age eighteen. At the time, they seemed perfect for each other. They felt secure in their identities and agreed on what they wanted from life. In the past three years, each partner has grown and changed so much, they feel almost like two different people from the ones who got married. What should Melissa and Joel do?

Managing After Divorce

OBJECTIVES

After studying this section, you should be able to:

- Explain how people adjust to divorce.
- Summarize the effects of divorce on couples and on their children.
- Describe challenges facing single-parent families.
- Compare blended families with nuclear families.
- Suggest ways for getting along in a blended family.

TERMS TO LEARN

adjustment
stability

At one time, sailing ships were the only way to cross the oceans. To make a safe passage, a captain had to be alert to a change in the winds. If their strength or direction shifted, he might need to tighten the sails or let them out. He noted his ship's response and changed course, if needed, to find smoother sailing.

Families facing divorce, or any other change, need to do the same thing. They must undergo a period of **adjustment**, working to change routines and feelings in order to function in a new situation. Adjusting to divorce is far from easy. All family members and their friends must deal with awkward and painful changes. They need a positive and determined attitude to handle divorce well.

THE DIVORCED COUPLE

Both partners have to rebuild their lives following a divorce. Each must cope with loneliness, anger, depression, guilt, and feelings of failure.

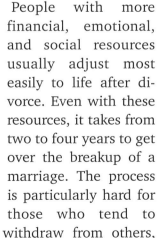

People with more financial, emotional, and social resources usually adjust most easily to life after divorce. Even with these resources, it takes from two to four years to get over the breakup of a marriage. The process is particularly hard for those who tend to withdraw from others, who lack self-confidence, and who are easily panicked or depressed.

Dealing with the everyday realities of caring for children can also make adjusting more difficult. Custodial parents must often

After a divorce, each person must adapt to life without the other. What changes might they face?

cope successfully with divorce, children must function on two levels. They experience unhappiness, yet are able to go on with daily life.

How Children View Divorce

Young children often imagine that a divorce is somehow their fault. Ten-year-old Wes heard his parents argue over how to deal with his rowdy behavior. By being "extra good," Wes concluded, he could save the marriage. When his parents separated anyway, Wes's disappointment and guilt made the breakup even harder to bear. Wes

stretch their resources. They also hide their own anger and sorrow to help children deal with their feelings.

Eventually, people learn to manage their feelings and make new lives for themselves. In building new relationships and solving problems on their own, they gain confidence. They start to heal the wounds of divorce.

CHILDREN AND DIVORCE

Without a doubt, divorce creates major changes in the lives of children. Even before children can understand the situation, they can sense the anger and tension as a marriage ends. Studies have found that to

Anger, resentment, and grief are typical feelings when a teen's parents divorce. Talking over the issues is healing.

Building Character

Optimism: A Quality That Counts

Optimism is a hopeful outlook on the future and the belief that things will work out well. It means having a positive attitude and seeing the bright side of events. A teen can practice optimism by:

- Seeing a parent's remarriage as a chance to build a bigger support system.
- Telling a friend that the adjustment to having a stepbrother can be worked out.
- Telling friends, after a long study session, that they're ready for a final exam.
- Giving others the benefit of the doubt for something unkind supposedly said.
- Believing in his or her abilities.

QUESTIONS

1. In what ways can optimism be helpful to you and your family?
2. Explain whether it's possible to be too optimistic.
3. In what ways have you recently shown optimism?

---

might have coped better had his parents made it clear that he didn't cause the divorce and couldn't prevent it.

Older children and teens understand that the situation is complex. Even after a divorce, however, some still hope their parents will reconcile. If the divorce ends an abusive home life, their relief is yet mixed with sorrow.

Children often model their parents' attitude to the divorce. If parents stress that divorce is the best way for all of them to have a better life, children tend to adopt this view. When parents cooperate on matters affecting their children, the children don't see themselves as coming from a broken home. Instead they see they have two homes with a loving parent in each.

The Need for Stability

Children cope best with divorce when they have **stability**, or few changes, in the rest of their life. Stability helps counteract the disruption of divorce. Living in the same home, going to the same school, and keeping the same friends gives reassurance that some things will stay the same.

Maintaining stable, loving relationships with both parents is important to a child's adjustment. If one parent drops out of the picture, a child's security is threatened. If partners are hostile toward each other, children often feel they must choose between parents. This sense of torn loyalty is perhaps the most stressful part of the breakup for children. Knowing that it's okay to love both parents softens the impact of divorce.

Effects of Divorce

How divorce affects children is a controversial subject. Research provides conflicting answers. Certainly the many circumstances surrounding the marriage and the breakup influence how well children adjust.

Experts basically agree that the period around the separation is the hardest on a child. It's a time of mourning the "death" of the intact family. A child may feel rage and frustration. Feelings of guilt, rejection, helplessness, and loneliness are also common. A child may need up to one year to sort out these feelings and adjust to the new life.

Studies of children of divorced parents have generally found that children can handle divorce. Emotional problems caused by the breakup tend to lessen with time. Having two loving, attentive parents helps minimize the negative impact. Some studies show no difference in school achievement, intelligence, or self-esteem between children from divorced and nuclear families. Divorce is often preferable to staying in a two-parent home filled with serious conflict. Children in families that suffer severe financial hardship usually fare worst after divorce.

Experiencing the realities of divorce firsthand often has long-term consequences for children. Often they are hesitant about deciding whether to marry, which may make them more careful in choosing a marriage partner. On the other hand, if their marriage falters, they are more apt to divorce.

Remarriage after a divorce signals hope for a new beginning. Realistic people know that challenges are ahead, too.

SINGLE PARENTING

The move to a single-parent family following divorce is one of change and challenge. The custodial parent must act as both mother and father for the child, earn the family's income, and manage the household. Even without the distress of divorce, these can be daunting tasks. The transition to single parenting often causes stress and problems for parent and child alike.

Money is frequently an ongoing problem in single-parent families, especially when that parent is a woman. Household incomes for single mothers tend to drop dramatically after divorce. If child support payments are late or unpaid, the situation gets worse.

Single parents who make good use of their support systems do best. They exchange help and services with family members and friends. They find community resources to help them.

REMARRIAGE

Most divorced people eventually remarry. They want the companionship and emotional intimacy that marriage offers. Divorced men remarry sooner and in greater numbers than women do. About one-fourth of divorced people remarry within one year; one-half marry within three years. The younger a person is at divorce, the greater the chance of remarriage.

Most experts suggest waiting at least four years after a divorce to remarry in order to heal the hurt caused by the breakup. People who remarry quickly to try to solve their problems rarely succeed. Unfortunately, in over 80 percent of all divorces, one partner remarries within two years.

People who do wait generally have happy second marriages. The couple is older and wiser for their experience, which increases the chance for stability in remarriage. Partners are more likely to understand what they want and need in a spouse. They usually have different expectations and more tolerance on such issues as housework and money, which may have caused major conflicts in the first marriage.

BLENDED FAMILIES

Over half of all remarriages create blended families. Estimates say that a majority of children born in the 1980s will live in a blended family at some point in their life.

Blended families differ from nuclear ones in significant ways. In a blended family, all

Calling Names. What's in a name? Quite a lot, when the name carries a positive or negative judgment. Blended families have long had this type of "image problem." Thanks to stereotypes and tales such as "Cinderella," the words "wicked" and "stepmother" go together in some minds. Positive talk can generate more positive feelings. To overcome negative thoughts about blended families, you can:

- Refer to children in a blended family as children, rather than distinguishing between "steps" and "own."
- Talk about having two homes instead of a "broken home."
- Call both parents' residences "home." Children don't "visit" a parent as if they were guests.
- Use a blended family member's given name, rather than "Dad's wife" or "their stepsister." Ask permission of adult family members first.

Try It Out. Think of two negative terms that come to mind regarding divorce and blended families. Rephrase each to make it less judgmental and use these positive references in your conversations with others.

members have "lost" an important relationship from the past. Important people in the lives of blended family members live elsewhere. The children have a parent somewhere else. A stepparent may have children living with the former spouse.

Also in blended families, the parent-child relationship is older than the couple relationship. In a nuclear family, the couple relationship is the first and older one.

Challenges of Blending

Life in any family has its challenges. The changes that occur as two families blend into one can present unique challenges, including:

- **Favoritism.** When favoritism occurs in a blended family, it's usually a parent favoring his or her own child over a stepchild. Some parents, however, are *more* demanding of their own children. Realizing that "fairness" is hard to achieve in any family can help everyone get along.

- **Discipline.** Children may have to adjust to new rules in the new family. Parents may need to work out conflicting views on discipline.

- **Resources.** Questions about dividing resources must be handled carefully. Sharing resources is basic to any family; however, some items might be kept for private use. All family members should be clear on which is which.
- **Values.** Rarely do all members of a blended family share the same values. They must learn to understand each other's views.
- **Previous Relationships.** Former spouses and children of previous marriages may not support the remarriage. They may interfere with new relationships. Child support payments, both incoming and outgoing, can be a source of conflict. Blended family members must accept the demands made by previous family ties.
- **Roles.** Roles in blended families take time to define. A stepfather, for instance, may at times act like a father, an uncle, or a teacher—but not *just* like any of them. Family members may need to base their behavior on the situation and people involved, instead of a set idea of what a person in a certain role is supposed to do.
- **Child-spouse competition.** Since the parent-child relationship is older than the couple relationship, the new spouse may feel excluded at first. A child may feel left out of the remarried couple's love and affection. Jealousy and competing for attention are normal responses. Spouses may need to make an effort to put each other first, while finding ways to show children that the parent-child relationship is as strong and important as before.

Like nuclear families, blended families must work at maintaining relationships. First, the couple must be committed to each other and the marriage. Their children should not come between them. Adjusting to life in a blended family may take three to five years. Love takes time to grow. Those who make the effort are likely to be rewarded with a successfully blended family.

SECTION 13-2 REVIEW

Check Your Understanding

1. How long does it commonly take people to recover from a divorce?
2. What is meant by stability? How is it helpful to children during divorce?
3. What long-term consequences might children of divorce experience?
4. Why might couples be happier in remarriage?
5. How can the issue of discipline be a problem in a blended family?
6. How can patience help people adjust to life as a blended family?
7. **Thinking Critically.** Why might a parent seem to favor a stepchild over his or her own child?
8. **Problem Solving.** Will is the only child of divorced parents. He always enjoyed visiting his father when they spent one-on-one time together. Now his father is dating a woman with three children, and they're usually there during Will's visit. Will's father wants him to get to know them. Will misses their private time together. What should Will do?

CHAPTER SUMMARY

- Marriages end for many different reasons, but certain factors have been identified that make divorce more likely.
- Marital breakup usually occurs in stages.
- Depending on their wishes and circumstances, a couple may legally end a marriage in one of three ways.
- A divorce, or dissolution of marriage, is the most common way to end a marriage. The process is regulated by state law.
- A divorcing couple must make decisions about children and finances. They may need the services of legal professionals.
- Since mothers are typically awarded custody of children, child support is usually a father's responsibility.
- People must make emotional and practical adjustments when a marriage ends.
- Most divorced people remarry. More than half of these remarriages result in blended families.
- To adjust to life in a blended family, members need to show each other tolerance, patience, and understanding.

REVIEW QUESTIONS

Section 13-1
1. How is the age of a bride and groom related to the chance for divorce?
2. Name and describe the stages that mark the end of a marriage.
3. Compare divorce and annulment.
4. What must a spouse do to obtain an adversarial divorce?
5. What are some advantages of joint custody?
6. Why is child support a difficult issue in many divorce situations?

Section 13-2
1. What challenges face people as they "recover" from divorce?
2. How can adults help children cope with divorce?
3. What challenges do blended families face?
4. What suggestions might help people in a blended family get along?

BECOMING A PROBLEM SOLVER

1. Anne's former husband has moved away and rarely sees their children. Anne hasn't received child support payments for three months. She can't afford to hire a lawyer to take legal action. What should Anne do?

2. Bret has been divorced for three years. He and Sonja would like to get married, but his children don't like Sonja or her children. He sees his children often and expects them to continue to be a big part of his life. What should Bret do?

THINKING CRITICALLY

1. **Compare and Contrast.** What are some advantages and drawbacks when a couple "stay together for the children"?
2. **Recognizing Cause and Effect.** What emotional benefits do family members gain when fathers pay child support as required?
3. **Predicting Consequences.** How do poor marriages affect society? What are the effects of divorce? Do you think making divorce difficult to obtain makes society stronger?
4. **Analyzing Arguments.** Liz's grandmother told her, "When I was your age, people only got divorced if something was terribly wrong in the marriage. And children didn't have as many problems as they do today." What is the grandmother's argument? Is it a valid one?

MAKING CURRICULUM CONNECTIONS

1. **Language Arts.** Imagine that your aunt and uncle are in a custody battle over their fourteen-year-old child. Your cousin tells you, "Can't they see what they're doing to me? Maybe you could tell them for me." Write a letter to your aunt and uncle explaining your cousin's feelings. Consider your relationship and their emotional state as you choose your words and tone.
2. **Math.** The judge has ordered a father to pay 20 percent of his after-tax income for child support. The father's take-home pay is $37,500 a year. How much should he pay each month?

APPLYING YOUR KNOWLEDGE

1. With your classmates, debate this issue: Divorce should not be allowed. In cases of physical or emotional cruelty, only separation should be permitted.
2. Working in a small group, make a list of reasons that justify divorce. Are you able to agree on the list? What issues cause the most disagreement?
3. In small groups, generate a list of positive points about living in a blended family.

Family & Community Connections

1. Survey 10 adults of various ages. Ask them, "Do you think divorce is taken too casually today? Why do you feel this way?" Compile your findings with those of your classmates. What is the overall result? Are there differences by age groups? What conclusions can you draw from this survey?

2. Write a short paragraph that begins, "Living in a blended family is (would be)...." Compare and discuss responses in small groups.

Handling Crises

IN YOUR OWN WORDS

What does the writer mean by "storms" and "sail my ship"?

Understanding Crises

OBJECTIVES

After studying this section, you should be able to:

- Distinguish the combination of elements that define a crisis situation.
- Explain the stages of reacting to a crisis.
- Locate resources useful in a crisis.
- Explain when and why intervention is needed.

TERMS TO LEARN

crisis
adaptation
shelter
intervention

The word *crisis* is used a lot these days. Hostilities between two nations grow into a military crisis. A devastating hurricane creates a crisis for aid workers trying to help victims. A social problem, such as violence in the schools or rising health care costs, is a crisis.

What does this word mean, that is used so often? A **crisis** (CRY-suss) is a situation so critical that it overwhelms the usual coping methods and causes great emotional distress. Some crises, such as a hurricane, hit quickly. Others, such as the effects of alcoholism, build slowly. Experiencing crisis is like dancing to music that gets faster and faster. At first you can keep up, but eventually you get short of breath, your legs feel rubbery, and you trip yourself up.

You can always choose to sit out a dance, but you can't sit out life's crises. They re-quire action. Fortunately, you have resources, people, and things to help you get on your feet and back in the dance.

WHEN IS IT CRISIS?

Not every serious problem is a crisis. Crises stand out by their overwhelming nature. The things you do to cope successfully with other difficulties don't work in a crisis. Specifically, three elements help determine whether a situation is overwhelming enough to be a crisis:

- **Hardship.** Certain events can create hardship. The greater the hardship, the more likely it is to bring on a crisis. A house fire, for example, causes loss of possessions as well as a place to live. Lives are seriously disrupted in such situations.

A crisis from natural disaster can occur without warning. This hurricane in the southeast destroyed many homes. How do people rebuild their lives after such an event?

- **Resources.** Handling any problem effectively requires resources. If you don't have the needed resources, a problem may become a crisis.
- **Attitude.** It's normal to be jarred when trouble strikes. If you give in to feelings of shock and helplessness, a difficult situation can turn unmanageable. If you can rebound and face a problem squarely, it's less likely to overwhelm you.

Some people seem to have many crises in their lives. Crisis-prone families often have inadequate resources to solve their problems. A lack of self-confidence makes people particularly anxious and fearful about life. Thus, they are more likely to define an event as a crisis.

Causes of Crisis

What kinds of events are likely to cause a crisis? Outside events, such as an accident, job loss, or a natural disaster, are candidates. Besides the hardship they can bring, such ordeals can seem overwhelming because they are beyond your control.

Crises frequently result from changes in family membership, including:
- The loss of a family member through death or separation, as by war or hospitalization.
- The unexpected addition of a family member. This includes an unwanted pregnancy or the addition of aged grandparents or blended family members.
- The loss of the family unit through nonsupport, abuse, addictions, delinquency, or events that bring disgrace.

Some crises result from a series of events. In one family, a child underwent life-saving, emergency surgery—just after the parents lost their income and medical insurance due to a job layoff. The strain of trying to cope with both events caused a crisis for the family.

REACTING TO CRISIS

Typically people react to crisis through a process that includes four stages. Time spent in each stage may vary, but the process is generally the same.

Stage 1: Impact

In this first stage, people experience shock and numbness. Whatever has happened hits them hard. Fear and helplessness are common emotions. During the impact stage, which may last a few hours or several days, a person may be too overwhelmed to even function. The first reaction a person normally has when diagnosed with a serious illness is an example of this stage.

Stage 2: Withdrawal and Confusion

In this stage, people pull back from the crisis situation. Some people act emotionally cold and withdrawn, as if they don't care about the things around them. Others maintain that no crisis exists. They busy themselves but accomplish little. They get confused and have trouble focusing on what they're doing.

"Confusion" describes Danielle's state at learning that her boyfriend had been killed in a car accident. She kept insisting there had been some mistake. She became very concerned about finishing a dress she was making for a dance they were to attend together.

Stage 3: Focus

People in this stage are ready to focus on the reality of the situation. They admit that a crisis has occurred and ask what action they must take to deal with it. Regaining some sense of control over emotions lets them see the problem more clearly. They can begin exploring options and making plans to take charge of the crisis.

A good example is Mrs. Dubinski's "plan of attack" after accepting that her son was an alcoholic. She called hospitals and clinics to compare treatment programs and decide which would be best for her son.

Tips & TECHNIQUES

Coping with Problems. How do you cope with problems? Some people pull into their shells as turtles do; some people run away. You can "get away from it all," at least for a little while, without leaving. Try experiencing calm by getting into nature—even without a forest or the ocean.
- Lie on your back and observe the trees and birds.
- Lie on your stomach and study the insects.
- Take a walk and use as many of your senses as possible to explore flowers, plants, rocks, animals, or an evening sky.

Try It Out. Think of a way that you could use nature to calm yourself. Use your idea the next time you're having trouble coping. Take that scene's spirit of wonder and calm with you afterwards.

She checked with her insurance company to see if they would pay any treatment costs. Finally, she asked her minister to recommend a support group to help her cope with whatever lay ahead.

Stage 4: Adaptation

The final stage in responding to a crisis is actually dealing with it. The plans made in Stage 3 are put into action. Through **adaptation** (ADD-ap-TAY-shun), people make changes that are practical and appropriate.

After managing the crisis successfully, life goes on, even though circumstances may be different.

Adaptation was important for Greg's family after a diving accident left him paralyzed. The family built a ramp onto the house to accommodate Greg's wheelchair. They turned the family room downstairs into a bedroom to replace Greg's upstairs room. Greg himself made arrangements for transportation to and from school. Adapting let Greg and his family get on with their lives.

Where Can You Go for Help?

Teachers and Counselors

Religious Organizations

RESOURCES FOR CRISIS

If there's ever a time that people need others, it's during a crisis. Recognizing and finding support gives a sense of control. Never be afraid to admit that you need help. Everyone does when crisis hits.

The family is a first source of help for most people. Friends are another possibility. Beyond those two groups, you might look to the resources shown below.

Remember that professionals have specific skills to offer. Many of these resources provide prevention services, as well as treatment and help. Most communities have clinics or health centers to treat physical, mental, and emotional conditions. Hotlines offer advice and support, usually twenty-four hours a day. They are staffed by trained volunteers. A **shelter** offers a safe place for those who experience physical violence or sexual abuse. Shelters give victims of violence protection from their abusers and time to consider their options. A shelter can be located by calling a hospital emergency room, the police station, or a local abuse hotline.

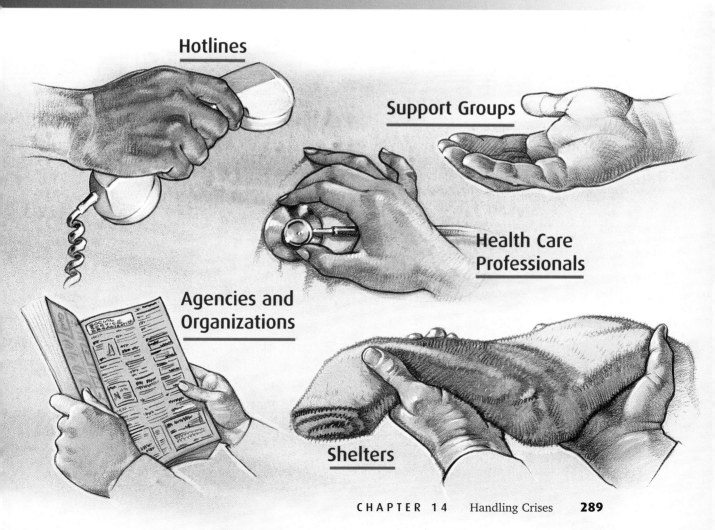

Hotlines

Support Groups

Health Care Professionals

Agencies and Organizations

Shelters

Career Success Stories

Ross Boyer: *Home Health Aide*

"Working for a home health care agency, I visit patients daily who are ill, elderly, or disabled. Each patient has different needs, so no two situations are the same. I help with personal care—bathing and dressing—and I even prepare meals. Some people need medical help. I might assist with medications and check vital signs. Sometimes I just give emotional support to the patient and family. I listen, share a glass of lemonade, and talk.

"The simplest things I do often give me the best feelings. I'm assigned to one home where the husband has Alzheimer's disease and the wife cares for him. You can't imagine what a responsibility this is for Margaret. I help however I can, and she leans on me for support. Right before one holiday, I could tell Margaret was upset. After I pushed her to talk, she said she makes a special nut bread every year for the family. Since she couldn't leave her husband alone, she hadn't been able to go out and buy the ingredients. I sent her right out to the store. It took only an hour of my time. Sometimes people don't think about how valuable an hour away can be to someone in Margaret's position.

"Many people say they couldn't do my job. It certainly isn't glamorous. I guess it suits me though. I feel like I've really helped someone after every visit and that makes *me* feel good."

CAREER PROFILE

Education and training: high school diploma

Starting salary: minimum wage

Job prospects: private and public home health agencies; hospitals; nursing homes

Important qualities: compassionate; personable; able to work independently; physical stamina

Plan Ahead

Would a career as a home health aide be right for you? If that's a possibility, try doing volunteer work in a nursing home. You may discover whether you have the qualities needed for the job.

INTERVENTION

In a crisis situation, something must be done. Who is more likely to intervene, a friend or a family member?

Intervention means taking direct action to cause change when someone else is in crisis. Why is intervention needed? Sometimes a crisis is beyond the ability of the person to handle or control. A child may be in danger or a person may be unable to think clearly. Only the caring action of another person can bring about a solution.

Intervening sometimes requires courage and resourcefulness. It takes the kind of person who cares enough to try. You have to be bold enough to risk interfering when the need is great. Friends and family members can begin the intervention process. Additional steps may involve the people and organizations named earlier. Intervention forces change that might not otherwise occur. As you will see in the next section, intervention can be critical.

SECTION 14-1 REVIEW

Check Your Understanding

1. What is a crisis?
2. An event is defined as a crisis by what three elements?
3. What are the stages of reaction to a crisis?
4. Identify five resources that can be helpful in a crisis.
5. What is intervention?
6. **Thinking Critically.** In what ways might changing the number of people in a family bring about crisis?
7. **Problem Solving.** Bruce suffered a serious spinal cord injury in a football game. His doctors told his family that he would need several months of intensive therapy in order to walk again and up to a year to recover fully. What resources would you recommend to Bruce and his family? How can these groups help?

The Crises People Face

OBJECTIVES

After studying this section, you should be able to:

- Identify the potential effects of physical or mental health problems.
- Identify prevention strategies.
- Recommend actions to take in cases of addiction, violence, and threats of suicide.
- Describe the importance of intervention in child abuse cases.

TERMS TO LEARN

addiction
drugs
alcoholism
violence
incest

In a poem by A.E. Housman, the narrator says that he faces trouble "as a wise man would; And train for ill and not for good." In other words, it's the bad times in life that you must prepare yourself to cope with. The good times take care of themselves. It's not easy to "train for ill," to think or talk about what can cause trouble. Some crises can't be prevented, so it's wise to be prepared. Learning about crises that challenge people will better prepare you to respond if needed.

PHYSICAL HEALTH PROBLEMS

When Victor's younger brother had the flu for three days, his parents each took one day off work to stay home with him. Victor took over his brother's chores. A minor illness caused minor inconvenience.

When illnesses, injuries, and disabilities are more serious, the impact on families is much greater. Some health problems can be prevented with safe and healthy habits plus good nutrition.

Effects on Family Life

As you may have noticed, things run more smoothly and people tend to be most comfortable when the regular routine is followed. When a major health problem hits someone in a family, routines and schedules can be turned upside down. People feel tense and unsettled.

Serious illness in a family can be a crisis no matter which family member is ill. Each member must adjust to different circumstances and to the extra efforts needed to fill the gap.

Depending on the family and health problem, certain adjustments must be made. Adjustments differ for each situation. One family may need a way to get a child to school when the person who usually drives is ill. When a father in another family spends evenings visiting the mother in the hospital, the family may have to decide how to provide dinner for the children. Through communication and cooperation, families work out problems like these. They often turn to extended family members and friends for help.

Financial Effects

Serious illness or disability commonly causes families financial problems. Income may be lost, even as medical bills—sometimes unbelievably high bills—pile up. If a family has no insurance, they may have no means to pay.

Such situations make it vital to think ahead about medical insurance needs. Even when health is good, a person never knows what's around the corner. Medical coverage should be purchased if not provided by an employer.

For people who face unmanageable medical bills, hospitals have personnel who counsel about such problems. Some social service agencies and religious organizations also provide financial counseling or assistance.

Emotional Effects

While financial effects are felt over time, the emotional impact of a family member's illness or disability is immediate. Everyone in the family responds individually. Those who must take on added responsibilities may feel the strain. Feelings of anger and resentment can even surface. Young family members may not understand what's going on. All have worries about what will happen to them and their loved one.

A parent may need to explain an illness to a young child to lessen fear. Teens can read about a disease to know how to react to the person who is ill.

What to Do

Empathy is a good guide when someone you know is challenged by physical health problems. Understanding what another person might be feeling helps you respond more positively. That response, from within the family or from others, may take the form of:

- **A touch or hug.** Physical closeness is comforting to many people, sometimes more so than words.
- **Offers to take responsibility for what needs doing.** Family members can share extra tasks according to their abilities. People outside the family can help also. Offers of specific help are most useful. "Why don't I take the kids for lunch?" is appreciated more than "Call me if you need anything."
- **Explanations.** Children need the reassurance of simple, honest, but positive explanations. They need love and attention more than ever.
- **Knowledge.** For teens and adults, learning about the health condition can give a sense of control. Knowledge can lessen fear by helping a person know what to expect and how to respond.

- **Openness.** Sharing feelings is beneficial. This outlet expresses your needs and reveals the needs of others.

MENTAL HEALTH PROBLEMS

Jeremy's Aunt Chloe wears youthful clothing, voices strong opinions at family gatherings, and gives expensive gifts for no special reason. Everyone agrees Chloe is a "character"—but is she mentally unbalanced?

Recognizing mental illness is not always easy. Anyone can have occasional mood swings or act irrationally at times. People may get used to someone's "colorful" personality and not think of it as "instability."

Two questions point to the possibility of mental illness: Does the person function normally on a daily basis? Do the person's actions routinely hurt or trouble others? If the answer is "no" to the first question and "yes" to the second, a real problem exists that needs attention.

Many people who realize that physical illness is not controllable think that mental illness is. This is not so. Mental illness is just that—illness. An ill person cannot "snap out of it." A mental disorder can be emotionally wrenching for the individual, family, and friends, but it's no one's fault.

Someone with a mental illness needs professional help. Psychologists, psychiatrists, and other sources of help, such as crisis hot lines, are listed in The Yellow Pages of the telephone directory under "mental health services." Counselors can assist people in gaining control of a minor problem before it becomes serious. Appropriate counseling and medication can keep a problem from getting out of control.

Ideally, a mentally ill person makes the decision to seek help. In extreme cases, family and friends may intervene to force the person into treatment. State laws vary on what actions can be taken.

ALCOHOL AND DRUG ADDICTIONS

Munching on a bag of your favorite snack food, you may joke, "I'm addicted to this stuff." True addictions, of course, are serious business. An **addiction** (uh-DICK-shun) is a dependence on a particular substance or action. It is a mental, and sometimes physical, need to have a substance or repeat a behavior in order to function.

Behavior addictions, often called compulsions, can cause problems in families. However, addictions to drugs more often reach crisis proportions. **Drugs** are chemical substances, other than food, that change the way the body or mind functions. Alcohol and nicotine are two examples. Few forces are as destructive to individuals and families as drugs.

Alcoholism

Alcohol takes control of people slowly. Many aren't aware of their addiction to alcohol, or **alcoholism**, until it is complete. They may deny their dependence on the drug. The people around them, having witnessed the gradual change in behavior and personality, know the truth.

Alcohol and other drugs cause many family crises. Financial problems, disability, and even death can result from use of either. What can family members do if a member is found to be addicted?

What distinguishes an abuser from a user of alcohol? Sometimes, nothing: an alcoholic may show no signs but is addicted just the same. More often, alcohol abusers exhibit definite behaviors. They drink often, sometimes alone, in the morning, or to face certain situations. They drink more over time. Drinking, or its aftereffects, may cause them to miss obligations, such as work or family outings. In its more serious stages, alcoholism leads to blackouts, periods when the person seems to be functioning normally, but later has no memory of events. Some alcoholics display only some of these traits. The stage of the disease is a factor.

Families know when alcohol is a problem. They know the embarrassment and frustration at the alcoholic's unpredictable behavior. They know the worry at the damage done to the person's health. They know the feelings of blaming themselves and resenting the alcoholic. Children often feel abandoned. Some families know the fear of being hurt by the drinker's violent actions. These emotions are like walls between family members. Alcoholism is often cited as a cause for family breakup and divorce.

Other Drug Addictions

Many drugs besides alcohol cause serious problems for individuals and families. Both medicinal and illegal drugs can be addictive. Chances are, you have already learned the dangers of drugs in a health class or drug awareness program. Over time, drugs destroy health. They seriously damage organs and systems of the body. They also distort thought processes and emotions, which, in turn, can lead to numerous other problems.

People with drug addictions may neglect their responsibilities to their employers, families, and to themselves. They may develop behavior problems that strain all their relationships. Violent and unpredictable behavior is often linked to drug use. Illegal drug use may result in criminal prosecution. These effects are an enormous burden on the family, as is the cost of drugs or treatment programs.

A person who abuses drugs may show some common signs of the addiction. He or

A teen, or any person, who has a drug addiction seldom realizes how his or her attitude and behavior have changed. Troubled relationships and school problems offer evidence.

Codependency

In families where someone has an addiction, such as alcoholism, other family members can develop a condition known as codependency. Codependents become wrapped up in the troubled person's problems. They take on responsibilities that the other person is neglecting, which may even help the addicted person hide the problem. For example, a codependent person might make excuses to others when the alcoholic spouse misses work or a family event.

Codependents try very hard to please people. They seek love and approval. Unfortunately, an addicted person is usually not able to give what the codependent needs. Giving and receiving are out of balance in the relationship.

Codependents often neglect their own concerns in trying to care for others. They get so caught up in helping that they ignore what they need from the relationship.

USING YOUR KNOWLEDGE

Trevor's mother is an alcoholic. Sixteen-year-old Trevor often comes home after school and finds her sleeping. He hides the empty bottles in the trash and straightens up so that his father won't come home to the mess. When his grandmother calls, he says that his mother isn't feeling well. What do you think is happening to Trevor?

she may miss school or work often and perform poorly when present. The person's behavior may not seem normal, marked by unpredictable moods. Aggression, attention seeking, and a poor attention span are other signs. Physical symptoms, including changed or unhealthy appearance, slurred speech, and poor coordination, may be evident. Of course, possession of drugs and drug paraphernalia is an obvious signal.

Taking Action

Intervention is critical in drug addiction. People who are close to someone with this problem must take action—for their own sake as well as for the addict. That might mean talking to a doctor to cut off access to prescription drugs. If illegal drugs are used, the police must be notified.

If you are ever in a position to help someone through an addiction, these suggestions can prove valuable:

- **Become knowledgeable.** Read about alcoholism or drug use. Talk to those who have accurate, up-to-date information.
- **Be thoughtful, not threatening.** No addict will seek help or stop using drugs until he or she is ready. Nagging is useless. A caring approach works best.

- **Be direct.** Call the problem "alcoholism" or "drug abuse" and describe in detail what it's doing to the person and to others.
- **Seek help for yourself.** Advice and support for those affected by another's addiction are offered by groups like Alateen. Look in the telephone directory under "alcoholism" or "drug abuse" for listings.
- **Learn about local resources.** Find out what resources are available in your community, so you'll be ready when the addict is willing. Many employers offer assistance programs for employees with drinking or drug problems. In some states alcoholics can be legally compelled to enter a treatment program.
- **Be optimistic.** Many families face tough situations brought on by addictions every day. If they are ruled by fear and embarrassment, they may never find a solution. If they believe, instead, that help is available and go after it with determination, a better life is ahead.

FAMILY VIOLENCE

Violence is physical force used to harm someone or something. Violent action can damage property, injure people, and even kill. Some violence occurs in one out of every two family homes each year. Police consider family violence calls among the most dangerous they answer. Any act of family violence impacts the whole family, not just the individuals involved.

Reasons that people act violently are complex and often unclear. One person might "snap under stress," yet another person under greater stress stays calm in a similar situation. People who use violence can always find explanations for their behavior. They might say, "The kid wouldn't stop crying," "I had to make him behave," or "She needs to know who's boss." Such reasons are only excuses. Violence is never justified, except in self-defense.

Violent behavior is often learned. Those who grow up with violence see it as a normal response. Unless they learn new ways to cope with stress and negative emotions, violence is passed to another generation, and the cycle continues.

Help is available in a crisis. Many agencies have people trained to help you find the assistance you need.

Most people who use violence don't really want to hurt others. They may want to behave differently, but they don't know how. To prevent violence-related crises, *any* signs of such behavior should be reported, investigated, and treated immediately.

Partner Abuse

Some violence between marriage partners occurs in one-fourth of all families. Abusive language may be part of the problem. Sometimes violence results in the breakup of a marriage. Other times, it becomes a destructive way of life.

Although some women are physically abusive toward men, violence directed by men against women is much more common. Men who batter women usually hold rigidly traditional views of gender roles. They tend to bottle their problems and their stress because they believe this is how men always act. Eventually, their rage explodes. Excessive drinking often contributes to partner abuse.

Why would a woman stay in an abusive relationship? She may not want to admit that abuse occurs. If she doesn't value herself, she may feel she deserves the abuse. A woman who was abused as a child is more apt to accept blows from a partner.

An abused woman may think she has no place to go. Perhaps relatives cannot or will not help, and she believes she can't support herself and her children alone. She may feel committed to the relationship; she wants to make it work.

Women who continue in an abusive relationship make a tragic mistake. Such relationships usually get worse, hurting children also. As you have read, many communities have shelters for these women and

No child deserves abusive treatment from adults. No reason excuses the behavior of an abuser.

children. Trained counselors can help a woman choose her next step and suggest ways to help the abuser.

Child Abuse

Abusive treatment of children takes several forms.

- **Neglect.** People neglect children when they fail to provide them with adequate food, clothing, shelter, supervision, or medical care. Young children especially cannot be left to care for themselves under any circumstances.
- **Emotional abuse.** The National Committee for Prevention of Child Abuse defines emotional abuse as a "pattern of behavior that attacks a child's emotional development and sense of self-worth." This includes name-calling and verbal

attacks, such as "You're no good" and "I wish you'd never been born." Withholding love is a type of emotional abuse. Any parent under stress may act in these ways at times, but patterns of such behavior indicate abuse.

- **Physical abuse.** Children who are physically abused are subjected to force that leaves an injury. Deliberately inflicted burns, cuts, and bruises mark this kind of abuse.

- **Sexual abuse.** Sexual abuse takes place when someone subjects a child, male or female, to fondling or rape, or lures the child to be part of some sexual activity. **Incest** is sexual activity between people who are closely related. The child usually knows the sexual abuser, who might be a parent, a stepparent, a sibling, or someone close to the family. Often, that person threatens or otherwise convinces the victim that secrecy is necessary.

Focus On ...

Emotional Abuse

Every day the media relay stories of child abuse. Most involve physical acts of violence that leave visible scars. Other damage is also inflicted on children every day, but it leaves no visible scars.

Emotional abuse is very destructive, causing invisible scars that can last a lifetime. It creates fears, personality problems, and sorrows that affect how children cope with relationships and living, even as adults. Research has identified five general types of emotional abuse toward children. They are:

- **Rejecting.** The adult actively avoids the child, sometimes refusing to see a child's needs. Verbal comments are belittling.
- **Terrorizing.** Threats of extreme or sinister punishment are made. The child is punished unreasonably.
- **Ignoring.** The adult is psychologically unavailable to the child.

- **Isolating.** Normal interactions with others are prevented.
- **Corrupting.** The child is encouraged to be antisocial or defiant, especially in the areas of aggression, sexuality, or substance abuse.

USING YOUR KNOWLEDGE

Nineteen-year-old Barry's earliest memories include those of his father's angry outbursts. Barry never knew what might trigger one. If Barry didn't do something just right, even when he didn't know what "right" was supposed to be, the rage appeared. It was followed by words that made Barry feel ashamed and worthless. How do you think these episodes have affected the way Barry is today?

Building Character

Courage: A Quality That Counts

When you have courage, you draw upon your mental and moral strengths in order to withstand danger, fear, or difficulty. Courage helps people get through their own crises in life, but it also enables them to step in when others need help. A teen can show courage by:

- Not letting a disability prevent him or her from developing talents.
- Coping with serious problems and not letting them be destructive.
- Stepping forward to encourage a friend in crisis to get help.
- Leaving a party where teens are drinking alcohol.
- Showing support for a friend whose father has died even though being there isn't easy.

QUESTIONS

1. In what ways do each of these actions show courage?
2. Why do you think some people have more courage than others do?
3. How can courage be developed?
4. In what ways have you shown courage?

Children who are sexually abused need to understand that they did nothing to encourage the activity. The abuser is totally responsible for the actions and must be stopped.

Breaking the Cycle

Child abuse of any kind may continue for years, leaving children in a state of daily fear, with lasting emotional scars. What's more, growing up with abuse may cause them to repeat the pattern with their own children someday.

No child or teen should have to live with any kind of abuse. When you know that abuse is going on, directed either at you or someone you know, you have to get help.

Talk to trusted people until someone listens. Family members, friends, or a teacher can help. Some adults, such as health and child care professionals, are legally required to notify police when child abuse is suspected.

Sometimes a family member doesn't want to hear accusations of sexual abuse. Nine-year-old Sage told her mother, with great difficulty, that her mother's new husband was touching her in bad ways. Her mother told Sage that she must have misunderstood. She even accused her daughter of lying. Fortunately for Sage, her grandmother was willing to take her seriously.

In abuse situations, intervention may be all that saves a child from a lifetime of anguish—or death. People who suspect child abuse can call the police department or the national abuse hotline. The local child welfare office, usually listed under the Department of Children and Family Services in the telephone directory, is another resource.

Sometimes family members must be separated for a while after abuse is reported. Although this can be difficult, it's in everyone's best interest. An abuser who learns how to control problem behavior may be reunited with the family later. Confronting the problem is unpleasant, but worth the effort when the result is a happier life.

People who are abusive, or fear they might become so, can be helped by Parents Anonymous, a national organization that sponsors support groups for parents throughout the country. Parents Anonymous is listed in telephone directories.

SUICIDE

Suicide has been called a permanent solution to a temporary problem. Although a suicidal person may not believe it, no problem is so overwhelming that it destroys any hope for future happiness. Every problem can be solved in some way. No problem is worth dying for.

Even when considering suicide, a person still wants to live. He or she sends out "distress signals." Take them seriously. You should act if you notice these signs:

- Discouraged remarks: "No one understands" and "There's no hope."
- Avoidance of, and withdrawal from, people and activities.
- Substance abuse and school problems.
- Creating artwork, poetry, or essays with themes of death.
- Purchase of a weapon, object, or substance that could be used harmfully.
- Giving away special possessions.
- Increasing depression and saying goodbyes.
- Uncharacteristic behavior changes.
- Extreme anger, sorrow, or despair.
- Sudden happiness, which often indicates that a decision has been reached.
- Threats and suicide attempts.

If you suspect someone is suicidal, don't be afraid to intervene. Say directly, "Are you thinking about suicide?" Ask what's wrong and listen rather than acting shocked or giving empty reassurances. Suggest alternatives and people and places that can help. Show that you care. Stay with the person, remove anything harmful, and seek help.

Some teens don't take the signs of suicide seriously when they see them in a friend. Would you pay attention and take action?

ENDING ON A HIGH NOTE

What you have just read is sobering, but remember this: the worst of times often brings out the best in people. Think of stories you've heard about a community that raised donations for a family who lost everything in a fire, or a determined individual who didn't let disability stand in the way of a long-cherished goal. Many people come through a crisis with a new appreciation for the caring of other people—and for their own fighting spirit.

Coming through a crisis can bring a family together. They learn what their strengths are.

SECTION 14-2 REVIEW

Check Your Understanding

1. How might people respond emotionally to the serious illness of a family member?
2. When should you be concerned about someone's mental state?
3. What are three common symptoms of alcoholism?
4. Describe five common signs of drug addiction.
5. What are four types of child abuse?
6. Would you worry if a friend who had been depressed for a long time suddenly acted cheerful? Explain.
7. **Thinking Critically.** Under what circumstances, if any, should a person be compelled to seek treatment for a mental illness or an addiction?
8. **Problem Solving.** Seventeen-year-old Aaron has a friend who started drinking beer two years ago. Now Olivia averages a few drinks nearly every night. Aaron has told her that she's got a drinking problem, but Olivia denies it. What should Aaron do?

Chapter 14
Review and Activities

CHAPTER SUMMARY

- When a crisis occurs, action must be taken in order to prevent further serious consequences.
- People usually react to a crisis in stages, which allows them to accept and deal with the situation.
- Many resources are available if people admit that they need help and seek it.
- Sometimes people must step in to help when someone is in a crisis state but cannot act alone.
- Health problems, either physical or mental, can cause a crisis for families.
- Alcoholism and other addictions can destroy individuals and families. These problems require appropriate action and treatment.
- Family violence may be directed at a spouse or a child. Help is available to victims of both types of abuse.
- A person who has thoughts of suicide can be helped by someone who recognizes the signs and cares enough to step in.

REVIEW QUESTIONS

Section 14-1
1. What makes a problem turn into a crisis?
2. How do hotlines help people?
3. What help can shelters offer people who are victims of abuse?
4. Why is intervention important?

Section 14-2
1. List suggestions that people faced with a serious illness in the family might do.
2. How might a person find help for a mental illness?
3. What is an addiction?
4. What is codependency?
5. List suggestions that the family of an alcoholic could follow.
6. What can a woman who is experiencing abuse from her spouse do?
7. How can a person help someone who is thinking about suicide?

BECOMING A PROBLEM SOLVER

1. Betsy and Emily were talking about a classmate they know but aren't close to. They realize they've both noticed the same things about him: he's usually alone; he draws strangely violent sketches in his notebook; he has a fascination for weapons; and he tells people how much he hates someone in the class. What should Betsy and Emily do?

2. Nathan was shocked when his friend Bryson came over after school one day with his CD collection. He gave the CDs to Nathan and said he wanted Nathan to have them because he didn't need them any more. What should Nathan do?

THINKING CRITICALLY

1. **Analyzing Behavior.** For some people, almost anything can become a crisis. Why do you think they react that way?
2. **Analyzing Behavior.** Why do you think some people are reluctant to seek help in times of crisis?
3. **Identifying Cause and Effect.** How does a woman's financial situation relate to her willingness to leave an abusive relationship?
4. **Predicting Results.** Why is intervention sometimes difficult?
5. **Identifying Cause and Effect.** What might cause a person in a crisis to refuse help when others offer?

MAKING CURRICULUM CONNECTIONS

1. **Science.** Research the immediate and long-term effects of alcohol on the human body. What biological processes are involved? How is the body affected? Write a report summarizing your findings.
2. **Math.** The Palos family must pay the first $200 in medical bills for each family member every year. This past year, Mrs. Palos had medical bills of $450, Mr. Palos had bills for $150, and their son had bills for $650. How much did the family have to pay?

APPLYING YOUR KNOWLEDGE

1. Working with a partner, identify a movie you have both seen that deals with a crisis. Briefly describe the crisis and evaluate how the characters coped.

2. Working in groups, list the examples of crises discussed in this chapter. Create two additional lists. First divide the original list into individual and family crises. Next, identify which crises may be preventable and which are not. For preventable crises, identify resources for, and methods of, prevention.
3. Working with a group, choose one of the crises in the chapter. Write a guide (perhaps a list) of what to do when faced with such a crisis. Compile group lists into a handout or pamphlet to share.
4. Suppose you took your child to the emergency room for an injury. Hospital personnel ask questions that indicate they are trying to determine whether you caused the injury. How would you feel? Why do they ask such questions? Explain your answers.

Family & Community Connections

1. Research your community to find out what resources are available to people who face crisis situations. With your classmates, compile a community resource guide that tells citizens where to go for help.

2. Find out the requirements for being a community volunteer. What kind of time commitment is required? What kind of training is provided? Share your findings with the class.

Chapter 15

Understanding Death

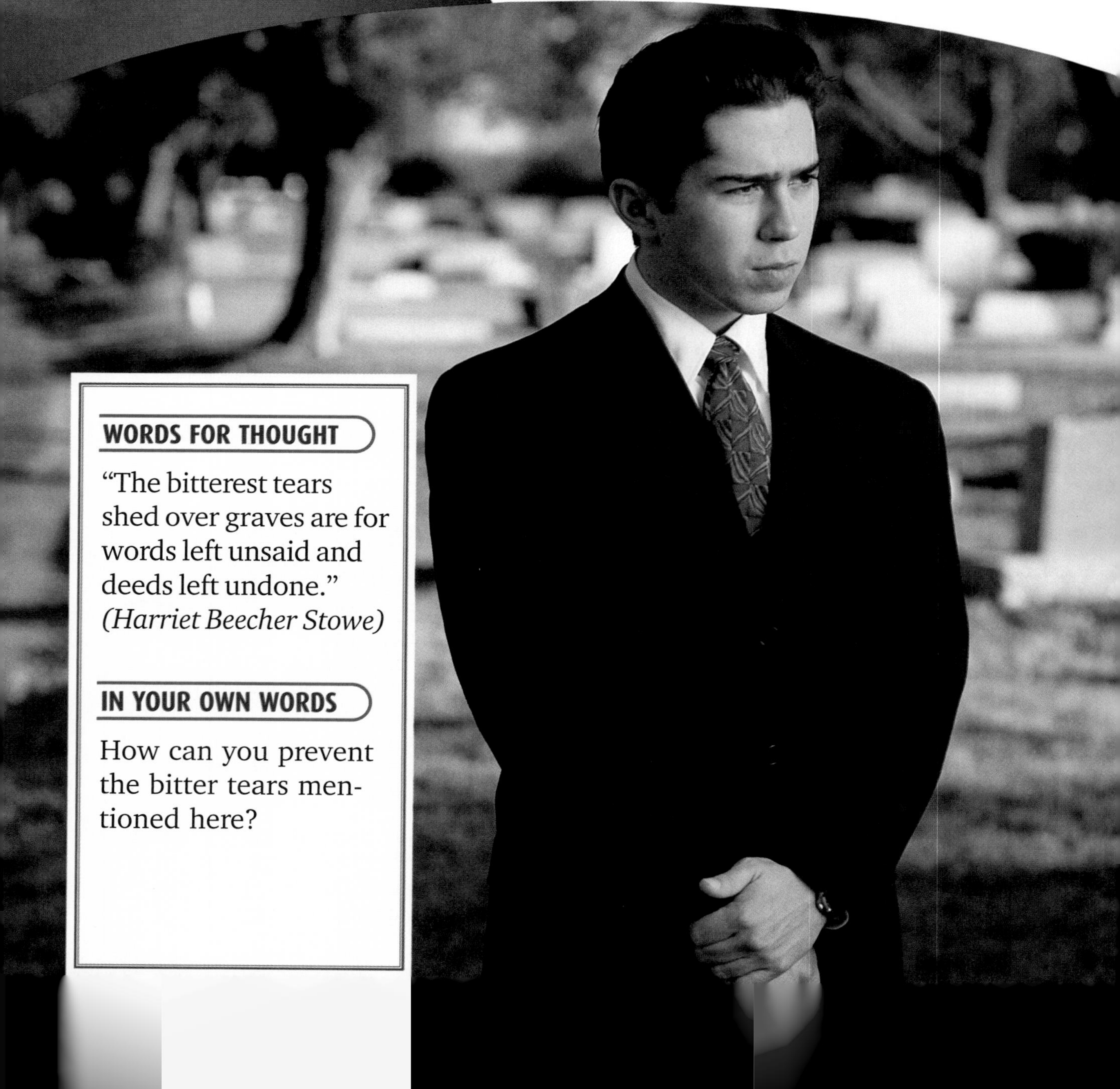

WORDS FOR THOUGHT

"The bitterest tears shed over graves are for words left unsaid and deeds left undone." *(Harriet Beecher Stowe)*

IN YOUR OWN WORDS

How can you prevent the bitter tears mentioned here?

Before Death Occurs

OBJECTIVES

After studying this section, you should be able to:

- Compare different circumstances of death and their effect on people.
- Trace the emotional changes in a dying person as he or she adjusts to death.
- Demonstrate ways people can support those who are dying.
- Describe the care offered by a hospice program.

TERMS TO LEARN

denial
isolation
hospice

If you ever want to quiet a noisy room, try saying, "Let's talk about death—no jokes, no polite phrases, just an honest discussion about dying." Chances are, no one will want to talk first.

For most people, death is a troubling subject. It involves a whole range of deep, mostly unpleasant emotions. It touches on very personal beliefs. Perhaps most disturbing, talking about death can lead to questions for which there are no easy answers. Avoiding the subject, of course, only makes it harder to deal with.

CIRCUMSTANCES OF DEATH

Death is as natural as birth. It's the opposite end of the event called life. Like birth, the physical process is the same for everyone, though the circumstances may differ greatly.

Death came to Charla's grandfather in a normal way. At age eighty-seven, he tired easily and needed some help meeting his needs, but was fairly healthy. As he grew weaker, he asked his family to visit more often. Some days he talked about the long life behind him. Other times, he took comfort in their silent company. One day he took Charla's hand, smiling, and whispered, "I'm not afraid, you know." Not long after that, he died.

Most people, if they think about it, might hope for a similar death. They want to experience all the stages of life. They want time to adjust to the idea of death little by little.

When a person has lived a long life, death is the next natural step.

A "natural" death also gives people the chance to put their lives in order to their satisfaction. They can make a will and pass on a special heirloom to the person they want to have it. To ease the burden on their family, some older people throw away things they have accumulated but no one wants and make their funeral arrangements. With all loose ends tied up, these people feel at peace when death finally comes.

Not everyone knows this kind of death, of course. Some people lose their lives suddenly or violently in accidents or wars, or to crime. Dying in this way leaves little or no time to think about death, let alone prepare for it. Whatever was unresolved in life remains that way.

Sometimes death comes early, but announced. Serious illness may force a person to come to terms with death without the experience of a long life.

COPING IN STAGES

When forced to face death unexpectedly, people everywhere share a similar emotional response. Psychiatrist Elisabeth Kübler-Ross' lifework was counseling dying patients and their families. She identified five stages of adjustment that a person must go through in order to accept the end of life.

Denial and Isolation

When first confronted with the news that death is approaching, a person goes into denial. **Denial** (dih-NEYE-uhl) is refusing to believe the facts, and therefore thinking and acting as if those facts don't exist. Sean recalled, "When my uncle found out he had terminal cancer, he went from one doctor to another, wondering why none of them could 'get it right.' It was like the truth was such a shock that his mind blocked it out. It would have been too painful to accept right away." Denial like Sean describes is a common reaction to any major loss.

Eventually, as the realization that death will occur sinks in, people experience **isolation** (EYE-suh-LAY-shun). They feel set apart from others and completely alone. Death, after all, is one thing that you can't experience with someone else. No one can share in another person's loss of life; no one can understand what it's like. A dying person may pull back from those who truly care, at least for a while.

Anger

With time, people accept the fact that they are dying, but they don't give in quietly. The second stage is one of great anger. Enraged by the thought of death, a person may lash out at everyone and everything. Doctors, family, and close friends may all be targets. People may be furious at a higher power, such as God, for letting them die. Their anger can be hard on loved ones.

When his uncle was dying, Sean said, "We had such little time left together, and we felt like he was wasting it by being so cruel. We didn't want it to end this way. We had to remind ourselves that he wasn't really mad at *us*—he was mad at what was happening."

Bargaining

At some point people who face death may try to bargain, to make a deal, in order to gain more living time. They may try to give up bad habits or act more kindly to others. Bargaining

is a dying person's attempt to gain control over the situation. Death is no longer denied, but hope remains that it can be postponed, if only briefly.

Depression

When people realize bargaining for time won't work, depression sets in. Now they genuinely realize that death cannot be avoided. Depression can aggravate the symptoms of the illness and sap a person's strength. If the cost of care causes the family financial problems, depression may be compounded by feelings of guilt. Most of all, people feel the impending loss of

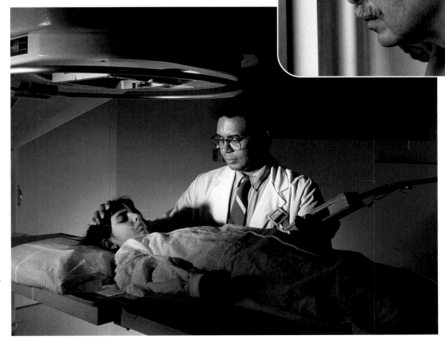

Even very young people face life-threatening illnesses. The adults who love them and take care of them have strong emotional reactions in such situations.

all they hold dear. This stage may seem almost unbearable to family and friends; however, their loyalty, love, and understanding are more important now perhaps than ever.

Acceptance

In this final stage, people come to terms with their situation. They can look back on life and acknowledge what was good but accept that it will soon end. The strong emotions that marked the first four stages of adjustment are quieted. The person is ready to face what lies ahead.

SUPPORT FROM OTHERS

As people work through these stages, they need love and support. Family members and close friends may be needed on an ongoing basis. Others can keep in touch and follow the family's advice regarding visits.

Supporting someone through death can be difficult. People may feel awkward or useless. They may fear hurting the person by saying or doing something inappropriate. Like the dying person, family and friends are also forced to admit that they are helpless to stop death from coming. In accepting someone else's death, they are reminded of their own.

These reactions are understandable. However, backing away from someone who is dying can make the experience harder on everyone. Rather than focus on their own feelings, people can take their cues on how to act from the dying person.

Sean described how his family supported his uncle in his fight with cancer: "When Uncle Marty felt like a new treatment was helping him, we told him how glad we were that he was feeling better. Sometimes, he'd say something like, 'I wonder what it feels like to die,' so we'd talk about that. Mostly, we talked about everyday things, things he liked—football or his dogs—and about ourselves. We all needed to put cancer in the background when we could and enjoy being together like everyone does. And if things got too heavy, we just held hands."

Support from family and friends may come in the form of just "being there," bringing everyday things into the patient's life, or just listening to the patient talk of the reality of death.

As a person becomes accepting of death, family and friends may grow more resistant. The person may need to express fears about dying and concerns about those who will be left behind. This conversation is most painful to loved ones, who may want to deny death when the dying person has reached the point of accepting it. Instead, they need to listen, calmly and thoughtfully.

Knowing that death is near is an opportunity, for the living and the dying. It gives a dying person time to do what might be put off otherwise. A person has the chance to examine values and act on them. Awareness of death can inspire people to say things they have long wanted to say. Relationships can be mended and strengthened for all time. Memories can be loving thoughts, not regrets.

HOSPICE PROGRAMS

Families that need help as death nears often turn to a hospice. A **hospice** (HOS-pis) is a program that provides physical care and emotional support to people who face death and to their loved ones. The hospice philosophy stresses managing symptoms, rather than extending life.

Building Character

Empathy: A Quality That Counts

Not everyone can see things from another's point of view. Can you? If so, you may have empathy. You can sense a person's feelings and thoughts as though they were your own. Empathy helps you figure out what people truly need. When you can respond correctly, that enriches your relationships and your life. A teen who shows empathy might:

- Visit a lonely relative in a nursing home.
- Send a personal note to the parents of a classmate who was killed in an auto accident.
- Bury a neighbor's cat when she was too grief-stricken to do it herself.
- Invite a neighbor whose spouse had died recently to a family holiday meal.
- Work late so a coworker can leave early to visit a family member who is in the hospital.

QUESTIONS

1. How are sympathy and empathy similar and different?
2. What other qualities can you cultivate to strengthen your ability to empathize?
3. Give an example of a time when you empathized with someone.
4. In what specific ways could you show more empathy in your family?

Career Success Stories

Mattie Williams: *Hospice Worker*

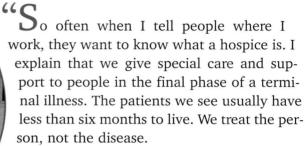

"So often when I tell people where I work, they want to know what a hospice is. I explain that we give special care and support to people in the final phase of a terminal illness. The patients we see usually have less than six months to live. We treat the person, not the disease.

"As a nurse, I'm part of a team that includes physicians, counselors, social workers, aides, clergy, and volunteers all working together. Our goal is to help the patient live as fully and comfortably as possible through the final days. Actually, we're there for the family and caregivers as well as the patient. We deal with lots of needs—physical, emotional, and spiritual.

"People wonder why I chose this kind of work. Actually, it can be hard. I have to be strong and able to separate myself from work when I go home. But it's also important and rewarding. Maybe because I'm continually faced with death, I see dying as a normal process. If you could have met Joseph, a patient I had last year, you'd see that hospice work isn't all gloomy. His spirit and sense of humor, and his family's too, were a bright spot for me every day. For the people who can't handle death this way, I try to be the bright spot for them."

CAREER PROFILE

Education and training: high school diploma; bachelor's degree

Starting salary range: minimum wage–$29,000

Job prospects: private and public home health agencies; hospitals; nursing homes

Important qualities: compassionate; desire to help others; good communication skills; physical stamina

Plan Ahead

Before 1974, hospice programs in the United States were almost nonexistent. Now there are programs in all of the states. Using the Internet and the telephone directory, locate a hospice that serves your area. If the work interests you, contact them for information.

Some hospices are facilities where people who are terminally ill can spend their last days. The hospice setting is more homelike and comfortable than a hospital or nursing home. Doctors, nurses, and physical therapists provide medical care. Psychiatrists, counselors, and chaplains attend to the emotional and spiritual needs of the dying and their family. The aim is to ensure the quality of whatever time the ill person has left.

Families often choose a hospice program because it recognizes their role in the person's death. Family members are encouraged to visit and taught to give medical care when possible. If a hospice facility is not an option, staff and trained volunteers can provide care in the family home.

Hospice programs help families cope with terminal illnesses. Care can be provided at home or in a homelike setting.

SECTION 15-1 REVIEW

Check Your Understanding

1. Why are older people often more accepting of death?
2. What is denial?
3. How can the second stage of adjustment be particularly hard on loved ones?
4. Why might a person experience depression when adjusting to the idea of death?
5. How can people know how to act when visiting someone who is dying?
6. What is a hospice program?
7. **Thinking Critically.** Why might people disagree with the hospice philosophy of end-of-life care?
8. **Problem Solving.** When Colleen's cousin Keith first learned he had cancer, he fell into a depression. Now he is excited about an experimental treatment that he read about. His doctors have warned that the treatment is unproven, but Keith is certain it will help, maybe even cure him. Colleen wants to support her cousin's hope, but fears the doctors are right. What should Colleen do?

Handling Grief

OBJECTIVES

After studying this section, you should be able to:

- Trace the stages of the grieving process.
- Recommend ways to help children deal with death.
- Demonstrate positive ways to comfort a grieving person.
- Describe practical decisions that must be made when someone dies.

TERMS TO LEARN

grief
bereaved
cremation
will

The death of a friend or relative is not an ending for those who survive. When someone dies, the impact he or she had on others continues to be felt. In memory and often with deep emotion, people live on in the hearts and minds of those left behind.

GRIEVING

Losing a special person to death brings emotions and physical feelings that can be very painful. These feelings are known as **grief**.

Because grief is so distressing, some people try to avoid grieving. Wanting to be strong, they push the pain deep inside, telling themselves they don't hurt.

Experiencing grief is painful but necessary. Feelings of grief are, to the mind, what symptoms of an injury are to the body. When you lose a loved one, your mind and spirit suffer a great blow. You can hide outward signs of grief, just as you can smile when you have a bad headache. The pain continues, however. Unless the reason for the suffering is addressed, greater problems will erupt later on. Some studies have linked unresolved grief to drug addiction, delinquency, illness, and even death.

The Process of Grieving

The grief process, also called "grief work" or mourning, includes three stages.

- **Stage One.** The first stage of grieving is shock and numbness, often coupled with denial. People in mourning, or the **bereaved**, may busy themselves with a flurry of purposeless activity. This stage helps them screen out the painful truth of what has happened.

- **Stage Two.** The reality of the situation sinks in during stage two. People feel an almost unbearable sense of loss and waves of great sorrow. Depression and anxiety are common in this phase.
- **Stage Three.** The final step in the grief process is recovery. In recovery, people face and bear the loss, and accept the loss as final. Hopes, dreams, and plans shared with the person who died are given up. The bereaved person makes the adjustments needed to go on with life.

How Long?

The time for grieving varies, but it's usually a lengthy process. The age of the person who died and the cause of death can affect the time needed. The closeness of your relationship to the person who died also makes a difference. Grieving may last up to two years after the death of a parent and from four to six years after the death of a spouse. A parent may grieve for eight to ten years after the death of a child.

Grieving has no timetable. Feelings of sadness can occur years after death. A photo, a song, or even a funny story may be a "flashback" reminder of the loved one and your loss of that person in your life.

Symptoms of Grief

Most people are unprepared for the severe physical and emotional reactions they feel in grief. Grief can affect any area of the body or mind.

When Elisa's brother was killed in an auto accident, Elisa felt she was holding up fairly well. She had trouble sleeping some nights, but she made up for it by getting more sleep later in the week. Her appetite was dull. Also, events seemed oddly unreal, which Elisa attributed to not getting enough sleep and food. Then her throat began to feel painfully tight, and she came down with the flu. Elisa described her symptoms to the doctor, who told her that all of them—eating and sleeping problems, feelings of unreality,

even throat pain—are physical signs of grief. Grief may also have led to her illness, since the number of disease-fighting white blood cells drops dramatically when a person grieves.

Emotionally, grief can be exhausting. Mixed emotions are common. Sadness and loss are the primary feelings; anger and fear are also common. If the dying process was very long or painful, the bereaved often feel relief when death comes. On the other hand, they may resent the dead person for leaving them. They may then experience guilt at feeling either relieved or resentful.

Emotions like these are normal. They soon disappear, and people should not worry about feeling them.

Working Through Grief

Grieving can't be rushed. By working with the process instead of against it, however, a person can begin recovery sooner rather than later. To work through grief, a person can:

- Accept the loss and try to understand the reality of the death. Viewing the body helps many people accept the finality.
- Give vent to emotions. There is no shame in crying or admitting to feeling lonely.
- Take time to heal. Important decisions and demanding projects should be put off, if possible.
- Hang on to good memories. Recalling even good times may be painful at first. Eventually, the pain fades and the memories live on.
- Ask for whatever support is needed from family, friends, medical professionals, and mental health counselors.

A funeral gives people, including children, a chance to face the reality of death and say good-bye.

SUPPORTING CHILDREN

Due to their incomplete understanding, children need special help in dealing with death. Up to age four, children can't understand loss through death. They understand feelings of separation and rejection, however. Young children must feel loved and secure in order to cope with death.

Between ages four and seven, a child sees death as temporary and reversible. At about age seven, the child begins to understand that death is permanent, but may believe that some body functions remain. At this age, death is viewed as something that happens to other people and families.

In the preteen years, a child comes to realize that death is the final and certain fate of everyone. Children who have experienced the death of pets, peers, or grandparents best understand this concept.

Talking About Death

When done appropriately, most children benefit from discussing death openly. Explanations should be simple but honest and suited to the child's age and ability to understand. To avoid confusion, questions should be answered clearly.

Jackson remembered these points when his wife died. Taking their three-year-old daughter Laine into his lap, Jackson told her: "Laine, I have to tell you something very, very sad. Mommy was hurt. She was too badly hurt to live. Now her body has stopped working, and it won't start again. Mommy has died, and she won't be coming back. We'll miss her very, very much, but Daddy is here. I love you a lot, and I'll take care of you." Jackson had to repeat his explanation more than once, but Laine was able to understand these basic facts.

Children also need simple, reassuring answers about the cause of death. You know that phrases such as "at rest" and "passed away" are pleasant-sounding substitutes for "died." Children, however, take words literally. Shortly after his father's death, one five-year-old began hiding every night at bedtime. Once in bed, he refused to stay. Would you be surprised to know that his aunt had told him his father had "gone to sleep"? The child was afraid of falling into the same type of "sleep."

Some families try to shelter their children from death. Parents may have trouble facing death or talking about it. This is unfortunate, because children need to have their questions answered. When children are given no answers, or incomplete ones, they often imagine things that are worse than the truth. Fears about death may deepen as they grow. A gentle discussion can help a child see death as a part of the cycle that all living things go through. Death is a sad time, but life, with its growth and new beginnings, goes on.

SUPPORTING FRIENDS

When Casey's mother died, his family was sustained by an outpouring of support. Neighbors brought over nourishing food when the family was too drained to fix a good meal themselves. Every day the mail brought cards and simple notes of condolence. Many friends made donations in his mother's name to her favorite charities. "What touched me most," Casey said, "is when people came up to me, at the funeral or at school. They'd hug me or shake my

Tips & TECHNIQUES

Music as Therapy. Music, and lyrics especially, can have a powerful effect on a grieving person. Music can lift or soothe the spirit, or bring further distress. To more fully understand this relationship, try this:

- Listen to your favorite radio station for half an hour. Imagine how someone who is grieving might feel after listening to the same music.
- Ask a religious leader or a funeral director to name songs that are often used at services. Review the lyrics of these songs. Why do you think they are frequently used?
- Identify instrumental music or lyrics that raise your spirits when you're depressed or feeling a sense of loss.

Try It Out. Create a therapeutic tape recording, using music that you find appropriate. Share your tape with a friend who needs a lift—after making a copy for yourself.

Decisions After Death

Many practical decisions must be made and actions taken soon after death occurs, when grief is strongest. That timing may seem unfair, yet the steps can help people cope with the shock of their loss. Families can turn to the funeral director for help with many of their questions and concerns.

Unless the deceased specified before dying, what will happen to the body is an early decision. Typically families choose between burial and cremation. **Cremation** (kree-MAY-shun) is the reduction of a body to ashes through intense heat. Arrangements must be made for either option.

Planning the funeral involves more decisions. For most people, a funeral is a necessary part of grieving. The bereaved need to honor the memory of the deceased and also mourn and say good-bye.

Funeral costs are a significant issue, since they can be very expensive. After a home and car, a funeral is often the third largest purchase a person makes. Together, family members can plan a ceremony that honors the loved one without causing financial problems. Reputable funeral directors guide families in spending an amount they are comfortable with.

If the person left a will, some decisions are already made. A **will** is a legal document that states how property is to be distributed after death. If no will was made, laws direct how property will be handled. Clothing and small, personal items are usually given to family, friends, or charity.

Many financial details must be addressed in the weeks following a death. Paying bills, filling out insurance forms, applying for life insurance or Social Security benefits, and changing names on car titles and bank accounts may need to be done. People and businesses may need notification of the death.

USING YOUR KNOWLEDGE

When seventeen-year-old Jim's father died suddenly, his mother was in shock. She said she couldn't make any arrangements. Despite his own grief, Jim knew he had to take some kind of action. What do you think he should do?

hand and say, 'I don't know what to say, but I'm really sorry.' I know how hard that can be. It was always good to hear that, even if I'd heard it a hundred times before."

As Casey learned, supporting a friend who is grieving doesn't take great gestures. Just being present and showing that you care is enough. Your first reaction to a tragedy may be to turn away, but these are the times when friends need each other the most.

Remember that grieving can take a long time. Months later, a friend might like to talk about the person who died. Bringing up a special memory that you have provides an opener if your friend wants to talk. Knowing that you haven't forgotten the loved one can also be comforting.

A MESSAGE FOR YOU

A lot of good can come from thinking and talking about death. You can realize that your reactions to death are typical ones. You can be ready to support others who face death or grief. What's more, you can discover a new appreciation for life. It is only as you consider the loss of life that you can begin to appreciate the wonder of living it fully.

Some teens have to help a young child cope with a death in the family. What can they do to be supportive?

SECTION 15-2 REVIEW

Check Your Understanding

1. Why is grieving important?
2. What are five symptoms of grief?
3. How would you talk to a child about death?
4. Why might you bring up the memory of a loved one who died to a grieving friend?
5. What are some practical issues that must be settled when a person dies?
6. **Thinking Critically.** In some cultures, a party is held to honor a person who has died. How might this custom be beneficial?
7. **Problem Solving.** When Bennett's father died, his best friend never acknowledged it. He didn't come to Bennett's home or attend the funeral. The first time Bennett saw him, his friend acted as if nothing had happened. What problems are occurring here? What should be done?

Chapter 15
Review and Activities

CHAPTER SUMMARY

- Death is often accepted more easily by those who have lived a long life.
- Death can come unexpectedly. When people know death is near, they can prepare for it.
- People who know they are going to die typically experience five stages of adjustment to death.
- Although it may be difficult for loved ones, a dying person needs their presence and support.
- Hospice programs help individuals and families deal with approaching death.
- Experiencing grief at the death of a loved one is difficult but necessary. People work through grief in stages.
- Grief has certain physical and emotional symptoms.
- Children need help from adults to build an understanding about death.
- Being present and listening to a grieving friend is the best way to show support.
- Certain practical matters must be dealt with when a person dies.

REVIEW QUESTIONS

Section 15-1
1. Contrast the different circumstances of death and the effects on the dying person.
2. Why do some people turn away from a dying person?
3. How can you give support to someone who is dying?
4. What is offered by a hospice program?

Section 15-2
1. Is grief the same thing as sorrow? Explain.
2. What can happen to people who refuse to grieve?
3. Describe the three stages in the grief process.
4. How long does the grief process normally last?
5. Would you tell a six-year-old that a deceased family member has gone on a long trip? Explain your answer.
6. How can you best respond to a friend who is grieving?

BECOMING A PROBLEM SOLVER

1. Cheryl's seven-year-old brother brought her a baby rabbit that their cat had caught. "Will he be okay?" he asked. Cheryl knew the rabbit wouldn't survive. How should she respond?

2. Franco feels that it helps him to talk about his father, who died a few months ago. When he tries to share some memories with his brother Luigi, however, Luigi says little. Franco is frustrated and worried by Luigi's response. What should he do?

THINKING CRITICALLY

1. **Compare and Contrast.** Would you want to know when you are going to die? If so, how long in advance? Explain your answer.

2. **Recognizing Values.** Do you think an expensive funeral does more to honor the deceased than a simple funeral? Explain your answer.

3. **Analyzing Behavior.** Hillary's mother died eight months ago. She still misses her mother deeply but manages to cope with daily living. Recently, she has started to feel like going out with friends again, though the thought of having fun makes her feel guilty. If you were Hillary, what would you do? What if you were her friend?

MAKING CURRICULUM CONNECTIONS

1. **Music.** Many classical and modern composers have written requiems or funeral masses. Locate and listen to selections of this type of music. What emotions is the composer trying to express or create in the listener? Why have many of the requiems of classical composers remained well known through the years?

2. **Language Arts.** Use the library or Internet to research funeral customs in other cultures. Choose a particular country or culture and write a report describing its customs and explaining their purposes.

APPLYING YOUR KNOWLEDGE

1. Research the costs of funerals or other memorial services in your area. Report your findings to the class.

2. Develop a list of phrases or sentences that would comfort someone who is dying or grieving. When could you use these phrases?

Family & Community Connections

1. List five things you would want to say or do if you knew that you did not have long to live. Ask two family members to make a similar list. Share your lists.

2. Working with a partner, write at least five questions that you would ask a funeral director if you had to make funeral arrangements. If possible, tour a funeral home or mortuary to learn about the services provided.

UNIT 5

Extending Your Relationships

Teen Views

Do you think teens should focus less on their friends and more on their families?

Luisa

"Not really. That's what high school is all about—to start being on your own more. You have to learn how to do things for yourself. You'll always need your family, but they can't take care of you forever. A lot of parents don't want to let go of their kids, even though that's the best thing."

T.J.

"I think you can spend time with your friends and still make room for family. Some of my friends don't spend much time at home. I think they're missing something. My friend Mitch complains all the time about not getting along with his parents, but he's never there long enough to try. Maybe they don't get along because they don't even know who he is anymore."

What's your view?

How do you think a teen should balance home and personal life?

Chapter 16

Working with Others

Working Relationships

OBJECTIVES

After studying this section, you should be able to:

- Distinguish a working relationship from others.
- Explain how certain factors contribute to good working relationships.
- Evaluate techniques for dealing with people in authority.
- Demonstrate positive behaviors for various working relationships.

TERMS TO LEARN

working relationship
cooperation
reciprocation
etiquette
authority

In the fashion world, a classic is a garment that's always in style and can be dressed up or down to suit different occasions. The ideas you're studying about relating to others are also classics. So far, you've seen them "dressed down" for the more casual relationships you have with family. In this chapter, you'll see how to "dress up" your interpersonal skills for the more formal working relationships in your life.

ELEMENTS OF GOOD WORKING RELATIONSHIPS

A **working relationship** is created to accomplish a task or goal. For teens, the two most common working relationships are those at school and on the job. You might also work with people in a neighborhood association, a church group, and other organizations.

As you grow older, you'll probably acquire more working relationships. In all of them, certain skills and attitudes come in handy. A good working relationship blends personal warmth with respect and courtesy.

A Friendly Attitude

Talk with Kirsten for even a few minutes, and you're likely to walk away thinking favorably of her and feeling good. Perhaps it's Kirsten's smile or the way she looks you in the eye and uses your name when she talks to you. You feel that she likes you, even if she doesn't know you well. Friendly people like Kirsten are a pleasure to work with.

The reputation you build in your working relationships sets the stage for the future. If a waitress gets along well with customers and fellow employees, how might that affect her next job?

Of course, no one can be friendly and upbeat all the time. Nearly everyone has times when they are down. Constant complaining and bad moods, however, bring the people around you down as well. Sometimes you can pull yourself out of a bad mood if you try. If you have a problem that needs attention, however, talk with someone who can help. When people solve serious personal problems, their work relationships are likely to improve.

Respect

Have you ever given a speech before a class, only to see some of your classmates talking, reading a book, or staring out the window? How did you feel? Respectful people don't do these things. When someone is talking, they listen. If another person has a problem, they show concern and a willingness to help. A respectful person takes other people and their opinions seriously.

Cooperation

The ability to work with others is called **cooperation**. Cooperation allows people to accomplish what they need. Owen, for example, worked weekends at a hospital. When he was named to attend a student government convention, Owen asked his supervisor for that weekend off. His offer to make up the time on other days showed cooperation, and his boss agreed to the plan.

Reciprocation

Good working relationships are based on giving and getting in return. This is **reciprocation** (ri-SIP-ruh-KAY-shun). People tend to get back what they give. If you approach people in a friendly way, they tend to be open to you. If you show that you respect others, they are more apt to regard you highly. If you show a willingness to cooperate, others are more likely to meet you halfway.

Etiquette

Good manners, or **etiquette**, are the rules of appropriate behavior in dealing with other people, both personally and professionally. Good manners are the oil that lubricates relationships. Dwayne, for instance, keeps his relationship with his dentist smooth by remembering his appointment date and arriving on time. At work he holds the door for others to enter and greets people as they arrive.

Just because family members spend so much time together doesn't mean good manners can be forgotten at home. Dwayne makes "thank you" a regular part of his vocabulary. He also lets people know where he will be when he's away from home.

All of these are common courtesies, but they're only a few. Etiquette rules can be found to go with all sorts of situations, both formal and informal. Books and the good examples of others can help you learn what to do. When in doubt, remember that good manners are based on treating people as you want to be treated. Ask yourself, "If that were me, what would I want someone else to do?"

UNDERSTANDING AUTHORITY

In most working relationships, someone has **authority**, or the right to give orders, make decisions, and enforce rules. Generally, people with authority have earned it through the qualities, skills, or knowledge they have. Their position may give them power. Teachers, bosses, and police officers are familiar examples, but anyone may hold a position of authority at some time. Have you ever taken care of young children? Then you had authority.

Building Character

Dedication: A Quality That Counts

Is there a topic or activity that holds your interest for hours at a time? If so, you're showing dedication. Dedication means devoting yourself to some purpose and making a commitment to something you value. Depending on interests, a teen could show dedication by:

- Rehearsing every night with the drama club for an upcoming musical.
- Becoming president of a group that supports a particular cause.
- Volunteering to work the Adopt-A-Pet days at an animal shelter.
- Going to a grandmother's 75th birthday party instead of out with friends.
- Delivering a package for a boss after working hours.

QUESTIONS

1. How does each of the examples above show dedication?
2. What are the benefits of being dedicated to something or someone?
3. To what are you dedicated? How do your actions show your dedication?

You have more control than you might think when it comes to working with people in authority. The way you handle the relationship affects the way you are treated. How can that work in both positive and negative ways?

Working well with others means learning to accept and get along with people in authority. This is easier to do if you remember that:

- **Exercising authority is often part of a job.** The person in authority is simply doing what's expected.
- **Authority is assigned to people to keep order, promote safety, and make sure jobs get done.** The purpose of authority is to make life easier and more efficient, not more difficult.
- **Like everyone else, people in authority have strengths and weaknesses.** Expecting no mistakes just because a person has authority is unfair.
- **Being in authority can be difficult.** As anyone who has cared for a five-year-old knows, managing the actions of others can be a challenge.
- **Authority is a responsibility.** People who are in charge are often held accountable for the actions of those under their authority.

Responding to Authority

Authority creates different responses in people. When faced with authority, some people try to please. They do what the person in charge wants. They don't like to "make waves."

In contrast, some people rebel at authority. They tend to do the opposite of what is asked of them. They may create disturbances when they question those in charge.

When carried to extremes, each of these approaches can be a problem. Pleasing others by following directions and doing your work, of course, is usually wise. A cooperative attitude and positive spirit reflect well on you and are appreciated by others. Occasionally questioning authority, however, is reasonable if done in an acceptable way. The result can be change and knowledge that benefit everyone.

Channeling Rebelliousness

Nicole had always had a rebellious streak. Since she didn't understand the purpose of the sanitation rules at the diner where she worked, she decided that she didn't need to follow them. This cost the restaurant a favorable rating when the health inspector made a surprise visit. Nicole nearly lost her job. From that experience, she learned to question the rules she didn't understand, rather than ignore them. She even turned her natural resistance into a positive quality when she found a more efficient way to organize the diner's supplies. Her rebelliousness, constructively channeled, became a force for improvement.

During adolescence, some teens feel like rebelling against authority. As teens form their own ideas, they may question what others expect of them. In the long run, however, everyone must live and cope with authority. Too much rebelliousness eventually hurts the rebel. A teen can learn to be an individual while still getting along with those who have authority.

BENEFITING FROM SCHOOL RELATIONSHIPS

Teens spend many hours in school. There they relate to other students as well as teachers, administrators, and support staff.

If a school didn't have rules and procedures to follow, what would happen? With chaos, learning wouldn't take place and students wouldn't be able to prepare for the future. Doing well in school often hinges on following rules. Therefore, those who cooperate do better in school than those who rebel. Teens should think about these questions: What happens when you break the rules? What happens when you follow them? Which behavior benefits you more in the long run? It's your choice.

Tasha reevaluated her choice while she was in high school. She said: "For a long time, I just wanted to do my own thing. I had an attitude. I didn't care about grades,

Awareness of Others. When you're riding in a car, do you think of other motorists as people or as "traffic"? Separated by the glass and steel of an automobile, it's easy to forget you share the road with real people.

The same situation can occur even when people are up close. How many people do you meet every day without really seeing them? Try relating with someone in a new way this week:

- Introduce yourself to someone you don't know in your neighborhood.
- Learn the names of people who offer you service—bus driver, cafeteria worker, clerk, paper deliverer, maintenance person. Call them by name when you see them.
- Smile at and say hello to students you pass in the hall.
- Ask casual acquaintances questions to learn more about them and their interests. Finding someone with common interests may be the beginning of a new friendship.

Try It Out. For one day, try to smile and say hello to people you see or meet. What reactions did you get? Was this an easy or difficult task for you? Explain.

rules, or what anyone thought. The way I acted got me attention, even though it was the wrong kind. My older sister had been the same way, but then she got in some serious trouble. I don't know if things will ever be right for her. When I realized I wanted something better for myself, that's when I started changing my attitude. Now I know I want a family and a good career someday, and I'm the only one who can make that happen."

When you're like Tasha and have the foresight to see how today affects tomorrow, you want to get along well at school. Making the most of school relationships can have long-term effects on a person's life.

HANDLING RELATIONSHIPS ON THE JOB

On the job, good relationship skills are often as important as good work skills. Some estimates say that almost 85 percent of people who are fired lose their job because they can't get along with others. As a worker, you have two basic relationships. One is with the boss; the other is with fellow employees.

Understanding Your Boss

A work supervisor actually has two basic responsibilities. The first is to get work done. The second is to take care of workers' needs. Often these responsibilities conflict.

Gretchen thought about her boss's position when she needed time off for a personal matter. She knew that if their project was held up because she couldn't finish her job on time, her supervisor would be held accountable. Gretchen took off only the time she needed and worked especially hard to finish her work by the deadline.

Although most bosses care about their employees' personal lives, the job is still critical to them. If work doesn't get done, businesses can't survive. People can lose their jobs. In order to meet their many responsibilities, bosses count on employees to show up, do the work as scheduled, and keep absences to a minimum. Bosses appreciate and reward those who make their job as supervisor less stressful.

Getting Along with Coworkers

Have you ever been around people who obviously didn't want to be around each other—perhaps friends who had a fight or a sibling in conflict with a parent? Then you can appreciate the

When you help someone learn a new skill or get a job done, you benefit, too. Can you think of some ways?

Getting Along with Coworkers

- ✓ We each do our share of the work.

- ✓ We willingly help each other get the job done.

- ✓ We give credit when others do well.

- ✓ We accept credit with humility.

- ✓ We recognize each other's good qualities.

- ✓ We make light of each other's weaknesses.

- ✓ We don't gossip about each other.

- ✓ We get along even when we're not close friends.

Why do coworkers who follow these principles build an effective work team?

value of working with people who get along. Good relationships make an enjoyable job more satisfying. Unpleasant tasks are easier to handle.

This was Eduardo's experience when he started work at a small advertising firm where everyone worked well together and pitched in to help each other. One night Eduardo stayed late to finish a Web page he was designing. Two coworkers brought take-out meals and urged him to take a dinner break. Refreshed by their kindness and company, Eduardo returned to his work re-energized.

As with all relationships, getting along with coworkers takes an effort. People who are liked by their fellow employees do their part and help others willingly. They lighten the work environment with a positive attitude. They look for strengths in people and make light of weaknesses. They avoid gossip. Remember, you may not like all the people you work with, but you can get along with them if you try.

EVERYDAY ENCOUNTERS

Hardly a day goes by that you don't relate to someone you don't know well—the receptionist at a medical clinic, perhaps, or a post office clerk. Winning the cooperation of these people is a good idea. You need their help today, and you may need it again in the future. Your manner may decide whether you and the other person finish your business on a high or low note. It can even affect the entire day. A considerate response is a cost-free way to improve the quality of someone's life.

YOUR INFLUENCE

Who influences your working relationships the most? You do. Your actions affect how others act. You can take the initiative to improve a relationship. Some people let pride or insecurity get in the way of taking action. They wait for others to make the first move. A strong, confident person is willing to reach out—and enjoys the results.

SECTION 16-1 REVIEW

Check Your Understanding

1. What is a working relationship?
2. How might you identify a respectful person?
3. Why do some people have authority over others?
4. What can students do to get along well in school?
5. Give advice for building a good relationship with your boss.
6. What are three suggestions for getting along well with coworkers?
7. **Thinking Critically.** Why might it be difficult for a pleaser and a rebel to change his or her behavior?
8. **Problem Solving.** Sheena is often late for work. However, she always stays late to make up for it. When Sheena was scheduled for a pay raise, her boss said he wouldn't increase Sheena's wages until she was more punctual. Sheena thinks this is unfair. What should she do?

Teamwork and Leadership

OBJECTIVES

After studying this section, you should be able to:

- Describe the qualities of an effective team.
- Judge a group's teamwork skills.
- Predict the success of a leader, based on leadership skills and style.
- Explain the relationship between the two basic leadership tasks.
- Explain the role of followers in team success.

TERMS TO LEARN

teamwork
leader
motivate
diplomacy
parliamentary
  procedure
bylaws

A group of ball players in matching uniforms take the field. Each player is a fine athlete; each is skilled in the basics of the game. Individual talents are not enough, however. Unless they play as a team, the group may be beaten by a band of less able players.

The same is true away from the sports arena. At any given task, the people who are most successful are not only good—they are good together. Achieving that kind of harmony is the focus of this section.

TEAMWORK

Sooner or later most people join with others in some kind of group. It may be an informal gathering of people with a common interest, such as a neighborhood poetry club. It might be a formal, structured group with a set purpose, such as a city council. Some groups dissolve after achieving their goal, as when Evan's mother sat on the school board committee that chose a new principal.

Whatever their reason for existing, the most effective groups are those that function as teams. **Teamwork** is cooperating to achieve a common purpose. A choral group, a marching band, and a football squad all need teamwork to perform effectively. Less obvious, but just as necessary, is the need for teamwork in the family and at work. What marks a group as a team? A team:

- Is a small group of people who regularly interact.
- Has common goals.
- Shows loyalty, enthusiasm, and a cooperative attitude.

Teamwork skills can be learned in many ways. When you do your part to get along well with a group of friends, you practice many of the same skills that you will use when working with others on a job or committee.

- Relies on contributions from all team members.
- Consciously coordinates its activities.

Qualities of Effective Teams

Because it's based on cooperation, teamwork satisfies people's need for companionship and positive interaction. Teamwork requires that people help each other, share information, and work together for their mutual benefit.

Team members find they can accomplish more by cooperating than each could individually. Joy said, "When we used to take inventory at work, each person was assigned one section of the storeroom. It took forever and got boring fast. Now, we tackle the whole job together. Each person has a different task. It's faster because we each focus on just one job. It's more fun because we all work together."

Teamwork takes an open flow of information. Sports teams obviously need to communicate on a play before they run it. Have you ever seen a basketball player pass the ball into the bleachers because the teammate who was supposed to take the pass wasn't there? Likewise, team members in a work setting must know what is happening, what is expected of them, and what resources they have to do their jobs.

Effective teams are built on give-and-take. Each person is involved in setting goals and making decisions; each participates in team activities. Members pitch in, even when it means sacrifices. No one person dominates. Rather, the contributions of all are valued.

Team members trust, support, and rely on each other. They appreciate each person's efforts. They champion each other's ideas. This mutual support helps them work together to accomplish their goals.

Teamwork Skills

Certain skills help people become valuable team members. *Cooperation* is probably most important. Working with and for one another is essential. Team players are strong contributors who help strengthen each other.

Effective *communication* skills allow information to flow freely among group members. Workers must know how to speak and listen, as Clay recalled with these words: "At the last place I worked, we didn't have a system for telling people what was going on. Sometimes two of us would find ourselves doing the same job! In this job, we all meet for ten minutes at the shift change and make sure everyone is clear about what's happening and what needs to be done."

Teams have a hard time functioning if they can't settle conflicts. Disagreements are inevitable when people work together.

Team members must use the skills of *conflict resolution* in order to get past difficulties and make progress.

Unselfishness is the hallmark of the best team members. Members are committed to the team's goals and do their best to help accomplish them. Getting credit for their contribution is less important than seeing the team succeed.

LEADERSHIP

Victoria loved to write. As a reporter for the school newspaper, she never missed a deadline and often stayed late to help with layout. She took time to help other staff members find information and solve problems. To Victoria's pleasure, she was named editor of the paper her senior year.

Victoria's devotion to the paper made her a leader on the staff. A **leader** is a person who guides or influences others. Like most

People admire those who support each other. While in their homerun race, Mark McGuire and Sammy Sosa gave credit to their teams and to each other. How did that make them strong leaders as well as team players?

Balancing Work & Family Life

THE CHALLENGE —

Coordinating Multiple Schedules

It's tough to keep track of family members when they're running in different directions. Families must make time for each other so they can communicate and stay healthy. Spending time together is easier when family members coordinate their schedules.

How You Can Help

To help your family organize schedules and spend more time together as a result, try following these tips:

- Keep a family calendar that's easy to read at a glance. Assign a different color pen to each family member. Ask them to use that color when writing appointments on the calendar.

- Encourage family members to tell each other when plans change.

- Create a family message system. Leave notes on the refrigerator or in a basket on the counter. Be sure all family members check daily for messages.

- Offer to help those who need it. Consider swapping favors. A teen could make brownies for a sister's party if she provides a ride to basketball practice. Be sure to give plenty of notice.

---

leaders who emerge from within the group, Victoria was highly involved with her team. As a major contributor, she was recognized as a leader by the other student reporters and advisors.

Leaders go by many names; captain, president, manager, and chairperson are a few. Whatever their title, leaders set the tone and direction of the group.

Leadership can be practiced at many different levels. Very high levels of leadership are shown by the president of a country and the officers of an international corporation. The student body president and the principal are leaders in your school. Even in a friendship between two people, one may take a leadership role, setting an example for the other and giving direction to their activities.

Depending on the situation, a leader may show any combination of useful traits. Some general skills, however, are useful to all leaders.

When students practice leadership, they prepare themselves for greater leadership roles in society. What might some of those be?

Technical Skills

The first type of skill good leaders possess is technical skill. A technical skill is knowledge about how to do specific tasks and the ability to do them. For example, Phil had to know how to use a cash register and balance the cash drawer when he was put in charge of the volunteer workers at the museum gift shop.

Katrina became the head coach of a softball team of seven-year-old girls when the other coach quit. An experienced softball player herself, Katrina had the skills to teach her players how to throw and hit the ball and run the bases.

People Skills

Leaders must be able to work effectively with people. They **motivate** others, or make people *want* to do things. They must also be able to communicate and resolve conflicts.

Nanette is the glue that holds her group of friends together. When an argument between two friends threatened their relationship, Nan stepped in: "Is this more important than the good times you've shared and the ones ahead too? Our group wouldn't be the same without you both. How can we help?" Nan appealed to each friend as an individual and as part of the group. She gave them reason to stay together. Her ability to work with people and help solve their problems makes her a natural leader. Can you think of other situations that would test Nan's skills?

Thinking and Planning Skills

Dealing with ideas is part of leadership. Good leaders are able to think critically and creatively and to make plans. As president of his school's computer club, Tim is responsible for setting the program of each meeting. He chooses projects suggested by club members or thinks of activities himself. Sometimes he must arrange for a guest speaker. This willingness to use his thinking skills has led members to call Tim the best president they've ever had.

CHAPTER 16   Working with Others   **337**

Communication Skills

Leadership Skills

Management Skills

Thinking Skills

Qualities of Leadership

What makes a good leader? The more of these qualities you show, the better your leadership skills:

✓ I enjoy working with all types of people.

✓ I get satisfaction from motivating others.

✓ I treat others with courtesy and respect.

✓ I am friendly and make it a point to learn people's names.

✓ I try to do my best.

✓ I am honest, sincere, and dependable.

✓ I have enthusiasm, a positive attitude, and a good sense of humor.

✓ I accept responsibility.

✓ I try to make thoughtful decisions.

✓ I have good oral and written communication skills.

✓ I am well organized.

✓ I treat others as I would like to be treated.

Using Your Skills

Think of a leadership position you'd like to hold. This can be in your family, with friends, on a sports team, or in a club. Identify at least three of the qualities listed above that you would need in this position. Do you have these qualities? Plan specific ways to develop or strengthen the qualities you've identified.

Leadership Styles

The way in which leaders use their skills is called leadership style. The three general styles of leadership are participatory, directive, and free rein.

With *participatory leadership,* the leader and group members work together to make plans and decisions about what they will do. Under this type of leadership, group members tend to show interest in their work and are most apt to become a team. Because they have input, they are enthusiastic about the group. They work with or without the leader's supervision. This type of leadership is most effective when group members are self-disciplined and responsible.

A *directive* leader sets the group's goals, and plans and controls all of its activities. Directive leadership is most useful when people must be told what to do or jobs must be done in a hurry. In stressful times or in emergencies, directive leadership is often best. If used inappropriately, however, members may be less motivated due to their lack of input.

A leader using the *free-rein* style allows the group members to work on their own to plan and organize their work. The leader only participates when asked direct questions. Free-rein leadership may be the best style to use when group members are trying to develop specific skills or when creative thinking is needed. A group of self-motivated people who have developed into an effective team may benefit from this type of leadership.

LEADERSHIP TASKS

Leaders of groups have two major tasks. The first is to accomplish the work of the group. The second is to promote teamwork. These two equally important tasks sometimes complement each other and sometimes conflict.

Accomplishing the Work

To get a team to accomplish its work, the leader motivates members to reach their goal. A leader must also coordinate schedules, solve problems, and manage resources.

Stuart was chairman of the committee to build sets for the school's spring play. After the designs were complete, Stuart planned how he and his team could finish the work by the play director's deadline. He made up and scheduled work crews based on members' skills and other commitments. He called to remind people when they were needed. Stuart made sure carpentry supplies had arrived and plenty of paint and brushes were available. When work sessions started to turn into social gatherings, Stuart urged people to stick to the task at hand.

What can a leader accomplish alone? Not very much. The leader needs a team with skills and dedication to get any job done well.

Promoting Teamwork

The second task of a leader takes social skills. The leader needs to increase the sense of team spirit and personal worth that people feel. By building good relationships, people want to put forth the effort it takes to reach team goals. Members who don't get along or feel good about their participation are apt to leave the group.

Even as Stuart was pushing committee members to finish the sets on time, he wanted to make them feel important and essential to the effort. He praised their work and let them know how glad he was for their help. His appreciation and enthusiasm motivated members to do their best.

Stuart showed skill in achieving both leadership tasks. He did this in part by using **diplomacy**, the ability to handle sit-

uations without upsetting the people involved. As a diplomatic person, Stuart used words in ways that didn't offend. For example, he said, "We only have one more day to get this done. What can I do to help you?" rather than, "Haven't you got that done yet?" Stuart also used qualifiers when he spoke. He began statements with phrases like "I think" and "It seems to me" to avoid sounding too judgmental.

FOLLOWERS

No team can exist, of course, without members, or followers. The right combination of leaders and followers is what makes a team effective. What's more, a team must have more followers than leaders in order to work well.

Everyone—even a leader—is a follower at times. A leader in one group is probably a follower in another. The leader of the debate team may be a follower in the math club.

A group's success depends as much, or more, on followers as it does on leaders. Without good followers, leaders accomplish little or nothing, unless they do all the work themselves. Leading a group is time-consuming. When followers are willing workers, a leader is more free to manage. The group can be more productive and is more likely to develop into a team.

Focus On ...

Effective Meetings

The work of a group, especially a formal one, often begins in meetings. Committees may be established and assignments made. People who have been given tasks may report on their progress.

To use meeting time effectively, many groups use rules of order, or **parliamentary procedure**. Parliamentary procedure is a method of running a meeting so that things go smoothly and all points of view are heard. *Robert's Rules of Order* is a widely recognized book that gives a detailed description of parliamentary procedure.

Another set of rules can help a group run an effective meeting. These are called **bylaws**. A set of bylaws is written and accepted by the group as the authority on how the group functions. Bylaws might tell how new members are brought in and officers selected.

USING YOUR KNOWLEDGE

The environmental group that Regan started a few years ago has grown from a handful of concerned citizens to several dozen. Meetings are getting disorganized as members try to plan activities and voice opinions. How can Regan help her club run its business more efficiently?

Team members must be good followers. What would the marching band's formations be like if each member decided to be a leader instead of a follower?

Many people prefer to be followers. They may lack the leader's time or commitment to the goal or may want to contribute in a specific way. That's fine. Whatever their involvement, however, all members must participate for the group to succeed.

Some people join a group only for what they can get out of it. They have fun but contribute little. These people are quickly recognized—and resented—by the rest of the group. When you join a group, plan to do your share. Each person works less when all work together.

Another common problem for groups is that some people are quick to criticize the leader, but would never accept a leadership role themselves. Many leaders are volunteers. Finding people to assume a leader's duties without pay can be difficult. How many people would stay in that role if they heard only criticism for their efforts? When you see people freely giving many hours to an organization, show them your appreciation. If you want change, volunteer your time and be part of the solution.

SECTION 16-2 REVIEW

Check Your Understanding

1. What are four traits that indicate a group is a team?
2. What are the benefits of cooperation?
3. What skills does an effective team member need?
4. Identify three types of leadership skills.
5. What does it mean to motivate people?
6. What is diplomacy?
7. Why are followers important in a group?
8. **Thinking Critically.** Can a group with a weak leader be an effective team? Explain.
9. **Problem Solving.** Jeri has enjoyed her two years working on the high school yearbook. Now other staff members are urging her to submit her name for the editor's job. Jeri is flattered by their support but isn't sure she wants the responsibility. What should Jeri do?

Chapter 16
Review and Activities

CHAPTER SUMMARY

- Good working relationships are based on respectful and courteous behavior.
- Certain people have authority over others in order to promote safety and help things run more smoothly.
- Learning when to accept authority and how to question it helps people deal with authority effectively.
- Appropriate behavior helps all students take advantage of the opportunities school has to offer.
- At work, good relationships with your boss and coworkers can be just as important as good work skills.
- You can make daily encounters with people more pleasant and rewarding.
- Effective teams develop certain skills that help team members work together.
- Leaders guide or influence others through practical skills, the ability to work with people, and thinking and planning skills.
- The success of any group depends both on leaders and followers.

REVIEW QUESTIONS

Section 16-1
1. What factors contribute to good working relationships? Why is each helpful?
2. Describe a useful attitude toward people with authority.
3. Does rebelliousness have any value? Explain your answer.
4. Why is getting along in school important?
5. What problem can bosses face in meeting their two main duties? How can employees help?
6. Why is getting along with coworkers important?

Section 16-2
1. Why should a team member be a good communicator?
2. Give examples of how a teacher might use general leadership skills.
3. Which leadership style would you choose when caring for a group of five-year-olds? Why?
4. How does diplomacy help leaders accomplish their two tasks?

BECOMING A PROBLEM SOLVER

1. Lara is leading a committee that is planning the homecoming dance and other events. After two meetings, they have gotten nowhere. Committee members don't agree on anything. Each has personal ideas to promote and won't accept others. Meetings have ended with yelling and even one person walking out. What should Lara do?

2. Michael is the president of his school's pep club. After years of lackluster leadership, membership and student interest in the club are down. What can Michael do to revive the club?

THINKING CRITICALLY

1. **Recognizing Alternatives.** Why are some people difficult to work with? What can be done to get along with these people?
2. **Problem Solving.** How should you react to people who misuse their authority?
3. **Identifying Cause and Effect.** Why do some people become pleasers and some rebels?
4. **Recognizing Assumptions.** How much of a role do you think popularity plays in leadership?

MAKING CURRICULUM CONNECTIONS

1. **Language Arts.** With your class, make a list of adjectives that describe effective team members and leaders. Then narrow the list to the top ten most useful traits for each.
2. **Art.** Create a poster that illustrates qualities of a good working relationship.
3. **Civics.** Using *Robert's Rules of Order* or another reference, create a sample agenda for the business meeting of a school club.

APPLYING YOUR KNOWLEDGE

1. List several ways you can develop a working relationship with someone you work with in your community.
2. Working in teams, demonstrate to the class the different types of leadership styles.
3. Hold a class meeting to discuss upcoming class activities. Use parlimentary procedure.

Family & Community Connections

1. Make a list of community groups that students could join. Discuss how each community group operates.

2. Many working relationships in the community have been replaced by technology. For example, automatic teller machines have replaced some bank tellers. Make a list of examples where technology has replaced human contact. What are the advantages and disadvantages of these situations? Do you think some people are more receptive to this technology than others are? Explain your answers.

Chapter 17

Relating to Older Adults

"It's not how old you are, but how you are old."
(Marie Dressler)

IN YOUR OWN WORDS

What is the difference between these two?

The Aging Process

OBJECTIVES

After studying this section, you should be able to:

- Explain two general theories on aging.
- Predict physical, mental, social, and emotional changes that older adults are likely to experience.
- Assess the impact of ageism.
- Recommend ways teens can better relate to older adults.
- Explain the merits of teen-older adult relationships.

TERMS TO LEARN

gerontology
disengagement
chronic diseases
ageism

One birthday card defines old age as "ten years older than we are." This message contains some truth as well as humor. With longer life spans and changing roles, people don't "get old" as fast as they used to. Traditional images of older adults are expanding. An older adult today may be a college student, athlete, or fast-food worker.

The expanded life span has also caused the older population in America to grow. As people born during the "baby boom" of the 1940s and 1950s reach retirement age, those numbers will increase even more rapidly.

Due to these two developments, older people are very likely to be part of your life—as educators, coworkers, neighbors, family, and more. Your understanding of this generation will increase if you have some idea of what it means to grow older.

THE THIRD AGE

A new way of looking at aging defines the period of life after age fifty as the Third Age. The first 25 years were devoted to developing as a person and the second 25 to career and family. The next 25 years—or more—focus on creative learning and personal exploration. These latter years can be productive and healthy when people make that happen.

Because the mature years can last so long, a single description of what people are like during this time doesn't fit everyone. People in their fifties and sixties are far from elderly. On the other hand, some eighty-year-olds are more vibrant than those much younger. The fact is people handle aging differently—for many reasons. Although aging brings change, for many people in the Third Age the effects may be hardly noticeable for a long time.

THEORIES ON AGING

Aging is a natural life process. The study of the aging process, or **gerontology** (jair-un-TAHL-uh-jee), has helped people understand the problems and rewards of growing older.

Two general theories sum up different approaches to aging. The first is the *activity* theory, which says, "Use it or lose it." In other words, active, involved people cope with aging more easily than do less active people. Physical, mental, and social skills remain strong through frequent use. Those who don't exercise—their bodies and their minds—eventually can't.

The second theory is called *disengagement*. **Disengagement** is withdrawal from others and from activity. This theory states that elderly people naturally become more solitary and sedentary. Social contacts are

Improving with Age

The Third Age can be the best, healthiest, and most productive time in a person's life. Research now shows that many stereotypes about mature adults are wrong.

Only 3 percent of adults age sixty-five to eighty-four are in nursing homes.

Computers

Retirement

Mature adults make up 70 percent of those traveling for pleasure in the U.S.

Mature adults spend more hours per week using computers than other age categories.

Travel

rarer and less important. Physical activity tends to diminish as the body weakens. Elderly people begin to focus more on themselves than on others.

Disengagement may seem like a logical progression as people age. Studies have shown, however, that disengaged people are less happy, healthy, and satisfied in almost every area of life than those who remain active and involved.

These theories appear to contradict each other. However, given the broad age range of older adults, it's possible that both theories are true. When older people stay inter-ested and active, life is healthier and rewarding. Much later, as they grow nearer death, disengagement may be a way of preparing to leave family and friends.

PHYSICAL CHANGES

The physical effects of aging are usually the most apparent ones. In general the body begins to change slowly. It seems to "shrink" as the tissues connecting the bones flatten and compress. Reactions and reflexes slow because the body doesn't replace old cells with new ones as quickly as

Health

What do you see that supports today's view of older citizens?

Of Americans over age sixty-five, 85 percent report their health as excellent to good.

Lifespan

A sixty-five-year-old today can expect to live another 17 years.

Adults over age fifty-five control $1 trillion in spending each year.

Money

As people age, they react to this time of life in different ways. Some people focus on the past, thinking about what was and what might have been. Others live for today, enjoying time with family and friends.

before. Many internal organs and systems work at a lower level. Muscles may become weaker, and bones break more easily. The senses don't respond as they do in younger people. Some loss of hearing and vision is common.

Some physical changes threaten good eating habits, especially in the elderly. A dulled sense of taste or smell can lead to a lack of interest in food. As a result, some people don't eat enough. Others try to add flavor by salting food heavily, leading to high blood pressure and heart disease. Tooth loss can interfere with eating enjoyment. Elderly people often have smaller amounts of saliva, making chewing and swallowing difficult. Physical problems

may make shopping for and preparing nutritious foods a challenge.

Dietary needs also change. Older people tend to need fewer calories, but greater amounts of some nutrients, than before. For example, increasing calcium intake can help prevent broken bones.

Chronic diseases, illnesses or conditions that occur repeatedly or never go away, are a fact of life for many older adults. Examples are arthritis, high blood pressure, and heart conditions. These illnesses become more common as the body becomes less able to deal with the stresses of aging.

Maintaining Physical Health

Some physical changes are unavoidable in older adults. Nonetheless, people can do a great deal to maintain their physical abilities. *Exercise* plays a part. Properly done, exercise is as beneficial and no more dangerous to older adults than to younger people. *Good nutrition* is also important. A poor diet worsens many physical problems. *Attitude*, too, can have a major influence on physical ability. When people realize that aging is not a disease and sickness is not inevitable, they are more likely to work at maintaining their health.

MENTAL CHANGES

The aging process affects thought processes also. The mind often slows, just as the body does.

Older adults sometimes have trouble with memory. Memory includes three functions: receiving information into the brain; storing it in short-term memory; and storing it in long-term memory. To recall and use information requires an organized effort from all three. In younger people, this interaction is fast and easy. In most older adults, all three parts of memory still function, but information may not travel between them as well. This is why older adults may have trouble calling up information quickly.

Whatever older adults lose in speed, they often make up for in thoroughness. Logic and understanding often improve. Older adults who are students may work longer and harder to learn new material than they did when they were younger, but they tend to learn more thoroughly.

Years after retiring as an assembly line supervisor, George Wysocki is still consult-

Tips & TECHNIQUES

Reminiscing. Reminiscing is more than recalling "the good old days." Focusing on happier times can bring pleasure to the speaker, especially as relief for current troubles. Reflecting on the past also helps older adults see meaning in their lives. To listeners, stories of past events offer insight and first-person accounts of history that they have only read about. Asking an older adult positive questions like these can spark a flood of memories:

- Who was your best friend? Why?
- What was the toughest decision you ever made? Did you make the right choice?
- When was the happiest time of your life?
- What was it like being a teen in the forties (or another decade)?
- What were some local, national, and world issues when you were young? How did they affect your life?

Try It Out. Arrange to visit an older adult. Make a list of questions and topics to explore. Conduct the interview, allowing time for digression and storytelling. (You might get permission to preserve your conversation on a cassette tape or videotape.) Write an essay describing some of the facts and insights you've gained.

Some older adults begin second careers after retirement. Selling original and family recipes over the Internet keeps this woman's mind active and alert.

ed when new methods are needed to improve productivity. George needs some time to completely understand the problem. Once he does, however, his experience and long-practiced reasoning skills help him make valuable suggestions.

Staying Mentally Healthy

The loss of mental abilities is not a necessary effect of aging. The greatest declines in thinking skills are probably due to outside factors, including depression, grief, poor health, poverty, and a lack of effort.

As with physical skills, older people use mental exercise to keep thinking skills sharp. Their activities should require active, not passive, participation. Some older people join clubs or become politically active. Others take part-time jobs, continue their education, or serve as volunteers. Many groups and activities offer discount rates to older adults and encourage their participation.

SOCIAL CHANGES

Older adults may see differences in roles and relationships. As some roles become less important, new ones often develop.

The greatest role change for most older adults is the loss of the work role through retirement. This loss is most difficult for those whose sense of worth is tied to their career. Men in particular can have trouble adjusting.

Friendships often gain importance as people age. Older adults tend to have more friends than any other age group except teens and young adults. One of the pleasures of being older is having more time for friends. As other family members die and grown children move away, friendships can become especially necessary and rewarding.

Older adults tend to keep the same types of social lives and interests as they did in younger days. People who have been less socially active continue in this pattern. For more outgoing older citizens, community centers and clubs offer companionship and sharing of interests, from cards to bird watching. When transportation is a problem, younger friends and special buses can fill the need.

Grandparenting

One significant role acquired by many older adults is that of grandparent. This role has become more important as people live longer. Over half of all older adults have great-grandchildren, making four-generation families fairly common.

Involved grandparents can enrich a child's life. Older adults give children a sense of family roots. They provide a sense of stability and safety, especially if divorce or other problems upset family life. Many grandparents find pleasure, satisfaction, and comfort in the role.

EMOTIONAL CHANGES

When Lurleen's husband of 42 years died, she thought she would, too. "I'd already lost so much," she said. "When my eyes started getting bad, I had to take early retirement. Then I had to stop driving at night. So many friends have died, and some have moved into nursing homes. I've started feeling lonely and useless."

Like Lurleen, some elderly people are depressed by the less pleasant realities of aging. Unless they find new meaning in their lives, they risk falling into despair. Medical treatment is available for people with this problem.

Preserving Emotional Health

Older adults who adapt to new roles find satisfaction. This alone seems to slow down the aging process.

A tendency toward disengagement must be balanced with activity and involvement. Contact with friends and family members is one of the best ways to maintain emotional health. When younger people talk to them and show appreciation for their wisdom and experience, older people remember that they still have something to offer. Older adults also need opportunities to talk

The often frantic pace of earlier years can lighten after retirement. Having time for hobbies and friends is a welcomed change for many older people.

Career Success Stories

Felix Morales: *Activities Director*

"I think I've always loved being around older people. I come from a big family, and our gatherings always included elderly aunts, uncles, and grandparents. It's just natural for me to enjoy them. In high school, I joined a group of students who visited a senior center each month. We played games with the residents, helped with craft classes, and just talked. A career involving older people was just the next step for me.

"When I was first hired as a nursing home activities director, they didn't offer any exercise classes, so I decided to start one. I used music from the '40s and '50s that I thought they would like. I planned exercises that could be done seated. At first only a few residents came to class, but eventually I had a room full. One woman couldn't lift her arms above her shoulders when class started, but eventually she could raise her arms over her head. Everyone felt more energetic, and even the staff noticed. The classes became so popular that I started offering them several times a week.

"Getting new residents involved can be a challenge at first. If I can spark an interest in even one activity, they start to meet people and want to be involved. I plan a variety of activities so there's something for everyone. These are my friends, so helping them stay happy makes me feel successful."

CAREER PROFILE

Education and training: bachelor's degree preferred

Starting salary range: $12-33,000

Job prospects: private and public nursing homes; hospitals; extended-care facilities

Important qualities: communication skills; good interpersonal skills; creativity; patience

Plan Ahead

You can learn about careers through volunteer work. With your class, list volunteer opportunities in your area. For each one, list associated careers that could be explored. What skills could you also gain?

about the past. Reminiscing helps them sort through their experiences and make sense of their lives.

IMAGES OF AGING

In some societies, old age is anticipated as a time for reflection and for receiving respect from younger generations. In others, it is feared as "the beginning of the end." Which of these attitudes prevails where you live?

To answer that question, look at the advertisements that use young adults to sell "fun" items from cars to potato chips. Count the products in supermarkets that promise to hide the gray, reduce wrinkles, and cover age spots. Youth is seen as desirable; aging generally isn't.

Progress is being made against this attitude, yet some people are still biased against older adults. They feel that older people cannot be as alert, intelligent, and capable as younger people. This belief is called **ageism** (A-jiz-um). Like any prejudice, ageism unfairly views all people as alike, instead of as distinct individuals. Ageism prevents older adults from living their lives to the fullest. It also denies others the chance to benefit from their talents and experience.

Moving Beyond Stereotypes

Understanding the aging process can help you understand older adults. You know the facts that disprove the stereotypes. You see that older adults are not all alike, any more than teens are.

Spending time with older people also gives a truer picture than stereotypes do. Teens have many opportunities to get involved in the lives of older adults. Perhaps you have older family members

Aging no longer means the rocking chair. Many senior citizens today feel healthier in retirement than they have for years. Why might that be true?

Older people provide a link to the past. When you spend time with them, you can learn facts about family history and past events. If you don't gather this information, who will?

living with you or near you. Would an older adult in your neighborhood appreciate your help and companionship? Your local or regional Agency on Aging can tell you what needs exist in your community. You might also ask about volunteering at a nursing home or hospital.

Older people have much to offer. Years of experience give them a unique perspective on life. When older adults talk about the past, teens can see how the world has changed and why. Listening to older adults recall challenges they have faced can provide insight into your own situation and give you new approaches to problems.

Older people can benefit from knowing you. Younger people can help older ones stay active, alert, and in touch with the community. Teens can provide a practical service, such as running errands and mowing the lawn. Regular visits can also give older adults a sense of security. They know they can count on someone in case of illness or accident.

SECTION 17-1 REVIEW

Check Your Understanding

1. What is disengagement theory?
2. How do eating habits often change in older adults?
3. In what ways do many older adults improve mentally?
4. What is the greatest social change for most older adults?
5. What can a teen gain from relationships with older adults?
6. **Thinking Critically.** Why do you think different societies hold different views on aging?
7. **Problem Solving.** Bailey is worried about her grandmother. The older woman has always been interested in the world around her but now has stopped taking the daily paper and no longer watches the news. She has dropped out of several clubs, so she doesn't go out much any more. What should Bailey do?

Concerns of Older Adults

OBJECTIVES

After studying this section, you should be able to:

- Assess the financial picture that many older adults face.
- Explain how medical care can present problems for older adults.
- Compare housing options available to older adults.
- Describe some primary safety concerns of older adults.

TERMS TO LEARN

fixed income
congregate housing
elder abuse

It's an obvious statement, but often forgotten: people are in this world together. What affects one generation eventually affects all. A problem solved for one group lightens the load on others. The reverse is also true. As you explore the following issues facing older adults, think of their impact on families and others of younger years—you and your classmates included. While these concerns are not problems for every older person, they are common enough to merit a closer look.

FINANCIAL CONCERNS

Louis and Anna, a married couple in their seventies, keep a close eye on their checkbook. Anna explained, "We have Social Security and our pension and a little savings. It's not the most comfortable living, but enough to get us by from month to month."

Many older adults share Anna and Louis' situation. They live on a **fixed income**, monthly payments that do not change whether or not expenses increase. This income is usually only a fraction of what a working person earns. People without other financial resources often have a hard time making ends meet. In fact, an estimated one-fourth of all older adults live in poverty. Women, members of minority groups, and those over age eighty-five are most likely to be poor.

Fears about the future can contribute to the problem. Since they can't predict how long they will live, some older adults live more frugally than necessary to save

Building Character

Caring: A Quality That Counts

Have you ever seen someone hurt and dejected, and wished you could take the pain away? Caring is concern for and interest in someone else, giving that person attention and support. Caring comes from liking people. A caring person truly enjoys reaching out to others. A teen can show caring by:

- Phoning a grandfather frequently to see how he is doing.
- Listening sympathetically when an older aunt talks about her most recent physical problems.
- Inviting a friend whose parents don't get along to a quiet family dinner.
- Taking a younger brother to a dental appointment when their mother is ill.

QUESTIONS

1. What rewards can come to a person who is caring?
2. Why might a lack of caring lead to conflict?
3. Describe a situation in which you showed caring.

---

money for later years. They may endanger their health by skimping on food, heating, and other basic needs. Lack of money can also be a major obstacle in receiving good health care.

Continuing to Work

Many people continue to work after "retiring." Some choose part-time work or jobs that are less physically or mentally demanding than those they held before. Many older adults enjoy the social benefits—the companionship and purpose the job provides—but most need or want the extra income. Pensions, Social Security payments, and personal savings may not be adequate and the wages are welcome.

As Clarence said, "I missed being with people after I retired, so I teach part-time at a vocational school now. I enjoy being around the students, and the paycheck makes my life quite a bit more comfortable."

As the number of retired people grows, the nation's Social Security system is expected to be strained. More people may need to work to make ends meet. Younger people are taking a serious look at how to start planning early for financial security in their older years.

MEDICAL CARE

The aging process and chronic illness take their toll on the body. Many older adults need more medical care, which can be very expensive, at a time that income is apt to be low. Although such government programs as Medicare help pay expenses, many older adults cannot afford adequate health care.

Over-medication is another problem. The dosage of medicine a person needs can change with age. People with several health problems can have different doctors prescribing medicines. One study found that the average older patient takes 13 different kinds of medicine a year. Some drugs are dangerous when mixed. Older adults may have trouble remembering which medicine to take and how much. These hazards make it especially important that doctors be informed about all medications an older person is taking and any negative side effects.

LIVING ARRANGEMENTS

Like teens, most older adults cherish their independence. The ability to care for themselves is basic to their sense of self-worth. Safety, however, is a greater worry as people age. Injuries are a major cause of death among people age sixty-five and older, and many of these occur in the home. Some simple steps can make housing safe for older people, especially those with disabilities. Furniture can be rearranged to create clear, easy traffic patterns, and skid-resistant strips can be applied to bathtubs and the backs of rugs.

Other, more extensive adaptations may be needed to meet changes in physical health. When Estelle began using a wheelchair, her kitchen was remodeled so she could reach the sink and appliances. Cabinets and storage spaces were lowered. Railings were installed in her bathroom.

For some older people, the death of a spouse or failing health prevents them from managing alone. Their choices in new living arrangements depend on their resources, their family, and their needs. Options include:

- **Shared housing.** Older adults may rent out rooms in their homes. Sometimes the renter is younger and helps with household tasks.

As people grow older, they may need more medical care. Why would this need cause problems for many aging citizens?

If an older person has health problems, the care and support of other people become important. What advantages are linked to moving in with other family members? Are there disadvantages?

- **Congregate housing.** In **congregate housing**, a group of people live in the same building and share meals and some living space while having their own rooms for privacy.
- **Living with family.** Older parents who can no longer manage alone may move in with an adult child's family. This arrangement takes adjustment on all sides. The parent has to adapt to being dependent on the adult child. The adult child must adapt to being responsible for the parent. All concerned lose some

degree of freedom, which may be offset by strengthened family ties.

- **Retirement communities.** These are housing units designed to meet the needs of older residents. Units are often arranged around a communal building where residents can meet for meals and social activities. Many retirement communities provide maintenance services and transportation to nearby health facilities and shopping centers.

Older couples often depend on each other. Many are happier together. Retirement housing that provides support services may enable them to stay together as long as possible.

Focus On ...

Choosing a Nursing Home

Selecting a nursing home for an older relative is a challenge for many families. Should your family ever face this responsibility, you can have more confidence if you:

- Discuss possible choices with the older adult's physician.
- Ask people who have relatives in a certain home for their impression.
- Choose a home that is near enough to visit.
- Meet with the administrative staff to find out about costs and services.
- Inspect the rooms, looking at size and attractiveness. Halls and other common areas should be clean and odor-free.
- Eat a meal at the home. Look for clean kitchen and dining areas and sanitary preparation and serving practices. Meals should be appealing and nutritious.
- Notice the residents. Do they appear clean, well cared for, and generally satisfied with the home?
- Observe how staff members treat the residents. Are they kind, capable, and respectful?
- Learn whether professionally staffed exercise and physical therapy facilities are available.
- View the home's recreational facilities and observe some activities.
- Make certain that special needs can be accommodated.

USING YOUR KNOWLEDGE

Geraldo's grandfather could no longer stay in his home alone, but his family had heard that the only nursing home close by wasn't good. What should the family do?

Nursing Homes

A nursing home may be the only option for a frail elderly person who needs skilled care. The percentage of older people living in nursing homes is small but rising. This increase is a result of several factors: the longer life span of women; a greater number of older adults who have no one to care for them; and an increase in the number of older people who have chronic illnesses.

Nursing homes vary greatly. Some resemble dormitories. One or two residents share a small room and bath. Common eating and entertainment facilities are provided. Others consist of small cottages or apartments. Some are designed for people needing a great deal of care and supervision.

The world becomes a better place when people look out for each other. Do you know any older people who could use your help and friendship?

Others are small communities of basically self-reliant adults. Regardless of services, the cost of a nursing home can be very high.

The decision to place a family member in a nursing home is not an easy one for most families. Lara's mother didn't want to go to a nursing home. Lara felt guilty, thinking she was neglecting her responsibilities as a daughter, but she couldn't give the care that her mother needed. In this case, a carefully selected nursing home was the only responsible choice.

SAFETY

Older adults are often very concerned with personal safety. Aware of their lessening physical abilities, they may feel vulnerable to crime and violence.

Elder Abuse

A growing concern in society today is **elder abuse**. Most often this is physical abuse directed at aging people by their adult children.

Caring for an aging parent—especially one who is ill—can create stress, a known trigger of violent reactions in some people. Those who take care of older relatives need a supportive network of people. All family members should share in the care, if possible. Community organizations that specifically address elders' needs are another resource. Anyone who observes this type of abuse must take action to end it.

Crime

According to U.S. Justice Department statistics, younger people are more likely to be victimized by crime than those age sixty-five and older. The effects of crime, however, can be far more destructive to an older person's quality of life.

Crime has a ripple effect among older adults, who are already sensitive to being targets. Seeing friends victimized by a crime, their own fear grows. Some refuse to leave their homes. Others move to a different neighborhood where they feel more secure. In reality, they may be less safe in unfamiliar surroundings.

Loss due to crime may hit older adults more sharply than others. The theft of $50 may be much more serious to a person on a fixed income than to a working person. If a television set is stolen, a homebound older adult may lose an only link to the outside world. Physical injuries received during a crime can be life threatening. An older body doesn't heal quickly.

RESOLVING THE ISSUES

As the older population increases, it's making its voice heard. Lawmakers and social agencies are working to resolve the concerns of older adults. The issues are complicated, however. So are the answers.

As with any social situation, not all solutions lie in government. Individuals need to care for each other. By taking some of the actions suggested in this chapter, you can improve the situation of the older people around you. Perhaps someday someone will do the same for you.

SECTION 17-2 REVIEW

Check Your Understanding

1. Why is a fixed income often a problem for older adults?
2. Why is getting adequate health care a particular challenge as people age?
3. What arrangements exist for older adults who can no longer live alone?
4. Describe the difficulty families may face when deciding to place an older relative in a nursing home.
5. What is elder abuse?
6. **Thinking Critically.** How do you think society's attitude toward aging affects the problems older adults face?
7. **Problem Solving.** Sheldon must find a nursing home for his father. One is close enough to his home that he could visit daily. The cost is low, but it isn't very clean and it seems to lack enough staff for the number of residents. Sheldon has more confidence in another home, but it's in a neighboring town and the cost is almost beyond his means. What should Sheldon do?

CHAPTER SUMMARY

- Teens may find opportunities to become involved in the lives of older adults.
- Older adults and teens can make valuable contributions to each other's lives.
- The physical effects of aging generally involve a lessening of ability.
- With old age may come memory problems, but also more thoroughness and insight.
- Older adults need to accept social changes in order to avoid depression.
- Even older adults who work after retirement may live on low incomes that make meeting basic needs difficult.
- Expense and over-medicating are two potential medical care problems for older people.
- Many older people can live independently. Modifications may be needed to make their homes safe and convenient.
- Elder abuse and crime are two safety problems faced by older adults.

REVIEW QUESTIONS

Section 17-1
1. Explain why both of the basic theories on aging may be true.
2. How does age affect thinking ability?
3. How does reminiscing benefit older people?
4. What are the consequences of ageism?
5. What can teens and older adults offer each other?

Section 17-2
1. How does the financial situation of some older adults affect their physical health?
2. Why is medication a particular concern for older adults?
3. What are some home modifications that might help an older adult live independently?
4. Briefly describe a quality nursing home.
5. What might cause elder abuse and how can it be prevented?
6. How can the concerns of older adults be addressed?

BECOMING A PROBLEM SOLVER

1. Hakeem's great-aunt seemed happy to sell her house and move into a nursing home. Six months later, she says she wants to "go home." What should Hakeem's family do?
2. Garth's father is newly retired. His mother still works. His father calls him several times a day. Garth loves his father, but the calls disrupt his work. What should Garth do?
3. Edna's elderly mother still lives in her own home, but is increasingly dependent on Edna's care. Edna's brother and sister both live in distant cities. Edna is starting to feel overburdened. What should she do?

THINKING CRITICALLY

1. **Recognizing Assumptions.** Discuss the meaning of this quote from George Bernard Shaw: "Youth is wasted on the young." Do you agree?
2. **Predicting Results.** How might understanding disengagement theory help a younger person relate to an elderly adult?
3. **Analyzing Behavior.** Dishonest and fraudulent businesses often target older adults as their victims. Why do you think this is so?
4. **Problem Solving.** What can parents, teens, and children do to promote adjustment when an older person moves in with them?
5. **Recognizing Points of View.** Why do you think some businesses prefer to hire older people as employees?

MAKING CURRICULUM CONNECTIONS

1. **Civics.** Select and research a law that relates to older adults, such as laws on mandatory retirement or drawing Social Security payments. Write a report summarizing the law and its impact on older adults and other citizens.
2. **Biology.** Research a chronic disease that affects older adults. What effects does the disease have on their bodies? Give an oral report to the class on your findings.
3. **Economics.** Using the Internet, magazines, and other sources of current news, learn about the fears regarding social security. Why are people concerned about this fund? What solutions have been suggested?

APPLYING YOUR KNOWLEDGE

1. Plan a day's menu for an older adult. Make it low in cost, easy to eat, nutritious, and appealing.
2. Write a few sentences that begin, "A grandparent is..." Share your writing in class, comparing classmates' expectations for grandparents with your own. What accounts for similarities and differences in images of grandparents?
3. Research three careers in the field of gerontology. What preparation is needed for each? What role does each play in improving life for older adults?

Family & Community Connections

1. List stereotypes that are associated with nursing homes. How do you think these stereotypes developed? How much truth is there to these statements? Discuss your ideas with your family members.

2. Find out what programs and services are available to older adults in your community. You may wish to compile a list to duplicate and share with older adults who may not be familiar with all of them.

Chapter 18

You and Your Friends

WORDS FOR THOUGHT

"You can make more friends in two months by becoming interested in other people than you can in two years of trying to get other people interested in you."
(Dale Carnegie)

IN YOUR OWN WORDS

Why is this true?

Friends in Your Life

OBJECTIVES

After studying this section, you should be able to:

- Explain what people gain from friendships.
- Distinguish the different kinds of friendships people can have.
- Demonstrate actions that promote friendship.

TERM TO LEARN

reciprocity

Have you heard anyone describe a friendship by saying "She's like a sister to me" or "We could be brothers"? Expressions like that clearly show the importance of friends: to many people, they are second only to family. It makes good sense, then, to learn how to develop and maintain these remarkable bonds.

WHAT FRIENDSHIP PROVIDES

If you were asked to explain why you are friends with a certain person, you might say, "We both like the outdoors," "I can be myself with him," or "When I have a problem, she always helps me find an answer." These are all specific examples of what friendship provides people.

More generally, people gain three important benefits from friendships:

- **Emotional support.** Friends supply comfort, reassurance, acceptance, understanding, and many other emotional needs.
- **Models for imitation.** Friends teach useful social and physical skills. They learn from each other.
- **Opportunities to practice roles.** Friends may try out different roles with each other. The teen years are a time for new experiences and growth. Friends provide an audience and feedback as you work to establish your identity.

ALL KINDS OF FRIENDS

When teens think of friends, they usually think first of people who are much like themselves. It's most comfortable to be with others who share your interests and outlook. Good friends, however, can be found in people of all types.

When you befriend a child, you have an opportunity to influence what that child becomes. Would you be proud to have a child mimic your attitudes and habits?

Friendships with Children

Friendships with children can benefit you and children both. Many families today are very busy, especially when all the adults are employed. Children who care for themselves part of the day often need an older friend.

Carl described his ten-year-old neighbor this way: "Tony is alone after school. He can't leave the house or have friends over. Sometimes he calls me for help with his homework. Once he was sure his gerbil was sick, but there wasn't anything wrong with it. Usually, there's nothing wrong at all. Tony just needs attention and someone to talk to. He feels better having me around for a while."

Younger children, always eager to grow older, look up to teens. They want to know what you like, what you do, and whether they can come too. They even try to imitate teens. This is a chance to teach them in positive ways. When you listen to children and take them seriously, you enrich their lives.

What can you gain from these friendships? First, you learn responsibility. When you're with children, they're in your care. You learn to respond to what they need. This knowledge may be useful if you decide to become a parent someday. Being with someone who admires you may inspire you to set a good example. Providing a model of behavior by doing what's right can be deeply rewarding. Your sense of self-worth, as well as the child's, grows.

Most teens have many opportunities to interact with children. Do you have younger brothers and sisters or nieces and nephews? Perhaps there are children in your neighborhood. Many schools need volunteer tutors and playground monitors. Park districts and other groups also need volunteers for children's programs. You may commit as much of your time, and of yourself, as you like.

Friendships with Adults

Just as a child can benefit from a teen's company, a teen can gain from friendship with adults. As a teen, Bernice was Lori's regular sitter. Now Lori is a teen and still profits from Bernice's experience. Bernice understands when Lori is excited about a party or upset with her parents, having gone through the same things herself not long ago. She is a trusted friend who can give Lori good advice.

As you've read, friendships with older adults can also be rewarding. Older adults can help you put this time of your life in perspective, and you can give them much appreciated companionship.

Friendship and Gender

Friendships between males and females tend to be different from those between people of the same gender. Females typically like to share personal concerns and intimate feelings with each other. Males tend to share interests and activities. A male-female friendship may combine both aspects. Such friendships often help you see issues from a different point of view.

Did you realize that no two snowflakes are exactly alike? The same is true of people, and that's what makes them interesting.

Other Backgrounds

Getting to know people of all races, nationalities, and economic levels can help you grow as a person. Think about it. Every encounter with someone is an opportunity to learn. Spending time with people who are different from you can bring insights and information that you wouldn't otherwise gain. How will you benefit? You will understand all people better. You will be more aware of how people think and feel, and why. Gaining knowledge of others and broadening your perspective makes you a more interesting person yourself.

In a world where so many diverse people mingle, it pays to be receptive to all. Your ability to relate to people of various backgrounds will serve you well in school, on the job, and in the community. Society can benefit from each effort to reach out to another in friendship. Fewer problems occur in communities where people like each other, and liking starts with understanding.

MAKING FRIENDS

How many people do you know who can sit down beside a stranger, chat breezily for a while, and walk away having made a new friend? Making friends is rarely that easy, for anyone. Shyness, low self-worth, and lack of experience make it especially hard for some people to make the first move.

If you feel unsure of yourself when making friends, remember two points. First, the other person may feel the same way. Also, you are worthy of being a friend. You have qualities and abilities that others will enjoy and benefit from. By polishing them, you become an even better candidate for friendship.

Admirable Traits

Friendships grow more readily when people are pleasant to be around and easy to get along with. What makes them that way? Here are a few ideas:

- **Positive attitude.** A positive attitude goes a long way toward building friendships. People enjoy those who look on the bright side and have a sense of humor. In contrast, self-pity and constant complaining drive people away.
- **Accepting.** No one wants to be criticized all the time. Someone who overlooks little faults is more fun to be with.
- **Caring and Courteous.** People respond to those who show they care. Just a friendly smile and a kind word make a difference. Brian recalled his first week at a new school this way: "I noticed Tim right off—because he noticed me. He saw me on my bike when I rode to school that morning and told me he liked it. I know it was a little thing, but it made me feel good."
- **Cleanliness.** People who are clean and neat are more pleasant to be around.

Tips & TECHNIQUES

Listening to Friends. As a friend describes an experience, you recall something similar that happened to you. You can't wait to tell your story. Sound familiar? In conversation, focusing on what to say next is often easier than listening to the other person, yet friendship thrives on hearing and understanding. To become a better listener:

- Listen with a purpose. Think to yourself, "I want to find out . . ."
- Relax while you listen. You'll often have time later to tell your own news.
- Encourage friends to talk. Use empathy in responding to what they've said.
- Aim to be supportive rather than "fix" your friends' problems.

Try It Out. Spend a day being conscious of how you listen to your friends. Even the best listener can become better. Think of two ways you could improve your listening skills. Put these into practice and evaluate the effects they have on your friendships.

Finding a Friendship

If you want to add friends to your life, what can you do? Here are some suggestions:

- Go where people are. Coworkers, classmates, teammates, and fellow volunteers are potential friends. Community events and school clubs offer possibilities.
- Smile and speak first to show friendliness and interest.
- Introduce yourself to people you don't know.
- Ask simple questions to start a conversation, listen to responses, and then offer feedback.
- Give compliments that are sincere.
- Give friendship time to develop. A smile today may become "hello" tomorrow and light conversation the next day. That's enough to get a friendship started.

USING YOUR KNOWLEDGE

Valerie knows plenty of people she would like to be friends with, but her efforts to win them over don't work. The friends she does have don't satisfy her. What would you suggest?

KEEPING FRIENDS

Often, building a friendship is easier than keeping it going. In fact, the oldest and strongest friendships require the most work. Long-time friends may begin to take each other for granted. Secure in the relationship, they may forget to be thoughtful.

Friendships are kept strong day by day through small gestures. Loaning a book, helping clean a room, and giving a small gift for no special reason—friends do these things for each other because they *want* to, not because they *have* to.

Of course, for friends to remain friends, each person must benefit from the relationship as well. An important quality of friendship is **reciprocity** (reh-sih-PROSS-ih-tee), or mutual exchange. Each friend gives to the relationship and also takes from it.

Each enjoys spending time together and sharing activities. Friends praise, appreciate, and listen to each other.

Friends are there for each other in bad times as well as good. When one friend experiences problems or a crisis, the other is ready with support. As Keisha said, "I wouldn't have made it through my parents' divorce without Kareem. He was there when I needed to talk and cry, even though he must have felt awkward. He'd just say, 'That's what friends are for.' "

Being friends doesn't mean always agreeing with each other. A solid relationship isn't threatened by differences of opinion. When honesty and respect provide the foundation, a friendship can withstand differences and even build upon them.

Communication Skills

Leadership Skills

Management Skills

Thinking Skills

Keeping Friendships Strong

Friendship is a delicate plant. It needs attention and care to thrive. Your friendships will flourish if you can honestly say:

✓ I accept my friends as they are. I don't try to nag them into becoming something they don't want to be.
✓ I encourage my friends in their goals and give praise when they accomplish them.
✓ I apologize when I hurt my friends and forgive them when they hurt me.
✓ I am loyal. I keep secrets and don't spread rumors.
✓ I work through problems with my friends, using the communication and conflict-resolution skills I have learned.
✓ I am reliable. My friends can count on me. I keep my promises.
✓ I willingly share my friends with others. I know that we grow through interaction with others.

Using Your Skills

Choose the statement above that describes you best and write it on a piece of paper. Choose the second-most descriptive statement and write it below the first. Continue until you have listed all the statements. What does this list tell you? What aspects of maintaining friendship do you need to work on?

SECTION 18-1 REVIEW

Check Your Understanding

1. What three benefits do friendships provide?
2. What can teens gain from friendships with adults?
3. Describe four qualities that make a person a better candidate for friendship.
4. What are five suggestions for getting a friendship started?
5. What does reciprocity mean to a friendship?
6. **Thinking Critically.** Why might some people make friends more easily than others?
7. **Problem Solving.** Melody moved to a new city before her junior year. She doesn't know anyone or where to meet people. What should Melody do to make friends?

Challenges of Friendship

OBJECTIVES

After studying this section, you should be able to:

- Recommend ways of dealing with peer pressure.
- Explain how gossip and competition affect friendship.
- Suggest strategies for handling loneliness.
- Explain the impact of a friendship that ends and how to cope with rejection.

TERMS TO LEARN

peer pressure
gossip

Having friends would be easy if nothing ever got in the way. Unfortunately, that's not real life. Friendships are challenged every day. Teen friendships may have a built-in obstacle: you have to nurture them at a time when your own personal concerns may seem like enough to handle.

Friendships are important to teens, however, because they help bridge the gap to independence. Building relationships with others means relying on family a little less, while handling life on your own a little more. Friendship is real-life education, with many issues to be approached and problems to be solved.

PEER PRESSURE

Peer pressure is an attempt to influence someone in a similar age group. It's one of the most challenging situations teens face.

When you want to join in an action or a belief because "everybody else is," you are feeling peer pressure.

Peer pressure may be positive or negative. If someone encourages you to do something helpful, that pressure is positive. Pressure that discourages you from doing something wrong is also positive. Problems come with negative peer pressure. Negative pressure pushes you to do something destructive. It might also tempt you away from the right actions.

Dawn felt negative peer pressure when she said she was training to be a peer mediator at school. "Everyone knows that's worthless," one friend hooted, "except to impress your parents." She felt positive pressure when another friend said, "Peer mediation really helped me. Don't let Donnie discourage you. You'll be a good mediator."

A teen exerts positive peer pressure when he encourages his friend to get an assignment done and even offers some help. How could negative peer pressure occur in the situation shown here?

Handling Negative Peer Pressure

Learning to handle peer pressure is a major task of the teen years. When you want to be part of the group, walking away isn't easy, especially for the sake of a principle.

What kind of person can actually stand up to negative pressures? First, you need a clear vision of what you believe. You also need the willingness to let your convictions show. You need the confidence to take a stand and not let reactions bother you. Finally, you have to want the satisfaction that comes when you do what you truly believe is right and is best for you and others.

Bowing to negative pressure may seem easier than bucking it. Who wants to face unpleasant reactions? On the other hand, who wants to live with the problems that could result? To bolster your confidence, think about this too: the people who stand up for what is right for themselves and others are the ones who are most admired in the long run.

GOSSIP

Gossip can destroy friendships. **Gossip** is conversation that includes rumors about others. You have two concerns where gossip is concerned. Will you spread it and how will you react to it?

Because it's often distorted and even untrue, gossip can do damage to others and turn people away from the one who spreads

Peer pressure has no power in and of itself. No one can *make* you do something you don't want to do. Teens, however, are very sensitive to their peers' criticism and acceptance. Often they have not yet formed a strong personal identity. They may not know exactly who they are and what they value. This uncertainty saps the inner strength to resist when people push them. Thus, peer pressure convinces them that they *want* to do what others are doing, even if deep down that isn't true.

In the disguise of friendship, peer pressure is dangerous. People who use peer pressure often know that what they want others to do is wrong. Getting friends to join them makes them feel important and in control; however, they are abusing one of the benefits of friendship. True friends don't ask each other to do what either one feels is wrong or unwise.

it. That's reason enough for not passing along information that could be false.

When you hear gossip, what should you do? Most can be ignored. If the information is important to you, however, you can look for the facts. Postponing a reaction is wise until you know what's really true.

COMPETITION

People face competition all through life—within the family, at school, at work, and elsewhere. In competition, one person gains something at the expense of another. Therefore, competition creates winners and losers.

Strong friendships allow for healthy competition, the kind that enables you to be gracious when your friend comes out the winner. Jerold and Logan were friends on the track team who both competed in the 1500-meter race. Only one could win the race, yet they usually walked off the track with arms across each other's shoulders. Their supportive friendship spurred each of them to do his best in every race.

If you let it, competition within friendship can create conflict. Admitting to feelings of rivalry helps defuse them. Wherever there is competition, there should also be good sportsmanship. Are you sensitive to a friend's feelings? When you win, you can

Focus On ...

How to Say No

When pressure to do the wrong thing makes you uncomfortable, remember these suggestions:

- Be assertive. You can be firm without offending others.
- Say no convincingly. Let the tone of your voice tell people that you mean it.
- Give reasons only if you want, but don't make excuses or apologize. You have the right to say no.
- Use facial expressions that indicate your seriousness. Look steadily at the person and don't smile.
- Use forceful body language. Avoid gestures that might indicate you are less than sure of yourself.

- Suggest an alternative activity. This puts the pressure on those who are pressuring you.
- If the pressure is too much, leave.

USING YOUR KNOWLEDGE

Bill watched as Troy took a little of the white powder and passed the bag to Eric. Bill knew Eric would pass it to him next, but he didn't want any part of this. What should Bill do?

Suppose two close friends begin to notice that one always seems to come out the winner in whatever they do. How might their friendship be affected? What should they do?

win with humility. Find ways to boost your friend's confidence. When you lose, be proud of your friend. In true friendship, a friend's joy is also yours.

LONELINESS

Everyone experiences loneliness, but not only when alone. You can feel lonely in a crowd if you're not connected with someone. Bouts of loneliness sometimes come for no apparent reason and leave just as quickly. This is common, especially among teens.

Due to personality, some people enjoy being alone. They may like to read or work on a hobby. For those who feel that friendship is missing, however, being alone too often can be painful.

Some loneliness grows from a fear of rejection. This fear may cause a person to withdraw, increasing isolation. Teens, who are still developing relationship skills, are prone to this type of loneliness.

Giving in to feelings of loneliness tends to deepen them. Hung Nguyen, for example, came to the United States from Vietnam when he was fourteen. His English was shaky and American customs bewildered him, so he didn't try to make friends.

Classmates, in turn, began to see Hung as a "loner." They didn't reach out to him. Hung's loneliness grew.

Coping with Loneliness

To break the cycle of loneliness, people need to see that they don't have to be something different than they are to have friends. True friends accept each other, including their weaknesses. Someone who tries to win friends by bragging or being phony actually drives others away.

Loneliness can be overcome with positive action. Relationship skills help you reach out to others. Practice good communication skills, especially listening. Ask others about their interests. As you build connections, you'll have a chance to share something of yourself as well. Rapport and empathy grow as you discover common bonds.

Sometimes, loneliness hangs on, despite what people try. This can be serious. Personal problems may interfere with a teen's ability to make friends. Talking to a trusted adult—a parent, older sibling, clergy member, or school counselor—can help. Covering up this kind of problem will not solve it. In fact, the longer it goes on, the worse it gets.

When you notice people who seem lonely, what can you do? Reaching out in friendship to someone who needs that contact can make you feel good. You won't necessarily become close friends, but your effort just might make a big difference in the other person's life.

POPULARITY

Popularity is envied by some teens, but what does popularity mean? A popular person is liked and accepted by many people. He or she usually has qualities that are widely admired. Popularity is sometimes linked to status. A football player who plays well might be popular for reasons that go beyond personal traits.

People who attach too much importance to popularity are most likely to make mistakes if they try to achieve it. In their desire to make friends and fit in, they may give in to negative peer pressure. That can lead to regrets.

"Why is it so easy for them, but not for me?" Loneliness can hurt. What advice would you offer this teen?

Popularity seldom lasts. When the school years end, popularity often does too. **What traits do you need for a lifetime?**

A better approach is to ignore your rating on the popularity scale. Realize that some people who are surrounded by admirers are sometimes longing for even one or two special friendships. That's what is really important.

THE END OF A FRIENDSHIP

Because people are constantly growing and changing, friendships do also. When friends grow in different directions and share fewer interests, the friendship may become strained. If the people involved feel the relationship is still valuable in their lives, they may work to repair it. They try to resolve the specific problems that have come between them.

Other times the individuals decide that the friendship isn't worth saving. They may simply let it die on its own of neglect. One person may take the direct approach, acting deliberately to end the friendship.

Sometimes people hang on to a friendship past the time that it gives much pleasure. When a relationship is no longer meaningful, the time to end it may have arrived. Some so-called friendships actually bring more harm than good, influencing your life in negative ways. Such friendships call for an ending.

Suppose a friendship is going in the wrong direction. **Would you have the courage to walk away even if that meant being alone for a while?**

Breaking off a friendship should be handled with tact and concern for the other person's feelings. This is easier when people agree that the relationship is over. When you must end a friendship, express your feelings without blaming or judging the other person. At the same time, don't allow yourself to be pressured into maintaining a relationship that you believe is better ended.

Handling Rejection

Feelings of rejection can surface when someone ends a relationship that you valued. The same feelings can be there when you try to begin a friendship with someone who doesn't seem interested.

People see rejection as failure. This is especially true for teens, whose self-worth is often closely tied to acceptance by peers. Like peer pressure, rejection is something teens must come to terms with. It hurts only as much as you let it.

To handle rejection, first look for opportunities to grow. Why were you rejected? If you need to change something about yourself, work for improvement. Don't be too hard on yourself—people are sometimes rejected for superficial reasons. When you can see no significant reason for the rejection, put the experience aside and move on.

When rejection comes after a longer friendship, you may feel anger or sorrow at the loss. You may want to blame yourself or the other person. These feelings are to be expected and must be worked through. Time helps ease the pain. Eventually, you can focus on your good times together and how the relationship helped you grow. Soon, you can begin to look forward to using your skills to build new friendships and discovering new rewards.

SECTION 18-2 REVIEW

Check Your Understanding

1. What are five tips for resisting peer pressure?
2. What can a teen do to combat ongoing feelings of loneliness?
3. What is the danger in valuing popularity too much?
4. Describe an attitude that can help you cope when a friend breaks off a relationship.
5. How can a teen handle rejection?
6. **Thinking Critically.** Why might people hang onto a friendship that is no longer rewarding?
7. **Problem Solving.** Teri and her friend Jordan are the two finalists in a scholarship competition. The last stage of the selection process is an interview with the judges. Teri handles interviews well; she knows Jordan gets flustered and self-conscious. Jordan has told her that if he doesn't get the scholarship, he won't be going to college. He hints that she should ease up on him during the interviews. What should Teri do?

Chapter 18
Review and Activities

CHAPTER SUMMARY

- Friendships make important contributions to people's lives.
- People of all ages and types can be friends with each other.
- Starting a friendship takes relationship skills and the confidence to reach out.
- People with whom you share things in common are the likeliest source of potential friends.
- Friendships are maintained by daily sharing and acts of kindness.
- Friendship is a give-and-take relationship.
- Peer pressure can be influential because teens want to be liked and admired by others.
- Teens who have a strong sense of themselves and of their values can stand up to negative peer pressure.
- Sensitive friends can manage and even benefit from competition.
- Loneliness can often be overcome by reaching out and connecting with others.
- When a friendship is no longer rewarding, a firm but kind ending is best.

REVIEW QUESTIONS

Section 18-1
1. What benefits come from friendships between teens and children?
2. What are the benefits of making friends with all types of people?
3. What might you say to support someone who is shy about making friends?
4. What are some ways to keep a friendship strong?

Section 18-2
1. Why is peer pressure both good and bad?
2. Are joking and pleading successful strategies for resisting peer pressure? Explain.
3. How should gossip be handled?
4. How should you respond to feelings of rivalry between a friend and yourself?
5. What attitude and actions can help people overcome loneliness?
6. How does a thoughtful person end a friendship?

BECOMING A PROBLEM SOLVER

1. Darcy and Sandy have been friends since they were eleven and twelve. They solemnly promised to keep in touch when Sandy left for college. In the six weeks since then, Darcy has written Sandy two letters, sent four e-mail messages, and talked to her answering machine twice, all without a response. What should Darcy do?

2. Every time Tom steps outside his house, eight-year-old Christian from next door seems to show up. He follows Tom, chattering and peppering him with questions. Tom is getting annoyed. What should he do?

THINKING CRITICALLY

1. **Compare and Contrast.** Which would you rather belong to: a small, close-knit group of friends or a large, loosely knit group? Why?
2. **Predicting Outcomes.** Some people believe that "you get the friends you deserve." Explain whether you agree with this view of relationships.
3. **Analyzing Behavior.** Many conversation starters among new acquaintances, such as "What school do you go to?" seem uninteresting. Why do people use them?
4. **Recognizing Evidence.** What signs do you see that other age groups are affected by peer pressure?

MAKING CURRICULUM CONNECTIONS

1. **Language Arts.** Write a description of an experience you and a friend shared that enriched you as friends or as individuals.
2. **Art.** Collect a variety of pictures—from magazine ads to photos of famous paintings—that you believe show friendship. What expressions, actions, or other elements of each picture suggest friendship to you?

APPLYING YOUR KNOWLEDGE

1. In small groups, develop and present a skit depicting one of the following situations: a person successfully handles negative peer pressure; two friends confront a problem in their friendship; one person breaks off a friendship with another.
2. Create a "top ten" list of qualities or characteristics you'd like in a friend. Then explain in writing which one is most important to you.

Family & Community Connections

1. Think of several people whose company you enjoy. List the qualities they have that make them likable. Write a specific "plan of action" for developing or strengthening these qualities in yourself.

2. Friendship and loneliness have been the subject of much poetry. Select a few examples from library resources. Read and study these, and share your interpretation with family members.

Understanding Love

"There is more hunger for love and appreciation in this world than for bread."
(Mother Teresa)

IN YOUR OWN WORDS

Why are these words true?

First Steps to Love

OBJECTIVES

After studying this section, you should be able to:

- Summarize in order the stages of learning to love.
- Explain the advantages of associating in groups.
- Explain how a relationship develops when two people become a couple.
- Describe qualities that characterize a positive couple relationship.
- Explain the role of commitment in a relationship.

TERMS TO LEARN

dating
rape
date rape
compatible

When people say something like, "I love warm apple pie with ice cream," you know what they mean. You don't wonder how serious they are or if their feelings will last. People toss around the word "love" in everyday conversation, yet they know that love's real impact and meaning is linked to relationships between people. This is also when the word causes the most confusion.

LEARNING TO LOVE

The idea of "learning" to love another person may seem strange. After all, isn't love just natural? Actually, the desire to love and to be loved is inborn in nearly everyone. You *learn* to love, however, as you learn to do other things—through experience and observation. You learn about love by receiving love from others and seeing the love relationships of others. Once you have received love, you can give it back and spread it to others. In this way, love multiplies. A person who has never experienced love can't give it.

Learning to love is a lifelong process that begins at birth and goes through a series of stages. Each stage helps you build a stronger foundation for future love relationships. Each new stage builds on the previous ones. If love relationships at one stage or another aren't satisfying, successfully going on to the remaining stages is difficult. With this in mind, take a look at the stages that people go through as they learn to love:

Babies learn to return the love they are given. What will happen to a child who doesn't get the caring attention needed?

- **Stage 1: Self-love.** A person's first love is love of self. Even this is learned. When babies' basic needs are met—they are well fed, diapered, kept comfortable and safe, and receive attention—they learn that they are worthy, lovable beings. These positive feelings are the first sensations of love.

- **Stage 2: Love of caregiver.** As babies are cared for and loved, they gradually gain trust and love for their caregivers (typically the parents). If babies' needs aren't fully met, they may never be able to give and receive love.

- **Stage 3: Love of peers.** As children interact with peers, they become attached to their playmates. They eventually develop a strong relationship with one or two best friends of the same gender. The feelings they have are one form of love. Friends become very important—and continue to be.

- **Stage 4: Hero worship.** As children grow older, they develop a loving admiration for an older person—a sibling or relative; a family friend; a coach or teacher; or even a celebrity. They imitate their chosen role model's talk, dress, and mannerisms. Through hero worship, children try out different qualities and traits, which helps them decide what they want to be like. They develop an identity. At the same time, they may hang pictures of their favorite opposite-gender movie, TV, or music personalities.

- **Stage 5: Love of the opposite gender.** During the preteens or early teens, children become interested in the opposite gender. At first, this attraction isn't specific; they are attracted to the opposite gender in general. Friends at this stage often tease each other about being "boy crazy" or "girl crazy." Girls like to talk about boys, and boys talk about girls. Later, they focus on one individual who catches their interest. These relationships are usually short-lived and based on observable qualities, such as appearance, popularity, or athletic ability. People at this stage focus on the thrill of being "in love" rather than the realities of love.

- **Stage 6: Mature love.** Mature love involves caring, sharing, respect, understanding, trust, and commitment. It develops over time and lasts. This is the stage that most people find the hardest to recognize and the most difficult to attain. Since people develop and mature at different rates, not everyone is prepared for a mature love relationship at the same age. Some people never develop enough emotionally to be capable of mature love.

In this six-stage progression, where do you think most teens are? They're probably in Stage 5. That stage covers plenty of territory, as you may already realize. During this period, young people typically go through steps that take them from group associations, to pairing, and eventually to commitment.

ASSOCIATING IN GROUPS

During the preteen and early teen years, most young people are involved in same-gender peer groups. During puberty, interest in the opposite gender builds, and groups expand to include both males and females. Parties, going to dances, and just spending time together takes place in groups.

Often these social groups continue throughout the teen years. The group gives protection in different ways. Socializing with the opposite gender can be less intimidating with friends close by. Sexual pressures are more manageable in a group. As long as the group is reliable, peer pressure can be positive. Parents, too, tend to feel more comfortable when teens associate in groups.

BECOMING A COUPLE

Eventually, people pair off as couples. Teens who spend time with a group may pair off informally within the group. Often no agreement exists, and the two people are free to see others. At some point, however, couples pair off more exclusively. The couple relationship becomes more important and other friendships less so.

Attraction

Couples are drawn to each other because of an attraction. Your reasons for liking someone are as individual as you are. Many people are first attracted to someone for a physical reason.

Children mimic the love they receive from caregivers. Since this child has been cared for lovingly, how will the puppy be treated?

You might react to a person's smile, physique, or skills. These are agreeable traits, but they alone don't make the person right for you.

Personal qualities are more important in a couple relationship, just as they are in marriage. Jermaine was thrilled when he started going out with Andrea. She was pretty as well as popular. He soon realized, however, that they had little in common. Because their interests were so different, they didn't enjoy their time together. Jermaine found that looks and popularity weren't enough to build a relationship.

It's also natural to be attracted to people your friends find attractive. However, what you like in a person won't be quite the same as what your friends like. What talents and personality traits do you admire? You are more likely to be attracted to those who share some of your interests. What else might attract you to someone?

What people find attractive in others varies greatly. While a friendly, outgoing smile beckons one person, a quiet, shy personality may appeal to someone else.

Dating

Once attraction takes hold, two people may begin to go out together. Over the years, this shared social activity has commonly been called **dating**. A date can be something as simple as studying at the library or as involved as going to the prom. Dating customs vary across cultures and generations.

What roles does dating have in personal development? Through dating, you can learn to understand others on a deeper level and improve your overall social skills. You prepare for adult life, including the possibility of marriage.

Especially in the early stages, dating is often awkward. As Blake recalled, "I used to start by talking about things I liked, because that made me feel comfortable. I was doing too much talking, so I started asking, 'What about you?' and 'What do you think?' The people I was with seemed to have more fun that way, and I did, too."

Blake's experience shows how you can improve your skills through dating, while you are also having fun. Like Blake, you will learn more about yourself and about getting along with other people. Your improved communication skills will help you in other types of relationships. Dating also requires that you take responsibility for what you say and do.

Dating on a Budget. It's hard to enjoy someone's company when you're worried about finances. Fortunately, dating is about spending time, not spending money. You may even get to know someone better by sharing simple activities. You and a partner might:

- Walk, hike, skate, or bike on public trails or swim at public beaches.
- Tackle routine tasks (cleaning the yard) or attempt creative projects (painting a room) together.
- Take advantage of the low admissions to school and community events.
- Watch for bargain days or reduced-admission times at sports or amusement centers, movies, and other entertainment.
- Enjoy "early bird specials" by going out for lunch or an early dinner, when restaurants tend to offer lower-priced meals.

Try It Out. Identify two activities that you and a partner might enjoy. Gather ideas for low-cost opportunities to take part in these activities. Look in newspapers and on community bulletin boards. Listen and watch for a community events calendar on local radio and television stations.

Dating poses certain risks. You may be rejected. You may be embarrassed by a mistake or confused by what people expect. A date that doesn't turn out as you hoped is disappointing. It takes self-confidence to put yourself on the line by dating. For most people, however, the chance to start a caring relationship outweighs the risks.

Starting to Date

When should couple dating begin? That's a common question for teens and parents. Family rules often dictate the age and conditions. Once a teen begins to date, new issues arise. Parents don't want dating to interfere with schoolwork and family responsibilities. They also don't want teens to deal with sexual pressures too soon.

Some people don't date until they are older. Since people mature at different rates, some are ready before others. Differences in

Readiness for dating is a personal issue. Some teens prefer to fill their spare time with hobbies and interests of their own. Dating stays in the background until the time is right for them.

maturity rates are especially noticeable during high school. Because females mature faster than males, more females than males may be interested in going out. This pattern tends to level off after high school.

Dating often causes concerns for teens. Some want to go out but can't bridge the gap with those who interest them. Some feel odd because they aren't interested in dating at all. What teens need to realize is that time takes care of most concerns. Concentrating on friends, activities, and school is better than worrying.

Dating Problems

While dating is fun, the smart teen is cautious. The possibility of abuse exists. Violence has no place in any relationship.

Physical Abuse

Physical abuse includes shoving, slapping, punching, or worse. Abusive people see violence as an acceptable way of solving problems. When disagreements occur, one person may try to frighten the other into compliance with violence or the threat of it. Abusers often feel sorrow afterwards and may promise never to do it again. If the abused partner doesn't take action, the cycle just begins again.

In Jane's words, "I guess I ignored Trent's temper and moodiness for a while. Then he hit me and acted like I deserved it. When it happened again, I quit seeing him. I got out while it was still easy. I don't need somebody who solves his problems by beating somebody down."

Ending a relationship is the only safe response when abuse surfaces. That ends not only the risk of injury, but also the chance of becoming more emotionally involved in a destructive relationship.

Emotional Abuse

Not all abuse is physical. Some is emotional. The person who cares less about the relationship controls it and may misuse that power. Lisann knew that Mitchell cared very much for her, but her interest was mild. She took advantage of his feelings. She "forgot" to return his calls and cancelled plans at the last minute. She thoughtlessly criticized him as well as things that were important to him.

Someone who constantly tears down another's self-esteem is abusive. Why would anyone put up with that kind of treatment? What would you do?

Focus On...

Avoiding Date Rape

Personal responsibility plays a large role in avoiding date rape. You can:

- **Avoid risky situations.** Be careful about where you go, especially with people you don't know well.
- **Set limits for yourself.** Know beforehand what behavior is acceptable and unacceptable, for both you and your partner.
- **Communicate.** Tell your partner about the limits you have set. Make sure your partner understands and accepts them. Speak up when you feel he or she is pressuring you to do something that goes against your values.
- **Recognize disrespectful behavior.** Learn to identify signs that your partner is not taking your standards seriously.

- **Be assertive.** If a situation makes you uncomfortable, say so forcefully, with verbal and nonverbal language. If it continues, get away or call for help.

USING YOUR KNOWLEDGE

Fiona was looking forward to her date with Kyle. Although she had heard some frightening things about him, she decided to give him the benefit of the doubt. He was so good looking, and Fiona wanted to be seen with him. What would you say to her?

With emotional abuse, a person routinely yells and belittles another, making the person feel worthless and fearful. Emotional abuse can lead to lasting problems. People owe it to themselves to leave such relationships.

Date Rape

Rape is forced sexual intercourse. It is an act of violence. Rape may occur between strangers or people who already know each other. **Date rape** is rape that takes place in a dating situation.

Date rape occurs more frequently than most people realize and often isn't reported. Teens in particular are reluctant to report date rape. They may mistakenly think it was their fault or that it isn't rape if they were on a date. Many think accusing someone of rape will create negative publicity and embarrassment for their family, and in the end, no one will believe them.

Rape can never be tolerated. In a threatening situation, teens must be assertive. They must leave the situation or call for help. Any rape, in any situation, must be reported. This will raise awareness of the problem. It may also prevent the rapist from repeating the act.

Looking for Positive Qualities

Every teen needs to be aware of problems that can occur in a dating situation. Awareness can enable you to help yourself in a troublesome situation. Fortunately, most dating relationships are safe. Many even lead to something strong and lasting.

Spending time with someone special gives you an opportunity to discover what that person is really like. Not surprisingly, you begin to look beyond the "big brown eyes" or the broad shoulders. The same qualities that characterize a good friendship become important. These include:

- **Compatibility.** People who can exist together in harmony are **compatible.** They share interests, values, and attitudes. As a couple, they see "eye to eye" on many things.

- **Honesty.** People in a positive couple relationship are honest with themselves and with each other. They can be themselves and express their feelings openly without fear of rejection or ridicule.

- **Respect.** Two people who respect each other honor and esteem one another and accept and appreciate their individuality. They take a sincere interest in each other's activities and listen to their ideas and opinions.

- **Mutual support.** In any good relationship, the people involved must be supportive. They help each other grow by giving encouragement.

- **Independence.** Partners enjoy time and activities together and apart. Neither partner tries to limit the other's interests or relationships with family and friends.

Other traits that mark a healthy couple relationship include trust, the ability to resolve conflicts, and a similar degree of devotion to the relationship. What other traits would you add?

COMMITMENT

When couples discover qualities they like, they may agree to date only each other. This is a commitment, but it may not be a long-lasting one. Younger couples may "commit" to one another only for the duration of the relationship. Once they discover that the relationship isn't right for them, the commitment ends. This is natural for those in the early stages of maturity.

Dating is a learning experience. You begin to discover what qualities you want in a partner. Do you think the qualities you admire now will be the same ones you value in a few years?

Building Character

Respect: A Quality That Counts

How do you act when you show respect for others? Respect is consideration for another person's feelings, beliefs, and rights. It means seeing another person's needs and wants as equal to your own. A teen can show respect by:

- Abiding by the curfew a friend's parents set when going out.
- Asking for a partner's suggestion about where to go for a date.
- Arguing calmly and reasonably in a dispute with a parent.
- Knocking on closed doors before entering a room.
- Obeying the law.

QUESTIONS

1. Explain how a person can show respect for things besides people.
2. How do you show that you respect others? How does this affect their respect for you?

SECTION 19-1 REVIEW

Check Your Understanding

1. How do people learn to love?
2. What stages do people go through as they learn to love?
3. What benefits are offered by associating in groups?
4. What roles does dating play in personal development?
5. Why does it often take self-confidence to begin dating?
6. If a teen is hit by someone she is dating, what should she do?
7. What are four qualities found in a successful dating relationship?
8. **Thinking Critically.** Why might emotional abuse be harder to identify and prove than physical abuse?
9. **Problem Solving.** Randy and Jewell are following the rules of courtship that their families approve. They care deeply for each other, but they don't spend time alone together and there is no physical contact between them. Although this is difficult, they like building their relationship on other more important grounds. Their peers make fun of their courtship. What should they do?

When Is Love Real?

OBJECTIVES

After studying this section, you should be able to:

- Compare the characteristics of infatuation to those of mature love.
- Explain how mature love develops.
- Evaluate reactions to the end of a love relationship.

TERMS TO LEARN

infatuation
mature love

Some kinds of love are like a rich pastry. They're wonderful while they last but have little to sustain you. Mature love, in contrast, satisfies and nourishes. It helps you grow stronger.

Telling one type of love from the others isn't always easy, especially for those just starting to develop love relationships. Some feelings of love are fleeting. The question "Is this the real thing?" is answered only over time. There are clues, however, that can help you recognize whether loving feelings might lead to a lasting love relationship.

INFATUATION

The first kind of love that most people experience is **infatuation** (in-FACH-yoo-WAY-shun). This is an intense emotional involvement that begins with a sudden, strong attraction based on physical appearance or other obvious traits. Infatuation might be triggered by another person's self-confidence, sense of humor, or manner of talking.

Infatuation is very real and very powerful. The infatuated couple want to spend all their time together. They want to share all their feelings—joys, sorrows, secrets, hopes, and fears. They are emotionally immersed in each other and overwhelmed by their own emotions.

While it lasts, infatuation is very enjoyable and satisfying. It is, however, self-centered. Partners focus more on how wonderful the relationship makes them feel and how it satisfies their own needs than on the feelings and needs of the other person.

Infatuation is exciting and thrives on special moments like this. What is daily life like for couples who stay together for a lifetime? Will infatuation work for them?

Infatuation is also unrealistic. It's a love of being in love. It's passion without reason. In their desire to be happy, infatuated people can overlook basic important differences between them and their partner. Problems, undesirable traits, and shortcomings tend to be ignored or glossed over. Infatuated people see only what they want to see.

Reality Sets In

Over time, the intense emotional high of the relationship dies down. When the attraction and emotions are not as new and strong, they no longer cloud the judgment. Reality begins to set in. The partners may realize that the attraction was superficial, based only on surface traits rather than something more meaningful and enduring. They may realize that the other person has traits or shortcomings they cannot accept, or that they have very little in common.

The dream, complete with an idealized partner with whom one can "live happily ever after," is over.

Louis and Kate were typical of infatuated couples. They were inseparable. They studied together, talked on the phone, and took long walks in the park. When they were together, nothing else mattered. They seemed to fulfill each other's every need. Within a few months, however, their feelings for each other cooled and then died completely. Without the intense emotion, they found they had little left. They had fallen out of love as quickly as they had fallen into it.

Infatuation is a natural type of love relationship. It can provide valuable experience when young people are learning what a truly loving relationship involves. In some cases, infatuation is the beginning of a committed relationship, a stepping-stone on the way to mature love.

Tips & TECHNIQUES

MATURE LOVE

Mature love is what most people have in mind when they think of real love. As the name implies, people who share a mature love have reached a high level of emotional development. They are secure and comfortable enough with themselves to commit to another person.

Mature love can begin with a sudden, strong attraction, but often it doesn't. Sometimes, in fact, the attraction builds slowly. As Alita said, "I didn't even like Rashid at first. He seemed kind of stuck up. We were lab partners in chemistry, so we started meeting to do homework and later went out to eat once in a while. We always had a good time together, but our relationship wasn't ever romantic. When his family

almost moved out of state, we realized how much we cared about each other. If you had told me I'd feel this way a year ago, I wouldn't have believed it."

Whether mature love begins slowly or quickly, it still has certain qualities that define it. These are what make it quite different from infatuation.

Recognizing Mature Love

Nearly everyone wonders at some point how to recognize true love. Although there's no chemical formula, you can look for a number of characteristics that help distinguish mature love from infatuation. Mature love is:

- **Secure and comfortable.** Partners are confident about the love that each feels.

They are trusting and faithful and don't need constant reassurances.

- **Based on shared interests.** The couple share certain interests that will allow them to have good times together.
- **Based on shared beliefs and goals.** They want basically the same things in life and want to work toward them together. Important issues won't come between them.
- **Highly focused on the other person.** Each person holds the other's well-being in high regard, sometimes ahead of self. Although neither one wants to lose personal identity in the relationship, each cares deeply about the other's point of view, emotions, health, and happiness and is willing to make sacrifices and compromises. Each wants to do things for the other to show caring and love.
- **Accepting but realistic.** Partners don't look at each other through "rose-colored glasses." In other words, they see the real person. They know how each reacts to boredom, frustration, stress, and crisis. They don't ignore or overlook undesirable traits, but they accept small imperfections. Before committing, they identify what they know would bother them over time and possibly interfere with a long-term relationship.
- **Responsible.** Partners take the relationship seriously. Each wants to contribute to the work needed to strengthen the relationship and build a good life.

- **Respectful.** Each has regard for the other as a person and wouldn't deliberately say or do things that are hurtful. They are proud of each other's accomplishments.
- **Able to put attraction in perspective.** Physical attraction is important but not the main focus. Partners enjoy each other's company.
- **Lasting.** The relationship stands the test of time. Few of the qualities described here can be determined without ample time to observe and analyze them.

With mature love, companionship is as important as physical closeness. How could this principle be tested in a dating relationship?

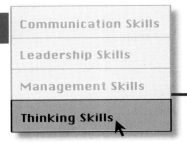
WHEN RELATIONSHIPS END

Even when people enter a relationship with hope, no one can tell what the future will bring. Discovering that mature love didn't develop may spell the end of a relationship. That can mean pain and heartache for one or both of the people involved. It's far better to end a relationship and move on, however, than to continue in one that isn't working for one or both partners.

If you're the one ending a relationship, a kind and gentle approach is best. Be straightforward, choosing words that aren't accusing and hurtful. You may wish to point out why you feel the two of you aren't right for each other. Sometimes the other person may be emotional, lack understanding of the situation, or be unwilling to accept what's happening. Taking a firm approach is better than leading the person on and giving false hopes when you know the relationship is over.

Your Own Recovery

Feelings of hurt, betrayal, and self-doubt are common when a relationship ends against your will. You may feel to blame. You may even vow to never get involved again. These are natural reactions that go away in time. Remember these ideas if you face such a situation:

- While exploring love, nearly everyone goes through relationships that end.
- Blaming yourself isn't realistic. Most relationships end because they simply weren't meant to be.

- A relationship that ends paves the way for one that's real. It's far better to accept another person's dissatisfaction and go on to look for a stronger relationship than to dwell on the loss or try to postpone it.
- Learn from the relationship. You'll probably have a better image of what you want and need in a partnership.

Regardless of why a relationship ended, you may go through a period of sadness. Recovery can be hastened in several ways. Some people write their thoughts in a journal. Just talking to a close friend who is supportive often helps. You might even pamper yourself a little.

You'll start to feel stronger inside if you determine to let the past go and move ahead with life. A new hobby, getting out with friends, reading a book—these are the kinds of things that can give you a fresh outlook. Remember that when people find real love, they are often thankful for what they've learned from past experiences. Recognizing true love is often easier.

The end of a love relationship is usually very painful. Some people think they have failed. They may even decide never to love again. Why is their thinking incorrect?

SECTION 19-2 REVIEW

Check Your Understanding

1. What is infatuation?
2. Why is infatuation said to be self-centered?
3. How does an infatuated couple respond to problems in the relationship?
4. How can infatuation be useful?
5. What does time have to do with identifying mature love?
6. How can you end a relationship appropriately?
7. **Thinking Critically.** What could happen if a person fails to see the negative qualities in someone he or she dates for a long time?
8. **Problem Solving.** Kenna was sick and missed two weeks of school. She needs to make up several assignments, but she's afraid of neglecting her relationship with Frank. She doesn't want to cut back on their time together. What should Kenna do?

Chapter 19
Review and Activities

CHAPTER SUMMARY

- People learn to love through experience and observation.
- Learning about love is a lifelong process. It progresses through stages, laying a foundation for love relationships.
- Getting to know each other is the first step in finding out if attraction can grow into love.
- Young people tend to associate in groups before pairing off as couples.
- Dating provides opportunities to learn skills that foster personal growth.
- Concerns in dating can include physical and emotional abuse and date rape.
- Infatuation is usually the first kind of love people experience. It either burns itself out or turns into something more long-lasting.
- Mature love means caring as much or more about the other person as you do about yourself.
- Important qualities in mature love are caring, responsibility, respect, and knowledge of one's partner.

REVIEW QUESTIONS

Section 19-1
1. Lamar was physically neglected as an infant. How might that affect his ability to love?
2. How does hero worship contribute to learning about love?
3. Is physical attraction a good basis for a long-term relationship? Explain.
4. What benefits, besides meeting a possible mate, can a dating relationship offer?
5. In what way might age affect a couple's commitment?

Section 19-2
1. Is infatuation realistic? Explain.
2. Describe six elements of mature love.
3. Can infatuation and mature love begin in the same way? Explain.
4. Can anything positive be said about a relationship that ends? Explain.
5. What can a person do to recover from a relationship that ends?

BECOMING A PROBLEM SOLVER

1. Derrick knows that Amy likes the way he spends money on her, but he thinks she likes him for more than that. Derrick now wants to cut back on expenses to save money for technical school. He worries about how Amy will respond. What should Derrick do?

2. Marti was sure that she and Drew had a lasting love. When they broke up, she was devastated. Now Marti doubts her judgment about people. She looks for hidden motives and is apt to take things the wrong way. She is disturbed by this change in herself. What should Marti do?

THINKING CRITICALLY

1. **Evaluating Evidence.** Is love at first sight possible? Why might people believe otherwise?

2. **Evaluating Behavior.** Evaluate each of the following situations. Which ones sound more like love and which like infatuation?

   • Craig began dating Marina because she was a cheerleader. He especially liked the envy he saw in other males when he was out with Marina.

   • When Cal's grades started to go down, Hailey suggested that they turn their dates into study sessions until Cal's grades improved.

   • Ma-Ling was moody for several weeks after her mother was laid off from her job. Jun sat with her at lunch and cheered her on at her volleyball matches as he had before.

MAKING CURRICULUM CONNECTIONS

1. **Literature.** Poems about love are among the most famous ever written. Locate and read a love poem, such as one of Shakespeare's sonnets or verses by Robert or Elizabeth Barrett Browning. Share the poem with the class. How does it describe love? How might a modern poet express those feelings?

2. **History.** Using library and Internet resources, research the history of love in relationships. Has love always been a factor in choosing a mate? What qualities were considered important for a successful relationship in different eras?

APPLYING YOUR KNOWLEDGE

1. As a class, debate the following statement: "Love relationships are more important to females than to males."

2. Analyze the love relationships depicted on a television show. Citing examples, explain whether these seem to be mature and satisfying to the partners.

Family & Community Connections

1. Write a short paragraph that begins, "Love is…" Compare your ideas with those of your family members.

2. Invite a clergy member who does premarital counseling to speak to the class. Ask the guest to identify those qualities that suggest the union will be a lasting, loving one.

Chapter 20

Understanding Sexuality

WORDS FOR THOUGHT

"Sex is never an
emergency."
(Elaine Pierson)

IN YOUR OWN WORDS

What is the warning
in these words?

Sexual Identity

OBJECTIVES

After studying this section, you should be able to:

- Explain what sexuality is.
- Explain how gender roles are learned.
- Compare changing attitudes towards gender roles.
- Distinguish influences on sexual identity and their impact.

TERMS TO LEARN

sexuality
gender role
sexual identity

The term "sexuality" is often misunderstood. It doesn't simply focus on whether you are attractive—or even male or female. **Sexuality** really focuses on how you handle your values and beliefs about sexual behavior. How do you act on those values in real situations? Children learn those values from your family, society, and religious beliefs.

Your earliest understandings of what it means to be a male or female came from observing how others define the genders. The behavior and characteristics expected of a male or female make up a **gender role**. Whatever is thought to be more acceptable for each gender becomes part of that role.

Gender roles can be viewed at two different levels—societal and individual. In other words, what does society say a male and female should be like? How does each person see these roles? The definitions found in society are not necessarily the same as those carried out by individuals.

If you had to make one list of words that describe females and another list for males, what words would you put in each one? Would you put any words in both lists?

The words you include in your lists would probably be very different from the ones previous generations would have used. You might also list words that differ from your friends. At one time societal gender roles were quite separate and distinct. Generally, women were homemakers, and men were wage earners.

Today, many clear-cut differences still exist in the expectations for male and female behavior. Some lines of distinction are blurred, however, and gender roles overlap more than before. These changes in ideas about gender roles can be a real source of confusion and conflict. Some people are troubled by the changes; others are more accepting. Examples of the problems that arise could fill this page. Who should a child's primary caregiver be—the mother or the father? Should males and females serve equally in the military? Should a female play football? Should a male wear an earring?

What Are Little Boys Made Of?

What are little boys made of, made of?
What are little boys made of?
Frogs and snails, and puppy-dogs' tails;
And that's what little boys are made of, made of.

What are little girls made of, made of?
What are little girls made of?
Sugar and spice and all that's nice;
And that's what little girls are made of, made of.

Mother Goose Rhyme

Over the years gender roles have changed.
Why wouldn't a person today be likely to write a poem like this one?

At one time becoming a professional athlete wouldn't have been part of a female's sexual identity. What else can these young women be and do that might not have been possible for their grandmothers?

People tend to be more open nowadays to those whose interests and actions differ from traditional gender roles. For example, when Thad first became a nurse fifteen years ago, he was one of just three males in his graduating class. Many of his patients felt uncomfortable being cared for by a male nurse. Today, most people don't seem to notice.

FORMING SEXUAL IDENTITY

In one study, people were observed while interacting with an infant. Some of the people were told the baby was a boy; others were told the same baby was a girl. Still others were told the gender of the baby was unknown. In each situation, the baby was treated differently. Those who didn't know the infant's gender were uneasy. They didn't seem to know how to relate to the child.

This study illustrates one way that children form their **sexual identity**, or the way people see themselves as males and females. Sexual identity develops as children acquire feelings and responses that are considered appropriate for their gender. They learn these ideas as they gain other types of knowledge. They earn approval for certain behaviors and disapproval for others. They observe and imitate what other people do. Also, as in the study described above, they draw conclusions from the way they are treated.

Children absorb information about gender from birth, most of it indirectly. They build a sense of themselves as males and females from informal contacts and experiences, such as the toys they are given and the games they play.

Often people are unaware of the subtle ways they shape a child's thinking. For example, when Seth mastered a basic math assignment, his teacher gave him extra, more challenging problems. Autumn also did well on the assignment. She was not given any extra problems to do.

Focus On...

Heredity or Environment?

Does heredity or environment have a greater effect on how people acquire gender traits? While the environmental, or external, influences play a part, people are less agreed on whether some traits are naturally present through heredity. For example, are males more aggressive and females more sensitive by nature, or do both result from society's conditioning?

Evidence for both possibilities exists. For centuries, men's physical strength has made them natural protectors and providers of the family. As mothers, females have handled the family's daily care. Psychologists note, however, that some behaviors are reinforced. When boys have a problem, for instance, they are often urged to solve it alone and to "stand up for themselves," even if it means fighting. Girls who have a problem are likely to get sympathy and help.

Also worth noting is that traits may take different expression over time. Some great-grandmothers might be surprised to see a hard-fought game between professional women basketball players. As young mothers in the Depression era, however, they might have been every bit as tough and competitive in keeping their families fed and their spirits up. Likewise, many older men never learned how to comfort a crying baby. Instead, they showed love by working long hours to provide a better life for that child.

Many traits are not as rigid today. Instead, positive traits and behaviors are encouraged in everyone. Blending and overlapping of roles is becoming more common.

USING YOUR KNOWLEDGE

Ezra likes to write poetry. He has kept this interest a secret for a long time because he's afraid his male friends will ridicule him. Now he really wants to test his skills through a school writing contest. Recognition, however, could cost him. What should he do?

Both children were "rewarded" for their accomplishment. Seth, however, was given the chance and expectation to achieve more. How might this difference affect each child's attitude toward math?

This subtle response is typical in many situations. Talent in mathematics traditionally has been viewed as a male trait, yet females are very successful in math, especially when given the same encouragement as males.

Influences on Identity

Of all the influences on a person's sexual identity, one of the strongest is the family. What it means to be female or male is first learned within the family setting. By the time they reach school age, children know a lot about the subject.

Learning about the roles of men and women continues through the grade school years. Children become more aware of the differences between the genders. They identify with behaviors of same-gender adults and copy them.

Peers are an important source of information as well. Children of all ages want to be like their friends. They naturally share activities that interest good friends. Copying friends' behavior and adopting their attitudes are quite common.

Television and movies are a major source of ideas about sexuality. Books, advertisements, and music videos all suggest what women and men should be like and how they should relate to each other.

Unfortunately, much of what people see and read in the media is not realistic. These portrayals of people, designed for entertainment, are often exaggerated and superficial. It can be easy to absorb ideas from fiction that cause problems in real life.

YOUR PERSONAL IDENTITY

As you can see, forming and expressing sexual identity is a complex matter. So many different images and models exist, and some ideas even contradict each other.

How you compare to someone else's definition isn't important. Sexuality is not a one-size-fits-all garment. No single standard fits every male and female.

Throughout life, you'll find plenty of people who appreciate you for the positive qualities you have rather than seeing you just as a male or female. Develop all the special talents and qualities you have, whatever they are. That can give you confidence and peace of mind.

SECTION 20-1 REVIEW

Check Your Understanding

1. What is sexuality?
2. What is a gender role?
3. Describe the two levels of gender roles.
4. What are four influences on sexual identity?
5. **Thinking Critically.** What do you think causes changes in society's view of gender roles?
6. **Problem Solving.** Deborah and her twin brother Daniel are looking at colleges to attend. Both are interested in out-of-state schools, but their parents are pressuring Deborah to stay at home and attend community college. She isn't satisfied with the courses the local school offers. What do you think Deborah should do?

Sexual Behavior

OBJECTIVES

After studying this section, you should be able to:

- Explain how rising sexual feelings can cause concerns during adolescence.
- Describe the symptoms of, and treatments for, common sexually transmitted diseases.
- Assess the effects of teen pregnancy on parents, children, and society.
- Plan ways of dealing with pressures to become sexually active.

TERMS TO LEARN

**sexually transmitted
     disease (STD)**
sterility
abstinence

You live in a time when talk and images of sexual behavior seem to be everywhere: in news shows, magazines, movies, and books. How much of the content is information, however? Of that information, how much is accurate and relevant to teens? Decisions about sexual behavior have always had great impact on people's lives. Today, such decisions can be a matter of life or death. If there was ever a time when it was okay to learn about sexual behavior by chance, that time has past.

EXPERIENCING CHANGE

With adolescence come physical and psychological changes that signal the beginning of adult sexual development. Sexual characteristics develop as teens become physically able to reproduce. Curiosity about sex and the opposite gender increases. Sexual daydreams and fantasies are common.

Males and females experience sexual desires differently. Males tend to be more easily aroused sexually by thoughts, jokes, and images. Their desire may not be associated with feelings of love for any particular female, yet this doesn't mean that adolescent males cannot feel affection or caring for a young woman. In females, sexual desires tend to be associated with feelings of love, romance, and tenderness.

Physical and emotional changes can be at least distracting, and often troubling.

Physical attraction typically comes with powerful feelings. Handling them is a new experience for teens. What can they do to prevent serious consequences?

Teens frequently feel pressure from within and from others to respond to what they feel. Messages about sexual behavior can be conflicting and confusing. Unless their values and goals are clearly in place, teens can have a difficult time knowing how to react to strong sexual feelings when they occur.

Saying yes to sexual pressures has serious consequences. When the time is right, a sexual relationship can bring much mutual pleasure. To those who are not ready for this step in their lives, however, sexual activity can bring major problems. Two of the biggest concerns for teens are diseases spread through sexual contact and pregnancy.

SEXUALLY TRANSMITTED DISEASES

A **sexually transmitted disease (STD)** is an illness spread from one person to another through sexual contact. Over twenty STDs have been identified. STDs are an epidemic in the United States, with over twelve million cases a year. Three million of these occur in teens.

STDs spread rapidly. When people have sex, in a sense, they are having sex with everyone their partner has ever been with before. Sometimes STDs are passed because a person is unaware that he or she is infected. By the time Chuck developed symptoms and was diagnosed with an STD, for example, he had also infected his girlfriend Courtney. Some irresponsi-

ble people don't care whether they infect others.

STDs tend to cause more pain and suffering in women than in men. Females may develop a painful general infection in the pelvic area known as *pelvic inflammatory disease* (PID). PID can damage the reproductive organs and leave a woman unable to bear children. Some STDs harm the baby during pregnancy.

Some STDs are easily cured. Others last a lifetime. A few are fatal. All STDs are preventable, and avoiding sexual activity is the best prevention. Some of the most common STDs are described below.

The most widespread STD is *chlamydia* (kluh-MID-ee-uh). Four million cases occur

Building Character

Self-Discipline: A Quality That Counts

Self-discipline is self-control. It means managing your emotions and thinking before acting. A person with self-control chooses wise actions over unwise ones, even when the alternatives are tempting. A teen might show self-discipline by:

- Ending a date at a reasonable hour, although it interrupts an enjoyable time.
- Respecting a partner's choice to refrain from sexual activity and not trying to undermine that decision.
- Planning a study session with a date when others are home, rather than when the home is empty.
- Walking away from an intense quarrel rather than using physical violence.

QUESTIONS

1. In what areas of life might a teen need to practice self-discipline?
2. How can self-discipline be strengthened?
3. What do you do when you feel yourself losing control?

---

each year. Pain in urinating is the most common symptom. Women may have pain in the abdomen, nausea, or a low fever. Many people, however, show no symptoms. Chlamydia can lead to **sterility** (stuh-RILL-uh-tee), which is the inability to have children. This disease is treated with antibiotics.

Genital herpes (HUR-peas) causes open sores on the sex organs. These resemble cold sores and heal in about three weeks. This STD cannot be cured. Anyone with an open sore can pass the disease to others. A woman with active herpes who gives birth can infect her baby during delivery, possibly causing brain damage or death for the infant.

Small growths on the sex organs are *genital warts*. They can cause discomfort and itching and can lead to cancer. There is no cure for genital warts, although a doctor can remove them.

Hepatitis B attacks the liver and causes flu-like symptoms. Most people recover without treatment; however, hepatitis B can lead to liver disease or cancer. It has no cure, but a vaccine that prevents the disease is available.

The germ that causes *gonorrhea* (gahn-uh-REE-uh) grows in warm, moist areas of the body. Symptoms include genital burning, itching, and discharge. In women, the disease can cause sterility. If a pregnant woman is infected, her child's eyes will be damaged at birth. Gonorrhea is treated with antibiotics.

Early symptoms of *syphilis* (SIF-uh-lus) include sores on the sex organs, fevers, rashes, and hair loss. Treated in time, syphilis can be cured with antibiotics. Untreated, it eventually affects the heart, eyes, and brain. It can lead to insanity and death.

Career Success Stories

Colleen McCoy: *Public Health Educator*

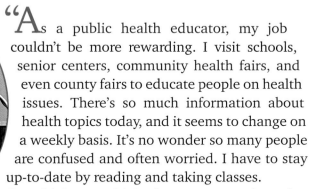

"As a public health educator, my job couldn't be more rewarding. I visit schools, senior centers, community health fairs, and even county fairs to educate people on health issues. There's so much information about health topics today, and it seems to change on a weekly basis. It's no wonder so many people are confused and often worried. I have to stay up-to-date by reading and taking classes.

"Wouldn't you think that most people today would be familiar with STDs and their effects? Well, they aren't. Educating the public about sexually transmitted diseases is one of my primary responsibilities. The more people I talk to, the more impact I can make in controlling the spread of STDs.

"It's the young people I worry about the most. Some of them have a carefree attitude, thinking nothing can happen to them. One of the most rewarding situations I've had involved a teen who came to see me when she was seventeen. She had already contracted three different STDs. She told me she had been in one of my classes two years earlier—but she hadn't listened. She wanted to share her story with young teens in my classes. Now she's a regular participant, who speaks from experience. I know she's made a real impact, and I'm so glad she wants to help."

CAREER PROFILE

Education and training: bachelor's degree in nursing or health education

Starting salary range: $25–29,000

Job prospects: public, state, and county health agencies and hospitals

Important qualities: excellent communication skills; enjoy working with people; organized; able to work independently

Plan Ahead

You can take more than one route to become a public health educator. Research this career and determine the path you would take if you decided to work in this job.

The AIDS Epidemic

One of the most frightening STDs is *AIDS*—acquired immune deficiency syndrome. In this disease, a virus called the *human immunodeficiency virus* (HIV) invades and kills the cells of the immune system. The body is then unable to defend itself from any number of diseases. HIV can live in the body many years before developing into AIDS. Once a person has AIDS, however, the outlook is not good. Death is often slow and painful, caused by pneumonia or cancer of the skin or glands.

HIV has been spreading rapidly among teens, but it's hard to know how many are affected. Because of the time lag between initial infection with HIV and the onset of AIDS, most infected teens will not show signs of AIDS until they are in their twenties. Meanwhile, they can pass the disease on to others.

How AIDS Spreads

AIDS is not spread through casual contact, such as holding hands or sitting next to someone. It isn't spread through saliva or tears, through the air (as from coughing), or through insect bites. Due to blood testing, AIDS is rarely passed through blood transfusions.

AIDS is spread through intimate sexual contact. Tiny rips or skin breaks in the sexual organs allow the HIV virus to enter the blood during sexual activity. Neither the male nor the female would normally be aware of these tiny breaks.

HIV can be transmitted in other ways as well. The virus can spread among drug users who share needles. An infected female can pass the virus to her baby if she becomes pregnant. This can happen

Young people everywhere are learning about the dangers of STDs. Many teens are taking these lessons very seriously.

through the exchange of blood between mother and child during pregnancy, during childbirth, or through the mother's milk while nursing.

AIDS has no known cure. Current medical treatment uses a combination of drugs to delay HIV from developing into AIDS. These powerful drugs do slow the progress of the disease, but they are expensive and have serious, negative side effects. Saying no to all high-risk behaviors is the only way to be safe from AIDS.

Getting Help

Younger teens and those with more than one partner are especially vulnerable to STDs, but anyone who is sexually active is at risk. Those who suspect they have a sexually transmitted disease should get medical help immediately. They will be required to give the names of their partners, so they can also be tested if necessary. Most treatment, however, is confidential.

Getting treatment for any of these diseases takes courage. The consequences of avoiding treatment, however, can be disastrous, for oneself and one's partner.

TEEN PREGNANCY

One million teens get pregnant each year in the United States. That comes to one teen every 26 seconds, or 56 children born to teens every hour. With figures like that, the United States has the highest teen pregnancy rate in the world.

What happens when teens become parents? Consider these results:

- **Education.** Many teen parents, both males and females, don't finish high school or go on for further education. This decreases their chance to get jobs that will support them and their children comfortably. Many teen mothers fall into poverty and stay there after their child's birth.

- **Health problems.** Many teen mothers don't get medical care during pregnancy. They are more likely to have complications in childbirth than are older women. Their babies are underdeveloped; some have physical and mental disabilities. Babies born to teens younger than sixteen are more apt to die in the first year of life than those born to older women.

- **Emotional costs.** Teens are still growing themselves. They are rarely prepared for the many responsibilities of parenting. Children born to teens are more likely to be abused, be abandoned, or require some type of foster care.

- **Child development.** Children of teen parents are often slow to develop. They tend to get lower grades in school and have more behavior problems. Failing or quitting school commonly results. These children typically become sexually active, marry at a young age, and divorce frequently.

- **Cost to society.** Many teen families are dysfunctional. As you know, families that

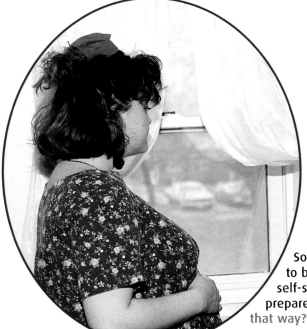

Some teens are determined not to become parents until they are self-supporting and emotionally prepared. Why don't all teens see it that way?

don't meet basic needs tend to produce people who cannot cope in society or make a contribution. A weak family weakens society.

Despite the strikes against them, some teens do make parenthood work. With sacrifice and great effort, from their families as well as themselves, these teens raise children successfully and improve their own situation. The reality of teen pregnancy and parenting, however, is that the negative possibilities far outweigh the "happy endings."

SEXUAL PRESSURES

Pressure to become sexually active is greater for teens today than ever before. Why, when the risks are so great, do so many young people choose a path that can cause such serious problems? The reasons are complex, and one teen's reasons may not be the same as another's.

Environmental Influences

First of all, you live in a society that sends sexual messages from every corner. In the media, people see sexual images that are much more explicit than they used to be.

The more people see something, the more acceptable it seems. What is accepted is likely to be imitated and, in being imitated, grows more acceptable to more people. When imitating the behavior of others, however, you're the one who has to deal with the consequences.

The media are only one source of sexual messages. People around you may also send them. Some teens, like Dawn, live in situations where teen pregnancy is a way of life. "My mom was seventeen when I was born," Dawn explained. "I heard warnings about getting pregnant, and I know from

The automobile has given many teens freedoms that they didn't have in the past. In what ways does the automobile contribute to sexual pressures? How can that be prevented?

Teens who feel the pressure to become sexually active have a decision to make. Do you think they can take a stand against the many negative messages on television and in the movies? Will the producers of such programs help you out if you get in trouble?

growing up that it's hard for the child. When I had a baby, Mom was really upset. She said she had hopes for me. A lot of my friends have babies. What's the difference whether you have a baby now or later?"

Dawn's words reflect a major obstacle in overcoming the cycle of teen parenting, and usually poverty. Teens in these situations must believe they can break the cycle, even though it isn't easy. They must also see that it's worth the effort. By not having a child too soon, a young person is free to get an education, go after an interesting career, and reach other goals. Thinking about what you *can* do and *can* become leads to a better life than just letting parenthood happen and take over.

Peers are a strong influence on sexual behavior. Some speak and act as though having sex is not only okay, but it's also what everybody's doing. Should you believe this? You have good reason not to. The talk you hear comes from some who exaggerate and others who take risks. Why follow their example?

Listening to certain people, you might feel "different" at times, but it's better to feel different for a little while than to regret something your whole life. Teens who think for themselves don't give in to pressure from others. These teens are often less vocal, however. They tend to let their silence and the example of their lives speak for them. You may have to pay close attention to receive their message.

Personal Pressures

Sometimes the pressure to have sex comes from within. A teen who feels lonely may see sex as one way of feeling loved. A person might believe sex is a way to hold on to a relationship. Sex may even seem symbolic of becoming "adult." None of these is a good reason for having sex.

A lasting relationship can't be based on sex, and a poor relationship can't be saved by it. A person who makes you feel that you must do something you don't want to is act-

When you face a challenge, what strengths can you draw upon? Self-esteem, confidence, and convictions about what you believe in and want for your future will all help you make the right decisions.

ing selfishly. Having sex is no proof of adulthood. A truer test is waiting until you're ready for all the responsibilities of sexual behavior.

Of course, the most basic pressure to have sex is simple, physical desire. Even teens who reject the outside pressures to become sexually active can have trouble resisting their own feelings. Sexual feelings are natural, and they can be strong. Your best defense against reacting without thought is to think before acting.

ABSTINENCE

Nearly any situation is more manageable when you plan for it. You are more likely to do what's right for you when you're prepared.

Because they recognize the risks linked with sexual activity and have stong values, many people choose **abstinence** (AB-stuh-nunts), which is refraining from sexual intercourse. You can make the decision on your own. You might write down your promise to yourself and keep it in a place where you can reread it often.

When you have a close relationship with someone, you can talk about your feelings before you get in an intimate situation. Make sure your partner understands your point of view clearly. Find out what your partner's thinking is, too.

Then stay out of the situations that could pose problems. Avoid being alone with your partner in empty houses, cars, or other private spots. Plan activities that involve others and take place in public.

This also gives you something besides sexual feelings to focus on. End evenings together when the planned activity is over. Intimacy tends to increase and willpower decrease as the night wears on.

Remember that you have the power to say no to any situation that doesn't feel right to you. Refusing to participate in something that you believe is wrong is your responsibility to yourself.

When you say no, be assertive. Don't send mixed messages. Sometimes one partner tries to say no, while still pleasing the other. When this happens, the negative message is too easily ignored.

If your partner is unsure about sexual behavior, respect his or her wishes. Pushing someone into activity that makes that person uncomfortable is a sign of selfishness and immaturity.

Finally, remember that building a loving relationship takes time. Partners need to get to know each other and to share experiences, thoughts, and feelings. Adding sex when it isn't wanted often kills a growing relationship.

No one can say that abstinence is easy. However, many find that alternative ways of showing love can be very fulfilling.

SKILLS CHECKLIST

Saying No to Sex

Many sound reasons exist for saying no to sexual behavior. Thinking logically, you can predict what could happen. Unfortunately, under pressure, logical thinking isn't easy. Recalling the reasons in the checklist below can help you and your partner think logically, making it easier to say no to sex.

✓ I don't want to be pregnant or get someone pregnant.
✓ I don't want to get an STD.
✓ My parents would be disappointed in me.
✓ It goes against my values.
✓ It would hurt my reputation.
✓ I don't want a sexual relationship to push me into an early marriage.
✓ I need time to know myself better.
✓ I want to learn to be more creative in expressing feelings of love and tenderness.

Using Your Skills

With a partner, discuss which three items in the above list you would be most comfortable using. Practice them in a dialogue with your partner.

Couples who fill their time together with planned activities are less likely to find themselves in situations with heavy sexual pressures. Fixing a pizza for friends, building a birdhouse—even a walk in the rain—all provide distractions.

Talking and joking, sharing dreams and interests—all can create a sense of intimacy and closeness. Bryce and Kelly liked to go window shopping together and plan for their future. They often spent their lunch hour having picnics together in a park near their workplace. On these outings, they read aloud from letters they had written to each other. Bryce and Kelly felt the deep satisfaction of showing their love, yet their actions didn't involve sexual behavior.

Love and affection can be shown in other nonphysical ways. Making dinner, buying a small gift, offering to do an unpleasant job, and other small sacrifices can express caring more than sexual behavior does. Sexual feelings can be shown in the tenderness and consideration you give someone you love. Respecting your partner's needs and goals, as well as your own, and choosing ways of expressing sexual feelings that feel right to you both, may be the sincerest—and safest—way to say "I love you."

The Right Time

When is the right time to have sex? "Now" is the easy answer for anyone who thinks he or she is in love. Remember, though, that love comes in many forms and may be experienced many times before it is real and deserving of commitment and marriage.

Most people want sex to be special. They want strong feelings of desire to go along with a strong bond to one beloved person. They are willing to wait, saving sex for the valued framework of marriage and family.

TAKING RESPONSIBILITY

Real-life stories point out what can happen to people who become sexually active too soon. They tell of lost self-esteem, of disease, of unplanned pregnancy, of abandoned hopes and dreams. These things happen when one thing is missing—responsibility.

What does it mean to be sexually responsible? It means knowing the facts about sexuality. It means thinking about the consequences of your decisions and actions to you and others. It means following the judgment of the mind, not the body. It means knowing yourself and your values—and living by them.

About Intimacy. Intimacy is a closeness between two people that allows them to share their deepest thoughts and feelings, to trust each other, and to show that they truly care. Intimacy helps a relationship last. Intimacy can exist without sex, but sex without intimacy is unrewarding and meaningless. How do you know whether a relationship includes intimacy? The following ideas can help you decide.

- Intimacy develops with day-by-day learning about another person.
- Your body and your feelings are among the most personal of possessions. A decision to share them that is dictated by chance or pressure is not intimacy.
- Intimacy is satisfying in memory. Before getting sexually involved, ask yourself "Is this a memory I want to be recalling in the future?"
- Intimacy increases as a relationship strengthens. If you value intimacy, you have nothing to lose by waiting to have sex, and much to gain.

Try It Out. Write a description of the qualities you would want in a person to whom you would trust yourself — the most valuable thing you have. This is the type of person you will want to trust yourself to when you commit to a sexual relationship in marriage.

SECTION 20-2 REVIEW

Check Your Understanding

1. How are STDs spread?
2. Describe the physical and emotional problems brought on by teen parenting.
3. What kinds of pressures to become sexually active do teens often face?
4. What situations should be avoided in order to deal with sexual desires?
5. **Thinking Critically.** If behavior reflects values, what values might abstinence illustrate? Sexual activity?
6. **Problem Solving.** Zain and Sally have noticed some very contradictory attitudes toward sexual behavior in their school. Some students don't give STDs a thought and their behavior reflects their attitude. Others are taking the threat very seriously. They are committed to abstinence until marriage. As a couple who think abstinence is best, Zain and Sally would like others to join in their thinking. How could they accomplish this?

CHAPTER SUMMARY

- Sexuality refers to how a person handles his or her values and beliefs about sexual behavior.
- Changing gender roles can be a source of confusion and conflict for people.
- Sexual identity is influenced by many factors, some environmental and some genetic.
- Saying yes to sexual pressures can have serious consequences.
- Sexually transmitted diseases are very dangerous, since some are incurable and even fatal.
- Sexual contact is the main way that AIDS is spread.
- Teen pregnancy can cause problems for the mother, father, child, and society.
- The pressure to become sexually active is very strong in society today.
- Choosing abstinence is the best way to deal with sexual pressures.

REVIEW QUESTIONS

Section 20-1
1. Is sexuality the same thing as sexual activity? Explain.
2. Are media images of sexuality positive models for real life? Explain.
3. When Quentin's brother teased him about being the only male in a cooking class, Quentin baked him a pie. What might this say about Quentin's sense of sexual identity?

Section 20-2
1. What are some possible long-term effects of STDs?
2. Explain how AIDS is, and how it is not, transmitted.
3. How can teens resist peers who pressure them to become sexually active?
4. What can young people do to express sexual feelings without physical sexual activity?
5. What is sexual responsibility?

BECOMING A PROBLEM SOLVER

1. Natasha told her best friend Sue, and no one else, that she is pregnant. She is determined to hide the pregnancy. Sue is urging Natasha to see a doctor soon, but Natasha refuses, saying that someone might find out if she does. Sue is concerned. What should she do?

2. Ever since he watched his older stepsister Andrea in a ballet recital, six-year-old Loren has been interested in dance. Andrea has given him some informal lessons and thinks Loren shows talent. Her stepfather, however, says he doesn't want his son to be a ballet dancer. What should Andrea do?

THINKING CRITICALLY

1. **Recognizing Points of View.** What do you believe are ideal gender roles for males and females? How do your ideas compare with those of classmates?
2. **Analyzing Behavior.** Does clothing send sexual messages? Explain your answer.
3. **Determining the Strength of an Argument.** Traditionally, females have had the greater responsibility to say no to unwanted sex. Explain whether you think this expectation is fair.

MAKING CURRICULUM CONNECTIONS

1. **Social Studies.** Research gender roles in various cultures. Compare gender-appropriate behaviors within those cultures.
2. **History.** Find information about a figure who was influential in changing societal views of men and women. Write a short biography of the person, highlighting his or her activities and the changes the person helped bring about. Explain how the person's life continues to affect people today.

APPLYING YOUR KNOWLEDGE

1. View your favorite music video. Decide what messages it sends and whether these are positive or negative. Relate your findings to the class.
2. In small groups, create a list of "lines" that some teens use to try to persuade a partner to have sex. Write at least one "No" response to each "line."

Family & Community Connections

1. Television shows that portray family life often reflect the ideal or generally accepted images of families of the times. Watch a television show that deals with family life. Look for ways in which gender roles are portrayed. Discuss your observations with your family members.

2. Research the incidence of STDs among teens in your community. What is the most common STD? What is the procedure when a teen is diagnosed with an STD? Is confidential HIV testing available? If so, how is it handled?

UNIT 6

Growing as a Person

Teen Views

What's the first thing you'd like people to say when asked to describe you?

Korey

"Probably that I'm a lot of fun. My brother always says what a nut I am, but he's just like me. For my birthday, he gave me the car I want—only it was a plastic toy. His birthday is today so I got him a joke book—but I cut out the punch lines and jumbled them up in an envelope. I think he'll have a pretty good time matching them up."

Juliana

"That I'm loyal. I don't like it when people let me down, so I don't do that. When I was on the debate team, my partner decided not to show up twice. I couldn't believe it! All that practice and hard work—just wasted. I wouldn't do that to anybody. If somebody's counting on me, I won't let them down."

What's your view?

How would you like to be described by other people?

Development Lasts a Lifetime

WORDS FOR THOUGHT

"Somehow we learn who we really are and then live with that decision."
(Eleanor Roosevelt)

IN YOUR OWN WORDS

How will you figure out who you really are?

Developing as a Teen

OBJECTIVES

After studying this section, you should be able to:

- Describe the major areas of human development.
- Explain how teens change in each area of development.
- Describe the impact of developmental changes on teens.
- Explain what influences development.
- Analyze your own growth in each developmental area.

TERMS TO LEARN

development
hormones
body image
temperament
life events

Have you ever looked at baby pictures of yourself and said, "I can't believe that was me"? An older relative might have remarked, "Even then, you were an interesting child. I remember once..." Fifteen years from now, if you find your high school picture or an assignment that you wrote last week, what do you think your reaction will be?

The process of growth and change over the course of life is called **development**. All areas of life are included: physical, intellectual, emotional, social, and moral. Development has already taken you a long way from childhood. It will take you further still in the years to come. In some ways, you may stay the same. In other areas, changes may make you look back and say, "I can't believe that was me." Will these changes bring you closer to the person you want to be? That remains largely up to you.

YOUR PHYSICAL SELF

Your physical self is the combination of your body's outward appearance and internal functions. Your basic body type and physical traits were inherited from your birth family.

During the teen years, the physical self undergoes rapid change—more than in any age except infancy. Changes in the body's production of hormones allow teens to develop the adult traits of their gender. **Hormones** are chemical substances that regulate cellular activity in the body. This process of physical change generally begins and ends a few years earlier in females than in males.

Body Image

Physical change in the teen years is normal and healthy, but it can be disturbing. A teen who develops more quickly or slowly than peers may feel especially awkward. This new awareness of the body can cause problems with **body image**, or the way you see your physical self.

Problems with body image start as people try to live up to some ideal, usually set by celebrities and models in the media. People may not realize—or care—that those images owe a lot to the wonders of skillful photography and makeup. The people in the posters and glossy magazine ads literally look better than life.

The pressure to live up to false images can cause teens to focus on so-called flaws. Overlooking their good points, they magnify what they believe is negative. One teen feels short. Another sees only a nose that is too big.

Strangely, the features that people dislike in themselves are usually not noticed by others. A winning personality tends to counteract any negatives. As people get to know each other better, in fact, physical traits seem to disappear. Think of the people you know and like. What makes you care about these people—the way they look or the way they treat you?

Making the Best of Yourself

Telling yourself that looks are only skin deep is one thing; believing it may be harder. What can you do? First, make the best of yourself physically. Following the principles of good health and hygiene and exercise puts you on the right track. Be realistic about what you can be and work toward that.

Second, learn to like what you see in the mirror. Everyone has good qualities. If your nose or your teeth are a problem, focus on your hair color or your eyes. Use positive self-talk. If you start to fall into negatives, stop and treat yourself to a compliment instead. Eventually, you'll boost your own body image.

From the beginning to the end of the teen years, physical change is dramatic. Continually seeing yourself as a "new" person can bring mixed emotions. What might some of them be?

"My feet are too big and my nose, well . . . ." Appearance means little when there's something special inside.

YOUR MENTAL SELF

The mental, or intellectual, self is the thinking self. You develop intellectually as you learn and use knowledge, logic, and reason. Understanding ideas and the relationships between them shows mental growth, too.

Some people mistakenly believe that mental abilities are shown only through school achievement. Actually, intelligence shows in many other ways as well. You might notice people who have musical talent, creative skills, and problem-solving abilities, to name a few. Obviously people don't all have the same strengths to the same degree. For example, Aaron is known as a genius with motors. He can listen to a lawn mower engine and quickly have ideas about what might fix it. His friend Paulie, however, wouldn't dream of fixing a lawn mower, but he plays the guitar well.

The dangerous looking moray eel is very shy and would rather hide than attack.

A teen grows mentally through many experiences. How can a part-time job or volunteer work spur mental ability?

During the teen years, you develop a more adult way of thinking. You come to understand that behavior has consequences. Sometimes these consequences are positive, sometimes negative. As your thinking matures, you are better able to choose appropriate behavior that brings rewards and satisfaction.

Predicting consequences improves your ability to plan. Young children can't anticipate the future; they learn everything by experience. When you understand the possible outcomes of actions, you can sometimes avoid problems or solve them before they occur. Your plans are more likely to succeed.

Learning Styles

All people learn through their senses. People learn by listening (auditory), by seeing (visual), and by doing (kinesthetic).

You learn in all of these ways, but one may be more effective for you than the rest. A preferred way of learning, or learning style, helps facts and concepts "stick."

Auditory learners excel at absorbing spoken messages. They benefit most from discussions and taped material. Visual learners understand written material most easily. They work well with computer programs, charts, exhibits, demonstrations, and videos. Kinesthetic learners do well with some type of physical action. It may be writing, speaking, performing skits, playing games, or running experiments. They might also learn by creating something through needlework, woodworking, or metal work.

Learning is reinforced if you use more than one style. When you take notes in class, for instance, you're both listening and doing. Viewing a movie involves seeing and hearing. Working on a computer means seeing and doing.

To take advantage of your preferred style, you may need to adapt information. Shannon learns best by writing. As she explained, "I redo my notes after a lecture and take notes when I read. If I'm trying to remember how to spell a word, it helps to write it in the air with my finger."

Understanding how you learn best can help you develop your learning abilities. You can apply your best learning style to the most important materials.

By discovering how you learn best, you can improve your mind—and your grades. **What learning techniques work best for you?**

YOUR EMOTIONAL SELF

Emotions are often pleasant, sometimes painful, and always necessary. They provide information that you can use to understand yourself and others.

There are eight basic emotions: fear, surprise, sadness, disgust, anger, anticipation, joy, and acceptance. Emotions can vary in intensity. Anger may be felt as mild irritation or red-hot rage. The basic emotions combine to make additional ones. Disappointment, for example, is a blend of sadness and surprise.

As a young child, you were naturally self-focused. You expressed emotions freely, often

> **INFOLINK**
>
> ### Controlling Emotions
>
> For more information on controlling emotions, see *Section 22-1*.

without much regard for the effect on other people. Part of growing up is understanding and managing your emotions. You begin to see that emotional control and tact are vital to getting along with others.

The teen years can present stumbling blocks to handling emotions. Not only do you feel new emotions, but hormonal changes in your body may also bring on mood swings. You may wonder why you feel lukewarm about some things—even though everyone else is excited—and passionate about others. How can you feel supremely happy one moment and very low the next?

Feelings themselves aren't right or wrong. Right or wrong enters in how you deal with your emotions. The ability to cope effectively with emotions is one sign of growing up, of being an adult.

YOUR SOCIAL SELF

Your social self is the side of you that relates to other people. Each person has an inborn style of reacting to the world and relating to others. Called **temperament**, this style is shown very early in life. Infants reveal temperament in how active and persistent they are, in how well they adapt to new people and experiences, and in how intensely they respond to their environment.

Some infants have an easygoing temperament. They adapt easily to new people, places, and changes in routine. In contrast, a baby with an excitable temperament is more sensitive to change and more easily upset by new faces and experiences.

A third type of temperament falls between the other two. Some babies react cautiously to their environment. When Carson first saw a wind-up car rolling toward him, he drew back and looked distressed. As the car passed harmlessly by, Carson watched with interest. A few minutes later he was giggling with delight.

Basic temperament is inherited. Its influence tends to persist throughout life, affecting the way people react to events and to others.

Inheriting a certain type of temperament, however, doesn't lock you into certain social behavior. You can learn effective ways to deal with people. An excitable person can learn to control reactions. A cautious person can work at trusting others. Someone with an easygoing nature can develop assertiveness.

YOUR MORAL SELF

Morally you are also developing. When you were very young, you had no concept of right or wrong. Your actions were driven primarily by self-interest. Gradually, you learned that some behavior is not acceptable. You discovered that what you do has an effect on others, a powerful consideration when making decisions about appropriate behavior.

As you know, moral principles are first taught within the family. A family impresses their values upon the younger members. Often religious teaching influences a person's moral code. Teens and young adults develop their ability to evaluate situations and issues according to these principles.

INFOLINK

Moral Development

For more information about moral development, see *Section 23-1*.

Moral development is vital, not only to individuals but to society as well. What happens when people have no regard for others?

Temperament shows at an early age. Whatever you inherit, however, you can shape as you grow.

Building Character

Honesty: A Quality That Counts

Honesty is more than simply not lying. It's being truth*ful*. That means being true to your feelings and beliefs, and giving your best, your honest effort. A teen could show honesty by:

- Telling the sales clerk after receiving too much change from a purchase.
- Writing a report for school rather than finding one on the Internet.
- Giving a coworker credit for a good job rather than accepting unearned praise.
- Telling details of weekend plans to parents, knowing that they might not approve.

QUESTIONS

1. Is it more difficult to be honest with yourself or with others? Why?
2. What might be some long-term consequences of dishonesty?
3. Is honesty always the best policy? Explain.
4. In what ways have you shown honesty?

What happens when they act on selfish impulses? You know how destructive the results can be. Only when each person strives to follow morally sound principles can people be strong together as well as apart.

INTERRELATED DEVELOPMENT

Areas of development are interrelated. What affects one area can affect them all. Jim felt this firsthand when he injured his spine in a fall while skateboarding. This event had impact reaching far beyond just his physical development.

First, Jim missed many months of school, delaying intellectual growth. Emotionally, however, he grew. He learned to manage his fear and anger after the accident. Recovering his physical skills taught him hope and patience. Jim's social development was set back at first when he missed out on activities with his friends. Relying on others and refocusing his life had a profound moral effect on him. Jim put new value on family, friends, and many things he had taken for granted before. He found ways to show these thoughts and feelings.

This one event in Jim's life changed him in every area of development. Situations that are less dramatic can also have far-reaching effects. For example, what happens if you become close to someone who has a strong influence on you? What else has an effect on the way you develop?

INFLUENCES ON DEVELOPMENT

You know, of course, that heredity has shaped part of what you are today. The environment also makes many contributions. These are some of the environmental influences you encounter every day:

- Technology influences your health, the information you have at your fingertips, and the way you handle work and free time.
- Economic conditions affect your health as well as the opportunities you have.
- Social factors have impact. For example, laws aim to protect you from discrimination. Changing gender roles allow you to have a wider range of opportunity than people of earlier generations had.

- **Life events**, the experiences that people have, can have strong impact on development. Injury or a health problem causes change. A teen who has a baby alters the future. What other events could change the direction of a person's life?
- Support from family and friends gives you a foundation for living and adds incentive to do well in life.

What's ahead for you? As you'll soon see, the path ahead, from now and through your adulthood, will be filled with change and opportunity. Your development has just begun. Right now you're setting the stage for adulthood. You can make decisions and plans that will give direction and purpose to your life.

Tips & TECHNIQUES

Building Confidence. Imagine your school principal asks you to head the organizing committee for a fund-raising project. Do you react with eagerness, dread, or something in between? Your response to new or difficult life events is a reflection of your confidence, your faith in yourself and your abilities. Few people, even those who are quite talented in some area, possess total self-confidence. Whatever your confidence level, these exercises can help you raise it:

- Stand up straight and look people in the eye when talking to them.
- Go out of your way to do something nice for someone.
- Learn a new skill through practice or instruction from someone.
- Make a plan for improving yourself as a student, employee, or family member, and carry it out.

Try It Out. List three situations where you feel most confident. Write down three things about those times that help you feel that way. Now list three situations where you feel least confident. Plan ways to incorporate the confidence-building aspects that you identified into those latter situations.

As a teen, you make choices about who your friends will be. How does this affect the person you are becoming?

Check Your Understanding

1. What effect do hormones have on development?
2. What can a person do to become more comfortable with his or her body image?
3. How are the three learning styles used?
4. What is temperament?
5. Why is the moral development of individuals so important to society?
6. **Thinking Critically.** How do you think certain body types and physical features become favored in a society?
7. **Problem Solving.** Morgan's efforts to be more outgoing are paying off as she makes new friends and gets involved in new activities. Now her best friend says Morgan no longer has time for her. She asks if Morgan has "outgrown" their friendship. Morgan still cares about her friend, but she likes what she is becoming too. What should Morgan do?

Life-Span Development

OBJECTIVES

After studying this section, you should be able to:

- Explain the concept of life-span development.
- Describe the life tasks of adolescence.
- Identify the stages of adult life and the life task of each.

TERMS TO LEARN

life-span development
life task
adolescence

Do you remember, as a child, wanting to be "grown up"? Actually, you may never reach that point. To those who remain open to learning and change, "growing up" can be a continual, lifelong process. Even if development in adulthood is less apparent than in younger years, it can be just as dramatic.

IMPACT OF LIFE-SPAN DEVELOPMENT

Have you ever had a good look at a tree that has been cut down? The tree's life story, year by year, shows in the cross section of rings in the trunk. The rings are not always evenly shaped or equally spaced. You see warps, scars, and discolored places. Each event the tree experienced—a summer of good rains or a spring of termites—has been imprinted in its very core. These events affected the tree's growth and health and left a lasting mark.

In the same way, each of your experiences leaves a lasting impression on you. You can't erase the scars from the past, any more than the tree can, but you can move beyond them.

In spite of past adversity, the tree continued to develop—and so will you. As Carli said, "I've made some bad decisions in my life—who hasn't? But I know I can change. Every day I get another chance to work toward being the person I want to be."

Carli is a firm believer in **life-span development**, the concept that change occurs throughout a person's life. All aspects of life—physical, mental, emotional,

Certain events mark significant moments of passage from one stage of life to another. This is one. Can you think of others?

social, and moral—enjoy ongoing growth and development. People are never "finished." They are always works in progress.

As you read the description of life-span development that follows, remember that it's only a guide to future development. It's not a blueprint. You will meet life's challenges and tasks in your own time as your life unfolds.

STAGES OF LIFE

Each person, in living, passes through various stages. Generally, these stages are infancy, childhood, adolescence, young adulthood, middle life, and late life. All people follow similar patterns of development. Particular development, however, is as unique as each individual's personality and circumstances.

Like development itself, the stages of life are interrelated. Each stage, with its own potential, traits, and problems, builds on the ones before it. Managing each stage successfully provides a solid base for the next. Within you are elements of the child you once were. These elements influence the teen you are now and the adult you are becoming.

The idea of life as stages is a useful framework for examining and measuring growth. On the other hand, it may suggest a precision that doesn't exist. Stages don't arrive and depart on schedule. You may enter a stage years ahead of another person, yet remain there longer.

Life Tasks

A **life task** is a challenge to be met at each stage of growth. It can be the skills, habits, knowledge, or attitudes you need to cope with the events in that stage. Accomplishing a life task inspires feelings of competence and success. You feel well positioned to meet the tasks of the next stage. In contrast, failure at a task leads to feelings of inadequacy, making success at future tasks more doubtful.

ADOLESCENCE

Adolescence (AD-ul-ES-unts) is the stage of life between childhood and adulthood. This is where you are now—the teen years. Like an agent in a spy film, you have missions to accomplish. They are the life tasks of adolescence.

Finding Your Identity

Before you can figure out what you want from life and how to get it, you must know who you are as a person. A secure sense of self gives you the confidence to deal with the demands made of you, to plan for the future and move toward adult responsibilities.

As a child, you were asked, "What do you want to be when you grow up?" As a teen, that question takes on new urgency. You start to ask, "What are my values and my goals? What do I want for the future?" With growth and experience, you form a solid understanding of yourself that you'll carry through life. In other words, you find your identity. Building a sense of identity is the main life task of adolescence.

The search for identity involves all facets of life. Growth can be uneven at times and frustrating, with progress made in some areas and not others. During these years, however, teens keep working, searching, learning, and growing. As they discover their unique goals, talents, and styles, they gradually begin to see who they are and where they fit in society.

Sloan described the feeling this way: "I've always been my parents' son and my sister's little brother. Somehow, I never seemed to stand alone. Last year, I took a graphic arts class and loved it. I think I can see myself as a Web site designer someday. I also won a seat on the student council. I feel like I'm starting to uncover pieces of myself that I didn't know were there."

Sloan's words show that he has begun another part of forming identity. He is integrating his personality, piecing together the various elements to create a unique identity. You integrate your personality as you gradually discover what interests you want to pursue as an adult. Your emotions stabilize and form a pattern for dealing with life. You mold your roles, talents, values, and attitudes into a cohesive whole.

Tips & TECHNIQUES

Thinking About the Future. Think back over the last three years. How have you changed? Can you see a pattern or process in your development? What do you think the future holds for you?

- Imagine you are opening fortune cookies. Write five fortunes that you hope or expect to be true for yourself. Base your predictions on the developmental tasks of young adults that you have read about, but personalize them to your own circumstances.
- Ask a friend to write five fortunes for you. (You could do the same for the friend.)
- Seal your ten fortunes in an envelope marked with a date for opening.

Try It Out. Follow the steps above. On the given date, open the envelope and see whether your predictions and your friend's were "on the mark."

Becoming Independent

A second task of adolescence is becoming independent. At some point, most people separate themselves from their parents. They leave home, symbolizing the end of childhood and adolescence. They earn their own money and control their own lives. The young person is seen as a separate, self-sufficient adult. Some young people struggle eagerly to break free. Others are in no hurry.

To live independently, you need problem-solving, decision-making, and management skills. Learning these skills prepares teens to depend less on parents.

Planning for Employment

Still another task of adolescence is planning for your life's work. Most years of adult life are spent earning a living, often in more than one job.

Generally, people who choose and prepare for careers are happier than those who take whatever comes along. To choose the right career, you need to know your talents and interests. Are you good at working with machines, or perhaps with people? Does an office setting or outdoor work sound more appealing?

Jobs that offer greater challenge, satisfaction, and income usually require preparation, and the teen years are the time to start. Daniel wants to be a chef. He knows he'll need training, so he's starting to investigate what schools are available and what he needs to do now to be accepted.

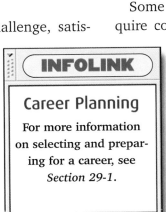

"Who am I? What will I be?" The search for identity can be frustrating at times, but it can also point you toward a bright future as you learn to know and respect yourself.

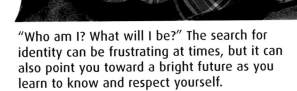

INFOLINK

Career Planning

For more information on selecting and preparing for a career, see *Section 29-1*.

Some fields that you might choose require college education. You need certain coursework in high school to be admitted. The better your grades, the better chance you have of getting into the school of your choice. Other fields offer on-the-job training through apprenticeships or company training programs. Technical training from a community college or trade school is required for other jobs.

Moving Through Adolescence

People move through adolescence at their own pace. Some seem to sail through their life tasks. Others find them more difficult. No one route through adolescence works for every teen.

Many people believe that adolescence is a time of turmoil and stress. The teen years are stereotyped as a constant clash with parents, siblings, teachers, friends, and employers.

Certainly some teens do find adolescence to be an uphill battle. Rapid change and development can bring problems in rela-tionships. Moving toward independence, teens are bound to clash at times with parents, who may be reluctant to let their care-giving role go.

For the majority of teens, however, adolescence is an exciting and satisfying age, a time of typical growth and development. They are able to build good relationships and form strong ties with family and friends. Most teens accept their parents' religious, political, and social views. They find ways to work toward independence without the conflict that some expect of these years.

Stages of Adult Life

Researcher Daniel Levinson described these life tasks that must be accomplished in each stage of adult life.

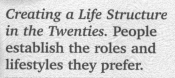

Developing Intimacy in the Twenties. To avoid loneliness, people build relationships. Some marry and form families.

Creating a Life Structure in the Twenties. People establish the roles and lifestyles they prefer.

Establishing Roots in the Thirties. Settling down brings stability. Focus may be on children, career, or community.

ADULT DEVELOPMENT

As teens slip into adulthood, the life tasks of adolescence should be gradually coming into place. Young people who have a sense of what they are and what they want to be are ready to be independent and move on with life. Many years and more life tasks lie ahead.

Most experts who study adult development have found a similar pattern that applies to most people. Each decade of life seems to be characterized by a basic life task. The illustration below shows what these are. Remember, of course, that exceptions always exist. Ages can vary and exceptions may occur. Each adult handles life tasks in an individual way.

As you enter adulthood, you will begin to establish a structure for your life. A life structure is based on three components. First are the *roles* you fill, such as parent, spouse, and worker. The second element is *relationships* with family members, friends, coworkers, and others. Finally, life structure includes the *physical world* in which you live, from your residence to your neighborhood and community. The ability you have developed to make sound decisions will help you adopt a life structure that suits you.

> *What might happen if a person doesn't accomplish the life task in a particular stage?*

Reevaluating Life in the Forties. Fearing time is limited, people question earlier choices. Opportunities and new interests are often seized.

Finding Stability and Peace in the Fifties. People have freedom from child-raising, more contact with friends, fewer money problems, and happy marriages.

Coming to Terms after Age Sixty. People look forward to retirement, anticipate life's end, and come to terms with how they've lived.

The directions people take in adulthood depend on their goals and interests. What directions are ahead for you?

What causes the life structure to change? Both external and internal influences have impact. Externally, a new job or a health problem could cause change. Internally, feelings of dissatisfaction or interest could cause a person to make changes.

Change gives adults opportunities for growth. Through change, they move on to the next life task. By handling each task as it comes, adults prepare themselves for the task ahead.

Throughout adult life, you will have times of stability and times of change. During stable periods, the life structure stays the same. In times of change, the life structure shifts. Changes can be major or minor. Will you take on a new role or leave an old one behind? Will you build a new relationship or end an old one? Will you move near or far?

AIMING FOR THE FUTURE

When you're a teen, imagining how you'll feel and what you'll think as a forty-, fifty-, or sixty-year-old seems impossible—even pointless. That's so far away. You won't wish you had done things differently in your youth, or will you?

Too often people do look back with regrets. Some are sorry they ignored certain rules. Some wish fervently that they had never started a bad health habit. Some wish they had tried harder to make a relationship work. Some wonder why they didn't plan for a career they would enjoy.

Ask any older adult how quickly life passes by, and the answer will probably be "very." It's a mistake to think you won't care how your life is going when you're older, because you will. You'll want to live an enjoyable life as a mature adult just as much as you do right now. In fact, with fewer years left to you, you may wish it even more.

You'll never be able to go back and change the past, but right now you're creating what will become the past. What an opportunity this is for you. You can make decisions and plans to give your life direction and purpose. You can aim for a good life throughout all your years, but you need to start right now.

Adulthood continues to be a time for personal growth. People master new skills and learn more about themselves. To make the most of the life you've been given, you can continue to improve and learn for many years to come.

SECTION 21-2 REVIEW

Check Your Understanding

1. What is life-span development?
2. How does each stage of life relate to the next?
3. What is a life task?
4. What are the three life tasks of adolescence?
5. What are the stages of adult life and the life task for each stage?
6. **Thinking Critically.** As you think about life tasks, what do you think might help an aging person be more at peace with the prospect of death?
7. **Problem Solving.** Darrin's father has decided to take a lower-paying, less demanding job so he can return to school for his college degree. Darrin plans to go to college when he graduates in two years. He wonders whether family financial help will be there for his own tuition, but he doesn't want to sound negative about his father's goal. What should Darrin do?

Chapter 21
Review and Activities

CHAPTER SUMMARY

- Physical changes in the teen years can be dramatic and disturbing.
- Mental growth occurs as teens learn to anticipate consequences and to plan.
- Identifying and using one's learning style can aid mental development.
- Emotional growth requires controlling and dealing with emotions appropriately.
- Teens grow socially when they learn to relate to people effectively.
- Moral growth, which continues in the teen years, is vital to both individuals and society.
- Life-span development stresses growth in all areas throughout life.
- Adolescence includes fulfilling certain life tasks that prepare a teen for adulthood.
- As adults develop in the early years, they establish a life structure.
- Adult life includes periods of stability and change in life structure.

REVIEW QUESTIONS

Section 21-1
1. How can media images of beauty affect a teen's body image?
2. Do all people show intelligence in the same way? Explain.
3. Why might a student who excels in the lab section of chemistry do poorly in the lecture section?
4. What emotional challenges do the teen years present?
5. What is the relationship between temperament and social growth?
6. How do people grow morally?

Section 21-2
1. Would you consider yourself to be fully grown at age twenty-one? Why or why not?
2. What information does a teen need to determine identity?
3. Is adolescence a difficult time for teens? Explain.
4. What is life structure based on?
5. How can young people avoid regrets during adulthood?

BECOMING A PROBLEM SOLVER

1. Nick learns best by doing. He has always struggled with literature and history classes, which involve mostly reading and lectures. What should Nick do to improve his grades?
2. At twenty-eight, Rochelle is happy and successful in her job. She enjoys volunteer work in the community; however, she has begun to feel a growing anxiety about being single at an age when most of her friends are married. Rochelle has close male friends but hasn't met anyone she would like to marry. What should Rochelle do?

THINKING CRITICALLY

1. **Recognizing Alternatives.** How might a person help others develop a positive body image?
2. **Drawing Conclusions.** Analyze your own development so far. How would you describe your progress in each area of development?
3. **Recognizing Stereotypes.** How do you think the teen years became known as a time of turmoil? Is this true for you or your friends? How might this stereotype affect the behavior of both teens and parents?
4. **Predicting Results.** Which stage of life do you think is, or will be, most difficult? Explain your answer.

MAKING CURRICULUM CONNECTIONS

1. **Language Arts.** Write a paragraph, short essay, or poem comparing human development to another type of growth or progress.
2. **Science.** Learn more about the hormones responsible for the physical changes that occur during the teen years. What factors can affect the timing and rate of these changes? Write a summary report of your findings.
3. **Language Arts.** Write a poem or an essay describing a life event that had a significant impact on your development.
4. **History.** Research the life of a historical figure whose life deviated from the typical pattern of development. Examples include Rosa Parks and Grandma Moses, whose historical accomplishments came in later life, and Mozart and Joan of Arc, who made an impact when they were young.

APPLYING YOUR KNOWLEDGE

1. Write a short paragraph that gives an example of personal development in one of the areas discussed in this chapter. Do not name the area. Read your example to the class and have classmates identify the area you are describing.
2. Research and write a report on ideas of beauty in other cultures or eras. Describe and explain why certain physical features are or were thought to be attractive. Compare them with the ideas of beauty that you see.
3. Choose a topic from the chapter. Plan to present the topic in ways that appeal to the three different learning styles.

Family & Community Connections

1. You can learn lessons from the experiences of others. Talk with an adult family member about the satisfactions as well as regrets the person has. How can you relate this person's experiences to your own life?

2. Many community resources offer services and support to people throughout life. Write these age categories as column headings: 20s, 30s, 40s, 50s, 60s, and 70+. Underneath each heading, list the community resources and services that might be most useful.

Chapter 22

A Closer Look at You

IN YOUR OWN WORDS

What is your focus?

Your Personality

OBJECTIVES

After studying this section, you should be able to:

- Compare the effects of heredity and environment on personality.
- Describe three types of traits that combine to make up personality.
- Demonstrate a process for gaining control of emotions.
- Compare extroverted and introverted personalities.
- Suggest ways to develop the personality you want to have.

TERMS TO LEARN

introverted
extroverted

Have you ever thought about what makes all the people you know so different? For that matter, what makes you different from all the people you know? Personality, each individual's unique blend of qualities and behaviors, is shaped almost like a sculpture: carved from a core material by countless strokes. There is a big difference, however. The sculpture has no control over how it turns out. You do.

ROOTS OF PERSONALITY

The processes that create personality are complex. Basically, personality is shaped by both heredity and environment. No one can say for sure which contributes more. Most likely, the two work hand in hand. Your environment molds the raw material you inherited—often in ways you don't notice.

Rachel, for example, had always been high-strung and impatient. These were inherited traits. As she matured, experience taught her the value of calmness and patience. That was the environment at work. She used her inherited intelligence to learn how to be more calm and patient. Support from family and friends—the environment again—helped her succeed.

Although both heredity and environment influence personality, you can't really blame either one for the problems you might have. That's because people have the ability to make changes. A personality that's causing problems can be fixed. It's much better to ask, "What can I do differently?" than to say, "I was born that way."

"He's his father's son." Expressions such as this point out the influence of heredity on personality. What else has an effect?

INFOLINK

Heredity and Environment

To review information on heredity and environment, see *Section 8-2.*

WHAT MAKES UP PERSONALITY?

Many different traits combine to make up personality. Each trait falls into one of three broad categories: emotional, social, and intellectual.

Emotional Traits

People experience more emotions than they can name. The eight basic ones you read about earlier are fear, surprise, sadness, disgust, anger, anticipation, joy, and acceptance. How strongly you experience each one and how easily and often they occur are part of your personality. For example, some people see humor everywhere. Laughter is more likely for them than shouts or tears.

Emotions are elements of personality that are easily seen but sometimes misinterpreted. Tyler, for example, had a fearful nature. He avoided meeting new people. His new classmates thought he was arrogant. Only after they knew him better did they realize how wrong their first impression was.

Controlling Emotions

As with other elements of personality, you have some control over your emotions. How you react is largely up to you.

Negative emotions, such as anger and frustration, are often the most difficult to control. Unfortunately, they can also do the most damage when you let them take over. If emotional control is a challenge for you, the following steps can help:

1. **Identify the emotion that's causing the problem.** Try to pinpoint exactly what you're feeling, whether one emotion or several. You may feel angry because you're disappointed. You may feel disgust for something frightening.

2. **Identify the cause of the emotion.** This could be an unpleasant person, event, or job. Once you have identified the cause, ask yourself what aspect you're reacting to.

3. **List what you can do to manage the emotion.** What steps can you take to change your reaction? What tools do you need? If you feel someone's actions are disgusting, getting to know the person better might change your opinion. If you're anxious about an upcoming event, you could put your mind at ease by learning about it.

4. **Take the necessary steps.** Once you've decided what needs to be done, take action. Talk to the person, rehearse the event, or do whatever else is necessary. Seek help from a knowledgeable friend or even a trained counselor if emotions are extreme and long lasting.

With this strategy, you gain more control over your personality. You can turn negative emotions into opportunities for growth and improvement. Anger over an injustice, for example, can motivate you to improve a situation. Sorrow for another person's loss may spur you to give support.

Of course, some negative emotional responses can't be changed. Some things will always be sources of irritation or anxiety. For these, you can use the stress management skills you've learned.

Emotions drive the way you interact with people. What emotions help you build positive relationships?

Social Traits

Social traits affect how you relate to others. All people show certain social personality traits. They may be polite or rude, obedient or rebellious, accepting or judgmental. Most people behave somewhere between the extremes. It's natural to express different traits in different situations. For example, you may tend to be more judgmental of people you don't know than of your friends.

Everyone relates to other people in his or her own way. In most individuals, however, social traits combine to form a personality that leans toward introverted or extroverted.

Introverts and Extroverts

Introverted means focused inward or on oneself. Introverts tend to prefer activities that allow them to concentrate on what you might call the "inner" life. Kyle, for instance, enjoys reading, listening to music, and sketching landscapes. Kyle isn't shy. He enjoys the company of others and relates well to them, but his need and appreciation for time spent alone is greater.

At the opposite end are extroverts. **Extroverted** means focused outward or on others. Extroverts prefer the company of people to being alone. They enjoy playing team sports, performing before an audience, and taking part in discussions. They are open with their feelings and opinions. Of course, they may also enjoy quieter activities as well.

Most mental health experts agree that a balance of introverted and extroverted qualities is desirable. Full social development means being able to enjoy time spent with others and time spent in quiet reflection.

Introverts are comfortable spending time alone. When does introversion become a problem for some people?

Managing Social Aspects

Like emotions, social aspects of your personality can be partially controlled and changed. Conner, for example, was naturally outgoing. He spent most of his free time with others. When a teacher talked one day about values and priorities, Conner realized he hadn't thought much about his. After that, Conner made it a point to find time for reflection. He began to read more and think about people's opinions. When he came across something that raised his curiosity, he learned more about it.

Conner began to understand why he felt and acted as he did. He felt more capable of deciding whether he was developing into the person he wanted to be. Conner still enjoyed activities with his friends but found it satisfying to take time for reflection as well.

Intellectual Traits

Intellectual traits deal with the mind and mental abilities. These skills include logical processes, such as making deductions and predicting consequences. Critical thinking skills are included—evaluating arguments and recognizing bias, for example. The intellect is also the source of the imagination, which expresses itself in any number of creative processes. Finding a better way to finish a task is creative and writing poetry is too. Your intellectual traits are in continuous use—when you read a book, decide what to eat for lunch, or understand a friend's joke.

You can do much to sharpen your mental skills. School provides a ready opportunity for intellectual growth, but almost any situation can be a learning experience. What possibilities for learning can you find in these everyday situations?

- An older shopper in the checkout line comments to you on how prices have risen.
- Your car needs an oil change.
- You spot an unusual rock while walking to school.
- You see a painting that you admire in a friend's home.

Building Character

Generosity: A Quality That Counts

How do you feel when a family member helps you do a job or a friend gives you a small gift? Generosity means giving your time, talents, and other resources without expecting something back. Being generous is part of the social aspect of your personality. A teen known for generosity might:

- Volunteer regularly at the American Red Cross.
- Donate older but wearable clothing to a clothing drive for the homeless.
- Help register voters before national and local elections.
- Include an elderly neighbor on a trip to the grocery store, shopping mall, or library.

QUESTIONS

1. Must a person have many resources to be generous? Explain your answer.
2. Is generosity contagious? Explain.
3. Is generosity more or less admirable if the person receives public recognition for giving?
4. Give an example of how you have shown generosity.

Some personality traits surface for certain reasons. A person who doesn't feel smart enough might try to look brighter by talking too much. Why might someone choose to be a "clown"?

Not everyone has the same capacity for mental growth. All people, however, can work at developing their mental abilities.

PERSONALITY AND PROGRESS

Personality is not static. Its emotional, social, and intellectual elements are always responding to internal and external influences. Personality grows and changes as a person does, intentionally or unintentionally. By being aware of this fact, you can work to shape the personality you want to have.

How you deal with your personality affects where you go from here. It's no contradiction to accept yourself yet try to improve at the same time. Self-improvement keeps you learning and growing over the years. Taking a closer look at your personality can help you understand how you got where you are. Then you can plan what you want for your future.

SECTION 22-1 REVIEW

Check Your Understanding

1. What are the two major forces that shape personality?
2. Personality is made up of what three types of traits?
3. Do you need to know the cause of a negative emotion in order to control it? Explain.
4. How do introverted and extroverted personalities compare?
5. What types of skills are considered intellectual personality traits?
6. **Thinking Critically.** What environmental factors might help create an introverted and an extroverted personality?
7. **Problem Solving.** Jonathan prefers to be alone or with one or two close friends. He feels tense in crowds or among strangers. He knows, however, that success in life depends on working well with others. What should Jonathan do?

Developing a Positive Attitude

OBJECTIVES

After studying this section, you should be able to:

- Explain what attitude is and where it comes from.
- Summarize the impacts of a positive attitude.
- Describe how an attitude can be changed.
- Relate meeting certain needs to self-esteem.
- Demonstrate ways to build a positive attitude.

TERMS TO LEARN

attitude
serotonin
self-esteem

William James said, " The greatest discovery of my generation is that a human being can alter his life by altering his attitude." Those who've had this experience would surely agree.

WHAT IS ATTITUDE?

Attitude is a person's basic outlook on life. An attitude is typically described as positive or negative. The automatic response you have to most situations, issues, and people tells you whether you have a positive or negative attitude overall.

Like other parts of personality, attitude has some basis in heredity. **Serotonin** (sir-uh-TOH-nun) is a brain chemical that affects mood and attitude. People who genetically have high levels of serotonin tend toward a more optimistic outlook. Those with low levels may be more easily depressed and discouraged.

Brain chemistry, however, tells only part of the story. People learn attitude from the environment, just as they do values and behavior. Your outlook is shaped by personal experiences at home, in school, and with friends. Anyone who is a role model also helps shape your approach.

THE IMPACT OF ATTITUDE

Negative attitudes need attention. If a person's attitude is negative most of the time, the cooperation and respect of others will eventually be lost. Sometimes the person acquires a reputation as a negative person. A

A positive attitude can often be seen.
What role do you think confidence plays in developing a positive outlook?

positive attitude serves a person better. It's desirable for several reasons:

- A positive attitude helps build relationships. Do you enjoy being around someone who always complains and expects the worst? Most people prefer upbeat, enthusiastic, and optimistic company.
- Positive thinking aids problem solving. You see more alternatives when you focus on solutions and find the spirit to tackle them instead of becoming overwhelmed.
- Thinking positively can help you reach goals. When you believe you can succeed, you make the effort to meet challenges. If you expect failure, any obstacle may be reason to quit trying.
- Positive thinking is better for your physical health. Studies have shown that optimistic people get sick only half as often as those with a more pessimistic attitude.

To put attitude in perspective, remember that a positive attitude can go astray if carried to extreme. If you're so bent on being positive that you can't recognize when something is truly wrong, that can get you in trouble too.

CHANGING YOUR ATTITUDE

Many people are looking for ways to improve their overall outlook. So much goes on in life to get people down that it's sometimes a real challenge to be positive. Like most personality traits, however, attitude can be improved. You may have to make an attitude adjustment one step at a time.

Focus On ...

Defeating Depression

Life's challenges can leave people feeling discouraged sometimes. Even unexplained, passing feelings of sadness are typical. Depression, on the other hand, is a long-lasting feeling of helplessness, hopelessness, or worthlessness that isn't normal.

About five percent of all teens experience depression every year. Such statements as "I can't seem to care about anything," "I don't have any energy these days," and "What's the point?" may be expressions of depression. Other signs include eating or sleeping too much or too little; difficulty in concentrating; unexplained physical ailments, such as headaches or upset stomach; carelessness about physical appearance; and talk or thoughts of suicide.

Depression often has no apparent cause. However, researchers believe they have identified several contributing factors. An imbalance of chemicals in the brain, such as serotonin, can make a person more prone to depression. Certain personality traits, such as a lack of self-confidence, may have the same effect. A tendency toward depression appears to be inherited in some cases. Stress can also trigger depression.

There is help for depression. A proper diet and adequate sleep and exercise provide the physical and mental fitness that wards off depression. Sharing feelings of sadness when they occur can prevent them from growing worse. More serious cases require the advice and care of trained professionals.

Depression is not cause for shame or embarrassment, nor a sign of weakness or mental instability. Like a fever, it's a sign that something isn't right and needs attention.

USING YOUR KNOWLEDGE

It was Friday as Michelle walked self-consciously down the hall of her high school. She couldn't wait to get home, where she would probably sleep most of the weekend. Maybe she wouldn't even come back on Monday morning, she thought, but who would notice? What would you say to Michelle?

Looking at Specific Situations

Your outlook shows in the way you view people, topics, issues, and even yourself. Think of a topic you feel very strongly about. You'll have three basic reactions. These combine to make up your attitude:

- **Mental.** You have beliefs about the topic that come to mind.
- **Emotional.** You sense feelings related to the topic.
- **Behavioral.** You behave in certain ways because of how you think and feel.

If you want to change an attitude, you need to tackle each of these components. Take little steps to make changes. Begin with the mental aspect. That's easiest to change because you can gather new knowledge and use logical thinking. Changing behavior takes willpower. If you learn something new, however, you may be able to change your behavior. Feelings resist change most of all.

Interestingly, behavior is often the most influential of the three parts in changing an attitude. When you act a certain way, thinking and feelings tend to follow.

Chris used this information to change his attitude toward his economics teacher. His grades were suffering because of his negative attitude. To change, Chris first gath-ered more information by talking with Mrs. Stewart. Getting to know her better helped him see her as a person and understand her point of view. He decided to make manageable changes in his behavior one at a time. On one day, he said nothing confrontational in class. On another day, he greeted Mrs. Stewart. Gradually, as he repeated the behaviors, Mrs. Stewart's responses to Chris changed. Over time, his feelings became less hostile and his attitude improved.

ATTITUDE AND SELF-ESTEEM

Having a positive outlook on life isn't easy if you don't feel good about yourself. Your feelings about self-esteem began in the family but are also influenced by other experiences in your life. How would you rate your own self-esteem? Use the checklist on the next page as a gauge. Remember that you *can* change how you see yourself.

High self-esteem is more than just feeling good about yourself. It is a tool you can use to push yourself to achieve new goals. You believe that you can achieve what you set out to do and you're willing to try. Failures are taken in stride, not dwelled upon.

People with low self-esteem often put themselves down, believing that they can't accomplish anything on their own. They attribute successes to luck. Failures just prove how inadequate they really are, or so they think. They often make excuses or blame others when things don't go well. They act as though life is beyond their control.

A feeling of connection with friends and family gives a person a sense of self-esteem. How can you help others feel worthwhile?

Improving Self-Esteem

If you could bottle and sell the formula for self-esteem, you might become wealthy. Since there is no such formula, however, those who need a boost will have to make a personal effort. A sense of self-esteem builds from meeting four emotional needs:

- **Identity.** Acceptance of yourself, flaws and all, makes you feel comfortable with who you are. Say to yourself, "I'm not like anyone else, and I don't have to be."

- **Belonging.** This is your connection to people. You can find one small way today to strengthen a tie to a family member, friend, classmate, or group. Every day you can find one more way.

- **Security.** In this sense, security is psychological safety. You know that others accept and respect you as you are. To feel secure, find someone who is accepting, reliable, and trustworthy. Then support each other.

- **Purpose.** Knowing what you want to be or achieve gives meaning to what you do every day. To gain purpose, set a few short- and long-term goals and start working right now to reach them.

Someone once said, "People will be happy in about the same degree that they are helpful." Do you think that's true?

just learning, so she wasn't discouraged. She made friends with an experienced counselor who was willing to help her.

As she developed her skills in working with the children, Amber became a trusted member of the camp staff. By the end of the summer, she felt that she would be welcomed back as a counselor the following summer. How did each of the four emotional needs build Amber's sense of self-esteem?

BUILDING A POSITIVE ATTITUDE

Imagine this scene. You wake up late when your alarm doesn't go off. You skip breakfast and barely make the bus to school. There you find that you've misplaced an important assignment that's due today. You're hungry, discouraged, and when you see the look on a friend's face, you realize that you forgot to call last night.

At this point, could you "look on the bright side"? Could you even find one? Some days challenge positive thinking. For those days, or any time, you'll need some ideas for putting a little sunshine back in your life.

- **Take positive action.** Remember that actions can change the way you feel. Just taking the first steps toward solving a problem can make you feel better.
- **Talk positively.** Dare to be an optimist. When you tell someone that you're sure things will go well, they typically do. If

When these four needs are met, self-esteem flows naturally. Success comes more easily. Amber's experience as a camp counselor shows how this works. Amber really wanted to work with children and help them. She landed the counselor's position on the second year of trying. Amber was nervous on her first day of summer camp, but she reminded herself that she was a competent, patient, caring person—all qualities that would help her work with the children.

Although she made some mistakes the first week of camp, Amber knew she was

things don't work out, remind yourself that such events often teach you the most. Instead of saying, "What a dumb thing I did today," say, "What can I do better tomorrow?"

- **Accept yourself.** Acknowledge weaknesses as well as strengths. Forgive yourself for mistakes and learn from them. Set reasonable goals and reward yourself for reaching them. Compare yourself *to* yourself, not to anyone else, and learn to measure progress in terms of where you are versus where you were.
- **Stay open to learning.** Mastering new skills and gaining knowledge increase your self-esteem. You also feel admiration and appreciation for the people who teach you.
- **Reach out to others.** Develop good relationships with a variety of people. Worthy friends come in all ages and sizes and from all backgrounds. Take positive

thinkers as role models. Remember that it's qualities that you want to imitate, not people. Trying to be exactly like someone else is not possible or desirable. Try helping others. Doing good for them makes you feel better about yourself.

- **Assert yourself.** You have a right to speak up and act on your beliefs. Preserve a positive atmosphere by saying what you think and feel in ways that aren't offensive.
- **Accept and respect others as they are.** Show that you value them. By treating people courteously, you show that you already think of them as worthwhile individuals.

A positive attitude can be a real asset in life. Doors will open for you. Other people will welcome you. When you know that someone else feels good about you, you can feel the same way about yourself.

SECTION 22-2 REVIEW

Check Your Understanding

1. What is attitude?
2. What influences the attitude a person develops?
3. How can positive thinking help you solve problems?
4. Describe three reactions that combine to make up attitude.
5. What are the needs that must be filled in order to have a good sense of self-esteem?
6. What are five tips for developing a positive attitude?
7. **Thinking Critically.** Does a positive attitude create a sense of self-esteem or does a sense of self-esteem create a positive attitude? Explain your answer.
8. **Solving Problems.** Madeleine is a worrier. Whether planning a school project or a family picnic, she's the first to find problems with an idea. She continually reminds others of what could go wrong. One day a friend told her, "Madeleine, would you lighten up? Things never turn out as bad as you think they will. You aren't going to have any friends left if you keep bringing everyone down." What should Madeleine do?

Chapter 22
Review and Activities

CHAPTER SUMMARY

- Heredity and environment are the two major influences that shape personality.
- Personality is composed of emotional, social, and intellectual traits.
- Negative emotions can be, and need to be, controlled.
- Personalities may be introverted or extroverted.
- Personality grows and changes as a person does. You have the ability to shape your personality.
- Attitude shows in the automatic responses you have to most situations, issues, and people.
- A positive attitude promotes mental, emotional, social, and even physical health.
- A negative attitude can be improved.
- Feelings of self-esteem thrive when you are secure in yourself and among others, and feel a sense of purpose.
- You can develop a positive attitude by thinking and acting optimistically toward yourself and others.

REVIEW QUESTIONS

Section 22-1
1. How do heredity and environment help shape personality?
2. Can a person have qualities of both an introvert and an extrovert? Explain.
3. How can you sharpen intellectual skills?
4. What is the value of analyzing and understanding your personality?

Section 22-2
1. Describe ways that having a positive attitude can improve life.
2. If you wanted to change your attitude, which aspect would you start with? Why?
3. Felicia has a strong sense of self-esteem, but Jackie doesn't. In what ways are they probably different?
4. How does having a sense of purpose contribute to a sense of self-esteem?
5. What role do others play in helping you build a positive attitude?

BECOMING A PROBLEM SOLVER

1. Chelsea needs people. If she's not with friends, she's talking on the phone with them. When she's alone, she feels moody. She can't even study well without a partner. Her mother says that Chelsea needs to learn to entertain herself. What should Chelsea do?

2. Evan has average grades. His parents earn a modest income. Still, Evan dreams of going to a top-ranked university. He studies hard and saves his money. Evan's parents warn him bluntly against getting his hopes up. Their negative attitude is an added burden to Evan. He wishes they shared his positive outlook. What should Evan do?

THINKING CRITICALLY

1. **Analyzing Behavior.** Do you think people need to control their positive emotions? Explain your answer.
2. **Forming Hypotheses.** Why might a person with few apparent successes in life still have a positive attitude?
3. **Drawing Conclusions.** How could having an inflated sense of self-esteem be a problem?
4. **Recognizing Assumptions.** Many people believe that an introverted person is insecure while an extrovert is brimming with confidence. Explain why this is not always true.

MAKING CURRICULUM CONNECTIONS

1. **Language Arts.** Find an article about a well-known person. Read the article to locate clues about the person's personality, attitude toward life, and self-esteem. Compare your findings to those of classmates. What qualities seem to link to success and happiness? Which ones have a negative effect?
2. **Science.** Learn more about serotonin and other chemicals that affect personality and attitude. How has an understanding of brain chemistry affected ideas about personality and treatment of mental and emotional stability?

APPLYING YOUR KNOWLEDGE

1. Working with classmates, make a list of things people can do to build positive attitudes in others.
2. Write a paragraph explaining whether you're more introverted or extroverted. Discuss what might account for differences in how people see themselves and the image they present to others.

Family & Community Connections

1. For three days, write down the negative things you hear people say about themselves. What faults do people seem to criticize most in themselves? What can be done to change this way of thinking?

2. Talk to a coach who uses positive imagery to teach others to visualize positive outcomes. How do players carry out these images? What effect does it have on their ability to play?

Developing Character

Moral Development

OBJECTIVES

After studying this section, you should be able to:

- Explain the importance of morality.
- Compare stages of moral development.
- Relate values to moral development.
- Suggest guidelines for making moral decisions.
- Explain how a code of ethics is formed.

TERMS TO LEARN

morality
conscience
code of ethics

When you teach a young child not to hit a playmate, when you write your *own* research paper in school, when you return the extra dollar you got in change, you are practicing morality. **Morality** is a system of conduct based on what is right and wrong. It contributes order and benevolence, or good will, to the world. Most people genuinely try to behave morally, but knowing which are right actions—and then taking them—can be a challenge at times.

WHY MORALITY?

Rules for behavior can seem like a burden at times, but ask yourself this: what would the world be like without them? Think of how you feel when you hear about a corrupt politician or a dishonest business person. How do you feel when you're treated unfairly? Experiencing the effects of someone else's immorality is enough to convince most people of the need for moral action.

High standards of morality are important to individuals and to a community. The morality of each member contributes to the moral strength of the group. Only when each person learns and practices moral principles can order and benevolence thrive. In addition, how you treat others greatly influences their treatment of you. Following a moral course, you gain self-respect as well as respect and cooperation from other people.

Myra Cauldwell: *Family & Consumer Sciences Teacher*

"After deciding to become a teacher, I chose Family and Consumer Sciences as my major because I wanted to teach practical skills the students could use every day. I like discussing subjects that improve the quality of life for individuals and families. Plus, trying to stay up-to-date keeps me on my toes. I have to know about everything from stress management to making a home safe.

"Each year my favorite assignment is the community service project we do. My students learn that people can make a difference. I encourage them to choose a project that will make our community a better place to live. As a team effort with all students receiving the same grade, they push each other to do their jobs.

"Last year my class organized a Thanksgiving food drive. They worked hard to get contributions, including bagging groceries at a local store for donations. It was a positive learning experience for everybody. The students felt good about helping so many families, and I was proud to be teaching the next generation of community leaders."

CAREER PROFILE

Education and training: bachelor's degree

Starting salary range: $22-25,000

Job prospects: public and private middle schools; high schools; vocational/technical schools; colleges and universities

Important qualities: good communication skills; able to motivate students; creative; organized

Plan Ahead

If a teaching career appeals to you, see if your school has a club for future teachers. If so, what opportunities does this club offer for students interested in teaching? Also, if you have student teachers in your school, interview them about the requirements of their college program.

MORAL DEVELOPMENT

People aren't born knowing right from wrong. They learn as they grow. Families teach children their earliest lessons in morality. Later influences include friends, religious leaders, and educators.

Morality thrives or dies by example. Only if teens and adults choose to teach morality and set good moral examples will children grow into adults who act justly and who raise their own children to do the same.

Studying moral development, psychologist Lawrence Kohlberg found that as the moral self develops, it advances through three general levels. Each level has two stages, for a total of six stages.

Morality is much more than following the laws of society. It's the way you conduct yourself all the time—even when you're alone.

Early lessons in morality begin with the idea of sharing. Do you think these children can understand such a lesson? How does a parent convince a child to share?

Preconventional Level

The first level of moral reasoning is the preconventional level. Children enter this level as preschoolers. At about age six, their conscience begins to form. A **conscience** (KAHN-chuntz) is an inner sense of what is right and wrong in a person's own behavior or motives. In healthy moral growth, the conscience grows with a person's experience and ability to understand concepts. An eight-year-old's conscience is far different from an eighteen-year-old's.

At the preconventional level, moral thinking focuses on the outcome of behavior. Acts are good or bad according to their results. A parent or other authority figure sets the rules.

Children obey because of what will happen if they don't.

In the first stage of this level, children obey rules to avoid negative outcomes. They have learned that some things are right or wrong, but they don't know why. They only know what will happen if they disobey. For example, three-year-old Mariah knows that if she throws a toy, her father will take it away.

At the second stage, children obey to earn rewards or to have favors returned. Again, children don't question the "whys" of right and wrong, but they know what behavior others desire. Jared's parents taught their five-year-old to dress himself by rewarding him with praise when he did so.

Conventional Level

Next in the development of the moral self is the conventional level, which includes stages three and four. At this level, the rules, expectations, and judgment of the group become the standard for behavior. The group may be family, classmates, or a unit of government. Most people have reached this level by age thirteen.

In stage three of the conventional level, people obey to avoid disapproval or dislike from others. Good behavior is whatever pleases other people. Those who give in to peer pressure are at this stage.

Obeying rules because they represent authority characterizes stage four. People accept that laws are to be upheld, not questioned, because they see that rules are needed for an orderly society. Ten-year-old Kit was riding with his father when they recognized a neighbor fly past in her car. Kit exclaimed, "Dad, Mrs. Epstein is speeding!" Later, they learned that she had been rushing to the emergency room after badly cutting her hand. "She still shouldn't have been speeding," Kit insisted.

Postconventional Level

In this last level, sometimes reached around age sixteen, moral beliefs are based on moral principles. People begin to evaluate customs, rules, and laws in terms of their personal standards of behavior.

At the conventional level, people have learned to respect authority. They know that society needs rules. If all people reached this level of morality, would society need security guards?

Contributing time and energy to help build homes for others is a sign of high moral growth. In what other ways do people demonstrate postconventional morality?

In stage five, people may decide that not all laws are good ones. They often work within the system to change laws they find unfair. In this stage, personal agreements between people gain moral importance. Decisions are based on the individual's idea of what is fair and fitting.

As a prank, Karl and A.J. dumped sacks of garbage in someone's backyard. A.J. was picked up by the police for trespassing and littering. When Karl found out, he turned himself in. He said, "It isn't fair for A.J. to take all the blame. We dreamed this up together and did it together." Karl's regard for his friend compelled him to accept responsibility for their mistake.

Morality in stage six is based on universal principles, such as the sacredness of life and the equality of all people. People in this stage adopt these principles as their own and act on them. At the highest degree of this level are those who devote their lives to others, such as Mother Teresa and Martin Luther King, Jr.

Like other aspects of personality, moral growth is not the same for everyone. Some adults show less advanced moral thinking than do some teens. Also, moral behavior is not always consistent. Even people who have reached the higher stages may act improperly at times. True moral growth is reflected in a person's attitudes and actions as a whole.

MORAL REASONING

Even if everyone reached the same level of moral development at the same time, they still wouldn't agree on every matter of right and wrong. People are raised differently. They learn different principles and values. Some values that you hold might not be the same as someone else's. You may both be certain of your beliefs, yet can you both be right?

Some situations are moral dilemmas. No option is entirely satisfactory. For example, people the world over believe in honesty as a moral value. However, might there be ex-

A clear code of ethics guides your actions at school, work, and play. Is making too many personal phone calls during work hours ethical? What principles should be in a person's code of work ethics?

guiding force in moral behavior; without them, many arguments can sound right, yet lead to a wrong choice.

Finally, think for yourself. It may be comforting to go with the crowd, even if "the crowd" is only one other person, but it may not be the right way for you. Strong moral convictions help you act with confidence.

ESTABLISHING A CODE OF ETHICS

One of your greatest allies when you make moral decisions is your code of ethics. A **code of ethics** is a clear set of rules or principles that guide actions and decisions. It is the real-life application of a person's values. It takes your welfare as well as the welfare of others into consideration. When you value honesty, for instance, part of your code of ethics says "It's wrong to lie."

A code of ethics is not created overnight. Rather, it takes shape as you confront the issues and problems of daily life. You build a code of ethics as you think and make decisions about what is right and what is wrong. A strong code of ethics is a mark of true moral development.

ceptions? Suppose Antoine sees a sibling doing something his parents have forbidden. Is not telling his parents dishonest? Does it matter whether he agrees with the rule? If you dislike a friend's new outfit, should you say so? Is it dishonest to steal food if a person is starving?

Difficult questions such as these will always exist. You will face your share throughout life. Moral reasoning is dealing with moral issues by using your reasoning skills. As with any decision, the goal is to understand the issue as clearly as possible and then make an informed choice.

First, ask questions to get the facts you need. Talk to those who can help you. Then, as you reflect on your options, consider how anyone might be hurt. Look for actions that do no harm, balancing the needs of others with your own well-being. Next, turn to the principles and values that you know are right. Positive values are the

Tips & TECHNIQUES

Recognizing Values. Character develops when you recognize and live by positive values. Some people will tell you what they value, but their actions speak louder than their words. Do you have a clear set of guidelines or principles for your life? To help you identify what's most important to you:

- **Look at your budget.** Where have you spent money in the last month? Purchases are one reflection of what you think is important.
- **Keep a log of how you spend your time over a week.** How do activities, and the time you spend on them, reflect your values?
- **Think about your favorite leisure activities.** What values are seen in these pastimes?
- **Survey your possessions.** Are the things you have a reflection of what is important to you?
- **Consider your relationships.** What does the company you keep say about your moral judgment?

Try It Out. Make a list of your values. Are these values the ones you believe are truly important in life? If not, how can you change your life to more closely reflect your values?

SECTION 23-1 REVIEW

Check Your Understanding

1. Why is morality important to individuals and society?
2. How does a conscience develop?
3. On what is behavior based at the preconventional level?
4. What is the main concern in the conventional level, stage three, of moral development?
5. Why can making moral decisions be difficult at times?
6. What is a code of ethics?
7. **Thinking Critically.** What does having a "double standard" mean? If all people have a double standard on moral issues, what might happen?
8. **Problem Solving.** James showed his sister the digital camera he had signed out from work for the weekend to take pictures of his daughter's first birthday party. His sister suggested that if James "forgot" to return the camera for a few days, she could use it to take photos for an art competition she had entered. What should James do?

Moving Toward Maturity

OBJECTIVES

After studying this section, you should be able to:

- Compare definitions of maturity.
- Distinguish qualities of mature people.
- Evaluate your philosophy of life.
- Assess the quality of your own character.

TERMS TO LEARN

maturity
conform
self-discipline
egocentrism
prejudice
philosophy of life
character

No one wants to be labeled "immature." The word conjures up images of temper tantrums, selfishness, and helplessness. Instead, they want to be known as mature, but how do they earn that distinction?

Someone once said, "Think of what others ought to be like; then start being like that yourself." Following this idea could put you well on the road to maturity.

MEANINGS OF MATURITY

Maturity (muh-TUR-uht-ee) is full growth or development. By this definition, maturity is never entirely achieved, because personal development never stops. It continues over a lifetime.

A person progresses toward maturity in all developmental areas—physical, mental, emotional, social, and moral—but not at the same pace or to the same degree. At age twenty, Bill had reached physical maturity. However, he still had trouble controlling his temper and getting along with others. How would you rate his emotional and social maturity?

When people use the term maturity to mean grown-up or adult, they usually mean having the qualities and traits needed for successful adult life. Some of these qualities are described in this section.

INDEPENDENCE

As people grow, they move from dependence on others to independence. Mature people have established their identities. They earn their own living and typically live apart from their parents. More important, they solve their own problems and make their own decisions.

Being allowed to drive is a turning point in the life of many teens. Is it a sign of maturity? How do teens demonstate maturity when driving?

Problem solving as an independent person becomes more complicated. As you get older, more of your decisions have a long-lasting impact. Alise wanted very much to work in a certain women's clothing store but applied at several other places too. When a gift shop offered her a job, Alise hesitated. Should she take the sure offer of the gift shop, or take a chance by waiting for the job in the clothing store? Alise didn't want to make a mistake that would affect her for a long time to come.

Rarely do you know exactly what will come from a particular decision or solution to a problem. Using the problem-solving process, however, helps mature people make thoughtful decisions. You can evaluate solutions before you carry them out. A good solution or decision for you is one that:

- Fills your needs and wants, not someone else's.
- Causes no physical or emotional harm to you or anyone else.
- Is based on fact, rather than on hope, wishes, or fantasy.
- Has acceptable short- and long-term results.

INFOLINK

Problem-Solving Process

To review the problem-solving process, see *Section 9-3.*

Handling Conformity

As you become more independent, you learn to think for yourself. You make decisions about when to follow your own ideas and when to conform. To **conform** is to follow the customs, rules, or standards of a group. Some conformity is needed for life and society to run smoothly. At other times individuality is acceptable and even preferable. Knowing what action to take in any given situation takes good judgment.

Kerry, for example, works in the mail room at the Federal Building. The dress code requires ties for all male employees. Kerry can't see how wearing a tie affects his ability to do the job. He follows the rule, however, because he values his job over making an issue about wearing a tie.

Having the self-discipline to stick to something leads to success. Can you stay with an assignment until it's done? Are you willing to practice a skill again and again in order to do it well? **These are signs of maturity.**

Self-discipline is needed to work toward long-term goals. Giving up today's pleasures for something you expect will happen months or years from now isn't always easy, yet showing self-discipline today can bring later rewards. The self-disciplined teen who makes sure schoolwork gets done before socializing has more career options as an adult.

RESPONSIBILITY

The word responsible is often linked to maturity. When you're responsible, you are dependable. People know you will do as you say and complete the tasks assigned to you.

Responsible people think about what their actions might cause. If something goes

SELF-DISCIPLINE

Self-discipline is the ability to direct your own behavior in a responsible way. Young children generally have little self-discipline, which is why they need the guidance of adults.

Developing self-discipline is one strong sign of growth toward personal maturity. You show this trait when you resist negative temptations and when you stick to a difficult job in order to get it done.

Some teens must be asked or told to do jobs for the family; others volunteer. Which approach do you take when family shopping, laundry, or cleaning needs to be done? Which shows maturity?

wrong, they accept their mistakes gracefully and follow up appropriately. They look out for other people as well as themselves.

Gerald often borrowed his stepfather's tennis racket. He noticed that several strings had frayed and would soon break. Gerald took the racket to be restrung. Since he had caused much of the wear on the strings, he felt responsible for having them replaced.

GOOD WORK HABITS

Good work habits show at home, at school, and on the job. Taking care of your responsibilities is easier if you have formed good work habits. You can develop a system of good work habits with these ideas:

- **Decide what you want to accomplish.** You're more apt to be motivated if you set meaningful goals.
- **Make time to get things done.** Instead of saying, "I just don't have time," find the time.
- **Make deals to motivate yourself.** If you have several jobs, save your favorite for last. Promise yourself some kind of treat after finishing an unpleasant task. You might make plans with someone to do something you strongly dislike. Committing to a specific date and time helps strengthen your resolve, and working with a friend can be fun.

SKILLS CHECKLIST

Communication Skills

Leadership Skills

Management Skills

Thinking Skills

Are You Mature?

The following checklist contains measures of maturity. How does your maturity rate?

✓ I accept responsibility for mistakes rather than make excuses for them.
✓ I accept what cannot be changed.
✓ I work to change what I believe needs changing.
✓ I control strong emotions when appropriate.
✓ I am open to other points of view.
✓ I am willing to do difficult or unpleasant jobs.
✓ I can do a job well, for its own sake, without recognition from others.
✓ I can wait for what I want when necessary.
✓ I am determined to overcome stumbling blocks.
✓ I keep my promises.
✓ I think for myself.
✓ I willingly put the needs of others ahead of my own.

Using Your Skills

Select one item above and identify three ways you could improve this aspect of maturity. Act on these ideas. Did you achieve the result you hoped for?

- **Make lists.** Write down your plan for doing the work. Include the steps you need to take and the rewards you've set out for yourself.
- **Tackle each task as if it were the most important.** Give a job your full attention and best effort, no matter how important it is.

RESPECT FOR OTHERS

One mark of maturity is the willingness to appreciate others and respect their needs and feelings. You can't do this if you're egocentric. **Egocentrism** is seeing life only from your own point of view. Children are naturally egocentric. Their reaction to a situation is primarily: "How does this affect me? What will I gain or lose?"

As they grow, children start to see that the world doesn't revolve around them. They learn to see what concerns other people and how they feel. As teens become more sensitive to others and develop empathy, they move past egocentrism and toward social maturity.

Rejecting Prejudice

Respect for others doesn't tolerate unfair judgments. An unfair or biased opinion is called **prejudice** (PREJ-ud-us). Prejudice is often directed at certain religious, political, racial, or ethnic groups. It's based on stereotypes, not on knowledge and facts. Stereotypes, in turn, thrive when people make assumptions about an entire group rather than get to know people as individuals.

Prejudice is a problem for society. People are ignored, challenged, injured, and denied fair treatment due to prejudicial attitudes. Once rooted, prejudice is a stubborn weed. To help stop prejudice from spreading, you can:
- Point out the unique qualities that make people individuals.
- Speak out against name-calling and avoid conversations that belittle people.
- Get involved with efforts to combat discrimination.

Excluding others shows that a person is immature, judgmental, and has a low sense of self-esteem. Including others shows that a person is mature, fair-minded, and has a strong sense of self-esteem. Which describes you?

Balancing Work & Family Life

THE CHALLENGE —

Understanding Other Viewpoints

When home, school, and work responsibilities keep you running, it can be hard to see that others are busy, too. Sharing opinions and feelings, however, can help family members solve problems. Understanding another's viewpoint makes families closer and stronger.

How You Can Help

To help yourself see another's point of view, try these tips:

- Start a "Day in the Life of . . ." session at dinner. As family members share the details of their day, listen and ask questions to find out how they felt about events.

- Ask a parent what it's like to raise a family. If your parent is employed, ask how it feels to work while raising a family.

- Change the scenery. Encourage family members to talk while taking a walk or car ride, doing a group activity, or completing chores.

- Play the favorites game. Ask family members to identify their most and least favorite memories, foods, games, songs, etc. Be sure to share reasons for choices.

- Help a grandparent, elderly relative, or family member with children with their daily routine. Report back to your family about how the relative is doing.

In becoming aware of prejudice, you may uncover some biases of your own. Confronting and working through these feelings is also part of social maturity.

COMPETENCE

People use many mental, emotional, and social skills in dealing with everyday life. Mature people have learned to use their skills competently, or effectively and capably.

With maturity, people recognize their own level of competence. They know when they have the ability to try something that could lead to success. They don't let pride and pressure lead them into situations they can't handle.

Mature people also know how to deal with repeated success. They don't become overly confident, nor do they live in dread of failure.

Growing Through Mistakes

Even the most competent person makes mistakes. Using errors as a means of improvement is a mark of maturity. How can failure work for you? It can:

- **Educate you.** You gain new information by discovering what doesn't work.
- **Push you in new directions.** You may work to improve skills or learn new ones.
- **Make you more realistic about what you can and can't achieve.** Perhaps you need to set a series of attainable goals to reach your ultimate ambition.

- **Give you freedom.** Having survived one failure, you feel freer to risk another. You know you can bounce back.
- **Bring others closer to you.** Supporting a friend through disappointment deepens the relationship and makes it more satisfying. It's harder to care about someone who rarely needs comforting.

Remember that there is a world of difference between failing and being a failure. In this competitive world, everyone fails at something. Failures and mistakes are nothing to be ashamed of. They only mean that what you did was not effective. What counts is how you react. If you can accept what happened and learn from it, you can use setbacks as a means to growth.

Building Knowledge

A competent person needs knowledge in addition to skills. Mature people value knowledge and the opportunities for gaining it. They know how to get needed infor-

Someone once said that "thoughts become actions, actions become character, and character determines your destiny." What is your destiny?

mation and apply it to problem solving, decision making, and resource management. They have prepared themselves for a job.

Practical knowledge is also needed. A mature, independent person knows where to license a car, how to file a tax return, how to choose nutritious foods, and other information that is useful for everyday living.

A PHILOSOPHY OF LIFE

As you become a mature person, you begin to develop a **philosophy of life**, the sum of your beliefs, attitudes, values, and priorities. This philosophy affects the goals you work toward, the personal traits you cultivate, and the way you treat others.

You may already have a philosophy of life without realizing it. Examine your thinking to find out. Try listing your values and ask yourself which are most important. Write down your goals, both short- and long-range. Are they consistent with your values? Think about the principles you follow. What things would you do? What would you avoid at all costs? When you can answer questions such as these, you are well on your way to understanding and developing your philosophy of life. You can then work to live by it.

DEVELOPING CHARACTER

Perhaps one of the highest compliments you can give a person is, "You have real character." People with **character** have moral strength. They think, judge, and act with maturity. Their code of ethics enables them to face life's challenges appropriately. Their personal philosophy guides them. Because of all this, they are admired. Do people see character in you? They will if you make it happen.

SECTION 23-2 REVIEW

Check Your Understanding

1. What does mature mean as it applies to being grown-up or adult?
2. How is conformity related to maturity?
3. What are four tips for developing good work habits?
4. How is egocentrism an obstacle to respecting others?
5. How is competence related to maturity?
6. What is a philosophy of life?
7. **Thinking Critically.** Do you think most people, as they leave their teens, are mature enough to handle adult life? Explain your answer.
8. **Problem Solving.** Melanie is a talented pianist who has won awards for her playing; however, she has trouble motivating herself to practice. Melanie's parents want her to try for a music scholarship for college since they can't afford the entire cost themselves. Melanie wants to go to college but dreads the thought of all that practice. What should Melanie do?

Chapter 23
Review and Activities

CHAPTER SUMMARY

- Morality allows individuals to live together in society.
- Moral development progresses through three general levels, which include six stages of development.
- Values help people make moral decisions.
- A person forms a code of ethics based on his or her values.
- Maturity is shown in certain qualities, including independence, self-discipline, respect for others, and competence.
- Mature people use good work habits to carry out responsibilities.
- Maturity includes combating prejudice in society, starting with oneself.
- A philosophy of life gives a person a framework for living.
- Character comes with moral development and maturity.

REVIEW QUESTIONS

Section 23-1
1. How does the group influence moral thinking at the conventional level of moral development?
2. What major changes in moral thinking mark the postconventional level?
3. Describe a process of using moral reasoning to guide decision making.
4. How does a code of ethics develop?

Section 23-2
1. Does maturity come automatically with age? Explain your answer.
2. How do self-discipline and maturity relate?
3. What can you do to stop the spread of prejudice?
4. What good, if any, can come from failure?
5. What can you do to clarify your philosophy of life?
6. Why is saying that someone has character a very high compliment?

BECOMING A PROBLEM SOLVER

1. In Kent's French class, students are assigned French works of literature to read and discuss in class. Kent knows that some students use English translations of the works, but he refuses to cheat. As a result, the others perform better in class. The instructor told Kent that he needs to improve to keep his grade. What should Kent do?

2. Jessie manages a small business. Cal, her newest employee, is a hard working, cheerful young man. However, his religious beliefs forbid him from working certain hours or joining coworkers in some after-work activities. Some employees complain that Cal is hard to get along with and doesn't do his share of the work. Jessie sees no proof of this and suspects they are acting out of prejudice. However, the business owner says to fire Cal because he's "bad for morale." What should Jessie do?

THINKING CRITICALLY

1. **Identifying Contradictions.** Royce became a teacher because he wanted to improve the lives of young people. When his son asks him to play catch or read to him, Royce is often busy planning lessons or grading papers. Does Royce have a consistent philosophy of life? Explain your answer.

2. **Evaluating Alternatives.** What role, if any, should public institutions, such as schools and government agencies, play in shaping a society's values?

3. **Arguing from Evidence.** How do you rate the general level of morality in society? Cite examples to support your answer.

4. **Applying Knowledge.** Although he dislikes making phone calls, Craig has agreed to call area businesses about donating items to the animal shelter's fund-raising auction. Suggest specific things Craig can do to finish this task effectively.

MAKING CURRICULUM CONNECTIONS

1. **Literature.** Read a "coming of age" story, in which characters undergo an experience that helps them grow toward maturity. Summarize the plot for the class. Explain how the events and the character's response to them aid that person's progress to adulthood.

2. **Psychology.** Learn more about the work of theorists who study morality. Two possibilities are Robert Coles and William Bennett. Share your report with the class.

APPLYING YOUR KNOWLEDGE

1. For three days, keep a log of the immature behavior you see. Share your observations with the class. Explain why you consider the behavior immature and what a more mature response would have been.

2. With your classmates, discuss how peer pressure affects the behavior of teens. What can teens do when this pressure encourages them to act in ways they believe are not right? Create a "tips" list for resisting peer pressure.

Family & Community Connections

1. What behaviors are encouraged, discouraged, required, and banned in a company's written code of ethics? Why do you think these acts were included in the code? Does the code seem fair? Is it reasonable? Is it too strict? Too lax? Describe any changes you would make.

2. Observe adults interacting with children or teens until you have seen three examples of the adult teaching habits that promote maturity. What concepts were being taught? How were they taught? Write a brief summary of the three examples.

Chapter 24

Supporting You Community

IN YOUR OWN WORDS

How can you tell that someone is "wrapped up" in himself or herself?

RECYCLING GUIDELINES
- Bin at curb by 7:30 a.m.
- No wet paper,

Citizenship

OBJECTIVES

After studying this section, you should be able to:

- Explain rights and responsibilities of citizens.
- Describe ways to stay informed about your community and influence its leadership.
- Relate respect for people and property to community strength.
- Demonstrate ways to prevent crime and care for the environment.

TERMS TO LEARN

citizenship
press conference
pollutants

Have you ever let a shopper with fewer groceries go ahead of you in a super-market checkout line? Has a stranger ever returned a lost item to you? Such actions show the spirit of citizenship. Citizens realize that "we're all in this together." A community—be it a neighborhood or a nation—survives and improves only if each person works to make it a better place for everyone. As you approach the end of your teen years and look forward to adulthood, you start to see how you can be part of this united effort.

WHAT IS CITIZENSHIP?

Citizenship is membership in a community that guarantees certain rights and expects certain responsibilities. Citizenship usually refers to a person's position in a nation or other large community. While you're not usually considered a "citizen" of your school, you can still practice the attitudes and skills of good citizenship there.

Citizens' Rights

Being a citizen provides you with certain rights. In the United States, these are listed in

only way of assuring rights, for you and for others.

Perhaps the most important duty of citizenship is participating in community events and government. Citizens who are involved in their community are often more satisfied with it. They are more apt to know how to work for solutions when problems arise.

When people think of citizen participation, they may think first of voting. Electing government officials and accepting or rejecting laws are important duties, as well as rights. Your vote influences the quality of life of the entire community. Ask yourself, for example: How much does my family pay in taxes? How often is garbage picked up? How available are parks, museums, and other community resources? Government affects daily life, and your vote affects government.

Staying Informed

To vote wisely and to preserve other rights in a democracy, citizens need information. They must know about issues that affect their community. They must learn about problems and possible solutions and understand their leaders' ideas for improving community life.

Most communities provide multiple sources of information to help citizens make responsible choices. The media—magazines and newspapers, television and radio news programs—report on issues and

the Bill of Rights, the first ten amendments to the U.S. Constitution, as well as in later amendments. These include the right to:

- Vote for government representatives.
- Express your opinion freely and publicly.
- Receive an education.
- Travel freely within the country.
- Receive a fair and speedy trial.
- Enjoy equal protection under the law, regardless of gender, race, or ethnicity.

Citizens' Responsibilities

The advantages of citizenship are balanced by its responsibilities. In fact, assuming the responsibilities of citizenship is the

the stands that government leaders take on them. At a **press conference**, political leaders answer questions from news media representatives. Government agencies hold public hearings on matters that they plan to act on. These hearings are opportunities for citizens to ask questions and voice concerns. Libraries and the Internet can help citizens learn more about issues and political leaders' record on them.

Another way to stay informed is through education. Schools teach skills and topics needed to make intelligent choices, including problem solving, resource management, history, and economics. Some activities promote community awareness, as when Natasha's high school band marches in the city's Founders' Day celebration. Student government gives young people an idea of what is involved in making fair, workable laws for a community.

Providing Leadership

Sometimes keeping informed and voting still doesn't bring satisfactory results. Then individuals have the duty to get more involved. Jonah's father thought his son's school should place more emphasis on writing and communication skills. Presenting his idea to the school board got no results, so he decided to run for a seat on the school board himself. There he was able to work for changes that he believed would improve education and the community.

Not everyone has the time or expertise to sit on a board, but anyone can learn what such boards are doing. You can attend board meetings, read accounts of the proceedings, and write or talk to board members. These people are greatly influenced by citizens, but they can give your view consideration only if they know what you think.

Some leaders stand before crowds to spread their message. Others provide leadership in less obvious ways. What are some examples?

RESPECTING PROPERTY

As a teen, you may own relatively little property—perhaps books, CDs, or sports equipment—but if you're like most others, you feel strongly about it. Some possessions cost you hard-earned money. Others have sentimental value. You want to be able to enjoy what is yours and get the best possible use from the items.

Just as your belongings are important to you, other people value theirs as well. You don't want your own possessions harmed, and neither does anyone else. Good citizens understand this, so they work to ensure everyone's right to enjoy their own property. Which of these actions show signs of respect for the personal property of others?

- Santiago cuts through his neighbor's yard when he is late for school.
- Becky borrows jewelry from friends and then forgets to return it.
- Tyrone saves chewing gum and candy bar wrappers until he finds a trash can.
- Carla asks her sister's permission before borrowing her car.
- Eva takes small items from work for her own use.
- Warren hangs framed posters throughout his apartment though the owner has asked him to avoid making holes in the walls.
- Mac organized a group of friends to clean up the graffiti that others had painted on a wall in his neighborhood.
- Shawanda leads her little sister away from the flowers she wanted to pick from the neighbor's flower box.
- Leroy borrows pencils and paper from classmates all the time and never offers any in return.

Respecting community, or public, property is also a duty of citizenship. This can be as simple as returning library books on time and in good condition. It can be more active, too, as when Herschel and his friends spent one Saturday morning picking up trash from the courthouse grounds. What other ways can you think of to show concern for the public property that's there for everyone to enjoy?

Some people destroy property and others make improvements. What kinds of people choose these separate courses? Why?

Caring for Property

Owning property is not something good citizens take lightly. They respect their possessions enough to give them good care in order to make them lasting assets in the community.

The Meyers own a large home in an older section of their town. They keep the house well painted. They mow the lawn, tend a flower garden, and make sure the fence is in good repair. By caring for their property, the Meyers enable others to feel positive about the community. They help protect the value of their own property as well as the value of their neighbor's property.

CONTROLLING CRIME

Good citizens understand the importance of obeying laws. They realize laws are necessary to protect the rights of everyone in the community. Not breaking the law yourself is a first step—but only a first step—to controlling crime.

Discouraging crime starts at home. For safety, follow these suggestions:
- Keep entrances well lighted at night.
- Lock doors and windows, especially when no one is home.
- Never hide a key under a mat or where it can be easily found.
- Don't allow shrubs to grow tall around entryways and windows.
- Never give out personal information to strangers on the phone about where you live and who is home.
- Keep expensive items in a safe place where they cannot tempt a thief.

By keeping a watchful eye on your neighborhood, you can prevent crime and be ready to help others. What might you notice that would cause you to take action?

Getting Involved

You can help keep your neighborhood safe as well. Get to know your neighbors and their habits. Stay alert for unusual activities, such as unfamiliar cars circling the neighborhood or strangers who don't seem to know their way around.

You may want to organize a formal or informal neighborhood watch, where neighbors promise to look out for possible criminal activity and help each other in emergencies. Jamal, for instance, knew his elderly neighbor Mrs. Higuera liked to walk her dog every afternoon. When he hadn't seen her in several days, he called her home and dis-

INFOLINK

Personal Safety

For more information on personal safety, see Section 25-2.

Good citizens see cultural differences as opportunities to learn about people. When you look beyond differences, you build bridges instead of fences. That's good for your community.

covered she was seriously ill with pneumonia. He called another neighbor, who drove Mrs. Higuera to the hospital.

When crime occurs, your response can help keep it from happening again. Report illegal activity when you see it. Cooperate with police officers. In the years ahead, contact elected officials to tell them you support their efforts to catch and prosecute lawbreakers.

The key to curbing crime is involvement. Crime breeds when people don't care about their neighbors or when they become afraid to get involved. Criminal acts hurt everyone: in higher taxes to hire more police; in higher prices to pay for stolen goods; in higher insurance costs; and in less trust and more suspicion among neighbors and strangers alike. Good citizens do what they can to prevent these damaging consequences.

A sad and puzzling phenomenon sometimes occurs when people witness crime in action. Some people, especially when they are with others, will stand by and do nothing. Entire groups have been known to watch someone being attacked without intervening or getting help. Personal safety is a concern, of course, but is there any excuse for not even calling the authorities or the 911 emergency number?

People need help when crime occurs. Compassionate, responsible action can literally be a lifesaver. Hoping that "someone else will do it" can be disastrous. A good citizen responds to such an urgent need.

PROMOTING UNDERSTANDING

Samuel's Aunt Rene can remember when she knew every family in her neighborhood. Young couples moved in, raised their children, and spent the rest of their lives in the same home. Now Rene sees regular change in her neighborhood. The Changs, who emigrated from Taiwan, are new neighbors next door. Selim Mataz, a schoolteacher from Armenia, just rented the house on the corner of her street.

As business and education grow increasingly international, you have a greater chance of coming into contact with a wider variety of people today than ever before. Your school, workplace, and community are made up of a number of different racial, ethnic, and social groups. Some individuals are American-born. Others were born in—and may be citizens of—other countries. This situation provides opportunity to learn more about people. Respect and understanding grow as you talk to people about their beliefs and customs.

CARING FOR THE ENVIRONMENT

Can you believe that every American produces an average of about 1,500 pounds of garbage each year, or that an estimated 46 million Americans breathe polluted air? These statistics are cause for concern. Such numbers are a direct result of individual choices. People who act responsibly care for the environment—both the home environment and the world environment.

Like preventing crime, preserving the environment begins by not making the situa-

The more you learn about the environment, the better prepared you'll be to help care for it. A good citizen learns first—and then takes action.

tion worse. You can make a difference. Buy products with minimal packaging. Choose recycled glass, plastic, and paper products, and reusable items over disposable ones. Reuse disposable items as long as possible.

Responsible people help protect the environment by conserving energy. Producing energy usually produces **pollutants**, or impurities in the environment. Using cold water when possible instead of hot, turning off appliances when not in use, and walking instead of driving a car are all ways of conserving energy. Recycling helps too, since it takes less energy to produce items from recycled material than from raw material.

Environmental concerns are world wide. What happens in one place eventually affects others. Find out ways people can help keep the world's benefits for generations to come.

THE COMMUNITY YOU CREATE

People want to live in strong, happy communities. They want to be able to walk the streets safely. They want a clean and healthful environment. They want friends, not enemies. Such communities exist only where people make them. The more people work to build up a community, the less tolerance is felt for those who would tear it down. A feeling of pride and satisfaction comes from practicing good citizenship, from contributing to the solutions instead of the problems.

SECTION 24-1 REVIEW

Check Your Understanding

1. What are three rights of United States citizens?
2. What are the benefits to citizens of getting involved with their community?
3. Why is information needed for good citizenship?
4. How is good citizenship demonstrated in the way people handle personal property?
5. Why do people form neighborhood watches?
6. How does conserving energy help protect the environment?
7. **Thinking Critically.** Give an example of how failing to assume a citizen's responsibility can result in losing a right.
8. **Problem Solving.** Tammy has noticed that a vacant corner lot in her neighborhood has become a collecting point for trash. Motorists stopped at the intersection sometimes toss fast-food wrappers and plastic cups from car windows. Bags of garbage appear overnight. The problem seems to be getting worse. What should Tammy do?

Service to Others

OBJECTIVES

After studying this section, you should be able to:

- Explain how you can benefit by volunteering.
- Distinguish qualities needed by volunteers.
- Identify specific volunteer opportunities.
- Suggest volunteer opportunities to suit people in various situations.

TERMS TO LEARN

volunteerism
altruism

Has a volunteer ever helped you? If you've used a library, played on a school sports team or in a band, or enjoyed activities sponsored by any number of youth programs, you've benefited from the generosity of volunteers. Although it's not always obvious, the spirit of **volunteerism**, of willingness to give service to others, is alive and well in many corners of your community.

WANTED: VOLUNTEERS

Volunteers are everywhere, yet they never seem to flood the market. The demand for them always exceeds the supply. Volunteers are needed because social service agencies, both public and private, have too few funds for too many jobs. Meanwhile, the need for their services is growing. When economic times are tight, programs are cut because salaries cannot be paid. The answer? Find someone who will work without pay. Find a volunteer.

Previously, women were a ready source of volunteer help. As more women have entered the work force, however, fewer are available for volunteer work. Retired people have filled the gap in part. Many older adults find that volunteer work gives continued purpose and meaning to their lives. Longer life spans and better health enable a growing number of retired people to contribute to their communities through volunteerism.

Teens, with their high levels of energy and enthusiasm, are an excellent volunteer resource. Often they have some time to spare, and want to do something more useful with it than sit in front of the television or talk for hours on the phone. The world of volunteering offers them plenty of opportunities—and personal satisfaction.

WHY VOLUNTEER?

Every community has needs that go unmet and jobs left undone. Filling these needs through volunteer work is one of the best ways for citizens to show commitment to their community. Most people see how important volunteers are to the organizations they help. Fewer people realize how giving time and talent enriches the life of the individual.

Practical Benefits

Doing volunteer work allows you to practice current skills and learn new ones. You enjoy the work more and do a better job if you choose a field where you feel confident. You may also expand your skills and knowledge into related areas. This can be an advantage when going after future goals.

Catch the Volunteering Spirit

Giving time to a recycling project.

The spirit of volunteerism is alive and well. Teens everywhere are pitching in to make a difference. Here's what some are doing.

Cleaning up a neighborhood park.

Caring for animals in a shelter.

Michelle, for example, is a talented artist. When she offered to help design an advertising campaign for a charity's fund-raising drive, she learned how to use a graphics program on the group's computer. Later, she found this skill valuable as she worked toward her goal of becoming an architect. People who are undecided about a career can learn what jobs they might be able to do by exploring their skills as a volunteer.

Volunteering lets you meet a great variety of people, which can be rewarding in your career hunt. New acquaintances can provide help and information about job openings, career opportunities, and workplace skills. Often volunteers can list people they work for as references on school, scholarship, and job applications.

Volunteer work can also help strengthen personal relationship skills. You improve your ability to work with others, follow directions, and communicate.

Finally, donating resources now can save other resources in the future. Randall learned that many convicted criminals return to prison because they lack the reading and writing skills needed to get jobs. He became a tutor for a literacy program at a state prison. His work not only helped the inmates but it may have also helped reduce the amount of tax money spent on crime.

How could you help?

Helping out at a retirement home.

Transporting patients in a hospital.

Reading to young children in a neighborhood center.

counter can be eye-opening, leaving you with greater sensitivity, empathy, and compassion for others.

Perhaps the greatest benefit to volunteers is the feeling of improving life for someone else. Volunteers often get to see the effects of their work. Gil volunteers at his church's day camp for children from poorer, urban neighborhoods. As he explained: "When I see those kids eating a good lunch and playing and learning new things like kids are supposed to, I know that I've made a positive difference in this world. What could be more important than that?"

THE QUALITIES YOU NEED

Except that you don't receive a salary, volunteer work is much like a paying job. When you volunteer, you make a commitment. Others count on you to be present and on time. They need your honest effort. To volunteer is to be entrusted with an important job. Letting down the organizers hurts them, your reputation, and the cause and people you were meant to serve.

Not surprisingly, then, good work skills can also come in handy when you volunteer. Depending on your situation, you may need leadership skills or the ability to work in a group. You might be needed for your technical skills and knowledge, anything from the rules of softball to experience with a computer, to the words in a nursery rhyme. As you use these qualities, you're also developing and refining them.

One trait shared by the most valuable volunteers is **altruism** (AL-troo-iz-uhm), or an unselfish concern for the welfare of others. Altruistic people are moved to help when they see a need. Altruism is a universally admired quality, as are many well-known people who display it.

Volunteer work that fits your interests is more enjoyable. This young woman matched her love of animals and the outdoors with work for the park service. **What would interest you?**

Emotional Rewards

Of course, volunteer work that doesn't enhance skills or advance careers is still a valuable experience. Learning new skills provides a feeling of personal growth and satisfaction. Working with others who share your concerns is a good way to make friends. As a volunteer, you may also come in contact with people you wouldn't otherwise meet: hungry people, homeless people, people who are simply lonely. The en-

Career Success Stories

Isacc Roberts: *Volunteer Coordinator*

"In the hospital where I work, we rely heavily on volunteers. It's my job to recruit them, coordinate their schedules, and make sure they know how much we appreciate them. Getting enough volunteers can be quite a task, so I make presentations to civic groups and college and high school clubs. I'm not shy about contacting any group that I think might be willing to help.

"The business part of my job takes a lot of time. During a typical day, I make many phone calls, meet with hospital administrators, and create schedules on the computer.

"After the work I put in to get volunteers, I don't want to lose them. Three years ago I spoke to administrators about holding a banquet to recognize our people. This event, now annual, is the only time during the year when we have the whole group together. The newspaper covers the banquet and our volunteer-of-the-year is featured. Even though I see the numbers on paper every day, I'm always amazed to see how large the group is in person. Our volunteers don't need recognition to keep going, but they deserve it. Making them feel proud of what they do makes me feel proud of my own efforts."

CAREER PROFILE

Education and training: bachelor's degree

Starting salary range: $15-25,000

Job prospects: hospitals; social service agencies; government agencies; associations

Important qualities: flexible; good organizational skills; personable; able to speak in front of groups

Plan Ahead

Recruitment is a responsibility in many careers. A corporation, for example, recruits new employees on college campuses. Name some other careers that would include recruitment as part of the job. Would you enjoy this responsibility?

WHERE TO VOLUNTEER

The opportunities for volunteering are too numerous to mention them all. Anywhere there are people needing help, there is probably a need for volunteers. Below are a few ideas. Others are shown on pages 484-485. You can probably name more.

- Children's sports leagues
- Religious organizations
- Music and theater groups
- School organizations and service learning programs, such as Y clubs and FHA/HERO
- Libraries
- Zoos

In addition, many national charitable groups may have local branches in your community. The American Red Cross offers a broad variety of services to people, from free blood-pressure screenings to food and shelter for victims of disaster. Big Brothers/Big Sisters pairs up children from single-parent homes with adults who act as friends and role models. Habitat for Humanity helps low-income families find decent housing by building new houses or rehabilitating older ones. The Salvation Army provides numerous services for the homeless, elderly, and others in need of aid.

To offer your services as a volunteer, first consider your interests, abilities, and the time you are able to invest. Then learn about the different organizations. Libraries often carry informational literature that is distributed by these groups. Some organizations have Web sites. To call a group directly, look in The Yellow Pages of the telephone directory under "social service organizations."

Local newspapers often have a regular listing of volunteer needs. Some larger communities have volunteer coordination services that can tell you what groups exist and what kinds of help are wanted. While looking into opportunities, consider persuading a friend to join you. You, your friend, and the organization will all reap the rewards.

WHAT'S RIGHT FOR YOU?

Is volunteering a tremendous obligation? Certainly you should take your responsibilities to a group seriously. Remember, though, that volunteering is a spirit as well as an activity. If you have the time, your involvement may include a regular commitment of hours and energy. However, once

Volunteering is a two-way street. You bring skills to the job, whether muscle power, musical talent, or an upbeat attitude. You come away with new knowledge and experiences that enrich your life.

Volunteering to serve people in need is a way of showing you care about your community. How could your schedule be arranged to include time for volunteering?

you start to think like a volunteer, you find little ways to serve in everyday life. Is there someone at home who needs you? Does a neighbor regularly need help with a task?

Volunteering comes in many sizes. You can find opportunities that fit your life when you say to yourself and to others, "Yes, I'd like to help."

SECTION 24-2 REVIEW

Check Your Understanding

1. What qualities make teens particularly suited for volunteer work?
2. How can meeting people through volunteering be professionally useful?
3. What types of skills are helpful to volunteers?
4. Where could you find information about groups that need volunteers?
5. What are eight organizations that might need volunteers?
6. **Thinking Critically.** What false expectations do people sometimes have about volunteering? How might these ideas affect their willingness to volunteer and their experience as volunteers?
7. **Problem Solving.** A student that Denise has always admired and would like to know better has asked her to help with a cleanup effort at a local park. Denise dislikes working outdoors, especially since the weather has been wet and chilly. What should she do?

Chapter 24
Review and Activities

CHAPTER SUMMARY

- Citizenship includes both rights and responsibilities.
- Good citizens stay informed and participate in the community.
- Good citizens are actively involved in preventing crime and in bringing lawbreakers to justice.
- Good citizens strengthen their community by caring for property and promoting understanding among people.
- Good citizens work to protect the local and world environment.
- Volunteers are constantly needed to provide many different services.
- By volunteering, you improve people's lives while you grow both personally and professionally.
- Volunteer opportunities are most rewarding when they suit your abilities and interests.

REVIEW QUESTIONS

Section 24-1
1. Why is voting an important duty and right of citizenship?
2. How could you determine whether a political candidate has changed his or her position on an issue?
3. How do property rights relate to citizenship?
4. How can citizens help control crime?
5. What actions can good citizens take to help protect the environment?

Section 24-2
1. Why are volunteers needed to help in the community?
2. What emotional benefits might you realize by volunteering?
3. Is volunteer work a less serious responsibility than paid work? Explain.
4. Why is altruism a valuable trait?
5. How would you respond to someone who said, "I like to help people, but with my schedule, it's hard to make a regular commitment"?

BECOMING A PROBLEM SOLVER

1. Audra read in the paper that only 11 percent of local voters turned out to elect school board members. She thinks this is disgraceful. What should Audra do?
2. Since she started volunteering at a soup kitchen, Christina has become more sensitive to the wastefulness she sees around her. At lunch, she scolds friends for throwing away food. When they go to the mall, Christina discourages them from buying unneeded, expensive clothes. Her friends are starting to avoid her. What should Christina do?

THINKING CRITICALLY

1. **Predicting Results.** When people destroy public property, who pays?
2. **Determining the Strength of an Argument.** People who neglect their responsibilities as citizens give many reasons, including those listed below. How would you respond to each one?
   a. "I just don't have enough time to get involved."
   b. "Politicians are only interested in their own careers. They don't care about the voters."
   c. "One person can't change anything."
3. **Drawing Comparisons.** How is successful community life like successful family life?

MAKING CURRICULUM CONNECTIONS

1. **Language Arts/Civics.** Write a letter to a government representative about a problem that you believe this person can help solve. Identify the problem and explain what you would like to see done.
2. **Math.** Contact the local election office to find out how many registered voters live in your precinct. How many of them voted in the last election? Calculate the percentage of registered voters who actually voted. Do you think this is an acceptable percentage? Explain your answer.

APPLYING YOUR KNOWLEDGE

1. Find information about the rights and responsibilities of citizens in another country. In a written report, compare these to those of United States citizens.
2. Research each of the following groups: Habitat for Humanity, Sierra Club, Special Olympics, Salvation Army, and Second Harvest. What is the purpose of each group? What role do volunteers play? Share your findings.
3. Find out where the garbage produced by your community is taken. Is it put in a landfill? If so, are alternative methods of disposal available or in planning?

Family & Community Connections

1. Interview a representative of a volunteer organization. Learn about the group's function and its opportunities for teens. Share this information with the class to compile a comprehensive list of community volunteer opportunities.

2. In newspapers, find information about upcoming meetings of local government or civic groups. Attend one of these meetings. In a brief written or oral report, explain how the meeting was conducted, what was discussed, and what was accomplished.

Moving Toward Independence

Teen Views

How mature do you think you and your friends are?

Austin

"I don't think we're all the same. I used to hang out with two guys who were always in trouble—with their parents, at school, even with the law. It kept getting worse until I saw my future slipping away. I had to get away from that. Maybe that makes me more mature. I don't know. All I know is that I'm headed for college now, and I like it that way."

Sui Lin

"I think most of us are pretty mature. Sometimes we're more mature than a lot of adults. You should hear my uncle scream if my cousin drops the ball in a Little League game. And my friend Carmel told me that a woman she works with goes in the back sometimes and takes naps. At least I know what's right."

What's your view?

What signs of maturity do you see in yourself and your friends?

Chapter 25 On Your Own

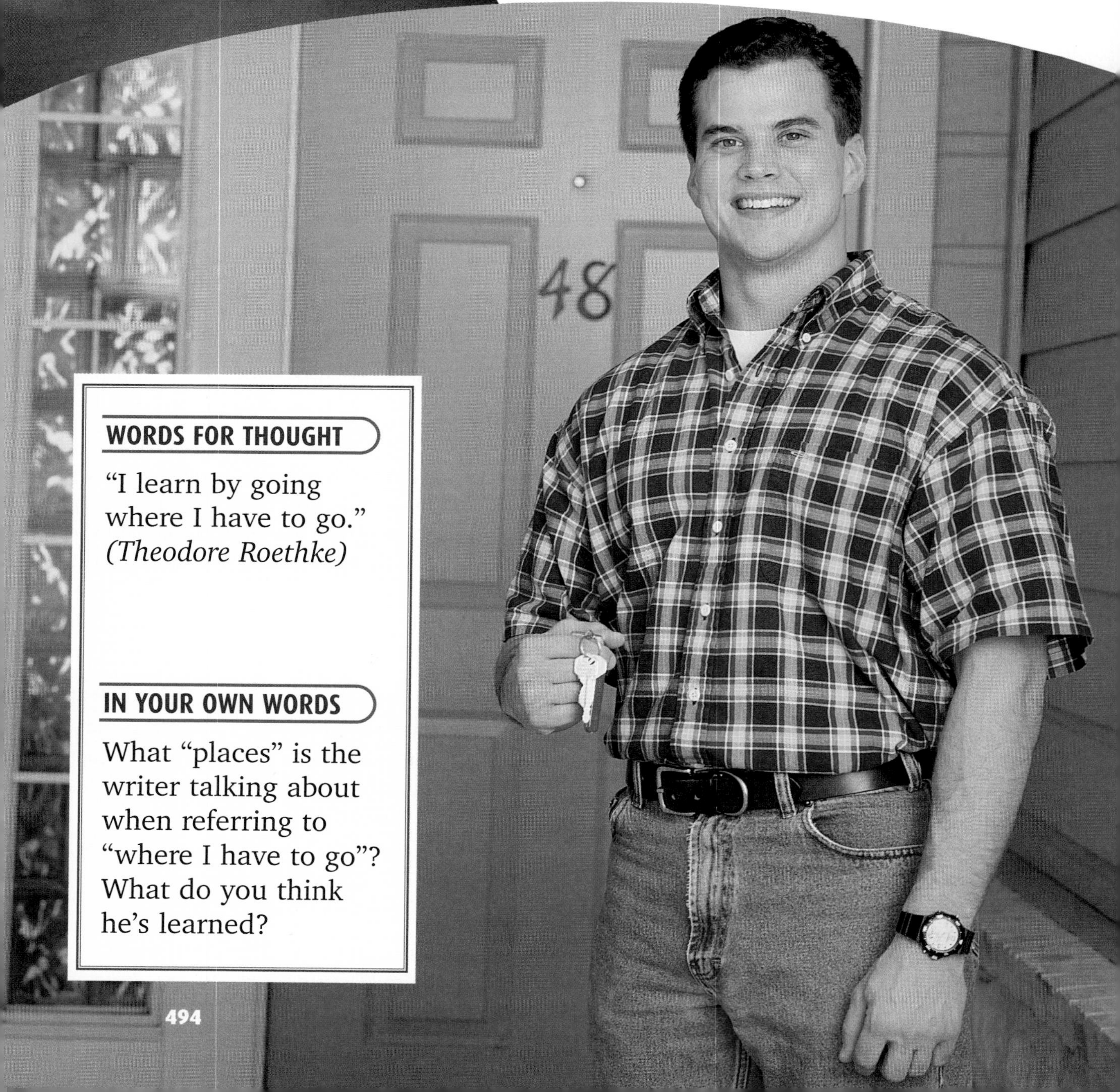

WORDS FOR THOUGHT

"I learn by going where I have to go."
(Theodore Roethke)

IN YOUR OWN WORDS

What "places" is the writer talking about when referring to "where I have to go"? What do you think he's learned?

Moving Away from Home

OBJECTIVES

After studying this section, you should be able to:

- Identify factors that affect the decision to leave home and your ability to live independently.
- Judge whether an apartment would be suitable for you.
- Compare housing options.

TERMS TO LEARN

security deposit
lease

"Leaving home." Does that phrase fill you with excitement, anxiety, or some of both? Mixed emotions are a natural response to the idea of moving out on your own. "Leaving home" means much more than finding a new place to live. In a broader sense, it implies that you are ready to live independently. Answering the following questions can help you assess how ready you are to meet the challenges of adulthood.

- Do you have a steady income sufficient to meet your housing, food, and clothing needs?
- Can you manage that money effectively to meet present and future needs?
- Do you have the knowledge and skills to eat nutritiously on your own?

- Can you clean and maintain a place of your own?
- Do you take responsibilities for your decisions and actions?
- Can you be happy spending time alone?

While you may not yet be able to answer *yes* to all these questions, you are building the skills you need. The feature about self-reliance on the next page suggests ways to practice independence.

CHOOSING INDEPENDENCE

When is the best time to move out on your own? That depends on you and your plans after high school. Will you join the working world? Do you plan to

Mixed emotions are typical when young people leave the family home. They might feel excited about independence but also a little apprehensive about managing on their own. How will you feel?

Building Character

Self-Reliance: A Quality That Counts

As an infant, you learned literally to "stand on your own two feet." As you become a young adult, you relearn this skill each time you practice self-reliance. Self-reliance is taking care of your own needs and meeting responsibilities with a minimum of help from others. Right now you might show self-reliance by:

- Buying clothes with money from a part-time job.
- Wearing a seatbelt and following safety rules when in a car.
- Using a personal checking account or credit card responsibly.
- Starting dinner for the family after getting home from school.
- Going to bed earlier in order to be alert in the morning.
- Arranging for transportation to school and extracurricular activities.

QUESTIONS

1. Can a person be too self-reliant? If so, in what way?
2. Does self-reliance strengthen or weaken family ties?
3. How do you show your self-reliance?

attend college or get other training? Perhaps you're thinking of joining the military. The option you choose will influence your decision about leaving the family home.

If you're like many young adults, you may delay the move awhile. Faced with the expenses of independent living, many people are seeing the advantage of staying at home for a few years after completing their education. Meanwhile, they work and save their money until they can better afford to live on their own. Also, people today are waiting longer to marry. Due largely to these two trends, more eighteen-to twenty-year-olds are living at home today than at any time in the recent past.

For these reasons, no time for moving out is exactly "right" for everyone. When you can support yourself financially and feel ready for the responsibilities of adult living, you'll probably be eager to make the move.

CHOOSING HOUSING

Your first big challenge after deciding to leave one home is finding a new one. Again, your choices are determined by your situation. Four-year colleges and universities generally require students to live on campus in dormitories for the first two years. Those entering the military typically live in barracks. Young adults in other circumstances have other options.

Apartment Living

Apartment living is the housing choice for many young adults. An apartment usually offers considerable privacy and freedom with minimal maintenance.

Locating an apartment can be an interesting and educational venture. Like many apartment hunters, Jacob checked the newspaper classified ads and inquired at rental agencies and real estate companies. He spread the word among family, friends, and coworkers in case they knew of available apartments. Along the way, Jacob gained some practical life skills. As he explained, "I learned that in rental ads, 'cozy' sometimes means 'tiny.' 'Convenient to shopping' may mean it's next door to an all-night convenience store."

Looking at apartments also gave Jacob a short course in economics. "I saw that some people don't have much choice in housing if they lack money. I also saw some places that were way out of my financial ballpark. It reminds you that you can't take things like a nice home for granted. You have to plan and work for them."

"Can I afford it?" By carefully weighing living expenses against potential income, you can evaluate whether housing is affordable. What other expenses will you have?

When looking for a place to live, think first about affordability and safety, then about suitability. An outdoor person, for example, might want a little space for growing flowers or vegetables—if possible.

Checking Out an Apartment

What do you look for when choosing an apartment? Questions that are commonly asked by apartment hunters include:

- **Can you afford the rent?** Most rental agreements require a **security deposit**, a one-time payment usually equal to one month's rent. The deposit is returned to you when you move out if you haven't damaged the apartment. Otherwise, the cost of any needed repairs is deducted from the amount. Sometimes the initial payment includes the first and last months' rent in addition to the security deposit.
- **Does the rent include utilities?** If not, ask what the average cost of utilities is for the apartment.
- **What are the terms of the lease?** A **lease** is a written agreement between the landlord (the property owner) and the tenant (the renter), spelling out the rights and responsibilities of each. It's wise to get these conditions in writing.
- **Does the apartment look and smell clean?** You won't want to rent sight unseen.
- **Is everything in good repair?** If not, don't sign the lease until promised repairs have been made.
- **What furnishings are provided?** Many apartments are equipped with larger appliances, such as a refrigerator and range.

- **Is the apartment safe?** What are the locks on the doors and windows like? Is any additional security provided? How safe is the neighborhood in general?
- **Is the location convenient to places you go frequently?** Additional transportation will add to your expenses.

You may have other concerns as well. If you have pets, will they be allowed? What parking and laundry facilities are available? You may want to make a checklist of the features you consider most important in an apartment.

Chances are, you won't find the ideal apartment, especially if your income is limited. Learning to live with noisy neighbors or a lack of storage space is part of maturity, too. Still, making an effort to find the most suitable apartment available is time well spent.

Furnishing Your Apartment

Have you ever thought about all the furnishings in your home that you use—not only larger pieces like a bed and microwave oven, but also smaller items like a can opener and lightbulbs? One of the challenges of life on your own is outfitting your apartment to suit your needs and tastes, usually on a tight budget.

Most first-time apartment dwellers gather furnishings from a number of different sources. Friends and family members might offer unused tables, lamps, or cooking utensils. Otherwise, check out thrift or discount stores, garage sales, auctions, or the classified ads.

Some furnishings can be made from existing items. A set of pillowcases can be transformed into curtains. Wooden and plastic crates make good storage containers.

When furnishing your apartment, choose according to needs. For a student, a sturdy desk and a good lamp for studying take priority over a plant stand.

Furnishing your apartment as you want it will take time. Let it be an opportunity to show your creativity and resourcefulness.

Other Housing Options

An apartment is just one option for independent living. A person might rent a *room in a private home*, often in exchange for performing certain jobs. This option can be helpful to both parties, especially when the homeowner is an older person. LaKeeta lives with Mrs. Beisser, who is eighty years old. In exchange for meals and housing, LaKeeta does some housekeeping and runs errands for Mrs. Beisser, who can no longer drive.

As LaKeeta explained, "It's a great arrangement for us both. Mrs. Beisser has a nice older house; it really feels like home. I have my job and my own social life, but I also like to spend time with Mrs. Beisser. I think she feels safer with someone around the house, too."

Not everything old is a bargain. Would furniture that's wobbly be a good buy? What about an antique?

Renting a *sleeping room* is a variation of home sharing, and often less expensive. A sleeping room is a single room, usually in a private home. The roomer shares bathroom privileges and may have kitchen rights.

You can get a taste of independence before committing to it fully by *housesitting*. Housesitters live in homes rent-free while the owners are away for extended periods. In exchange, they agree to be responsible for watching and maintaining the property until the owners' return.

Living with a Roommate

Sharing an apartment or a house with a roommate has its advantages. It's usually less expensive than living alone, and many people enjoy the companionship.

As with any relationship, successfully sharing space with a roommate takes communication and cooperation. To get along with a roommate:

- Decide beforehand how to divide expenses and household tasks.
- If you buy furnishings jointly, decide who gets them if one of you moves out.
- Agree on a code of conduct. Define what behavior is expected in your home.
- Respect each other's privacy. Sharing space doesn't mean giving up all personal possessions. Don't read your roommate's mail. Ask before borrowing items.
- Show consideration. Think of each other's needs, wants, and responsibilities before acting. Ask for input before making a decision that affects a roommate. Respect each other's wishes.
- Keep a sense of humor. Problems are bound to arise, but the right attitude can defuse potential conflict and turn it into an opportunity for growth.

MOVING BACK HOME

Many young adults, after living on their own a while, decide to move back home. For some, it's a matter of economics: they simply can't meet expenses on their own. Others decide they need more guidance to better handle the challenges of independence. Some people move home to recover from the stress and pain of divorce. A lengthy illness or disabling injury can send people home for physical and financial healing.

Some of the best friends don't necessarily make good roommates—yet some do. Talking about rules offers clues about compatibility. Why is this useful before the move?

Some problems can come when an adult returns home. When Alex moved back after a year of living alone, it was agreed that he would pay room and board and do his own laundry. At the same time, his mother and stepfather expected Alex to tell them when he was going out and when he would return, and to call if he would be late. Can you see the contradiction in these expectations and their potential for causing conflict?

When adult children move home, all family members need to recognize that their roles and relationships have changed. Clear communication about responsibilities and expectations is essential. Adjustments and compromise may also be needed.

Very few people live permanently with their parents. Typically, moving back home is a temporary arrangement, lasting just until young adults get their bearings, emotionally or financially, and strike out on their own again.

Some young adults who move back home do so to help the family. Whether temporary or long-term, the arrangement will go more smoothly if they talk over what each expects.

SECTION 25-1 REVIEW

Check Your Understanding

1. What factors affect the decision to move out on your own?
2. Name three resources for locating available apartments.
3. What is the purpose of a security deposit?
4. What is one advantage of housesitting?
5. Why might a young adult move back home?
6. **Thinking Critically.** What are some tenants' rights and responsibilities?
7. **Problem Solving.** Maribeth, age twenty-two, has always lived with her parents. She works full-time, pays rent, and does her share of household tasks. Although everyone is happy with the arrangement, Maribeth's parents worry because she doesn't socialize beyond work and family gatherings. They are pressuring her to find her own place, hoping this will encourage her to meet more people on her own. What should Maribeth do?

Managing on Your Own

OBJECTIVES

After studying this section, you should be able to:

- Describe practical concerns that single people face and how to address them.
- Demonstrate ways to protect yourself when living independently.
- Recommend ways to develop good relationships as a single person.

TERMS TO LEARN

autonomy
investing

When you were a child, your parents may have let you decide whether they should buy the toothpaste with the blue flecks or the one with the green gel. As a teen, you're probably more than capable of deciding which toothpaste to buy, when and how to use it, and whether to switch brands to one that you like more.

Now suppose one of your parents asked you to pick a dental plan to supplement an employer's health insurance package. That's a more weighty issue for a teen, yet single adults make similar decisions, alone, every day. Such choices are part of **autonomy**, the ability to direct your life independently. For singles, autonomy is a responsibility, but a potentially rewarding one.

FINANCES

Single adults are usually their own—and their only—source of income. They are also their own money managers. They make sure the bills are paid. They decide whether remaining money is saved or spent, relying on their own values and priorities.

Singles need to plan for the future as well. About ten percent of all single people will remain so for life. Many people who are now married will be single at some point due to divorce or the death of a spouse. Therefore, people have to be prepared financially for a time when they may be on their own. They must make decisions about:

- **Insurance.** This coverage protects health and possessions.

- **Savings.** People may have savings accounts, savings bonds, and certificates of deposit. Savings are essential for emergencies and luxuries alike. A savings plan is also needed for major purchases like a house or a car.

- **Investments.** Investing is using money to earn money. People invest in real estate, in the stock market, and in other funds designed to return more money than is put into them. Many young people think of investing as something to do when they're older and more established financially and professionally. Even before you have money to invest, however, is not too soon to plan for long-term financial security.

INFOLINK

Managing Money

For more information on spending and saving money, see *Section 27-1.*

NUTRITION AND HEALTH

When she first moved out on her own, Brenda had every intention of continuing the healthful habits she'd begun as a teen. She soon discovered much that she hadn't counted on. Deciding what foods to buy was actually harder with only herself to please; she had so many more choices and didn't always make the right ones. The flood of new responsibilities threw off her routine. She had to stay up late or get up early to finish everything. Exercise was something she fit in when she had the

time and energy. When she had a bad cold, she had to decide whether to go to work, call in sick, or see a doctor.

Eventually, Brenda got a handle on her health habits. She picked up pamphlets on choosing healthful food from the county health department and regional Cooperative Extension Service. She read articles on time management and listened to time- and money-saving tips from older relatives and coworkers. She asked her pediatrician

Planning meals, buying groceries, and eating alone are new experiences for many young adults. How would you make each of these go successfully for you?

to recommend a family practitioner. By taking charge of her own life, Brenda also improved her mental health.

As a single adult, you'll face the same responsibility for your well-being. Taking this course is one way that you're preparing for that day. Other classes in foods, fitness, and health are resources for making such decisions in the future.

TRANSPORTATION

Many young adults who live at home have access to an automobile. They might use the family car or share rides with friends when they need transportation. When they move out, however, getting from here to there can test resourcefulness. A single person may have to buy a car, use public transportation, ride a bicycle, or walk.

INFOLINK

Health and Wellness

For more information on health and wellness, see *Chapter 26*.

Owning a car is a great convenience, but upkeep is an ongoing expense. Gasoline, insurance, and maintenance can be costly. You can cut costs by learning to do regular maintenance and make minor repairs yourself. Community colleges, and even service stations, sometimes offer courses on auto care.

When Julio moved out, his parents sold him the older family car at a price he could afford. While he felt lucky to have the car, Julio had never been responsible for the work and money involved in its upkeep. Washing the car and changing the oil were time-consuming tasks. Besides gasoline and insurance, Julio paid for new spark plugs, a new tire to replace a flat, and a new taillight after someone hit his car in a parking lot. He soon decided that the television he had been hoping to buy would have to wait.

ENRICHMENT

What attracts many people to the single life are the opportunities for personal growth. Without a spouse or children, singles are free to commit more fully to careers, volunteer work, travel, and continuing education. They typically have more time for friends and family as well as hobbies and social events. Creating a personally pleasing home environment—hanging the artwork and preparing the foods you enjoy—is another form of enrichment that couples and parents often must compromise on.

Are you comfortable spending time alone? That's a big part of single living.

Your Personal Safety

As a single adult living alone, you'll need to be aware of your personal safety. These guidelines can help:

- Make sure your home's doors and windows have reliable, working locks.
- If you suspect someone has broken into your home, leave immediately. Call the police from a neighbor's phone.
- Know your neighbors. Recognizing those who live nearby will not only help you identify strangers but will also give you someone to turn to if you need help.
- Be familiar with your surroundings. Notice anyone or anything that seems unusual or out of place.
- If you're out after dark, walk and park your car in well-lit areas. Lock your car when you leave it and have your keys ready when you return.
- Always check the back seat of your car before getting in.
- If you think you're being followed, on foot or in a car, go to a well-lit place where there are people. Report the incident to the police.
- Tell the police if you often receive odd or disturbing phone calls or "wrong numbers."

USING YOUR KNOWLEDGE

Garson comes home for lunch every day to let his dog out of the house. Several times this week, he has noticed a strange car with two people in the front seat parked across the street. The car leaves soon after Garson arrives. What should Garson do?

If they wish, singles can also spend ample time alone. Reading, listening to music, or reflecting on life while working a jigsaw puzzle—such quiet pursuits can deepen a person spiritually.

RELATIONSHIPS

Building satisfying relationships can be a challenge for singles, especially if they live alone. Getting to know others may take more effort and creativity.

Toby, for example, started a new job in a new city. The workplace wasn't the best place for socializing, and people in his apartment building seemed busy in their own routines. Toby decided to try volunteer work and discovered a local chapter of Habitat For Humanity. He got to know a diverse group of people from his community while contributing to the community's strength. His sense of belonging increased as feelings of loneliness faded.

Clarisse took a different approach to solving the same problem. An avid baseball fan, she signed up for a bus trip to a ball game in a nearby city, organized by some of her coworkers. In the casual setting of a bus ride and ballpark, Clarisse and her coworkers got better acquainted and began to build friendships.

Both Clarisse and Toby overcame isolation by reaching out to others. They used their interests and talents to build relationships. Other similar opportunities for involvement include those listed below. How else can singles meet and make friends?

- Presentations and lectures on topics of interest at libraries and universities.
- Groups and activities sponsored by religious organizations.
- Volunteer groups, such as the American Red Cross or Big Brothers/Big Sisters.
- Parents Without Partners, a group for single parents.

- Groups related to occupations.
- Community theater and musical groups.
- Sports activities, such as joining a recreational bowling league.

DEVELOPING A WAY OF LIFE

When Lauren got her first job, she saved her money until she could make a down payment on a duplex located near a fitness center and the city swimming pool. She walks to work, travels twice a year, and spends time with her family and friends.

Harland lives very differently. He and a friend share an apartment in an older building. He spends much of his spare time working with disadvantaged youths and enjoys quiet evenings at home listening to music and reading books. Harland regularly sends money home to help his family.

Lauren and Harland have each developed a way of life. Taken together, their decisions about different parts of life—where to live, how to spend time and money, even what clothes to wear—form a pattern that says something about them.

It only takes an invitation to involve people in your life. Simple entertainment is fine. Just enjoying snacks and a ballgame on television can help build the bonds of friendship.

City life appeals to some young singles, while others prefer a rural setting. Wherever young adults live, they face similar challenges in managing their new responsibilities with success.

As a single, independent adult, you'll face the same decisions. The kind of life you choose will be based on your values and your heritage. Your experiences with family members and others will also influence the way you live.

Finding a way of living in which you feel comfortable and confident—and finding people to share it—is the essential challenge and opportunity of living on your own. It means successfully managing life in all areas: work, health, finances, and relationships. Fortunately, you have a great number of resources available, from the global span of the Internet to the down-to-earth advice of the special, trusted people in your life, to help you prepare. The more you know now about what awaits you, the better you can use the time that lies ahead.

SECTION 25-2 REVIEW

Check Your Understanding

1. What three areas should be included in a single adult's financial plan?
2. How is time management important to caring for your health?
3. What can you do to stay safe when traveling by car?
4. What transportation challenges do independent young adults face?
5. What opportunities for involvement can single people take advantage of?
6. **Thinking Critically.** Many people believe that young adults today expect too much, too soon in terms of finances, housing, and transportation as compared to previous generations. Do you agree? If so, is this trend necessarily negative?
7. **Problem Solving.** Hope would like to insure her TV, computer, and some other possessions against theft or damage because she knows that she couldn't afford to replace them. On the other hand, the insurance premiums will strain her budget. What should Hope do?

CHAPTER SUMMARY

- The right time to move out varies according to each person's situation.
- Several housing options are available for independent living.
- Moving back home temporarily is common for young people today.
- Managing finances includes meeting current expenses and also providing for the future.
- Young adults need to take precautions to protect their personal safety.
- Owning a car is a convenience and a responsibility as well.
- Life as a single can be full, rich, and personally satisfying.
- It may take a greater effort, but singles can build satisfying relationships.
- The single life is most rewarding if you develop a way of life that fits you and your values.

REVIEW QUESTIONS

Section 25-1
1. What is the "right" time to move out on your own?
2. What qualities should you look for when choosing an apartment?
3. How can you furnish an apartment on a budget?
4. Compare advantages and disadvantages of home sharing with renting a sleeping room.
5. What issues should people agree on before becoming roommates?

Section 25-2
1. Jeri pays her bills and saves a little for unplanned expenses. Are her financial concerns met? Why or why not?
2. What obstacles to caring for their health must single people deal with?
3. Why should you be familiar with your neighborhood and your neighbors?
4. How can singles meet people and build relationships?
5. What is meant by "developing a way of life"?

BECOMING A PROBLEM SOLVER

1. Candy works and goes to school part-time. She can't afford a car, and public transportation isn't convenient, so Candy rides a bike. After the weather turned cold, a neighbor she doesn't know well started offering her a ride. Candy said no but is tempted to accept the next time. What should Candy do?

2. Rick is ready to sign the lease for an apartment. The secretary in the rental office explained the terms, but Rick would like to read it himself. The language is so complicated, however, that he thinks he wouldn't understand it. What should Rick do?

THINKING CRITICALLY

1. **Predicting Results.** Adam, age seventeen, said: "I can't wait until I'm eighteen. Then I can move out and live the way I want to." Based on this statement, do you think Adam is prepared for living independently? Give reasons for your answer.
2. **Recognizing Assumptions.** Do you think employers should make judgments based on marital status when hiring and promoting employees? Explain.
3. **Recognizing Stereotypes.** Some people think that those who choose to stay single are selfish and trying to avoid responsibility. Do you agree? Explain your answer.
4. **Comparing and Contrasting.** What are some advantages and disadvantages of living in a group setting, such as a dormitory or barracks?

MAKING CURRICULUM CONNECTIONS

1. **Math.** Money management experts recommend spending about 25 percent or less of your gross income (income before taxes) on rent. Given this formula, what is the most you should pay in rent per month if you grossed $20,000 a year? $30,000 a year?
2. **Civics.** Investigate local and state law concerning renters' rights and responsibilities. What are tenants' options if they have a disagreement with their landlord?

APPLYING YOUR KNOWLEDGE

1. On a sheet of paper, make a list of responsibilities involved in living independently. Using a scale of one (lowest) to ten (highest), rate yourself on how well you think you would handle each one. Write a short paragraph explaining whether you feel ready for independence, based on your ratings.
2. Find ads in magazines and newspapers showing some aspect of single living. What products seem aimed at single people? How are their lives depicted? Describe for your class the image of life as a single that you found.

Family & Community Connections

1. Talk to an owner of rental property about a landlord's concerns. What risks and expenses do owners have? What are some of their responsibilities? What can renters do to make the landlord-tenant relationship a success?

2. Contact the local police, fire department, or sheriff's office for information on personal safety. Use the information to create an educational display.

Chapter 26

Health and Wellness

WORDS FOR THOUGHT

"Little and often make much."
(Anonymous)

IN YOUR OWN WORDS

How do you think this comment relates to health and wellness?

Influences on Health

OBJECTIVES

After studying this section, you should be able to:

- Explain why people are healthier in general today than 50 years ago.
- Explain how personal choice contributes to health.
- Describe what is meant by wellness and how it influences all parts of your life.
- Identify what you can do throughout your life to promote and protect your own good health.

TERMS TO LEARN

vaccines
pathogens
antibiotics
cardiovascular diseases
wellness
preventative medicine

Imagine that it's 6:45 a.m. and you struggle up through a fog of sleep to shut off your alarm clock. Staying up until 1:00 a.m. watching television was a mistake, one that you've made twice this week. Breakfast is a caffeine-laced soft drink. At school you go through your first-hour class in a daze. Later, you confide to a friend, "I'm tired of feeling tired all the time."

Whether or not this scene fits you, it's one that many teens recognize. The daily actions people take have an effect on their health. How much sleep do you get? What do you eat and drink? Is exercise part of your routine? These are all related to the way you look and feel, and you'll soon see how.

IMPROVEMENTS IN HEALTH

Overall, people today are healthier than they've ever been. There are several reasons why.

Vaccines have helped reduce the rate of many illnesses. These preparations are actually made from **pathogens** (PA-thuh-juns), the viruses and bacteria that cause diseases. When administered, vaccines prevent people from getting certain diseases. Whooping cough, diphtheria, polio, and measles were common in the past but are now controlled by the widespread use of vaccines.

Antibiotics, special medicines that destroy disease-causing bacteria, have con-

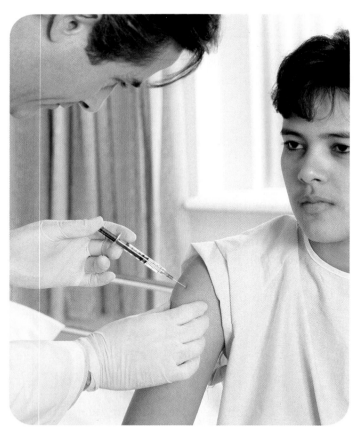

Vaccinations have virtually eliminated certain diseases in society. Most vaccinations are given from infancy through early childhood, but some require later booster shots.

Felix, for instance, has health insurance through his employer. He's protected from financial losses in case of serious medical problems. Having insurance makes him more likely to seek medical care when he needs it.

PERSONAL CHOICES ABOUT HEALTH

Even though the overall level of health is better than it used to be, not everyone enjoys good health. Serious illnesses today include obesity, heart disease, cancer, and strokes.

According to the National Cancer Institute, cancer is second only to heart disease as the leading cause of death in the United States. People who die from lung cancer lose an average of 15 years of life. Smoking is directly linked to lung cancer. **Cardiovascular diseases** (car-dee-o-VAS-kyuh-lur)—heart-related diseases, such as strokes and high blood pressure, are the leading cause of death in the United States. Smoking, poor eating habits, lack of exercise, and stress are linked to heart illnesses.

Dustin learned about the link between health habits and disease the hard way. As the manager of a growing firm, he worked long hours, ate fast food on the run, and seldom exercised. Under pressure, he smoked more than ever. Some nights he had trouble getting to sleep, so he took sleeping pills. Although Dustin got by for a number of years with these poor habits, he began to have health problems. Finally, a heart attack caused him to take a close look at his habits. He was lucky to have a second chance.

tributed greatly to treating many diseases. For example, tuberculosis and meningitis, which were once incurable, can be treated successfully with antibiotics. Many common bacterial infections are also treated with these medications.

Finally, the overall standard of living today has made a difference. With better housing and sanitation, people enjoy better health. In general, people have more money to spend on health care, including health insurance. In 1940, less than ten percent of the population had health insurance. Today, about eighty-five percent do.

It took something serious for Dustin to see the importance of wellness. With his doctor's help, however, Dustin adopted new health habits. Although it wasn't easy, he gave up smoking. He started taking his own lunch to work—a sandwich with lean meat on whole-grain bread and fruit or a vegetable salad. He began to walk every evening and play racquetball twice a week. To relieve stress, he took time to read a good book and spend time with his family.

Dustin never realized how much he was damaging his own health until he discovered what it was like to feel good. Now he not only feels happier, but he also has more energy.

WHAT IS WELLNESS?

What happened to Dustin doesn't have to happen to you. You can prevent many health problems by choosing wellness. **Wellness** is a positive state of physical and mental health. It's more than just the absence of disease or sickness. A commitment to wellness means you've made a decision to live in a way that promotes good health.

With the right attitude toward health, your behavior changes. You take responsibility for adopting good health habits. You might call this using **preventative medicine**. That means you find out what health experts say about how to stay healthy. Then you make these actions part of your routine.

Wellness pays. When you're healthy, you not only look and feel good, but you also feel good about yourself. What's more, you save money. Health care is expensive. A serious illness can create thousands of dollars in medical bills.

Many illnesses can be prevented when people make good choices related to their health. No one else can make these choices for you.

Young people show maturity by making responsible health decisions. Besides figuring out how to get needed rest, what other decisions do you have to make?

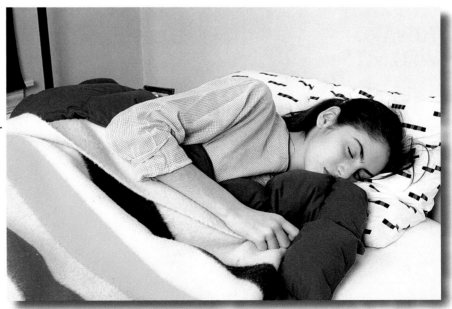

The Role of Mental Health

To be well, your mental health is as important as your physical health. Stress, crises, and other mental strains affect the body, causing both physical and mental illnesses. In fact, some researchers estimate that about half of those who seek medical treatment suffer from physical illnesses directly related to emotional stress.

JoAnn, for example, made it through five intense days of final exams and then caught the flu because her immune system was weakened. When sixteen-year-old Ned's parents divorced after several difficult years, they fought over where everyone would live and how property would be divided. Feeling constant worry and pressure, Ned started having headaches frequently. Both of these situations show how emotions can affect physical health.

Stressful feelings often go away after exercising or taking time for an activity you enjoy. What are you risking if you don't include exercise and relaxation in your daily life?

WORKING TOWARD WELLNESS

When it comes to wellness, you're in the driver's seat. Just as you're in charge of following the rules of the road when you drive, you're also in charge of following good health habits. Nothing comes with guarantees, but statistics show that you have a much better chance on the highway when you drive safely. You also have a much better chance for good health when you practice wellness.

Adults and teens alike often make the mistake of thinking, "I won't get sick. I've always been healthy." That may seem true, but until the first time something happens, it's easy to say it never will. When will you first develop a serious health problem? With good health habits, your chances of avoiding that possibility are likely to increase tremendously.

Looking at Limitations

Of course, you can't control everything that affects your health. Some health conditions, such as heart disease and diabetes, run in families. Due to inheritance, the chances of getting the disease go up. Also, certain diseases seem to be more common in one gender than the other.

That doesn't mean good health habits aren't needed, however. For people with a family history of a certain illness, good health practices may be even more important in reducing the risk of developing a disease. If you can, finding out about your family's health history can give you helpful information for the future.

Another limiting factor is economic condition. Unfortunately, people who have lower incomes tend to have more health problems. They might not eat as well, or they might lack necessary health care. In this situation, people must use resources very carefully to maintain good health.

Angie finds inexpensive ways to stay fit. She plays on her school volleyball team for exercise. She also signed up for a class at the community center to learn about fixing inexpensive but nutritious meals and snacks. Despite her family's limited budget, Angie plans to stay healthy.

Wellness Tips

In the next section of this chapter, you'll take a closer look at some recommended health habits. Before you read on, however, take note of these ideas that can help as you aim for wellness:

- **Practice cleanliness.** Many contagious illnesses can be prevented by washing your hands several times a day with soap.

Building Character

Self-Respect: A Quality That Counts

Self-respect means valuing yourself as a person. You care enough about yourself to do and be your very best. It also means avoiding what could hurt you. You can show self-respect by:

- Exercising daily to take good physical care of your body.
- Taking a walk to release anger and stress constructively.
- Joining a school club to help overcome shyness.
- Making the decision not to use drugs.
- Practicing a skill daily to develop a talent.

QUESTIONS

1. In what ways does each of the above actions show self-respect?
2. How do you think a person develops self-respect?
3. How do you show that you respect yourself?

Luisa Ramirez: *Wellness Specialist*

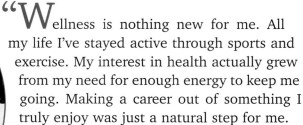

"Wellness is nothing new for me. All my life I've stayed active through sports and exercise. My interest in health actually grew from my need for enough energy to keep me going. Making a career out of something I truly enjoy was just a natural step for me.

"When I say that I'm a wellness specialist, many people assume I only deal with physical fitness, but wellness is much more than that. We address mental health as well as physical. My job is to plan and carry out wellness programs in our company and encourage everyone to participate. Each year I survey employees to find out what they want. Weight loss, stress management, and stop-smoking programs always seem to make the list. Sometimes I arrange for an employee to get special help through outside services.

"When you work in a corporate environment, the bottom line is often dollars—how much will it cost? I try to emphasize what we're saving. I was really pleased when management noticed that the average number of absences per employee decreased by 1.5 days per year after the wellness program started. The company is paying less for health care and missed work. On a business level, that's the most satisfying thing for me. On a personal level, I like seeing that people are healthier and happier overall."

CAREER PROFILE

Education and training: bachelor's degree

Starting salary: about $25,000

Job prospects: schools; hospitals; health and fitness clubs; corporations

Important qualities: energetic; caring; good communication skills

Plan Ahead

Several paths could lead a person to a health career. What are three careers that deal with each of the following aspects of wellness—physical, mental or emotional, and social?

- **Get regular dental and medical check-ups.** Problems are more easily managed when detected early.
- **Become knowledgeable.** The news is full of new developments in the health field. You can locate books and magazines that will keep you up-to-date.
- **Be wary of false information.** You'll hear about many remedies and treatments, weight loss programs, and health supplements that are totally worthless. Investigate before you believe.
- **Link with people who will support you.** Religious organizations and school clubs are good places to start.
- **Make your own decisions.** If people close to you have poor habits, you don't have to imitate them. You can choose your own path to wellness.

You can get exercise in ordinary ways. Even washing the car stretches muscles as you reach and scrub. Besides that, you can burn 70 or more calories in half an hour.

SECTION 26-1 REVIEW

Check Your Understanding

1. What are four diseases that are controlled by the use of vaccines?
2. How have antibiotics changed medical care?
3. What is preventative medicine?
4. Why can thinking that you'll never get a serious illness be a problem?
5. What are five tips for helping maintain wellness?
6. **Thinking Critically.** Matthew bought a car right after graduation. He takes excellent care of it so it will run well. Matthew skips meals, doesn't exercise, and eats lots of sweets and fried foods. What inconsistency do you see here?
7. **Problem Solving.** Simone's sister orders all sorts of herbal supplements from catalogs in order to prevent illnesses and treat minor conditions. She suggests that Simone start using them, too. What should Simone do?

Building Positive Health Habits

OBJECTIVES

After studying this section, you should be able to:

- Identify basic guidelines for healthful eating.
- Describe the causes and symptoms of eating disorders.
- Summarize the health benefits of exercise.
- Explain the impact that sleep, stress, and drugs can have on health and wellness.
- Identify personal and community resources that can help you stay healthy.

TERMS TO LEARN

anorexia nervosa
bulimia
compulsive eating
endurance
aerobic exercise
strength
flexibility
sleep deprivation

If healthy habits aren't part of your life so far, then you have a great opportunity ahead. Even if you practice wellness now, you can always find ways to improve your approach.

EATING RIGHT

You may have heard this said before: "You are what you eat." All this means is that food choices count when it comes to your health and development.

A poorly nourished body has a lower resistance to illnesses and takes longer to heal when injured. A poor diet can also lead to tooth decay. Do you know anyone who has difficulty concentrating or is irritable? The reason just might be poor diet.

On the other hand, a good diet while you're young helps you grow and develop normally. Throughout your life, good nutrition will remain important to wellness. Eating right can help fight heart disease, weight problems, diabetes, and some types of cancer.

Here are some basic nutrition guidelines to help you stay healthy:

- Follow the United States Department of Agriculture MyPyramid suggestions for healthy eating.
- Study good nutrition. Find out your nutrient and calorie needs.
- Read the labels on food packages and learn what the nutritional information means.
- Eat regular meals instead of grabbing snacks that aren't nutritious.

MyPyramid

MyPyramid is a symbol and food guidance system developed by the U.S. Department of Agriculture (USDA). It is designed to encourage consumers to make healthier food choices and to be active every day.

MyPyramid.gov
STEPS TO A HEALTHIER YOU

Five food groups are represented by color bands in the MyPyramid symbol. Foods from all groups are needed each day for good health. The five groups are:

Grain Group. Bread, pasta, oatmeal, breakfast cereals, tortillas, and grits are examples of grain products. Grains are important sources of dietary fiber, several B vitamins, and minerals, including iron and magnesium.

Vegetable Group. This group includes any fresh, frozen, canned, or dried vegetables, eaten raw or cooked, as well as vegetable juice. Vegetables are important sources of potassium, dietary fiber, folic acid, vitamins A, E, and C, and other nutrients.

Fruit Group. Any fruit or 100 percent fruit juice counts as part of the Fruit Group. Fruits are important sources of many nutrients, including potassium, dietary fiber, vitamin C, and folic acid.

Milk Group. This food group includes milk and many foods made from milk, including yogurt and most cheeses. Foods in the Milk Group provide calcium, potassium, and vitamin D.

Meat & Beans Group. All foods made from meat, poultry, fish, dry beans or peas, eggs, nuts, and seeds are considered part of this group. They supply many nutrients, including protein, B vitamins, vitamin E, iron, zinc, and magnesium.

Designing an eating plan based on the food groups is easy and flexible. You can adapt your choices to your own food preferences, eating patterns, family circumstances, and cultural traditions. Some foods, such as pizza, include foods from several groups.

- Don't fill up on "empty" calories from sugary foods and soft drinks.
- Limit sodium and fats by eating fewer fried foods and fatty meats. Most fast food is high in both fat and salt and should be eaten in moderation.

Maintaining a Desirable Weight

Excess weight is a common cause of many diseases. High blood pressure, arthritis, heart disease, and diabetes are more apt to strike those who are overweight. Being underweight may not be healthy either. It can weaken the body and make fighting off illness harder.

For the best health, your weight should fall within the range shown for your gender and height in current, standard weight tables. Remember to consult your physician before trying to gain or lose weight.

Eating Disorders

Eating disorders are psychological problems related to food and eating. They result in abnormal eating behaviors. Often these disorders are related to issues of power and control. Stress and crisis may also be involved. The teen years are a time of high risk for eating disorders. In most cases, professional help is needed to overcome these problems.

The slender image of many celebrities can cause teens to worry too much about weight. How can you avoid this trap?

Anorexia nervosa (an-uh-REX-ee-uh ner-VOH-suh) is a mental disorder that shows itself in a fear of being fat. The patient, usually female, refuses to eat enough to maintain a healthy body weight. In anorexia nervosa, the patient overcontrols the body. This mental illness can cause death because of malnutrition and the strain put on the body. Patients must often be hospitalized for treatment.

Patricia was twenty pounds overweight in the eighth grade. She decided to lose the extra weight before high school. When she did, Patricia felt so much more confident and successful that she didn't want to stop. Soon she was dieting simply to feel in control. After catching a bad cold that developed into pneumonia, Patricia spent a week in the hospital recovering. Through support from her physician and family, she learned how to feel successful and improve her self-worth without destroying her health.

Bulimia (buh-LIM-ee-uh) is an eating disorder that involves "binge" eating. A person who has bulimia eats huge amounts of food in a short period of time and then induces vomiting or uses a laxative. Females are more likely to suffer from bu-

Balancing Work & Family Life

THE CHALLENGE —

Managing Mealtimes

Television shows of the past often showed the family gathered around the dinner table enjoying a meal together. Many busy families today miss that kind of sharing. Families are stronger when they find time to spend together, and mealtime can be the perfect setting.

How You Can Help

To help make mealtime a shared event that your whole family can look forward to, try these ideas:

- Suggest that your family choose a regular time to have at least one meal together each week.

- Offer to help plan the meal, buy the groceries, and prepare the food, or pick it up from a carryout service. Meals don't have to be fancy. You might choose a regular theme, such as pizza night.

- Be there for the designated meal.

- Keep conversation light and positive. Plan something special. Each person might bring a joke or take turns telling something good that happened that week.

- Avoid distractions. The television and radio can be turned off. Telephone calls can be delayed.

- Clean up together. Work is easier and more fun when people do it together.

---

limia. This disorder is not usually life threatening, but can lead to unhealthy body weight and damage to the teeth and esophagus from vomiting.

A third type of eating disorder is **compulsive eating**. Sufferers are unable to resist food and cannot stop eating. Like bulimia, compulsive eating is a lack of control over eating habits. A response to emotional distress, such as depression, anger, or anxiety, is usually the cause. Compulsive eating plays a major role in obesity.

EXERCISING

Exercise helps keep your heart strong, your muscles toned, your lungs working well, and your blood circulating smoothly. Nutrients and oxygen can move more easily to all parts of your body.

With cross-training, you include different kinds of exercise throughout the week. A ballet lesson on one day might be combined with a bike ride and a walk with friends on other days. What are the advantages of this approach?

If you exercise regularly, you're apt to feel better and have more energy. Your immunity against illness increases. Without exercise, your muscles, including your heart, weaken, and your breathing becomes more shallow.

An effective exercise program builds:

- **Endurance. Endurance** is the length of time you can work or exercise. You build endurance through **aerobic exercise** (uh-ROE-bik). This is strenuous activity that raises the heart rate and increases the amount of oxygen taken into the lungs. Walking, swimming, jogging, and cycling are great ways to build endurance. Experts suggest at least thirty minutes of aerobic exercise three to four times a week.

- **Strength.** Your ability to apply force is known as **strength**. Strength training, which is also called weight training, builds strong muscles and bones. It also helps prevent the loss of muscle that oc-

curs with age. Machines are available to use in strengthening all the major muscle groups. Although these are expensive to buy, you may find them in schools, Y's, and health clubs. Weights and stretchy bands are commonly used and can be purchased at lower costs.

- **Flexibility.** With **flexibility**, you are able to move your muscles to a great extent, sometimes to their fullest extent. Stretching exercises promote flexibility by keeping muscles long and limber. Stretching helps muscles relax. Short, tight muscles cause stiffness and pain. When you stretch, gradually increase the stretch without straining the muscles and hold for 10 to 15 seconds. Bouncing while you stretch tends to cause small tears in your muscles.

Working on all three areas every time you exercise isn't necessary. Alternating types of exercise on different days allows muscles to rest and may prevent you from becoming bored with exercise. No matter what the exercise, always warm up first to prevent injury.

Before beginning a serious exercise program, you should see your doctor. Simply adding more exercise to everyday activities, however, is generally safe and helpful. For example, Sam increased his activity level by using the stairs whenever he could and walking instead of driving short distances. He also started parking his car in the far corner of a parking lot rather than looking for a space close to the door. Where in your daily schedule could you include exercise?

GETTING ENOUGH SLEEP

Many people try to get by with too little sleep. With the right amount of sleep, you should awake feeling restored and alert for the day.

Recent research confirms that most people do need close to eight hours of sleep each night. Although some manage with less, some need more. Heredity and health influence the amount of sleep you need.

The study of sleep disorders is gaining attention today. **Sleep deprivation** (de-pruh-VAY-shun), not getting enough sleep, affects health. Often people don't even

SKILLS CHECKLIST

Your Sleep Habits

Getting a good night's sleep isn't always easy. What can you do when you're tired but sleep won't come? The following checklist of ideas is based on suggestions from scientists who study sleep:

✓ I exercise regularly in the morning or late afternoon, but not just before going to bed.

✓ I go to bed and get up about the same time every day.

✓ I sleep only enough to feel alert and rested.

✓ I skip caffeine (as in soft drinks) after 4:00 p.m.

✓ I don't take sleeping pills unless a doctor prescribes them. Then I take them only as ordered.

✓ If I feel hungry at bedtime, I eat only a light snack. I don't go to bed hungry or directly after eating a big meal.

✓ I use my bed only for sleep, not for reading, watching TV, or working.

✓ I do something relaxing just before going to bed.

✓ I keep my bedroom at a temperature that helps me sleep best.

Using Your Skills

Use the checklist as a class survey. Is there a correlation between the number of ideas that people follow and how well they sleep? What do you conclude?

You may enjoy exercising more when friends join you regularly. Why does this increase motivation?

Relaxation helps control stress. Dean relaxes to music. In his words, "I can relax just by putting on my headphones and listening to my favorite music. When I'm tense, I let myself go with the music. Listening to music can actually get me out of a bad mood."

Physical activity also relieves stress. Tension and nervous energy disappear and you improve your physical condition as well.

realize why they're so tired, can't concentrate, and are perhaps even depressed. Researchers have found that chemical factors can affect how much sleep people actually get. Depression, stress, and tension may also cause sleep interruptions. A growing number of sleep clinics now diagnose and treat sleep problems.

DEALING WITH STRESS

As you read earlier, too much stress can interfere with daily activities and lead to medical problems. Fortunately, you can reduce stress in your life.

First, look at how you manage. Review what you've learned about setting priorities and organizing your time and activities. By seeing yourself as successful, you can aim for a healthy perspective.

REJECTING HARMFUL DRUGS

Staying away from harmful drugs is your right as well as your responsibility. Your wellness depends on the choices you make.

Drugs typically affect the mind and influence behavior by changing feelings, mood, and perception. They can lead to addiction and have destructive effects on the lives of those who take them and the people around them.

Depending on the drugs used, long-term damage can include permanent injury to the liver, heart, kidney, lung, and brain. Depression, severe mood changes, and mental illness are common. Harmful drugs can cause permanent damage that may prevent you from ever being healthy again.

Tobacco

Tobacco use is a leading cause of illness. Smoking is the most common preventable cause of death in the United States. Smoking is linked to cancers of the lungs, throat, mouth, esophagus, pancreas, and bladder. Heart disease, emphysema, chronic bronchitis, and strokes are also related to smoking. Cancer of the lip and mouth has been linked to pipe smoking and the use of smokeless tobacco. Cigar smoking is also dangerous.

When Ralph's father had a stroke, the doctor said it was a combination of an increased heart rate, high blood pressure, and narrow blood vessels. These were all related to his smoking habits.

Alcohol

Alcohol causes serious problems. Brain damage, heart disease, liver damage, cancer, ulcers, and gastritis have been linked to alcohol use. Just as devastating, alcohol use is also linked to poor mental health for drinkers as well as their families.

About half of all fatal car accidents in the United States are related to alcohol use. This is because alcohol affects the brain, slowing reflexes and causing poor judgment.

RESOURCES

Wellness can't be taken for granted. To preserve wellness, what can you do? You have your own strengths to turn to, and you can also look for help around you.

Tips & TECHNIQUES

Finding Health Resources. A comfortable feeling comes when you know where to go when you need help. When you have a problem, where will you turn? Name a specific person or group for each of the following situations:

- Who would you see if you had a leg injury?
- Who would you go to for a toothache?
- Who could help you deal with overwhelming stress?
- Who would you talk to if you thought you might have an eating disorder?
- Who could help you if you needed to give up smoking?
- Who could help you learn about prostate cancer if your grandfather develops it?

Try It Out. Make a list of the people or groups who provide health care or services for you. Share resource ideas with the class so that everyone can have a comfort zone when it comes to needing help.

Personal Resources

Emmy Lou expressed thoughts similar to many other teens when she said: "I can tell you the important facts about nutrition and how you should eat, but sometimes I just don't seem to do the right thing. Passing up a jelly donut isn't easy, especially when everyone else is having one. As for exercise, I know I need more, but it always seems like work to me."

Poor health is typically preceded by excuses. How can you overcome them? You can try a number of ideas. First, be a leader. If others around you are making weak decisions, you can be the one to suggest something different. Look for ways to exercise that are fun. A dance class or talking with a friend while you take brisk walks may not seem like exercise at all. Apply your management skills to your health by setting goals and making a written plan. Involve a friend or relative who also wants to make health improvements. You can work together.

When you're committed to making wellness a priority in your life, excuses won't get in the way.

Most communities have organizations that help people with health concerns. Where could you go in your community?

Finding Insurance

Like everyone else, young people can have illnesses and medical emergencies. When Justine fell and broke her leg, the medical bills quickly added up. There was one for the emergency room, one for the lab technician who took X rays of the leg, and another for the X rays themselves. There was a bill for the doctor who set the leg, and even one for the crutches Justine used while recovering. Can you imagine the consequences without insurance?

Health insurance is a resource that gives you financial protection from resulting bills. Assuming you won't need insurance is very risky. Teens are typically covered under a parent's policy, but such coverage doesn't last when you're on your own. If you don't have insurance where you work in the future, you'll want to get trustworthy advice about buying coverage.

Community Resources

Managing your health won't seem out of reach if you take advantage of community resources, too. These are some that are available:

- **Health care services.** Doctors, nurses, hospitals, and clinics help when you are physically ill. Some clinics even offer free or low-cost services ranging from medical care to treatment of mental illness.
- **Recreation facilities.** Public parks, tennis courts, and swimming pools provide opportunities for exercise. The YMCA and YWCA also have good programs. Belonging to a health club and participating in an organized recreational program are other ways to enjoy exercise.
- **Government health programs.** Most counties have public health departments that provide health-related services. Two major federal health programs are Medicare, for older adults, and Medicaid, a government program to help low-income people with medical bills. Other

federal programs are offered through the Department of Health and Human Services. These cover many areas of health care, such as research on diseases and their cures, mother and child health services, and programs to prevent and control the spread of disease.
- **Nonprofit service organizations.** They are devoted to raising awareness about health issues. These organizations include the American Cancer Society, American Red Cross, Kidney Foundation, American Heart Association, and many more.
- **The library.** In the public library, you'll find books and magazines as well as health-related programs. Many libraries also offer use of the Internet. A librarian can show you how to use the resources.

Maintaining wellness doesn't have to be difficult. By combining personal and community resources, good health habits can gradually become a way of life for you, just as they have for many others.

SECTION 26-2 REVIEW

Check Your Understanding

1. What are five ways to maintain wellness?
2. Why is eating a variety of foods important for good nutrition?
3. Describe the different types of eating disorders.
4. How is aerobic exercise different from other types of exercise?
5. What are three suggestions for controlling stress?
6. What is the leading preventable cause of death in the United States?
7. **Thinking Critically.** What impact does self-discipline have on a person's health?
8. **Problem Solving.** In order to have more time to work and be with friends, Melissa decided to train her body to need less sleep. Gradually, she has decreased the amount of time she sleeps each night. She now has afternoon slumps and often feels groggy. What should Melissa do?

CHAPTER SUMMARY

- Many of your daily actions affect your health. Once you are independent enough to control these actions, you become responsible for your own health.
- Medical advances have controlled the spread of many diseases, but those related to poor living habits are becoming more common.
- You can do much to achieve wellness.
- Good eating habits are needed for growth and development, resistance to disease, and maintaining a desirable weight.
- There are simple, easy ways to increase the amount of exercise you get each day.
- Getting enough sleep and reducing stress help people feel their best.
- Harmful drugs can destroy both physical and mental health.
- Personal and community resources can assist you in achieving and maintaining good physical and mental health.

REVIEW QUESTIONS

Section 26-1

1. What are three factors that have contributed to an improved state of health today?
2. How do personal health habits relate to disease?
3. What does wellness mean? What are its benefits?
4. In what ways are physical and mental health related?
5. If money is limited, can people still be healthy? Explain.

Section 26-2

1. What are five basic nutrition guidelines?
2. You've read that the mind and body work together where health is concerned. How does this apply to eating disorders?
3. If a friend was having trouble sleeping, what six suggestions would you offer?
4. What three elements should be included in a well-rounded exercise program? Why is each necessary?
5. How can tobacco and alcohol affect people physically?

BECOMING A PROBLEM SOLVER

1. Caitlyn has decided to start running each day. She has the time, but finds it hard to get motivated. What should Caitlyn do?

2. Kevin is on the wrestling team. In order to meet weight requirements, he often forces himself secretly to vomit before weighing in. He tried to get into a higher weight class, but his coach says he needs Kevin at the lower weight. What should Kevin do?

THINKING CRITICALLY

1. **Drawing Parallels.** How does this saying relate to health: "An ounce of prevention is worth a pound of cure"?
2. **Drawing Conclusions.** Many people don't live with their biological family and may not know them. What impact might this have on their approach to wellness?
3. **Analyzing Behavior.** Why do you think some people disregard the potential harm from tobacco, alcohol, and other dangerous drugs?
4. **Drawing Conclusions.** Does more information about diseases help people or make them overly sensitive to their health? Explain your answer.

MAKING CURRICULUM CONNECTIONS

1. **Language Arts.** Write a creative, humorous essay entitled "An Unhealthy Day in the Life of…" In it, describe what happens to a person with an irresponsible attitude toward health and wellness.
2. **Health.** Research the problems related to bacteria that have become resistant to antibiotics. What are the implications of this for the treatment of disease? What impact might this have on the overall health in society?
3. **Physical Education.** Design an exercise program for yourself that includes activities to build endurance, strength, and flexibility. Select activities that you would enjoy doing. Try out the exercise program for a week.

APPLYING YOUR KNOWLEDGE

1. Join with a team of classmates to plan a teaching lesson on one of the following topics: nutrition; exercise; sleep problems; drug use; stress and mental health; health insurance. Narrow the topic to a more specific subtopic and locate additional information. Present your lesson to the class.
2. Investigate the effects of caffeine on the body. What physiological changes does it create? Find out how much caffeine is in your favorite drink. How much caffeine do you drink a day? What effect does this amount of caffeine have on your body?
3. Research a specific health-care field. What training and skills are needed to work in this field? What new technology is used in the field?

Family & Community Connections

1. Create a list of community resources that could contribute to wellness. Do you think wellness is a priority in your community? Explain your answer.

2. If you were the owner of a business, how would you promote employee wellness? Plan ideas with a partner.

Managing Money

IN YOUR OWN WORDS

Why might borrowing money be harmful to a friendship?

Spending and Saving Money

OBJECTIVES

After studying this section, you should be able to:

- Explain what money means to people.
- Describe two basic approaches to spending money.
- Explain methods for handling everyday expenses.
- Describe credit options and explain their wise use.
- Explain the function and importance of savings accounts.

TERMS TO LEARN

debit card
credit
interest
down payment
balance
loan

What makes a person "rich"? Is it money—or is it something else? Your response tells a lot about you. It shows what you value and what your priorities are.

ATTITUDES ABOUT MONEY

Managing daily life is certainly easier when you can pay for the necessities and perhaps some extras, but what do people truly need in order to be happy? This question has provoked many debates and always will. Without a doubt, some people put more value on money than others do. What do you think?

Often attitudes toward money spring from emotional needs rather than practical ones. One teen might bolster low self-esteem by buying designer clothes or the latest sound equipment. Another person might save everything in order to feel more secure. To feed a desire for power, one person might manipulate people by paying for favors and buying loyalty. Still another might buy gifts in order to keep a friend and feel appreciated and loved.

Dawn always spends money on her friends. She buys them gifts and pays for movie tickets. In Alison's words, "I don't know exactly why, but Dawn keeps spending money on me. If she thinks that's why we're friends, she's wrong. I really like Dawn, but not because of the money. I keep telling her that she doesn't have to buy friendship."

SPENDING STYLES

Money "burns a hole in the pocket" of some people. Spending money as fast as you get it reveals a spending style—in its most extreme form. These two basic spending styles can be seen in people:

- **Present-oriented.** With this approach, people tend to buy what they want sooner rather than later. They typically do less financial planning and saving. They're also less likely to consider how their spending habits affect the family. On the other hand, they may enjoy life a bit more because they worry less. In extreme cases, these spenders can go into debt and be devastated by an emergency.
- **Future-oriented.** People who focus on the future think more about saving. They rarely lose sight of goals, making purchases carefully in order to reach those goals. These spenders are prepared when something unforeseen happens. If the future-oriented style is carried to extreme, a person might be reluctant to spend money at all and be unwilling to chip in for purchases. This can be frustrating to family and friends.

Which style most reflects your approach to spending? Very few people are purely one style or the other. Instead they are a mixture, with one style more dominant. Whatever style fits you, you'll need to blend it with good management principles in order to avoid money problems.

HANDLING EVERYDAY EXPENSES

Most teens are financially responsible for only part of their expenses. Adults usually take care of housing, food, medical care, and at least some clothing and entertainment. What do you pay for?

As you become more independent, you take on more financial responsibility. At some point, you'll discover that keeping enough cash on hand to pay all your bills isn't safe or convenient. With a checking account, however, your money is safe yet ready to use when you need it.

Using a Checking Account

With a checking account, you deposit money in a financial institution. You could use a bank, savings and loan association, or

"I love this hat, but I won't have any money left if I buy it." If Kimie is a future-oriented spender, what will she do? What would you do?

"It balanced!" To manage a checking account, you need to know how to make your records agree with the bank statement. If you haven't learned this skill yet, who could teach you?

credit union. The institution holds your money safely until you're ready to use it. You can withdraw it in person, electronically, or by writing checks.

Checking accounts can give more than one person access to the money. If you open an account in your name, you're the only one who can use it. Joint accounts give another person access. Bart and his father can both write checks on Bart's account. As Bart said, "Dad's never written a check, but he's on my account in case of an emergency."

Although convenient, checking accounts can be abused. Sometimes people write checks for more money than they have in an account. When that happens, the check is said to "bounce." In other words, the check is returned unpaid to the person cashing it. The check writer will still have to pay for the item, however. In addition, most businesses charge a fee for bad checks to help cover the cost of collecting their money.

Writing bad checks is illegal. It amounts to stealing. A person who writes bad checks can be arrested.

ATMs

Most financial institutions have automatic teller machines (ATMs). These machines are convenient because you can access your account when the institution isn't open. Some ATMs are available 24 hours a day. You can withdraw cash from your account and make deposits. To do this, you need an ATM card and a personal identification number (PIN), assigned by the institution.

Money you withdraw from an ATM is subtracted from your account immediately. You should keep accurate records of ATM transactions so you'll know how much is in your account.

Debit Cards

Another way to pay for purchases with checking account funds is with a **debit card**. These are much like credit cards in look and use. The difference is that money is deducted from your checking account without you writing a check. Unless you keep very good records of what money has been taken out, overdrawing the account can easily happen.

Debit cards need safe keeping. Rebecca described what happened to her: "I loaned my debit card to someone I thought was a friend. The next thing I knew, the bank called to say I was overdrawn. Getting that all straightened out with her and the bank wasn't fun."

TYPES OF CREDIT

Credit means borrowing or using someone else's money and paying it back later. Larger purchases, such as houses and automobiles, are typically bought this way. Credit, however, allows you to buy all kinds of goods and services today and delay payment for them.

Credit is "rented" money. Any time you rent something, a fee is involved. **Interest** is what you pay to use someone else's money. After adding interest, the cost of what you buy goes up.

The three main types of credit are credit cards, installment buying, and loans.

Credit Cards

Credit cards are the plastic cards used to buy goods and services without cash. Many different credit cards are available. American Express, Visa, Mastercard, and Discover are accepted by a variety of businesses. A single-use card can only be used with the business that issues it. Department

SKILLS CHECKLIST

Managing Credit

Credit is easy to use and misuse. You need to manage the way you use credit, just as you manage your use of cash. If you do the following, you'll be using credit wisely:

✓ I use credit only when necessary and make sure that the benefits outweigh the costs and risks.

✓ I shop for the best bargain by comparing terms and interest rates.

✓ I go to a bank or credit union first because their rates are usually lower than most other sources of credit.

✓ I pay off installment loans and credit card debts quickly because these are expensive sources of credit.

✓ I assume no more credit than I can repay out of my current income.

✓ I limit my credit payments to no more than 20 percent of my take-home pay.

Using Your Skills

Create a brochure that will help teens manage credit when they are on their own. If possible, design and produce your brochure on a computer. Plan a way to distribute the brochure to older teens.

Career Success Stories

Perry Walton: *Debt Counselor*

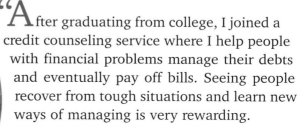

"After graduating from college, I joined a credit counseling service where I help people with financial problems manage their debts and eventually pay off bills. Seeing people recover from tough situations and learn new ways of managing is very rewarding.

"The people who come to me have usually waited until the bill collectors are at the door. I talk with clients about what they earn and what they owe. Then we work together to develop a financial plan they can live with.

"Credit cards can be a real problem. People run up debts without ever thinking about how they'll make the payments. I've had clients with four or more cards charged to the limit at 22 percent interest. I often help them consolidate their debts into one bill. Through consolidation, I can help them lower the interest rate to as low as 9 percent, a huge savings in the long run. Then I ask them to bring in all their credit cards and cut them up. If they don't, it's too tempting to misuse them again.

"Recently, I began working with young people in what I call a 'preventative medicine' program. We discuss the pitfalls of credit. They learn about investing money early. I hope they'll start saving even a small amount of money. If young workers invest early, chances are they'll never need my services."

CAREER PROFILE

Education and training: bachelor's degree

Starting salary range: $18-24,000

Job prospects: banks; savings and loan associations; credit institutions; insurance companies

Important qualities: good communication skills; persuasive; good math skills

Plan Ahead

Would you be a good candidate for a job like this one? Check out your skills regarding math and money management. If you're interested, investigate other job possibilities, too, such as accounting, business management, and actuarial science.

stores and gasoline companies often issue single-use cards.

Some credit card accounts start collecting interest immediately after you make a purchase. Others don't charge interest if you pay the full amount due each month. The amount of interest charged varies among cards. Rates are typically very high. Information about interest rates is included in the material sent out with each card and should be read carefully. Interest may not be the only cost with a credit card. Many have annual and late-payment fees, too.

If you get a credit card, be sure to write down the number of the card and the telephone number of the company. Keep these numbers in a safe place where you can find them. If your credit card is lost or stolen, call the company immediately. Someone there will take steps to prevent anyone else from charging items on your card.

Installment Buying

Not everything you want to buy can be purchased with a credit card. Larger items, such as cars, furniture, and appliances, may be bought with an installment plan. Getting installment credit from the dealer who sells a product is often more expensive than other types of credit. Check carefully before making a commitment.

With installment buying, you make a partial cash payment, called a **down payment**. You then sign a contract to pay the **balance**, or remaining amount, in monthly installments. Many people judge installment plans by how much their monthly payment will be, which can be misleading. You need to look at the interest rate as well as other possible costs.

High interest rates are typically linked to low monthly payments. For how many months will you make payments? Multiply the number of months times the payment. How does that compare to the cost of the item? Before signing, look for the annual percentage rate (APR) and what that will be in overall dollars. With this kind of information, you can decide whether buying on the installment plan is worthwhile.

When using an installment plan, read the contract before signing. If you miss a payment, will the whole amount come due? If you cannot pay, will the dealer take back the item? Will you lose all the money you have already paid? A clear understanding helps you make better decisions.

With a credit card, you can conveniently order catalog items, make hotel reservations, and even charge phone calls. What happens to your future income, however, every time you use credit?

"Six months, same as cash." To encourage buying, some businesses charge no interest if you pay by a certain date. What will happen if a buyer can't pay the full amount at that time?

Loans

When you borrow money and agree to pay more than the borrowed amount back, that's a **loan**. You can get a loan from many places—at varied costs and terms.

Banks and credit unions are common sources of low-cost loans. Some people borrow from family or friends at good rates. Expensive sources of cash include small loan companies, cash advances on credit cards, and pawnbrokers. Erica said, "I thought getting cash advances on my credit card was an easy way to borrow money. When I added up the fees and interest I was paying, I learned fast that it may have been easy, but it wasn't cheap."

Federal laws control the information supplied when you borrow money. This helps you compare costs and terms on different loans. Analyze a loan contract in the same way you would an installment agreement. What is the time frame? Do you pay in installments or one lump sum? Before signing, be sure you understand what's expected. Find out what the consequences will be if you can't meet those expectations.

APPLYING FOR CREDIT

When you seek credit, businesses want to know that you'll be willing and able to pay. You'll have to fill out a credit application that typically asks about employment, including how long you've been on the job. Other questions may concern how many people are in your family, what other sources of credit you have, whether you rent or own a home, and how much money you already owe.

The company then does a credit check either on their own or through a credit bureau. Credit bureaus keep files that show what credit people have and how their accounts are handled. Based on your credit history and the information you provide, the company then decides whether to extend credit to you. Note that if a credit bureau provides incorrect information, you have the right to get the error corrected.

USING CREDIT WISELY

Buying on credit is an easy way to get what you want, but purchases are quickly made and forgotten—until the bills start coming in. Debt problems are extremely common, and they lead to many serious consequences. Stress, family problems, and loss of property are just a few.

Why do people get themselves in such situations? Here's a typical example of how trouble escalates. Anna received many offers of charge cards in the mail, so she kept them and started using them. She liked buying all the nice things she wanted with no need for cash. Remembering what and when she bought didn't seem to matter.

Eventually, Anna's income didn't cover even the minimum payments on her bills. She couldn't get ahead because the interest kept piling up, so she borrowed money to pay some bills. Without cash for anything, she kept charging. The problem worsened until she took out another loan.

Worries about bills added to Anna's problems. Finally, she went to a professional credit counselor, who showed her how to pay off the bills and how to keep from making the same mistakes in the future. It was a long road back for Anna, but she vowed not to make the same mistakes again.

With debt problems, Anna ran the risk of ruining her credit record. Without a good credit record, you may not be able to buy a car or house or get other credit you may want. Learning how to manage money well is the best insurance for protecting your credit record.

Using Credit Wisely— or Not?

"Credit cards are easy to get. I have twelve."

"I pay off my bills every month to avoid interest."

"Interest rate? I'm not sure what the rate is on my card."

"I really want a new sweater, but I'm not going to charge it."

SAVING YOUR MONEY

Regardless of your spending style, saving should be part of your plan. Saving money for the future isn't easy. You might have to give up some things, but the benefits outweigh this drawback.

Money in savings earns interest. As the account grows, you build a fund for emergencies or some special goal. When people face illness, accidents, unemployment, or any unexpected major expense, they realize the usefulness of savings. Experts suggest that you keep at least three times your monthly salary in an emergency fund.

Regular savings accounts are convenient. Most banks, savings and loans, and credit unions allow unlimited access to these accounts. With a few restrictions, you can deposit and withdraw money as you like.

Interest rates on regular savings accounts are typically low. If you're willing to tie up your money for longer periods of time, you can earn higher rates. Certificates of deposit (CDs) and government savings bonds offer higher rates of interest. Your money, however, is not available for a specific period of time without some penalty. Find out more about other accounts at your bank, savings and loan, or credit union.

Who in this group might have a problem with credit? Why?

"This credit card bill is high. Did I really charge all that?"

"How did my payments get this way? My whole paycheck won't cover them."

"I closed a credit account because I didn't like the terms.

"I only use my credit card for travel. The rest of the time I pay cash."

When you buy stock, you own part of a company. If the company does well, your stock increases in value. When buying stock on the Internet, you need to be sure the seller is reputable.

Some people keep an emergency fund in savings and put additional amounts in other investments. Such investments as the stock market come with a risk of loss. On the other hand, if extra funds are used, the opportunity for greater earnings may be worth the risk. A smart, well-studied approach to investment and all of money management contributes to satisfaction in life.

SECTION 27-1 REVIEW

Check Your Understanding

1. How would two people, with basically different approaches, handle spending?
2. What methods can you use to pay bills with the money in your checking account? How do they work?
3. What is credit?
4. How does installment buying compare to getting a loan?
5. Why is saving money necessary?
6. **Thinking Critically.** Why do you think so many people have trouble managing credit cards?
7. **Problem Solving.** When Jeri got a part-time job, she couldn't cash her paycheck. The bank wouldn't cash it since she didn't have a checking account there. The supermarket charged $5.00 to cash the check, but Jeri hated to spend that every time she got a paycheck. What should Jeri do?

Making a Financial Plan

OBJECTIVES

After studying this section, you should be able to:

- Explain what a financial plan is.
- Identify and describe the five basic steps in creating a financial plan.
- Explain specific concerns when working out a family financial plan.

TERMS TO LEARN

financial plan
fixed expenses
flexible expenses

"Making ends meet" is seldom easy. With a financial plan, however, managing money goes smoothly. Also known as a budget, a **financial plan** guides spending and saving so that money makes life enjoyable rather than upsetting.

CREATING A FINANCIAL PLAN

Jana wanted a career that would allow her to have spending money, so she knew she had to make that happen. She decided to save money for education and training as a dental hygienist. She needed a plan that would guide her spending and saving.

Five basic steps can lead Jana—and you—to a financial plan. Each step takes effort and honesty in order to be workable. As you look at where your money goes and how to spend it, keep your values and priorities in mind, just as Jana did.

You'll need to look at both short- and long-term goals. What do you want to do with your money? What expenses are necessary and which are luxuries?

Estimate Income

The first step in creating a financial plan is to estimate income. Estimating conservatively is wise. If you're employed, base your income on take-home pay rather than on your hourly wage or salary. If your hours are irregular, estimate what your average pay is. Remember that money for taxes, so-

Managing money well can be like moving through a maze. You'll meet obstacles, but with determination you can find your way to success.

cial security, and any company benefits is deducted from a paycheck. Add any allowance and other regular income.

Record Expenses

Secondly, you need to determine exactly what your expenses are. You'll need to keep records. Try carrying a small notebook to jot down the cost of everything you buy. Keeping accurate records will help you see where your money really goes.

For Howard, keeping records was difficult. He didn't think he would ever get into the habit of writing down what he spent. In time, however, he began to see how useful the exercise was, and it became easier.

Analyze Spending

Third, analyze your spending habits. You'll probably be surprised at how much money you spend. For example, how much do you think you spend each month on these: snacks, candy, and gum; magazines; personal products; clothing; CDs?

Once you're aware of the leaks in your spending, you can decide what to do about them. Some expenses may be important enough to include in your plan. Where could you cut back most easily?

As you look at your records, you'll notice certain regular expenses. These are called **fixed expenses**. They might include a car insurance payment or school activity fees. When you're still living at home, you probably don't have as many fixed expenses as you do when you live on your own. Later, you might have rent and utility payments, among others.

Next, look at **flexible expenses**. These don't occur regularly. They may be nonessentials, such as a birthday gift, or necessities, such as a textbook for school. Flexible expenses can be adjusted. For example, if you need a new pair of shoes but don't have the money, you might try to include them in the budget for next month.

Plan for Spending and Saving

The next step in making a financial plan is deciding how to spend your money. List and total fixed expenses. Include savings as a fixed expense, even if the amount is small. Then subtract that total from your income.

The remaining money is what you have for flexible expenses. You'll want to set up categories for these, such as school supplies, clothing, transportation, and enter-

Building Character

Resourcefulness: A Quality That Counts

With resourcefulness, you use what you have to get what you need and want. You use resources creatively and even substitute one resource for another when necessary. A teen could show resourcefulness by:

- Finding a way to earn extra money to pay for some lessons.
- Making a gift instead of buying one.
- Offering to tutor a friend in exchange for help with painting a room.
- Asking the history teacher to recommend sources for a research paper.
- Planning tomorrow's dinner menu while waiting in line at the store.

QUESTIONS

1. What resources are available to you? List as many as possible.
2. Why should money be used resourcefully?
3. How can you share or exchange resources with others to benefit everyone?

---

tainment. Based on what you've been spending and what you would like to spend, assign a financial limit for each category of flexible spending.

To carry out your plan, use it to guide and control your spending. Continue to keep track of expenses, staying within the spending limits you've set.

Evaluating Your Plan

If you've done a good job setting up your financial plan, you'll be able to live with it. As the final step in managing the plan, you'll need to make periodic checks to see how well it's working. Remember that a financial plan is personal. What works for you might not be right for someone else.

As you use the plan, make adjustments to fit your changing situation. If you save

money in a category, you can boost your savings and maybe have money for something extra. A carefully thought-out plan can set the stage for good money management for life.

THE FAMILY FINANCIAL PLAN

The principles of personal financial planning can be applied to making a family plan as well. Like an individual, each family has an income and expenses. Although some expenses are common to all families, others are based on the particular family's goals and priorities.

As you might imagine, a family's financial plan is probably more complex than an individual's. After addressing the basic family needs of shelter, food, and clothing, par-

Focus On ...

Financial Danger Signals

Would you recognize a financial problem in the making? When you do, you can take steps to get your finances back on track before things get out of hand. Some financial danger signals include:

- Paying only the minimum amount due on credit accounts.
- Paying regular monthly bills with loans or savings.
- Using credit to pay for items that are normally paid for with cash.
- Not knowing how much your total debt is and how much interest you're paying.
- Depending on irregular income, such as overtime or tax refunds, to pay bills.

USING YOUR KNOWLEDGE

For the third week in a row, seventeen-year-old Eddie asked his brother to borrow a little cash "just to get by." His brother was annoyed, asking where his paycheck had gone. Eddie wanted to go out on the weekend, too. He started thinking about who else might loan him some money. What would you suggest to Eddie?

ents must put priorities on everything else. The many expenses connected to taking care of a family add up quickly.

Making Financial Decisions

In the Carson family, not everyone always agrees on how money should be spent. Seventeen-year-old Spencer can think of plenty to spend money on. His parents, however, are conservative spenders and have reasons for saving. Does this difference of opinion fit anyone you know?

Usually teens and younger family members don't have a clear picture of the family's financial obligations. Without knowing the complete picture, it's easy to disregard insurance payments, medical bills, and the high cost of groceries. Only when you're in the "driver's seat" do you fully understand how well income is covering expenses.

How a parent decides to distribute any extra income may not always be a teen's choice. Discussion may make the decision clearer. Beyond that it's best to look at the situation objectively. Try to see other points of view and look at long-range impacts. Remember that decisions about spending aren't easily made. That old saying, "life isn't fair," may even apply.

You can show cooperation and understanding and hope that someday, if you're a parent, you'll receive the same.

Planning for Family Development

As the family passes through each stage of family development, the special qualities of each stage alter how they spend money.

When a couple forms a family, both partners may be employed. They spend money on items for their home and the activities they enjoy. As children join the family, they need supplies and equipment. All the expenses of raising children are added to the financial plan. In addition, one parent may cut back on work to be at home.

Probably the time of greatest financial pressure is when children are teens. Costs for education, transportation, and personal care can be high. Financial pressures typically lessen as children are launched and become independent. Adults in their middle years are often at the peak of their earning power. During retirement, when income usually decreases, adjustments must again be made. Adults who have planned financially for retirement can feel secure at this time.

Dreams come true when families stick to a financial plan. A new home became a reality for this family. What financial goals would you set for your family of the future?

Without a financial plan, a family is likely to find frustration and disappointment throughout life. With one, they have a rudder to keep them on a reliable course.

SECTION 27-2 REVIEW

Check Your Understanding

1. What is a financial plan?
2. What are the five basic steps in creating a financial plan?
3. What's the difference between fixed and flexible expenses?
4. What personal relationship skills are essential to preventing conflict when dealing with family finances?
5. **Thinking Critically.** Do you think a future-oriented spender needs a financial plan? Why or why not?
6. **Problem Solving.** Linc lives with his father, who doesn't save money. Linc tends to be the same way. He wants to go to a technical school but doesn't think the money will be available. What should Linc do?

CHAPTER SUMMARY

- Money means different things to different people. For some, it's tied to emotions.
- A checking account offers a safe, convenient alternative to paying in cash, but it must be used responsibly.
- Buying goods with credit allows you to have items now and pay for them later.
- Different types of credit include credit cards, installment accounts, and loans.
- A financial plan outlines future spending based on income, expenses, and priorities.
- By creating a financial plan, you devise a way to manage your spending and saving.
- Making a financial plan for a family can be more difficult than making an individual plan because each family member may have different values and priorities about money management.
- Effective, usable financial plans reflect the needs, wants, and resources of the family's stage of development.

REVIEW QUESTIONS

Section 27-1
1. What does money mean to different people?
2. When does a check "bounce"? What are the consequences?
3. What precaution can you take to help if your credit card is lost or stolen?
4. What can happen to get a person in credit trouble?
5. What are six tips for managing credit use?

Section 27-2
1. What is the purpose of a financial plan?
2. What usually happens to fixed expenses as a teen becomes an adult?
3. Why is record keeping an important step in making a financial plan?
4. What are three financial danger signals?
5. How does the typical financial situation of a family change throughout life?

BECOMING A PROBLEM SOLVER

1. Ted was excited when he got his first credit card. He charged several items that he'd been waiting to purchase. Then he hit his credit limit. When the credit card bill came, however, Ted wasn't so excited. He could barely make the minimum payment. When he saw the amount of interest charged on his second bill, he knew he had a problem. What should Ted do?

2. Nona typically spends all the money she has. In fact, she never seems to hold onto it for very long. She'd like a car of her own, but she wonders if she could even save enough for a down payment. She also worries about making regular payments. What should Nona do?

THINKING CRITICALLY

1. **Recognizing Assumptions.** Can people be happy with very little money? Explain your answer.
2. **Identifying Cause and Effect.** How can past experiences, including those of other family members, affect a person's attitude toward spending money?
3. **Predicting Results.** Do you think it's a good idea for teens to have their own credit cards? What potential benefits and risks are involved?
4. **Analyzing Behavior.** What personal traits are necessary for making and following a financial plan?

MAKING CURRICULUM CONNECTIONS

1. **Math.** Maureen bought new bedroom furniture on an installment plan. The price of the furniture was $1500. She paid 10 percent down and must pay the remainder in 16 monthly installments of $100 each. How much total interest will she pay?
2. **Civics.** Investigate the laws that control the use of credit in your state. What is the highest interest rate that can be legally charged? Are there any limits on the fees that can be assessed? What happens when people can't or don't pay their bills? Write a report of your findings.

APPLYING YOUR KNOWLEDGE

1. Collect information on different credit cards. Compare their interest rates and how the interest is figured.
2. Investigate electronic banking through the personal computer. What equipment is required? How does it work? Does this sound like an option you would be comfortable with? Why or why not?
3. Learn about money management software. How would these programs help people plan and control their finances?

Family & Community Connections

1. With your family members, create a financial plan that you would like to try, using the steps outlined in this chapter.

2. Find out what the interest rate would be on a car loan at a local bank, credit union, finance company, and car dealership. Why would someone pay the higher rates when lower rates are available elsewhere?

Chapter 28

Consumer Skills

Being a Good Consumer

OBJECTIVES

After studying this section, you should be able to:

- Explain how skillful consumers judge quality and price.
- Explain what "comparison shopping" means.
- Describe impulse buying.
- Give tips for saving money.
- Recognize and explain different ways advertisers try to get you to buy their products.

TERMS TO LEARN

consumer
bargain
unit price
comparison shopping
warranty
impulse buying
direct advertising
indirect advertising

One pleasure of earning money is buying what you need and want. Do you ever want more than the budget allows? Businesses entice you in many ways—with clever advertising, attractive packaging, and determined salespeople. Whether *you're* in charge is your choice.

TRAITS OF SKILLFUL CONSUMERS

A **consumer** is simply a person who purchases goods and services. To be a skillful consumer, you must:

- Become familiar with available products, prices, and standards of quality.
- Read and do research to learn what features to look for or avoid in products.

- Use self-discipline to resist society's message to buy more than you need.

You can learn the skills you need to be a smart consumer, but first you have to want to do so. When you're serious about making the most of your dollars, you'll be inspired to discover how.

JUDGING QUALITY AND PRICE

A cautious consumer wants to get top quality at a fair price. Do you look at how well something is made before you buy? How do you know if the price is reasonable? These are skills that consumers need.

What Is Quality?

You may have heard an older relative say something like this: "They just don't make them like they used to." This lament says that some products are poorly made today. Looking for something that has quality—it's well-made, works right, and will last—can save frustration and money.

Experience teaches about quality. For example, Victoria bought a new shampoo. After using it, her hair was oily and limp. Victoria concluded, "I'll never buy that brand again!" Unfortunately, learning by experience can be costly. Most people want to know ahead that a product or service is worth buying.

You can learn about quality by reading what consumer advocate groups and magazines say about the product you want and the manufacturers who produce it. Two groups that test products in laboratories and then report to readers are Consumers Union, which publishes *Consumer Reports*, and Consumers Research, which publishes *Consumers Research Magazine*.

Information is also available at public libraries. You can ask the reference librarian to help you find what you need. By exploring the Internet, you'll find more good information if you choose reliable sources.

A Fair Price

No one wants to pay too much for an item, yet deciding which is the best quality for the price isn't easy. Sometimes the lowest price isn't the best buy.

While shopping, Ramona bought several packages of an inexpensive panty hose. The first time she wore a pair, they snagged and ran quickly. Her "bargain" hose were no bargain after all. Four conditions make a purchase a true **bargain**:

- The product is one you need, want, and will use.
- The item's quality is suitable.
- The product sells at a price you're willing to pay.
- A reliable dealer sells the item.

The marketplace is full of choices. Would you pay extra for a brand-name item that your friends are buying, or would you save money by choosing something else?

Shopping Savvy

If you saved a dollar a week by making careful purchases, in a year you'd have $52 to invest or spend. Saving more would give you even greater spending power. Here are some ideas for making that happen:

- Take advantage of sales, advertised specials, and markdowns.
- Try private brands, lesser known brands, house labels, and discontinued models.
- Shop at discount stores rather than neighborhood or convenience stores.
- Buy basic quality; avoid deluxe models.
- Shop at garage sales, thrift stores, and through the want ads when you can judge quality.
- Pay cash since credit costs.
- Use coupons unless quality house brands are cheaper.

- Check the **unit price**, a measure of the cost per unit of weight or volume, to compare prices on different sized packages.
- Don't be fooled by eye-catching, convenient packaging. Items like small cans of pudding with pull-top tabs are handy but costly.

USING YOUR KNOWLEDGE

Max has a $.75 coupon for a brand-name toothpaste that costs $3.45 without the coupon. The house brand, which is the same size, costs $2.65. Which should he buy?

COMPARISON SHOPPING

To find good quality at the lowest price, you can go **comparison shopping**. This means you look at the same item in several stores to compare quality and price before you buy.

When shopping, you can compare prices on everything from small grocery items to major purchases, including cars, furniture, and large appliances. With large items, the amount saved can be substantial. On the other hand, regularly saving a little can add up. When Dylan buys detergent, for example, he checks the cost of different brands on the shelf. By comparing quantities and prices, he saves money with very little effort.

Tips for Comparing

When you do comparison shopping, following a few suggestions leads to satisfying results:

- **Know what you want.** Before you begin, write down the features you want in something you're going to buy. Look for these and avoid features you don't need.

For example, if you want a CD player that holds five disks, why pay for one that holds many more? The more features, the more you're likely to pay.

- **Use the telephone.** If you know what you want, why not call several stores? You'll learn who has the item and how much it costs at each. Calling first can save you time.
- **Compare similar items.** Read labels carefully so you can tell whether the products are comparable. For example, don't compare the prices of silk and cotton shirts.
- **Check any warranty.** The **warranty** is a written guarantee. Is there a warranty and what does it cover? If it covers parts, check *which* parts. Labor for repairing the product may be covered. Also, check the length of time the warranty is in effect.
- **Compare credit terms.** As you have learned, costs can vary greatly.
- **Check the return policy.** Be sure to find out whether the store or company backs its products.

IMPULSE BUYING

"I just couldn't resist." How many shoppers have come home with this explanation for some unexplainable purchase? Have you?

Impulse buying is purchasing items without previous consideration or thought. You see something you like, so you buy it. Impulse buying is typical of present-oriented spenders, who often buy without thinking.

Retailers promote impulse buying in the store layout. Items they want you to grab are often close to the front of the store, so you see them as you enter. They're also placed near checkout aisles. People see them while waiting and are tempted to buy.

The phone is handy when shopping for a service. What information would you gather before ordering a cake for your parents' anniversary party? What questions would you ask?

Controlling Impulse Buying

To control impulse buying, you must know what you truly need and can afford to pay. A shopping list will help you focus on what you intend to buy when you start out. As Adrienne said, "I decide what I'm going to get when I make my shopping list. While I'm at the store, I keep my eye on the list. That way I'm looking for something specific rather than just looking."

Take only enough money to cover what you've planned to buy. Impulse shoppers find it easy to spend "extra" money they're carrying.

ANALYZING ADVERTISING

Advertising can be very helpful to consumers. You keep up-to-date on new and existing products. Advertising gives you price information and tells you when sales occur. You learn where to find products and services. Being a good shopper would be much harder without advertising.

A wise consumer, however, is also cautious about ads. Since the purpose of advertising is to get you to buy more goods and services, businesses use it to create needs and wants that didn't exist before.

Advertising is everywhere—on television and radio; in newspapers and magazines; and on buses, subways, and billboards. It's even on clothing and the Internet. If you're careful, you'll use advertising and not allow it to use you.

Advertising Techniques

Companies advertise directly and indirectly. **Direct advertising** tries to convince you to buy a particular product by appeal-

A "treasure" that's bought impulsively may seem like a mistake later. Why do auctions lead some people to impulsive buying?

ing directly to your values. One common approach focuses on glamour. Health, happiness, success, good looks, and love are other values that advertisers promote.

Indirect advertising is more subtle. For example, celebrities are often associated with products even though they aren't selling them. The hero of a movie drinks a well-known soft drink. The star in a television series gets on an airplane from a major airline. Companies pay to have their products featured in this way.

Another form of indirect advertising is the printing of company or product names on clothing. If you have a sweatshirt with a brand name on it, you're advertising every time you wear the shirt. What other examples of indirect advertising come to mind?

A Critical Eye

To use advertising successfully, you need a critical eye. Analyzing the situation with these suggestions helps you decide whether buying is wise:

- **Learn to separate fact from fiction.** Advertising isn't always a reliable source of information. For example, an ad for calcium pills that claims to have the highest amount of calcium of all pills tested may refer to a test that included only two other brands.
- **Recognize "no-promise" promises.** Beware of conditional words in ads, such as "can" and "often." If your cold medicine promises to "relieve symptoms for up to 12 hours," does that mean one hour, 12 hours, or something in between?
- **Watch out for below-cost sales.** When an ad says, "Price is less than our cost," remember that stores must make a profit to stay in business. Are they really selling at less than cost? If so, why? If you've compared prices, you'll be able to tell whether the price is truly low.
- **Be careful of percent-off ads.** If a store raises its prices, then advertises "30 percent off selected items," you may pay more "on sale" than you would otherwise.
- **Get the whole story.** Advertised prices sometimes don't include other fees or the cost of everything else you'll need. For example, Mitzi was interested in a computer. When she saw one advertised at an incredibly low price, she went to check. The advertised price was for the computer only. When she added the price of the monitor, keyboard, printer, cables, and programs needed to make the computer run, the advertised price was no bargain. Mitzi was lured to the store, but she used her head before making a purchase. The practical consumer always tries to do the same.

Advertisers offer coupons to entice you to buy. You save money if you really need the item. **How does the producer benefit?**

Tips & TECHNIQUES

Garage Sales. A garage sale is a good place to find a bargain. If you decide to shop at one, look for items that are truly worth buying and that you can use. Otherwise, the item may end up in a garage sale again. While shopping at garage sales, try to determine why the merchandise is for sale.

- **Can you find evidence of impulse buying?** You may notice "cute" but useless items for sale. Some clothes may still have the original price tags attached.
- **Are there hardbound books that were read once and discarded?** You might find alternatives to paying a high price for something you aren't going to keep.
- **Do clothing and home furnishings have out-of-style colors and designs?** Some styles and designs last longer than others.
- **What kinds of items are in very good condition?** They may show a fad or gimmick that disappeared quickly.
- **Do you see the same item for sale at many garage sales?** A home appliance, decoration, or piece of exercise equipment that everyone is selling may have been heavily promoted but not that useful.

Try It Out. Write a set of "rules" or guidelines that would help you and others get true bargains at garage sales.

SECTION 28-1 REVIEW

Check Your Understanding

1. What are three traits of a good consumer?
2. What conditions make a purchase a bargain?
3. What is a warranty?
4. How can a person control impulse buying?
5. Describe two types of advertising techniques.
6. **Thinking Critically.** Why do you think many people buy and wear clothes with advertising logos and designs?
7. **Problem Solving.** After returning from a shopping trip, Olivia lined up her purchases on the bed for a look. Already she had second thoughts about several items. Again, she wondered why she keeps buying things she doesn't need and seldom uses. What should Olivia do?

Consumer Rights and Responsibilities

OBJECTIVES

After studying this section, you should be able to:

- Describe the four major rights of consumers.
- Explain the responsibilities consumers have.
- Describe effective ways of making consumer complaints.
- Identify resources consumers can use.

TERMS TO LEARN

Better Business Bureaus
Consumer Action and Advisory Panels
small claims court

Patty Lynn showed her friend the new hair dryer she was returning to the store. "It doesn't get hot," she said, "so I'm taking it back. And I'm taking back this shirt, too. I brushed my pen against the sleeve, and now it's got an ink spot on it." Something's wrong with this picture. If you can't tell what, this section will give you ideas.

Consumers have both rights and responsibilities in the marketplace. State and federal laws protect consumers' interests, or rights. At the same time, however, consumers also have responsibilities. To earn your rights as a consumer, you have to live up to your responsibilities.

CONSUMER RIGHTS

Consumers have four major rights: to safety; to be informed; to choose; and to be heard.

Consumers have a right to products that are *safe*. Some goods that are hazardous to health or life may be banned by law. In other cases, labels provide warnings that the product *can* be dangerous. Specific directions are given for the safest possible use. If you buy the product, it is your responsibility to read, understand, and follow the directions in order to prevent the dangers of misuse.

Consumers have the right to be *informed*. Several federal agencies work to be sure that companies provide accurate information about products, both in advertising and labeling. Lars, for example, is allergic to dairy products. He reads the list of ingredients on food packaging to help him select products that fit his special dietary needs.

Consumers have the *right to choose*. Under the American economic system, fair competition is encouraged for providing goods and services. As a result, you can choose from an array of similar products and purchase any you want.

Finally, consumers have the right to be *heard*. If you're not satisfied with a product or service, you should receive a full hearing and fair treatment. Also, the government considers consumers' interests—everything from safety to pricing—when making decisions that affect the public. Consumers must make their views about products and services known to their representatives and to government agencies.

CONSUMER RESPONSIBILITIES

Consumers have responsibilities as well as rights. They must be *careful, considerate shoppers* who treat merchandise as carefully as if they owned it. While grocery shopping, Theresa saw a package of "frozen" beans sitting in a puddle of water on the bread shelf. Can you see how someone's thoughtlessness cost the store—and eventually the shoppers, too?

Consumers have the responsibility to *pay* for all merchandise. Shoplifting is illegal. Losses cut into a store's profits and are

Today's technology makes letter writing easier. A letter composed on a laptop or sent by e-mail can quickly relay consumer concerns to government representatives and agencies.

passed along to shoppers in higher prices. Shoplifters will pay higher prices, too, for items they buy. A shoplifter may pay an even higher price with an arrest record for theft on his or her permanent record.

The consumer is responsible for *saving sales records and receipts*. Then records will be available if a product needs to be returned or exchanged.

With the manufacturer's instructions, you are expected to put a product together and use it correctly. Accepting this responsibility earns you the right to be heard if the item doesn't work.

Consumers are responsible for *following product instructions*. Vernon was very disappointed with the wax he bought for his car. When he complained at the store, the manager asked if he'd waxed the car in the sun. Vernon said yes. The clerk explained that the brand he bought worked only when used indoors or in complete shade. If Vernon had read the directions more carefully, he could have avoided wasting much time and energy.

CONSUMER COMPLAINTS

Filing a consumer complaint when you have a problem with goods or services is both a right and a responsibility. You have the right to be treated fairly and honestly, and you have the responsibility to save others from unfair treatment if you can.

Refunds and Replacements

Returning unsatisfactory merchandise for a refund or replacement is common. Handled correctly, these situations are usually resolved successfully.

As with any consumer problem, first write, call, or visit the business involved. You'll probably have the best success if you go in person with the product and your receipts. State your problem and explain clearly what you want done. Do this as often as needed until you are able to get the issue resolved.

Alvin bought a pair of pants. The seams came apart the first time he washed them. He returned them to the store, saying politely, "I wore these only once, but the seams came apart when I washed them. I'd like to return them for a refund." The clerk offered to exchange them for another pair. Alvin declined and asked to talk to the store manager. Again he was polite but firm about what he wanted. When she, too, pushed for an exchange, Alvin complained to the vice president for consumer affairs of the company that made the pants. Ten days later, he received a check for the price of the pants. It paid to be persistent.

Remember that two points of view exist on an issue. Many stores have to deal with irresponsible shoppers. A person who buys a dress, intending to wear it once and then return it to the store, for example, is dishonest. A worn or damaged garment can't be sold, which costs the store money. The loss is passed along to other consumers through higher prices.

Returning an item is fine, as long as the reason is a good one. Stores that have to deal regularly with deception may seem strict with their policies, but the cause may be consumers themselves.

Most businesses require a receipt for returns. You can store receipts in a file or box. Then if something goes wrong, you'll always have the receipt you need.

Writing a Letter of Complaint

Sometimes writing a letter of complaint is the most practical approach when you have a problem. Information that comes with a product may tell you where to send such a letter. Most of the time, the letter should be written and sent to the head of the consumer relations department. If you don't have an address, check the library or the Internet. Type or write carefully and clearly, and make certain your spelling is correct.

Be sure the letter is as businesslike as possible. Be reasonable and logical without attacking the company. State the problem and what you want the company to do. Include copies of your receipts and any other information that would support your case. Keep a copy of the letter.

Building Character

Diligence: A Quality That Counts

Diligence is doing things completely, giving them your full attention and care. When you're diligent, you are thorough, making sure that all details are covered. A teen practices diligence by:

- Following through in writing a letter of complaint and getting a refund for a backpack with a buckle that won't close.
- Carefully researching features, repair records, and gas mileage before shopping for a used car.
- Comparing prices at different stores before making a major purchase.
- Double-checking to be sure a school assignment has been done correctly.
- Following through on all home responsibilities, doing jobs promptly, completely, and well.

QUESTIONS

1. How could you be more diligent in using consumer skills?
2. In what other parts of your life might diligence be a helpful habit?
3. When do you show diligence?

Billing Problems

Incorrect billings try the patience of many consumers. People may be billed for items they didn't buy. Their payments may have been credited to the wrong account. The combination of human error and the widespread use of computers sometimes makes these problems difficult to solve. Be sure, however, that the problem is corrected as soon as possible. If incorrect information goes to credit reporting companies, you may have trouble getting credit later.

Merle was billed on his credit card for a purchase made by someone in a town 2000 miles away. He'd never even been there. Merle didn't pay the charge but wrote to the company explaining the situation. In the meantime, the credit card company charged him interest on the unpaid amount. It took three months to remove the charge from the bill. Another two months went by before the interest was removed. By contacting the company, however, Merle avoided paying for something he had not purchased.

When you report a billing error in writing, the company is required by law to investigate your complaint. It must reply within 90 days of the date your letter was received. If you're right, the billing will be corrected and any interest charges removed. If you're wrong, you're expected to pay the disputed bill within ten days.

RESOURCES FOR CONSUMERS

As a consumer, you have many resources to help with problems. The government operates some. Businesses and industries run others.

Government Agencies

The federal government and all state governments have consumer affairs offices, although they may have slightly different names in each state. Many county and city governments also have agencies that deal with consumer problems.

These agencies are more concerned with the serious problems of fraudulent goods and services than they are with shoddy merchandise and poor service. They are, however, available to every citizen and may be able to help with your problem. The attorney general of each state enforces consumer protection laws.

Business Organizations

Reputable businesses insist on treating customers fairly. They recognize that satisfied customers are the reason they're in business. Many businesses and industries have established organizations to police themselves.

Better Business Bureaus are independent organizations sponsored by businesses in a community. They monitor advertising and keep files on local companies. The information on file may include how long a company has been in business, how often complaints have been made against a company, and how a company handles complaints. Better Business Bureaus do not advise consumers but will share information with them. Citizens can make a complaint or get information by calling them.

Consumer Action and Advisory Panels (CAP) are organizations formed by specific industries to help solve consumer problems. The appliance, automobile, moving, travel, magazine publishing, and direct marketing industries all have some type of CAP. In fact, most industries do. If you have a problem with a business, a CAP may be able to help you.

If you can't solve a consumer problem alone, you may need the help of professionals. Alone or with help, you'll need to gather the information that states your case.

Focus On ...

Identifying Consumer Fraud

Consumer fraud occurs every day. Your best defense against fraud is to become knowledgeable. Learn to be wary of situations like these:

- A telephone solicitor calls you (you haven't placed the call) and offers an item at a good price. He wants your credit card number.
- A person at your door is "taking a survey" and wants to come in for a moment.
- A telephone caller wants you to donate money to a charity or give money for any purpose that you're not sure about.
- A mail solicitation looks too good to be true. You may have won a "prize" or you get something "free."

USING YOUR KNOWLEDGE

Karen received an item in the mail that looked very official. Inside, the large print said that she was already the winner of a very nice prize, either an automobile or a large-screen television. All the papers in the envelope confused her. She thought she needed to reply and place an order to win her prize. What should Karen do?

Small Claims Court

Sometimes consumer disputes are resolved through **small claims court**. These courts handle cases that don't exceed the money limits set by each state. In addition, you can't sue for more than the actual cost of the time or services lost. Most consumers use small claims court only as a last resort because of the time, cost, and effort that are involved.

To use small claims court, you must file a complaint and pay a filing fee. There may be other fees as well. The clerk of the court will help you understand the procedures used in your state and explain what is expected of you. You may wish to visit small claims court and watch a few cases before your own comes up.

Lawyers are not required in small claims court. In some states, they aren't allowed. The judge works to bring out the facts of the case and to understand the issues. You'll need to take all the evidence concerning your case. The decision will either be announced immediately or mailed to you.

Judgments in small claims court aren't always well enforced. The judge may order one party to pay, but the person refuses. You may have to spend more time and effort to collect what's owed to you.

A small claims court can help if you're trying to recover a small amount of money. For large amounts, however, an attorney is needed to take your claim to a higher court.

SECTION 28-2 REVIEW

Check Your Understanding

1. What are the four major consumer rights?
2. What are four consumer responsibilities?
3. If you have a complaint about a defective product, what should you do first?
4. What is the purpose of government consumer agencies?
5. How could a small claims court help you?
6. **Thinking Critically.** Should consumers be able to claim their rights if they don't live up to their responsibilities? Explain.
7. **Problem Solving.** When Cody got his credit card bill, it included a charge he hadn't made. He decided not to pay it but didn't have time to write a letter to the company explaining the situation. The next month, the credit bill contained a finance charge in addition to the original charge. Cody thinks it's unfair that a finance charge was added for a charge he didn't make. What should Cody do?

Chapter 28
Review and Activities

CHAPTER SUMMARY

- A consumer must make responsible, informed shopping decisions.
- To be a good consumer, you must know how to determine the quality of a product and the fairness of its price.
- Comparison shopping is a good way of getting the best quality for the best price.
- Advertising gives consumers important information about products, services, and store hours. Information in advertising, however, must be carefully evaluated.
- Many consumers' rights are protected by state and federal laws.
- Consumers are responsible for acting in ways that protect businesses and other consumers from loss.
- Filing a consumer complaint is a right and a responsibility that helps ensure fair treatment for all. Many government and private agencies exist to help consumers who believe they have been treated unfairly.

REVIEW QUESTIONS

Section 28-1
1. What is a consumer?
2. What two resources could you use to learn about product quality?
3. Can price alone show whether an item is a good buy? Explain.
4. What are four tips a skilled comparison shopper might suggest?
5. In what ways does advertising both help and hinder?
6. To analyze advertising, what four things can you do?

Section 28-2
1. What information on product labels helps ensure consumer safety?
2. Why are shoplifters a problem for businesses as well as consumers?
3. How would you write an effective letter of complaint?
4. How do Better Business Bureaus help consumers?
5. What can you gain if you take a company to small claims court?

BECOMING A PROBLEM SOLVER

1. Savannah's friend Hayley often buys from a television shopping channel. One day, Hayley calls to tell Savannah to turn on the shopping channel. An actress they like is selling jewelry, and Hayley thinks Savannah will want to buy some. What should Savannah do?

2. Don is getting tired of the constant phone calls from people who want to sell him something. They call his home every day during meals, when he is sleeping, and when he's in a hurry. Don feels tense and aggravated after each call. What should he do?

THINKING CRITICALLY

1. **Recognizing Assumptions.** Many people seem to believe that happiness comes through possessions. Do you agree? Support your answer with examples.
2. **Predicting Consequences.** Some people admit to being "shopaholics." When does this trait become a problem?
3. **Analyzing Behavior.** Have you ever bought an item that you saw advertised? Think about foods, small personal appliances, clothing, and cosmetics. How much impact did the ad have on you? Why?
4. **Identifying Evidence.** To prevent dissatisfaction after a purchase, what clues would you use to tell that you're dealing with a reputable business?

MAKING CURRICULUM CONNECTIONS

1. **Language Arts.** Imagine that you have purchased a defective product. Write an effective letter of complaint, using the tips in this chapter.
2. **Math.** A 16-oz. jar of brand name applesauce costs $1.59. The supermarket house brand is a 14-oz. jar for $1.09. What is the cost per ounce of each jar? Which is the better buy? Why? Where in the supermarket can you find this calculation already done for you?

APPLYING YOUR KNOWLEDGE

1. Find a product comparison in an issue of *Consumer Reports* or another consumer publication. Using the publication's findings, decide which product you would buy.
2. Find five examples of advertisements. Identify the techniques and appeals used in each. Share your findings.
3. Suppose you were going to market the class you're taking right now to younger students. With a group of classmates, create an advertising campaign that would "sell" the class.

Family & Community Connections

1. Investigate the consumer laws in your state. What protections do they offer? What are the penalties for breaking these laws? Write a summary of your findings.

2. Interview the manager of a retail store to learn about examples of irresponsible consumers. How do their actions raise prices for other consumers? What can be done about this problem?

Thinking About a Career

Chapter 29

WORDS FOR THOUGHT

"To love what you do and feel that it matters—how could anything be more fun?"
(Katharine Graham)

IN YOUR OWN WORDS

Can you imagine spending your life in a career that you don't like? How can you prevent that?

Preparing for a Career

OBJECTIVES

After studying this section, you should be able to:

- Compare various tests used to evaluate interests and skills.
- Describe the services offered by career counselors.
- Compare the training and education offered by vocational schools and universities.
- Relate goal setting to career planning.

TERMS TO LEARN

career
aptitude
career counseling
apprentice
career path

Imagine sitting with friends in the cafeteria on the first day of a new school year. Everyone is sharing stories of how they spent the summer: volunteering in a senior center; supervising children's games and crafts in the park; working as a receptionist in a real estate office.

You listen with interest as each person talks. Some of your friends are thinking about related careers. As you wonder about your own plans for the future, you ask yourself: What do I want to do with my life? Where will I be in five or ten years? You realize that it's time to start thinking.

that question with "a firefighter," "a baseball player," or "a nurse." The teen years are a prime time to ask that question again. You now have a more realistic view of the world of work. Your working years are still ahead—but rapidly approaching. If you don't plan and set goals now, then when? People who don't think about where they want to be in ten or fifteen years often drift from one unsatisfying job to the next.

Personal satisfaction is one reason to plan for a **career**, or the kind of work you do over a period of years. Financial security is another. The well-being of you and your future family may depend on the decisions you make today. A good job offers a family more than a way to pay the bills. It gives them oppor-

PLANNING YOUR FUTURE

"What do you want to be when you grow up?" As a child, you may have answered

tunities to make choices in life—about where and how to live. It provides power and control and supports their efforts to remain strong.

As Brenda said, "When my husband died, it was a terrible time for all of us. At least I had a good job that let me take care of the kids. If I'd had to sell the house and make the kids change schools, it would have made a rough time even worse."

As what happened to Brenda shows, you can't predict the future, but you can plan for it. When a career plays such a large role in your future happiness, it makes sense to plan carefully. If you don't start now, time and circumstances may make it more and more difficult to achieve your goals.

EVALUATING YOUR INTERESTS AND ABILITIES

Have you ever noticed that when you're doing something you really enjoy, it doesn't seem like "work"? Think of how satisfying it would be to have a career that you like and are good at, too. What are your skills and interests? Can they be channeled into a worthwhile occupation? A number of resources are available to help you answer those questions.

Tests

Certain tests identify interests and abilities and match them to fields of employment. Except for intelligence tests, these tests have no right or wrong answers. Some tests reveal broad, general skills, while others focus on specific, job-related talents. Commonly used tests include:

Now is the time to begin planning for a career. Teens who have a part-time job can save money for education or training and try out different work environments at the same time.

- **Intelligence tests.** These rate mental abilities, such as reasoning and problem solving.
- **Aptitude tests. Aptitude** is a natural talent and capacity for learning a certain skill. Aptitude tests can cover many areas, such as mechanical understanding or physical coordination.
- **Activities preference tests or interest tests.** This type of test helps you translate your likes and dislikes into specific work preferences. You select activities you like best from lists. Test results show

patterns of interest. You can then compare these patterns to career descriptions to see what you might enjoy doing.

- **Job preference tests.** This test lists pairs of tasks and asks you to choose between them. When the test is scored, you're given a list of jobs that should suit your interests.

These tests are useful, within limitations. They can't tell you what job to pursue or guarantee happiness and success. Their purpose is to point out careers that indicate a likelihood for success.

Career Counseling

Career counselors are another source of assistance in pinpointing skills and interests. **Career counseling** helps people choose and succeed in their work. School guidance counselors often serve as career counselors. Counselors are also found in employment agencies and private firms.

Career counselors talk with clients about their interests, talents, and career and personal goals. They are trained in interpreting tests, such as those described here, to help you discover your work strengths.

Career counselors are also good sources of information about careers, as Dane found when he visited his school counselor's office. Dane wanted a career that would make use of his love for skiing and hiking. The counselor gave him pamphlets and government publications about jobs that might fit that description. She de-

scribed the current job market for each occupation in different regions of the country. She pointed out which career fields were likely to grow and which were apt to shrink. She gave him reading and reference lists so he could research particular careers on his own.

The counselor was also able to answer Dane's questions about the education or training needed for specific jobs. She gave him brochures from schools that offered such training and suggested others that he might contact.

Private career counseling is also available but can be costly. The fee may be worthwhile, however, if you want the personal attention and added resources of a specialist.

Aptitude and interest tests help you choose a career that blends with what you like to do and what you do well. People are sometimes surprised by what they learn from these tests.

DECISIONS ABOUT EDUCATION AND TRAINING

What are your plans after finishing high school? If you say "to go to work" and you have or can find a job that suits you, you're set. Good workers are needed and appreciated everywhere. Remember, though, that you need a long-distance view of work. The job you have or can get now may not support an independent adult. You may "outgrow" a job and wish for something that interests you more—and perhaps pays you more, too.

People often find that they need education or training past high school to qualify for the jobs they'd *really* like to have. The amount of education you receive depends on your interests; your work goals; your financial situation; what your family expects of you; and what you expect of yourself. You need to weigh all of these factors, and more, to make decisions about education that are right for you.

Perhaps you already have an idea of the kind of career you want, and you know

you'll need special training. You can obtain education or training in several ways.

Career or Technical Schools

If you know what job you want and are ready to prepare for it, you may choose a career or technical school. These schools provide specialized training for a specific career, such as culinary arts, cosmetology, or electronics. Courses consist of both classroom study and hands-on experience. Programs are intensive and shorter than other types of education since students receive training only for that particular occupation.

Apprenticeships

For many occupations, including plumbing, painting, and carpentry, you can receive on-the-job training through an apprenticeship. As an **apprentice**, you receive training from a skilled worker in a trade. As you learn, you gain experience and earn money at the same time.

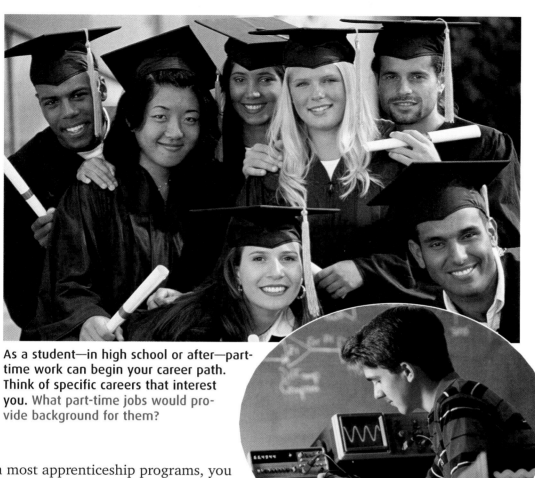

As a student—in high school or after—part-time work can begin your career path. Think of specific careers that interest you. What part-time jobs would provide background for them?

In most apprenticeship programs, you must register with the state or federal government. You then work as an apprentice for a set length of time, usually four to six years. At the end of that time, you may have to take written and practical tests to prove your knowledge and skills. You are then certified or licensed by the United States Department of Labor or the trade's apprenticeship program.

Requirements and other details of specific apprenticeships vary. The career counselor in your school can help you find out more about programs in your area.

Colleges and Universities

Maria has loved to read ever since she learned how. Her career plans have always included some sort of job involving literature, perhaps teaching English. With this goal in mind, Maria enrolled in a four-year university. There she took a variety of courses, with an emphasis on literature and education.

After two years, Maria decided that while a good story excited her, she didn't have the patience for teaching. A discussion with a counselor opened her eyes to the range of jobs in writing and communication. With an eye toward future job growth, Maria chose

Communication Skills

Leadership Skills

Management Skills

Thinking Skills

Paying for Education

The high price of higher education—college, university, or vocational school—is a concern for many students. Use this checklist to see if you're doing all you can to help manage the cost of additional education:

✓ I've looked into taking advanced placement courses to earn college credit without taking college courses.

✓ I'm keeping up my grades and getting involved in extracurricular activities, which can help me earn a scholarship.

✓ I've chosen a course of study to take advantage of scholarships that are for those preparing for a particular career.

✓ I've learned about government financial aid and whether I'm eligible.

✓ I've asked about tuition breaks for weekend and summer classes and other discounts at the schools I may attend.

✓ I've considered attending a community college for my first two years of study.

✓ I'm saving money from my part-time jobs.

Using Your Skills

Identify the suggestions above that you haven't already taken. Choose three that seem best for you. List the steps you need to take in order to carry out each suggestion.

a career in television news. Now in her first job after college, Maria is a researcher and writer for a news program. Her ultimate goal is to produce features for a national television news magazine.

Maria's experience illustrates one advantage offered by two-year community colleges and four-year colleges and universities. People who aren't sure of a career can study a number of subjects to learn what brings them pleasure and success. Tuition at these schools can be expensive, and the course work itself demands effort. Most people try to reach a decision within a year or two to avoid spending time and money needlessly. Of course, many people attend

college because they need a university degree for the work they've already chosen.

Education and Training Costs

Getting a vocational school or college education takes money—sometimes a lot of money. One year at a private, four-year university can cost more than what some families earn in that same year. Tuition, fees, books, and possibly living expenses—all of these items must be counted in the price of education.

These expenses, however, are investments in your future. The more education you have, the more money you are likely to earn over the course of your lifetime. Additional training can help you get a job and be promoted. Lindsey was named supervisor of the medical records department of a hospital after working there only a few years. Although she's the youngest person in the department, she has specific training in medical records and in the computer program used to manage them. The money Lindsey spent on her education has already paid off.

SETTING CAREER GOALS

As in any area of life, setting goals is important for career success. Career goals help you focus on what you need to do. You can identify resources and develop a plan to prepare for the kind of work you want.

In establishing career goals, your interests and skills can guide you. You should also consider that changes in the job market, in your family situation, and in yourself might cause you to switch jobs and even careers. Workers today average six or seven job changes over their lifetime. Your goals, both long- and short-term, should help you stay flexible as well as focused.

Madison remembered these two points as she set some work-related goals for herself. She was interested in medicine and chemistry. Her final career goal was to work in pharmaceutical research for a drug company. Her first short-term goal was getting a part-time job in a pharmacy to help her learn more about various medications and their uses. Longer term, Madison planned to attend a university with a re-

Focus On ...

Family Living Careers

Since you're studying about families, you might like to take a look at related careers. Many careers let you work with families and provide services for them. You'll need good communication skills and a concern for others to be successful.

Although this list is by no means complete, here are some family-related career areas that you might explore: *child care; social services; counseling; religion; law enforcement; education and teaching; and health care.* A little investigating can produce a great deal of information about careers in these and other areas.

USING YOUR KNOWLEDGE

Aiden is an outgoing, energetic student with a talent for inspiring and organizing others. He was a main force behind the senior class blood drive. Aiden thinks a career in family living would be rewarding but doubts that he has the patience for the everyday problem solving of jobs in counseling or child care. What advice would you give Aiden?

search hospital, where she could work and explore several types of medical research. These goals would lead Madison to her chosen career, while preparing her for jobs in related fields at the same time.

Choosing a Career Path

Thinking about flexibility as you set career goals helps you see how one career can lead to another. This connection is called a **career path**. Figuring a career path can be part of setting your career goals. Madison's career goals, for example, include a career path through the fields of pharmacy and research.

At this point in your life, you may not be able to lay out a career path. What you do need are some career plans and goals to give you focus over the next few years. As the years unfold, you can adapt or change your goals to match your changing interests and circumstances.

What's ahead for you? A college degree? Technical training? The type of work you want to do will tell you how to prepare.

Check Your Understanding

1. Why are the teen years a good time to think seriously about a career?
2. What is the difference between intelligence and aptitude tests?
3. What do career counselors do?
4. What are the main types of institutions that provide career training?
5. What might cause a person to change careers?
6. Why should your goals help you stay flexible?
7. **Thinking Critically.** Should a person ever choose a career that doesn't match aptitudes and interests? Why or why not?
8. **Problem Solving.** Anthony, age seventeen, is a top student and a talented saxophone player. His dream is to earn a living as a jazz musician. He has been offered an academic scholarship by one college but wants to attend a performing arts school where he could focus on his music. Anthony's parents think he should accept the scholarship. What should Anthony do?

Getting a Job

OBJECTIVES

After studying this section, you should be able to:

- Compare sources of information about job openings.
- Fill out a job application form correctly.
- Demonstrate ways to prepare for a job interview.
- Compare concerns of entrepreneurs with those of employees.
- Define and explain the value of professionalism.

TERMS TO LEARN

resume
application form
references
interview
notice
entrepreneur
professionalism

The best-laid plans for a brilliant career won't do much good unless you can reach that early, all-important goal: get a job. Job hunting is where the ideas on paper or in your head meet real life. From your first look at the "help wanted" ads to your first day at work—and beyond—finding a job can challenge your energy, enthusiasm, and self-confidence. Tracking down and landing a job can seem like an imposing assignment. As the old Chinese proverb reminds you, however, "A journey of a thousand miles begins with a single step."

LOCATING JOB POSSIBILITIES

Pounding the pavement. Knocking on doors. Leaving no stone unturned. Phrases like these, used to describe job hunting, give a good image of the work and effort the process sometimes involves. Jobs don't come looking for workers; you have to know where to look for them.

Want Ads

One of the first places many people think of when looking for a job is the newspaper want ads. While they take up a large part of the classifieds, "help wanted" ads are usually an ineffective way of matching job seeker to job. One study found that over a twelve-month period only one-fourth of all employers in a typical city hired anyone as a result of a want ad. These ads are brief, so you'll have to follow up on any promising jobs to learn whether you're suited for them.

Personal Contacts

Many people are surprised to learn that one of the best ways to discover job openings is through others. If you're looking for a job, tell family members, friends, neighbors, and acquaintances. Describe the work you're looking for and ask them to let you know if they hear about such a job.

Businesses

Another effective, but challenging, tactic for finding jobs is to visit places of business and ask whether they're hiring. This approach takes courage. You may be disappointed if no jobs are available.

The more contacts you make, however, the better your chance for success. Your interest and initiative may impress a possible employer. The Chamber of Commerce or The Yellow Pages in the telephone book can guide you by providing an overview of local businesses.

Some job seekers identify businesses they'd like to work for, then send each company a letter asking about jobs and a resume. A **resume** is a written account of qualifications, including education or training and experience. Generally, this isn't enough for finding a job. A business may receive hundreds of resumes for every job offer it makes. Many have a policy of not responding to unsolicited letters.

Placement Offices

School placement offices are another source of information about jobs. Job openings are usually posted. Counselors may be able to help you identify firms to approach for the type of job you want. Community colleges often have active placement offices. Even if you aren't attending the college, you can visit the placement office to see what information is available.

Employment Agencies

Employment agencies provide job listings, counseling, and testing. State-funded agencies offer these services for free; however, they place only about one-third of the people who apply. Private agencies charge a fee for their services, and their placement rate is even lower than that of public agencies.

Imagine the jobs in a city like this. Finding the right one isn't easy without good help. Where would you turn for help in finding a job?

If you decide to use a private agency, be sure you understand the contract terms. Donovan wished he had when he found a job through a private employment agency. He and his employer each paid half the fee. The match wasn't a good one. Donovan left after only one month. When he tried to get his money back, he learned that the agency had earned its fee when he accepted the job. The contract said nothing about the length of the job.

Internet Sources

The Internet is a growing source of job leads. Most major newspapers offer their want ads on-line, allowing you to check job openings in distant cities. Local, state, and national job banks are also available.

Community facilities often provide the public with access to the Internet. Jack, an apprentice plumber, used the computer at the public library to see what jobs were available in the city where he wanted to move. Accessing a national job bank, Jack entered his trade, job requirements, and the city name. To his surprise, fifteen openings appeared. His hour at the library led him directly to a job he enjoys.

APPLYING FOR A JOB

When you find a job opening that sounds promising, you'll probably be asked to fill out an **application form**. This form gives employers basic information about job candidates. They can quickly compare applicants to find the most promising ones.

The application form is the first impression you make on a possible employer. You'll want to be sure it's a good one. Read

Matching people to jobs is a career in itself. Some employment services place people in temporary positions that can lead to full-time employment.

and follow all the instructions carefully. Answer every question, printing neatly in black or blue ink. If a question doesn't apply to you, write "not applicable" in the space given. Be sure to have your social security number, your employment record, and all other needed information.

Most application forms ask for references. **References** are people who will recommend your ability and character to a potential employer. Be sure to ask these people for permission before including their names as references. Take their names, addresses, and telephone numbers with you for the application form.

John will always remember filling out his first application. First, he had to borrow a pen. Then he had trouble understanding a question. He grew tense and frustrated; his writing became hurried and sloppy. For one question, he scratched through his answer. Then he had to ask for a phone book because he had forgotten his list of references. Needless to say, he didn't get the job. How do you think he prepared when he applied for his next job?

INTERVIEWING SUCCESSFULLY

Promising applicants are usually asked for an **interview**, a face-to-face meeting between an employer and a potential employee. Many job seekers approach the interview with anxiety—and no wonder. First impressions in an interview are important. What you say and how you act can make the difference between acceptance and rejection. If you know what to expect and prepare for it carefully, you can calm your nerves and make the interview work in your favor.

To help convince the interviewer that you're the best candidate, plan ways to explain what you have to offer. Show self-confidence. Ask any questions you have about the job. Asking about wages and benefits is acceptable, but avoid giving the impression that they are your main concern.

Making the Most of an Interview

"You've got the job." If that's what you want to hear, then you need to stand out from the rest when you interview.

Check the tips here and then talk to someone with interviewing experience. What other pointers are offered?

Prepare to talk tactfully about your strengths.

Learn about the business.

Arrive a little early.

Dress neatly; be clean and well groomed.

Bring information you might need.

LEAVING A JOB

Sooner or later, most people leave a job. When you do, for whatever reason, it's a good idea to leave on a positive note. You never know when you may need the contacts you've made.

It's good workplace etiquette to give your employer **notice**, an official written statement that you're leaving. A letter of resignation is the most common type of notice.

Depending on the job and the business, your employment may end at the time you resign. In other cases, you're expected to work a period of time after giving notice to allow your employer to hire a replacement.

Your reputation strengthens when you help someone learn your job.

BECOMING AN ENTREPRENEUR

When her son turned two, Tina decided to return to work but couldn't find reliable child care. She opened a child care center in her home instead. Scott started typing and formatting classmates' papers to earn money in college. He bought software that allowed him to make elaborate graphics, and his customer list kept growing.

Building Character

Perseverance: A Quality That Counts

When told by nature to head in a certain direction, an ant will climb up walls, over rocks, and even across you, to get where it must. That ant is a model of perseverance: it keeps working at its task, despite difficulties or obstacles. You show perseverance, too, when you strive for a goal with unrelenting effort, ignoring discouragement and opposition. A teen could demonstrate perseverance by:

- Filling out job application forms even when businesses say they aren't currently hiring.
- Taking summer school classes to achieve a grade point average high enough for acceptance into a training program.
- Running every morning before school in hopes of making the track team.
- Always speaking cheerfully to a withdrawn, reserved neighbor who rarely returns the greeting.

QUESTIONS

1. In what situations is perseverance often needed?
2. What is the difference between perseverance and stubbornness?

Tina and Scott are entrepreneurs. An **entrepreneur** is someone who organizes and runs a business. Like many successful entrepreneurs, Scott and Tina saw a needed service and decided to provide it. Both were highly motivated, self-confident, and willing to develop the business and personal skills needed to run a business.

Entrepreneurship can be demanding. You often work long hours, at least to start, with no guarantee of success. The financial risk is great because the failure rate of new businesses is high, about fifty percent. You must be willing to sacrifice the security of a regular paycheck for the deep personal satisfaction and good income that working for yourself can provide.

Many possibilities for entrepreneurs exist, especially in ways that serve families. As families get busier, they're more willing to pay others for tasks they usually do themselves.

DISPLAYING PROFESSIONALISM

Finding a job and succeeding are two different things. Having a good attitude toward your work is essential for success. How you think and feel about your job affects your job performance, as well as that of fellow employees.

The most valuable workers develop a spirit of **professionalism**. That is, they

Entrepreneurs enjoy the freedom of being their own boss. To get a business off and running, however, usually takes long hours and enormous effort. What type of person becomes an entrepreneur?

show a positive attitude and a sense of commitment. They use ethical behavior on the job. Employees with professionalism take pride in their work, whatever it may be. They carry out their duties cheerfully and to the best of their ability. Their actions on the job reflect high moral standards. Self-discipline, responsibility, and the ability to work without supervision are attributes of a professional worker.

Kadar, a waiter in a restaurant, understood the importance of professionalism to himself and to others. Kadar arrived early, in a clean uniform. He was patient and helpful even to difficult customers. He followed food safety and sanitation rules and encouraged coworkers to do the same. As Kadar explained, "It's just a matter of doing your job as well as you hope other people do theirs. Besides, if the restaurant loses customers and the owner loses money, what would happen to me?"

You can start to develop a professional attitude now. By taking your "job" as a student seriously and striving to give your best effort, you're developing skills that can take you far in whatever career you choose.

SECTION 29-2 REVIEW

Check Your Understanding

1. Why are classified ads a poor source for finding a job?
2. How can using the Internet help you locate jobs?
3. Why should you be careful when completing a job application form?
4. What is the purpose of a job interview?
5. What qualities are helpful to entrepreneurs?
6. How does a worker show professionalism?
7. **Thinking Critically.** How can a person talk about personal strengths in an interview without sounding arrogant?
8. **Problem Solving.** After six months on the job, Jordan gave notice. Although he did his job well, his personality clashes with the boss were difficult for everyone. Jordan knows he is largely responsible for this and doesn't blame anyone. He wants to leave his job on a positive note. What should Jordan do?

CHAPTER SUMMARY

- Since work is such an important part of life, now is the time to start thinking about a career and how to prepare for it.
- Various types of tests can help you select a career.
- Career counselors can advise you about job possibilities in different fields.
- Advanced career training can be acquired from vocational schools, apprenticeships, and colleges and universities.
- Setting goals and choosing a career path can help you advance in a career and change careers if you choose.
- Filling out an application and interviewing for a job are opportunities to present your best self to potential employers.
- Professionalism shows in your commitment to a job and in your ethical behavior.
- For those with the skills and resources, entrepreneurship can be rewarding.

REVIEW QUESTIONS

Section 29-1

1. How do career counselors help you choose a career?
2. What advantages are offered by vocational schools and apprenticeships?
3. What are the advantages and disadvantages of attending college when you aren't sure about what career to pursue?
4. In what ways should career goals help prepare you for your future work life?
5. Why is a career path valuable?

Section 29-2

1. What ways to learn of job openings would you recommend to a friend? What ways would you discourage?
2. How can you make a good impression when completing a job application?
3. How can you use an interview to show you're the best person for a job?
4. How does your professionalism benefit your coworkers and employer?
5. What are some advantages and challenges of becoming an entrepreneur?

BECOMING A PROBLEM SOLVER

1. Bret's friend told him about some difficult questions that he was asked at a job interview. Bret realizes that the questions would give him trouble, too. He has a job interview scheduled for next week. What should Bret do?
2. As a salesperson, Jerry helps customers find items, even if it means recommending a competitor's store. The high-pressure tactics used by others on the sales staff bother him. Jerry works partly on commission, however, so his approach is costing him income. Also, Jerry's boss has hinted that his job is in danger unless he becomes more "productive." What should Jerry do?

THINKING CRITICALLY

1. **Recognizing Alternatives.** Besides testing, how can you decide if your present interests are ones you would like to base a career on?
2. **Comparing and Contrasting.** What are some benefits and drawbacks of working for a time after high school before continuing your education?
3. **Recognizing Values.** Which do you think is more important, doing work you love or having a career with a good income? Why?
4. **Predicting Results.** Name five common first jobs for teens. What valuable experiences do these jobs offer?

MAKING CURRICULUM CONNECTIONS

1. **Language Arts.** Research a job or career that interests you. Write a one-page summary describing the job, its training or educational requirements, and other qualifications.
2. **Economics.** Research the educational or training requirements for three levels of employment in the same career; for example, preschool, elementary, and high school teacher. Compare the added education needed with the salary for each position. Are the costs of the education a good investment? Why or why not?
3. **Language Arts.** Using library and Internet resources, develop a resume.

APPLYING YOUR KNOWLEDGE

1. On a sheet of paper, list ten interests and abilities that you have. Then list three jobs or careers that would allow you to combine two or more of these skills and interests.
2. Working in pairs, conduct mock job interviews in front of the class. Have the rest of the class evaluate the strengths and weaknesses of each applicant's performance.
3. Locate at least three Internet sites that post job listings. Combine your sites with those of your classmates to create a list of job-related Internet sites that could be used by those looking for work.
4. Locate a teen entrepreneur in your school. Ask him or her to talk to your class about motivation, opportunity, and how to get started in a teen venture.

Family & Community Connections

1. Bring job applications from at least two different places of employment to class and fill them out. Use the suggestions in the chapter.

2. Survey ten workers of various ages. Ask how long they have held their current job and how they first learned that it was available. Compile findings with classmates, noting both the source of the job lead and the year.

UNIT 8

Forming Your Own Family

Teen Views

How will you know whether someone is the right marriage partner for you?

Maceo

"It kind of scares me, because I wonder if you can really be sure. My parents got divorced when I was in preschool. I couldn't believe it when my mother said they'd only known each other a few months when they got married. That's one thing I'd never do. I'd make sure I really know the person."

Kelley

"Some of my friends are on another planet. They see guys that are drop-dead gorgeous and that's all they care about. When it comes to marriage, the way a person looks shouldn't be that important. I want someone kind, who'll treat me with respect. My cousin married a great-looking guy, but she had to leave him because he was always hitting her."

What's your view?

What qualities are the most important in someone you might marry?

Chapter 30

Selecting a Partner

WORDS FOR THOUGHT

"Love at first sight is often cured by a second look." *(Anonymous)*

IN YOUR OWN WORDS

What often happens after that second look?

Understanding Attraction

OBJECTIVES

After studying this section, you should be able to:

- Compare theories of partner attraction.
- Explain the value of knowing about theories of attraction.

TERMS TO LEARN

homogamy
complementary needs
propinquity

In folk tales, the poor but decent woodsman can find happiness with the lovely but lonely princess. In real life, how long do you think this match would last? Would they even meet in the first place?

Folk tales don't talk about why people are attracted to each other and whether they would make a good match. On the other hand, you're probably very interested in this information. How does a friendship develop into a long-term commitment and eventually a solid marriage? The answer could have an impact on your future.

THEORIES OF ATTRACTION

Hoping to ensure your own future happiness in marriage, suppose you asked long-married couples for their secret of success.

You start by asking, "What attracted you to each other?" Someone might say, "He made me laugh" or "It was love at first sight." These responses may be true, but they don't tell you much.

Scientists who study human behavior take a detailed, elaborate approach to developing theories of mate selection. Their research has produced several useful theories. No one theory explains all relationships, but each one gives insight into what causes people to choose as they do.

Homogamy

"Like attracts like." Studies that focus on dating and marriage partners have found this saying to be true over and over. This is the basis of the **homogamy** (huh-MAH-guh-mee) theory.

The theory of homogamy says that attraction is based on similarities. Do you think inner or outer similarities are better indicators that an attraction might last?

Homogamy means sameness. This explanation for attraction says that people choose partners who are more like them than different from them.

Some scientists have suggested that people desire three levels of homogamy: in outer qualities, inner qualities, and ideas about roles.

Outer Qualities

First, people are attracted to those who share their outer qualities. This makes sense, for similarities create comfort, rapport, and ease in beginning relationships. Race, age, religion, education, and family background are some common traits that many couples often share. You may know couples who have striking differences, but in these basic traits many are alike.

Gimel's experience illustrates the impact of shared outer traits. Gimel worked on the assembly line of an auto plant. His parents were immigrants who work in the same plant. All three lived in an extended family with strong ties to relatives in their native country. One evening, Gimel went out with Mara, a student at the university in town. Mara described her studies as an art major and her summer of touring art museums in Europe. She talked about her father's job as legal counsel to the mayor's office in a large city and admitted that she was having trouble getting along with her father's third wife. How well do you think Gimel and Mara related to each other?

Goals, Interests, and Values

Couples who share outer qualities next look for homogamy in goals, interests, and values. People who like and want the same things in life are more apt to develop positive feelings for one another. Agreement in values makes acceptance of the other person easier.

Homogamous goals and values are more common among people with similar outer traits. For example, two people raised in the same religious faith are more likely to hold similar values about moral issues. People who have received the same type and level of education are likely to relate well.

Roles

As couples become more serious about each other, their need to agree on roles gains importance. What are the responsibilities of each partner in a marriage? What should each person be as a parent? The more similar the answers are, the more likely the relationship is to progress and remain strong.

Roles became an issue for Charles and Pamela. Pamela dreamed of having children, several of them, and soon. She wanted to stay home while the children were young. Charles, meanwhile, thought that if he and his future wife both had careers, they could travel and enjoy the benefits of two incomes. Any children could possibly come much later. With very different expectations, the couple eventually decided to end their relationship, knowing they would never see eye-to-eye on some very critical issues.

Complementary Needs

Whoever coined the expression "opposites attract" may have noticed a pattern of attraction called **complementary needs**.

A shared interest can bring two people together. What might happen to the relationship if one person adopts an interest only to please the other?

This theory suggests that people select others who complement (complete) and meet their personality needs. Each partner's psychological strengths balance the traits of the other. For instance, an outgoing, emotional person may be attracted to someone who is thoughtful and serene. A strong leader may choose a supporter.

At first glance, the theories of homogamy and complementary needs seem to contradict each other. Actually, they work together. People are drawn first to those like themselves. From among this group, they

People who spend time together on a job, in school, or in an activity tend to form attractions. If you're looking for someone special, why are clubs and volunteer work often recommended?

themselves what they want in a mate, in terms of material resources, personal qualities, and skills. Then they look at what they can offer in return.

According to this explanation, you tend to choose someone who brings you the best "package" of practical and emotional rewards at a fair cost to yourself. People select and develop those relationships that give the most "value." For example, Deon is a successful businessman who can provide a family with a comfortable living. He wants a wife who will enjoy entertaining clients. Judy is a professional musician who spends much of her time traveling and rehearsing. Her husband manages her career and schedules her tours.

Since people tend to be more comfortable with others who offer qualities equal to what they can return, social exchange parallels homogamy. The idea of exchange may seem somewhat calculating, but it's seen in many happy relationships. You and your friends probably practice some kind of social exchange, yet your friendship is more than an accounting of favors given and received.

seek someone who can help them meet their psychological and emotional needs. Ideally, both types of attraction lead people to choose a partner who affirms and reinforces their sense of self and basic philosophy of life.

Social Exchange

In some cultures, families arrange marriages between young people based on what each family can offer the other. Some researchers believe that people select their mates on the same idea of social exchanges. They ask

INFOLINK

Rewards and Costs in Relationships

To review information on the rewards and costs of relationships, see *Section 5-1*.

Propinquity

Libby and Bryan met and became close in high school. After graduation, however, Bryan enrolled in a local community college, while Libby went to a university out of state. The long-distance phone calls and weekend visits were expensive, time-consuming, and not enough to keep their relationship going. Eventually they lost interest because the relationship took so much effort.

Libby and Bryan's relationship illustrates the propinquity theory. **Propinquity** (pro-PIN-kwit-ee) is nearness in time or place. People are more apt to meet, get to know, and stay with others who are physically close by. Propinquity reinforces social exchange because the relationships are more convenient. They bring rewards without the costs of a long-distance relationship, including time and money, and such emotional costs as loneliness.

Ideal Mate

Have you ever thought that a devoted, loving couple were "made for each other"? The ideal mate theory takes that expression to heart. According to this theory, people have a mental image of an ideal mate, based on appearance, character, or other traits. They measure potential partners against this ideal and are most attracted to those who come closest to "perfection."

Some people have a very clear image of their ideal; they can envision the mate's hair color and how that person would act on a date. Others take a different approach, saying, "I can't quite describe it, but I'll

---

Building Character

Dependability: A Quality That Counts

Suppose you and two classmates are working on an economics fair project together. You and Bryce have come to all three meetings so far, but Angelina has missed two and been late to one. Who is dependable? Dependable people can be counted on. They've proven themselves worthy of trust by keeping their word and meeting responsibilities. A teen can show dependability by:

- Showing up for an assigned shift at a volunteer event.
- Starting dinner on time so it's ready when the rest of the family gets home.
- Staying late at the library to finish part of a group presentation for class the next day.
- Turning in an article for the school newspaper before the deadline.
- Making an effort to be patient and sympathetic when friends need support.

QUESTIONS

1. Why is dependability important in a marriage partner?
2. What behavior might you see in a person who is not dependable? How does lack of dependability affect relationships?
3. Give an example of how you demonstrate dependability.

know it when I see it." Often the image of an ideal mate is based on parents. A person may idealize the parent of the opposite gender—or the exact opposite, depending on how that person feels about the parent.

When people imagine the ideal partner, what do they see? A sense of humor? Stability? **What would you look for?**

THEORIES AND REALITY

While these ideas about attraction do not neatly describe every situation, they do offer "food for thought." Typically, people find themselves in serious relationships without ever having considered what traits they value. Knowing why you find a potential mate attractive helps you see the "magic" of the relationship more realistically. Also, as you think about the qualities you seek, you may start to ask what qualities you can bring to a marriage.

SECTION 30-1 REVIEW

Check Your Understanding

1. In what three areas do couples seek homogamy?
2. How does the idea of complementary needs seem to contradict the homogamy theory?
3. According to social exchange theory, what is a person's goal when choosing a mate?
4. What is the basis for relationships according to propinquity theory?
5. How can understanding theories of selection be helpful?
6. **Thinking Critically.** Do you think people are generally aware of the forces of attraction that are at work within them? How could an increasing awareness be helpful?
7. **Problem Solving.** When Jalen met Lakisha, they were immediately attracted to each other. They seemed to have so much in common. Slowly, Jalen began to notice differences, so he told Lakisha about his doubts for their future together. She pointed out that differences make relationships interesting, and now Jalen is uncertain. What should he do?

Choosing the Right Partner

OBJECTIVES

After studying this section, you should be able to:

- Relate readiness factors to success in marriage.
- Predict potential marital problems based on certain factors in a relationship.
- Evaluate whether an attitude toward marriage is realistic.
- Explain why belief in the institution of marriage is important.

TERMS TO LEARN

readiness
institution of marriage

When two people believe that they have fallen deeply in love, that isn't the best time to begin asking, "Are we ready for this?" They are not likely to make an objective decision. Questions about **readiness**—certain qualities and conditions that indicate whether a person is prepared for marriage—need to be answered before then. Some should be asked even before a relationship is in sight.

SIGNS OF READINESS

The idea of readiness is simple: the more readiness factors partners have or take time to acquire, the more tools they have for creating a long and rewarding marriage. Of course, no formula guarantees success—not in marriage or in life. However, you can give yourself a much better chance by thinking ahead.

Age

Until the late twenties or so, the older two people are at the time of their wedding, the more likely the marriage is to be stable. Added years bring more life experiences, often leading to greater maturity and to better jobs and incomes. All of these circumstances tend to contribute to stronger marriages.

This effect levels off at about age twenty-seven for men and twenty-five for women. A thirty-two-year-old woman, then, is no more apt to be successful than a woman of twenty-nine.

"Jimmy and I decided to wait until we were at least twenty-five to get married. It's a good thing, because this is DeAndre, and we wouldn't have found each other if I had married too soon."

Independence

People who can't stand on their own aren't able to support someone else. When examining your own level of independence in preparation for marriage, you might ask questions like those below. If the answers are "yes," chances are you are well on your way to independence:

- Do I have the practical knowledge I need to survive on my own?
- Do I make good decisions?
- Can I make decisions without turning to family for help?
- Am I comfortable with the idea of living apart from the family that raised me?
- Can I support myself financially?

Remember to ask the same questions about a potential partner. A successful marriage takes two self-sufficient people. One person may rely too heavily on the partner otherwise, or both may depend too much on their families.

Although bonds with parents and other family members should remain strong, a marriage is meant to form a new family. Partners who are not ready to transfer their first loyalty to each other are not ready for marriage.

Parental Approval

Parental approval shouldn't be a main reason for choosing a mate. However, parental input can be very informative. Because parents genuinely want their children to be happy, they often have good reasons for disapproval of a potential partner. Perhaps they are bothered by qualities in the person that their son or daughter missed. They may see that the timing isn't right.

In most cases, couples are wise to postpone marriage if parents object, even if their worries seem unfounded. Over time the troublesome situation may be resolved, and true love will wait. Secretive meetings only make matters worse.

Sometimes parents come to support their child's choice of partner. By the same token, many couples eventually see their parents' reasons for concern and decide against marrying. When the issue is a partnership for life, spending a little extra time to make the decision is a worthy investment. Marrying against parents' wishes greatly stresses all relationships involved.

When parents approve of a prom date, they believe a teen will be in safe company for an evening. What does their approval mean when a couple becomes engaged?

Knowledge of Each Other

In one study of 1000 marriages, researchers found that partners who had known each other for at least five years before marrying were the happiest. Five years is not a magic number. The point is that taking time to know your partner well before making a lifetime pledge is essential to success.

Couples who marry after a very short time together simply don't have the chance to learn about each other and talk over important issues. The same may be true of couples who are separated prior to marriage. You can be more sure that your relationship will last if you have experience facing life's ups and downs together.

To discover a partner's views on relevant topics, many couples use prepared checklists designed for this purpose. Counselors

Experts say that a partner for life should be someone you can spend ordinary time with and still enjoy the relationship. **Why is this necessary?**

and clergy members have them, or you can find them in resource books and magazines. Going over such checklists together, a couple may confront questions about marriage that hadn't occurred to them, such as the role of religion in their future family's life. Talking these over can bring greater understanding and confidence to the relationship.

A Sense of Responsibility

Think of all the responsibilities the adults in your family have. Just meeting the family's physical needs for food, clothing, shelter, and more is a serious duty. Meeting emotional needs may be harder still. For a marriage to succeed, partners must be willing and able to take on these and many other responsibilities.

Supporting a family takes financial responsibility. Before getting married, partners should be earning enough money to pay their expenses, even if they have to delay marriage to finish their education or establish themselves in a job. Low income often contributes to marital instability. In fact, fights about money are the most often

A married couple has many responsibilities to fulfill. **What is likely to happen if one person can't or won't participate?**

Differences

Too many differences can threaten a relationship. Before two people think seriously about commitment, they might ask each other:

- **What role does religion play in your life?** If one person feels more strongly than the other, the couple may eventually have trouble reconciling the difference.
- **Will age make a difference?** A significant age difference presents a problem when two people can't relate to each other.
- **Will cultural differences be a problem?** A couple may need to examine how their backgrounds have affected their attitudes, values, and expectations.

named cause of divorce. Financial preparation and planning help prevent added stress.

Spouses have other important responsibilities to one another. Practically speaking, they must be willing to share routine household tasks. Emotionally, they must be ready to support each other.

Friendships

When a person has friends, the ability to build a successful marriage typically increases. That's because the relationship skills needed to build friendships are the same ones that contribute to a strong marriage. Those who don't have good relationships before marriage will likely have the same problem later.

When Eric started dating Chauncy, he was impressed by the number of friends she had. As he got to know her, he saw why. Chauncy was bright and funny, a good listener with natural enthusiasm for life. Her popularity confirmed Eric's positive impression of her. Sharing her with so many people was sometimes difficult, but Eric asked himself, "Could I care about someone no one else wants as a friend?"

Likewise, having siblings can influence a person's readiness for marriage. Learning to get along with brothers and sisters is valuable training for life as a spouse. Close relations with friends and siblings contribute to a happy childhood, which is something else that favors a happy marriage.

People need to look at a potential partner realistically. You can admire a person for looks, talents, social status, and many other qualities, but how do these balance against such qualities as kindness, honesty, and reliability?

A Realistic Attitude

Does having all of the qualities and conditions described here make someone ready for marriage? The answer is, not entirely. People can be prepared for marriage in many ways, yet still have an unrealistic attitude toward married life. They may expect too much from themselves, from their partners, or from the relationship. They may not realize that choosing the right partner is only the first step toward a successful, long-term relationship.

The following points can help you think realistically about marriage and potential marriage partners:

- **Marriage is not a cure-all.** Some people see marriage as a means to some other end. They marry for social status, financial security, or to have children. They want marriage to get them out of a destructive home environment or into a stable relationship with a permanent partner. Some people feel pressure from family to marry. Marriages made in response to a problem aren't typically strong. People are more interested in finding a partner who meets a particular need, rather than one who is right for them in many ways.

- **Love is different from, and more than, sexual attraction.** Ideally, a strong, physical attraction would complement a strong, loving marriage. When the sensual aspect becomes the focus of the relationship, couples may fail to deal with other areas that are important to married life. Sexual excitement tends to lessen with time; then unresolved differences and problems can drive couples apart.

- **What you see is what you get.** Planning to change a partner's habits after marriage is a mistake. If a person cannot or will not change before marriage, why should he or she change afterwards? A person may "reform" before the wedding but slide into old ways later. It's wiser to marry someone whose traits you already find appealing.

- **Don't expect a perfect partner.** You can't be one, and you aren't going to find one.

Choosing whether to marry—and whom to marry—are among the most important decisions you'll ever make. Having realistic ideas about married life and a real understanding of your possible spouse gives you an advantage in making your marriage happy.

WARNING SIGNS

Just as some conditions can encourage couples to move ahead with their relationship, other factors should make them put the brakes on. These signs warn of problems that are likely to prevent a relationship from being healthy or successful.

Abuse

Abuse has no place in a loving relationship. It shows a partner's inability to handle problems in a mature way. If abuse occurs, the couple should stop seeing each other. If they want to consider salvaging the relationship, they need outside help to make that decision. On their own, abusive relationships rarely improve and usually get worse.

Abuse, you'll remember, may be physical or emotional. Charlotte and Damon never raised a hand to each other, yet Damon could be incredibly critical toward her. Charlotte hoped that Damon would become more sensitive as they grew closer. Instead, he grew worse. Every day he found something to complain about, some way of trying to make her feel incompetent or inferior. Fortunately for Charlotte, she had the self-respect to realize that Damon had the problem, not her. Although it was difficult, she broke off the relationship.

Tips & TECHNIQUES

Alone and Together. Some people feel incomplete without a marriage partner. How would you feel?

- Write down six to eight ways in which marriage partners enrich each other's life, such as having someone to share problems with.
- If you never married, how would you handle each of these areas?
- Would any important need go unfulfilled for lack of a mate?
- What can you do to develop your abilities, skills, and confidence so that you can manage your life on your own?

The "need" to be married can press people to make unhappy matches. A marriage between partners who know they can live without each other, but choose to share their lives, is the most secure.

Try It Out. Identify three skills you need to develop in order to manage life on your own. Choose one and plan ways to learn or improve this skill. How does becoming self-sufficient allow you to bring more to a relationship?

Some problems in a relationship can be settled and put aside. Others can't. Do you think strong feelings of jealousy can be "cured"?

Substance Abuse

A partner's abuse of alcohol or other drugs will promise a rocky relationship. Substance abusers often have emotional problems that make it hard for them to stay in an involved, committed relationship. Substance abuse also decreases self-control, making the abuser more prone to acts of physical or emotional cruelty.

Few people knowingly marry someone with a substance abuse problem. Partners often hide their addiction, especially early in the relationship. Getting out of such a relationship can be difficult. A partner may feel that he or she is abandoning the other person just when the need for support is greatest. Abusers must solve the problem themselves, however. A partner can still be a supportive friend yet make it clear that a long-term relationship is possible only when the abuser has control over the problem.

Jealousy

When Laurie began dating Andy, she was flattered by his constant attention. The closer they became, however, the more possessive Andy was. He was no longer satisfied with working to build their relationship; instead, he wanted to cut off Laurie's other friendships as well.

Andy was acting on feelings of jealousy. Like most jealous partners, Andy was insecure about himself and the relationship. He was afraid of losing Laurie to someone or something else. By trying to gain control of her life, Andy was guilty of emotional abuse.

To some degree, such emotions are normal in a relationship's early stages, when neither partner is sure of how the other feels. In a mature, committed relationship, however, feelings of jealousy and uncertainty are rare.

Arguments

No relationship is without disagreements. If a couple spend much of their time arguing, however, they should seriously reconsider their relationship. One or both of them may still need to develop the qualities of a mature relationship, including communication, compromise, and respect for differences. They may not be as compatible as they thought.

Argument is different from discussion. Discussion is honest, thoughtful, respectful, and sticks to the subject. It leads to compromise and the resolution of problems. Argument is emotional, poorly reasoned, and can be hurtful, even leading to physical abuse by some. Argument doesn't solve a problem. It becomes one.

A BELIEF IN MARRIAGE

Strange as it may sound, love is not enough for a successful marriage. Love alone won't enable you to solve the problems and tackle the situations that married life brings. To do this, you must have a strong belief in the **institution of marriage**, or marriage as a way of living. You must value marriage itself and believe it's worth preserving in society.

People who believe in marriage as an institution have added incentive to do what it takes to make a marriage work. Only with this commitment is readiness for marriage possible.

When people truly believe that marriage is a commitment, they know they can and will make every effort to keep the marriage strong. Reaching that understanding is part of readiness.

SECTION 30-2 REVIEW

Check Your Understanding

1. How is age a factor in readiness for marriage?
2. What is the value of a prepared marital checklist?
3. Why are people with many friends more likely to have happy marriages?
4. What often happens when people look to marriage as a way to solve a problem in their life?
5. Is jealousy a good quality in a potential partner? Why or why not?
6. How does belief in the institution of marriage affect marital success?
7. **Thinking Critically.** How would you advise someone who is "holding out" for a partner who fits every point of the description of readiness in this chapter?
8. **Problem Solving.** Sarah and Ian will graduate from college in a few months. They plan to marry shortly afterwards. They will have little money, but both have been offered jobs with good pay. Sarah's parents want to loan them some money to help them pay expenses until they're on their feet financially. What should Sarah and Ian do?

CHAPTER SUMMARY

- Partners are frequently attracted to each other by homogamy in both outer and inner traits.
- Complementary needs and social exchange explain that partners choose one another because each one fills certain needs for the other.
- People tend to choose partners from those who are close by.
- Some people seek a mate who resembles their ideal.
- Mature, independent couples who are willing to accept responsibility tend to have happy marriages.
- A strong marriage requires understanding of one's partner and of married life and a commitment to marriage itself.
- Such signs as abuse and jealousy should warn couples that the relationship needs help and perhaps should be ended.

REVIEW QUESTIONS

Section 30-1
1. How do the three levels of homogamy progress from outer to inner qualities?
2. How do homogamy and complementary needs work together?
3. Compare the complementary needs theory with social exchange.
4. How might a person's strong sense of an ideal mate help with finding a partner? How would it interfere?
5. How can theories of attraction help you when considering a potential partner?

Section 30-2
1. Why should a parent's opinion matter when choosing a partner?
2. Why is a sense of responsibility needed in a successful marriage?
3. Describe a realistic attitude toward marriage.
4. Why does the text state that "love is not enough for a successful marriage"? What else is needed?

BECOMING A PROBLEM SOLVER

1. Danielle and Mike are planning their wedding, although Mike's father opposes the marriage. Mike told Danielle that his father won't attend the ceremony. Danielle knows that Mike and his father have grown very close since his mother died. What should she do?

2. Stacy's mother and great uncle are both recovering alcoholics. Stacy hasn't told her serious boyfriend about her family history, but she's starting to feel guilty about holding back. What should Stacy do?

THINKING CRITICALLY

1. **Analyzing Behavior.** How do you explain successful relationships between people who seem to have very little in common?
2. **Recognizing Contradictions.** According to this chapter, independence from parents is important for a successful marriage, yet so is parental approval. How do you explain these seemingly contradictory statements?
3. **Analyzing Decisions.** Why would someone marry with plans to change the other person later?
4. **Comparing and Contrasting.** If you were allowed to base your selection of a partner on only one theory of attraction, which would you use and why?

MAKING CURRICULUM CONNECTIONS

1. **Language Arts.** Today's society is very mobile. Explain in writing how this trend toward movement and travel affects mate selection. Include references to homogamy and propinquity.
2. **Science.** Identify ways that technology has opened new avenues of communication and contact between people, such as Internet chat rooms and video dating services. For each means of contact, draw conclusions about the advantages and drawbacks to finding potential partners and pursuing relationships. Share your findings and ideas with the class.

APPLYING YOUR KNOWLEDGE

1. Write down five traits that you find desirable in a partner. Combine your list with those of classmates. Make separate lists for male and female students. On the board, list the five most popular traits for each gender. Discuss their similarities and differences and the effects these traits have on relationships.
2. Locate a checklist that evaluates couple relationships. What kinds of information might the checklist reveal to a couple about their relationship?

Family & Community Connections

1. Interview married couples from different generations—your own, your parents', and your grandparents', if possible. Ask: How did you meet? What traits did you look for in a spouse? What did you expect marriage to be like? Summarize their answers in a short report.

2. With your family members, debate this statement: Marriage can survive on love alone, because loving partners put their relationship first.

Chapter 31

Choosing Marriage

IN YOUR OWN WORDS

What should a person do to *be* the right person?

The Engagement

OBJECTIVES

After studying this section, you should be able to:

- Describe the purposes of an engagement period.
- Determine when breaking an engagement is a wise choice.

TERMS TO LEARN

engagement
premarital counseling

If you look up the word *engaged* in the dictionary, you'll find among its many meanings: *attracted, involved,* and *intermeshed*. All of these definitions describe the progress of an engaged couple. First they become attracted to each other. Then they are involved with preparations for life. Over time they become increasingly intermeshed.

As you will see, these preparations include more than picking out a wedding dress and changing the names on a checking account. Those details, while important, are still secondary to the essential work of the engagement period.

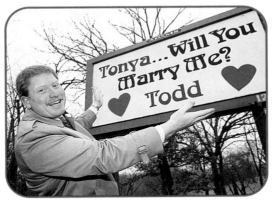

PURPOSES OF ENGAGEMENT

The first official step on the way to saying "I do" is the engagement. An **engage-**ment is a promise or intention to marry. Partners declare themselves ready to accept the commitment and responsibilities of marriage.

The engagement period is a time to prepare for the wedding. Even more important, it's a time to prepare for marriage. This crucial period of work and transition leads to the exchange of vows and the joining of two lives into one future. In various ways, engagement allows the couple to address the issues that will affect the success of their life together.

LEARNING ABOUT EACH OTHER

"I thought I knew all I needed to know about Paul before we got engaged," Greta recalled. "Then I started noticing little things, like how he throws away the end slices of a loaf of bread. I think that's so wasteful! I realized how much more we still had to learn about each other before we got married."

Like Paul and Greta, couples benefit by using their engagement as a time to make sure they really know each other. Each should know and be comfortable with the other's spending patterns, cleanliness habits, and food preferences. Getting well acquainted in this way before the wedding tends to leave fewer surprises that could cause problems during marriage. Some experts recommend an engagement of six to twelve months to provide enough time for this discovery process.

Identifying Differences

Perhaps the greatest fact-finding value of an engagement is in allowing a couple to identify and deal with differences. They can then decide whether this diversity will enhance their relationship or undermine it. What effect do you think the following differences might have on a marriage?

- Tia prefers fast food. Scott is a vegetarian.
- Martha would like to have two children once she and Glen are financially secure. Glen wants to have four children, beginning right away.
- Tanya and Barry have strong, opposing political views.
- Marcus dislikes socializing and Tabitha loves to party.

Only the couple themselves can judge whether the differences between them are enough to threaten the success of their marriage. This decision is clearer when each partner is sure about his or her values and expectations for the relationship.

Even food can be an issue for a couple. How might these opposing views be handled: a love of fast food versus eating nutritiously; a desire to eat out all the time versus having meals at home?

Practical Matters

Many engaged partners know "about" how many children they want and that one of them "ought to" stay home with them "for a few years." More definite plans would be wise. Practical matters that need to be addressed include:

- Where will you live? Will you rent, buy, or move into the other's home?
- How will you manage money? What are your spending and saving priorities? Who will be responsible for buying and bill paying?
- Do you want children? If so, when? How many? Who will care for them at home?
- Will you both have outside careers? If so, will one be more important than the other? Whose?

- How will you handle issues involving in-laws? Will they stay with you when they visit? Where will you spend holidays?

USING YOUR KNOWLEDGE

Whenever Michelle and Walter talk about their plans for married life, Walter has few opinions. When Michelle asked him about this, Walter replied, "Why are you surprised? I'm just trying to be agreeable." Michelle still feels uneasy. What should she do?

Generally, problems caused by differences are more easily solved before rather than after marriage. Working together to deal with the issues strengthens the relationship and sets a pattern for the future. In this sense, engagement is a testing ground for marriage. It allows couples to work together on the problem-solving techniques that they will use in married life.

Many couples believe that living together before marriage is a good way to find out if they are truly compatible. This seems to make sense; however, recent studies have shown that couples who try this arrangement are less satisfied with their marriage than those who do not. They are also more likely to divorce.

DEVELOPING TEAMWORK

On a basketball team, the most valuable player isn't always the one who scores the most points. It may be the one who passes the ball to other players who have a better shot at the basket. That kind of teamwork is a model for engaged couples. During this time, they start to think as "we" rather than "I" when setting goals, making plans, and solving problems.

A couple need not be exactly alike to make a good team. In fact, their different strengths and qualities can combine in an effective working partnership. Someone who can generate a lot of ideas quickly, for instance, would benefit from a partner who can think critically and insightfully.

Using Teamwork Skills

Trust is important to developing teamwork. Engaged couples need to have honest discussions on serious, personal issues. They must confide in each other for a deeper understanding to develop. Partners also count on each other to do their part in maintaining the relationship.

Good communication skills are also necessary. Couples have a lot to discuss. As Trisha said, "Phil and I talked about everything we could think of: how to handle housework, what we expected parenting to be like, earning and managing our money, religion, volunteer work—you name it. We wanted to be sure we heard all the ideas and understood each other's thinking before the wedding."

Finally, compromise is essential to teamwork. As a couple plan for the future, they must be thinking about what is best for *both* of them, as well as any children they might have. Ensuring the survival of their partnership will take some giving in on each side. A willingness to meet each other halfway is a sign of commitment to making the marriage work.

ESTABLISHING NEW RELATIONSHIPS

During the engagement period, families and friends develop a new relationship with the couple. As a future family member, the prospective spouse is often included in family activities to let family and friends meet and accept the new addition.

A growing number of engagements today are between partners who have been married before and may have children.

Conversation between two engaged people needs to include plenty of exploration. They should share opinions about children, money, roles, and careers. What other topics would you add?

A stepfather-to-be can start to build a bond with his stepson well before the marriage. **What actions will help build that bond?**

These situations are more complex because they involve more family members than first marriages—not only the couple and their children, but former spouses and grandparents who are still connected to the couple by the children. Emotions, and stress levels, can run high.

In these cases, the engagement period can be valuable for dealing with everyone's personal concerns. Children especially need patience and reassurance to cope with the stress of adjusting. When Eugene and Jolene told his six-year-old son Trace that they were getting married, Trace seemed saddened. He explained to his father, "I like Jolene okay, but I don't think I want a stepmom." The couple used the engagement period to help Trace understand what their relationship would be and to get used to the idea of them becoming a family.

SEEKING ADVICE

Some partners seek the counsel of trained professionals prior to their marriage. In fact, some religions require such **premarital counseling** before the couple can be married in the faith.

Good premarital counseling helps couples focus on their reasons for marrying by addressing questions about their relationship. They might be asked:

- How or why did you fall in love? Was it quick and unexplainable, or did it occur slowly for reasons you both understand?
- What, right now, is your partner's most endearing trait? Is it a long-lasting quality? If so, will it still seem as appealing in the future?
- When you're with your partner, do you naturally "put your best foot forward"? Do you have to remind yourself to show respect and courtesy?
- Do you and your partner reveal your weaknesses, fears, and mistakes to each other? Are you both accepting of each other?

Premarital Counseling. Imagine that you do premarital counseling. Your job is to lead couples to a better understanding of each other, in part by helping them identify and discuss potential trouble spots in the relationship.

- List five topics or questions that you think are most important for the couple to "get out in the open" through discussion.
- Explain how you go about determining if the couple fit well together in each of these areas. Besides obvious disagreement, what do you look for? What questions do you ask?
- What advice would you give a couple who disagreed on some of these issues? Would you discourage the marriage?

Try It Out. Compare your ideas with those of your classmates. Based on your collective "counseling," try to write some general guidelines for determining compatibility.

Counseling usually helps reveal potential trouble spots. Knowing their particular points of disagreement enables a couple to handle them better and often resolve them before marriage.

Some engaged couples take advantage of community resources to learn more about marriage and each other. Religious organizations, social service agencies, and other educational groups may offer classes or information on marriage issues.

Well spent, the engagement period is a unique opportunity for couples to gain a deeper understanding of themselves and their relationship. Such insight is the backbone of an enduring marriage.

BROKEN ENGAGEMENTS

When a couple becomes engaged, people tend to assume that marriage automatically follows. Actually, about one-third of all engagements are broken before marriage, and often with good reason.

As their engagement proceeds, some couples find that they don't love each other enough for marriage. They care for one another, but not enough to willingly accept the needed sacrifices and compromises. Likewise, couples may encounter too many problems in meshing their personalities. Conflicting traits that were tolerable while dating are felt more sharply as the couple try to draw closer.

Separation can strain a relationship, as different experiences cause people to grow in different directions. Annessa and Lamar got engaged just before Annessa enlisted in the Navy. Six months later Annessa came home on her first leave. She had changed so much that she seemed like a stranger to Lamar. He, too, had made new friends and found new interests. With so little in common, they rethought their engagement.

Parental opposition ends some engagements. The couple may dislike the strain put on the family, or they may become convinced that the parents are right.

Recovery from a broken engagement can take time. Some people want to stay active and be with others. Some want to reflect and have time alone. Both approaches help the healing.

Breaking an engagement can be a painful experience. Both partners may grieve for the loss of an important relationship. They sometimes feel a sense of failure. Returning gifts, with explanations to family and friends, can be awkward. Breaking the ties is easier if the couple can act with dignity and treat each other with respect.

Whatever the difficulties of a broken engagement, they are far less than those of a troubled marriage or a divorce. Marriage is meant to be a lifetime commitment. It should be entered only when both partners are convinced that they can live happily with the decision.

SECTION 31-1 REVIEW

Check Your Understanding

1. Why is the engagement period important to a successful marriage?
2. What are some things a couple can learn about each other during the engagement period?
3. What is the purpose of premarital counseling?
4. Why might an engagement be broken?
5. **Thinking Critically.** Why do you suppose that living together before marriage might actually worsen a couple's chances for success?
6. **Problem Solving.** Two months into her engagement, June confided to her mother that she was having second thoughts about marrying Daniel. Her mother called this a case of "cold feet" and assured her daughter, "All couples feel this way before a wedding." What should June do?

Making Wedding Plans

OBJECTIVES

After studying this section, you should be able to:

- Explain the societal significance of weddings.
- Compare the types of contracts people make when they marry.
- Explain laws and customs connected to weddings.
- Suggest ways to handle common concerns when planning a wedding.

TERMS TO LEARN

contract
prenuptial agreements

In some ways, planning a wedding is a preview of how a couple will work together in marriage. They make choices and accept compromises. They try to accommodate each other's friends and family. They see each other under stress. The details of a wedding are many and varied. Partners may be more concerned with choosing their attire than with getting a license. However, less obvious preparations are sometimes most important.

A CEREMONY WITH SIGNIFICANCE

Few occasions in people's lives are treasured the way weddings are. For centuries, cultures around the world have created and carried out different rituals to stress both the joy and the seriousness of the event.

All weddings, whatever their form, share important purposes. They mark the personal and often spiritual union of a woman and a man. In addition, they are a formal, legal expression of commitment and the creation of a new family. This public declaration is significant because society has an interest in promoting stable relationships between couples. Marriage provides the structure for having and raising children. Within the framework of the family, children are nurtured. They are also absorbed into the culture. In this way, society continues.

CONTRACTS AND CUSTOMS

When a couple marry, they enter into at least one contract with each other. A **contract** is a binding agreement between two or more people. Marriage itself is a contract overseen by the state and made official with a marriage license. A couple can make other contracts before marriage.

In addition, couples often include regional, ethnic, or family traditions in the wedding ceremony. These customs show the societal aspect of marriage and give a sense of continuity with past generations.

Marriage Laws

Society has a stake in marriage and enacts laws to help ensure successful ones. Marriage laws often include restrictions regarding minimum age, mental soundness, and certain diseases. In some states, marriage may be forbidden among people with certain close blood ties, such as cousins.

In the United States, marriage is regulated by each state. Couples must be sure they meet the requirements of the state where the ceremony will be performed. Their marriage will be valid in every state, however.

Before issuing a license, many states require a blood test. Blood tests check for many types of sexually transmitted and other communicable diseases. The purpose is to ensure that couples know about conditions, not to prevent marriage.

Each state has a time frame for obtaining a license. For example, at least three days but no more than 30 days before the ceremony. A marriage ceremony must be performed by an authorized person and be witnessed. The license becomes valid when signed by the person who marries the couple and the witnesses. The marriage contract between two people then becomes legal, and they are bound by the marital laws of that state.

All states require a license to marry. Where do people in your community obtain a license? What is the cost?

Prenuptial Agreements

The laws spell out certain requirements, procedures, and protections in marriage. Couples who have special concerns may make additional agreements before the wedding. These are called **prenuptial agreements** (pre-NUP-shull). Some couples have lawyers draw up prenuptial contracts.

Partners may write agreements on any topic they wish. However, prenuptial agreements typically deal with three main issues: protecting property within the marriage; establishing ownership in case of marital breakup; and defining the roles, rights, and duties of each partner.

- **Protecting Property.** A prenuptial agreement to protect property is a contract most often used in remarriages. A partner may want money or possessions from a first marriage to go to children from that marriage. Kaitlyn used a prenuptial agreement in this way. She explained, "I set aside payment from my first husband's life insurance for our two children. I was saving it for their college education. When I remarried, I wanted it clear that the money was for my children's education."

- **Establishing Ownership.** Some prenuptial agreements make provisions for dividing property if the marriage ends. Such contracts are ordinarily used only when the couple has many assets. To many people, starting a relationship by preparing for its end signals a lack of commitment. Others feel more secure with the protection the agreement provides.

- **Defining Roles.** Finally, a prenuptial agreement can spell out partners' rights and responsibilities in marriage. The agreement may state who will take time off from work to raise children; who will manage the money; how major decisions will be made; or how much freedom each partner will have. This type of agreement is less apt to be a legal contract.

For most couples, the biggest advantage of crafting a prenuptial agreement is discussing and deciding important issues. Writing an agreement clarifies each partner's personal views and responsibilities.

When two people are in love, they may not want to think about the business side of a marriage. Why do some couples take a practical approach with a prenuptial agreement?

Some people plan to have part or all of a wedding ceremony outdoors. Why would a backup plan be smart?

Ceremonies

If you've been to many weddings, you know that the ceremony can be as individual as the people who do the planning. The bride and groom often tailor events to their own wishes.

Certain conditions must be met, however. The ceremony must fulfill the legal requirements described earlier. Most religious faiths require that a certain form be followed as well. Also, the wedding and other festivities must fit within a family's budget.

Depending on the couple's preference, a wedding ceremony may be either civil or religious. Civil ceremonies are performed by a judge, justice of the peace, or other appropriate official. They may take place almost anywhere: in a home or a courthouse, on a beach or on horseback. This type of wedding is usually less formal than a religious ceremony and is often personalized to suit the couple.

Because family life is central to most faiths, marriage is also an important religious ceremony. Many people choose to be married in a religious ceremony, which usually is held in a house of worship. A religious official, such as a minister, rabbi, or priest, performs the ceremony. The readings, music, and vows all reflect the couple's beliefs. While services are usually less flexible than civil ceremonies, partners may be allowed to include personal reflections and music that they find meaningful.

Weddings are often followed by some type of reception. Here the bride and groom are "received" by family and friends and their wedding celebrated. Like the ceremony, receptions can be simple or very elaborate.

Customs

Wedding customs vary according to ethnic background, religion, and even geography. The couple may choose to follow customs and rituals with widely accepted meanings. These have both symbolic and practical value.

- The exchange of rings is a traditional symbol of marriage and sometimes engagement. As an unending circle, the

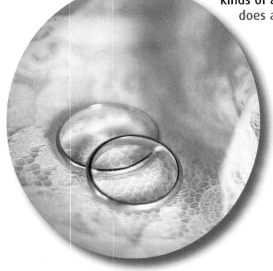

In ancient history a ring was used to seal many kinds of agreement between people. **What does a ring symbolize today?**

the ceremony on the wedding day. Today, photographs—including those of the couple together—are frequently taken before the wedding so everyone is free to enjoy the entire reception.

WEDDING CONCERNS

State and church laws dictate some aspects of a wedding. Except for the simplest of services, however, weddings require a great deal of planning to go smoothly. Deciding about arrangements can be complicated and time-consuming, yet such preparation is essential to a successful wedding.

Managing Expenses

Traditionally, the bride's family paid the costs of the ceremony and reception, and the groom's family paid for the rehearsal dinner the evening before. Today, expenses may be split more flexibly. The groom's family may contribute to the cost of the wedding. If a partner's parents are divorced, costs may be divided in nontraditional ways. With more couples postponing marriage until they are older, many can and want to pay part or all of their own expenses.

Usually, parents who are not paying toward the cost of the wedding are not involved in the planning. Out of courtesy, however, their ideas should be sought and considered.

At any income level, a wedding can strain the budget. Thoughtful couples keep plans and expectations realistic. They know

ring represents unity and timelessness. Gold is often chosen for wedding rings for its great value, strength, and enduring quality.

- Family members or close friends often give engagement parties, or showers, for the couple. The couple's friends and their parents' friends celebrate the engagement and upcoming wedding together. Typical gifts are items the couple will need to set up a household.

Couples can customize the wedding ceremony in other ways, within the limits of law and religion. Some choose a special location. Some express their commitment in a personal way by writing their own vows. In these cases, a couple should try to choose a place and words that will remain meaningful throughout their lives. Self-written vows should be checked with a religious or civil authority to make sure they are legally binding.

Many older customs are no longer followed. You may have heard that it's bad luck for partners to see each other before

The cost of any single item for a wedding may not seem like a problem. By the time you put all the expenses together, however, the total can be amazing. Why is a wedding budget useful?

much as possible. Some couples find themselves in the middle of conflicts between families or family members.

Planning can avert some problems. For instance, complications can arise involving divorced or remarried parents. Couples can avoid hurt feelings by thoughtfully wording announcements and invitations and carefully planning photograph and seating arrangements. The advice of a professional wedding planner and photographer can help. A couple can sometimes sidestep a conflict by explaining that "this is how the professionals handle things."

Good communication is also needed to minimize conflict. Those involved with the wedding should be kept informed, especially about any changes, to avoid unpleasant surprises. Family members who don't

that parents may be tempted to go "all out" to make their children's wedding a beautiful occasion. They don't pressure parents to give them an extravagant wedding that will take years to pay for.

Managing Conflicts

Holly recalled planning her wedding: "Dan and I joked that the only way to please everyone was to have three weddings. Since we could only have the one, we did what pleased the most people, starting with the bride and groom. After all, our parents *had* their weddings. This was our turn."

Many couples would echo Holly's words. They want to please their families, especially those members who are helping to pay for the ceremony. A wedding is meant to express the couple's tastes and values, however. They want to follow their own ideas as

Plans for a wedding typically begin very early, sometimes as much as a year ahead. The day is less stressful for everyone involved when each detail has been thought out in advance.

take part in the planning may especially appreciate being remembered with updates.

Couples hope that family members will put aside differences at times like this and show a cooperative spirit to help make the occasion the happy one that it should be. If relatives refuse to bend, however, the couple may have to be assertive. They must make decisions thoughtfully, explain them calmly, and then stand by them. The saying "You can't please everyone" is worth remembering.

At the same time, sensitivity and generosity can help make the event meaningful for everyone. When Noah and Elise were planning their wedding, Noah's mother mentioned that she had always hoped for a daughter to wear a special pendant that she had worn as a bride. However, she only had sons. Elise offered to wear the pendant, although she had planned on different jewelry. Elise knew this day was special for her future mother-in-law, too.

Keeping Perspective

Everyone wants a picture-perfect wedding. All the planning and rehearsals, however, can't prevent some unforeseen problems. By keeping a sense of humor and perspective, a couple can keep difficulties from becoming disasters. They can focus on what's really important: the love they feel for each other and the commitment they are making before family and friends. In years to come, the bride who trips walking down the aisle and the groom who passes out at the altar will have the most entertaining wedding stories in the family.

Most people look back on their wedding day as a high point in their lives. If they have selected the right partner and used the time during their engagement wisely, their wedding can be the beginning of a long and happy life together.

A happy wedding day is the bridge to a new life together. With effort from both husband and wife, the couple can make the years ahead happy, too.

Building Character

Commitment: A Quality That Counts

Do you think of commitment as a promise you have made or as dedication to a cause? Both imply integrity—being true to your word and to your values. A committed person acts on important beliefs, even at a cost. A teen could show commitment to:

- A strong family, by visiting with older relatives who drop in unexpectedly.
- A future family, by thinking about values and goals in order to choose a partner who shares them someday.
- An education, by reserving some time for study each night.
- Friends, by sticking by them when they make mistakes.
- The environment, by carpooling and recycling.

QUESTIONS

1. What are some good and poor reasons for refusing to make a commitment?
2. Can people expend resources on something they are not committed to? If so, how can you tell when this is the case?
3. Identify one thing that you are committed to. What specific actions could you take to strengthen your commitment?

SECTION 31-2 REVIEW

Check Your Understanding

1. What legal restrictions does society place on marriage?
2. What are the main reasons for writing a prenuptial agreement?
3. How might a couple personalize their wedding ceremony?
4. What is a wedding shower?
5. What conflicts do some couples face when planning a wedding?
6. **Thinking Critically.** With the strain of planning a wedding, what might a bride and groom do to be sure they aren't too tired to enjoy the celebration?
7. **Problem Solving.** Due to financial pressures, Austin and Emily have decided to have a small wedding. Austin's mother, however, keeps thinking of more people who should be invited. What should Austin and Emily do?

Chapter 31
Review and Activities

CHAPTER SUMMARY

- Partners can use the engagement period to prepare for marriage.
- By learning more about each other, a couple can make problems in marriage less likely.
- An engaged couple need to see themselves as a team.
- The engagement period gives the couple's family and friends time to accept and adjust to their upcoming marriage.
- Many couples seek counseling before marriage as further assurance that they are making the right decision.
- Wedding plans can be called off during the engagement period if a person has serious doubts.
- Weddings are important to society as well as to individuals.
- Marriage is a legal contract with certain rights and restrictions. A couple may make other contracts to cover personal concerns.
- Couples may choose from among types of wedding ceremonies and customs.

REVIEW QUESTIONS

Section 31-1
1. How should a couple spend their engagement period to help ensure a happy marriage?
2. How do couples develop and show a sense of teamwork?
3. How can an engagement period be particularly helpful to someone who has a child from a previous relationship?
4. If a couple discover differences during premarital counseling, should they call off the wedding? Why or why not?

Section 31-2
1. Why is a wedding valued in the eyes of society?
2. What requirements must be met for a marriage to become legally binding?
3. Why might a couple decide to have a prenuptial agreement?
4. What are the differences between civil and religious wedding ceremonies?
5. How can a couple successfully manage financial concerns and conflicting ideas when planning a wedding?

BECOMING A PROBLEM SOLVER

1. Katrina's mother is angry that Katrina has invited her father's new wife to her wedding. Her father says if his wife is not welcome, he won't attend. What should Katrina do?
2. Sierra gets along with everyone in Gabe's family except his father, who seems critical of everything she says and does. Gabe assures Sierra that his father's behavior will change as he gets to know and accept her. Sierra dreads visiting Gabe's family and usually has a headache afterward. What should Sierra do?

THINKING CRITICALLY

1. **Recognizing Alternatives.** How long do you think the engagement period should be? Why?
2. **Recognizing Assumptions.** The bride traditionally receives more attention than the groom in wedding preparations. Why do you think this is so? What change, if any, would you make in this custom?
3. **Predicting Results.** Do you think people treat each other differently before marriage than they do afterwards? How might a person guard against surprises?
4. **Recognizing Values.** Which do you think is better, a simple wedding or an elaborate one? Explain.

MAKING CURRICULUM CONNECTIONS

1. **Civics.** Research the marriage laws of your state. What requirements and restrictions govern marriage?
2. **Math.** Research possible reception costs, including catering, hiring a band, and renting a hall. Add up those costs also. Assume you invite a certain number of guests to the reception. What would be the average cost per guest?
3. **Language Arts.** Assume that you have just been married and are sending thank you notes for gifts. Write a note thanking someone for a particular gift. Share your thank you note with the class.

APPLYING YOUR KNOWLEDGE

1. Locate a bride or groom's checklist outlining a schedule for planning a wedding. Explain how using this checklist might make wedding planning easier.
2. Describe to the class any unusual wedding ceremonies that you have seen or heard about. Why do you think people choose such ceremonies? How, if at all, might they reflect a couple's view of their relationship and of marriage?

Family & Community Connections

1. Interview someone who does premarital counseling. Ask the person to identify the most important issue that couples must address in preparing for marriage. What issues commonly cause problems? How does the person help couples work through them?

2. Discuss ways in which technology has changed weddings and how they are planned. How can technology make wedding planning more convenient? How can it increase stress?

Building a Strong Marriage

WORDS FOR THOUGHT

"It takes two to make a marriage a success and only one to make it a failure."
(Herbert Samuel)

IN YOUR OWN WORDS

How can one person make a marriage fail?

Qualities of a Strong Marriage

OBJECTIVES

After studying this section, you should be able to:

- Distinguish characteristics of a strong marriage.
- Explain the pattern of marriage satisfaction.

TERMS TO LEARN

marriage commitment
U-shaped curve

If they've worked to build a strong relationship, an engaged couple have an edge in building a solid marriage. Their time together up to the wedding has been like "training camp" for a sports team. Marriage is the actual season.

Next comes the couple's chance to put into action all they've learned and practiced. This is where they show day-in, day-out dedication, their devotion to "the game." Marriage is when the work is hardest, the stakes are highest, and the rewards are greatest.

WHAT MAKES A MARRIAGE STRONG?

What is your idea of a "beautiful" painting? Is it a dramatic scene, depicted in brilliant colors and bold strokes? Is it a sparse, abstract image of simple lines and muted colors?

Just as everyone has different ideas about what makes a painting meaningful, each couple has a different idea of what makes a marriage satisfying. In a strong marriage, partners work with each other to fulfill what each wants from the marriage. Their way of interacting might be far different from another couple's, yet both couples may be equally happy in their marriage.

For Bill and Francine, their quiet conversation over a dinner of cold sandwiches is a moment of real closeness and sharing. In contrast, Jon and Margo feel the strength of their relationship most while joking and exchanging good-natured put-downs as they bustle about the kitchen making dinner.

Often it's the everyday situations that lead to problems in marriage. Suppose one person believes that cooking should be shared, but the other expects to be served. What may happen?

What is it that makes such different types of relationships rewarding ones? Certain traits underlie all strong, happy marriages, whatever their differences. A few of the most important ones are described in this section. All are necessary, but none comes without effort, even sacrifice. Couples who are willing to cultivate these qualities can look forward to—and someday, back on—a happy married life.

Realistic Expectations

When Erik and Beth were first married, Beth left the school where she taught by 4:00 p.m. so she could be home before Erik and fix dinner. Eventually, she returned to the typically long hours that teaching demands. Erik was troubled by this. He expected to find Beth at home when he arrived, and he felt she was putting her work ahead of him. Beth, meanwhile, didn't understand why Erik couldn't start dinner before she arrived, so her irritation grew.

Erik and Beth never spoke of their dissatisfaction. They both assumed that each would know what the other was thinking and feeling without being told. Neither partner had expected to be unhappy.

Like Beth and Erik, many people enter marriage with higher expectations than can be met. Each partner has ideas about how the other is supposed to be and act, about *what* should be done as well as *how* it should be done. When a partner, for whatever reasons, doesn't meet those expectations, the relationship feels its first strain. This is unfortunate because, in many ways, what you expect of a marriage is the single most important factor in whether yours is a happy one.

Couples who communicate and who know each other well before the wedding are more apt to have realistic expectations about what their life together will be like. They have asked questions and listened to responses. They are less likely to be disappointed as the excitement of a new marriage wears off and life settles into a routine. Their satisfaction with each other strengthens the relationship.

Commitment

When partners truly want and expect the relationship to last, they act to make this happen. They work together to overcome obstacles, and they take satisfaction in finding solutions. Such couples have a high level of **marriage commitment**, the desire to make a marriage work.

A strong commitment to marriage means that partners put each other first—before work, extended family members, and even their children. This firm commitment is one thing that helps hold a marriage together through stressful times and even through crises. It can help prevent some problems as well.

How will you know whether someone can make a commitment to marriage? You might look at how well the person does with other types of commitment. What would some of these be?

Sometimes a couple must make a deliberate decision to give their relationship highest priority, as Lynette's words show: "Our son Mitch has a learning disability, so I work with him every evening to help him keep up in school. Sometimes it's hard for me to remember that my first loyalty is to my husband. When Roy asks me to go for a walk, I try not to say, 'I can't. I have to help Mitch.' I realize Roy's love and support are important to me. Our time together keeps our marriage strong. It also helps me be relaxed and patient with Mitch."

Acceptance

Acceptance is part of dealing with any aspect of life. Partners in a strong marriage accept each other for who they are. They see that they both have strengths and weaknesses; both have attractive and unattractive points. They are tolerant of the differences between them, resisting the urge to show their partner the "right" way—their way—to act or think or feel. Over time, these differences may become endearing traits.

As you have read, married couples sometimes try to "improve" their parners. Some even enter the marriage with this idea, though this approach rarely works. People change only if *they* want to, not because some-

INFOLINK

I-Messages

To review I-messages and other communication skills, see *Section 6-2.*

one else tells them they should. Attempts to "redo" a spouse are often met with anger and disappointment. How would you feel if the person you loved and had married no longer found you "good enough"?

Certainly advice and constructive criticism can have a place in a marriage, especially if one person's behavior is damaging or dangerous. Loving partners, however, think of the other's feelings when expressing displeasure. They save criticism for issues that are serious enough to risk offending their spouse. They use I-messages that express personal feelings, rather than you-messages that might be perceived as an attack.

Flexibility

Flexibility regarding change is another part of building a strong bond. Neither you, nor your partner, nor the marriage itself will stay the same. Changes in jobs, values, and ways of living can threaten a couple's commitment over the years. Those who accept change and learn to make the most of the opportunities offered have a better chance of maintaining a strong relationship.

When Kyle and Della married, Della was just out of high school and waiting tables in a pizza restaurant. A few years later, Della became discontented with her job. She wanted to go back to school to study computer programming. Kyle became worried. Della didn't seem like the same person he had married. She hadn't cared about education before. He wondered how she would feel about him if she got a degree and went off to some corporation to work.

At first Kyle's attitude about Della's goal was firm. He was against the idea. As they discussed the plan, however, Della helped Kyle see the advantages as well as her need. His attitude changed, and in the months ahead he found ways to help Della reach her goal, and he became proud of her efforts. His flexibility helped strengthen their marriage.

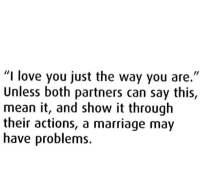

"I love you just the way you are." Unless both partners can say this, mean it, and show it through their actions, a marriage may have problems.

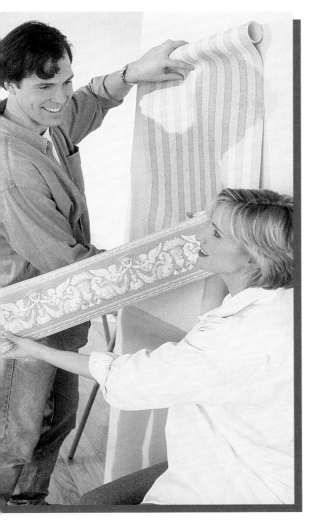

Decisions are an everyday part of married life—everything from deciding what to eat, to home decorating, to how to raise children. Why are decisions easier to make when people are flexible?

support your partner. Consider how these couples showed thoughtfulness:

- Brenda turned off the television show she was watching when Peter needed to talk about a problem.
- Colin slipped an encouraging note into Anne Marie's coat pocket on her first day at a new job.
- While Felice studied for a final exam, Alejandro occupied their young son by coloring pictures with him.

THE U-SHAPED SATISFACTION CURVE

Many newlywed couples believe that the excitement and intimacy of their engagement and wedding will last indefinitely. Very few marriages maintain that level of happiness, leaving people disappointed.

Many family scientists have studied happiness and satisfaction in marriage. Looking at marriage over the years, they identified a pattern called the U-shaped curve. A **U-shaped curve** describes something that starts at a high level, drops as time progresses, and then rises again, forming the letter "U."

During the first years of marriage, a couple establish their daily pattern of living—in activities, making decisions, and adjusting to each other's needs, habits, and

Thoughtfulness

A dating or engaged couple typically work hard to please each other. They buy small gifts or do unexpected favors. These gestures of caring may gradually decrease after the couple marry, yet such acts of thoughtfulness are continually needed to build and maintain a strong marriage.

Thoughtfulness, of course, is more than just giving things. It involves showing empathy and concern when your partner has a problem. It means making an extra effort to

Building Character

Supportiveness: A Quality That Counts

Think of all the types of support you've seen: walls support a roof; parents support a toddling child; citizens support a candidate. When you give support, you help hold a person up, keep someone moving forward, or help someone reach a goal. Support can be a word of praise or sympathy or help with a difficult task. Married couples show support when:

- Each listens uncritically as the other describes a difficult day at work.
- One encourages the other to apply for a higher position at work.
- They both follow a healthful diet when one wants to lose weight.
- One calls from work to ask how the other is feeling after the death of a grandfather.

QUESTIONS

1. How do people feel when they give and receive support?
2. How can giving support sometimes mean taking risks?
3. Give specific examples of how giving and receiving support are part of your life.

---

personalities. They tend to enjoy a high level of satisfaction. Because many people "put their best foot forward" during dating and engagement, there may be some surprises during this time. In general, however, the newly formed union is a happy one.

Typically, marital satisfaction begins to decline with the birth of the couple's first child. When such resources as time and money are stretched, the parents usually participate in fewer activities together. The demands of parenthood can interfere with the closeness they previously enjoyed. However, the stress of parenting doesn't cause a drop in overall life satisfaction. The joys gained from raising children may more than offset the drop in marital happiness.

Marital satisfaction "bottoms out" when children are school age. The two lowest points tend to come as children enter school and when they are teens.

When children start to leave home and resources become more plentiful, marital satisfaction begins to rise again. It continues to increase into middle age, equaling or surpassing the satisfaction that is felt by newlyweds.

Understanding the pattern to marital happiness enables a couple to cope better with its decline. They realize that the marriage is not in a downward spiral. Relying on the qualities of a strong relationship, they can work to minimize the decline and look forward to the better times that lie ahead.

The things that make a marriage satisfying may not be quite the same for all couples. What do you think every couple might need in order to be happy over the years?

SECTION 32-1 REVIEW

Check Your Understanding

1. In what ways are all strong marriages alike?
2. What is marriage commitment?
3. How do thoughtful partners handle giving criticism?
4. Is gift giving the best way to show thoughtfulness in a marriage? Why or why not?
5. Describe the U-shaped curve of marriage satisfaction.
6. **Thinking Critically.** Often the problems that come between a couple have built slowly, and sometimes been barely noticed, for many months and years. How can this be prevented?
7. **Problem Solving.** Abigail told Harlan that she feels taken for granted now that they are married. "You hardly compliment me any more, or say thanks for the special things I do for you, or bring me little gifts like you used to." Harlan replied, "Be realistic. No one can do those things forever." What should Abigail do?

Skills and Resources in Marriage

OBJECTIVES

After studying this section, you should be able to:

- Explain how certain relationship skills contribute to a strong marriage.
- Recommend resources that can help keep a marriage strong.

TERMS TO LEARN

intimacy
estranged
mutual

A new car rolls off the assembly line in fine working order, but it doesn't stay that way by itself. The motor oil gets dirty and the battery runs low. An owner who changes the oil and buys a new battery is rewarded with many miles of safe motoring.

Marriages also need maintenance. Couples need certain skills and resources to keep the relationship running smoothly. The more they refine these skills and use these resources, the more rewarding is their journey together.

SKILLS FOR MARRIAGE

In Units Two and Three, you read about skills for strengthening relationships. The building blocks of good relationships—communicating, resolving conflicts, managing resources, and making decisions—

also form the basis of a strong marriage. At its best, marriage is a lifelong relationship that uses all of these skills.

Communicating

The ability to communicate well is vital in marriage. It makes every other skill possible. A practical reminder to stop at the store communicates a message, but a marriage needs more. People must feel free to say what they think and how they want things to be. They must be willing to listen in return. They must be able to make mistakes and explain their worries without fear of judgment or ridicule. Communication allows partners to build each other up through praise and affirmation.

Ideally, communication in marriage occurs in an atmosphere of complete trust. Partners know that private discussions will be kept private and that information won't be used to hurt each other or anyone else. To do so would be a betrayal—a violation of trust—and damaging to the relationship.

The demands of children, work, and household tasks constantly challenge communication in marriage. Good communication habits can be lost. Couples may need to set aside specific times to talk, perhaps in the morning or at night when children, neighbors, and television are not distractions. Making this effort shows their commitment to keeping the marriage strong.

Resolving Conflicts

Skillful communication is perhaps most useful when resolving conflicts. Positive conflict resolution is one pillar of a strong marriage.

Every couple knows conflict, but not every one deals with it well. Some people believe that truly happy couples never disagree and that any conflict is a sign of a troubled marriage. As a result, they avoid disagreement of any kind. Do you think this strengthens their marriage?

At the opposite end are couples whose every disagreement erupts into conflict. You'll recall that excessive arguing is a warning sign in a relationship, signaling basic incompatibility as well as deeper problems.

A healthy relationship avoids both extremes. Couples deal with disputes as they arise. They decide whether a difference is worth pursuing. They try to be sensitive to

When people tune each other out, communication isn't possible. How can you tell when someone really needs to be heard?

each other. They use reason, compromise, and other conflict-resolution skills to come to a decision that satisfies both.

As in any relationship, resolving conflict in marriage should be a balance of give-and-take. When one partner does most of the giving while the other mostly receives, the marriage is rarely happy. "Keeping score," giving only as much as you feel you get, isn't a loving approach either.

Sharing Intimacy

Talking about problems you wouldn't share with anyone else, listening to a favorite song together, going for long walks, holding hands and saying nothing—all of these express intimacy. **Intimacy** is closeness that develops from a personal relationship. It's part of a healthy marriage.

Intimacy may be expressed through sexual activity, but many other ways are just as valuable. A warm and loving conversation that shares deep feelings shows intimacy. A touch, hug, or look that says "I care" is an intimate moment. Daily intimacies such as these are like a spring that waters a garden, keeping it fresh, healthy, and vital.

The Need for Intimacy

Partners may not have the same need for intimacy. Someone who wants to share every personal feeling can overwhelm a more reserved spouse. This isn't a fault in a marriage, but couples do need to talk about their needs and find a level of intimacy that satisfies them both. A person may need to give a partner some space at times, while the spouse can learn ways to express feelings. Such is the give-and-take of the marital relationship.

Communication Counts

Does anything guarantee a successful marriage? Good communication may top the list.

Listen instead of tuning out. Eliminating distractions helps.

Make time to talk, so that you grow closer.

Hold back on judgments. Criticism and ridicule are destructive.

When intimacy is shown in many small ways within a marriage, sexual intimacy follows more easily. Partners feel an emotional closeness that makes sexual expression meaningful. When sex is linked to intimacy in this way, and not to physical pleasure alone, sexual attraction can last the lifetime of the marriage.

Intimate expression in a marriage can break down for many reasons. One person may lose trust or a sense of commitment to the marriage. Another person might let day-to-day life interfere with closeness. Sometimes people simply forget that others need to be shown or told that they are loved.

When partners stop making an effort to be close, whatever the reason, they begin to feel **estranged**, or alienated. Expressions of intimacy decrease. Sexual relations can be strained.

As you can see, what couples think and feel affects how they act, and how they act affects their thoughts and feelings. Emotional support leads to intimacy, yet intimacy provides emotional support. The wise couple know how this cycle works, and make it work for them.

As the years go by, do you think these communication suggestions become easier or more difficult? Why?

Voice appreciation and love. People need to hear such expressions.

Choose kind words. Say "Thanks for dinner" instead of "You never fix anything I like."

Show trust. Private discussions are just between the two of you.

The amount of touching people need isn't the same for everyone. What could happen if one person wants to hold hands or hug and cuddle more than the other does?

Sharing Decisions

As partners in marriage, two people have many major decisions to make together—where to live, whether to have children, and more. By sharing decisions, partners work toward the same goals in their marriage. Discussing and comparing options lets them choose the one that seems best for both of them. Decisions that are **mutual** (MYOO-choo-al), or agreed to by both partners, are more apt to be carried out by both husband and wife.

Different couples have different decision-making styles. Some make all major decisions together. Others divide decision making between husband and wife. When convenient, styles may be combined. Because Colette buys most of the family's clothes, she decides how much to spend. When the family needed a new car, however, Colette and Patrick together chose the model to buy.

In making decisions for themselves and their family, a couple strive for the fairest outcome possible. This doesn't mean that both partners must feel equally satisfied with every decision. Individual decisions are often more favorable to one person than to the other. On the whole, however, each partner should feel that the sacrifices and benefits even out.

Common Values

A couple who recognize their commonly held values have an advantage in making decisions. Knowing that your spouse cares about the same things you do helps you

Deciding who will do what can be confusing for a couple. For example, when both parents are employed, who takes care of a sick child? Why does planning ahead help?

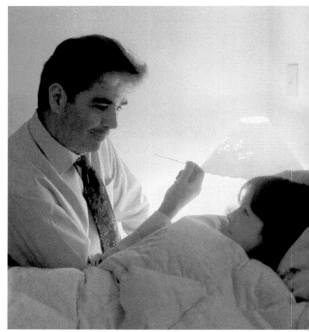

identify options that will be agreeable to you both. Recognizing shared values is especially important if one partner is entrusted with deciding a matter that also affects the other partner.

Managing Resources

As in many marriages, money was a resource in short supply for Darren and Anya. Finding enough money for the things they wanted was a challenge. Fortunately, the couple were skilled at managing the resources they did have.

Darren, a talented carpenter, repaired second-hand items they bought at garage sales. Anya used her organizing ability to clip and use money-saving coupons on groceries. For entertainment, they took advantage of free community programs. As they worked together toward their common goal, the couple developed a sense of unity and togetherness. Rather than let a lack of resources strain their marriage, they forged closer bonds through shared sacrifice.

Family Finances

Conflicts over money are a leading cause of marital breakup. To manage this resource while avoiding arguments, a couple can:

- **Talk about money.** Before marriage, discuss spending habits and attitudes about money. Will two incomes be pooled? Will each partner have some money for personal use? After marriage, talk about your financial state. Is one partner spending too much? Can you afford to "splurge" on something or to make a major purchase?
- **Make a financial plan and stick to it.** Decide how much money is available for family expenses, and how much—if

Few issues cause more disagreements in families than money matters. By working together toward compromise and agreement, a couple can minimize such problems.

any—will be kept for individual use. Make sure both partners feel the plan is fair. Include the value of unpaid work.
- **Establish priorities.** Distinguish between needs and wants. Compromise about what is essential and what is a luxury. Decide on financial goals as well.
- **Assign financial responsibility to the one who handles it better.** This could mean that one person makes all the financial decisions. It could mean division of money management responsibilities. For example, one person might keep track of the budget, while the other pays the bills.
- **Always save something.** Even a small amount set aside regularly adds up. More important, it gives a feeling of security and allows the couple to work toward shared goals.

Spending Time Together

To married people, time can be a more valuable resource than money. You can build a strong relationship without spending much money on each other, but you must spend time with each other. Doing activities together, whether work or play, expresses love and builds closeness.

As with communication, family and household needs can interfere with time spent together. Many couples turn work into pleasant, shared experiences.

Sam and Rebecca, for example, spent part of a Saturday afternoon raking leaves together. A job that would have taken three hours for one person took half the time, leaving them with enough time to fix a pizza together for dinner. The jokes and conversation they shared while working made the afternoon pass quickly and brought them closer together.

Of course, a marriage must also allow room for individuality. Clinging to a partner can be a sign of jealousy and insecurity. Happy, satisfied couples know they can spend time apart without threatening their relationship. They appreciate a partner's interests, even if not shared.

RESOURCES FOR MARRIED COUPLES

For building a strong marriage, a couple's first resource is themselves. To reach some goals, however, they need help from others. To manage their lives and maintain a rewarding relationship, couples can turn to a number of outside resources.

Family and Friends

Like everyone, married couples can benefit from the help of families. Parents can

Tips & TECHNIQUES

Blending Lives. If you think about it, your life is full of things to do and people to see. Try listing all the activities that make up your schedule, including: school and work obligations; time spent with friends and family; volunteer work; regular hobbies and events; and important holiday and family celebrations.

Now imagine that you're married, and your spouse's schedule must mesh with yours. You can't be in two places at the same time, so you make choices. Which in-laws do you visit on the holiday? Whose friends do you invite over? Couples make decisions like these by communicating, managing time effectively, and solving problems creatively. Above all, they remember the advice that applies to thoughtful partners as well as careful drivers: right of way is something you give, not take.

Try It Out. In a small group, each of you write down five activities that couples might have on separate slips of paper. Fold slips and mix them. Take turns pulling out and reading two slips aloud. Have all group members suggest ways partners might respond if those activities conflicted in a couple's schedule.

Most every partner comes with family and friends. How will they be included in the couple's life? Agreement will make a big difference in their happiness.

give advice based on their own years of experience. Siblings may be eager to help with child care. Extended family members may be willing to provide financial assistance. These acts of support can benefit both the couple and their families.

At the same time, ties with family members and between the couple can be strained if partners routinely turn to family for help. Marriage means accepting the responsibility of building a life with a partner, which includes dealing with problems. Working out problems on their own, a couple develop the teamwork needed for a strong marriage.

As a newlywed couple focus on each other and on establishing their relationship, friendships often become less important. Most partners soon rediscover the value of good friends, however. Spouses usually can't meet all of their mate's emotional needs.

Marriage Enrichment

A variety of programs to strengthen marriage are available to couples. Their purpose is not to "fix" broken marriages but to make average or good ones better.

Many marriage enrichment programs are sponsored by religious groups. Others may be offered by colleges or mental health centers. They may be a series of sessions held over several weeks or intensive, full-day,

weekend "retreats." Topics covered include improving communication, solving conflict, and developing intimacy.

Marriage Counseling

As the latest divorce statistics attest, a marital relationship can run into trouble. A couple may lose their closeness or be worn down by a conflict that resists resolution. Their frustration at not knowing how to improve the relationship can threaten their commitment. These couples often save their marriage through counseling.

By acting as a "referee" and advisor during sessions, a marriage counselor helps couples learn to solve their own problems. Since most problems involve a breakdown of communication, this is often where counselors begin. Couples may also need help in understanding and overcoming anger, resentment, and guilt.

Alice King: *Family Counselor*

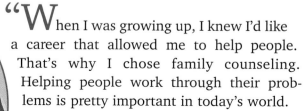

"When I was growing up, I knew I'd like a career that allowed me to help people. That's why I chose family counseling. Helping people work through their problems is pretty important in today's world.

"I usually meet with clients for several one-hour sessions. The particular problem, the client's commitment, and the insurance company's willingness to cover costs determine how many sessions we have. When working with couples, I may see them individually or together. I have to be a good listener and have a good memory since I conduct as many as thirty sessions each week. Keeping extensive notes helps."

"In counseling people, I've learned to accept and understand their emotions. People get into difficulty when they try to control their feelings instead of their actions. Some successes are obvious, as when a runaway child moves back home or a couple learn to talk more openly.

"I try to give a fresh, objective point of view. We all seem to see other people's problems more clearly than our own. Admitting there's a problem, getting help, and taking responsibility for working things out are bold steps. I'm always encouraged when a couple or a family take these steps. It's sad to realize that so many people never even try."

CAREER PROFILE

Education and training: usually a master's or doctorate degree

Starting salary range: $20-25,000 in hospitals and governmental agencies; about $5-10,000 less in some private agencies

Important qualities: concern and empathy for others; the ability to objectively look at a situation; good listening skills

Plan Ahead

If you think you might like this type of work, ask your school counselor about taking an aptitude test. You can verify whether you fit the characteristics needed for someone who works closely with people who have problems.

Due to a lack of state regulation, some so-called "marriage counselors" are not competent. Finding a skilled counselor can take some effort. Local family service and health care agencies may be able to locate a qualified professional. Sometimes these groups provide counseling at a low cost. Many clergy members have training or experience in counseling couples.

Marriage counseling works best when both partners want to improve their relationship and are willing to work at it.

BUILT TO LAST

A well-built marriage is like a well-built home. The marriage offers warmth, security, and protection to individuals and promotes stability in society. It is founded on a firm commitment that doesn't shift over time. Practicing the skills that built a couple's relationship, from dating to engagement to marriage, will keep it standing for a lifetime.

Closeness builds when couples share serious moments as well as silly ones. A good balance between work and play is worth aiming for.

SECTION 32-2 REVIEW

Check Your Understanding

1. Why can communicating well in a marriage be a challenge?
2. How can intimacy be a problem for married couples?
3. What does fairness mean in decision making?
4. Give some tips to help couples manage their money.
5. What resources can couples use to maintain their relationship?
6. When is marriage counseling most successful?
7. **Thinking Critically.** When one partner in a troubled marriage refuses counseling, experts urge the other partner to seek help alone. What are some advantages and drawbacks to this approach?
8. **Problem Solving.** In an effort to save money, Bart and Rose have worked out a budget. However, Rose often buys little gifts for Bart that cost enough to put the couple over the agreed-upon spending limit. Rose says, "I can't help it. When I see something I know you'd like, I want you to have it." What should they do?

Chapter 32
Review and Activities

CHAPTER SUMMARY

- Having realistic expectations about a spouse or married life can help prevent disappointment.
- People need to be committed to marriage.
- Partners in a strong marriage accept each other as they are.
- Flexibility allows people to adapt to new situations in a marriage.
- Marital satisfaction tends to vary predictably over the years.
- Communication, thoughtfulness, and expressions of intimacy help build closeness between marriage partners.
- As in any relationship, conflicts occur and must be resolved for a marriage to stay strong.
- Managing resources and making decisions together can give a married couple a shared sense of sacrifice and purpose in their marriage.
- Resources are available to help couples improve their marriage or solve problems within it.

REVIEW QUESTIONS

Section 32-1
1. How can expectations cause problems as a couple adjust to marriage? What is a solution to this problem?
2. What does having a commitment to marriage mean?
3. How does trying to change a partner affect marital strength?
4. How can flexibility be helpful in a marriage?
5. How can knowledge of the marriage satisfaction curve be helpful to couples?

Section 32-2
1. Why is communication so important to a marriage?
2. Is intimacy the same thing as sexual activity? Explain your answer.
3. How can sharing decisions bring couples closer?
4. What are the similarities and differences between marriage enrichment and marriage counseling?

BECOMING A PROBLEM SOLVER

1. After their two children were born, Maria became a full-time homemaker. Ben supported the family on his salary, working overtime as much as possible. Six years and three children later, the couple have little time or energy for each other. Worse yet, they are starting to feel that they have little in common. What should Ben and Maria do?

2. Greg and Ann are good friends with another couple. When the four are together, Ann discusses any trouble or argument she and Greg have had. Greg says he doesn't want others to know their business. Ann says that sharing problems makes her feel better and may bring a solution. This difference is becoming a problem. What should they do?

THINKING CRITICALLY

1. **Drawing Conclusions.** According to the chapter, is it true that "little things mean a lot" in a successful marriage? Why?
2. **Recognizing Alternatives.** What are some ways a couple can combat the routine of married life in order to remain close?
3. **Making Generalizations.** What amount of time do you think is reasonable for each marriage partner to spend on personal hobbies and activities at home and away?

MAKING CURRICULUM CONNECTIONS

1. **Social Studies.** Analyze images of married life among movie stars or famous athletes. Do you find these images favorable or unfavorable? Based on these portrayals alone, what recommendations would you have concerning marriage?
2. **Literature.** Ideas of what makes a strong marriage have changed greatly over time, as reflected in the literature of different ages. Choose a novel, short story, or play that features a marital relationship. Is the marriage strong or weak? What actions or details does the author show to convey this? How might this description of and attitude toward marriage be representative of that era? Share your ideas in a short report to the class.

APPLYING YOUR KNOWLEDGE

1. Debate this statement: Since "actions speak louder than words," a marriage partner should not have to be told that he or she is loved.
2. Working with a classmate, make a list of ways that marriage partners can show thoughtfulness toward each other. Compare your list with others.
3. Discuss this question with several classmates: What are advantages and disadvantages of having children later in a marriage?
4. Without giving names, describe a successful marriage familiar to you. Identify what makes the marriage a good one. How are these qualities expressed?

Family & Community Connections

1. Identify three community activities that a couple might attend or take part in. Explain how these activities could contribute to a strong marriage.

2. Use a newspaper to look up the number of divorces granted compared to the number of marriage licenses issued. What conclusions can you draw from comparing these figures?

Examining Parenting

OBJECTIVES

After studying this section, you should be able to:

- Evaluate reasons for and against having children.
- Compare challenges and rewards of parenthood.
- Explain the options available to infertile couples.
- Give reasons why people choose adoption.
- Compare advantages and disadvantages of adoption procedures.

TERMS TO LEARN

parenting
genetic diseases
infertility
fertility
adoption
closed adoption
open adoption

Imagine you decide that you want to be a truck driver. Driving a truck looks exciting. Besides, can it be much different from driving a car? You hop into the cab of a tractor-trailer, staring at the array of switches and gauges. You turn the ignition. The dashboard lights up and the cab vibrates as the motor rumbles powerfully. You frown uncertainly as your hand wavers over what looks like a gearshift. What will the outcome be? You can probably think of some unpleasant possibilities.

Every day in the real world, countless people put themselves in the driver's seat of a family by becoming parents—without training. Raising a child looks exciting and not that difficult. This approach to parenting can also produce some painful results.

CHOOSING PARENTHOOD

For some people, parenthood just happens. They don't ask themselves whether having a child is the right thing to do, nor do they prepare themselves for the responsibilities.

Having a child isn't something you can walk away from—emotionally, legally, or morally. You can quit a job or end a friendship. Parenthood, however, can't be undone. It has a long-lasting impact on parents—and children. People who are not prepared to love and care for a child properly may make more mistakes. Whatever goes wrong, the child also pays a price, perhaps for a lifetime.

When a couple choose to have a child, they're usually better prepared to give the necessary love and care. **Why do some people mistakenly *think* they are ready?**

the role. Children born to parents who are ready and know how to raise them stand a better chance at becoming happy, productive individuals.

Pressures to Have Children

In many ways society promotes the idea of having children—and with good cause. A society can't continue without future generations. Society's approval of parenthood shows in everything from income tax deductions for children to half-price meals for children at restaurants.

Children, too, learn the expectation of parenthood as they grow up. Small children practice parenting by playing "house." Adults tell children, "When you have kids of your own…" Such comments imply that parenthood is automatic.

Among married couples, pressure to become parents may be more personal. The couple's parents often look forward to grandchildren and may hint, sometimes strongly, that they're eager to become grandparents.

Peer pressure can also be strong in encouraging a couple to start a family. As friends have children and talk of the fulfillment of parenting, a childless couple can feel left behind, out of step, or selfish.

People need to be aware of all the pressures to bear children, whether obvious and convincing or otherwise. They need to realize that children should be born because parents honestly want them and are willing to make a commitment to their up-

The high pregnancy rate among teens is evidence that parenthood is taken too lightly. However, anyone who has children without forethought risks the same difficult outcomes.

There is a better way to look at parenthood. People need to view **parenting**, the process of caring for children and helping them grow and learn, as a choice. Then they can make thoughtful decisions about whether, when, and how to parent. They can find and use the parenting information they need.

Consciously choosing parenthood in this way is a gift you give yourself and your child. As with any goal, you are more apt to succeed as a parent when you've chosen

bringing. Having a child for any other reason is a shaky start to parenting. Children are a source of joy and fulfillment to many people, but rarely to those who want them for the wrong reasons.

Pressures to Remain Childless

Because of the widespread opinion that people should have children, most pressure to remain childless comes from the couple themselves. About ten percent of people of childbearing age choose not to have children. They make this choice for reasons like these:

- Some couples take a global view of the issue. They believe the world already has too many people competing for limited resources. They may worry about bringing a child into a world troubled by international conflict and environmental problems. Those who have such broad concerns tend to have few, if any, children.

- Some people simply don't enjoy children. Megan, for example, grew up in a big family. Years of caring for siblings taught her that parenting wasn't for her. Her mother warned that she would be lonely in her old age, but Megan said, "Children aren't insurance policies. You don't have them now to benefit from them later. Besides, suppose my child wants to travel or settle in a different part of the country?"

- Some people have values and goals that conflict with parenting. People with career ambitions may decide that children would interfere with their professional success. Many people enjoy travel and activities that are difficult to do with children.

- Some people avoid having children because of diseases that run in the family. Such **genetic diseases** are passed from parent to child, although not every child may be affected. Genetic diseases include diabetes, hemophilia, sickle cell anemia, cystic fibrosis, and Tay-Sachs disease. Through genetic testing or counseling, couples with a family history of such a disease can learn their chances of passing it to a child.

The image of a happy, settled family with children can make people want that for themselves. Why might having a child too soon actually prevent people from reaching such a goal?

Thoughtful Decision Making

In the past, married couples were expected to have children unless they were physically unable to do so. Today, modern methods of planning births allow choices about if and when to have children. This ability to choose carries the responsibility to choose wisely.

As in all decision making, the best choices come when all the options and consequences are thoughtfully weighed. You need to recognize the values, circumstances, and pressures that influence your choice about whether to have a child. Sorting through all the facts and reasons can help you make decisions about parenting that are right for you.

Life without children can be a choice today, just as choosing to have them is. Do you think a teen can know for sure that he or she will never want to have children?

Only you can decide whether you want to parent. Your choice, however, has broad implications for your future and that of your children. Making the right choice now helps ensure a happy, satisfying life for yourself and for any children you might have.

INFOLINK

Meeting Children's Needs

For more information on meeting children's needs, see *Section 34-1*.

CHALLENGES OF PARENTING

As with any job, you need a job description to think intelligently about parenting. Raising healthy, well-adjusted children takes certain skills, plus lots of time, energy, patience, and understanding. Parents must supply *all* of a child's needs. They are responsible for making sure a child is safe, loved, educated, socially adjusted, and guided. Handling these duties well can challenge even the most dedicated and loving parent.

Financial Responsibilities

Raising a child is expensive. Conservative estimates set the cost of raising a child at two and one-half to three times the family's yearly income at the time the child is born.

Where does the money go? Food and clothing are two regular expenses that grow as the children do, and children grow rapidly. Costs for medical care, child care, education, and recreation cannot be overlooked either. Having a child may mean that a family needs a larger home, bringing higher utility bills and rent or mortgage payments. To

Building Character

Thinking Realistically: A Quality That Counts

"Be realistic." That advice has saved people from many a foolish action. Has it also discouraged people from achieving a dream? Having a realistic outlook means seeing life as it is—not as you'd like it to be nor as you fear it might be. When you're realistic, you base decisions on facts and make the facts work for you. A teen shows a realistic attitude when:

• Observing that babies are lovable but that caring for them takes work.
• Practicing patience now in order to be a better parent someday.
• Talking to a counselor about the education needed for a desired career.
• Saving money for unexpected expenses.
• Letting self-critical thoughts go after simple mistakes.

QUESTIONS

1. How can having a realistic attitude help prevent problems in life?
2. Which do you think is the greater danger when trying to be realistic: being too positive or too negative? Explain your answer.
3. Do you think you view life realistically or not? Give some examples to support your answer.

---

cover these costs, a couple may have to lower their standard of living—going out less, buying fewer and less expensive clothes, and finding inexpensive leisure activities.

Personal Costs

As substantial as the financial costs are, the personal costs of having children can be even greater. These include the time and energy it takes to provide all the care that babies and children need, as well as the personal sacrifices involved.

Women tend to take on more parenting duties than men do. They are more likely to give up or modify career goals. Sharing parenting roles helps spread the personal costs of raising children more evenly between fathers and mothers.

The combined drain on parents' time, energy, and finances often leads to feelings of lost freedom. Parents may notice they have less time and energy left for themselves and each other. As Traci said, "Whenever Wayne and I think about going someplace, we have to decide whether we can take the baby. Is getting everything ready to go worth the effort? If we pay for a babysitter, can we still afford to go out? It's never just a matter of getting up and going. Nothing is that simple anymore."

Often a fascination with babies inspires pregnancy. What people sometimes forget is that a baby very quickly becomes a child, and children come with long-term challenges and responsibilities.

REWARDS OF PARENTING

For many parents, of course, the rewards of having children make all the challenges worthwhile. To some couples, a family is not complete without a child to share in their love and affection.

Another reward of parenthood is the stimulation children provide. Playing with a child can be great fun, for both parent and child. Seeing the world through a child's eyes—whether

a tiny, scurrying insect or a bolt of lightning in the sky—can be a learning experience as well. Parents may find a renewed appreciation for all the wonders of the world and of life itself.

Parenthood can also bring a sense of fulfillment. Parents can take pride in caring for the needs of their children and watching them grow. Those who know the satisfaction of helping a child develop into a happy, well-adjusted, responsible adult often consider it to be a success equaled by no other.

Helping a child develop can bring joy and fulfillment to a parent's life. What interests would you possibly share with a child someday?

CHOICES AND INFERTILITY

Infertility, or the inability to have children, affects about one in five married couples. A couple is said to be infertile if pregnancy doesn't occur after a year of intercourse without using birth control.

Fertility, the ability to have children, peaks in a person's twenties. Thus, infertility is most common among couples in their thirties and forties.

Some couples who have fertility problems still have choices about whether to have a child. About half of these couples can have children with medical help. Complete medical histories and a series of special tests can reveal the exact reason for the couple's inability to conceive. Once the source of the problem is found, treatments can be started. Certain procedures are morally unacceptable to some couples, however.

Some couples who choose medical treatment find it a test of their commitment to having a child. They are asked to share details of the most private part of their life together with a number of medical professionals. Several years and several thousand dollars worth of treatments may yield no birth, one birth, or multiple births. A couple must be willing to take such risks and live with the results.

Adopted children are truly "chosen." The parental love and pride is no less than what a biological parent feels. When birth parents want to reclaim a child, what do you think the law should say?

CHOOSING ADOPTION

Adoption is the legal process of taking a child of other parents as one's own. The parents and child are bound in every legal way until the child reaches age eighteen. Birth parents give up all rights and duties of parenthood.

People adopt for many reasons. Infertile couples may not have success with medical treatment or may be opposed to its use. Some adoptive parents fear passing on serious genetic diseases to biological offspring.

Sometimes people who can safely have children of their own prefer to adopt. They may be concerned with overpopulation or want to help a child who might otherwise not have a home. Such couples often adopt children considered "hard to place"—those who are older or have health problems or disabilities. Some single people who strongly wish to parent also choose adoption.

Open and Closed Adoptions

The issue of identity is a sensitive one in adoptions. Birth and adoptive parents who believe in privacy choose **closed adoption**, where identities are not revealed. Closing adoption records, however, can make it difficult to obtain vital personal and medical information. In addition, the uncertainty can create anxiety. Adopted children with few facts about their birth parents may be bothered later by questions. Birth parents worry whether the child is happy, healthy, and loved.

Open adoption, in which identities are known, is becoming more popular. In open adoption, personal information may be contained in files. The birth mother and adoptive parents may meet and remain in contact over time. Open adoption removes some of the doubt and uncertainty. It can provide the child with a sense of continuity and identity. However, involving several parents in raising a child can cause problems and confusion.

USING YOUR KNOWLEDGE

Michael and Juanita adopted their son in a closed adoption due to the birth mother's wishes. Jared, now ten years old, is asking questions about his birth parents and background. The couple feel threatened and worried about violating the birth mother's privacy. What should they do?

Adopting an Infant

Many couples adopt infants in order to enjoy the experience of raising a child almost from birth. The supply of infants available for adoption, however, cannot meet the demand. The wait for a healthy infant or toddler averages five years and can stretch as long as ten years.

Some couples who are determined to have a baby turn to international adoption. They give a home to an orphaned or abandoned child from another country. International adoptions are very expensive. They require patience and perseverance. Many risks are associated with this type of adoption.

Adopting an Older Child

Because the demand is higher for infants and toddlers, the wait to adopt an older child is usually shorter. The adoptive parents, however, must be prepared for special challenges. An older child may have emotional scars from losing birth parents or from lack of a stable, loving home life. A child who has a disability may require added patience, new skills, and other adjustments for the couple.

For parents who see both the limitations and the possibilities, however, raising a "hard to place" child can be a great joy. LaJean recalled when she and her husband Abe adopted four-year-old Craig: "He reminded me of a stray puppy. Craig was malnourished and he'd been abused. He'd scream and thrash around if you tried to hold him. It took a year, but gradually Craig started to smile and trust people again. To see him learn to love and be loved gave us the greatest feeling in the world."

Whether through birth or adoption, children are a cherished addition to a family.

Arranging Adoptions

About three-fourths of all adoptions take place through public, state-approved agencies. These agencies are concerned with serving the child, the birth parents, and the adoptive parents.

Placing a child for adoption is usually a difficult decision, but a loving one, for the birth parents. These parents, often teens, realize that they cannot provide the kind of home and upbringing a child needs. They want their child to have a better chance at a healthy, happy life than they can offer. Adoption agencies help with this decision by counseling birth parents to make sure they understand all their options. Medical records and other information about them and the child are collected for the adoptive parents.

Meanwhile, prospective parents are screened and counseled to confirm that they are ready and able to care for a child.

Once parents are approved, the agency tries to match them with a suitable child. That child is given to the parents for a trial period. At the end of this time, if both the parents and agency are satisfied that the match is successful, a court awards permanent custody.

Private Adoptions

Adoptions can also take place privately. Clergy, doctors, and lawyers arrange these adoptions, often more quickly than a public agency can. The adopting couple typically pays the medical, hospital, and legal fees, and in some cases, the birth mother's living expenses. "Buying" the child is illegal.

Private adoption carries certain risks. Steve and Becky's physician arranged their adoption of baby Rachel. When Rachel was

Raising a child has many rewards for those who are ready. A close bond between parent and child builds when people wait until the time is right.

six months old, the couple learned that her birth father was seeking custody. The father had never given written consent, but Becky and Steve hadn't realized this was significant.

Without consent from both parents when a baby is adopted, the adoption decree isn't final. Although Steve and Becky were the only family Rachel had ever known, her birth father's rights took precedence over theirs. In their joy at becoming parents, they hadn't obtained legal advice to protect their interests. Rachel's father had.

However a person becomes a parent—whether "naturally," with medical aid, or by adoption—the basic truth of parenting is the same. Raising a child involves risks and rewards, sacrifice and satisfaction. Are the pleasures worth the challenges? For those who see the reality of parenting and who love children enough to choose it, the answer is a definite *yes*.

SECTION 33-1 REVIEW

Check Your Understanding

1. What is the difference between parenthood and parenting?
2. Describe some pressures to have children.
3. What financial costs are associated with having children?
4. What are some of the rewards of parenting?
5. What options are available to an infertile couple who wish to become parents?
6. How do adoption agencies help ensure the success of their matches?
7. **Thinking Critically.** Are parents who go through a lengthy adoption process or expensive medical treatments to have a child apt to be better parents? Explain.
8. **Problem Solving.** Amber and William have learned that Amber is unable to have children without lengthy, expensive medical treatments. Amber is willing to try this course in order to have a child of her own. William thinks they should put the time and money toward adopting a child. What do you think they should do?

Preparing for Parenthood

OBJECTIVES

After studying this section, you should be able to:

- Assess your personal readiness for parenthood.
- Predict what might happen to mothers, fathers, and infants who aren't ready for parenting.
- Suggest ways to learn about children and parenting in preparation for parenthood.
- Distinguish measures that contribute to a healthy pregnancy.

TERMS TO LEARN

parenting readiness
child development
conception
sperm
ovum
prenatal

What's the hardest thing to do in sports? Some say it's hitting a baseball. If you misjudge the ball's arrival at home plate by even a split second, you'll swing the bat too early or too late. Without good timing, the most powerful hitter on the team can strike out swinging.

Fortunately, success in daily life rarely takes such precise timing. Nonetheless, as you've probably learned from experience—when you just miss catching the bus or when you're the right caller in a radio listener contest—sometimes timing is everything.

LOOKING AT READINESS

Studies in life-span development show that *when* an event occurs in life has as much impact as the event itself. Losing your job is almost always a negative event, for instance, but it's apt to make a bigger impact if you're a forty-year-old parent and spouse than if you're sixteen and in high school.

Likewise, having a child is a life-changing event, since responsibilities increase and some sacrifices may have to be made. These demands are best handled when the stage of life you've reached allows you to meet them.

How can a couple decide whether they'll be able to handle the changes and responsibilities that come with parenting? They need to examine their **parenting readiness**, their degree of preparation for parenting. Here's some of what they need to consider:

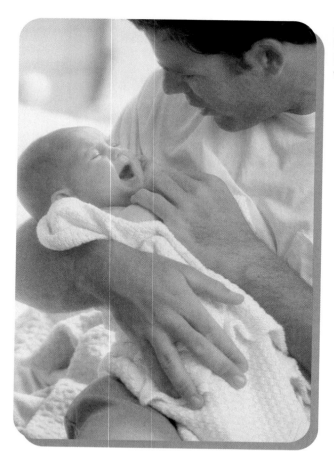

A baby doesn't cry to cause trouble. Crying is the infant's only way of communicating discomfort. How does emotional maturity help a parent cope with crying?

goals. Children can cause their plans to change. Deciding when to have children is the best insurance against having to give up something important.

- **Age.** In a sense, age is the best indicator for judging parenting readiness. Age affects the other factors. Older parents tend to be more emotionally and financially stable. They have had more time to reach their goals. The experience and wisdom they have gained are resources for dealing with the many challenges of parenthood. As you will read, the impact of age is far-reaching.

Looking at the elements of readiness is more than just helpful when thinking about parenthood. It can also prevent serious lifelong effects on the mother, father, and child.

Effects on Mothers

A woman's age and physical maturity affect her readiness for motherhood. Teens run a greater risk of complications in pregnancy and delivery than adult women. For instance, they are twice as likely to die from miscarriage or excessive bleeding.

Early motherhood and education usually don't mix. Women who have a baby while in high school or college are less apt to graduate than those who wait. Strained by caring for a child and working to support themselves, many women drop out of school. Without an education, they cannot hope to get good jobs. Therefore, young mothers tend to have low incomes.

- **Emotional maturity.** Emotional maturity brings the patience, confidence, sense of responsibility, and other traits that good parents need. Since teens are still developing, these qualities may not be in place yet. Since they're still learning to take care of themselves, they may not be ready to assume total responsibility for another person.
- **Financial readiness.** Would-be parents need to look ahead to future expenses and income. No one wants to feel financial burdens and stress. Careful planning before children enter the picture can make a difference.
- **Goals and expectations.** Couples should think about what will happen to their

Examining Readiness. Pilots in training use computer flight simulators to practice flying skills before taking a real plane up. You can use the same principle to practice your parenting skills and interests before you commit to raising a child. Which of the following "trial runs" are most feasible for you?

- Shadowing a relative or neighbor with young children to learn about routine parenting situations.
- Leading a children's story hour at the public library.
- Helping at various children's holiday activities.
- Inviting children into your classroom for a play school experience.
- Helping supervise children in an after-school program at an elementary school.
- Reaching out to a youngster in your neighborhood.

Try It Out. Survey your community and create a list of opportunities to work with young children. Arrange to take part in one that seems interesting to you and begin learning about your readiness to be a parent.

The earlier a woman has a baby, the more apt she is to have other children soon after. The baby's and mother's health suffer for this. Also, supporting and caring for several children increase the pressure of an already demanding role. Teen mothers have been found to have very high levels of stress compared to their nonparenting peers.

Lastly is the frustration factor. A younger mother may feel frustrated when she skips right from being taken care of to taking care of someone else. Missing that period of independence, growth, and socializing that young single people enjoy can be disappointing. If a woman has already managed her own money and reached some goals, she can usually accept the restrictions of child raising more easily.

Every mother wants to have a healthy baby. What impact does her age have on her baby's health?

More and more fathers are realizing that their children need them—emotionally as well as financially. How can a father benefit from a close relationship with his child?

Effects on Fathers

Physically, fathers can walk away from parenthood more easily than mothers, but the law holds them equally responsible. A father is legally bound to support his child until the child turns eighteen—regardless of the father's age or whether he is married to the child's mother or whether he ever sees his child. Fathers as young as fourteen have been sued for child support.

As with mothers, young fathers may have to interrupt their education, sometimes dropping out of school, to meet their financial obligation. Some are able to resume their education later, but usually under a double burden of work and study.

Also, like teen motherhood, teen fatherhood tends to lead to low-paying, unskilled jobs that offer less security and chance for advancement. Earning money becomes a life long worry.

Teens who are also fathers often find that they don't quite fit into either the teen world or the adult one. Their responsibilities isolate them from their more carefree peers, yet they can't fully relate to adults. They may feel lonely and confused about their roles.

Effects on Infants

When sixteen-year-old Annalea learned she was pregnant, she did what many teen mothers do: she denied it. She told no one. She went on a diet, trying to hide her pregnancy from family and friends. She finally saw the doctor when she started to "show," about five months into her pregnancy.

By then, Annalea's poor eating habits had harmed her unborn child's health. The baby was born seven weeks early and weighed only three pounds. Annalea thought she could face pregnancy alone but didn't have the maturity to handle it.

As Annalea's experience shows, infants are also affected by a parent's lack of readiness. Babies born to teens face greater health hazards than those born to older mothers. They are likely to be premature, with low birth weight. Even full-term infants tend to be smaller and weaker. The younger a mother is, the more likely her baby is to die before celebrating a first birthday.

Sadly, infants born to young parents are at greater risk of abuse. Teen parents often don't understand infant development. They underestimate the baby's needs and overestimate the baby's abilities. Some teens, unrealistically, expect an infant to love them very much and to cry very little. When heaped upon parents who are not yet adults themselves, these disappointments and other strains of parenthood can lead to child abuse.

PREPARING YOURSELF

Some parents will tell you that trying to learn about parenting by reading books is like trying to learn to swim on dry land. It's true: there is no substitute for experience. By the same token, however, you don't learn to swim by diving into the pool. First, you get used to the water temperature; then you learn to float. Along the way, you decide whether swimming is for you.

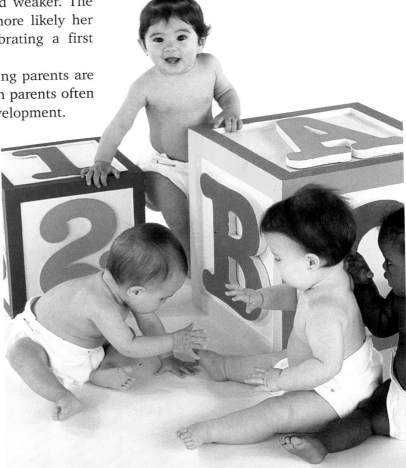

Babies are happy and healthy for good reasons. What are some of those reasons?

Learning About Children

People who have prepared themselves by learning about children assume the parental role most easily. Future parents need to know about **child development**, or how children grow and change at each stage from birth through the teen years.

Understanding what children can typically do at different ages helps parents respond to them in the best way. Parents can be more patient and realistic. They can feel more confident about providing what the child needs. Parenting produces less stress and greater satisfaction.

Gaining Experience

One of the best and simplest ways to learn about children is to spend time with them. For people from large families, that's easy. The trend toward smaller families, however, means that people may need to find other ways to be around children. Many teens babysit to earn money. The practice they get in caring for children may be more valuable than the pay.

Some people do volunteer work with children. Loy helped supervise a play park at a community center. Watching children play together taught him a lot about their physical, emotional, and social skills. Teaching a Sunday school class, coaching a sports team, and getting involved with the Big Brothers/Big Sisters program once you turn twenty-one can also give insights about children.

Some parents learn only through experience. Although preparation doesn't provide all the answers, parents can gain information and confidence for dealing with the lively, challenging energy of a child—or two.

Likewise, there are ways to prepare yourself for parenting before you have a child. Getting a truer picture of parenting now allows you to develop realistic expectations about what's involved. You'll be better equipped to handle parenting problems and to really appreciate the joy and wonder that raising a child should be—if you decide to parent someday.

Watching children and parents in public places can be both interesting and informative. How do parents handle both good and poor behavior effectively? Observing can give you ideas about good parenting.

Learning About Reproduction

Learning about pregnancy and childbirth can help people prepare to be parents. The more a woman understands the physical changes taking place in her body, the more comfortable she will be with them. The father can be a supportive partner.

Pregnancy begins with **conception**, the union of the male and female reproductive cells. The male cell, called the **sperm**, and the female cell, the **ovum**, each contain half the genetic information needed to create a new human being. During pregnancy, the cells divide, grow, and develop.

A Healthy Pregnancy

A woman who is healthy and physically fit before pregnancy will likely experience an easier **prenatal** period, the time from conception to birth. Her body will be able to nourish the baby and cope with the stress of pregnancy and childbirth. Her baby will probably be healthier, too.

Good medical care during the prenatal period is vital to the health of mother and child. Teresa saw Dr. Sanjo often during her pregnancy. Dr. Sanjo monitored the baby's growth and development and Teresa's weight gain and overall health. She urged Teresa to eat healthfully, exercise regularly, and get enough rest. When Teresa developed high blood pressure, as many pregnant women do, Dr. Sanjo prescribed a treatment that was safe for both her and the baby.

Pregnant women should avoid substances that can be harmful to a developing child. Tobacco, caffeine, and drugs, including alcohol, are all potential dangers.

You can find many ways to learn about children. Acting as a big brother to neighborhood children is just one way. What are others?

Career Success Stories

Eugene Norris: *Parent Educator*

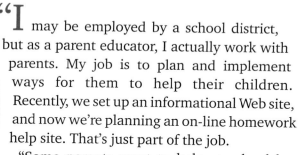

"I may be employed by a school district, but as a parent educator, I actually work with parents. My job is to plan and implement ways for them to help their children. Recently, we set up an informational Web site, and now we're planning an on-line homework help site. That's just part of the job.

"Some parents want to help at school but think they don't have the necessary knowledge or skills. Through our *Parents as Teachers* program, I prepare volunteer parents to serve as teacher assistants, tutors, and speakers. Recruiting busy parents to talk to classes about their work is part of my job. Kids need to see how school links to the work world. When a carpenter tells about using geometry on the job or a sales representative describes the written reports to be done, students start to see how important education is.

"As another part of this program, I help parents develop the skills to teach their own children. Since reading is so critical, we emphasize that. When parents tell me that reading to their children has become a special part of the evening routine, I know those children will benefit. Their ability to read fuels success in every subject area. I'm lucky because my work is varied, interesting, and rewarding. A career doesn't get much better than that."

CAREER PROFILE

Education and training: bachelor's degree minimum; master's degree preferred

Starting salary range: $22-25,000

Job prospects: school districts

Important qualities: able to instruct others; organizational skills; good communication skills; problem-solving skills

Plan Ahead

For whatever career you choose, you'll need many of the skills you're learning today. With your class, list familiar careers. Share ideas about how what you study in school links to these careers.

RESOURCES FOR PARENTS

People who want to learn more about parenthood have many resources. Courses on parenting and child development are a good place to start. You can find them offered by high schools, community colleges, social and mental health agencies, religious organizations, and hospitals.

Many couples take childbirth classes during pregnancy. There, expectant parents learn what occurs during pregnancy and birth. They practice breathing and relaxation exercises to ease the pain and stress of the birth process. Hospitals and clinics usually sponsor these classes.

Parenting books and magazines are other sources of information. Reliable Web sites of parenting and child development organizations may also be useful. The card catalog at the library or an Internet search will, no doubt, supply more references than you can read. If you choose to become a parent someday, these and many other resources can help you prepare for the job.

Where can you learn to be a parent? Libraries have books and magazines to get you started, at no cost to you.

SECTION 33-2 REVIEW

Check Your Understanding

1. Why is emotional maturity necessary for parenting readiness?
2. What physical risks do teen mothers face?
3. Why are infants of teen parents more likely to experience abuse?
4. Why is knowledge of child development helpful to parents?
5. Why is prenatal care important for a healthy pregnancy?
6. What are some sources of information on parenting and related topics?
7. **Thinking Critically.** Imagine you volunteered to help with an arts program for children. What might this experience teach you about children?
8. **Problem Solving.** At seventeen, Charlie left school to work full-time to help support his child. He rarely sees his friends from high school, and the older men he works with don't accept him as an equal. He is feeling increasingly alone. What should Charlie do?

CHAPTER SUMMARY

- Having a child permanently changes a person's life.
- Pressures to have children come from society and sometimes family and friends.
- Parenthood is a major responsibility. It requires financial and personal sacrifice but also offers many rewards.
- Infertile couples may try to have children through medical help.
- Some people become parents through adoption.
- Several factors should be examined to determine readiness for parenthood.
- Having a child before parents are ready has long-term negative effects on the lives of the mother, father, and infant.
- Learning about children, child development, and parenting can help prepare a person for parenthood.
- Women who care for their health during pregnancy help ensure that their baby will be healthy also.

REVIEW QUESTIONS

Section 33-1

1. What are some advantages, to parents and to children, of becoming a parent by choice?
2. How can having a child change a person's life?
3. What factors should an infertile couple weigh when deciding whether to use medical help to have a child?
4. Why might people who are physically able to have children choose to adopt one?

Section 33-2

1. What are some factors that affect parenting readiness? Briefly explain their impact.
2. How does parenthood affect teen mothers and fathers?
3. What are some benefits of learning about parenting, children, and reproduction?
4. What can a woman do to help ensure having a healthy baby?

BECOMING A PROBLEM SOLVER

1. Bob and Kim's lawyer has an infant for them to adopt. However, the birth mother insists on meeting them and wants an open adoption. The couple is uneasy at having that much contact with the mother. They worry about her involvement in the future. What should Bob and Kim do?

2. Deb and Alan are happily married thirty-year-olds. They enjoy careers and life together. Recently, however, they've felt a certain emptiness and dissatisfaction. They wonder if a child is what is missing from their lives. What should Deb and Alan do?

THINKING CRITICALLY

1. **Assessing Outcomes.** Why does having a child tend to strengthen an already solid marriage but weaken an already troubled one?
2. **Recognizing Assumptions.** Is it natural for people to want to have children? If so, is it unnatural to not want children?
3. **Predicting Results.** What would happen if a person wants to have a child when the spouse is strongly against it? How might this situation be prevented?
4. **Analyzing Decisions.** Should an adopted child have access to the identity of birth parents? Why or why not?

MAKING CURRICULUM CONNECTIONS

1. **Math.** Interview the parent of an infant to learn the costs of caring for the child. Make a list of all expenses and compute the average monthly cost of care. Compare results with others in the class.
2. **Social Studies.** Investigate the trend of international adoptions. What rules govern such adoptions? What are some advantages and hazards? Write your findings in a report for the class.
3. **Science.** Research a medical procedure used to help infertile couples. What is involved? What's the success rate? Are there negative consequences? Report your findings to the class.
4. **Science.** Learn what progress has been made against a genetic disease. Have scientists learned the cause of the disease? What treatments are being tried? What is the outlook for the near future? Write a summary of your findings.

APPLYING YOUR KNOWLEDGE

1. Write a pledge to any future children you might have, explaining what you will do to prepare yourself for their birth.
2. Working with a partner, identify five behaviors that are common in infants and young children. Use these behaviors in a chart that shows how parents might respond if they are knowledgeable about child development.
3. Write down three short-term and three long-term goals that you have for yourself, including the time by which you hope to reach them. Write a short essay describing how having a child now would affect whether you would reach those goals.

Family & Community Connections

1. Interview three people of various age ranges—for example, your own age, early twenties, and late twenties—to learn their feelings about having children and parenting. Has each person's opinion changed in the last five or ten years? If so, how? What happened to affect his or her thinking?

2. Find out what organizations offer parenting and childbirth preparation classes in your community. Create a list of educational opportunities for prospective parents.

Chapter 34

Skillful Parenting

WORDS FOR THOUGHT

"To bring up a child in the way he should go, travel that way yourself once in a while." *(Josh Billings)*

IN YOUR OWN WORDS

What point is made with this statement?

Promoting Children's Development

OBJECTIVES

After studying this section, you should be able to:

- Explain the importance of mothers and fathers in parenting.
- Describe patterns of physical, intellectual, emotional, social, and moral development in children.
- Demonstrate ways to promote development in children.

TERMS TO LEARN

motor skills
monitor

Deciding to have a child is only your first parenting decision. It opens the gate to countless others. By becoming a parent, you agree to think for at least two people—yourself and your child. Although children are born with minds of their own and the will to use them, making choices that keep them safe and healthy is the parent's job.

PARENTHOOD AS PARTNERSHIP

Have you ever thought of everything a parent is to a child? A parent is a provider, protector, teacher, counselor, nurse, chef, chauffeur, and more.

With both mother and father present, parenting duties can be shared. The benefits go beyond having help with the cooking or laundry. Recent studies indicate that children have needs not easily met by one parent alone. Mothers and fathers are both important because each parent responds differently. Each offers special strengths that are complementary. They also bring different personal interests, skills, and qualities.

When children have two loving, involved parents, their development tends to be more well-rounded. Children need adult attention to develop to their fullest in all areas—physical, mental, emotional, social, and moral.

PHYSICAL DEVELOPMENT

A pregnant woman cares for herself physically in order to have a healthy baby. This commitment to good health, by both parents, continues as a child grows. Parents see that children are properly fed and clothed. They encourage play as well as rest. Parents protect children from harm. Through physical care, children first become aware of their parents' love for them.

Nutrition

To children, a "good" diet might be plenty of their favorite food—and nothing else. Fortunately, parents have the means and the knowledge to serve healthful, balanced meals. Physical growth gallops along in childhood. Children need nourishing foods to help them develop strong, healthy bodies.

To provide a child with an adequate diet, you must know about their nutritional needs and eating habits. For example, small children have small stomachs. They frequently don't eat enough at one meal to last them until the next. Therefore, parents must be ready with wholesome snacks, such as fresh or dried fruit, cheese and crackers, and fruit juice.

Also, foods must be prepared so the child can eat them safely and willingly. Do you recall, as a child, refusing to eat foods that touched each other on the plate? Skilled parents know how to satisfy these quirks without creating a finicky eater.

Clothing

"Put on your shoes." "Don't forget your mittens." Keeping children dressed appropriately often includes reminders like these, yet protection from the elements is not a parent's only concern. Clothing must be durable and safe for an active child. Garments should be comfortably cut to allow freedom of movement. However, large or baggy clothes can interfere with play, catch on play equipment, or cause a child to trip and fall.

Children tend to follow the example parents set. If the parent eats a nutritious breakfast, the child learns this good habit. If you had a child who wanted sugary cereals, would you have the willpower to say no?

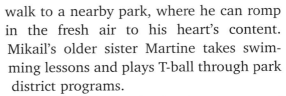

The message that exercise is fun teaches a child to choose active play over watching television. How will a child benefit from regularly making this choice?

walk to a nearby park, where he can romp in the fresh air to his heart's content. Mikail's older sister Martine takes swimming lessons and plays T-ball through park district programs.

Jana understands the importance of exercise to children's physical and mental health. Physical activity lets children release pent-up energy. Given plenty of opportunities for exercise, children develop strong bones, muscles, and motor skills. **Motor skills** are the abilities that depend on the use and control of muscles, especially those in the arms, legs, hands, and feet. Picking a flower, throwing a ball, and pedaling a tricycle are all motor skills.

Rest

A child's active, rapidly growing body needs plenty of rest to replenish energy supplies. Tired children often don't learn well. They are more prone to illness and irritability. Parents make sure children have regular opportunities to rest and nap through the day. They teach good sleep habits by sticking to scheduled bedtimes. They use calming techniques to help children get to sleep—and get back to sleep—on their own.

Medical Care

Concerned parents make sure children receive good medical care, from before birth and throughout childhood. Dental

Suitable children's clothing also encourages self-dressing. Parents look for articles with elastic waistbands, snap closures, Velcro® fasteners, and other features that help children dress themselves. Accomplishing this task promotes feelings of competence and independence. The resulting pride that children feel aids their emotional development.

Exercise

Jana and her children live in a small apartment with no room for indoor active play. The apartment complex has no outdoor play area. Jana and her son Mikail

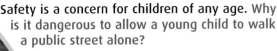

Safety is a concern for children of any age. Why is it dangerous to allow a young child to walk a public street alone?

A Safe Environment

As soon as his son started to crawl, Seth covered all the unused electrical outlets with plastic plugs. He knew that the holes were just right for the prying fingers of a curious infant, who had no idea of the danger of electric shock. Seth also put child-proof locks on all the cabinets. This kept his son from the many items that were off-limits to a child, from the bleach, to the garbage, to the good china. These measures were in addition to the steps Seth already took to keep his family safe, including locking doors and windows and keeping a fire extinguisher near the kitchen.

Childproofing a home as Seth did is one way that parents create a safe environment for children. No home can be made safe enough for an unsupervised child, however. Children are impulsive. They have no idea what their actions may bring. They are aptly described as "accidents waiting to happen."

Children, therefore, need monitoring. To **monitor** is to keep close watch over. Young children need constant attention. A three-year-old, eager to test physical skills, can easily climb from a chair onto a counter—and just as easily fall. Infants have been known to drown in half a bucket of water.

Children need less monitoring as they gain experience and develop thinking skills. Parents prepare them to take responsibility for their own safety. A skillful

care begins as soon as a child has teeth to look after. Regular physical and dental checkups help ensure that children are growing as they should. Problems can be detected early, lessening the impact.

Parents also seek prompt medical attention when a child is ill or injured. In addition, infants and children need a series of vaccinations to protect them from certain diseases, including polio, measles, and mumps.

In order to obtain quality care, parents make health insurance a priority. However, public health clinics assure needed services to families who can't afford them.

Balancing Work & Family Life

THE CHALLENGE —

Caring for Young Children

Young children require plenty of time and attention. When parents and family members are busy with work, school, and problems, they sometimes overlook the family's youngest members. Pitching in to care for young children is a good way to build family relationships and ease tension at home.

How You Can Help

To help care for a young child in your family, try these ideas:

- Offer to pick up a child from a scheduled activity or play date.
- Talk, play, or share a hobby with a child while your parent is busy.
- Fix a snack for a child who stays home alone after school.
- Offer to help with homework.
- Accompany a child to the library to read or study.
- Teach a child routine skills, such as how to prepare simple snacks, replace a button with needle and thread, or operate a microwave oven without help.

---

parent knows when and how to teach a child about recognizing and avoiding dangerous substances and situations. Parents and children often practice responses to emergencies.

Monitoring shouldn't end entirely until children reach maturity. Even in the teen years, parents need to know where their children are and what they are doing, since new threats emerge. Teens who are monitored have lower rates of drug and alcohol abuse, running away, and delinquency.

Self-Care

Parents help children take over some of their own physical care gradually. When children are old enough, parents show them how to keep teeth and gums healthy by brushing and flossing regularly. They teach children to wash their hands before eating and after toileting to prevent the spread of germs. The child acquires healthful hygiene habits and also a sense of independence.

INTELLECTUAL DEVELOPMENT

Volumes have been written on how children learn, but many questions remain. When you think that babies come into the world knowing nothing, you can appreciate the marvels of the human mind. Parents have the great responsibility of spurring and guiding learning, yet the task isn't overwhelming. In fact, it can be fun.

Providing Learning Experiences

As nutritious foods fuel physical growth, learning experiences nourish intellectual growth. By knowing how children learn, parents can provide experiences and activities to suit their child at each age and stage of development.

Young children learn through their senses and actions. They discover how things work with hands-on exploration and investigation. Thus, parents promote learning by

Nurturing a Child's Brain

To become a thinker, a child needs many sensory experiences. Make a list of ways to provide them.

A newborn's brain contains billions of cells. During the first two years of life, brain weight doubles as neurons connect. The more connections, the better the brain functions.

exposing children to the sensory experiences the world offers: bright colors; a range of sounds; and intriguing smells and textures. Active and quiet play are also occasions for learning. For example, what thinking skills might a child use to paint a picture?

Children draw upon experiences to form ideas about the world. Outings to museums, zoos, parks, band concerts, and fairs give them a greater understanding of the people, occupations, and events that make up their world.

Around age seven, children begin to think logically. They are able to classify objects into broad categories. They still learn best through direct experience, however. Manipulating and organizing objects strengthens their ability to compare and contrast. Collecting items from rocks to trading cards to figurines is an enjoyable learning experience at this age.

Research shows that caregivers cause brain connections to form by stimulating a child's senses—sight, hearing, smell, taste, and touch. With every positive interaction, the brain wires for thinking.

Simple actions count—talking, playing games, giving affection. Although the first few years of life are the most critical, brain circuitry strengthens throughout childhood.

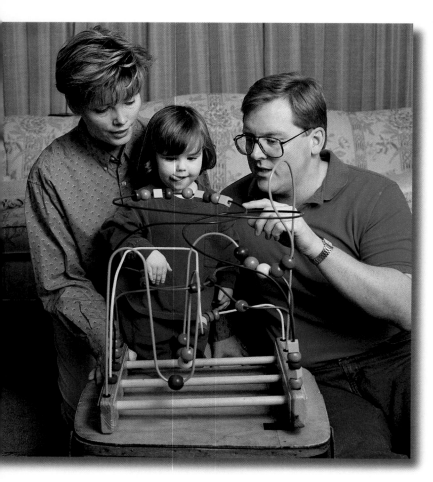

A child's mind expands with every new and positive experience. Fancy toys are fine, but you don't have to have them. What everyday items around a home could help a child learn?

cold. Now it's getting warm. Doesn't that feel nice? Now it's getting hot—ouch!" When Kurt learned that "hot" was unpleasant, he kept his distance from a "hot" stove. He also avoided all things labeled "ouch"—kitchen knives, a rose bush, and an angry family cat.

Learning Language

The ability to use language opens up whole new worlds for children. Throughout life, verbal skills are vital for sharing ideas. Intellectual, emotional, and social growth are all enhanced by the ability to communicate with words.

Parents nurture language development from the day a child is born. When Jorge was a baby, his parents talked to him as they fed, bathed, diapered, and dressed him. They named everyday items: crib, chair, banana, blocks. They pored over pictures in storybooks, describing what each character was doing. Jorge delighted in their silly songs and rhymes, making language fun. Wherever they went, his parents pointed out sights and activities.

All the while Jorge was absorbing the rules of language. He had amassed an impressive vocabulary even before he could speak. As he developed speech skills,

At age eleven or twelve, children begin to think abstractly. That is, they use imagination to predict what might happen in the future and to suggest causes for what has happened in the past. This allows children to solve some problems with thought alone.

Parents teach best by tailoring "lessons" to their child's gradually developing thinking skills. For example, Bree knew that warning about burns wouldn't keep her two-year-old son Kurt from touching a hot oven. Instead, she taught him about temperature while washing his hands. As they held their hands under the running water, Bree noted, "This water is cold—brrr, that's

Jorge became an avid talker, with several thousand words at his command. If he didn't always use them properly, his parents didn't correct him. They simply modeled proper usage and pronunciation until Jorge caught on.

EMOTIONAL DEVELOPMENT

A growing child experiences a widening range of emotions, both positive and negative. Part of guiding emotional growth is helping children identify these feelings and express them acceptably. By kissing and cuddling an infant, for instance, a parent teaches the child how to show love and affection.

Parents need to teach children how to handle negative emotions. Beginning around age two, parents set rules about which actions aren't permitted. A parent might tell a five-year-old who is having a tantrum, "I know you're angry that you can't go to the park, but screaming isn't allowed. You can punch a pillow or run in the yard. Sometimes running helps me when I'm angry."

Accepting negative emotions is one way to help children feel emotionally secure. Children see that they are loved even when they feel unloving. This sense of unconditional love—of being loved "as is" and "in spite of"—is essential to healthy emotional development. Children who doubt their parents' love will grow up doubting themselves. They may fear

losing that love by not living up to certain expectations. This undermines a child's sense of self-worth and confidence.

In contrast, parents help build children's self-worth by giving love, attention, and encouragement. They offer children many chances to succeed, according to the child's abilities. Self-dressing, as you read, is a chance for a two-year-old to feel successful. An older child might know success by helping prepare a meal.

Equally important, parents recognize and praise a child's accomplishments. Sincere praise enhances self-worth and encourages children to take on new tasks and challenges.

When children have trouble mastering a skill, parents need to model persistence by not letting children give up. Leigh's six-year-

When you see teens and adults who can't control anger, you begin to understand why children need to learn this skill early in life. Why is a calm and patient approach best when helping children manage anger?

old son Jacob struggled with handwriting. She told him, "I know this isn't easy for you. Some things are hard to learn, but just because something is hard is no reason to give up. I know you can do this."

Leigh praised every improvement she noticed. She shared Jacob's pride as his letters became clearer. When one of his practice papers earned a gold star from his teacher, Leigh stuck it on the refrigerator. With Leigh's support, Jacob learned a lesson that was just as valuable as how to form letters: difficulty—and overcoming it—is part of life.

Helping children learn mental skills needed for independence also promotes feelings of competence. You can strengthen decision-making skills by giving them limited choices about what to wear, what to eat, and what activities to try. Letting them handle their own money teaches them to weigh options and manage resources. When giving children choices, parents must be sure that everyone can live with the consequences if the child makes a bad choice. This too is part of independence.

SOCIAL DEVELOPMENT

Social development begins at birth, as infants are held, fed, and calmed by a soothing voice. Babies thrive socially and emotionally on the love and attention they receive from parents and others.

Showing babies affection doesn't spoil them. By two or three months of age, they show how much they enjoy the attention by offering coos, gurgles, and smiles in return—smiles that will be an important part of relationships for a lifetime. Games of "peek-a-boo" and "pat-a-cake" and other pleasing interactions between parent and child also contribute to social growth.

By talking to children to encourage language skills, parents also promote social development. Children come to enjoy people. Communication is an important skill for entering into relationships.

As children grow, parents' expectations and attitudes about social behavior remain a chief influence on social growth. A parent's smile or praise encourages children to repeat desirable behavior. A frown or

Tips & TECHNIQUES

Discipline Demonstrations. Books and articles on raising children can make discipline seem simple. What's the real story? To get a better idea, observe in real life.
- Choose a public place where parents and children often go, such as a restaurant, library, or a supermarket.
- Observe three or four incidents of a child showing positive or negative behavior.
- Note the parents' response and the effect on the child.
- Based on what you've learned, did the real-life situation go as you would expect, or did the results surprise you?

Try It Out. Volunteer to take care of a child for a few hours. Respond to the child's behavior in positive ways. Evaluate your approach and the child's reaction. How could you improve your technique?

scolding discourages other actions. In this way, children learn how to act in order to get along with others.

All the positive exchanges that take place within the family are good for social development. Children learn relationship skills by watching and interacting with parents and other family members. They carry these skills outside the family to build strong relationships throughout life.

MORAL DEVELOPMENT

As you may recall, infants and young children don't understand principles of right and wrong. They look to parents to tell them whether behaviors are good or bad. In a sense, a parent who takes a spoon from an infant who repeatedly throws it across the room is teaching a subtle moral lesson.

As children grow better able to relate to others, moral development takes on a strong social element. Again, children may not understand why they should treat others a certain way. By showing approval or disapproval, parents encourage children to act with kindness, generosity, and other positive social traits. As children see the benefits of this behavior, they accept kindness and generosity as values to act on.

At around age six, children begin to develop a conscience. Certain actions trouble them because they have learned that these behaviors are not right. Their sense of judgment and self-control are still developing, however, so they need parents to set rules

Children learn first within the family and then transfer lessons to the outside world. With close, loving interaction at home, children trust that people beyond the family circle can be worth knowing, too.

and limits. Although children will probably dislike some rules, they are generally grateful for them. In rules, they sense parental love and concern for their well-being.

As with other types of development, parents guide moral growth by adapting their standards to a child's abilities. They might expect truthfulness from a six-year-old who has begun to develop a conscience. At the same time, they know that children this age are very imaginative. Fact and fiction sometimes blur in their minds. They may spin tall tales without being intentionally dishonest. Parents who are sensitive to this difference may decide that the child needs help in separating fantasy from reality, not punishment for lying.

CHILDREN WITH SPECIAL NEEDS

Some children face added challenges in development due to physical impairments, emotional problems, or learning disabilities. They must work harder to master physical or intellectual skills. These children have the same basic needs as others but require extra attention to reach their fullest potential.

Likewise, parents of special needs children require the same skills as other parents, but to an added degree. Parenting these children may demand more time, energy, and patience. Parents may have to work with doctors, therapists, and educators to plan and carry out developmental goals.

As with any child, raising one with special needs can take extra effort. Frequently, however, where the demands are great, so are the rewards.

A child with special needs can have a charm that brings great joy to family and friends. Early diagnosis is needed for successful treatment and management of any condition.

SECTION 34-1 REVIEW

Check Your Understanding

1. What are the advantages when the mother and father in a family are both involved in parenting?
2. What health benefits do good nutrition and adequate sleep offer children?
3. How does a skillful parent monitor a growing child?
4. How is learning language important to overall development?
5. Why should parents accept a child's negative emotions?
6. What added challenges do parents of special needs children face?
7. **Thinking Critically.** Based on what you've read, how would sharing in a family meal promote a child's development?
8. **Problem Solving.** Jetta is a single mother of three-year-old Cameron. Jetta's mother watches Cameron while she works. When Jetta gets home, she's usually too tired to take Cameron where he can play with other children, and often it's too late. Jetta is worried that this lack of socialization is hurting her son's development. What should Jetta do?

Guiding Children's Behavior

OBJECTIVES

After studying this section, you should be able to:

- Compare the three basic parenting styles.
- Demonstrate ways to encourage good behavior.
- Explain the proper use of limits in guiding children's behavior.
- Distinguish appropriate methods of dealing with misbehavior.
- Suggest guidelines for disciplining children.

TERMS TO LEARN

authoritarian style
authoritative style
permissive style
discipline
time-out

In one recent survey, parents said that of all parenting skills, they had least confidence in their ability to discipline their children. Shaping the behavior of a child isn't easy, but learning some basic principles is a first step toward building this parenting skill.

PARENTING STYLES

The way a parent approaches discipline is closely linked to a parenting style. A parenting style is a pattern of relating to children that reflects a person's idea of what the parent-child relationship should be. Parenting style is shaped by personality, childhood experiences, and a person's basic attitude toward children and child rearing. Societal influences also have impact. There are three basic styles of parenting:

- **Authoritarian.** The **authoritarian style** of parenting expects children to trust and obey without question or hesitation. Parents set rules and goals to channel behavior. Rules and goals are clearly and firmly stated, often with little or no discussion. Failure to meet expectations is dealt with swiftly and firmly.

- **Authoritative.** Greater flexibility shows with the **authoritative style**. Parents consider a child's desires, abilities, and ideas when setting rules and standards. Children are allowed a certain amount of independence and decision making within the established limits. In this style, parents tend to give children reasons for the rules and decisions they make.

- **Permissive.** Parents who use the **permissive style** exert minimal authority and provide limited structure. Children are allowed to set many of their own goals, rules, and limits. They may act within broad guidelines as long as they are willing to accept the outcomes of their decisions.

Skillful parenting often involves blending the basic styles, since what works in one situation may not work in another. Any one style or combination of styles may be used successfully, as long as parents provide love, attention, security, and support.

DISCIPLINE

Discipline is the process of helping children learn to behave in acceptable ways. It helps children conform to the expectations of the family and society. More importantly, discipline helps children gradually learn to control their own behavior. This is called self-discipline.

Many people confuse discipline with punishment. In fact, punishment is only a small part of effective discipline, to be used only when necessary. Discipline is more accurately called *guidance*.

Effective guidance is a balance of three parenting skills: encouraging good behavior; setting and enforcing limits; and dealing with misbehavior.

Encouraging Good Behavior

One of the best ways to encourage good behavior is to set a good example. Much of a child's learning comes from watching others. Children are great imitators, adopting many of the beliefs and behavior patterns they see around them.

The way a parent guides a child's behavior shows parenting style. How might a parent use each of the three basic parenting styles to handle cleanup after this project?

Some parents wonder why children misbehave, until they examine their own behavior. A child who hears kind words will use them, too. A child who sees thoughtfulness will return it. *What else will a child mimic?*

When thinking about the example they set, parents should remember that "actions speak louder than words." For example, Chen didn't go to school one morning, telling his father it was a teacher in-service day. When his father learned the truth, he grounded Chen for the weekend. He then called the school secretary and explained that Chen was home with a fever. What example did Chen's father set for his son?

Positive behavior is also encouraged by praise. A vague "Good boy" doesn't tell Riley what he did to earn praise. He may wonder and worry why he was "good" at that time but not at others. Saying, "You did a good job picking up the toys," is more helpful. Children who understand the *action* that was good are more apt to repeat it even without praise.

Setting and Enforcing Limits

Parents set limits to tell children what's acceptable, appropriate, and safe. Limits may be physical restrictions, such as permitting a child to play only in the yard, or rules for behavior. Useful limits are simple and clearly stated. They are reasonable and appropriate for the child's age. Rules that emphasize what children should do rather than avoid doing are most effective.

As children grow older, they need fewer limits, especially when they've shown themselves to be responsible and faithful to parents' rules. Parents, therefore, should revise rules and limits as necessary. Frustrating children with needless restrictions often creates feelings of resentment and defiance.

Dealing with Misbehavior

Unfortunately, all problems aren't prevented by encouraging good behavior and setting reasonable limits. Children, like everyone, behave inappropriately at times. Parents choose an effective response based on the child and the misbehavior.

Sometimes children "act up" only to get attention. Ignoring harmless misbehavior—and praising good behavior—often resolves the situation. Other times, a simple warning or reminder is enough to keep a child from repeating a misdeed.

In some cases, you can let children experience the natural consequences of their behavior. Deron dawdled while getting ready for school; he was only half-dressed when the school bus arrived. Deron rode to school still wearing his pajama top, with his shirt in his backpack. Until he could change in the rest room, his embarrassment was punishment enough for his actions.

Sometimes parents need to impose consequences to show displeasure. A young child may be given a **time-out**, removed from the presence of others or from the activity for a short time. This gives children—and parents, if needed—a chance to regain self-control. Children can think about why their behavior was unacceptable.

Revoking privileges can also be effective, especially when related to the misbehavior. This technique is most appropriate for older children, who can make the connection between the action and the consequences. Suppose a child left a bicycle lying in the yard overnight after repeated reminders to bring it in. What privilege might be denied?

Making the positive moments outnumber the negatives ones should be every parent's goal. Why is this true?

Building Character

Patience: A Quality That Counts

Children are not known for patience, so parents need enough for both of them. Patience is the ability to tolerate delay and trouble. Patient people are willing to move slowly toward goals. A teen could show patience by:

- Making encouraging remarks while waiting for a four-year-old sister to put on her own socks and shoes.
- Reading a young brother a favorite story over and over.
- Passing the time with conversation while waiting in a busy restaurant.
- Explaining a math problem several times to a confused classmate.

QUESTIONS

1. What physical reactions might occur in people who are impatient?
2. What might a person do to become more patient?
3. Are you a patient person? How or when do you show patience?

Whatever punishment occurs, it should match the offense. A parent may need a cooling-off period to avoid overreacting. When her son was very late arriving home, Penny grounded him for a month. Within a few days, she realized that the punishment was too severe. If she decided to reduce the punishment, she would have to carefully avoid such situations in the future so that her words would still be taken seriously.

Frequently, using a combination of disciplinary methods works. The Kimbroughs were trying to teach two-year-old Shawnell to share. They pointed out how they shared things and talked about how good it felt. When Shawnell grabbed toys from his playmates, they removed him from the activity for a few minutes, then coached him on how to ask for a toy politely. They showed their pleasure when they noticed Shawnell sharing with others.

Experts vary in their opinions on spanking. Some feel strongly that spanking should be avoided. They point out that spanking doesn't help children learn desirable behavior and teaches them that hitting is acceptable. Others believe that in certain situations using an open hand to strike a child's bottom without causing physical injury is permissible. Getting the attention of a child who is out of control is cited as one of these situations.

Whatever their views, experts agree that spanking should not be done too hard or too often. Other positive guidance techniques offer effective alternatives. Parents should never use spanking to vent their anger or frustration.

The lessons children learn when they're young last a lifetime. A parent who misses opportunities to love and guide and teach can't go back and make them up.

TAKING ACTION

Advice on guidance may seem overwhelming, but doing nothing is a poor option. Parents may not discipline perfectly, yet a confident and loving approach to guidance is needed. The following tried-and-true basics can help parents teach good behavior:

- **Start early.** Good habits are easier to instill when children are very young and exposed to fewer outside influences. If inappropriate behavior is left uncorrected in a young child, it may be deeply rooted and hard to change when the child is older.
- **Be consistent.** Children can't learn what parents want if they react differently to the same behavior. Parents need to decide what is and isn't appropriate and respond in a similar way each time the behavior occurs. The same reward or punishment every time may not be practical, but children should know whether an action will bring positive or negative consequences.
- **Present a united front.** When more than one person handles discipline, they need to agree on rules, limits, and guidance techniques. Otherwise, approaches may be confusing or inconsistent. Children are quick to take advantage when parents disagree on basic points of discipline.
- **Follow through.** Commands and warnings are meaningless unless misbehavior is met with action. For instance, telling a child not to pick the flowers is pointless if you don't supply a consequence for disobeying.

All parents want children to behave well. Family life is much more enjoyable for all members when behavior is under control. Should you someday choose to have children, you will do a much better job if you prepare yourself now with clear thinking about guidance techniques.

Even though children do misbehave, they want and respect parental guidance. When discipline is properly balanced with loving support, children can thrive.

SECTION 34-2 REVIEW

Check Your Understanding

1. What is meant by "parenting style"?
2. What is the purpose of discipline?
3. What three parenting skills are needed for effective discipline?
4. Why do parents set limits?
5. Why should parents think carefully before choosing a punishment?
6. What are four basic rules for guiding children's behavior?
7. **Thinking Critically.** What problems might result if parents threaten consequences that they can't carry out?
8. **Problem Solving.** Stan thinks his wife Belinda is too strict with their children. Stan tolerates some behaviors that Belinda disapproves. He rarely hands out a serious punishment. As a result, the children are confused, and Belinda feels Stan is undermining her authority. What should Stan and Belinda do?

Chapter 34
Review and Activities

CHAPTER SUMMARY

- Meeting children's physical needs includes promoting growth, health, and safety.
- By providing sensory experiences, parents aid a child's intellectual development.
- By encouraging language development, parents stimulate both learning and social skills.
- Through family relationships, children learn to get along with others.
- Parents are one of the earliest and strongest influences on their children's moral development.
- Most parents use a blend of parenting styles.
- Parents teach good behavior by example and praise.
- Parents set limits to help children avoid inappropriate and unsafe behaviors.
- To discipline effectively, parents must be consistent and predictable in using guidance techniques.

REVIEW QUESTIONS

Section 34-1
1. Is it possible for one parent to be "a mother and a father" to a child? Why or why not?
2. What can parents do to promote physical development?
3. How do childproofing and monitoring work together to provide a safe environment for childern?
4. How can parents promote intellectual development as children grow?
5. How do parents help their children grow emotionally?

Section 34-2
1. Compare how decision making is handled with the three basic parenting styles.
2. How is discipline related to punishment?
3. Is all praise equally helpful for encouraging good behavior in children?
4. What could a parent do to deal with a child's misbehavior?
5. Why is consistency important when guiding a child's behavior?

BECOMING A PROBLEM SOLVER

1. Lourdes is concerned about her four-year-old son Elias. He is very shy and clings to her when he is around other children. Lourdes knows Elias will need to be comfortable with his peers when he starts school. What should Lourdes do?

2. Taylor and Ben's three-year-old Donnell is mentally disabled. When Taylor helps Donnell with tasks, Ben warns that she doesn't let him do enough for himself. Taylor replies that Ben is refusing to accept their son's disability. What should Taylor and Ben do?

THINKING CRITICALLY

1. **Identifying Resources.** Give examples of how financial readiness helps parents meet needs in various areas of development. What are the limitations of money in helping children develop?
2. **Recognizing Alternatives.** In a two-parent family, should one parent be in charge of discipline or should responsibility be divided? Give reasons for your answers.
3. **Recognizing Ambiguous Statements.** Suppose a parent tells a child, "Don't stay out after dark" or "Come in before it gets late." Are these effectively stated? Why or why not? How would you state the rule?
4. **Identifying Cause and Effect.** Children need a sense of self-worth, but they also have to learn that the world doesn't revolve around only them. How can parents instill a balance between these two perspectives?
5. **Predicting Consequences.** Suppose a parent is too busy, too tired, or too insecure to apply consequences when a young child misbehaves. What could happen in the near future and in the years ahead?

MAKING CURRICULUM CONNECTIONS

1. **Health.** Develop a recipe book of healthful snacks for children. Try to include all food groups.
2. **Science.** Learn more about one special need that a child might have. How can children with this condition be helped to reach their potential? What are the most recent advances in treating this condition? Report your findings to the class.

APPLYING YOUR KNOWLEDGE

1. As a class, debate the possible advantages and drawbacks of each parenting style. Does any one style seem superior to the others, or is a certain style preferable in a certain situation?
2. Bring in a children's book for the class to evaluate. What kinds of words are used? How many pictures are there compared to words? What subjects seem most popular? Compare these points in books for younger and older children.
3. Watch one hour of children's television programming. What skills do these shows teach, intentionally or otherwise? By what methods?

Family & Community Connections

1. Read several advice columns in parenting magazines. What problems seem most common? How do experts recommend handling them? On what issues do experts agree and disagree? Is their advice consistent with what you have read in this chapter?

2. In small groups, use telephone books and newspapers to locate resources for children with special needs and their parents in your community. Share your findings with the class.

Glossary

A

abstinence. Refraining from sexual intercourse. (20-2)

adaptation. Making changes that are practical and appropriate. (14-1)

addiction. Dependence on a particular substance or action. (14-2)

adjustment. A period of working to change routines and feelings until everything feels normal again. (13-2)

adolescence. The stage of life between childhood and adulthood. (21-2)

adoption. Legal process of taking a child of other parents as one's own. (33-1)

adoption, closed. An adoption procedure in which the identities of the birth parents and adoptive parents are not revealed to each other. (33-1)

adoption, open. An adoption procedure in which the identities of the birth parents and adoptive parents are made known to each other. (33-1)

adoptive family. A family in which parents have gone through a legal process to make children a part of the family. (3-1)

advertising, direct. Advertising that is aimed at you in an obvious way. (28-1)

advertising, indirect. Subtle advertising of a product through celebrity use or clothing logos or labels. (28-1)

aerobic exercise. Strenuous activity that raises the heart rate and increases the amount of oxygen taken into the lungs. (26-2)

affirmation. Positive input given to help others feel appreciated and supported. (8-1)

ageism. Prejudice against older people. (17-1)

alcoholism. An addiction to alcohol. (14-2)

alimony. Financial support of an ex-spouse. (13-1)

altruism. Unselfish concern for the welfare of others. (24-2)

annulment. A decree stating that a legal marriage never took place because of some prior condition at the time of the marriage. (13-1)

anorexia nervosa. An eating disorder that shows itself in a fear of being fat. (26-2)

antibiotics. Special medicines that destroy disease-causing pathogens. (26-1)

application form. A form that asks for basic information about a job seeker. (29-2)

apprenticeship. A position in which you receive paid on-the-job training from a skilled worker in a trade. (29-1)

aptitude. Natural talent or capacity for learning. (29-1)

assertive. Communicating ideas and feelings firmly and positively. (6-2)

assimilation. Adopting the habits, customs, and patterns of a new culture. (4-2)

attitude. A person's basic outlook on life or a specific topic or issue. (22-2)

authoritarian style. A parenting style based on the belief that children should obey their parents without hesitation or question. (34-2)

authoritative style. A parenting style with which parents set limits, standards, and goals but base their expectations on children's abilities and stage of development. (34-2)

authority. The right to give orders, make decisions, and enforce rules. (16-1)

autocratic style. A family decision-making style with which responsibility for decision making is in one person's hands. (3-2)

autonomy. The ability to direct your life independently. (25-2)

B

balance. Remaining amount due on a financial account. (27-1)

bankruptcy. A legal process that declares a person unable to pay debts. (12-1)

bargain. A good-quality product you need, want, and will use that is sold by a reliable dealer at a price you are willing to pay. (28-1)

bereaved. Suffering the death of a loved one. (15-2)

Better Business Bureaus. Independent organizations sponsored by businesses in a community. (28-2)

body image. The way you see yourself. (21-1)

bulimia. An eating disorder involving binge eating followed by vomiting or laxative use. (26-2)

bylaws. Rules established by a group. (16-2)

C

cardiovascular diseases. Heart-related diseases, such as strokes and high blood pressure. (26-1)

career. The kind of work you do over a period of years. (29-1)

career counseling. Helping people choose and be successful in their work. (29-1)

career path. The connections between the various jobs that make up a career. (29-1)

character. Being morally strong, with the ability to think, judge, and act with maturity. (23-2)

child development. A description of what children are like at each stage of growth. (33-2)

chronic diseases. Illnesses or conditions that occur repeatedly or never go away. (17-1)

citizenship. Membership in a community that guarantees certain rights and expects certain responsibilities. (24-1)

code of ethics. A clear set of morally sound rules and principles that guide actions and decisions. (23-1)

commitment. A pledge to support something of value. (8-1)

communication. The process of creating and sending messages and of receiving and evaluating messages from others. (6-1)

communication channel. The way in which a message is sent. (6-1)

communication, nonverbal. Sending messages to others without words. (6-1)

communication, verbal. Spoken words. (6-1)

comparison shopping. Looking in several stores to compare quality and price before buying. (28-1)

compatible. Existing together in harmony. (19-1)

competition. A struggle for superiority or victory. (7-2)

complementary needs. An explanation for attraction based on partners who meet and complete each other's personality needs. (30-1)

compromise. Giving in on some points in a disagreement and having your way on others. (7-1)

compulsive eating. An eating disorder involving an inability to resist food and control eating. (26-2)

conception. The uniting of the male and female reproductive cells. (33-2)

conflict. Disagreement or struggle between two or more people. (7-1)

conflict resolution. An approach to solving disagreements. (1-1)

conform. To follow the customs, rules, or standards of a group. (23-2)

congregate housing. An arrangement for a group of people who live in the same building and share meals and some living space while having their own rooms for privacy. (17-2)

conscience. An inner sense of what is right and wrong in one's own behavior or motives. (23-1)

consequences. The outcome or results of decisions and actions. (9-3)

consumer. A person who purchases goods and services to fill needs and wants. (28-1)

Consumer Action and Advisory Panels. Organizations formed by specific industries to help solve consumer problems. (28-2)

contract. A binding agreement. (31-2)

control. Directing another person's behavior. (7-1)

cooperation. The ability to work with others. (16-1)

credit. Borrowing or using someone else's money and paying it back later. (27-1)

creditors. Those to whom a debt is owed. (12-1)

cremation. Reduction of a body to ashes through intense heat. (15-2)

crisis. An unstable or critical situation where the outcome will make a decisive difference for better or worse. (14-1)

cultural heritage. The beliefs, customs, and traits that are passed down among generations. (4-2)

culture. The traits and customs of a specific group of people. (4-2)

culture shock. The difficulties and feelings of uneasiness people have when exposed to another culture. (4-2)

custody. A legal decision about who has the right to make decisions that affect children and who has the physical responsibility of caring for them. (13-1)

D

date rape. Forced sexual intercourse that takes place in a dating situation. (19-1)

dating. Shared social activity between two people. (19-1)

debit card. A card that automatically deducts money from your checking account when it is used for buying. (27-1)

decision. A choice that is made. (9-2)

delegate. To assign responsibility to others. (11-2)

democratic style. Responsibility for decision making is shared. (3-2)

denial. Refusing to believe facts, then acting and thinking as if the facts don't exist. (9-1 & 15-1)

dependent. Relying greatly on others. (3-2)

development. The process of growth and change over the course of life. (21-1)

diplomacy. The ability to handle situations without upsetting or offending people. (16-2)

discipline. The process of helping children learn to behave in acceptable ways. (34-2)

disengagement. Withdrawal from others and from activity. (17-1)

diversity. Varied differences in people. (4-2)

divorce. Legal action that ends a marriage. (13-1)

divorce, adversarial. A divorce in which the spouses become legal opponents. (13-1)

divorce mediator. An impartial third person who helps the divorcing couple work out an agreement. (13-1)

down payment. A partial cash payment paid when buying an item with credit. (27-1)

drugs. Chemical substances, other than food, that change the way the body or mind functions. (14-2)

E

economize. Finding ways to spend less money. (12-1)

egocentrism. The inability to see life from anyone's viewpoint but your own. (23-2)

elder abuse. Physical abuse directed at aging people. (17-2)

emotional support. Everything that people do to help meet the emotional needs of others. (2-1)

emotions. Feelings created in response to thoughts, remarks, and events. (2-1)

empathy. The ability to put yourself in another person's situation. (5-1)

empty nest. The home with children grown and gone. (3-3)

enculturation. The process by which each generation passes along what it has learned to the next. (4-2)

endurance. The length of time you can work or exercise without stopping. (26-2)

engagement. A promise or intention to marry. (31-1)

entrepreneur. Someone who organizes and runs his or her own business. (29-2)

environment. The surroundings, people, and experiences that shape development. (8-2)

epinephrine. A hormone produced during stressful situations. (12-2)

estranged. Alienated from each other. (32-2)

ethics. The moral rules of society. (9-2)

ethnocentrism. The belief that a person's own culture is the best or most natural. (4-2)

etiquette. Rules of polite behavior. (16-1)

evaluate. Studying the results of actions to determine their effectiveness. (9-3)

exploitation. Using another person unfairly for personal benefit. (5-1)

extroverted. Focused outward or on others. (22-1)

F

family, blended. Husband and wife, at least one of whom has children from a previous relationship. (3-1)

family, extended. Family group including relatives other than parents and children. (3-1)

family, nuclear. Family consisting of a mother, father, and their children. (3-1)

family system. Family members acting together with their different roles and personalities. (8-2)

feedback. A response to a message, indicating that the message was understood correctly. (6-2)

fertility. The ability to have children. (33-1)

financial plan. A plan for spending and saving money. (27-2)

fixed expenses. Regular expenses, often of the same amount. (27-2)

fixed income. Monthly payments, such as social security or a pension, that do not change. (17-2)

flexibility. The ability to move your muscles to their fullest extent. (26-2)

flexible expenses. Expenses that do not occur regularly. (27-2)

functions. Purposes. (1-1)

futurists. People who study and predict what may happen in the future. (10-2)

G

gender role. The behavior and characteristics expected of a male or female. (20-1)

genetic diseases. Illnesses passed from parent to child through heredity. (33-1)

gerontology. The study of the aging process. (17-1)

goal. Something a person plans to be, do, or have, and is willing to work for. (3-2)

goal, long-term. A goal that requires considerable time to achieve. (9-2)

goal, short-term. A goal that requires a short period of time to achieve. (9-2)

gossip. Conversation that often includes rumors about people. (18-2)

grief. The painful emotions felt after experiencing loss. (15-2)

grounds. A marital crime, such as mental or physical cruelty, desertion, adultery, or insanity, used as reason for divorce. (13-1)

H

heredity. The genetic traits received from parents at birth. (8-2)

high self-esteem. Self-confident people who see themselves as capable and of worth. (2-1)

homogamy. An explanation for attraction based on similarity between partners. (30-1)

hormones. Chemical substances that control body processes. (21-1)

hospice. Programs that support and care for people who face death. (15-1)

household work. Tasks done in the home to keep up with day-to-day living. (11-1)

I

ideal. Perfect. (3-1)

identity. A view of yourself as a person. (12-1)

images. Mental pictures of what something is like. (3-1)

impulse buying. Purchasing items hastily, without consideration or thought. (28-1)

incest. Sexual activity between people who are closely related. (14-2)

income-producing work. Tasks done to earn money. (11-1)

independence. The ability to take care of yourself. (2-1)

infatuation. An intense emotional involvement that begins with a sudden strong attraction based on physical appearance or other obvious traits. (19-2)

infertility. The inability to have children. (33-1)

institution of marriage. Marriage as a way of living. (30-2)

interdependence. A feeling of mutual reliance. (3-2)

interest. The money paid to use someone else's money. (27-1)

intervention. Taking direct action to cause change and provide help when someone else is in a crisis. (14-1)

interview. A face-to-face meeting between an employer and a potential employee. (29-2)

intimacy. Closeness that develops in a personal relationship. (32-2)

introverted. Focused inward or on oneself. (22-1)

intrusive. Enters your life without your invitation or willingness. (10-2)

invalidation. A negative response to another person, including accusing and belittling the other. (13-1)

investing. Using money to make money. (25-2)

isolation. A feeling of being set apart from others. (15-1)

L

launching. The process that sends children out on their own. (3-3)

leader. A person who guides or influences others. (16-2)

lease. A written agreement between the landlord and tenant, spelling out the rights and responsibilities of each. (25-1)

leave of absence. Time off from work (usually unpaid) to use for a specific purpose. (11-2)

legal guardian. Person who has financial and legal responsibility for a child. (3-1)

life events. The experiences that people have in life. (21-1)

life-span development. The concept that change occurs throughout a person's life. (21-2)

life task. A challenge to be met at each stage of life. (21-2)

listening, active. Participating in the message exchange to understand what the speaker is feeling and what the message really means. (6-2)

listening, passive. Responses that invite the speaker to share feelings and ideas. (6-2)

loan. Money lent to someone else to earn interest. (27-1)

low self-esteem. Doubt in personal abilities and worth. (2-1)

M

management process. Using resources effectively to achieve goals and solve problems. (9-2)

marriage commitment. Desire to make a marriage work. (32-1)

mature love. Love that has reached a high level of emotional development. (19-2)

maturity. To be fully developed. (23-2)

mediator. A person who leads those in conflict to solutions without taking sides in the controversy. (7-1)

monitor. To check and keep track of. (34-1)

moral code. The principles of right and wrong that a person lives by. (2-2)

morality. A system of conduct based on right and wrong. (23-1)

motivate. Making people want to do things. (16-2)

motor skills. Abilities that depend on the use and control of muscles, especially those in the arms, legs, hands, and feet. (34-1)

mutual. A decision upon which both partners agree. (32-2)

mutuality. When both people contribute to the feelings and actions that support a relationship. (5-1)

N

needs. Requirements for a person's survival and proper development. (2-1)

negotiate. To deal or bargain with another person. (7-1)

notice. An official, written statement that you are leaving a company. (29-2)

O

obsolete. Outmoded, or replaced by more advanced technological devices. (10-2)

optimist. Someone with a positive point of view. (1-2)

options. Possible courses of action. (9-3)

ovum. The female reproductive cell. (33-2)

P

parenting. The process of caring for children and helping them grow and learn. (33-1)

parenting readiness. Degree of preparation for parenting. (33-2)

parliamentary procedure. Rules of order that describe how to run a meeting. (16-2)

pathogens. The viruses and bacteria that cause diseases. (26-1)

peer pressure. An attempt to influence someone in a similar age group. (18-2)

permissive style. A parenting style in which parents tend to let children set their own goals, rules, and limits. (34-2)

personality. The characteristics that make a person unique. (2-1)

pessimist. Someone with a negative point of view. (1-2)

philosophy of life. The sum of a person's beliefs, attitudes, values, and priorities. (23-2)

pollutants. Impurities in the environment. (24-1)

power. The ability to influence another person. (7-1)

prejudice. An unfair or biased opinion, often about certain religious, political, racial, or ethnic groups. (23-2)

premarital counseling. Getting advice from trained professionals before marriage. (31-1)

prenatal. The period from conception to birth. (33-2)

prenuptial agreement. An agreement regarding special concerns made by a couple before their wedding. (31-2)

press conference. When political leaders answer questions from news media representatives. (24-1)

preventative medicine. Finding out what experts say about how to stay healthy, and making these actions a part of your routine. (26-1)

prioritize. Ranking things according to importance. (9-2)

problem. A situation in which something must be solved or worked out. (9-1)

procrastination. Putting something off. (9-1)

professionalism. A positive attitude toward, commitment to, and ethical behavior on the job. (29-2)

propinquity. Nearness in time or place. (30-1)

R

rape. Forced sexual intercourse. (19-1)

rapport. A feeling of ease and harmony with another person. (5-1)

readiness. Certain qualities and conditions that indicate whether a person is prepared for marriage. (30-2)

reasoning. Thinking logically to reach a conclusion. (9-2)

reciprocation. Giving and getting in return. (16-1)

reciprocity. Mutual exchange. (18-1)

references. People who have agreed to discuss your ability and character with a potential employer. (29-2)

reimbursements. Money paid back. (11-2)

relationships. Connections with other people. (5-1)

resourceful. Able to recognize and make good use of resources. (9-2)

resources. All those things that are used to solve problems, make decisions, manage life, and reach goals; they can be human, material, and community. (9-2)

respect. Showing appreciation or esteem for another. (7-2)

resume. A written account of qualifications for a job, including education or training and experience. (29-2)

risk. The possibility of loss or injury. (9-3)

role. A pattern of behavior associated with a person's position in society. (5-2)

role, chosen. A role that is deliberately selected. (5-2)

role conflict. A disagreement over role expectations. (5-2)

role expectation. Anticipated behavior. (5-2)

role, given. A role that is automatically acquired. (5-2)

role models. People who shape your thinking and from whom you learn appropriate behavior. (5-2)

rotation. Doing certain tasks for a specified period of time, then switching assignments. (11-2)

S

security deposit. A one-time payment to cover costs of potential damage to an apartment. (25-1)

self-discipline. The ability to direct your own behavior in a responsible way. (23-2)

self-disclosure. Telling about yourself. (5-1)

self-esteem. The way you feel about yourself. (22-2)

serotonin. A brain chemical that affects mood and attitude. (22-2)

service industries. Businesses that provide services to others, including information processing. (4-1)

sexual identity. How people see themselves as male or female. (20-1)

sexuality. How a person handles values and beliefs about sexual behavior. (20-1)

sexually transmitted disease (STD). Illness spread through sexual contact. (20-2)

shelter. A safe place to go in the event of physical violence or sexual abuse. (14-1)

siblings. Brothers and sisters. (8-2)

sleep deprivation. Not getting enough sleep. (26-2)

small claims court. Courts that handle cases that do not exceed certain money limits set by the state. (28-2)

socialization. The process of learning to relate to others and get along with them. (2-1)

sperm. The male reproductive cell. (33-2)

stability. Having few changes in your life. (13-2)

stereotype. Standardized idea about the qualities or behavior of a particular category of people. (5-2)

sterility. The inability to have children. (20-2)

strength. The ability to apply force and support weight. (26-2)

stress. Physical, mental, or emotional strain or tension. (12-2)

stress management. Techniques that help a person cope responsibly and comfortably with the pressures of daily life. (12-2)

subculture. A culture shared by a group of people who live with a larger, different culture. (4-2)

support system. A group of resources that provide help when needed. (9-3)

T

teamwork. Cooperating to achieve a common purpose. (16-2)

technology. Using scientific knowledge for practical purposes. (10-1)

telecommute. Using modern technology to perform a job at home. (10-1)

temperament. An inborn style of reacting to the world and relating to others. (21-1)

time-out. A disciplinary method involving removal of a child from the presence of others or from the center of activity for a short time. (34-2)

traditions. Customs that are followed over time and often passed from one generation to another. (8-1)

trend. A general direction or pattern of change over time. (4-1)

trust. A belief that others will not reject, betray, or hurt you. (5-1)

U

unemployment. Not having a job. (12-1)

unit price. A measure of the cost per unit of weight or volume. (28-1)

U-shaped curve. A pattern that describes something that starts at a high level, drops as time progresses, and then rises again. (32-1)

V

vaccines. Chemicals developed to protect against specific diseases. (26-1)

values. Beliefs and principles that are based on ideas about what is right, good, and desirable. (2-2)

value system. The set of values a person has. (2-2)

violence. Physical force used to harm someone or something. (14-2)

volunteerism. Willingness to give service to others. (24-2)

W

wants. Things that are desired but are not essential. (2-1)

warranty. A written guarantee. (28-1)

wellness. A positive state of physical and mental health. (26-1)

will. A legal document that states how a person's property is to be distributed after death. (15-2)

work ethic. An attitude toward work that says, "I value honest work, and I want to work hard to take care of myself and my family and to have a good life." (11-1)

working relationship. A relationship created to accomplish a task or goal. (16-1)

Credits

Cover Design:
Greg Nettles, DesignNet

Cover Image:
FPG International

Interior Design:
Greg Nettles, DesignNet

Infographic Design:
Greg Nettles, DesignNet, 162-163, 208-209, 238-239, 346-347, 434-435, 632-633, 670-671

Allsport USA
Jonathan Daniel, 118
Harry How, 401
Vincent Laforent, 335
Archive Photos, 66
Aristock, Inc.
Alex Bieri, 498
Jim Chatwin, 422, 480
Fitz, 479
Robb Helfrick, 611
Novastock, 466
Vincent J. Ricardel, 421
Michael A. Schwarz, 457, 518
John Slemp, 653
Arnold & Brown, 71, 93, 108, 136, 146, 183, 217, 234, 252, 271, 273, 290, 312, 352, 407, 409, 458, 487, 516, 526, 535, 578-579, 613, 638, 660
Ron Brown, 189
Keith Berry, 75, 644, 649, 682
Ken Clubb, 36, 37, 47, 130, 190, 198-199, 260-261, 288-289, 331, 400, 484-485, 519, 538-539, 578-579
Corbis Images/Westlight, 381
Corbis Westlight, 170, 348, 350, 355, 357, 399
Steve Chenn, 23, 520
Dennis Degnan 339, 388, 404
Walther Hodges, 22, 465
Michael Pole, 414, 522, 639
Bob Daemmrich Photography, Inc., 59, 459, 476, 478, 489
Digital Stock, 148, 149, 238, 239, 346, 347, 434, 632
Laura Dwight, 272
FPG International, 239, 346
Mark Adams, 14, 434, 497
Tony Anderson, 447, 540
Burgess Blevins, 481
Gary Buss, 517, 556, 633
Ron Chapple, 435, 633
Ken Chermus, 502
Jim Cummins, 307, 435, 506
Michael Goldman, 601, 630
Mark Harmel, 375
Michael Krasowitz, 309, 326, 430, 549, 614, 617
Rob Lang, 553
Kevin Laubacher, 239, 313
Bill Losh, 571, 594, 618
Eric O'Connell, 507
Richard Price, 608
Stephanie Rausser, 495
Stephen Simpson, 499, 596, 671

Telegraph Colour Library, 434, 435, 670, 671
Arthur Tilley, 262, 429, 441, 632
John Terrance Turner, 486
Curt Fischer, 67
Food Pix, 666
David R. Frazier Photolibrary, Inc., 35, 99, 341, 436
Index Stock Imagery, 162, 267, 348, 365, 366, 665, 680
Index Stock Photography, 260, 446, 511, 533, 612, 615, 616, 646
International Stock
Cliff Hollenbeck, 617
Earl Kogler, 166
Richard Pharaoh, 174
Patrick Ramsey, 275
Jay Thomas, 11, 360, 376, 470, 571, 661
Dusty Willison 148, 249
John Langford Photography, 1, 26, 44, 64, 88, 106, 124, 140, 158, 180, 206, 224, 246, 266, 284, 306, 324, 344, 364, 380, 398, 420, 440 456, 474, 494, 510, 530, 548, 566, 586, 604, 622, 642, 664
Joe Mallon Photography, 67, 563, 651
Masterfile
Dale Sanders, 333
Pierre Tremblay, 412
Larry Williams, 412
Ted Mishima, 45, 276, 294, 315, 443, 475, 576, 629, 672
Morgan-Cain & Associates
Timothy Fuller, 104, 105, 178, 179, 322, 323, 418, 419, 492, 493
Steve Torregrossa, 24, 25, 244, 245, 584, 585
Cristin Nestor, 513
PhotoDisc, 145, 148, 149, 208, 209, 238, 239, 346, 347, 632, 633, 670-671

Models and fictional names have been used to portray characters in stories and examples in this text.

Index

Nursing homes, 359–60
Nutrition, 518–21
    for children, 666
    and health, 349, 503–4

O

Older adults. *See also* Aging
    process
    caring for, 356
    financial concerns of,
        355–56
    living arrangements for,
        357–60
    medical care for, 356–57
    safety, 360–61
Open adoption, 650
Optimism, 39, 277
Options in problem solving,
    197–201
Others, respect for, 468–69
Over-medication, 357
Ovum, 659

P

Parenting, 81–82, 643–64,
    644
    challenges of, 646–47
    choosing, 643–46
    as partnership, 665
    preparing yourself for,
        657–59
    readiness for, 653–57
    rewards of, 648
    styles of, 677–78
Parents
    communication with,
        169–70
    relating to, 167–71
    resources for, 661
Parliamentary procedure,
    340
Participatory leadership, 338
Partner abuse, 299
Passive listening, 129, 131
Pathogens, 511
Patience, 682
Peer mediation, 371
Peer pressure, 371–73, 644
Peers, love of, 382
Pelvic inflammatory disease,
    405
People skills, 337

Permissive parenting,
    677–78
Perseverance, 580
Personal identification num-
    ber (PIN), 533
Personalities, 49, 441
    and birth order, 172–74
    differences in, as source of
        conflict, 143
    emotional traits in,
        442–44
    environment versus hered-
        ity in, 172
    in families, 73–75
    intellectual traits in,
        445–46
    and progress, 446
    roots of, 441
    social traits in, 444–45
    and stress management,
        257
Personal resources, 526
Personal safety, 505
Pessimism, 39
Philosophy of life, 471
Physical abuse, 300, 386
Physical development,
    347–49, 666–69
Physical health, 292–94, 349
Physical needs, meeting, 50
Physical reactions, 151
Physical self, 421–22
Pierson, Elaine, 398
Placement offices, 576
Polio, 511
Pollutants, 482
Popularity, 375–76
Population, aging, 89
Positive attitude, 221, 368,
    447–53
Positive discussions, 134
Positive qualities, 388
Positive self-talk, 263
Positive thinking, 448
Positive view, 39–41
Power struggles, 143
Pregnancy, 659
    teen, 409–10, 656–57
Prejudice, 468–69
Premarital counseling,
    609–10
Prenatal period, 659
Prenuptial agreements, 614

Press conference, 477
Preventative medicine, 513
Price, determining fair, 550
Pride, culture as source of,
    101
Prioritize, 189
Privacy, 161, 218–19
Private adoptions, 651–52
Problems, 144, 181
    attitudes toward, 185–86
    coping with, 287
    identifying, 184, 196–97
    impact of, 181–82
    overcoming, as team,
        164–65
    simple, 181
    social, 182–83
Problem solving, 31–32
    carrying out plan in, 202
    evaluating, 202–3
    looking to future, 203
    making plan in, 201–2
    options in, 197–201
    resources in, 188–91
    skills for, 29, 187–95
Procrastination, 184, 185
Product obsolescence, 215
Professionalism, 580–81
Property, 478–79
Property settlement, 272
Propinquity, 590–91
Purpose and self-worth, 451

Q

Quality, 550

R

Rapport, 111
Readiness, 593
    for marriage, 593
    signs of, 593–99
Realistic thinking, 647
Real-life families, 66
Reasoning, 194
Rebelliousness, 328–29
Reciprocity, 326, 369
Recreation facilities, 527
Recycling, 482
References, 577
Refunds, 558–59
Reimbursements, 240